T0294838

From Oil to Gas and Beyond

A Review of the Trinidad and Tobago Model and Analysis of Future Challenges

Edited by
Trevor M. Boopsingh and
Gregory McGuire

UNIVERSITY PRESS OF AMERICA, ® INC.
Lanham • Boulder • New York • Toronto • Plymouth, UK

Copyright © 2014 by
University Press of America,® Inc.
4501 Forbes Boulevard
Suite 200
Lanham, Maryland 20706
UPA Acquisitions Department (301) 459-3366

10 Thornbury Road
Plymouth PL6 7PP
United Kingdom

Library of Congress Control Number: 2013957828
ISBN: 978-0-7618-6328-1 (clothbound : alk. paper)
eISBN: 978-0-7618-6329-8

∞™ The paper used in this publication meets the minimum
requirements of American National Standard for Information
Sciences—Permanence of Paper for Printed Library Materials,
ANSI/NISO Z39.48-1992

The book *From Oil to Gas and Beyond* is dedicated to the memory of the late Trevor Michael Boopsingh, the founder and first Chairman of the Association of Caribbean Energy Specialists Limited (ACES). It was indeed his brain-child to review and analyse the transformation of the Trinidad and Tobago energy sector and to provide a blueprint for the future.

During his long and distinguished career Trevor Boopsingh received numer-ous accolades and honours for his outstanding service to the local and regional energy sectors. From 1988 to 1998, he served as a Senior Lecturer in the Faculty of Engineering at the University of the West Indies at St. Augustine, Trinidad. During this period he completed several major studies on Petroleum Management and presented papers on a wide range of local, regional and in-ternational energy matters including Regional Energy Security (2004), Energy Modernization (1996), From Oil to Gas in Trinidad and Tobago (1995) and Downstream Possibilities in CSME (2005). 1990 he wrote the seminal classic "OIL, GAS and DEVELOPMENT–A View from the South." He also held numerous leadership positions in the public and private energy sectors and served as Permanent Secretary in the Ministry of Energy and Natural Resources in the Govern- ment of Trinidad and Tobago from 1981 to 1987. During this period he was deeply involved in a series of complex and historic negotiations re. exploration and production licenses; natural gas contracts and production sharing contracts.

Trevor Boopsingh was the consummate Caribbean intellectual. He served as Chairman of the Engineering Institute at U.W.I, St Augustine from 1994 to 1998. He was honoured as a Distinguished Graduate by UWI, Mona, Jamaica at their 50th anniversary celebrations in 1998. In 2000 he became a Distinguished Member of the International Society of Petroleum Engineers and in 2002 he was awarded the prestigious Chaconia Medal (Gold) in the annual National Awards for long and meritorious service to the Republic of Trinidad and Tobago.

Contents

List of Figures

List of Tables

Acknowledgments

This book would not have been possible without the generous support and encouragement of several of the major players in the energy sector in Trinidad and Tobago.

On behalf of all researchers and authors, the editors which to acknowledge the substantial contributions of The Petroleum Company of Trinidad and Tobago; The National Gas Company of Trinidad and Tobago and BG Trinidad and Tobago Limited. Your support has enabled us to record, for the use of current and future generations, several key elements of a truly amazing story of the emergence of the Trinidad and Tobago energy sector.

Introduction

In 2008, Trinidad and Tobago celebrated one hundred years of commercial oil and gas production. For most of the twentieth century, Trinidad and Tobago's economy was dominated by oil. By the turn into the twenty-first century, however, gas had overtaken oil as the country's main source of revenue, making Trinidad and Tobago the world's first gas-based economy.

This book focuses on the petroleum industry and the overall economy of Trinidad and Tobago, which, in the aftermath of the global financial crisis of 2008, proved to be the most resilient of the English-speaking Caribbean.

Given the pivotal role that oil and gas are expected to play in the life of the twin-island nation for decades to come, the hope of the authors is that this book will provide some guidance for those charged with the responsibility for guiding the future of the petroleum industry as well as for the country.

From Oil to Gas and Beyond brings together the combined experience and expertise of a broad range of respected energy sector professionals. Each essay is devoted to a pertinent aspect of this dominant global industry: from its critical geosciences, to its complex engineering; from its unique taxation methods, to its environmental challenges. Also addressed are the geopolitical issues of the Caribbean region in the context of critical global energy security concerns, as well as the complex socio-economic and structural issues that, inevitably, arise as a result of the levels of wealth generated by mineral exploitation.

The first four chapters of *From Oil to Gas and Beyond* survey the evolution of the industry and the economy of Trinidad and Tobago over the past century. The opening chapter moves very quickly through the exploration period that followed the drilling of the first oil wells in 1856, to the successful efforts that led to the start of commercial oil production in December 1907. After reviewing early pioneering initiatives, from the first refineries to the efforts that helped fuel the Allied war efforts in World War II, Chapter 1 presents a detailed overview of developments since Trinidad and Tobago attained its political Independence from Britain in 1962. This is presented through a review of five case studies, which include the story of the entry and exit from Trinidad and Tobago of Texaco and Amoco, two of the giant multinationals of the last century. Neither has survived; Texaco was absorbed by Chevron in 2001 while Amoco was acquired by BP in 1998.

Among selected case studies are the Government of Trinidad and Tobago's failed attempt to establish a commercial gas-producing platform, and the development and evolution of PCS Nitrogen, one of the larger fertilizer production operations at Pt Lisas.

The five case studies provide the contextual background for Chapter 2 which describes Trinidad and Tobago's rapid expansion in natural gas output at the end of the twentieth century, its emergence as a major exporter of Liquefied Natural Gas (LNG) and its development of a domestic platform fabrication industry.

Trinidad and Tobago has benefited from at least three periods of economic boom in the first century of its oil industry. The first occurred during World War II when, as a result of its location, refineries and fuel production, the colony of Trinidad became an asset of immense strategic value to the British Empire. The second was a brief but memorably rapid rise and fall in oil production in the late 1960s, as US oil companies took over the numerous ageing and very fragmented oil companies on the island. The third occurred in 1973/74 when OPEC pricing power triggered a global shift in control over oil-producing assets, reverberating in the transfer of key elements of control and taxation to the Government of Trinidad and Tobago.

By the end of the first oil century, signs of a fourth boom-and-bust period were beginning to emerge. This was the result of the global financial/credit crisis of September 2008 which triggered a collapse of oil and gas prices from the record highs in July 2008, leading to a sharp fall in government revenues, particularly from the natural gas sector.

As in the 1970s, the downturn of 2008 came amidst sharply rising; unsustainable levels of boom-time State expenditure on construction and social welfare programmes. However, this time around, a more strategic management ensured a respectable level of international savings. Thus Chapter 3 reviews the management of the economy from the mid-1970s to the mid-2000s, beginning with background data and analysis for 1974 to 1986, which was a period of increasing oil production up to 1978, accompanied by increasing oil prices from 1974 to 1981. This was followed by a period of shrinking Government revenues as oil production progressively declined from 1979 to 1986 and beyond, while oil prices fell four-fold from its high of $US40 per barrel in 1981 to less than US$10 per barrel in 1986.

Chapter 3 also analyzes the data for the first decade of the twenty-first century which, from 2000-2007, registered a steady increase in natural gas output and prices until the disruption of September 2008 when the global financial crisis sharply curtailed US demand.

In the unfolding scenario of declining income, the chapter discusses Trinidad and Tobago's legislative framework for savings and the peculiarities of the country's unique situation as the only gas economy in the world. It also addresses the implications of dependence on natural gas, perceived as the bridge to the future for a world desperate for more climate-friendly energy. Also examined are the strengths and weaknesses of the petroleum economy, and the implications of the increased dependence on natural gas.

The formation of the National Gas Company (NGC) in 1975 was a significant step in the evolution of national participation in, and control of the petroleum industry. Chapter 4 details the fledging steps in creating gas pricing policies that led to the development of a domestic industry based on natural gas. The chapter focuses on how, with the collapse of oil prices in 1986, the State, through NGC, adjusted its pricing policy to create a flexible gas pricing. This strategy was adopted in order to assure new investors in the downstream gas industry that their investments would not suffer from changing and variable market conditions for their products, which were then mainly ammonia and methanol.

Chapter 5 covers National Ownership and the supporting framework, including the development of a domestic business sector, training of nationals and related policy positions adopted by the Government to extract maximum value from the energy sector. For many newly emerging petroleum-producing countries, national development requires critical and realistic assessments about equity positions and risk; it also requires the development of skill sets and other training. For such countries, the Trinidad and Tobago experience offers a powerful case study of how, despite small size, a natural resource endowment can be exploited in a manner consistent with one's national aspirations, history and level of education among other things.

By 2010, Trinidad and Tobago held direct control of an estimated one third of the total assets of the country's petroleum industry through equity. However, despite some level of domestic private investment over the period 1990-2010, the majority of the country's total energy assets were in the hands of international capital through private equity and guaranteed debt which have been attracted to Trinidad and Tobago as a result of the sector's phenomenal growth in the post-Independence period.

Given the high level of foreign investment, Trinidad and Tobago's economic independence has required the development of an integrated sectoral plan that takes into account local content, the use of domestic energy services, exposure of nationals to new technologies, new management techniques and new skill sets, particularly those at the leading edge.

Trinidad and Tobago is blessed with petroleum, largely because of its geographic and geologic identity with the South American mainland whose eastern Venezuelan tip can be seen with the naked eye from Icacos on Trinidad's south western peninsula. For centuries, such close proximity has been the basis for a long and natural relationship which, over the last century, has evolved to include their respective petroleum business interests.

Chapter 6 links the important geopolitical role that Trinidad and Tobago, as a founding member and only significant energy exporter of CARICOM, must play in the energy security of the region. Additionally, as one of the world's largest gas and gas-based commodity exporters, it explores the role Trinidad and Tobago must play in meeting the challenges of global energy security challenges.

In more geo-technical terms, Chapter 7 lays out the possible future hydrocarbon resources of the country with, by 2010, some 60 percent of marine acreage still not under license or lease and almost all of the entire land acreage unexplored at depths in excess of 10,000 feet.

Chapter 8 seeks to widen the vision to include greater efficiencies in the use and development of energy resources and to make room for renewable and alternative energy resources. It also identifies the challenges if the country is to retain the global leadership position it has attained in the natural gas industry.

Chapter 9 reviews the status of the vision developed by the domestic petroleum industry in 2003 as part of a wider Government planning exercise titled "Vision 2020." A scorecard of the achievements and challenges encountered over the period 2003-2008 captures how reality has deviated from the stated vision, including the impact of the unexpected and phenomenal increases in oil and gas prices between 2004 and 2008, and its many consequences.

Chapter 10 turns the focus inward to the very important role of petroleum development on the oil-producing communities throughout South Trinidad. The petroleum dilemma of "blessing or curse" is reflected in references such as "the devil's excrement" or, to quote one Caribbean politician "a dose of salts," which reflect the sometimes unenlightened and injudicious management of heightened public expectations in response to rapid revenue increases. Petroleum companies are often aware of the stark contrast between their own highly capital-intensive and sophisticated knowledge-based operations and the often rural and disadvantaged communities where they extract and process petroleum. Despite powerful examples of successful symbiotic relationships between them, Trinidad and Tobago's long history nevertheless demonstrates that the lessons of the past have not always guided the present in the management of social and human issues that accompany industrialization and its distribution of wealth.

Chapter 11 defines these issues in terms of modern environmental concerns, with particular focus on the impact of emissions from industrial activity in a pair of lush tropical Caribbean islands and the related legal and environmental issues.

The following chapters review the challenges that face Trinidad and Tobago's energy sector, including the size, shape, direction and sustainability of the industry. Chapter 12 begins with a look at Petroleum Taxation and defines the method by which the State collects petroleum rent, which has its principal and consistent source of funding since Independence. It also addresses attendant challenges posed by current taxation methodology and discusses the role of the State in shepherding domestic private capital into the mainstream of the domestic energy sector.

The final three chapters, Chapter 13 to Chapter 15, treat with the challenges facing Trinidad and Tobago's energy sector, in particular, and the economy in general as the country moves into the second decade of the twenty first century. The technical challenges are the focus of Chapter 13 as it explores the short and the medium-term constraints, and outlines the case for policy reformulation and further institutional development.

Chapter 14 turns to the communication challenge of bridging the gap between the energy industry, and the general population for whom the country's energy resources are part of the national patrimony. The quality of communication can make the difference in whether these contending interests collide or become aligned.

From Oil to Gas and Beyond concludes with a discussion of the critical challenge of leadership in Chapter 15. Facing a world that is so vastly different from the first oil century, Trinidad and Tobago and its energy industry will require a different kind of leadership if both are to extract maximum benefit from the country's natural resources while providing energy security for future growth and prosperity. This chapter traces the development of professional competence among nationals in the petroleum industry, the availability of talent and leadership, and the phenomenal growth of the domestic petroleum industry, both in size and complexity. It also discusses the increasing globalization of talent and leadership that is a feature of the modern petroleum industry.

If this book assists, in any way, to better inform Trinidad and Tobago's approach to the energy agenda of the future, it would have served its purpose.

Chapter One

From Walter Darwent to Atlantic LNG Train 4

Trevor M. Boopsingh

"The presence of oil and asphalt in Trinidad could not escape the observation of the earliest visitors from Europe. San Fernando hill, the mountain of Annaparima, was an obvious landfall, the approach to which, through the Boca de Serpiente, was located so close to La Brea that the early explorers could not fail to notice the pitch accumulations which must have been of great use to those early mariners."—(Penny and Harris 1955)

In 1595 Sir Walter Raleigh landed in Trinidad and caulked his ships at the La Brea Pitch Lake, a place of wonder to early Spanish settlers who, being far more interested in gold, considered to be little more than a mess of black, stickiness. Two centuries later, in 1797, the Pitch Lake aroused fresh interest in Lieutenant Ralph Abercromby and Lord Thomas Cochrane after the island exchanged hands with the routing of the Spanish by the British. This led to Dr Nicholas Nugent, an eminent member of the Geological Society, being despatched to Trinidad in 1807 for the specific purpose of studying the Pitch Lake. An account of his investigation was published by the Geological Society four years later.

For almost fifty years, there was no follow-up of Dr Nugent's efforts. Then in 1855 arrangements were made for a geological survey of Trinidad, with specific reference to the Pitch Lake. The survey was conducted by Georges Parkes Wall and James Guy Sawkins who published "A Report on the Geology of Trinidad" or "Part I of the West Indian Survey" in 1860 (Wall and Gay 1860). The survey stimulated great interest in the possibility that oil might be produced from the pitch of the lake or from formations surrounding the lake itself.

Records show that the Merrimac Company, registered in 1857, attempted to produce oil by distillation of pitch and in that same year drilled a well to a depth of about 280 feet from which oil was produced. This well was deeper than Drake's well in Pennsylvania, and preceded it by two years.

Around 1865, however, the pioneering American civil engineer Walter Darwent, succeeded in convincing a number of merchants in Port of Spain to float the Paria Oil Company. In May 1866, having drilled a dry hole somewhere near San Fernando, the Darwent group completed a successful well at a depth of 160 feet in the Aripero estate. According to Penny and Lonsdale Harris, historical records provide sufficient detail "to identify what is perhaps the first recorded fishing job" (Penny and Harris 1955).

Darwent's untimely death in 1867 brought an abrupt end to this earliest phase of the Trinidad oil industry, but according to Penny and Harris, there was growing excitement about the possibilities of oil:

> ....planters and proprietors of estates and lands in Moruga could not fail to be aware of the extensive oil seepages in that locality. Another hunter brought a sample of oil to one of those planters, Mr Randolph Rust. It was thus that a life-long interest in oil was aroused in an energetic and far seeing personality. His enthusiasm was contagious and eventually he and businessman John Lee Lum, began operations in 1901 at Aripero.

Rust and Lee Lum, who owned adjacent properties in south-east Trinidad, began the long uphill fight to develop Guayaguayare into a commercial oil-field in 1901, with the backing of Canadian finance.

One can only imagine the practical difficulties of getting equipment into such an area which was accessible only by boat. Equipment, material and supplies had to be ferried around the island from Port of Spain on the north western coast to Guayaguayare on the south eastern coast. Rust and Lee Lum, however, triumphed over their many difficulties, including bouts of ill health, to begin their first well in May 1902, using the Canadian Pole System of percussion drilling. The well was completed three months later at a depth of 1,015 feet, with oil being produced at the rate of 100 barrels a day. Eight more wells were drilled with reports in the early drilling logs indicating that, in some cases, rotary drilling was used at depths below 600. Ultimately, after five years of sustained effort, Rust and Lee Lum's pioneering initiative was overwhelmed by a lack of funds. Guayaguayare was abandoned without making a single commercial shipment after it proved impossible to transport the oil out of the field.

One result of Rust's early efforts was a decision by the Government in 1904 to hire eminent geologist, Edward Hubert Cunningham-Craig to map the geology of Trinidad, with the primary objective of locating oilfields. This decision paved the way for the arrival of yet another dynamic personality, Arthur Beeby Thompson, an engineer with experience with British oil companies in Russia. He arrived in January 1906, at a time when the great oilfields of the Middle East and Venezuela had not yet been discovered and the greater part of world oil production was divided about equally between the USA and Russia.

Cunningham-Craig's survey had directed interest to the Point Fortin region, prompting Beeby Thompson to start building a base there for the Trinidad Oil Syndicate in late 1906. Conditions were unhealthy with staff and employees suffering severely from malaria and yellow fever. However, drilling commenced in May 1907, yielding a number of shallow producers in 1907 and 1908 by percussion drilling. History records FW 3 in Point Fortin as the first well to produce oil in commercial quantities. Given its December 1907 completion date, 1908 is recognised as the first full year of commercial oil production in Trinidad and Tobago. The success of FW 3 could not have been more timely. The Admiralty, whose new ships were almost entirely oil burners, was becoming anxious to secure oil. According to Penny and Lonsdale Harris:

> Due to the anxiety of the Admiralty about oil fuel supplies for the Navy and their insistence upon British control, discussions continued in London. At a conference in Downing Street on February 1909 there were present Lords of the Admiralty and their Adviser, Sir Boverton Redwood, representing the Colonial Office, Governor Designate of Trinidad, Sir Geo. Le Hunt, G. McCarthy and John Cadman (then Inspector of Mines) from Trinidad, Alexander Duckham, Solicitor Carson and Beeby Thompson representing the Trinidad Oil syndicate.

In early 1910, Trinidad Oilfields Limited was formed as a public company. By then Beeby Thompson had secured more acreage including the area known as Parry Lands. In 1911–12 a number of prolific wells were drilled in this area, one of which flowed 10,000 barrels per day from a depth of 1,400 feet. Thus, Trinidad's first commercial success was achieved by Trinidad Oilfields Limited. In 1913, some of those properties were taken over by United British Oilfields Trinidad Limited (UBOT), a majority-owned subsidiary of the Shell Oil Company.

The first well to be drilled entirely by the rotary drilling method was Parry Lands No. D4 completed to a depth of 580 feet in 1914, the year of the outbreak of World War I. By then, a number of other exploration companies had emerged in the Trinidad landscape including Trinidad Leaseholds Limited (TLL) which was founded in 1913. In 1914, TLL brought in Helena 1, the discovery well for Forest Reserve which would later become Texaco Trinidad. Among the other newcomers was Trinidad Central Oilfields which was formed as a private company in 1911, with headquarters in Tabaquite. In 1914, Trinidad oil production passed its first one million-barrel mark.

The pioneering adventure of Trinidad's early oil production was merely the first stage of the complex petroleum business chain which includes storage, transportation, refining and marketing. The early method of crude oil storage in Trinidad utilised underground earthen tanks. Rust records 300 bbls being stored in one of these tanks in the early days in Guayaguayare, where according to reports, a pony fell into one and drowned. In 1914, a report showed 30,000 bbls of crude stored in earthen tanks in Forest Reserve. Few details of storage tanks exist prior to this time, although in 1910 six large 64,000 bbl tanks were erected in Brighton.

On the refinery side, the first small crude unit was established at Point Fortin in about 1910, followed by another in Brighton. Dr Bridget Brereton notes in The History of Modern Trinidad 1793–1962 that "Point Fortin became the first centre of oilfield operations as a port and a developing township. After UBOT took over in 1913, a refinery, a jetty, houses, railways and pipelines were constructed and a crude, but flourishing town sprung up. Point Fortin was in fact 'the town that oil built'" (Brereton 1982).

The first export cargo of crude oil was loaded from Brighton in 1910. Seven years later, in 1917, a pipeline was laid to transport crude oil from Forest Reserve to Pointe-a-Pierre while another was constructed to carry light crude from Tabaquite to Claxton Bay.

Over the course of almost one hundred years, the Forest Reserve field, one of the many identified in Cunningham-Craig's geological mapping survey, has produced more than 500 million barrels of crude, helped along by productive enhanced oil recovery methods. To this day, its discovery well, Helena 1, still produces a trickle. Addressing the 1960 meeting of the Petroleum Association of Trinidad and Tobago, A.L. Downs presented the following vivid description of the period as he recounted an episode involving the Admiralty tanker Masconomo on arrival in Trinidad on August 16, 1916:

The captain, on-going ashore and inquiring of the manager whether there was any oil was told: "Not at present, but if you care to wait a day or two, we're drilling a well and we'll give you all it's got—if it gets any!" The captain and some of his officers were then taken on a trip to Forest Reserve to see the well brought in. "Fortunately, the initial flow was sufficient to complete the cargo, and oil was pumped straight from the well into the ship, no doubt plus water and sand."

This incident occurred at Pointe-a-Pierre, a community initially settled by the Spaniards and the French after the Cedula[1] in 1783 and which was a thriving community long before oil due to the many successful sugar estates in the area- Bon Accord, Bonne Aventure, La Carriere and Concorde, to name a few. Its fortunes received a further boost with the Trinidad Government's decision in 1882 to build a railway to link San Fernando to Port of Spain via

Pointe-a-Pierre. Trinidad Leaseholds Limited's decision to establish a small refinery here in 1916-17 increased the economic potential of the Pointe-a-Pierre/Plaisance Village area. Like all refineries of the period, it utilised the horizontal boiler-type crude stills.

In 1922, a rather primitive form of the cracking plant was introduced at Pointe-a-Pierre with some rather dire consequences as the following description would indicate:

> Trees in the vicinity of the plant, when it was in operation, exhibited glorious autumn tints as a preliminary to dying, birds passed away in the atmosphere of hydrocarbon vapours and hydrogen sulphide, silverware turned black with prolific deposits of silver sulphide, and the whole neighbourhood was rendered uninhabitable.

By the 1920s, oil exploration and discovery were having a dramatic impact on south Trinidad. Several new companies emerged on the horizon, including Apex, Kern and Trinidad Petroleum Development Co. (TPD). This last, registered in 1918, secured a solid footing in the industry and by 1930 had built a small refinery at Santa Flora to produce casing head gasoline from light crude discovered in the Palo Seco field. TPD became the key component of British Petroleum (BP) which established its head offices at Santa Flora as it took control of the many oilfields in the surrounding areas of Siparia, Palo Seco, Fyzabad and Moruga.

Similar progress was being recorded along the island's south eastern coast leading to the successful development of Guayaguayare as an oilfield in 1925. However, Guayaguayare's prime and peak output was not to be achieved until Texaco took over those leases much later in the 1960s.

The discovery of the Penal oilfield by UBOT in 1936 transformed that village from a rice and cocoa producing community to an oilfield town and linked it by pipeline to the refinery at Point Fortin. The Barrackpore field which had been discovered by the Venezuelan Oil Company in 1911 and acquired by TLL had already converted that village into another oilfield town.

World War II brought Trinidad and its oil output and refineries fully onto the global stage, as the two refineries became critical refuelling depots for the Allied forces. Trinidad was not merely a critical link in the provision of fuel for the British forces; it was the only source of fuel on this side of the Atlantic Ocean, as Allied forces sought to interrupt the flow of Axis attacks from Nazi submarines against cross-Atlantic shipping. The strategic value of Trinidad's oil and location made the north eastern port of Chaguaramas a prized asset in the land leases-for-destroyers exchange between the USA and Britain before the infamous Japanese attack on Pearl Harbour pushed the Americans into that war.

By the time Trinidad and Tobago embarked on self-government in 1956, the new petroleum multi-nationals of the world were beginning to dominate the colony's post-War economy with the industry itself expanding beyond the island's terrestrial boundaries into the marine offshore areas. The three biggest names were British Petroleum, then operating under the name Anglo Iranian Oil Company, TLL (later to become Texaco) and UBOT (Shell). Together the three formed a company called Trinidad Northern Areas Limited (TNA) and acquired a licence for offshore exploration under one hundred feet in the Gulf of Paria between the west coast of Trinidad and Venezuela. To encourage its marine exploration initiative, TNA was granted the Submarine Well Allowance, a special fiscal incentive with an accelerated depreciation provision to reduce the investment risk.

In 1954, TNA (later Trinmar) struck it big with High Seas Well 1, now known as Soldado 1, which over fifty years later, remained one of the country's most prolific and enduring producers.

By 1956, crude oil imports stood at 70,000 barrels of oil per day (bopd) for a total refinery throughput of 165,000 bopd. Total Gross Domestic Product for a population of under three quarter million people rose to an estimated TT$764 million or just over TT$1,000 (US$500) per capita. The colony, whose economy had begun in sugar and later flirted with cocoa, had become the first oil economy of the Caribbean.

Figure 1.1 shows the history and evolution of the oil industry, from the first commercial production of oil in 1908 to the formation of Petrotrin, a fully

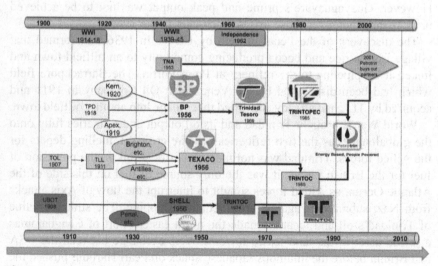

Figure 1.1.   Evolution of Petrotrin.

state-owned petroleum company. The five case studies that follow examine the role of the multi-national oil companies that were vital in taking Trinidad and Tobago from oil to gas and beyond. They also trace the critical policy decisions that have guided the development of the petroleum-based economy to phenomenal success over the course of one hundred years.

CASE STUDY 1: FROM TEXACO TO PETROTRIN

The year 1956 saw the advent of self-government in Trinidad and Tobago and the rise of a new nationalistic political party that was anxious to lift the mass of the population out of historical dispossession. Across the Atlantic, the US oil industry was expanding to global proportions due to the appetite for gasoline and aviation fuels in the boom following World War II. 1956 was also the year that the American oil giant, Texas Oil Co, later known as Texaco, arrived in Trinidad having acquired the assets of Trinidad Leaseholds Limited (TLL) and other smaller companies through negotiations conducted mainly in London and New York. However, whatever frostiness this overseas transaction might have triggered between the multi-national company and the new government was quickly warmed by the special relationship that developed between the Texaco chairman Augustus Long and Dr Eric Williams, the new Premier of Trinidad and Tobago who would lead his country to political independence in 1962.

Texaco's acquisitions in Trinidad included those previously held by TLL as well as other smaller associated companies such as the two at Brighton, Antilles and Brighton, the latter having offshore and deviated land wells, as well as the small refinery distillation units. The refinery at Pointe-a-Pierre was also a key part of Texaco's purchased assets, as was the one-third share of TNA (Trinmar). The TLL-operated oilfields in Forest Reserve, Vessigny, Palo Seco, Penal, Barrackpore and Guayaguayare all became part of Texaco's producing portfolio. Guayaguayare, in particular, was revisited, and the oil-fields there so intensively drilled and exploited that by 1968 more than 70,000 barrels of oil per day were being pumped from the oilfields under Texaco's control, pushing Trinidad and Tobago's crude oil production to its highest ever level of 186,000 bopd in that year.

Increased production brought new matters of concern for technical staff of the fledgling Ministry of Petroleum and Mines. Among them were the large quantities of gas being wasted in producing oil, especially from the Guay-aguayare fields, and the issue of whether maximum ultimate oil recoveries were being achieved.

Texaco's refinery at Pointe-a-Pierre was at the same time under constant upgrade. By 1965, there was a host of new additions to the refinery including a new catalytic reforming unit, another crude distillation unit, a hydrotreater, production facilities for benzene, toluene and xylene (BTX), an aromatics fractionation unit, a lube oil complex and a normal paraffins unit. By 1968 the refinery was running at throughput levels of more than 300,000 bopd; by 1970 it had peaked at 354,369 bopd.

By 1973, three Merox treating units for kerosene manufacture and a de-sulphurization unit had been added along with a single point mooring. Crude imports also peaked in 1970 at 331,300 bopd with crude distillation at Pointe-a-Pierre exceeding 400,000 bopd in that year. Crude came from Indonesia, Saudi Arabia and from Venezuela, to name three of the large sources, as Texaco combined its global assets to make the Trinidad refinery operation the largest crude distillation site in the Western Hemisphere.

Such accelerated growth in the multi-national petroleum sector, however, was occurring within an increasingly restive socio-political environment. In 1970, mass protest erupted on the streets of the capital, Port of Spain, as the disillusioned post-Independence generation staked its claim to respect, representation, equity and a bigger piece of the national pie.

The impact of Trinidad's Black Power Revolt reverberated throughout the island including the oil industry. Oil companies found themselves under pressure by the Government to create new jobs and Texaco responded by hiring a substantial number of persons at the Pointe-a-Pierre refinery. By 1973–74, as OPEC shifted the balance of pricing power from multinational companies to producer countries, the Trinidad and Tobago Government introduced new petroleum tax legislation establishing the Ministry of Finance as the entity to set tax reference prices and throughput fees. It also made the refining, producing and marketing divisions into separate taxable entities by law. Neighbouring Venezuela, then a leading member of OPEC, began nationalizing its oil industry, creating Petroleos De Venezuela S. A. with the consequence that Texaco soon lost control of its Venezuelan operations and its crude production in that country.

In 1975, the Government of Trinidad and Tobago tried to persuade Texaco to deepen its refining processes beyond distillation of offshore crude and urged the company to build some additional petrochemical units. Linear alkyl benzene and maleic anhydride were two petroleum-based products that had been studied in some detail. Ultimately, the Government decided to take over Texaco's retail marketing operations in Trinidad and Tobago.

That year, a major strike by the workers at Pointe-a-Pierre forced the government to deploy the Trinidad and Tobago Defence Force to ensure the delivery of petroleum supplies to the public. The Government also attempted to persuade Texaco to sell a majority holding of its operations to the State but Texaco showed little interest in Government participation. After peaking in 1970, crude oil production from Texaco's fields suffered a dramatic decline, dropping by an estimated 66 percent to 32,745 bopd in 1978. Texaco's Pointe-a-Pierre refinery suffered a similar fate with a drastic decline in throughput to 183,000 bopd due to an estimated 50 percent decline in crude imports which, in 1978, was down to 152,000 bopd.

In this climate, the government's introduction of a new system of taxation using tax reference prices caused consternation among the international producers. The big three—Texaco, Tesoro and Amoco—all protested. For the national Treasury, however, the new fiscal measure was highly lucrative. Amoco which had first brought its oil production on stream from off the east coast of Trinidad in 1972, was producing at a peak of 138,000 bopd in 1978 with total country production of crude oil reaching an historic high of 240,000 bopd in February of that year, making Amoco Trinidad the single greatest generator of tax revenues to the Government of Trinidad and Tobago. The total take in tax and royalty revenues from all oil companies rose spectacularly, from approximately TT$53 million in 1972 to TT1,735 million in 1978 (Ministry of Finance 1980).

Given the radical developments in the international oil market, the key stakeholders in Trinidad and Tobago—Texaco, the Oilfields Workers Trade Union (OWTU) and the government—recognised that given the changing role of international oil companies, large "offshore" refining centres such as the Texaco refinery of the 1960s, were no longer viable methods of operating. This was particularly so because certain fiscal disadvantages for operating refineries in the USA were being eliminated, and because of the emergence of the Louisiana Offshore Oil Port (LOOP) for direct imports into the USA via large crude carriers.

In 1979, the Government's response, prompted in large part by the OWTU's concern about the effect of the changes on labour, resulted in the appointment of a Presidential Commission of Inquiry into the operations of Texaco in Trinidad and Tobago. In a letter dated March 30, 1979, the General Manager of Texaco told the Secretary of the Commission that Texaco was "confident that the Commissioners will, after reading and hearing the company's submissions, understand the need for implementing a return to a conventional corporation tax system, together with appropriate incentives to the oil industry generally."

In a 31-page memorandum, Texaco's principal antagonist, the OWTU, accused the company of a multitude of improper practices including "poor environmental practices, both in the atmosphere and in the waterways; contravention of the Trinidad and Tobago Government's position on trade with South Africa; running down of plant and machinery; damage to producing fields e.g. the Navet field in Guayaguayare; deliberate lowering of refinery

throughput levels; poor industrial and human relations through the contract
system; widespread health and safety hazards and retrenchment by attrition"
(Oilfield Workers Trade Union 1982).

The union cited the decline in employment from 6,872 persons at the end
of 1975 to 6,036 at the beginning of 1979.

Scores of witnesses, including foreign experts and government officials,
testified over a period of more than two years. When it closed, however,
the Commission of Inquiry into Texaco's operations provided no substantial
recommendations for resolving the impasse between the union, the company
and the Government. In the meantime, the Government undertook a thorough
review of the petroleum taxation system, largely because of a 1976 ruling by
the US Internal Revenue Service on foreign tax credits for petroleum-producing companies. In 1981, new petroleum tax legislation that was retroactive to
January 1980, eliminated the use of tax reference prices and substituted fair
market values while introducing a Supplemental Petroleum Tax (SPT). Refining, producing and marketing were, however, still to be treated as separate
taxable entities.

In addition, through the use of a Production Allowance, smaller fields and
fields with predominantly natural gas reservoirs, benefited from an effective
lower tax rate, allowing natural gas fields to be developed at relatively lower
gas prices.

At first, since the changes were effected after much consultation and
exchanges of expert advice between the companies, foreign tax authorities
and Government experts and officials, the new legislation was accepted as a
reasonable compromise. However, as oil prices entered their decline phase in
late 1981 and accelerated into a breakdown of the official pricing mechanisms
of OPEC by late 1982, three significant responses emerged. These were:

1. The Tesoro Petroleum Corporation offered to sell its shares in the joint
   venture Trinidad-Tesoro Petroleum Company to the Government of Trinidad and Tobago.
2. Texaco offered to sell its refining operations in Trinidad to the Government.
3. Amoco indicated that falling crude prices and the SPT system of taxation
   were limiting cash flow to such an extent that exploration activities had
   to be discontinued.

In an 80-page memorandum submitted to the Government on September
20, 1982, the OWTU called for the nationalization of the oil industry and
urged that Texaco not be paid on the nationalization of its operations.

At around the same time, Trintoc produced a comprehensive plan to
upgrade the old Shell refinery at Point Fortin which required Government

approval and financing. Given its limited financing capability, however, the government deferred the Point Fortin upgrade as well as a proposed aluminium smelter, opting instead to approve the construction and financing of a fully State-owned methanol and urea plant. Texaco, meanwhile, had warned the government that any attempt to upgrade Trintoc's Point Fortin facility would threaten the continued operations of the now non-viable Pointe-a-Pierre refinery.

In 1983, under mounting tension, Texaco and the Government began to negotiate the terms of disengagement. By 1984, the OWTU upped the ante, calling on its members to strike. Faced with the prospect of a nation-wide gas shortage, the government secured an Emergency Order and brought in Defence Force personnel to drive gasoline tankers and deliver supplies to all retail outlets. After protracted negotiations in 1985, Texaco sold all its refining assets, land holdings, land-producing properties and some of its offshore holdings in Trinidad (excluding its one-third share in TNA and its 50 percent shareholding in a production-sharing contract with Tenneco) for approximately US$185 million. These assets were initially managed by Trintoc and eventually merged into a greater Trintoc.

Later that year, the Government also purchased Tesoro's assets in Trinidad, paying in fuel-oil shipments to an estimated value of approximately US$150 million. Trintopec, the new entity created from the purchase, was retained as a separate State oil-producing enterprise until 1994 when it was merged with those of the expanded Trintoc to form Petrotrin.

The merger of Trintoc and Trintopec to create Petrotrin was legally consummated in January 1994. Most of the vast real estate holdings were retained by the State in an existing company called Palo Seco Agricultural Estate Limited with the exception of the lands directly under oil-producing leases and the acreage surrounding the two refineries at Point Fortin and Point-a-Pierre. The merger was prompted by the fact that Trintoc and Trintopec had suffered combined losses of approximately TT$300 million in 1993 due in part to the losses incurred in a failed state venture into gas production (See Case Study 5: TRINTOMAR) as well as refining losses incurred by operating two export refineries well below operating capacity. Beginning in 1992, Trintomar was effectively isolated and some of its key assets transferred to Enron which was the first new international entrant to Trinidad and Tobago since Tesoro in 1968.

In April of 1994, twenty years after the future of two old multi-national refineries was placed on the agenda, Petrotrin took the decision to shut down the Point Fortin refinery and keep only the Pointe-a-Pierre Refinery in operation. The cost of this delay was enormous given that for several years (1982–1994) crude and semi-finished products had been diverted to keep the two refineries going, both carrying large annual operating deficits due to excess labour, insufficient crude supplies and ageing plant and equipment. The first upgrade of the Pointe-a-Pierre refinery, which had begun in 1991 (the first new plant to be built since the desulphurization facility two decades before), was completed in 1996.

Much of the merger activity in the period 1993–95 was an exercise in change management and strategic communications. External change management consultants were employed, a single company newsletter titled "One Voice" was established, and new management was selected from within the company. A merger sub-committee of the Board was established with a focus on industrial relations, organizational development and communications. The debt incurred by the failure of the Trintomar gas-producing venture, the operating losses at the refineries and the Inter American Development Bank's loan of US$400 million for repairing, correcting and modernizing the Pointe-a-Pierre refinery, were treated as a "Burning Platform," a graphic simulation of the adverse economic circumstances of the time. A voluntary severance package was made available to all with emphasis on the refining segment after selected Point Fortin personnel were relocated to Pointe-a-Pierre.

A key component of the communications strategy was the "town hall" meetings which were held throughout the company in 1993 and 1994. The format consisted of a "deep-cut" selection of personnel that included every level of the hierarchical structure of both companies, from senior executives to the most junior employees. The plan also included several innovative strategies in sport and culture to establish a sense of unity and common purpose between both sets of employees, and between them and the surrounding communities.

The success of the transition was immediate and impressive. In its first year of operation, Petrotrin was returned to profitability; by 1995 it had posted more than $200 million in after-tax profit. All this occurred in a year in which employees of the Pointe-a-Pierre refinery went on strike, leaving management to man the refinery's operating control rooms for about seven weeks. In 2001 Texaco's offshore Gulf of Paria operation was finally merged into Petrotrin with the sale of its one-third share of Trinidad Northern Areas (TNA) which was by then an environmental liability with its ageing offshore platforms and pipelines.

Texaco, however, held on to its 50 percent shareholding in a production-sharing contract off the east coast of Trinidad which it had initially entered into with Tenneco as operator in 1974, and in which more than 2 TCF of natural gas had been discovered. In the early 1990s, Tenneco sold its Trinidad and Tobago interests to British Gas (BG) allowing BG to begin gas production from that concession in 1994. Texaco, which had started off with the famous Spindletop well in Texas, passed into history after Chevron bought out the global company that had once proudly proclaimed itself the "Star of the Nation" in advertisements in Trinidad.

In the post-1974 period, as Texaco had found itself entering uncharted and troublesome waters, Amoco, the new and very significant crude oil producer in Trinidad and Tobago emerged as arguably, the country's most important oil company. Amoco enjoyed this status largely as a result of its contribution to the Treasury under the terms of the Petroleum Subsidy and Levy Act.

The 1974 enactment of this Act alongside the Petroleum Taxes Act retained the practice of having all petroleum product prices from the refineries (the ex-refinery price) in line with international market prices. However, prices at retail outlets in Trinidad and Tobago continued to be set by the Government at lower levels as a political choice to provide "a direct benefit to the people to whom the oil belonged." The difference between the ex-refinery prices and the retail sales prices was computed for all products sold locally including gasoline, diesel oil and LPG. The total cost of this subsidy was pro-rated on a per-barrel basis and borne as a cost of operation of each domestic crude oil producer. Consequently, as crude oil prices rose in the 1970s and as domestic petroleum product consumption rose, the subsidy rose to levels that had never been anticipated. The full cost of this fell to the producers who took pains to point out that this cost was unlimited and not within their control.

Figure 1.2 shows the extent of the subsidy between 1974 and 1992. As crude prices fell in the 1980s, the effect of the subsidy was tempered by the increase in gasoline prices at the pump and the devaluation of the TT dollar.

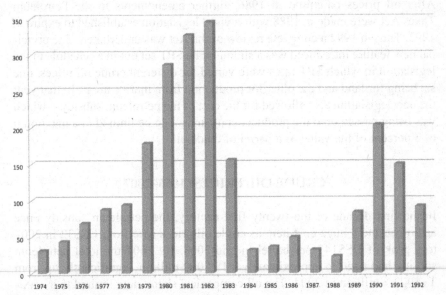

Figure 1.2.   Petroleum Subsidy 1974–1992.

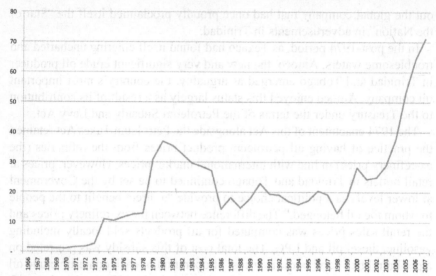

Figure 1.3.   Crude Oil Prices 1966–2007.

Over the course of the 1980s several amendments were made to the Petroleum Taxes Act 1980. First, it reduced the SPT in Land Areas from 35 percent to 15 percent in 1983 in an effort to stimulate drilling and production activity. One year later, the SPT in the marine areas was, among other measures, also reduced to 55 percent with royalty allowed as a deduction for both provinces. After oil prices collapsed in 1986, further amendments to the Petroleum Taxes Act were made in 1988 with revised legislation established to expire in 1992. Thus in 1992 a complete review of the Act was undertaken. The principal new feature introduced was a sliding scale SPT set out in a schedule to the legislation in which SPT rates were varied for different crude oil prices, one set being for land and the other for production from marine areas. In that year the new legislation also allowed for the cost of the petroleum subsidy—which was being passed onto the producer companies—to be limited to a maximum of 3 percent of the value of a barrel of crude oil.

CRUDE OIL PRICES: 1966–2007

In the first decade of the twenty first century, the petroleum subsidy once again became a huge cost item as crude oil prices rose from US$32 in 2004 to a peak of US$147 per barrel in mid-2008. By 2007 the total petroleum subsidy had risen to approximately TT$2,000 million, significantly up from TT$922.7 million in 2004. The oil companies' share, now limited to a maximum of 4 percent of the value of a barrel of crude oil, was approximately TT$900 million in 2007.

As the oil production company of highest significance in terms of contribution to the Treasury, Amoco is worth having two elements of its experience examined as case studies. The first, reproduced here as Case Study 2, discusses how Amoco entered the T&T arena and how it evolved to become the acquisition target of a larger multinational which had returned to Trinidad to become the country's largest gas producer.

CASE STUDY 2: FROM AMOCO TO BPTT

Even as BP and Shell as consortium partners in Trinidad Northern Areas drilled the first exploratory well, High Seas # 1, offshore Point Fortin in 1954, oil was already being produced from shallow waters of less than 100 feet in both the Gulf of Mexico and Lake Maracaibo, Venezuela. Smaller players had also noted that in the search for oil to meet the world's growing appetite for petroleum, offshore acreage would play a major part in future oilfield discoveries. By 1961, with cracks appearing in the West Indies Federation, and Trinidad and Tobago moving towards political independence, Pan American Oil (PATO), Sun Oil and Pure Oil obtained exploration rights to a large chunk of offshore acreage on the east coast of Trinidad extending up to the 600-foot contour in the Atlantic Ocean. Sun Oil and Pure Oil withdrew after the first two unsuccessful wells. After failing to get other partners, PATO drilled the next two wells on its own and hit the vein of black gold: OPR 3 was a gas discovery and OPR 4 found oil in commercial quantities.

PATO became the Amoco Trinidad Oil Company and after a review of the fiscal regime under which deeper water oilfields of more than 100 feet were to be developed, successfully argued the case for the fiscal regime to provide an additional capital allowance through the Submarine Production Allowance (SPA). Production from the Teak field, the first of three new large oilfields, began in May 1972. In 1971 the Samaan oilfield had been discovered and the following year, a third oilfield, Poui, was identified. This was Amoco's first venture outside the USA and it proved to be wildly successful as new oil production from the licensed area offshore the East Coast of Trinidad came into full production, almost in sync with the massive new oil price increases triggered by OPEC's oil embargo in October 1973. In spite of the fact that almost all of the petroleum-bearing reservoirs in the three fields consisted of a very fine, talcum-like, unconsolidated sand which proved difficult to contain behind the well bore, oil production rose from 9.3 million barrels in 1972 to a peak of 50.3 million barrels (138,000 bopd) in 1978, carrying Trinidad and

Tobago that year to its highest ever annual crude oil production of 83.8 million barrels (228,000 bopd).

With crude oil prices rising from 1973–74, the light, sweet crude found in the east coast fields rose from an estimated value of US$3.50 per barrel at the start of production in 1972 to an estimated US$14.58 per barrel in 1978. By 1981, Amoco's crude was estimated by the US Customs at US$41 per barrel. US Customs routinely evaluated the crude imports brought in by Amoco from Trinidad as two of Amoco's refineries in the US had been modified to maximize the product output from the crude's peculiar chemical composition. By 1985, Amoco produced its 500 millionth barrel from the east coast of Trinidad. Its production was now down to just over 90,000 bopd, which was, however, still more than 50 percent of the country's total production.

Two other outstanding features characterized Amoco's crude oil production over that period. Firstly, the high quality of the crude produced by Amoco attracted premium prices from international buyers. Also, because of the prolific nature of the wells with the highest productivity ever seen in Trinidad (except in the early days of uncontrolled blowouts), Amoco's output rose rapidly. These two factors combined to make it become, by far, the single largest contributor to Government revenues for more than two decades.

For many years Amoco provided more than two thirds of total petroleum revenues to the Treasury. Figure 1.4 shows total revenues from oil, as well as the payments made by Amoco (gas revenues were negligible then), peaking

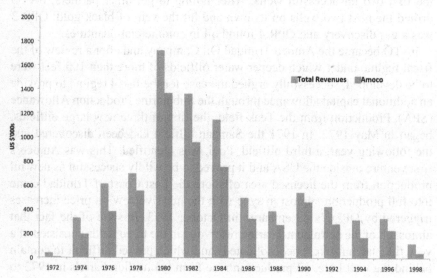

Figure 1.4.   GOTT Petroleum Revenues: 1992–1998.

at US$1,725 million in 1980 when Amoco's fiscal contribution peaked at US$1,369 million. In 1986, when oil prices collapsed, total revenues from oil were still in excess of US$1 billion.

In 1990 when total revenues to Government rose again to US$545 million because of the effects of the first Gulf War, Amoco's contribution was US$464 million, representing 85 percent of the total. The situation changed dramatically after February 1998, when the Asian financial crisis sent prices plummeting to less than US$12 per barrel, yielding a mere US$120 million in total revenues from petroleum. The price collapse marked a double whammy for the government since 1998 was also the year before the commissioning of Atlantic LNG Train 1 whose construction had been facilitated by a number of tax concessions. Revenues fell that year to their lowest since the pre-OPEC year of 1972, with Amoco's revenue contribution falling to 34 percent of total revenues.

The second feature which prompted Government action was the volume of associated natural gas that was wasted as estimated by this author from Ministry of Energy annual reports and other data, as shown in Figure 1.5.

In 1975, the Government had established The National Gas Company (NGC) to purchase and sell natural gas to industrial users on the west coast of Trinidad. The first customer was a new ammonia plant, Tringen that had been commissioned as a joint venture between W. R. Grace and the Government of Trinidad and Tobago. Then, in an agreement fulfilling an obligation in its licence to build a refinery in Trinidad and Tobago, Amoco agreed to establish

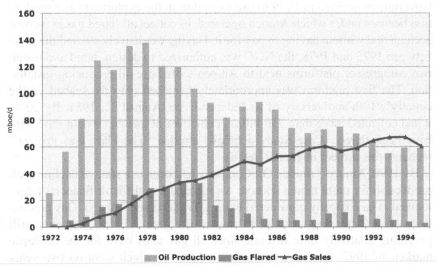

Figure 1.5.   Amoco Oil and Gas Output 1972–1995.

another joint venture with the Government to use gas to produce ammonia and urea. Fertrin, as the company responsible for the purchase and construction of the two ammonia plants was then named, made its first ammonia for sale in 1981. Case Study 3 details the history of this joint venture as well as its sale, resale and expansion.

The time-frames for producing oil to generate revenues, and then for developing commercial uses in Trinidad and Tobago for the associated natural gas that was produced in the process of doing so, were not aligned. In the early 1970s, the Government of T&T had rejected the export of natural gas as LNG, as had been proposed by Amoco and Peoples Gas of Chicago. Instead, in January 1975, the government convened a large gathering of international companies, industrialists and public officials at a conference called *The Best Uses of our Petroleum Resources*. Amidst the planning and negotiations with sundry investors for building the infrastructure of port, harbour, industrial estate, pipelines, electric power and water supplies, associated gas production continued to increase and was largely wasted through flaring.

In 1980 Trinidad and Tobago's annual gas production as recorded by the Ministry of Energy was 195.7 million cubic feet per day, of which 101.2 million cubic feet per day was flared into the atmosphere. These volumes did not, however, take into account gas either produced or flared in Amoco's operations. Ninety-five million cubic feet per day of the gas produced by the other companies was used, most of it (87 percent) as fuel in the fields and refineries. Flaring at Amoco's oilfields in that year is estimated by this author to have been well in excess of 300 million standard cubic feet per day. The Government decided in 1979 to use its option in the exploration and production licenses under which Amoco operated, to collect all flared gas at its own account and without having to pay for it. Having extensively studied the issue between 1975 and 1978, the NGC was authorized to design, build and install two compressor platforms next to Amoco's offshore oil-producing installation. The first platform was appropriately launched onto the seabed on the country's 19th anniversary of its Independence, August 31, 1981. By 2008, it had collected more than 750 billion cubic feet of gas that would otherwise have been flared. (Case Study 4 below, entitled "The Flare Gas Project," recounts this project in greater detail).

By 1990, Amoco Trinidad Oil Company had been in a state of declining oil production for more than a decade. An increasingly difficult financial future loomed. The company considered exiting Trinidad and Tobago. Gas production, while increasing steadily, as shown in Figure 1.5, was, however, still providing relatively little revenue since all gas sales were for the domestic market. In 1992, the Government invited Enron, which went on two years later to become the first new alternate supplier of natural gas to the NGC.

British Gas followed shortly thereafter as the second new gas supplier to the country, with the first gas from a Production Sharing contract coming on-stream in 1996.

Over the years, however, Amoco had discovered large natural gas fields in its exploratory drilling programme, and with the incentive of new provisions in the revision of the petroleum tax laws in 1992, had identified even more natural gas reserves by the mid 1990s. During the period 1993–1998, Amoco had consistently achieved an exploratory success ratio of 60 percent in finding gas, adding an estimated 13 TCF of new gas reserves through the drilling of 21 exploratory wells between 1993 and 2000. Much of this gas had been tentatively identified in the exploration programmes of the previous two decades.

Amoco Trinidad's next big contribution came with the recognition that the next major step in its evolution required a change from being an oil company, to being a company in the gas business. By this time, Amoco had acquired considerable experience and gas reserves in fields off the Rocky Mountains in the USA. By 1998 it had become the first and sole supplier of natural gas to the LNG plant at Point Fortin, the first to be built in the Western Hemisphere in 20 years. It had, however, come to this opportunity as a reluctant bride.

An article in the Wall Street Journal, March 2001, entitled "How Trinidad Became a Big Supplier of Liquefied Natural Gas to the U.S." notes as follows: "Amoco's senior management was not convinced that this gas business could work in Trinidad, says Robert Riley now head of bpTT, which became the successor to Amoco after BP took over Amoco in 1998." The article notes that the "company's chairman and chief executive, Larry Fuller, worried that even if LNG demand in the US were strong enough, Trinidad wouldn't have enough gas to satisfy the demand" (Barrionuevo 2001). The article continues:

> In the fall of 1993, Trinidad's Dr [Kenneth] Julien (then Chairman, National Gas Company) accompanied Prime Minister Patrick Manning to Amoco's Chicago headquarters for a final sales pitch. Mr Fuller was still worried. "This was a big gamble for us," he recalls. But Mr Fuller was impressed by what he calls Mr Manning's "forceful" arguments. "I still had reservations after the meeting," Mr Fuller says, "but everybody left committed to go forward with the arrangement."

The article then notes that beyond "agreeing to supply the plant with gas, Amoco acquired a 34 percent stake in the facility, for $340 million. The other original major investors were Cabot, British Gas, and the Trinidad government." This was after Amoco had done some extensive studies on Trinidad and Tobago's gas resources, and had concluded in 1996 that there were indeed enough reserves offshore Trinidad and Tobago to support six LNG trains, each of 450 mmscfd capacity. The initial Train 1 of Atlantic LNG

(Case Study 7) went into production in 1999. Furthermore, when BP bought the entire Amoco operations worldwide, the studies for its expansion to include two more LNG trains and supply the markets that Repsol brought as a partner, were well underway under Amoco. Repsol had already committed in principle to working with Amoco on LNG, in exchange for a 30 percent share of the gas-producing operations and, therefore, later became the other partner in the gas producing operations now called bpTT, offshore the east coast of Trinidad.

It is ironic that BP became the winner in the acquisition business since, in the early 1990s, Amoco had spent considerable time and money evaluating candidates for acquisition, one of which was BP. Another was Arco. With John Browne replacing Robert Horton as CEO of BP, growth became an urgent objective. BP's motivation to acquire Amoco was probably its gas fields in Egypt, Indonesia and Trinidad and Tobago, as the company sought not only to grow, but to change direction for a future which, it recognized, would require a shift into the cleaner and greener fuel of natural gas. Amoco disappeared as an oil company within Trinidad and Tobago as well as globally. However Amoco has retained its name in the gasoline retailing business in certain states of the USA. Subsequently, rebranding to "Beyond Petroleum" followed.

The discovery of commercial quantities of natural gas by Amoco Trinidad Oil Company as far back as 1968, (the South East Galeota (SEG) field, now known as the Cassia Field), allowed the Government of Trinidad and Tobago to pursue several options for the use of these resources. One option was resource-based industrialization alternatives that would diversify the economy away from oil. Until the early 1970s, natural gas was largely utilized by oil companies as a pneumatic driver for gas-lifting of crude oil from wells, as gas injection in secondary oil recovery and as fuel. Its use in electrical power generation began at the Penal Power station in 1953, which was followed by its use in other industries including as a fuel in cement manufacture in 1954 and in the manufacture of fertilizer by Federation Chemicals Limited (Fedchem), a subsidiary of W. R. Grace, in 1959.

Electrical power generation in that year has been estimated at a total of 33 megawatts of installed plant. Gas was expanded for commercial usage on a national level, beginning in 1964 at the Port of Spain power plant. This was preceded by the milestone event of 1964—the construction of a 16-inch pipeline from Penal to Port of Spain as the first dedicated pipeline for the transmission of natural gas.

In 1975, in order to implement the recommendations of the "*Best Uses of our Petroleum Resources*" conference, Cabinet approved the natural gas pricing principles to be incorporated into a contract between Government or its designated agency, and Amoco Trinidad Oil Company for a natural gas supply agreement (Government of Trinidad and Tobago 1975). In March 1975, the designated agency became the National Gas Company of Trinidad and Tobago Limited (NGC). NGC's role was the purchase and sale of natural gas to commercial and industrial customers in Trinidad and Tobago.

As early as the 1975 conference, several conference participants had highlighted the merits of a fertilizer industry relative to other uses for natural gas. The case for doing so included the following points:

- Agriculture is the single largest industry in the world, yet less than 50 percent of the world's inhabitants had enough food to eat
- Regionally, Trinidad and Tobago would be in an excellent position to service its own nitrogenous fertilizer needs as well as those of its Caribbean neighbours
- In contrast to other projects, only hydrocarbon gas is required for the production of nitrogenous fertilizers as a raw material
- The fertilizer industry is a proven success in Trinidad as evidenced by W. R. Grace's operation in Trinidad from 1959 to 1974
- Each project had potential downstream or supportive industries of great economic benefit to Trinidad and Tobago.

Overall, the commercial potential of nitrogen fertilizer projects looked attractive with the prospect of significant revenue for the Government. Persuaded by the demand for fertilizer imports by nearby territories, W. R. Grace entered a joint venture with the Government of Trinidad and Tobago for the construction of a new and larger ammonia manufacturing plant.

TRINGEN

The conference report from "The Best Use of Our Petroleum Resources" forum laid the basis for several policy initiatives. Eight projects were identified for further detailed study:

1. rapid expansion of the electrical power system
2. upgrading of the petroleum refinery sector
3. establishment of an aluminium smelter
4. establishment of an iron/steel complex
5. expansion of ammonia and urea production through the building of new plants
6. construction of a methanol plant
7. upgrading and expansion of cement production
8. LNG for export to the USA.

The aluminium smelter, upgrading of the refining sector and LNG did not survive the appraisal stage, but others did. A new project, the Flared Gas Project, went into the development stage.

By 1978, crude oil production reached a peak of 228,000 bopd, with gas sales of 82 mmscfd. With the commissioning of the first Tringen plant, ammonia production began its upward climb, reaching 500 thousand metric tonnes per annum. However, refinery throughput was now well below its peak and, at 235,000 bopd, GDP was now at a level of TT$8,550 million or just under TT$9,000 (US$3,700) per capita. Power generation had expanded to more than 510 megawatts of installed capacity with the population having grown to just over one million.

CASE STUDY 3: FERTRIN TO PCS NITROGEN

Fertrin, a joint venture between the Government of Trinidad and Tobago and Amoco, was established on January 28, 1978. The business decision was based on the final feasibility study for the manufacture of ammonia, which was prepared in 1975 by the Government/Amoco Project negotiating team and which included Kellogg & Company in Houston, Texas. This had been preceded by a joint Government and Amoco urea feasibility study. For the government, urea production was a significant component of the ammonia project in terms of maximising value-added from the investment. For Amoco, however, the primary objective was the monetization of natural gas, if not as liquefied natural gas, then through some form of primary processing. Ammonia production offered itself as appropriate for achieving this goal.

Fertrin was originally established as a joint venture partnership on October 5, 1977 on the basis of a 51-49 shareholding split between the Government and Amoco. Point Lisas was selected over Brighton as the site for the ammonia plant. In the case of the urea plant, however, the Government would ultimately have to go it alone with a 100 percent investment in the Trinidad and Tobago Urea Company (TTUC) after Amoco passed on this project.

By 1976, with most of the natural gas now coming from the east coast of Trinidad, the Government, through the Ministry of Petroleum and Mines, undertook the construction of a 37-km (23-mile) long, 61-cm (24-inch) diameter pipeline from Beachfield to Picton. The NGC also constructed 8 km (5 miles) of 51-cm (20-inch) diameter pipeline, "Spurline," from the main 40-cm (16-inch) T&TEC pipeline at Phoenix Park, through the industrial estate in Pt Lisas, with its terminal point at the T&TEC power station. Both pipelines were completed in 1977.

Given the growth in natural gas consumption and the range of user categories, the government appointed a Ministerial team to review and recommend a pricing policy for natural gas sales in Trinidad and Tobago. There were several reasons for this. For one, it was difficult to justify applying the natural gas price that was given to customers in the domestic market, to those in export markets. For another, natural gas customers operated with differing cost of production structures and would therefore be affected differently by the cost of natural gas as fuel versus feed stock. Finally, in line with the Government policy of natural gas being the basis for industrialization, priority had to be given to those activities with greatest benefit to the domestic economy.

After its formation on January 28, 1978, Fertrin negotiated and concluded agreements to purchase two units, each producing 1,000 metric tonnes per day of ammonia, from Pan Canadian Petroleum Limited and Agrico Chemical Company. These were previously manufactured but uninstalled process plants which, although they had been built using pre-1974 conversion technology, helped expedite implementation. Cost of acquisition, modification and shipping to Trinidad came to US$45 million. The project was financed through a US$66 million loan from US ExIm Bank, commercial bank loans of US$96 million from three co-manager banks (Citibank, Barclays International and Royal Bank of Canada), a US$18 million bridge loan from Royal Bank of Canada and a TT$1 million overdraft facility from Trinidad and Tobago's National Commercial Bank.

Despite Amoco's reluctance to participate fully in the project, the company provided support through a purchasing services agreement during construction, as well as a project management contract and an ammonia marketing agreement. Amoco International Sales Company (AISC), a wholly-owned subsidiary of Amoco which was specifically created for the project, entered into an exclusive agreement with Fertrin, dated June 12, 1979. AISC was responsible for the marketing and transport of the ammonia sold for export to foreign markets outside the Caribbean Common Market (CARICOM). AISC earned revenue through a commission of 3 percent of the FOB Trinidad port value, and a chartering commission for ocean transport arrangements.

With downstream development proceeding apace, the government moved to formalise the institutional framework for managing the process. In 1979, the National Energy Corporation (NEC) was created as the supervisory company for various state investments in the petroleum and energy-based industries. Its responsibility was mainly to formalize the activities of the Coordinating Task Force which had been NEC's predecessor in energy sector development.

> The role of the National Energy Corporation is to guide the development and management of oil, gas and other mineral resources of Trinidad and Tobago; to assist the Government in the formulation of energy and industrial policy and strategy; and to increase public participation in decision-making in key areas of the resources and entry-related industries. (National Energy Corporation 1980)

On September 19, 1981, the first Fertrin plant was formally commissioned after some construction delays and cost overruns. The first production of ammonia took place on October 9, 1981 followed by the first shipment aboard the *MV Wiltshire* on November 20, 1981.

Even at that early stage, the Fertrin 01 plant experienced a delay in full production because of problems associated with the supply of natural gas from Amoco. The problem stemmed from a delayed investment for the development of Amoco's Cassia field following the renegotiation of the natural gas supply contract between Amoco and NGC. The commissioning of the second Fertrin plant (02) was also delayed. It was held up until July 12, 1982 due to problems in getting an adequate water supply for the cooling towers.

The State-owned urea plant was commissioned by the NEC on December 2, 1983 following first production in November. The plant was operated by Fertrin on behalf of NEC and was brought fully on stream on January 16, 1984 following repairs to problems that had been identified during start-up. This plant was also shut down for four months, from February to June 1984, after the NEC and Fertrin failed to settle on the operating and ammonia supply agreements.

The fall in global petroleum prices, combined with declining oil production locally, led to a severe reduction in Government revenue, the major contributor to the country's foreign exchange earnings. Accompanying this decline was the consequent fall in commodity prices of methanol, ammonia and urea. Combined with the technical difficulties being experienced at the Iron

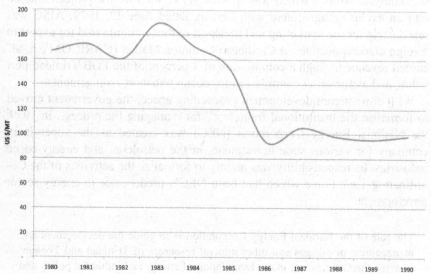

Figure 1.6.	Average Ammonia Prices 1980–1990.

and Steel plant, prices posed a major problem for the newly commissioned plants under the NEC. Ammonia prices declined by 30 percent: moving from US$150 per metric tonne in 1983, to US$100 per metric tonne in 1991. Particularly difficult periods were Q2 to Q4 1986 when average ammonia prices fell to US$88 per metric tonne, and Q3 1989 to Q2 1990 when average ammonia prices were as low as US$74 per metric tonne.

With very large debts to service and mounting utility bills, NEC was unable to look to the Government for support. Oil prices continued to decline, dropping to US$15.97 per barrel in 1988, while oil production continued its decline to 155,000 bopd in the same year. Fertrin itself suffered losses for five of its six years in operation over the period 1981 to 1986, as shown Table 1.1

At the end of 1986, a new government took office and identified as one of its first imperatives for 1987, the organization of financing for the state enterprises sector, including public utilities. A plan for capital restructuring—including divestment or capital enhancement, training, production expansion, changes in management style and accountability—was to be developed for each enterprise, as appropriate. Divestment was selected as a tool for structural transformation to address the Government's need for financial resources for debt servicing, investment re-allocation and economic transformation. However, the strategy to utilize natural gas for industrial expansion remained vital in the quest for economic development. Called into question however, was the extent to which the strategy was supported by the price of natural gas for industrial users. By 1986 also, the urea plant's on-stream factor had improved to 94 percent, with production at 443,376 metric tonnes. By November 1987, following anti-dumping investigations into urea exports to the European Economic Community, it was agreed that Trinidad and Tobago would limit its urea sales to Europe. This commitment, signed by the NEC, would limit the annual volume of urea sold to 75,000 metric tonnes of fertilizer for the next five years. At the urea plant, the focus was on reducing the incidence of shutdown time which yielded encouraging results with a 44 percent increase in output to 490,311 metric tonnes (83 percent capacity

Table 1.1.   Fertrin Profit/Loss Statement

Year	Net Profit/Loss TT$ Million
1981	(6)
1982	(87)
1983	(32)
1984	(42)
1985	(118)
1986	(32)

utilization) in 1986. Urea prices, however, continued to fall, dropping to the mid-US$80/mt by year-end. The overall impact was somewhat mitigated by declining ammonia prices, especially in the second half of the year when they fell to US$88/mt. Falling product prices suggested the need to shut down the urea plant in order to contain losses. However, supply commitments made plant closure very difficult, if not impossible.

From the point of view of operation, 1988 was a hallmark year for urea. The output of 538,023 metric tonnes was just over the nameplate capacity of 535,000 metric tonnes. In addition, it achieved the production feat of two million tonnes on December 24, 1988. With urea prices once again rising, the company earned net cash income that year. This favourable cash position allowed the Urea Company to settle a number of its significant payables; by year-end, payment for raw materials supplied by Fertrin had become current. Within the first four years of operations, the Urea Company, having lost an average of TT$75 million per annum after finance charges, realized a net profit of TT$6 million in 1988. The change in financial fortunes even resulted in the company being awarded an export award in two consecutive years, effectively removing the threat of plant closure.

In 1991, the domestic economy began to contract anew after a short period of recovery due to higher oil prices caused mainly by the impact of the first Gulf War on global energy markets. In addition, the energy sector faced challenges related to the failure of the Trintomar platform (Case Study 5) and declines in petroleum production. To obtain much needed foreign exchange, the Government divested some of its petrochemical companies, including Fertrin and TTUC (Trinidad and Tobago Urea Company 1991). Tables 1.1, 1.2 and 1.3 provide information on profitability.

Fertrin's losses shown in Table 1.3 were due mainly to the combination of depressed ammonia prices which, on average, were below US$100 per metric tonne, and high interest expenses. Interest expenses were TT$83 million in 1988, TT$74 million in 1989 and TT$42 million in 1990. Over the period shown in Table 1.3, production surpassed plant design capacity each year by an average ratio of 1.16, due mainly to de-bottlenecking conducted in earlier years, as well as efficient plant operations (Fertrin).

Table 1.2.   TTUC Profit & Loss Account

	1989	1990
Gross Sales	256	252
Operating Profit	22	30
Net Profit/(Loss) TT$ Million	(2)	12
Unit Cost of Production TT$/Mt	428.64	410.73
Sale Price, TT$/Mt	497.90	522.10

Table 1.3. Fertrin Profit & Loss Account

	1988	1989	1990	1991	1992
Net Sales	366	347	344	362	314
Operating Profit	75	39	31	54	32
Unit Cost of Prod., TT$/Mt	411.30	425.70	403.40	383.18	357.87
Sale Price, TT$/Mt	388.58 (est)	395.25	408.00	477.70	n.a.

Source: Annual Meeting 1990, TTUC Financial Statements, March 21, 1991; Annual Technical Meeting, FERTRIN, 1988 & 1991, March 19, 1992; January 26, 1989

With First Boston Corporation as financial advisor to the Government of Trinidad and Tobago and Amoco Corporation, 100 potential buyers in North America, Europe and Asia were invited to make offers for Fertrin and the Urea Company of T&T. In November 1992, first round bids were received from 11 companies. After a period of negotiations, Fertrin and TTUC were sold to Arcadian Partners LP for a total purchase price of US$175 million. Trinidad and Tobago's 51 percent stake in Fertrin and 100 percent ownership of the TTUC plant brought the country 75.15 percent of the gross proceeds, with a final receipt of US$90.97 million after payment of its share of outstanding loans. At the point of signing, the transaction marked the largest divestment initiative in the Caribbean. Arcadian Partners had been formed in 1989 through the consolidation of five nitrogen companies, becoming the largest nitrogen company in terms of production and distribution in the USA. The company had its headquarters in Memphis, Tennessee, and was operated by Arcadian Corporation. At that time, its annual sales were approximately US$600 million from a range of primary products including ammonia, urea, ammonium nitrate, nitrogen solutions, phosphates and nitric acid.

The sale of Fertrin and TTUC to Arcadian Partners was completed on March 24, 1993, and allowed the corporation to become the largest producer of nitrogen chemicals in the Western Hemisphere, with TTUC being its first granular urea facility. The closure of several nitrogen-producing facilities in the USA, from early 1990s (because of uncompetitive production costs due

Table 1.4. Fertrin Annual Production and Production/Design Capacity

YEAR	Annual Production (000 Metric Tonnes)	Production/Design Capacity*
1988	836.7	1.20
1989	796.1	1.16
1990	775.9	1.13
1991	803.8	1.17
1992	788.0 (est)	1.14

* Design Capacity—689,000 metric tonnes

28   *Chapter One*

to rising feedstock prices), made the Fertrin and TTUC purchase a strategic acquisition for the company. It provided Arcadian Partners with access to ammonia and urea at competitive costs due to favourably priced natural gas at the Trinidad location. The sale resulted in very little change in staff size as Arcadian Partners moved into a period of significant plant capacity growth.

Following the 1993 acquisition, the first capacity addition to the existing Fertrin facilities was the 2003 ammonia plant. This involved the relocation in 1994 of an original C. F. Braun design, with a capacity of 750 tonnes per day which was constructed in 1965 in Brea California. Minor modifications allowed a production rate increase to 830 tonnes per day. By 1994, ammonia prices began a recovery to US$173 per metric tonne in 1994 peaking at US$200 per metric tonne in 1995. Following construction, start-up and commissioning, first production of ammonia from the 03 plant was delivered in June 1996. This was quickly followed by the start of construction of a fourth ammonia plant. Ammonia prices remained above US$166 per metric tonne in 1997 until a decline to US$90 per metric tonne in 1999.

However, Arcadian Partners was not to see the start-up and commissioning of the plant. In mid-1996, through an agreement to purchase Arcadian Corporation, Potash Corporation of Saskatchewan (PCS) acquired the assets of the ammonia complex at Pt Lisas. In March 1997, PCS completed the acquisition of Arcadian Corporation through the merger of Arcadian into a wholly-owned PCS subsidiary; PCS Nitrogen Inc. PCS was the world's largest potash company, the third largest phosphate producer and the second largest nitrogen producer in the world.

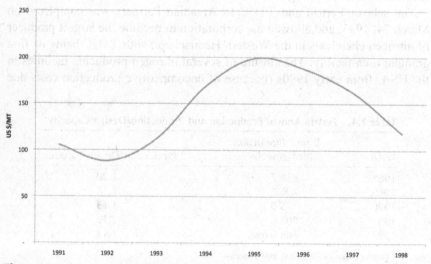

Figure 1.7.   **Average Ammonia Prices 1991–1998.**

Under new ownership, the 03 turnaround was completed in September 1997, resulting in a more reliable and efficient ammonia production unit. Construction of the 04 plant continued apace towards mechanical completion on January 22, 1998. The entire project was completed in 23 months under the coordination of the PCS project team, PCS operations and Kellogg Pan American Corporation (KPAC). The 04 plant was now one of the world's largest ammonia plants constructed well within schedule and with an unblemished safety record of 2.8 million man hours without lost time. The main contractor for the project was M. W. Kellogg and the plant's capacity was 1,850 metric tonnes per day. The plant utilized the most advanced technology available at that time which was the natural-gas-efficient Kellogg Advanced Ammonia Process (KAAP). The PCS Trinidad complex became the largest consumer of natural gas in Trinidad and Tobago, utilizing approximately one-third of the natural gas produced at the time.

In 2008, in an effort to increase the sustainability of Trinidad and Tobago's agricultural sector, the Government of Trinidad and Tobago agreed to grant PCS Nitrogen Trinidad Limited a lease of approximately 75 acres of land in central Trinidad. This grant was for the purpose of establishing the PCS Nitrogen Trinidad Limited Model Farm Project. It was anticipated that the PCS Model Farm would benefit the national community by:

- building the human capital in the agricultural sector;
  improving the efficiency and competitiveness of our agricultural sector
- contributing to the socio-economic development of the agricultural communities near Pt Lisas
- introducing the farming community to revolutionary crop production and management techniques

Despite earning significant foreign exchange, the profitability of the two joint-venture fertilizer projects with Amoco and with W. R. Grace plummeted as international ammonia prices followed the trend in oil and gas prices in the late 1980s. In 1991, Norsk Hydro—Norway's largest publicly-owned company and a world leader in the manufacture and sale of mineral fertilizers—purchased all of W. R. Grace's shares in Fedchem along with its 49 percent shareholding in Tringen. A major upgrade of Tringen I was done in 1996 following which its production rate rose to 1,365 metric tonnes/day. Another major upgrade was completed in 1998 which resulted in an overall capacity increase of 300,000 metric tonnes/year. Later, in 2004, the company was re-named Yara Trinidad following the separation of Norsk Hydro's fertilizer assets from its other operations.

The Iron and Steel plant, ISCOTT, which was commissioned in 1981, was subject to anti-dumping charges by the mid 1980s as the US steel industry took aim at the upstart steel producer from Trinidad and Tobago. Consequent market challenges coupled with production problems resulted in a significant shortfall in steel product which ultimately led to ISCOTT being leased in 1988 to ISPATT, an iron and steel company based originally in India and owned largely by the Mittal family. Increasingly buoyant methanol and urea prices helped both of these fully state-owned companies to become the early success stories of the gas-based Point Lisas Industrial Estate.

The sharp turn in the country's economic fortunes after the oil price collapse of 1986 had several implications, each with varying consequences. First, the Government changed, leading to a review of all new policies, some of which were implemented. One of these was a more open approach to the use of private capital as in the case of Clico (Colonial Life Insurance Company) Energy which was born out of the need to develop new competitive strategies in response to the socio-economic downturn of the 1980s. Another factor which inspired this transition into the oil and gas sector was the need for greater local involvement and ownership in the sector. Formally established in 1989, Clico Energy was charged with the responsibility to develop and manage new projects in the energy sector.

Like Clico, another local company willing to spread its wings into the international arena was Tucker Energy Services. Both received some level of indirect support from the Government, but their success was in large part due to their own creativity and independent initiatives. Tucker—one of the oldest oil service companies in Trinidad—accelerated its investments in overseas operations so as to diversify risk after the collapse in oil prices in 1986. In the process, it became a mini multinational company.

In the case of Clico Energy, Colonial Life Insurance Company employed a liberal interpretation of the regulations governing the insurance industry and expanded into the global energy landscape, taking local gas-based industry plant operators along into the Middle East.

As noted earlier, the National Gas Company signed a 20-year gas supply agreement with AMOCO in 1975 for the supply of up to 300MSCF/D, initially using production from the Teak D offshore platform. In 1979, acting on the instruction of the Government, NGC also undertook a Flare Gas collection and compression project as a gas conservation measure. The Flare Gas Project included the construction of two gas-compression platforms in the Teak and Poui fields and the associated sub-sea pipelines (Herbert). This project is the subject of Case Study 4.

CASE STUDY 4: THE FLARE GAS PROJECT

The Government of Trinidad and Tobago, using its authority under the Petroleum Act, and after reviewing the feasibility of capturing flared natural gas, directed the National Gas Company in 1979 to determine the feasibility of installing two compressor platforms at Amoco's Teak and Poui fields to collect and compress the associated gas which was being wasted there.

This was a conservation measure and, under the Exploration and Production Licenses held by Amoco, the Government had the right to collect any flared gas without cost. At that time, the gas was projected to last 10 years on a declining basis and was deemed sufficient to support compression capacity of 60 mmscfd at Teak and 48 mmscfd at Poui.

The platforms were to be installed in 190 feet of water and within 250 feet of the Amoco production platforms, with a main deck, an upper deck, a utility deck, two-storey living quarters and landing areas for helicopters. Four reciprocating compressors were installed on the Teak platform and five at Poui. The compressors were designed to compress the inlet gas from 20 psig to 1000 psig, a compression ratio of approximately 30:1, with the compression to be carried out in three stages. Due to the uncertain quality of the gas and the variability of inlet suction pressures, a choice was made in favour of more rugged low-speed reciprocating machines over high-speed centrifugal ones.

Bridges with walkways were also required to connect the platforms to the Amoco producing platforms. Supporting the compression process on the platforms were generators, natural gas- and diesel-driven, fire water pumps, one crane, a potable water maker, instrumentation systems, gas and fire detection systems, escape capsules and communication systems.

The fabrication of the jackets and the packaging of the compressors were done in Louisiana, USA. These were installed in 1981 using hollow 42-inch diameter steel piles driven 210 feet into the seabed, the decks being lifted in two pieces and welded onto the jackets. Subsequently, the bridges, vent boom and utility module, as well as the living quarters and helideck, were set in place. Technicians were trained at Ingersoll Rand, the vendor of the compressors. In March 1982, the Poui platform was commissioned and three months later, Teak was also brought into operation.

Initial production from Poui averaged 33 mmscfd while that of Teak averaged 27 mmscfd. At peak, the total volume being conserved reached 115 mmscfd. In late 1986, after it became clear that the project would have adequate gas well after its projected 10-year life span, Petro Marine Inc was contracted by NGC to design and project-manage an expansion project to fill out the space on the Teak platform. Three solar turbine-driven compressor trains with a design capacity of 33 mmscfd were selected for service. In March 1988, this compressor package was installed, One month later it was commissioned.

The investment of approximately US$105 million was extremely successful. Apart from conserving approximately 100 million standard cubic feet of gas per day for more than 25 years—which would otherwise have been flared—it provided the NGC and the country with considerable economic benefit since this gas has proved to be the cheapest source of natural gas to NGC. With the help of secondary recovery and other life-prolonging efforts in these fields, compressed gas from these two platforms in 1996 still represented 18 percent of NGC's gas supplies, with output volumes of the compressors still holding at 105 mmscfd. Over the three-year period to 2008, an average of 83.5 million standard cubic feet per day of gas was still being compressed on the platforms. It is estimated that over the life of the project more than 900 billion standard cubic feet of gas was saved, compressed and utilized, or sold.

The NGC, essentially a transporter and monopoly buyer and seller of natural gas, now with a flared gas collection of approximately 100 mmscfd, had by 1990 also commissioned a 650 mmscfd gas processing facility as a joint venture with Conoco. The venture called Phoenix Park Gas Processing Liquids plant was expanded three times to treat the increasing volumes of natural gas being sold on the island.

In 1988, NGC, together with Trintopec and Trintoc, sought to break the Amoco stranglehold on gas supplies in the country by investing in a new gas-producing platform offshore the east coast. This venture was called Trintomar. The Case Study of Trintomar which follows is essential to understanding some of the events which unfolded in Trinidad and Tobago in the decade of the 1990s.

CASE STUDY 5: TRINTOMAR

The Trinidad and Tobago Marine Petroleum Company Limited (Trintomar) was formed in 1988 for the purpose of developing a portion of the licensed area previously held by the South East Coast Consortium (SECC) known as the Pelican Field. Development of the Pelican Field was proposed to offset projected natural gas shortfalls to industrial users which were expected to have occurred in 1990.

In a paper by Boopsingh and Ramsaran presented in 1994, it was noted that "over the past two (2) decades, four offshore platforms in Trinidad and Tobago have been economic failures (Boopsingh and Ramsaran 1994). Two (2) of them were offshore the East Coast of Trinidad, one by Amoco and the other by Trinidad Tesoro, and two (2) others in the West Coast marine areas of the Gulf of Paria, both under Texaco's purview. All of these were decisions taken and implemented by major international oil companies. The fifth and most recent economic failure was undertaken by a consortium of state-owned companies, in an effort to meet a shortfall in natural gas supplies which was then dominated by one offshore supplier."

The Pelican Field was discovered in 1977 and three wells, Pelican 1, 2 and 3, were drilled during the exploration phase. The gas field lies offshore the east coast of Trinidad approximately 25 miles south east of Point Galeota, at the south-eastern tip of Trinidad, in 230 feet of average water depth.

During the period of project development and implementation, several pertinent changes took place in ownership of the acreage and in the political life of the country. The licensed area was, up to 1985, called the South East Coast Consortium and Texaco Trinidad, Inc. was the operator. Tesoro Petroleum Corporation, together with Texaco, sold their interests in the acreage to the Government during that same year. In 1986, as a result of general elections, the implementation of the project was deferred so as to allow the new Government shareholder representatives to evaluate the project.

Throughout the period, a reputable international financial adviser guided the project and assisted the Government in raising the required project finance. Trintomar's shareholders were:

Trinidad and Tobago Oil Company Limited (Trintoc): 40%
T and T Petroleum Company Limited (Trintopec): 40%
National Gas Company (NGC): 20%

The project entailed the design, fabrication and installation of a platform and production facilities and the drilling of six wells, initially for producing natural gas and condensate to meet a specified gas contract schedule. Three exploratory wells had been drilled; one tested gas and condensate while the other two experienced mechanical problems. The development was based on reserves for the field, which were estimated at 740 BCF gas and 21 MMbbls condensate. The revised original estimated capital expenditure for the project was US$151.1 million.

The project failed to achieve any of its economic objectives after a cost overrun of US$40 million for a total estimated cost of US$191.1 million as at December 1992, and with 11 wells drilled instead of the six originally proposed. The objective sands of the first well were wet, foreshadowing the series of problems which plagued the project to its end in 1993, when it was declared to be uneconomic.

The conclusions arrived at by Boopsingh and Ramsaran were:

1. The estimated proven gas reserves of 740 BCF (1986) for the Pelican Field was certified to be 204 BCF in 1992 after the project was implemented.
2. The original revised estimated development cost for the project was US$151.1 million vs an actual cost of US$191.1 million.
3. The reserves estimate was based on insufficient quality data to support a project of such importance and high capital expenditure.
4. The difference between the initial proved reserves, 740 BCF, and the sales demand forecast, 665 BCF, was too small to be comfortable if the initial data quality, risk and uncertainty were taken into account.

5. The drilling results of the first well, PA-1, was the first additional conclusive information to indicate that the initial reserves estimates were too
   high, and should be reduced.
6. Re-running the 3-D Seismic for improved data quality would have improved the interpretation.
7. Project completion was never achieved, even with a cost overrun of
   US$40 million.
8. Delineation drilling and testing prior to the investment decision would
   have altered the project scope because of better interpretation of the
   structure and gas deliverability. Such additional information could have
   led to a review of other options for meeting the demand forecast.
9. After the drilling accident (*one well had been drilled into another*) it was
   clear that the project's objectives would not be achieved. Even at that
   stage, it would have been more prudent to stop and re-evaluate the impact
   and consequences of continuing the project. With reserves already down-
   graded, incurring further costs would merely increase debt repayment.
10. The drilling accident did not cause the project's failure.
11. The facts available after the accident on PA-7 indicated there was no
    sound technical or economic justification for proceeding with the project
    along the chosen path.
12. Water production problems from all the wells placed a constraint on well
    deliverability, indicating that the demand forecast could not be met.
13. Poor quality, limited data and the US$151.1 million investment required
    that this project be classified as a high-risk venture at the time of the
    decision.
14. Critical analysis of the investment decision would have questioned the
    need for the State companies to bear the full risk of the project.
15. The assumption of low-risk very probably influenced the State compa-
    nies' decision to undertake the project.
16. This failed project cost US$191.1 million, which is more than one third
    of the combined assets (1993) of Trintoc and Trintopec.
17. A joint venture partner should be considered in such high-risk, high-
    capital expenditure projects in order to spread the risk.
18. Energy Security issues need to be more critically evaluated with the most
    affordable option being quantified.

In summary it can be said that:

a. The reserves estimate was based on insufficient quality data to support a
   project of such importance and high capital expenditure.
b. The results showing the first well was wet provided conclusive evidence
   of significantly reduced reserves.

c. Delineation drilling could have changed the scope of the project, and
d. One hundred percent State ownership was based on the project apparently being assessed as a low-risk development project.

The world was undergoing some major changes at around the time that the investment decision on Trintomar was made. Among the significant events were the development of the futures markets, the collapse of oil prices and its impact on the Soviet economy, the Chernobyl disaster, and the fall of the Berlin Wall in 1989 with the parallel dissolution of the former Soviet Union. There was turbulence in Trinidad, too, with an attempted coup in July 1990.

Against the background of dramatic change in international markets, the increasing importance of capital, technology and markets had to be balanced against the critical role of energy in economic development, and the role of the State, particularly in a petroleum-based economy such as Trinidad and Tobago. It should be noted that the first large injection of foreign capital following the change of government in 1986 was a large Inter-American Development Bank loan in 1991 for upgrading the refinery at Pointe-a-Pierre.

Until then, the role of the private sector in petroleum in Trinidad and Tobago had been guided by two principal factors:

• the relatively short period during which the country had exercised independent control over its resources; and
• the small size of the country with its very limited human resource pool in a population of just over one million people.

Since the early years of the oil century, limitations of size, including capital accumulation and the small domestic capital market, had required the continuous presence of the foreign private sector in petroleum. Exploration was a capital-intensive and high-risk business. The Trintomar experience had shown just how risky energy projects—even one involving natural gas development—could be. Towards the end of 1991, a new government assumed office but made no conscious attempt to identify the critical factors that had caused the Trintomar failure. Instead, as suggested by then Minister of Finance Wendell Mottley in his 2008 publication *Trinidad and Tobago—Industrial Policy 1959-2008*, in the context of the factors outlined earlier, including a large and pressing debt repayment schedule, the Finance Ministry had a clear bias towards increasing foreign private capital in the energy sector as well as privatization or sale of State-owned assets (Mottley 2008).

The country's energy policies were therefore re-assessed in the context of global energy trends. In addition, several new policy initiatives in energy were introduced in 1992/3 in response to the economy's high level of dependency on crude oil and natural gas.

As previously mentioned, the Petroleum Taxes Act was amended to allow for lower pre-determined Supplemental Petroleum Tax rates to be applied for lower oil prices. This allowed for greater certainty in the planning process in respect of applicable taxation rates in the future. Exploration activities therefore increased and gas reserves expanded. Private capital was now critical to expansion of the energy sector as financing of public expenditure for State enterprises, including the utilities that were in need of urgent attention, came from the sale of State assets. Fertrin, as was mentioned in Case Study 3, was sold in 1994 to Arcadian. To treat with the failure of Trintomar and the continued dominance of Amoco as a gas supplier, Enron and British Gas were now brought in as gas producers.

Increasingly critical was a reliable electricity supply to support future development of industry. By December 1994 the divestment of the generation assets of the Trinidad and Tobago Electricity Commission was effected, and a new company, Powergen, was formed to operate these plants. The initial main shareholders of Powergen were the Trinidad and Tobago Electricity Commission (51 percent); Southern Electric International (39 percent) and Amoco (10 percent). Mitsubishi later became the majority owner after it purchased the company from Mirant International, a subsidiary of SEI. PowerGen sells bulk power to T&TEC under a 15-year Power Purchase Agreement (PPA) under a commitment to provide 819MW of capacity and 100MW of spinning reserve at a specified heat rate. The PPA specifies the prices to be paid by T&TEC.

Figures 1.8 and 1.9 feature information sourced from a presentation made by T. M. Boopsingh, *Financing Energy,* World Energy Congress, 1995, and

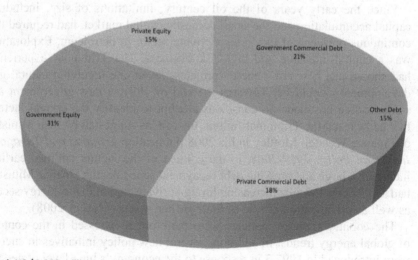

Total: US $3,300 million

Figure 1.8.   Capital Expenditure on Energy: 1975–1985.

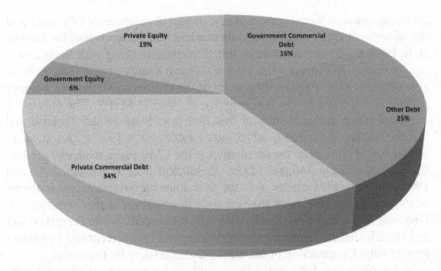

TOTAL EXPENDITURE: US $3,200 million

Figure 1.9.   Capital Expenditure on Energy 1986–1996.

show the sharp reduction in Government equity during this period compared to the 10 years of the post-1974 oil boom (T. Boopsingh 1995). It is, however, noteworthy that much of the make-up funding was not sourced directly from the private sector but through private sector-backed debt.

In 1992 the NGC, after merging with the National Energy Corporation, was also mandated to promote further natural gas development. New gas

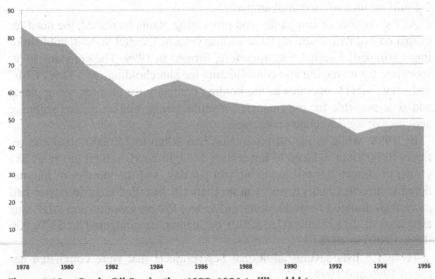

Figure 1.10.   Crude Oil Production 1978–1996 (million bbls).

purchase contracts were signed and new project developments followed using the same flexible gas pricing formula that had first been adopted for Tringen II. In 1993, CL Financial made its initial investment along with foreign partner Ferrostaal AG in the Trinidad and Tobago energy sector. This partnership ultimately led to the establishment of the Caribbean Methanol Company (CMC) which has a production capacity of 500,000 MTPY. The only other methanol plant in the country at that time was State-owned Trinidad and Tobago Methanol Company which was established in 1989 with a capacity of 460,000 MTPY. With the installation of the CMC plant, methanol production increased from 460,000 MTPY to 960,000 MTPY between 1989 and 1993. This, as noted earlier, was the first domestic private sector initiative of its kind in the history of the country's downstream energy industry. CL Financial had a majority shareholding of 64.9 percent, while Ferrostaal AG and Metallgellshaft commanded shareholdings of 25.1 percent and 10 percent respectively. Construction of the plant was undertaken by Ferrostaal.

In the years that followed, Clico established a number of strategic partnerships with various foreign stakeholders, mainly from Germany. In 1997, both Ferrostaal AG and CL Financial had full ownership of TTMC after the State sold its interests in the company. In 1996, TTMC built a second plant (TTMC II) which, again, was constructed by Ferrostaal AG and had a capacity of 550,000 MTPY. In 1998, yet another methanol company, Methanol IV Company Limited (MIV) was constructed, and the plant also had a capacity of 550,000 MTPY. The shareholding of this company was distributed among Clico Energy, Ferrostaal, Helm, and the GE Capital Group. These three companies, CMC, TTMC and MIV produced a combined total of approximately 2.2 million tons of methanol annually.

As the number of companies and processing plants increased, the need for deeper co-ordination among these entities became inevitable. Methanol Holdings (Trinidad) Limited was, therefore, formed in 1999. The company is responsible for managing and consolidating the shareholdings of TTMC, CMC and MIV. MHTL operates as the holding company for all processing plants and is responsible for the financial, manufacturing, marketing and shipping activities of the associate companies.

By 1998, while crude oil production had fallen to 150,000 bopd and refinery throughput reduced to fewer than 110,000 bopd, natural gas sales had grown to almost 700 million cubic feet per day, and the number of international companies had grown to more than 10. Installed electric power had more than doubled from 20 years earlier to 1170 megawatts, and GDP was estimated at TT$33,000 (US$5,300) per capita, as compared to $TT9,000 (US$ 3,700) in 1978.

Table 1.5 lists several additional new projects that were completed between 1996 and 1999.

Table 1.5.   Projects Completed during 1996–1999

Project	Completion Year
Clico Methanol IV	1998
Farmland / Miss Chem Ammonia	1998
PCS (Arcadian) Additional Ammonia Plant	1998
ISPATT—DRI expansion	1999
Cliffs Circored HBI plant	1998
Expansion of Phoenix Park of Gas Processing	1998
Atlantic LNG Plant Train 1	1999

Total capital expenditure for these projects amounted to approximately US\$3,000 million, if offshore exploration and producing and gas transmission expenditures are included. Almost all of the expenditure for gas transmission was financed through the international capital market using foreign private equity as the base. In addition, in 1999 T&TEC entered into a 30-year PPA with Inncogen Ltd. (now Trinity Power Management Limited) to supply 195 MW. Trinity Power's total installed capacity is 225MW.

By 1999, therefore the industry had entered a new phase of development, the pace of which accelerated in the subsequent decade.

NOTE

1. The Cedula of Population was a decree by the King of Spain in 1783 which allowed anyone of the Roman Catholic faith who would swear loyalty to the Spanish Crown to "take lands of up to 3,000 acres (12 km^2) free of charge" to settle in Trinidad.

BIBLIOGRAPHY

Barrionuevo, Alexei. "How Trinidad Became a Big Supplier of Liquified Natural Gas to the U.S." *Wall Street Journal* (Wall Street Journal), 2001.

Boopsingh, Trevor. *Financing Energy.* World Energy Congress, 1995.

Boopsingh, Trevor M, and A Ramsaran. "Review of Trintomar: Technical, Economic and Management Perspectives." 1994.

Brereton, Bridget. *History of Modern Trinidad and Tobago 1783-1962.* New Hampshire: Heinemann, 1982.

Central Bank of Trinidad and Tobago. *Annual Economic Survey.* Central Bank, Various Issues.

Fertrin. "Presentations to Annual Technical Meetings with Ministry of Energy." Various Years.

Government of Trinidad and Tobago. "Best Use of Our Petroleum Resources." 1975.

Herbert, Mc Nicholls. "NGC Flare Gas Project." *GASCO News.*

Mottley, Wendell. *Trinidad and Tobago—Industrial Policy 1959-2008.* Ian Randle, 2008.

National Energy Corporation . "Annual Report." 1980.

Oilfield Workers Trade Union. "Memorandum to the Government of Trinidad and Tobago on Nationalization of the Oil Industry." 1982.

Penny, W.F, and J. Lonsdale- Harris. *A History of Trinidad Oil.* London: London Committee of Trinidad Oil Companies, 1955.

Trinidad and Tobago Urea Company. "Financial Statements." 1991.

Wall, Parkes Georges, and Gawkins James Gay. *Report on the Geology of Trinidad: or, Part I. of the West Indian Survey.* Printed for H. M. Stationery off., 1860.

Chapter Two

The Last Decade—
Liquefied Natural Gas and Its Impact

Trevor M. Boopsingh

Trinidad and Tobago's decision to develop a natural gas-based sector marked the advent of several downstream industries including methanol, ammonia, urea, fertilizers and LNG. By the turn into the twenty-first century, the country was home to some of the world's largest chemical processing plants, and had emerged as the leading global exporter of methanol and ammonia. Buoyant commodity prices, coupled with increasing global demand in the mid 2000s, significantly increased national revenue. By 1996, natural gas production had exceeded oil production (based on energy equivalent), signalling Trinidad and Tobago's transition from oil to a gas-based economy. The transition was fully effected in 2001 when gas revenue surpassed revenue from oil.

The early 2000s registered several notable milestones such as the commissioning in 2001 of Titan Methanol, a new and independent methanol company, and the expansion of Atlantic LNG Trains II and III in 2002 and 2003 respectively. By then, Clico Energy, a methanol producer, had begun diversifying into ammonia production with the establishment of Caribbean Nitrogen Company (CNC) and Nitro 2000 in 2002 and 2004, respectively. CNC and N2000 jointly produce 1.3 million tonnes of ammonia annually, which is exported primarily to the US Gulf Coast and Midwest. The initial shareholders of these two plants were Clico Energy, MAN Ferrostaal, Koch Nitrogen and EOG Resources.

In 2005, Methanol Holdings (Trinidad) Limited embarked on the construction of the world's largest methanol manufacturing facility. The methanol plant, M5000, was constructed at an estimated cost of US$450 million with a capacity of 5400 MT of methanol per day (approximately 1.97 million MTPY). The five plants represent a total investment of over US$1.5 billion. As at 2010, over 300 persons were employed by MHTL. Clico Energy, through its main subsidiary Industrial Plant Services Limited, managed and operated the five methanol plants. Methanex of Canada, the largest global methanol producer, entered Trinidad by purchasing Titan and its successor plant, Atlas (bpTT-36.9 percent) and together with the five plants under MHTL increased the export capacity of Trinidad and Tobago to 6.5 million tonnes, thereby raising the country's profile to that of the world's second largest exporter of methanol.

The most significant expansion in natural gas output, however, came with the introduction of LNG, the first train coming into production in 1999. ALNG is, therefore, central to understanding how Trinidad and Tobago became a gas economy. Case Study 1 highlights Atlantic LNG.

CASE STUDY 1: ATLANTIC LNG

In 1992 the Government of Trinidad and Tobago was approached by a small Boston-based LNG importer, Cabot LNG, to discuss the development of an LNG export project. In that year a new government was also in the secondary stages of implementing a structural adjustment programme—establishing a floating exchange rate, divesting State-owned assets and encouraging foreign investment. In keeping with its programme, the Government published a Green Paper on energy policy which contained key permissive elements for the development of an LNG industry. In its election manifesto, the governing party had reversed its previous position on the use of natural gas for export and was now championing the use of gas from the North Coast Marine Areas (NCMA) as source gas for LNG.

As previously noted, Amoco and the Government of Trinidad and Tobago began negotiating with Peoples Gas of Chicago for an LNG project in the late 1960s. The effort was aborted following the OAPEC embargo when the Trinidad and Tobago Government decided to use natural gas to develop domestic industry instead of exporting natural gas in its raw form. The second unsuccessful attempt at LNG was initiated by Tenneco in the early 1980s. However, with the fall of oil prices from its $40 per barrel levels in 1980, the pricing of LNG became a major issue. After considerable expenditure and time the project was discontinued in 1983.

ATLANTIC LNG—THE BEGINNING OF AN ERA

Cabot LNG was a small-scale Boston-based LNG supplier to the volatile but lucrative New England market. Faced with the twin challenges of fierce competition and limited supply, Cabot sought opportunity in Trinidad and Tobago where it joined forces with Amoco, BG and NGC in establishing an LNG plant.

BG, which had hopes of proving up additional large gas reserves in the Dolphin field off Trinidad's east coast, also held Tenneco's stake in the NCMA gas discoveries that had been established in 1975. BG needed to monetize these reserves since domestic gas sales was not an option at the local market prices. NGC effectively had the monopoly rights regarding the purchase, transmission and sale of gas, and was a key partner in the project.

The Atlantic LNG consortium (ALNG) was formally established in 1995 by the founding sponsors of the LNG project, namely, Amoco Trinidad (LNG) B.V., British Gas Trinidad LNG Ltd., Repsol International Finance B.V., Cabot Trinidad LNG Ltd. and NGC Trinidad and Tobago LNG Ltd. (Amoco's shareholding was later owned by bpTT, LNG B. V. and Cabot's holdings by Suez LNG Finance S. A.) The plant is located at Point Fortin in the south-west of Trinidad, with its administrative office located in Port of Spain. Train I, a 3-mmtpa capacity train, was commissioned in late 1998 with its first shipment in 1999. The project was initially developed as a single train plant but the resounding success of the first venture prompted the partners to expand the facility. Trains II and III began construction in 2000 with the first cargo from Train II being shipped in August 2002, while the first production from Train III was delivered in 2003. Both trains each had a capacity of 3.3 mmtpa and 5,000-6,000 bpd of natural gas liquids. In 2003, the Government signalled its interest in supporting a fourth train. The first cargo from Train IV was shipped on January 8, 2006. This train had a capacity of 5.2 mmtpa and 12,000 bpd of NGLs, but for a variety of reasons did not operate continuously at full capacity until mid 2007.

The trains are operated by ALNG but the ownership structure of each train varies. The shareholder percentages in 2010 are illustrated in Table 2.1.

Table 2.1. ALNG: Percent Shareholding

Train I	Train II/III	Train IV
British Gas Trinidad LNG (26%)	British Gas Global Investments B.V. (32.5 %)	British Gas Trinidad LNG (28.89%)
Repsol LNG Port of Spain B.V. (20%)	Repsol Overzee Financien B.V. (25%)	Repsol Overzee Financien B.V. (22.22%)
BP Trinidad LNG B.V. (34%)	Amoco Trinidad LNG LLC (42.5%)[4]	BP (Barbados) Holding SRL (37.78%)
NGC Trinidad and Tobago (10%)		NGC LNG (Train IV) Ltd (11.11%)
Suez LNG Finance S.A. (10%)		

ALNG TRAIN I: SUCCESS IN THE FACE OF CHALLENGES

Initial discussions between Cabot and NGC revealed that Cabot required around 2 mmtpa of LNG and proposed a much smaller scale plant than was considered optimal. However, feasibility studies concluded that a plant size closer to 3 mmtpa was required for economic viability. The increase in size beyond Cabot's needs required a new buyer/market for the additional output. The Spanish company, Repsol, signed on as a partner of the joint venture because it needed to diversify the sources of Spanish gas.

Given the lack of experience of ALNG's business partners in the LNG field, several experts predicted the failure of the project. As Alexi Barrionuevo, staff reporter of the Wall Street Journal noted in his article "How Trinidad Became a Big Supplier of Liquefied Natural Gas to the U.S.":

POINT FORTIN, Trinidad:
"When energy executives gathered on this small island in May 1994, the notion of building a profitable liquefied-natural-gas plant here drew scorn. Martin Houston, then head of British Gas PLC's Trinidad operations, recalls a competitor commenting, 'If you build an LNG facility in Trinidad, I will eat my shoes.' Two years later, at the ground-breaking ceremony for just such a facility, Mr Houston suggested to the crowd that 'the sceptic be sent a little bit of hot pepper sauce for his shoes.'" (Barrionuevo, 2001)

The article notes that "much of the credit for Trinidad's unlikely ascension in the LNG field goes to two persons. The first was identified as Gordon Shearer, a determined geophysicist born and raised in Scotland. In the late 1980s, Mr Shearer was asked by his employer, Boston-based Cabot Corp., to revive the company's struggling LNG business." Mr Barrionuevo goes on to report that:

Mr Shearer considered Nigeria and Venezuela as sources but ultimately set his sights on Trinidad. Critical to this decision was a seaside lunch in June 1990 in Laguna Nigel, Calif., with Cliff Davis, an industry veteran who had tried for nearly a decade to pull together an LNG project on the island. Mr Davis, then chairman of Midcon Corp., pointed out that Trinidad's potential gas supply was large, and proximity to the US would lower transportation costs. Additionally, natural gas fetched a relatively high price in New England because of the high transmission tariff to move it by pipeline to New England from the South West and other gas-rich regions. For unrelated reasons, Mr Davis's Midcon had abandoned any Trinidad ambitions, and he turned over valuable files and contact information to a grateful Mr Shearer.

Mr Shearer first came to Trinidad with one of Mr Davis's former colleagues at Midcon in 1991 to meet the key people in energy on the island.

The second person identified in the WSJ article was "Kenneth Julien, Chairman of Trinidad's National Gas Company, who had been working to develop the island's gas resources since the mid-1970s."

The tall, burly Dr Julien was the chief architect of the Point Lisas Industrial Estate, a coastal collection of some 20 natural-gas-fuelled plants that help make Trinidad the world's largest exporter of methanol and ammonia, both of which are used in the chemicals industry. Dr Julien, now 68, says he felt a kinship with Mr Shearer: "We were both small guys who had to deal with the massive Amoco and British Gas," Dr Julien explains. Mr Shearer, he adds, "had an obsession that the LNG business was going to happen [in Trinidad], and he wanted to be a part of it." (Barrionuevo, 2001)

The sponsors' ingenuity and willingness to be a part of the new LNG business in Trinidad were critical to the eventual success of this effort. Among the many achievements were drastic cost reductions. Analysis had suggested that a 2.3–2.5 mmtpa plant would cost roughly US$1 billion; there were, however, major economies of scale to be gained from expanding to a 3-mmtpa train. Project costs were also reduced by encouraging competition among its contractors. Of all the paths to cost reduction none had a greater impact than the "dual FEED" strategy. The design of the plant had been based on the APCI (Air Products) process but after working in Alaska, Bechtel believed there could be significant benefit to be had from using the Philips Cascade technology in the plant. The sponsors agreed to accept the additional cost of running parallel FEED exercises to determine which method was more efficient. The two FEEDS were run alongside each other followed by a competitive bidding process. The bid was won by Bechtel's use of the Philips Cascade process which proved to be far more efficient than the APCI process in this project.

On the marketing side, Cabot had come to the project knowing that the niche market in which they were a major supplier—Boston—would provide a premium market that could support the costs of marketing LNG c.i.f. in Boston. The closest profitable market for LNG after Boston was Europe where gas prices were well above those in the US at Henry Hub but below Boston prices. Repsol decided to take the risk. Spain's high dependence on gas from a single source, Algeria, put it at gas supply risk; it needed to diversify its gas sources. The company had at first contracted Nigerian LNG, but consecutively missed deadlines from that project. In scouting for another supplier, Repsol found Trinidad.

In 1995, the sponsors agreed upon selling terms and contracted Cabot to purchase 60 percent of production while Repsol was contracted for the other 40 percent[7]. Buyer flexibility terms were also accepted along with agreement on Repsol's active stake in the LNG project. LNG was sold on an f.o.b basis on two long-term (20-year) contracts, with 60 percent contracted to Cabot at Lake Everett while the other 40 percent was contracted to Gas Natural of Spain at Heulva Terminal in south-east Spain.

Two of the sponsors, Amoco and BG, planned to supply the plant with gas from their upstream operations. Given the vulnerability of profits in a new venture, it was agreed that BG would not supply gas from its NCMA block off the north coast because of the high cost of development. That left only the prospect of Amoco and BG's east coast reserves. Amoco had already completed much of the appraisal drilling which concluded that it had adequate reserves for supplying the entire project. BG, however, was unable to prove its gas reserves in a timely manner. Project completion thus mandated that Amoco supply the entire project, while granting BG the right to supply 50 percent of the gas needed in the event of an expansion.

The challenge of transporting the gas extracted from the east coast was resolved by NGC, who agreed to lease the pipeline responsible for feeding the plant to be built by BP. The result of structural negotiations is illustrated below. For Train I the gas supplied by the upstream shareholders was transported through the NGC pipeline to the LNG plant where it was processed and then shipped to its respective buyers.

The Trinidad project required large-scale financing because of the small size of two of its sponsors. Banks gave their commitment in June 1996 in the form of a Heads of Agreement. The reported cost of the plant and its facilities was US$965 million, well below the project cost of a 2-mmtpa plant. The plant was financed by US$365 million from equity and retained earnings, as well as US$600 million from debt. The lead managers of the loan included ABN Amro, Citibank and Barclays.

The project (Train I) benefited from the Fiscal Incentives Act and was granted a number of incentives including the following:

• Standard tax holiday of 10 years
• Relief from taxes on dividends and other distributions
• VAT exemptions on imports
• Concessions on import duties
• Relief on withholding tax

The finished project, though not very labour intensive, created 140 permanent jobs of which 120 were held by nationals of Trinidad and Tobago.

LNG: TRAINS II/III

Amoco and BG had found gas reserves well in excess of those required by Train I and both were eager to expand ALNG to monetize these reserves.

Discussions with the Government of Trinidad and Tobago began in 1999, and approval for expansion of the plant was granted in 2000. It should be noted that the project owners did not seek a tax holiday, given the greater-than-expected success of Train I as a result of high US gas prices and economies of scale from which the expansion to Trains II/III would benefit. At the time of expansion several factors seemed to favour the shareholders. In the first instance, gas prices in the US were on the rise, making expansion more profitable than in the early 1990s. Further, there appeared to be growth in the European market which could not be adequately supplied by Nigerian LNG or Algerian LNG. Additionally, there were economies of scale to be gained since the site on which Train I was built was designed to accommodate the construction of more trains.

BP and Repsol formed a joint venture to develop an LNG terminal in Bilbao, Spain, as well as an associated gas-fired power plant that required roughly 800,000 mmtpa of LNG. The venture assured ALNG access to a larger European market. The Bilbao terminal was groundbreaking in that it provided terminal and re-gasification services without purchasing the LNG. The output produced by Trains II/III was split among several buyers. Most of the LNG was to be sold in the US but there were other buyers with con-tracted amounts outside the US. Train II output was sold to BG (1.66 mmtpa), Tractebel (0.23 mmtpa), Repsol directly (0.68 mmtpa) and Gas Natural (0.76 mmtpa). Train III capacity was sold to Repsol (1.74 mmtpa), BG (0.83 mmtpa), Gas de Euskadi (0.76 mmtpa).

The difficulties posed by this expansion had little to do with financing but with project structure and conflicts of interest. Both BP and Repsol needed more LNG for their Bilbao venture so these two shareholders were pushing for the expansion. On the other hand, BG had not yet proven the reserves necessary for supplying 50 percent of Train II as stipulated by the agreements for Train I. Cabot and NGC had borrowed funds for investment in Train I which had not yet come on stream, so they saw little urgency in expansion. In addition, the new government had a different view of the risks NGC would be exposed to, as an equity partner, in such a large venture. Given these mis-aligned objectives it was clear that all five shareholders would not be able to negotiate for expansion and that the ownership would have to be restructured. Hence, both Cabot and NGC withdrew from the expansion in return for finan-cial compensation. As a result shareholder percentages in Trains II/III of the Atlantic LNG Company of Trinidad and Tobago Unlimited were distributed among BP (42.5 percent), BG (32.5 percent) and Repsol (25 percent).

The producers were attracted to a quasi-tolling plant structure for this ex-pansion under which the natural gas which was owned by the upstream sup-pliers, namely BP and BG, would be converted to LNG for a set processing fee. Train II is supplied partly by BP from its east coast reserves (50 percent) and partly by BG from its north coast reserves (50 percent). Train III receives

75 percent of its gas from BP and the remaining 25 percent is supplied from both the NCMA and the east coast acreage held by BG and Chevron Texaco. BG had to construct a new 24-inch pipeline to transport gas from its north coast reserves to the Point Fortin plant. Once the LNG is processed, the upstream suppliers were free to sell their output individually, all output being sold on an f.o.b. basis. It should be noted that in contrast with Train I, Trains II/III were able to secure a greater variety of buyers. As part of the agreement for sanctioning this project expansion ALNG funded a tertiary level institute, the Trinidad and Tobago Institute of Technology, for the training and development of nationals in specialized technical fields.

ALNG TRAIN IV

In 2003, the Government granted approval for the construction of Train IV at the ALNG complex in Point Fortin. The train has a capacity of 5.2 mmtpa and 12,000 bpd of NGLs. A new 56-inch pipeline was constructed to carry gas from the fields to the LNG plant, the largest of the three pipelines developed for the LNG project. At the time of construction Train IV was one of the largest single-train LNG projects in the world. Ownership of this train was divided as follows: BG (28.89 percent), BP (37.78 percent), Repsol (22.22 percent) and NGC (11.11 percent). The starting point of negotiations for shareholder stakes with Train IV, as with Trains II/III, was the initial equity share percentages of Train I. As before, each shareholder had the option of receiving the same share percentage with any rejected share being proportionally divided among the remaining members. Once more, Tractabel did not participate. Its share was taken up by NGC representing the Government which, by then, was once again in the hands of the PNM, political party that had formed the Government when the decision was taken for Train I.

The train was supplied with upstream gas by bpTT, BG and other suppliers. Train IV was designed to use processes that were very similar to those used in the previous trains but modified for expansion in an updated and more efficient manner. The technological advances of the Philips Cascade process made it possible to construct a train of the magnitude required for an 800 mmscfd plant, compared to the earlier plants which were of the magnitude of 450 mmscfd each.

A pure tolling arrangement was adopted for Train IV under which the natural gas supplier retained ownership of the gas up to the point of sale and paid a toll fee to the LNG plant owners for liquefaction and re-delivery of gas. In the case of Train IV, the upstream suppliers were bpTT, BG and EOG Resources. Their gas is processed in return for a toll, after which it is sold to the respective buyers: BG, BP, Repsol and TTLNG (representing NGC).

Train IV's output was targeted at seven destinations including Puerto Rico; Dominican Republic; Lake Charles, Louisiana; Elba Island, Georgia; Cove Point, Maryland; Everett, Massachusetts and Spain.

With Train IV, the Government instituted new provisions that were designed to capture a greater portion of additional revenues created by destination flexibility and cargo swaps. The Government prevented transfer pricing and ensured that the State would earn revenues when LNG marketers diverted cargoes, destination premiums and spot cargo transactions. Train IV was expected to earn more revenue for the country than all the previous arrangements. In his 2008 book, Trinidad and Tobago—Industrial Policy 1959–2008, Wendell Mottley estimates Government revenue from Train IV at approximately US$1.73 per mscf at a Henry Hub natural price of US$5 per mscfd. That would amount to TT$3.1 billion from Train IV alone. At a Henry Hub price of US$3 per mscf, he estimates the Treasury would have collected TT$1.3 billion from Train IV alone.

ALNG AND THE ECONOMY

In 1999 the first of four LNG Trains came on stream. It is useful to review the impact of this multi billion-dollar investment on the economy of Trinidad and Tobago.

Figure 2.1 shows Trinidad and Tobago's rapid economic growth, with increasing levels of GDP following the start of production of gas for LNG

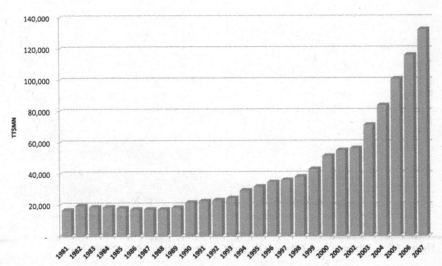

Figure 2.1.   Trinidad and Tobago GDP $ TT Millions 1981–2007.

in 1999. Further examination reveals that large increases in annual GDP coincided with the start of various LNG trains. In 1999, the year the first train came on stream, Trinidad's GDP was recorded at TT$43.3 bn. Construction on Trains II and III began in 2000, with those trains coming into production in 2002 and 2003, respectively. In 2003, GDP had increased by more than 50 percent, over TT$22.9 billion, over the level recorded in 1999, when only one train was in operation. By the time Train IV's first cargoes were shipped in 2006, GDP was at TT$122.1 billion, nearly three times the figure reported for 1999. It is no coincidence that GDP growth for that year was 12.2 percent, given that Train IV was one of the largest LNG trains in the world up to then.

The development of ALNG has had a profound impact on the structure of the economy. The country is still largely dependent on the oil and gas sector but ALNG has effectively shifted the base of the economy from crude oil to natural gas.

Figure 2.2 shows the oil and gas production data for Trinidad and Tobago over the past 100 years in barrels of oil equivalent. Despite this shift to a greater reliance on gas, the oil industry is still a critical and very profitable industry from which Trinidad and Tobago earns substantial revenues, especially when oil prices are high.

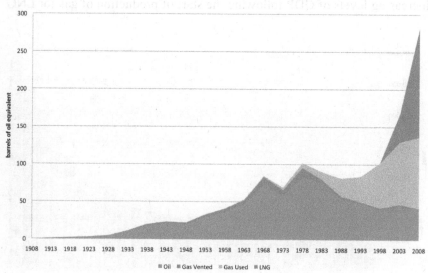

Figure 2.2.   Trinidad and Tobago Oil and Gas Production 1908–2008 (boe).

CORPORATE SOCIAL RESPONSILITY

Since its inception, ALNG has adopted a policy of social responsibility, manifested in the company undertaking several projects of benefit to the citizens of the country.

The company is involved in:

- programmes that focus on children and education;
- programmes that develop the skills of young people in the community;
- partnering with community organizations to improve infrastructure that supports community life.

The agreements to establish Train I and the subsequent Train II/III expansion project entailed certain obligations from ALNG to support the development of skills among nationals for energy and energy-related industries. With initial financing of TT$82 million and annual injections of TT$2.5 million for a period of 20 years beginning in 1999, ALNG ensures that each year the National Energy Skills Centre (NESC) and the Trinidad & Tobago Institute of Technology (TTIT) deliver on the goal of increasing the pool of skilled nationals. In 2004, TTIT became the foundation from which the University of Trinidad and Tobago was launched.

There are, however, some unresolved issues. The community of Point Fortin where the plant is located bears the brunt of the company's externalities. Residents have often complained to the media about their suffering as a result of construction work at ALNG and the day-to-day running of the plant. Some members of the 300 or so families who live downwind of the ALNG facility have claimed to suffer from asthma and other respiratory and skin complaints, excess noise and dust, sleeplessness and stress as a result of the plant. With respect to the physical environment, residents have not forgiven or forgotten the destruction of the Clifton Hill beach, a favourite recreational space for the community, during the laying of the pipeline to the plant in 1998–99.

Sustainable development was a very important issue for many, especially after the idea of a fifth train surfaced, completely in line with the Government's Vision 2020 goal. Some critics opposed additional LNG trains on the basis of concerns about exhausting the country's natural gas resources. Feasibility studies were conducted by the Government in collaboration with BG and Petronas in order to assess the practicality of an additional train, whether independently as Train X or as part of ALNG. The positive outlook for the future of LNG has fuelled discussions about one of the two modes for future expansion in such a way as to capture a larger share of the growing global demand based on the need for clean energy:

Liquefied natural gas (LNG) is one of the fastest growing sectors of the energy market. It is expected to almost double in size between 2005 and 2010, delivering around 40% of global gas supply growth in just five years (International Energy Agency 2006).

Atlantic LNG has made a major impact on Trinidad and Tobago in three different ways. It facilitated the development of a more diversified and stronger economy. It facilitated the development of a new industry—Platform Fabrication, as shown in Case Study 7—and it reversed the fortunes of the people of the borough of Point Fortin and its environs which had been in a state of almost terminal decline since the refinery at Point Fortin was shut down in 1994, after some 80 years of continuous operation. In this regard, apart from the significant reduction in unemployment in the construction and post-construction stages, Point Fortin has experienced some renewal of investor confidence, including from among small businesses and the services sector. There have been increased training opportunities for the youth people of the community.

Over the period 1992–99 five new production platforms were commissioned for offshore petroleum fields off the country's north and east coasts. By way of contrast, as shown in Table 2.2, between 2001 and 2007, 14 offshore platforms were commissioned. In part this was largely because of Atlantic LNG Trains I, II, III, and IV coming on stream between 1997 and 2007, and in part because new oilfields were being developed by BHP-Billiton off the east coast of Trinidad between 2004 and 2005.

The pace of platform construction will in the medium-term future be consistent with the country's new gas production plateau. While the pace is expected to be maintained as producers pursue their optimal depletion strategies in the near to medium term, it is not expected to increase significantly because of a fall-off in exploration activities. Thus, Case Study 2 seeks to illuminate the new business to Trinidad and Tobago which has arisen in the first decade of the 21st century: Platform Fabrication.

CASE STUDY 2: PLATFORM FABRICATION

As previously mentioned, during 1976–1983, the second effort to build an LNG plant in Trinidad was given serious consideration by the Government, Tenneco and Amoco among others. An interim report from 1978 conducted to pursue further development for the establishment of a joint venture platform fabrication facility with George Wimpey and Company Limited, stated that, based on the needs of the local gas-based industry 11 to19 additional

Table 2.2.   Offshore Platform Installation: 1992–2007

	Platform	Year Installed	Owner
1	Flamboyant	1992	bpTT
2	Immortelle	1993	bpTT
3	Mahogany 'B	1997	bpTT
4	Mahogany 'A	1998	bpTT
5	Amherstia	1999	bpTT
6	Osprey	2001	EOG Resources
7	Hibiscus	2002	BGTT
8	Kapok	2003	bpTT
9	Cassia 'B'	2003	bpTT
10	Parula	2004	EOG Resources
11	Angostura CPP	2004	BHP-B
12	Kairi A	2004	BHP-B
13	Kairi B	2004	BHP-B
14	Canteen	2004	BHP-B
15	Aripo	2004	BHP-B
16	Cannonball	2005	bpTT
17	Oilbird	2006	EOG Resources
18	Mango	2007	bpTT
19	Cashima	2007	bpTT

platforms would have been required to meet the new demand for the production of gas for LNG than was then expected to be in production by 1985.

The report concluded that the viability of a platform fabrication facility in Trinidad and Tobago depended to a large extent on the establishment of LNG facilities, as the volume of gas for such a facility would provide the critical mass for successive platform construction. The timing of an investment decision on LNG should be such that the fabrication yard facilities had the capability to capture as many as possible of the platforms required to meet the supply needs for the LNG.

HISTORY

George Wimpey Caribbean Limited (Wimpey), had entered Trinidad in 1957 to construct a multi-well drilling platform for the consortium of BP, Shell and Texaco (TNA) for use in the offshore licensed areas off Point Fortin called Trinmar Limited. The development of offshore work resulted in the rapid development of the Soldado oilfields where Wimpey was contracted to construct multi-well offshore drilling platforms with production platforms interconnected with bridges, large gas compressor stations, single-well protective structures, riser platforms and numerous other offshore structures.

In view of the continued expansion of both offshore and onshore activities Wimpey decided to open a steel fabricating works. As such, seven hectares of land were purchased at Goodrich Bay near Couva and existing buildings were modified and expanded to facilitate major fabrication works. The fabrication yard was adjacent to the sea and had a wharf which could berth vessels drawing up to 3.5 metres of water, and fabrication steel units of up to 170 tons were loaded out for installations. It had successfully carried out a wide variety of contracts, including jetty and dock components, mooring dolphins, single-well protection jackets, several multi-wall production platforms, block station and associated work.

In June 1977, a contract was awarded to George Wimpey Caribbean Limited for the construction of the Trini-Tes platforms B and C for the Trinidad Tesoro Petroleum Company, for installation off the east coast of Trinidad in less than 100 feet of water. The project began when the first shipment of steel arrived on the site on September 21, 1977, and was successfully completed on April 19, 1978.

The peak total manpower employed for the platform fabrication project was 337, taking into account 350 individuals at Wimpey and 27 as subcontractors, excluding suppliers of materials and equipment. Brisco Services Limited provided electrical and instrumental installation, whereas non-destructive testing was contracted to Trinidad Inspection Services.

Some of the personnel who were available locally to complete Trini-Tes Platforms B and C were as follows: draughtsmen, plant operators, fabricators, assemblers, machinists, welders, riggers, sand-blasters, pipe fitters, carpenters, painters, electricians, technicians and apprentices. The specifications to which the platforms were built were as shown in Table 2.3.

PLATFORM SPECIFICATIONS

In 1978, Wimpey Offshore Limited proposed to develop a fabrication yard to facilitate the development of offshore fields. They provided three options to the Government of Trinidad and Tobago:

1. The Government could set up a fabrication yard and operate it using its own resources entirely.
2. The Government could pursue the traditional option of having the oil companies use competitive bids from foreign yards which would result in maximum cost-effectiveness. However this option would give little benefit to employment, transfer of technology to nationals and the involvement of other local support industries.

Table 2.3.   Platform Specifications

	Trini-Tes Platform B 20 wells	Trini-Tes Platform C 14 wells
1. Height of Upper Deck above Sea Level	135 ft	140ft
2. Depth of Water	75 ft	82 ft
3. Length of Piles	280 ft	285 ft
4. Weight of Steelwork		
• Jacket	350 tons	360 tons
• Lower Deck	105 tons	105 tons
• Upper Deck	260 tons	260 tons
• Piles	535 tons	500 tons
Total	1250 tons	1225 tons

Source: Trinidad Tesoro Petroleum Company Limited

3. The third and most beneficial alternative to the citizens of Trinidad and Tobago was the purchase of the structures from a fabrication yard established
   locally in which the Government would have the controlling interest.

Unfortunately none of these options was pursued.

In 1995, after the third attempt at seeking to establish an LNG plant in
Trinidad, ALNG was formally started up, and the earlier reports at evaluating
the feasibility of establishing a fabrication yard became once more relevant.
Natural gas development consists of long term supply contracts from many
relatively large fields, resulting in the ability of producers to space out field
development over time. This results in the platform fabrication demand occurring over an expanded period of time. With the estimate of future platforms
expected over a period of 15 to 18 years because of the increased demand for
natural gas, the result was the development of the local content initiative and
investment in the capacity to design and fabricate platforms locally.

The Government had been developing the La Brea Industrial Estate for the
purpose of sitting the LNG facility and maximizing the use of one of only
two natural deep-water harbours on the island of Trinidad (the other being at
Chaguaramas near Port of Spain). In 1995, the Government recognized that
the presence of very old oil wells on the site and the existence of near-surface
faulting, posed a serious hazard to any LNG plant on the site near to the harbour. ALNG was, therefore, relocated to Point Fortin. Alternative uses then
had to be found for the harbour portion of the site. The wells were abandoned
and all the oil facilities decommissioned.

Development of the La Brea Industrial Estate by Labidco (La Brea Industrial Development Company), which had begun in 1995, cost approximately
TT$133 million to its shareholders (the National Gas Company and Petrotrin).

The Estate's business activities were redirected towards the development and leasing of industrial lands, logistical services for offshore services and port operations, in support of offshore platform construction, bio-remediation services for oil waste and pipe import storage and coating.

Most platform fabrication projects for the east coast fields were, before then, contracted to companies in the Gulf of Mexico and then shipped to the offshore oilfields of Trinidad and Tobago. For the east coast fields, platforms fabricated by these foreign companies were generally quite large in terms of size and weight, consisting of the basic components, namely jackets, caissons, piles and topsides, each ranging from 600 to 2,500 tonnes each.

In 2004, 25 acres of the industrial estate were allocated to the construction of a fabrication yard facility costing an estimated $80 million, with 17 acres as a common yard space and two four-acre blocks for a long-term lease by fabrication contractors. The common yard and dock are leased on a short-term basis to facilitate the import of components, materials and the load out of finished structures.

PLATFORM FABRICATION

Offshore platforms such as those being contemplated for use offshore the east coast of Trinidad in water depths of more than 200 feet, and at locations as many as 50 miles offshore, are constructed to facilitate drilling, production and living quarters for the individuals working on the structure. Some of the key project activities involved with platform fabrication are: engineering design, steel fabrication and assembly, equipment and vessel installation, piping fabrication and installation, electrical instrumentation and equipment, protective coating and cathodic protection, function testing, procurement, construction management, logistics, and project management.

As an example, a platform may involve the fabrication of jackets weighing 2500 tons, piles weighing 1800 tons and topside decks weighing 2500 tons, with equipment such as well control panels, generators, compressors, water treatment modules, manifolds, tanks, separators, fire detection and suppression units, survival capsules, cranes, helidecks, vent and flare booms. On the other hand, with the minimal platform concept and in the hub-and-spoke model, as was later proposed by bpTT, where there is the Gas Gatherer-type platform, reduced weight of the producing platform structure allows it to be loaded off from the LABIDCO docks into less deep waters with jackets, piles and topsides weighing 900 tons, 600 tons and 900 tons, respectively.

In 2002, BPTT commissioned a study on the status of the local fabrication industry. Three categories of resource requirements were analyzed viz:

expertise, facilities and commercial requisites. The findings were presented to industry service companies in order for them to prepare for participation in a fabrication initiative being promoted by bpTT. Below is a summary of findings for each category.

1. EXPERTISE
    - Adequate skills and expertise
    - No single contractor has a full range of expertise to undertake a complete project
    - Availability depends on market experience primarily in onshore projects and upgrades and modifications
    - Limited experience in high value areas such as project and fabrication yard management
    - Adequate capabilities for the Gas Gatherer-type platform
2. FACILITIES
    - Critical pieces of equipment now unavailable, can be easily acquired
    - Potential fabrication yard sites exist
3. COMMERCIAL
    - Characteristics of many local fabrication companies:
        ◦ Small asset-based turnovers
        ◦ Funding mainly from external sources
        ◦ Transparency issues in governance and financial management

Initially, the idea of offshore platform fabrication in Trinidad and Tobago was considered a major constraint to the local content objectives of the Government (Ministry of Energy and Energy Industries 2004). This was because of the immense size and weight of the structures which were unable to get off the island, especially with platforms such as the Amherstia platform (bpTT) producing at least 1 BCFD and weighing 3,500 tonnes on the topside with a 2,400 tonnes jacket. Another constraint which existed was the lack of design engineering skills which resulted in increased design and construction engineering costs for exploration and production companies. Thus, for the business of platform fabrication to be successful in Trinidad, these two major constraints would have to be managed.

PLATFORM FABRICATION BUSINESSES

(1) Damus Limited/Gulf Island Fabrication Inc.

Damus Limited was founded in 1973 and is the largest construction contractor in Trinidad and Tobago and the eastern Caribbean. The company provides diversified mechanical engineering and support services, particularly to the petrochemical, manufacturing and marketing sectors. It is locally-owned, by the Mahabir family, and is managed by a team of experienced employees. The predecessors of Damus were heavily involved in tank fabrication. The company has, however, diversified into piping fabrication for both chemical and industrial plants including field installation and mechanical installation of static and rotational equipment. In addition, Damus is involved with the installation of offshore pipelines in the west coast, installing pipes in manageable lengths out to the offshore site.

In 2003, BHP Billiton awarded a fabrication contract to Damus Ltd. and Gulf Island Fabricators Inc. of the United States for the Kairi 1 platform in Trinidad to support drilling and production in the Angostura field. Damus Ltd. successfully constructed the 600-ton Kairi 1 topside, fabricated and installed the process piping, equipment packages and the E&I scope, along with the hook-up work of the Kairi 1 platform and the central processing unit.

The Kairi 1 was one of the largest platforms ever fabricated in Trinidad and Tobago and the first to be constructed at LABIDCO. As such, the technology transfer and training of Damus engineers by Gulf Island Fabricators Inc. were essential elements in developing the domestic platform fabrication business. Furthermore, the investment in new welding equipment and the use of flux core welding techniques by local welders would have increased productivity and the transfer of skills to industries outside of the oil and gas industry.

Also in 2003, Damus Ltd. was contracted by bpTT to fabricate the 400-ton Bombax gas pipeline subsea manifold and to undertake the Beachfield gas manifold modifications in developing BP's gas resources from Trinidad's east coast. The subsea manifold was one of BP's largest offshore marine structures in Trinidad and Tobago and was expected to double the production and transportation of gas from 1.5bscfd to 3.0bscfd. The Bombax pipeline formed the initial link of a long-term expansion plan, and was essentially a loop of the existing 40-inch pipeline system. The project consisted of 63 km of offshore pipeline and was BP's widest diameter pipeline in the world.

The subsea manifold which was completed within approximately 160,000 man-hours, was fabricated on site at Chaguaramas Terminals. It was the first of its kind to be built in the country and was praised by bpTT's Business Unit Leader and CEO Robert Riley as a project which strengthened the company's belief in raising the bar on local content, and transforming Trinidad and Tobago into a world-class upstream oil and gas province.

Joint ventures with experienced foreign design engineering and fabrication companies assisted the development of Damus Ltd. tremendously through the interaction with local engineers in executing tasks more efficiently in terms of the project management techniques and systems.

(2) Summit Engineering and Construction/Fluor Daniel S. A. Ltd.

Summit E&C, a Trinidad and Tobago-based company, was established in 1999 to provide services of engineering management, project management and engineering design, along with construction contracting to industrial customers in Trinidad and Tobago. Summit's workforce was comprised of engineers, technicians and construction personnel who provided customers with design engineering services, planning and scheduling of projects, procurement, contracting, cost control and overall construction management.

In 2003, the foreign design and engineering company Fluor Daniel South America Limited and Summit Engineering and Construction of Trinidad and Tobago formed a strategic alliance to provide bpTT with EPCM services for its drive towards local content with its first group of locally designed, engineered and fabricated offshore platforms. With the alliance between Fluor and Summit, local designers, engineers and technicians were trained for bpTT's offshore platform development work. The exercise was developed using the BP Cannonball and introducing the "minimal platform concept," along with the standard models of the Cannonball. The creation of smaller satellite ("next field") platforms—BP Mango and BP Cashima—in effect reduced the need for contracting foreign design engineering companies and developed the local content initiative by allowing the majority of the design engineering tasks to be carried out locally by Summit Engineering and Construction. The Fluor Summit strategic alliance was created to assist high-valued EPCM services by utilizing the resources and capabilities of Fluor's global offices in training and employing Trinidadians in filling the gaps in the domestic industrial sector.

On the bpTT Cannonball project, 25 Summit employees were placed for approximately six months at Fluor's engineering execution centre in Texas, where they received extensive technical training, and participated in designing a number of bpTT's major projects. In the process, Summit's employees were exposed to Fluor's work processes, design standards, systems, practices and its organizational network.

The Cannonball project team involved 30 Fluor EPC execution specialists and 30 Summit employees, who were then transitioned to the Trinidad office at the beginning of 2004 to complete the project. Keith Narayansingh of Summit Engineering and Construction posited that the bpTT/Fluor/Summit alliance represented a paradigm shift from the traditional approach of "getting the job done" to developing sustainable capability for doing work.

To support the development of local content, bpTT entered a seven-year "Greenfield" service agreement for the Fluor-Summit Alliance team. Under this agreement, Fluor-Summit would execute the offshore platform EPCM projects associated with their "next field developments" and use of the "minimal platform concept." To ensure the sustainability of this alliance, bpTT encouraged Fluor-Summit to seek additional engineering design contracts from other local clients.

In turn, the availability of the services provided by Fluor-Summit prompted the local company Weldfab Ltd to form an alliance with Gulf Island-based Chet Morrison Inc. to create TOFCO, the Trinidad Offshore Fabrication Unlimited.

(3) Weldfab Ltd/Chet Morrison Inc.

Trinidad Offshore Fabricators (TOFCO) began operation in January 2003 at a 20-acre site near the Gulf of Paria in south La Brea where marine access is unrestricted by navigational height and width considerations. It offered offshore services and repairs, and had a staff of one expatriate manager and 17 nationals comprising welders, fitters, fabricators and a project manager. (By 2008 there was a record of 900 employees including administrative staff, with only eight experienced expatriates being employed.)

The business is an equal joint venture between Weldfab Ltd., a local services company of Trinidad, and Chet Morrison Contractors Inc. (CMC) of the USA.

The initial project undertaken by the company involved the fabrication of the BHP Angostura Bridge and Flare Boom which was successfully completed and loaded out to La Brea onto the cargo barge CMS 1264. However, it was not until October 2003 that TOFCO began its first major contracted project for the BP Cannonball platform. The project was completed in March 2005 and equipped by BP as a fully automated system featuring state-of-the-art technology which increased efficiency, improved safety and remote access to platforms and reduced operational costs.

Robert Riley, then Chief Executive Officer of bpTT, noted that Cannonball had built a legacy of sustainability through the creation of distinct indigenous businesses in two sectors: platform design and engineering, and fabrication, thus demonstrating Trinidad and Tobago's ability to deliver a major project from start to finish. The Cannonball platform, named after a local tree with multi-coloured flowers, was located 35 km off the coast of Galeota Point, Mayaro, in water depths of 231 feet. It was the second drilling platform constructed in Trinidad and Tobago and the first ever to be built from bottom up. The completion of the Cannonball platform proved to be a milestone in Trinidad and Tobago's history of economic and social achievements by providing a catalyst for its local content initiative and promoting the further development of its platform fabrication business. Using the minimal platform concept, TOFCO constructed bpTT Cannonball's topside and jacket, each weighing 800 tons.

The third major project contracted to TOFCO was the construction of the EOG Oilbird platform, a 1,000-ton deck with a 1,300-ton jacket. The project began in March 2005 and was completed in June 2006. The Oilbird platform was a partnership among EOG, NGC, Petrotrin and the Neal and Massy Wood Group Ltd. The EOG Oilbird was the first offshore process facility designed in Trinidad and Tobago with an estimated 74 percent local workforce, making it yet another local content initiative.

The fourth project undertaken by TOFCO was the fabrication of the BP Red Mango and BP Cashima platforms, both clones of BP Cannonball. In 2007, TOFCO was contracted by BG to construct the BG/Fluor Poinsettia which was completed in October 2008. With a deck weighing 4,000 tons, it was the largest platform deck structure at the time of unveiling. This was followed by the EOG Toucan and the BP Savonette platforms.

General Manager at TOFCO, Suresh Gangabissoon noted that the initial services offered by the company ranged from offshore fabrication to the provision of upkeep and maintenance, which later evolved to a larger role in the actual fabrication of platform structures. He emphasized the ability of local fabrication companies to compete fully with their foreign counterparts in the Gulf of Mexico, the traditional location for platform fabrication. He said once training in advanced welding techniques and platform management was provided, Trinidad and Tobago would enjoy national competence in this field, thus increasing the extent of local content in the oil industry. In addition, he emphasized that the joint venture with Chet Morrison Contractors Inc. provided the technical capacity and knowledge to perform at high levels and has accelerated the growth of the company's capability. The key challenges resulted from having to import steel, electrical and installation equipment and

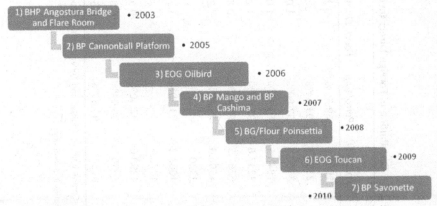

Figure 2.3. Tofco Platform Fabrication Project Completion Timeline.

Table 2.4.   Distribution of Foreign Direct Investment by Sector 1992-2004

Year	Total FDI	Petroleum	Food, Drink & Tobacco	Chemicals & Non-Metallic Minerals	Assembly Type & Related Industries	Distribution	All Other Sectors
1992	1003.8	89.59%	-0.29%	0.18%	0.18%	0.94%	9.41%
1993	2194.6	93.64%	0.51%	0.03%	-0.11%	1.13%	4.80%
1994	3120.3	52.80%	1.09%	24.70%	-0.37%	0.19%	21.57%
1995	1848.1	89.96%	1.08%	0.57%	-0.14%	2.10%	6.43%
1996	2237.6	93.94%	1.21%	0.64%	0.20%	1.23%	2.78%
1997	6267.5	95.46%	0.84%	0.23%	-0.01%	0.31%	3.17%
1998	4596.3	76.47%	1.24%	0.30%	-0.01%	0.27%	16.26%
1999*	2320						
2000	4063.2	93.80%	-3.26%	0.28%	-2.81%	0.26%	15.59%
2001*	4870.5						
2002	4290.6	92.40%	0.52%	0.22%	1.17%	-0.10%	5.79%
2003	3656	88.04%	0.82%	0.33%	0.91%	0.38%	9.52%
2004	6128	93.55%	0.59%	0.23%	0.89%	0.28%	4.07%

Source: Central Bank of Trinidad and Tobago Annual Economic Survey Various Issues, http://www.central-bank.org.tt

*Information not available

from the demographics of the workforce with its high percentage of younger employees who required more training and management skill.

In his Budget Speech of 2004-05, the Prime Minister and Minister of Finance indicated his Government's intention to review the Petroleum Tax Legislation which had worked so effectively in stimulating Foreign Direct Investment, particularly in exploration and in the downstream natural gas-based industries, since the tax law changes of 1992.

The 2004–2005 Budget Speech noted that the 1992 tax regime was predicated on an oil-based economy but that natural gas had long since (1996) surpassed it as the major energy form being produced in the country in barrels-of-oil equivalence. After some delay, the new petroleum legislation was passed in Parliament in 2006 and made effective retroactive to 01 Jan 2005. However, its focus was on collecting the windfall profits that were accruing to the gas producers while seeking to harmonize the tax code as it applied to both the E&P License and the Production Sharing Contract (PSC) by formally legislating a taxable PSC.

In the meantime, the National Gas Company had completed a 56-inch cross-island pipeline to provide the transmission capacity to supply ALNG Train IV as well as additional industries earmarked for the La Brea and Union Industrial Estates, the latter having been relocated east of the original site. An offshore 36-inch pipeline had also been constructed in 2006 to increase the company's transmission capacity to 1.4 bcfd. Further, the gas processing

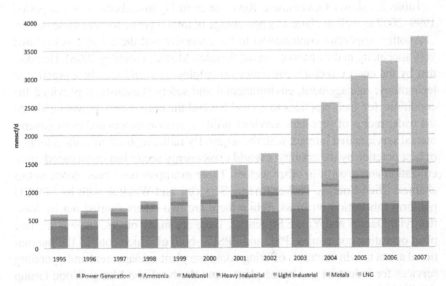

Figure 2.4. Natural Gas Production and Utilization.

capability at Phoenix Park Gas Processing Ltd., of which NGC is a 39 percent partner, was expanded steadily to 1350 mmscfd.

NATURAL GAS PRODUCTION AND UTILIZATION

By 2007 crude oil production had slipped to 115,000 bopd. Refinery production had stabilized over the previous decade at approximately 160,000 bopd, with a further very costly upgrade initiated at the Pointe-a-Pierre Refinery. The new upgrade sought principally to produce the more demanding gasoline quality required by the environmental standards of the premium markets of the USA. Natural gas sales had, however, increased dramatically to 3,800 million cubic feet as LNG came on stream. Installed electric power had grown to 1,594 megawatts with plans for another 700 megawatt IPP, well on the way to meeting the requirements for an aluminium smelter. By 2007, Gross Domestic Product had jumped to TT$102,000 (US$16,500) per capita, a significant increase over the per capita level of US$5,300 just 10 years before.

This was due in large part to the conflation of three factors: the sharp increase in natural gas sales as LNG Trains I, II, III, and IV came on stream (see Figure 2.2); the increase in the international prices for energy in November 2005 which saw natural gas prices at Henry Hub reaching US$15 per mcf with Far East buyers of LNG in 2007 paying almost US$20 per mcf, and finally, the petroleum taxation changes effective January 1, 2005.

Table 2.5 shows Government Revenue from Hydrocarbons over the period 1999–2007 as well its share as a percentage of total revenue for that same period.

Another important contribution to the economy and the country is captured very succinctly in the observations of Wendell Mottley (Mottley 2008). He notes that by the energy sector's insistence on employing worldwide best practice in technology, management, environmental and safety standards, it provided the conditions for such practices to spread beyond the core energy players and into the wider radius of suppliers, services, utilities, subcontractors and even governmental services that interact with the sector. By radiating outwards, the adoption of best practice by the country's world class energy sector has encouraged modernization and growth in other sectors. Three examples have been noted in this chapter: Clico Energy, Tucker Energy Services, and Weldfab with its TOFCO platform fabrication business. While there are two others singled out by Mottley, viz: Damus and Yorke Structures, there are many others, such as the two plant operating companies IPSL and PPSL—both of which entered the international arena to win contracts offering complete plant management and operating services for industrial gas-based plant—and the Neal and Massy Wood Group (NMWG) joint venture. Thus, even companies in the basic services sector aspired to world class status.

Table 2.5. Government Revenue: Petroleum and Total 1998–2006 ($TT Mn)

Year	Total Current Revenue (TT)	Petroleum Revenue (TT)	Petroleum Rev as % of Current Revenue
1998	9629.4	1706.9	17.7
1999	9613.2	1999.7	20.8
2000	13006.7	4475.6	34.4
2001	13379.9	3693.5	27.6
2002	14517.2	3931	27.1
2003	17852.6	6904.7	38.7
2004	20624.7	7641.1	37.0
2005	29008.7	13360.4	46.1
2006e	38479.6	21385.3	55.6
2007e	40034.0	20079.2	50.1

Source: Central Bank of Trinidad and Tobago Annual Economic Survey Various Issues www.central-bank. org.tt, and Gregory McGuire

BIBLIOGRAPHY

Barrionuevo, Alexei. "How Trinidad Became a Big Supplier of Liquified Natural Gas to the U.S." *Wall street Journal* (Wall Street Journal), 2001.

International Energy Agency. "Natural Gas Review." 2006.

Ministry of Energy and Energy Industries. *Local Content and Participation Policy Framework.* GOTT, 2004.

Mottley, Wendell. *Industrial Policy in Trinidad and Tobago 1959-2006.* Kingston: Ian Randle, 2007.

Chapter Three

Managing the Resource-Based Economy in Times of Plenty

Gregory McGuire

INTRODUCTION

The comparatively poor economic development outcomes of natural resource-rich developing countries relative to their resource-poor counterparts are well documented in the economic literature. The cyclical and volatile nature of commodity markets makes countries that are dependent on resource exports vulnerable to boom and bust economic cycles. The phenomenon, often referred to as the "Resource Curse," was first used by Auty to describe how countries rich in natural resources were unable to use their wealth to boost their economies and how, counter-intuitively, their growth rates are lower than those of countries without natural resources (Auty and Gleb 1986). While not an extreme case, the Trinidad and Tobago economy offers one example.

Blessed with significant reserves of hydrocarbons, the Trinidad and Tobago economy experienced two periods of economic boom in its post-Independence history. The first, from 1974 to 1982, was followed by a period of economic decline that extended for a decade; the second, from 2002 to 2008, came to a very abrupt end with the global recession of 2008, triggered in part by the financial crisis in the industrialized countries of the world. Both periods were marked by record increases in hydrocarbon output and prices that, together, generated windfall revenues for Trinidad and Tobago. On the basis of these higher inflows, Government increased spending on both economic and social fronts in order to meet its broad development goals. This was reflected, at first, in relatively high economic growth rates for the period of boom, followed thereafter by stagnation and decline and, ultimately, by a large fiscal deficit with its attendant problems. Whether Trinidad and Tobago made the most of its hydrocarbon windfall is subject to conjecture. However, when history repeats over a period of thirty years, questions should be asked.

In this case, the effectiveness of the Government's macro-economic management strategy for avoiding the "resource curse" needs to be placed under review. This essay examines macro-economic management in the Trinidad and Tobago economy, with an emphasis on the seven-year period 2002–2008 and with comparison to the first boom period of 1974–1982.

The essay is laid out as follows: The opening section reviews some of the theoretical and empirical studies on macroeconomic management of hydrocarbon-based economies. This is followed by a description of the Trinidad and Tobago experience over the two periods of boom. Next, Government choices in the aftermath of the second boom are evaluated against some of the policy guidelines developed by local and international experts. This assessment covers the choices made between consumption and savings, the distribution of expenditure among competing ends, and the provision made for the future. The final section proffers some conclusions and takes a look at the unique challenges posed by the gas economy as opposed to the old oil economy.

THEORIES OF THE PETROLEUM ECONOMY

Much of the theoretical and empirical work on the management of oil wealth post-dates the first oil boom (1974-1982). Perhaps it was precisely the post-boom experience that motivated Richard Auty, Jeffery Sachs and Andrew M. Warner and others to address the issue. In an excellent survey of the literature, Paul Stevens traces the evidence, transmission mechanisms and mitigation measures of the resource curse (Stevens 2003). For empirical evidence, he cites the work of Sachs and Warner which examined the relationship between natural resource-based exports and economic growth in the period 1970 to 1990 from a sample of 95 developing countries (Sachs and Warner 1997). They found only two countries in the list of resource abundant developing countries—Malaysia and Mauritius—that sustained even a 2 percent per annum growth between 1970–1980. Sachs and Warner concluded that "resource abundance does have some innately damaging effects on economic performance." Several other studies by Auty, Lal and Myint and Sachs and Warner support the case that countries that benefit from a large endowment of natural resources often perform worse than those without natural resources (Auty 1993), (Lal and Myint 1996), (Sachs and Warner 1997).

Several hypotheses have been offered for the persistent macro-economic imbalances in resource-rich developing countries. George Soros posits three instrumental factors: exchange rate appreciation, the disruptive effects on the economy of highly volatile commodity prices, and the effects on political conditions (Sachs, Humphries and Stilglitz 2007).

The most popular explanation for the resource curse phenomenon may be the "Dutch Disease" hypothesis. Developed by economists W. Max Corden and J. Peter Neary in 1982, the Dutch Disease hypothesis was based on the experience of the Netherlands following the discovery of oil and gas in the 1960s (Corden and Neary 1982). According to their model, an economy may be conceptualized as having three major sectors: a booming resource sector, a lagging (non-booming) tradeable sector—such as agriculture and manufacturing—and a non-traded goods and services sector (construction). Under such conditions, a resource boom will affect an economy in two ways. Firstly, it will increase demand for labour and wages in the booming sector thereby causing a shift in resources towards the booming sector and away from the lagging sectors, such as agriculture as in the case of Trinidad and Tobago. The second effect is more powerful. The boom provides Government with windfall revenues that support the expansion of expenditure in non-tradable sectors like construction and public services. As demand for labour in these sectors increases, resources drift from other productive sectors to the non-tradable sector. Increased demand in the economy causes prices and costs to rise, thereby further eroding the competitiveness of the lagging tradable sector. The result is a decline in output and employment in the lagging sectors—a phenomenon described as de-industrialization—leaving the economy structurally weaker than in the pre-boom period.

While the resource curse hypothesis has gained currency over the last three decades, questions remain about its validity as an explanation of the problems faced by resource-rich underdeveloped countries. A case can be made that the root cause of the problem might lie in institutional and structural deficiencies rather than in commodity price swings or revenue mismanagement.

Nearly two decades before the chronicling of the Dutch Disease concept, Dudley Seers sought to explain the problem in a seminal essay, "Mechanisms of an Open Petroleum Economy" (Seers 1964).The Seers model posited that the petroleum sector dominates the economy in terms of export earnings and Government revenues. The dominant sector causes distortions in wage, income and pricing levels to the detriment of other sectors in the economy. The large inflows of foreign exchange during boom conditions mask underlying weaknesses in the Balance of Payments. In addition, chronic social and economic inequalities are ignored during boom conditions but are made manifest in the immediate aftermath of the boom, often triggering economic hardship and social unrest.

A third strand of inquiry hypothesises about the nature of the "Rentier Economy" (Beblawi and Luciana 1987). For Beblawi, the oil rentier economy is defined by three main characteristics:

1. Rent is the predominant income
2. The origin of the rent is external; and most importantly

3. A minority of the population is engaged in the generation of the rent while the majority is involved in the distribution and utilization of it.

In the oil rentier economy, the industry is essentially an enclave. It contributes massive amounts of external rents in the form of foreign exchange paid to Government as taxes and royalties. The State becomes the major intermediary between the oil sector and the rest of the economy and state expenditure drives the rest of the economy. Without budgetary constraints, the Government embarks on large capital-intensive projects, some of which have little commercial or social viability, typically characterized by short-term employment benefits but longer term costs in terms of maintenance and debt.

The rentier economy nurtures a huge counter-productive force in the rentier mentality, which results in a break of the cause-effect link between work and reward. This is fed by the Government's short-term unemployment relief-type programmes which become entrenched. There is a profound loss of productivity as increasing numbers seek to capitalize on available rents by doing as little as possible and embarking on rent-seeking activity. The demand for imports spirals while domestic goods decline, both in terms of competitiveness and output. Consequently, as the boom draws to a close, foreign exchange reserves quickly dissipate, and with the productive sectors destroyed, the economy is unable to sustain growth.

There is no intention here to debate the merits or demerits of these hypotheses. What can be said conclusively, however, is that the economy of Trinidad and Tobago evinced features of each of the foregoing theoretical explanations, to varying degrees over the period of the two booms.

Economists—both institutional and private—along with others have been just as prolific in prescribing solutions to the phenomenon. In the main, solutions revolve around expenditure restraint, increased savings, productive investments, increased transparency, fiscal rules and economic transformation. Jeffery Sachs contends that the key to avoiding the resource curse and promoting development is an investment strategy in public goods that is growth focused with long-term objectives (Sachs, Humphries and Stilglitz 2007).

For Sachs a successful development strategy should have three components:

1. A time path of public investments suited to national circumstances
2. An economic policy framework to support private sector economic activity
3. A political framework to ensure the rule of law and macro-economic stability

Sachs' key recommendation is that oil income should be turned into public investments rather than into increased private consumption. Developing public goods such as infrastructure, health care and education, directly benefits the population while simultaneously facilitating private investment, both local and foreign. Controlled investment spending would avoid squeezing the non-oil tradable goods sector and create minimal and limited exchange rate effects.

The experiences of some resource-rich countries such as Norway, Botswana, Chile and UAE have given credence to the view that part of the solution to avoiding the resource curse is to save windfall earnings, typically to support any one of three purposes: future earnings, short-term revenue stabilization or investments. The first decade of the twenty-first century saw a proliferation of sovereign wealth funds, both resource and non-resource based. The Sovereign Wealth Institute lists 58 SWF as at September 2009. While this mechanism has grown increasingly popular, Sachs is of the view that this may not be the most appropriate choice for poor countries.

"In essence, policy makers face a choice among four kinds of long-lasting assets: oil in the ground; financial assets (e.g. foreign exchange reserves), physical assets (e.g. roads, hospitals) and human capital. For an oil-rich country like Norway with extensive physical and human capital already in place, the best choice may well be to accumulate financial assets to cover long-term costs of the public pension system. For poor countries, however, it is likely to make much more sense to turn oil earnings quickly into physical assets and human capital" (Humphreys, Sachs and Stiglitz, 2007 pps.189-190).

Revenue Watch Institute (RWI) and the Extractive Industries Transparency Initiative (EITI) have recommended institutional strengthening to foster greater transparency in payment and spending of oil revenues, as a means of avoiding the resource curse. For RWI, many of the problems of oil-rich developing nations stem from a lack of transparency which breeds widespread corruption.[1] The work of the RWI is supported by the EITI which aims to have oil companies disclose publicly the amount of taxes and royalties paid to governments.

The International Monetary Fund has tended to focus on fiscal rules to manage the influx of new revenue flows. Sachs points to five recommendations of the IMF, namely: minimize the risks of Dutch Disease; seek enhanced growth in the short to medium term; promote good governance and reduce corruption; prepare an exit strategy; and regularly reassess the appropriate policy mix (Humphreys, Sachs and Stiglitz, 2007, pps. 191).

In the specific context of Trinidad and Tobago, as the economy entered the second boom of the period under review, which was based initially on natural gas expansion, there was widespread national concern that mistakes of the past would be repeated. As a result, policy prescriptions were volunteered on the management of the gas windfall from local and foreign sources.

An IMF Staff paper recommended that the "sustainable non-energy overall deficit of the central Government which will ensure that energy wealth and total debt remain constant over time is 8% of non energy GDP under the base case assumptions and varies between 6% and 10% with changes in interest rates and the level of reserves" (Velculescu and Rizanvi 2005).

In 2005, Lloyd Best and Eric St Cyr advanced proposals for a macro-economic framework designed to manage the economy during periods of boom while engaging in the task of long term transformation. For Best and St Cyr, the imperative was to build the onshore economy since, as they saw it, the off-shore economy was based on depleting assets that would sooner or later come to an end (Best and St Cyr 2005). Key elements of Best's proposals were:

1. Budgeting based on fixed price of oil and natural gas, based on the long-run average. At that time a price of US$25/bbl for oil and $3.25 for gas was suggested.
2. The establishment of four separate funds to which budgetary allocations were to be made:
   a. The Heritage Fund: future generations' share of the national patrimony
   b. The Provident Fund: for building the stock of economic and social capital
   c. A Stabilization Fund: to smooth the flow of revenue over time. For Best, all surpluses over and above the Budgeted energy revenue were to be placed in the Fund
   d. A Sterilization Fund: a holding place for money in order to regulate the flow of liquidity to the system so that the volume of currency in circulation bears the desired relation to the real resources available. In short, financial flows must match productive capacity.
      According to Best, "the objective of these Funds is not to limit Government spending but to redirect it away from excessive current consumption to planned long term investment" (Best and St Cyr, 2005, pps. 28–29).
3. Emphasis on onshore transformation. Best argued that the imperative for the Government was to meet the legitimate demands for equity while avoiding waste-expanding capacity and promoting transformation towards sustainability. In sum, surpluses earned in the offshore energy sector should be used to transform the onshore non-energy sector seeking to free it from its historical dependence on foreign exchange earned offshore (Best and St Cyr, 2005).

The Vision 2020 Sub-Committee on Macroeconomics and Finance found some common ground with both Staff papers highlighted above. The Committee noted that Vision 2020 required a much faster growth rate of GDP than the country had ever experienced. It cautioned, however, that for such growth rates to be sustainable, an appropriate macro-economic framework needed to be put in place.[2]

The Committee urged the establishment of rules or guidelines for fiscal, monetary and incomes policy. Six rules of fiscal policy were prescribed:

1. The Budget must be based on long-term prices of both oil and gas set at a conservative number of say US$22.00 /bbl (WTI) and $3.00/mmbtu for LNG f.o.b Trinidad for an extended period of five years
2. A balanced Budget should be achieved after allocation to the Revenue Stabilization Fund and the Heritage Fund
3. The ratio of Government expenditure (recurrent plus capital expenditure) to GDP should not exceed 30 percent of GDP over the medium term
4. Reductions in taxation must pass the test of sustainability, which would take into account the projected growth of expenditure and the variability of revenue from the energy sector
5. The ratio of Total Debt to GDP must be reduced to no more than 50 percent within five years
6. The Government should not be directly involved in activities which can be handled by the private sector or non-governmental organizations, except in the case of strategic investments, where Government investments should typically be time and size-bound.

While the above prescriptions were not binding on the Government, they provided a broad framework for pursuing macro-economic policy and a useful basis for assessing the efficacy of macro-economic management.

THE FIRST BOOM 1973–1982: A BRIEF RECAP

Trinidad and Tobago and other oil exporters experienced unprecedented increases in oil revenues in the period 1973 to 1982. In general, the windfall revenues were fuelled by a sharp increase in oil prices. Between 1973 and 1974 there was a near four-fold increase in oil prices, from US$2.71 to US$9.76. This was followed by smaller increments until 1979 when the Iran-Iraq War contributed to another big jump from US$17/bbl to US$28/bbl in 1980. In the case of Trinidad and Tobago, price increases were supplemented by growth in oil production. Crude oil production increased steadily from 166 thousand barrels per day in 1973 to a peak of 229 thousand barrels per day in 1978, before declining to 159 thousand barrels per day in 1983.

The period 1974 to 1982 was one of tremendous prosperity for Trinidad and Tobago. Government revenue increased from a meagre TT$495 million in 1973 to over TT$6 billion in 1982. Expenditure increased along with higher revenues, moving from TT$492 million in 1973 to TT$5.9 billion in 1982.

Table 3.1. Selected Economic Indicators 1973–83

	1973	1974	1975	1976	1977	1978	1979	1980	1981	1982	1983
Changes in GDP (1970 Constant prices)	1.70%	3.80%	1.50%	6.40%	9.10%	10.00%	3.60%	10.40%	4.60%	4.00%	-9.20%
Crude Oil production (000bbls/d)	166.2	186.7	215.4	212.2	229.1	229.6	214.3	212.2	189.3	177	159.8
Crude Oil prices (US $/bbl)	2.7	9.76	10.72	11.51	12.4	12.7	17.26	28.67	32.5	33.47	29.31
Current Account Surplus/ Deficit	-50.7	576	715.9	618.5	414.5	97.1	-87	1132.2	956.4	-1615	-2464
Inflation	14.9	21.9	17.1	10.3	11.8	10.2	14.7	17.5	14.3	11.4	16.7
Unemployment	12.8	12.6	13.2	12.5	11.2	9.5	8.3	8	8.6	8.1	9.1
Foreign Exchange Reserves US$	34.23	340.63	755.81	870.94	1335.04	1646.17	2015.75	2640.29	3202.58	2983.38	2082.67
Import Cover	1	4.4	12.2	12.1	16.3	16.6	15.9	15.8	19.5	12.9	9.9

Source: Central Bank of Trinidad and Tobago: Handbook of Key Economic Indicators 1989 GOTT; Central Statistical Office various reports.

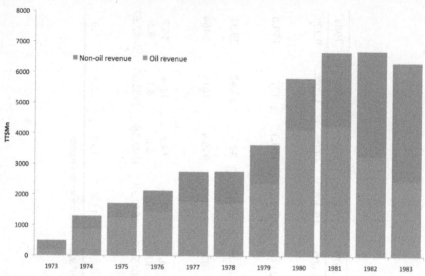

Figure 3.1.   Oil – Non Oil Revenue 1973–1983.

Buoyed by increased Government expenditure, the economy experienced continuous growth in GDP, averaging 5.9 percent per annum, with peaks of 10 .4 percent in 1978 and 1980. In an expanding economy, unemployment fell from a high of 21 percent in 1974 to about 8 percent in 1982. The higher value and volume of oil exports generated rising current account surpluses and a healthy balance of payments position, with foreign exchange reserves climbing from just US$340 million in 1973 to a peak of US $3202.58 million in 1981 (Table 3.1).

Mindful of the potentially temporary nature of the boom, macroeconomic policy in the early years was manifestly very cautious. In 1978, the Government's concern about the level and distribution of expenditure of its fortuitous oil bonanza resulted in the appointment of a committee under the chairmanship of then Central Bank Deputy Governor, Dr. Euric Bobb, to review and make recommendations on patterns of Government expenditure. (Government of Trinidad and Tobago (GOTT) 1978).The Bobb Committee noted three significant shifts in the pattern of Government expenditure:

1. Greater involvement in economic activity or directly productive services. The advent of windfall revenue and the simultaneous availability of abundant natural gas reserves prompted the Government to embark upon a deliberate strategy of resource-based industrialization, marked by the development of the Point Lisas Industrial Estate and the establishment of several energy-based plants with significant state equity.

2. Increasing emphasis on capital expenditure. The Government's capital expenditure outside of its direct industrialization programme was aimed at improving the much maligned public utilities, the overburdened, grossly inadequate infrastructure, and social services. There was heavy expenditure on highways and secondary roads, improvements on ports, utilities, transportation, the national airline and education through a stepped-up school expansion programme.

3. The emergence of welfare expenditure as a major area of budgetary outlay. Transfers and subsidies were increased in several areas as a deliberate policy of sharing the oil wealth with citizens. Government welfare expenditure took the form of heavy subsidies to both producers and consumers, and to public assistance programmes. In 1973, for example, rice was subsidized. By 1978, the subsidy programme had extended to embrace a wide range of basic foodstuffs including flour, cooking oil, copra, poultry meat and poultry feed. The cost of food subsidies increased from $3.2 million in 1973 to $62.6 million in 1978. In addition, Government continued subsidizing petroleum fuels, public utilities, transportation, electricity and water. The petroleum fuels subsidy amounted to a total of $168 million in revenue foregone between 1974–78. The young and vulnerable were also singled out for attention with the introduction of the school feeding programme and free bus transport for school children and senior citizens.

The Bobb Committee noted that "the allocation of budgetary resources showed a very strong and undesirable preference for satisfaction of current consumption as opposed to improvement of the economy's productive potential." The Committee recommended moderation in the rate and direction of Government expenditure. Further, it recommended that:

1. No new welfare programmes be added
2. A moratorium on tax reductions; and
3. Review of the tax regime and utility tariffs with a view to increasing rates.

However, against a background of further increases in oil prices in 1979 and 1980, the Government accelerated its expenditure along the pattern set in the first five years. Annual growth of current expenditure which averaged 27 percent per annum in the first five years, accelerated to 34 percent per annum between 1979 and 1982. The Bobb Committee had expressed concern about the size of transfers and subsidies, which at that time accounted for 14 percent of Government expenditure. By 1981 it had swollen to 25 percent of Government expenditure.

An attempt was made to spread expenditure over time through the creation of a number of special funds—Funds for Long Term Development—into which budgetary allocations were made for specific projects. In 1980, there were 47 such funds including: Culture, National Parks, Transportation, Primary Schools, Fisheries, Drainage, Airport, etc. Total appropriation was TT$5,360 million (Table 3.4).

When oil prices began to slip in 1983 the weaknesses in the economy were immediately evident, along the lines suggested by Seers. In 1982–83 both the current account and the fiscal account moved into deficit. The stock of foreign exchange reserves quickly dissipated. Unemployment began to rise again as the State could not maintain its previous rate of injections into the non-oil economy.

Notwithstanding criticisms in some quarters (Auty and Gleb, Oil Windfalls in a Small Parliamentary Democracy. Their Impact on Trinidad and Tobago 1986), one of the positive legacies of the first boom period was the State's investment in economic infrastructure, which laid the foundation for the successful transition to a natural gas-based economy. In the period 1975 to 1985, the Government invested some US$3,300 million in gas-based projects, mainly at the Point Lisas Industrial Estate. Table 3.3 shows expenditure on gas-based projects including those that did not materialize over the 1974–82 period. These projects did not yield any short-term payout, resulting in adverse comment from many quarters. By the following decade, however, gas production had exceeded that of oil on a barrel of oil equivalent basis, and within another 10 years would begin to contribute more to the Trinidad economy than oil. The foundation for this growth was established in the 1974–83 period.

THE SECOND BOOM 2001–2008

Unlike the first boom period, the coming of the second energy-inspired economic boom was easily foreseen. The advent of ALNG Train I in 1999 and the signing of agreements for ALNG Trains II and III in 2000 meant the near doubling of natural gas production. This would, potentially, place Government revenue over the medium term on a completely new platform. ALNG Trains II and III came on stream in 2002 and 2003 respectively, followed by ANLG Train IV in 2005. In five short years, therefore, the LNG investments had added another 2.2 bcf/d to natural gas consumption. Growth in ammonia and methanol capacity also contributed to annual growth of natural gas output, from 0.54 tcf/yr in 2001 to 1.35 tcf/yr in 2008, an increase of 250 percent. Meanwhile, crude oil production also increased after BHP Billiton brought

Table 3.2. Trinidad and Tobago Fiscal Position 1974–1983

TT$ Millions

	1973	1974	1975	1976	1977	1978	1979	1980	1981	1982	1983
Current Revenue	495	1300	1715	2131	2755.1	2772.2	3643.8	5819.4	6671.8	6705.5	6322.8
of which Oil	197	889	1254	1447	1770.5	1733.5	2371.1	4136.5	4253.7	3274.2	2461.4
Non Oil	298	411	461	684	984.6	1038.7	1272.7	1682.9	2418.1	3431.3	3861.4
Current Expenditure											
Wages	227.4	343	374.1	469.3	614.6	737.9	1039.4	1213.5	1342.6	2970.6	2698.9
Transfers and Subsidies	119.6	162.2	241	349	271.9	541.2	936.1	1340.4	1593.2	2411.5	2981.5
Goods and Services	111.4	113.3	185.7	204	211.5	251.7	403.5	396.1	378.9	363.4	747.4
Interest	34.5	51.2	47	43.5	42.6	80.3	125.7	125	179.4	160.6	197.1
Total Current Expenditure	492.9	669.7	847.8	1065.8	1140.6	1611.1	2504.7	3075	3494.1	5906.1	6624.9
Current Account Surplus/Deficit	2.1	630.3	867.2	1065.2	1614.5	1161.1	1139.1	2744.4	3177.7	799.4	-302.1
Capital Expenditure	108.5	287.5	353.2	805.1	979.1	1281.4	1686.2	2391.3	3181.1	3583.6	2540
Total Expenditure	601.4	957.2	1201	1870.9	2119.7	2892.5	4190.9	5466.3	6675.2	9489.7	9164.9
Current Prices GDP	2564	4192.7	5300.1	6090.5	7532.8	8549.6	11045.8	14966.1	16438	19175.5	18461.4
Expenditure/GDP	23.46%	22.83%	22.66%	30.72%	28.14%	33.83%	37.94%	36.52%	40.61%	49.49%	49.64%
Debt											
Internal	370.20	387.20	413.50	484.60	557.60	599.10	637.10	661.80	631.20	760.40	1034.80
External	255.70	241.40	222.20	128.90	499.60	756.50	898.50	1047.90	1083.50	1338.10	1551.00
Total	625.90	628.60	635.70	613.50	1057.20	1355.60	1535.60	1709.70	1714.70	2098.50	2585.80
Debt/GDP Ratio	24.41%	14.99%	11.99%	10.07%	14.03%	15.86%	13.90%	11.42%	10.43%	10.94%	14.01%
Foreign Exchange Reserves (US$ Millions)	34.23	340.63	755.81	870.94	1335.04	1646.17	2015.75	2640.29	3202.58	2983.38	2082.67
Import Cover Months)	1	4.4	12.2	12.1	16.3	16.6	15.9	15.8	19.5	12.9	9.9

Source: Central Bank of Trinidad and Tobago: Handbook of Key Economic Indicators. 1989

Table 3.3. Expenditure on Energy Based Projects: 1974–1983 (TT$ Mn)

	1974	1975	1976	1977	1978	1979	1980	1981	1982	1983	Total
Payment for Shell T'dad Ltd.	69,631.20	23909.3				150	171				93,861.50
Loan To Trintoc	637.8					2500					3,137.80
Registration of Trintoc	25.1	77.7									102.80
Payment to Commonwealth Fund For Technical Corporation re Energy-based Projects	500										500.00
Gas Transmission 24"		15,597.70	6,778.40	9068.1	1443.9	732.6					33,620.70
Fertrin Fertilizer JV (Amoco)			13.6	66.6	5406	49510.3	17850	62440	12240	55080	202,606.50
Regional Aluminium Smelter		250	150	364.3	464.9	16					1,245.20
Polyester Fibre			18.8	40.3							59.10
Petrochemical Complex			75.5	178	68						321.50
*Iron and Steel Project		987	7,670.00	82,725.10	169,741.00		242,015.80	78,406.00	349,060.00	140,000.00	1,070,604.90
*National Gas Company		77.1	3,154.80	70,436.20		7,999.20	37,715.30	167,574.40	47,196.50	90,023.80	424,177.30
*Tringen	1074.4		96,041.00	20,555.70	1,687.10						119,358.20
*Texaco – Part Purchase			10,250.00	11,448.80					9,500.00	1,960.20	33,159.00
*Point Lisas Development			1,100.00	654.1	82.6						1,836.70
Point Lisas Power Station			27,974.80	18,806.10	22,198.90	85,139.10					154,618.90
*PLIPDECO	500	100	3,300.00	5,500.00	1,118.60	3,458.20		10,000.00	3,773.40	14,259.90	41,510.10
*New Generating Plant at Penal			13,575.00	3,170.00	810	1,090.00			33,840.00	2,826.00	55,311.00
*Point Lisas–Sir Solomon Hochoy Highway			526.4	23.8		2,481.60					3,031.80

											Total
*National Energy Corp.						2,000.00	8,518.00	112,979.00	159,036.80	148,871.40	431,405.20
*Urea Project						1,200.00			57,388.00	53,942.00	112,530.00
*Trinidad Cement Ltd.					2,380.00	8,353.20	65,269.20	80,490.90	16,611.00	16,864.40	189,968.70
*Liquid Natural Gas Project					511.4	1,415.70					1,927.10
*Trinidad Cement Ltd. – Upgrade									11,690.50	46,864.40	58,554.90
*Second Cross-country National Gas Pipeline									25,000.00	32,945.00	57,945.00
*Second Offshore Gas Pipeline–Advance NGC									47,100.00	108,972.20	156,072.20
*ISCOTT–Construction of Dock Facilities at Point Lisas									5,548.00	5,034.40	10,582.40
*NEC Methanol Plant Mgm't Information Systems									53,800.00	46,950.00	100,750.00
*NEC–Equity Injection re Construction of Point Lisas Harbour									14,000.00		14,000.00
*Point Lisas Industrial Estate–Diversion									3,773.40	4,300.00	8,073.40
Point Lisas– Phase II–Supply & Installation of 33B MW Generating Plant									1,174.00		
TOTAL	71,868.50	41,498.80	170,628.30	223,037.10	206,062.40	166,066.90	371,368.30	511,890.30	850,731.60	768,893.70	3,380,871.90

Source: GOTT Accounting for the Petrodollar, 1982

Table 3.4. Special Fund for Long Term Development: 1974-1983

	Fund	Date Created		Fund	Date Created
1	Food and Agriculture	1979	25	National Parks development	1977
2	Fisheries Development	1974	26	Co-operative Societies Development	1976
3	Public Transport	1979	27	Tobago Development	1977
4	Petroleum Development	1974	28	Land Acquisition	1977
5	Primary School	1979	29	Local Government Areas Development	1977
6	Building Projects	1974	30	National Shipping Services	1977
7	Infrastructure Development	1975	31	Sewerage	1978
8	Caribbean Integration	1975	32	Airport	1978
9	Education	1976	33	Equipment	1978
10	Port Development	1976	34	Library services	1978
11	Water Resources	1976	35	Construction Materials	1979
12	Roads	1976	36	General Industrial Development	1978
13	Housing	1976	37	International Marketing Organisation	1978
14	Sports	1976	38	Private Housing Estates Sites and Services	1978
15	Drainage	1976	39	Joint Services Staff College	1978
16	Telecommunications	1976	40	School-Feeding Programme	1978
17	Electricity Development	1976	41	Participation in Commercial Enterprises	1979
18	Health	1976	42	International Year of the Child	1979
19	National Training	1976	43	University Medical Complex (Mt. Hope)	
20	Recruitment and Settlement of Nationals	1976	44	National Institute for Higher Education (RST)	
21	Air Transport	1976	45	Racing Authority	
22	Culture	1977	46	Fire Protection and Fire Fighting	
23	Pre-Investment	1977	47	Less Developed Countries (Caricom) Disaster Relief	
24	Social and Community Development Projects	1977			

the Angostura field on stream. Oil production climbed gradually from 114 thousand barrels per day in 2001 to peak at 144 thousand barrels per day in 2005. On the basis of hydrocarbon production alone, therefore, Government revenue in the period 2001–2008 would have been substantially higher than five years earlier. However, from 2002, the fortuitous and simultaneous increases in the prices of all major commodity exports provided a further boost to Government's fiscal position (Table 3.5).

When the PNM administration took office in 2002, it articulated its vision of making Trinidad and Tobago a developed nation by 2020. By 2004, the Vision 2020 National Development plan was completed providing the Government with a roadmap. As in the boom of 1974–1982, a flood of additional revenues removed fiscal constraints to development. The Government, therefore, moved expeditiously to implement programmes to meet the goals of Vision 2020 which required a growth rate of not less than 9 percent per year. This was the context within which fiscal policy would be played out during the period 2004 to 2008.

Over the period 2001–2008, the State collected TT $225 billion in revenue, of which the energy sector—i.e. mainly E&P companies taxed under the Petroleum Taxes Act—contributed 45 percent or $102.9 billion. If the energy sector is defined to include the petrochemical sector and downstream processing plants, the share of energy sector revenues then rises to 51 percent or $130 billion. Total Government expenditure amounted to $177 billion, with recurrent expenditure taking the lion's share of 85 percent of the total. Expenditure climbed at an annual average rate of 13 percent per year, compared with revenue growth of 20 percent per year (Table 3.9). The increases in revenue were particularly steep in the years 2007 and 2008, when all commodity prices hit record levels. Between 2002 and 2008, the price of oil increased by 381 percent, natural gas by 264 percent, ammonia by 378 percent and methanol by 274 percent. Government expenditure patterns reflected some of its Vision 2020 priorities. Overall, whereas wages and salaries had constituted the largest share in the first boom period, they now played second fiddle to transfers and subsidies, which accounted for 41 percent of Government outlays.

In delivering the 2007–8 Budget in his capacity as Finance Minister, Prime Minister Patrick Manning provided a comprehensive accounting statement on the distribution of expenditure over the six year period 2002–07, as captured in Table 3.7

The picture that emerges is one in which Government transfers—broadly defined to include the three categories of transfers (households, state enterprises and educational institutions) the Unemployment Relief Programme (URP) and the Community Environmental Protection and Enhancement Programme (CEPEP)—were the dominant features of expenditure. This in

Table 3.5. Selected Economic Indicators: 2002–2008

	2001	2002	2003	2004	2005	2006	2007	2008
Changes in GDP (2000 Constant prices)	4.3%	6.8%	13.2%	7.9%	5.8%	13.5%	4.6%	2.3%
Oil production (Bbls /Day)	113.5	130.6	134.6	122.9	144.4	142.7	120.6	114.3
Natural Gas Utilization (tcf/yr)	0.54	0.63	0.92	1.04	1.11	1.34	1.40	1.35
Crude Oil prices (WTI US$ /bbl)	25.98	26.18	31.08	41.51	56.64	66.05	72.34	99.67
Natural Gas Prices (Henry Hub)	4.05	3.37	5.49	6.18	9.01	6.98	7.11	8.90
Ammonia (US$/tonne Caribbean)	138.0	111.0	201.0	252.0	281.0	278.0	291.0	420.0
Methanol (US$/tonne)	203.0	164.0	257.0	265.0	284.0	376.0	434.0	450.0
Current Account Surplus/Deficit (US$Mn)	946.0	76.0	985.0	1647.1	3598.0	7270.5	5364.3	8791.9
Inflation (%)	5.5	4.2	3.8	3.7	6.9	8.3	7.9	12
Unemployment (%)	10.8	10.4	10.5	8.4	8	6.2	5.5	4.6
Foreign Exchange Reserves (US$)	1858.0	1907.4	2241.8	2976.8	4771.4	6760.6	7038.6	10021.0
Import Cover (mths.)	5.1	4.9	4.6	6.9	7.9	9.9	9.4	11.5

Source: Central Bank of Trinidad and Tobago: Annual Economic Survey. Various Issues.

Table 3.6. Distribution of Government Expenditure

	1974–83	2001–08
Wages and Salaries	43	25
Transfers and Subsidies	39	41
Goods and Services	12	15
Interest payments	3	14

Source: Table 3.2 and Table 3.9

part reflects the considerable importance placed on ensuring that the energy wealth was distributed in a manner that would improve the quality of life.

The Government's social investment programme placed heavy emphasis on education, health, housing and the widening of the social safety net.

In the field of education, the Vision 2020 goal of increasing the number of nationals trained at tertiary level from 4 percent to 45 percent of the population by 2020 was vigorously pursued by the establishment of the University

Table 3.7. Distribution of Government Revenue 2002–07

Head	Amount $TT	Notes
Revenue		
Total Revenue	$162 billion	Energy = $ 69.7 billion Non Energy = $ 93 billion
Expenditure		
Wages and Salaries	29.2 billion	Includes two rounds of salary adjustments for public servants
Goods and Services	17.1 billion	Medicines, school books, computers, materials, etc
Interest Payments	14.9 billion	Payments on local and foreign debt
Subsidies	6.1 billion	Includes Gasoline subsidy – $3.9 billion and sea and air bridge to Tobago $1 billion
Transfers to educational Institutions	5.3 billion	Payments to UWI, UTT, Secondary Schools, GATE
Transfers to Households	15.5 billion	Public Officers pension, social security grants, social assistance, disability grants
Transfers to State Enterprises	18.8 billion	Largest recipients BWIA, CARONI, WASA, Airports Authority
Tobago House of Assembly	5 billion	
Unemployment Relief	1.5 billion	
CEPEP	1 billion	
Total	125 billion	

Source: GOTT Ministry of Finance Budget Speech 2007-8

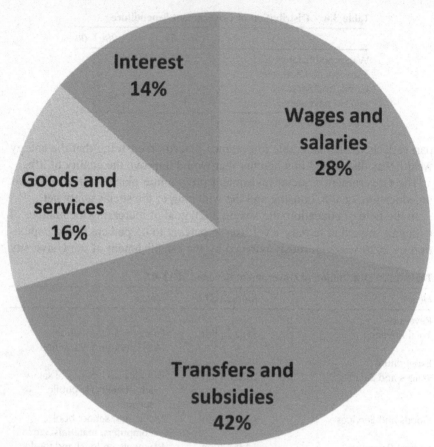

Figure 3.2. Distribution of Govt Expenditure 2002–2008.

of Trinidad and Tobago (UTT), increased intake at the University of the West Indies (UWI) and the provision of financial support for tertiary education through the Government Assistance for Tuition Expenses (GATE) and the Higher Education Loan Programme (HELP). Multiple avenues for Technical and Vocational skills training were also introduced over the period, as the Government attempted to enhance the national human capital. Table 3.8 provides a listing of the major programmes primarily focused on youth and single women. According to World Development indicators, the number of males enrolled in tertiary education in Trinidad and Tobago increased from 4.94 percent of the male population in 2000, to 10.8 percent in 2005. Total student enrolment in UWI doubled from 8,667 in the 2000-01 academic year to 16,094 in 2008/09. The development of a seamless education system from nursery to tertiary was another of the Government's Vision 2020 goals in

Table 3.8. Skills Training Programmes

Skills Training Programmes 2001–2009

Programme	Full Name/Purpose	Persons Trained 2005
OJT	On the Job Training	5234
MUST	Multi Skills Training	1330
HYPE	Helping Youth Prepare For Employment	
CCC	Civilian Conservation Corp	3697
YAPA	Youth Apprenticeship Programme in Agriculture	2617
YTEPPP	Youth training and employment Partnership programme	6029
PCA	Patient Care Assistant Programme	N.A.
GAP	Geriatric Adolescent programme	825
NTST	Non Traditional Skills Training for Women	
MiLAT	Military Led Academic Training	
MIPART	Military Led Programme of Apprenticeship and Reorientation Training	

Source: Conrad Enil; Accounting for the Resources: 2005

education. This spurred the construction of over 90 Early Childhood Care and Education centres across the country.

The Government's investment in health also featured multiple programmes aimed at reducing the cost of, and improving access to health care for citizens. These initiatives included the Chronic Disease Assistance Programme (CDAP) which provided free medication to people suffering from diabetes and hypertension among other ailments, free eye and other elective surgeries and improvement to cancer treatment facilities. The Government's housing programme was arguably the most ambitious and visible element of its social investment strategy.

Pursuant to the Vision 2020 goal of ensuring access to adequate and affordable housing[3] for all citizens, the Government set a target of constructing 8,000 housing units per year beginning 2004. As at fiscal 2008, 32,000 units had been delivered, sold to citizens at subsidized prices under soft mortgage terms. Home ownership was further facilitated by the introduction of the Rent to Own programme and the provision of Home Improvement Grants to those who could not afford to purchase a new home immediately. However, an accelerated housing development programme, along with an Urban Development Programme and other major infrastructure works, stretched the productive capacity of the construction sector beyond its limits, creating shortages and bottlenecks and fuelling inflationary pressures reminiscent of the first boom period.

Table 3.9. Trinidad and Tobago Fiscal Position 2001–2008 (TT$ Mn)

	2001	2002	2003	2004	2005	2006	2007	2008
Current Revenue	13379	14495	17852	22020	31910	38553	40210	46677
of which Oil	3508	3668.7	6904.6	8159.3	15851.8	21111.5	19365.9	24331.8
% share	26.22%	25.31%	38.68%	37.05%	49.68%	54.76%	48.16%	52.13%
Non Oil	9871	10826.9	10947.9	13860.7	16058.6	17441.9	20844.3	22345.8
Current Expenditure								
Wages	4091.2	4140.7	4627.8	4998.2	5304.4	5492.6	6576	6352.7
Transfers and Subsidies	3157.4	3525.7	4148.8	6268.1	8177.3	10756.6	10371.1	12609.5
Goods and Services	1481.6	1753.8	1952.1	2440.4	3004.5	3742.4	4168.1	4177.1
Interest	2311.4	2409	2493.8	2396.3	2541.5	2453.3	2698.1	3016.1
Total Current Expenditure	11041.6	11829.2	13222.5	16103	19027.7	22444.9	23813.3	26155.4
year on year increase		7.13%	11.78%	21.78%	18.16%	17.96%	6.10%	9.84%
Current Surplus/Deficit	2337.4	2665.8	4629.5	5917	12882.3	16108.1	16396.7	20521.6
Capital Expenditure	861.1	671.6	844	1645.3	3135.9	4757.8	8407.5	7225.6
Total Expenditure	11902.7	12500.8	14066.5	17748.3	22163.6	27202.7	32220.8	33381
Current Prices GDP	56700	56290	70718	79826	100682	115951.2	132280.8	163324.9
Expenditure/GDP	20.99%	22.21%	19.89%	22.23%	22.01%	23.46%	24.36%	20.44%
Debt								
Internal	9953.50	10729.00	11104.20	11501.60	11457.70	11855.80	13249.9	14802.4
External	10495.17	9759.33	9783.90	7878.78	11721.78	8159.76	8770.86	9089.64
Total	20448.67	20488.33	20888.10	19380.38	23179.48	20015.56	22020.76	23892.04
Debt/GDP Ratio	0.36	0.36	0.30	0.24	0.23	0.17	0.17	0.15

ECONOMIC IMPACT

The increase in investment, output and spending reverberated in the performance of the economy. Over the period 2002 to 2008, the economy grew at a rate of 7.7 percent/yr., which was among the highest in the world. Near full employment was achieved as unemployment fell to an all-time low of 4.6 percent in December 2008. Foreign construction firms and workers helped to bridge the gap in manpower availability and productive capacity. The local manufacturing sector appears to have responded well to the stimulus of increased Government expenditure. The all-industry index of domestic production (excluding the energy sector), recorded an average growth of 12 percent per annum over the period 2004–08, thus showing no evidence of "Dutch Disease." Huge surpluses on the Balance of Payments current account accumulated foreign exchange reserves of US$10 billion, up from US$1 billion in 2002.

In this context, the sudden reversal of the economic outlook in the aftermath of the global economic crisis of September 2008 and the crash of commodity prices came as a shock to many. In reality, however, the economy had been showing signs of slowdown since 2007. The optimistic story told by the positive trends in macro-economic aggregates such as GDP, employment, and foreign exchange reserves was an incomplete one. It is a conclusion

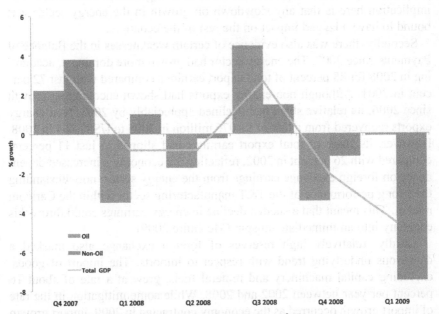

Figure 3.3.   Trinidad and Tobago Quarterly GDP Growth Rates.

that emanates from an orthodox classical view of the economy as a cohesive whole, functioning in the same way as, say, Japan or France. Such an approach fails to be informed by the theoretical frameworks of Seers (1964) or Best (2005) that seek to explain the unique characteristics and functioning of the Trinidad and Tobago economy. Under the Seers model, arguably the most important macro-economic aggregate is the Balance of Payments, a thorough examination of which gives a different picture of the economy and holds the key to understanding the severity of the impact of the external shock of 2008.

For Best, the Trinidad and Tobago economy has two distinct parts, the "offshore" energy sector and the "onshore," which covers the rest of the economy. A proper assessment of the state of the economy at any point, therefore, compels us to look behind the aggregate data to discern how each segment of the economy is performing, to identify the main drivers—internal and external—and to assess whether the economy is on the road to sustainable transformation.

First, while overall economic growth was an impressive 7.7 percent over the seven-year period, most, if not all of the impetus came from the energy sector, which recorded an average growth of 11.5 percent, fuelled by new investments amounting to over US$3.5 billion. The average non-energy growth rate was 5.4 percent, with the leading sectors being those that were fuelled by Government expenditure and/or energy sector investments. These were construction (8.6 percent), distribution (9.7 percent) and manufacturing (8.9 percent), a significant component of the latter being construction related. The implication here is that any slowdown on growth in the energy sector was bound to have a lagged impact on the rest of the economy.

Secondly, there was also evidence of certain weaknesses in the Balance of Payments since 2007. The energy sector had grown more dominant, accounting in 2008 for 88 percent of total export earnings compared with just 72 percent in 2001. Although non-energy exports had shown encouraging growth since 2006, its relative share had declined appreciably by 2008. Non-energy exports recovered from a low of $1,076 million in 2005 to US$2,204 in 2008. However, its share of total export earnings had slipped to just 11 percent, compared with 26 percent in 2002, reflecting the economy's increased dependence on foreign exchange earnings from the energy sector, notwithstanding the strong performance of the T&T manufacturing sector within the Caricom market. This meant that a sudden decline in energy earnings could throw this economy into an immediate tailspin (Mc Guire 2009).

Thirdly, relatively high reserves of foreign exchange also masked a dangerous underlying trend with respect to imports. The import of goods, excluding capital machinery and mineral fuels, grew at a rate of about 16 percent per year between 2002 and 2008. While some mitigation in the rate of import growth occurred as the economy contracted in 2009, import growth

Table 3.10. Selected Balance of Payments Indicators: 2002–2008 (TT$ Mn)

	2002	2003	2004	2005	2006	2007	2008
Energy Exports	2874	4244	5143	8596	12955	11650	16482
Non Energy Exports	1046	962	1260	1076	1262	1741	2204
Current Account Balance	76	984.7	1647.1	3594	7271	5364	8792
Capital Account Balance	326.7	-505.7	-1115	-2118	-6152	-3823	-6086
Overall Surplus/ Deficit	84.9	334.2	532	1476	1119	1541	2706

Source: Central Bank of Trinidad and Tobago: Annual Economic Survey: Various Issues

was likely to outpace export earnings and had the potential for leading to a deterioration of the Balance of Payments, if there was no recovery in prices. An economic slowdown triggers fears of depreciation in the external value of the currency. Such fears encourage hedging on the part of importers who purchase early in order to protect against the depreciation/devaluation risks. This scenario is highly probable in a liberalized foreign exchange market, as evidenced by the sharp increases reported in sales of foreign exchange by the Central Bank to the commercial banks during 2009.

Fourthly, the Government was increasingly dependent on rent proceeds from the energy sector. This is reflected in the explosion of the non-energy fiscal deficit which moved from 8.61 percent in 2002 to a peak of 25.54 percent in 2006 before reverting to 18 percent of non-energy GDP in 2008. The decline in the latter years is due to rising non-energy revenue from the petrochemical sector which itself benefited from record high prices.[4] Over the period 2002–08 the non-energy deficit averaged 16 percent of non-energy GDP, 3 percent higher than during the period 1974–82. An IMF staff paper had recommended that, in order to maintain expenditure at a sustainable level, Government should restrain the non-energy fiscal deficit to between 8–10 percent of non-energy GDP (Velculescu and Rizanvi, 2005). The obvious implication of such a high level of dependence on energy revenues is that when prices cycle down, the Government is hard-pressed to maintain the level of expenditure. The experience of the first boom period indicates the Government resisted making the adjustment in expenditure by running a deficit Budget financed first by borrowing, then sale of assets, followed by devaluation and then salary cuts. There can be no denying that the Trinidad and Tobago Government has been spending money on services directly related to the mass of the population. What, then, might be the problem?

The problems with Government expenditure of oil (energy) wealth stem from several sources. The ones that stand out are perhaps the quality, impact and the balance between spending today versus saving for tomorrow. The quality of the expenditure relates to the value derived from the amount of money spent. In other words, are citizens getting value for money? In the case of both capital and recurrent expenditure the answer is likely to be negative, even from members of the cabinet. Examples abound: a deficient health care system, escalating crime, worrying school performance data, shoddy workmanship and incomplete projects. The prime example is the Tarouba Stadium in south Trinidad, which remained under construction for years after its scheduled opening for Cricket World Cup 2007, and at double the initial cost. Like so much else, the Tarouba Stadium was, in part, a victim of the Government's accelerated development thrust which stretched productive capacity and created resource constraints and bottlenecks, driving up the cost of labour, material and real estate in general.

Secondly, Government expenditure becomes problematic when its macroeconomic impact yields undesirable results. The impact of Government expenditure on inflation in Trinidad and Tobago has been perhaps the most glaring example. While no one can deny the significant role of high imported food prices on the domestic inflation rate, it would be imprudent to ignore the impact of Government expenditure. Other regional economies that faced the double problem of high food and energy prices have been able to maintain inflation rates below that of T&T. In Barbados, for example, the inflation rate over the period 2002 to 2008 was on average 2.5 percent below the rate in Trinidad and Tobago, despite the removal of fuel subsidies in the former.

Thirdly, Government expenditure becomes problematic when it rises to a level, and at a rate that is unsustainable. Notwithstanding prior knowledge of the temporary nature of natural resource booms, expenditure increases over the period absorbed not only the extra revenue derived from output increases but, more significantly, the windfalls generated by the sharp price increases of 2007 and 2008, as well. Moreover, the expenditure increases were directed towards consumption rather than investment. In fact, whereas direct state investment in creating new productive capacity was a major component in Government spending in the first boom period, it was virtually absent in the second.

FRAMEWORK FOR EVALUATION

Drawing from the large body of theoretical and empirical work and taking into consideration the state of economic and social development in Trinidad and Tobago, the following seems to be a useful framework for evaluating the performance of the Government in managing the hydrocarbon wealth earned over the period 2002–2008. The evaluation framework is based on five criteria: fiscal responsibility, economic transformation, investment in public goods, investment in human capital and savings.

Fiscal responsibility: At the minimum, this requires Government to avoid the trap of pro-cyclical expenditure. That is, Government should tailor recurrent expenditure to sustainable levels of revenue, avoiding as much as possible dependence on windfall revenues derived from volatile price swings. The technique of budgeting on the basis of an agreed long-term average price offers one means of avoiding the lure of high prices. Failure to restrain expenditure during the boom period often translates into budgetary strains, deep expenditure cuts, increases in unemployment and deterioration in the external account, when the boom ends. The growth in Government expenditure should also be related to the productive capacity of the economy. Too rapid an expansion often leads to supply bottlenecks and rising material and labour costs, setting off an inflationary spiral. Government performance can be measured against three benchmarks suggested at the initial stages of the 2003–2008 period.

The second criterion of the evaluation framework is economic transformation. In the context of the inevitable depletion of non-renewable natural resources, it is imperative that Governments of resource rich states create conditions for nurturing growth in the non-energy side of the economy. According to Lloyd Best, "economic transformation requires the development of a vibrant and sustainable non-energy industry onshore, capable of earning foreign exchange and paying its way in the world" (Best and St Cyr, 2005). This may be measured by budgetary provisions for the development of non-energy sectors, new policy initiatives, infrastructure and legislative developments. The success of Government interventions will be reflected in growth in the non-energy sectors' contribution to macro-economic variables such as GDP, foreign exchange earnings and employment.

Investment in public goods is the third criterion in the framework. Public goods are goods and services that benefit the society as a whole, not only those who are willing to pay for it. These include health, education, sports and entertainment infrastructure, national security, utilities, and transportation. Given the country's state of development, future growth hinges in part on the condition of its social and economic infrastructure. What is important is not just the level of investment but also the quality of products or services derived from investments. The intent is that such investments will contribute meaningfully to a general improvement in the quality of life of citizens (Sachs, Humphries and Stilglitz 2007).

The level of investment in human capital development is the fourth evaluation criterion. Empirical evidence has demonstrated that a well developed human capital base of a nation can play an important role in economic development. Natural resource rich states are acutely aware of the imperative of converting "black gold" into "human gold." Being a public good, State expenditure on education is a means of providing equal opportunities for all citizens and ensuring that all share equally in the wealth provided by nature. Expenditure on education is arguably the best mechanism for long term reduction of poverty and income inequality.

Finally, the amount of windfall earnings saved is the last measure to be examined. There are two powerful drivers for saving in a natural resource-based economy. The first is the inherent volatility of commodity prices which would suggest that some current earnings be saved for stabilization purposes, in order to ensure an orderly pattern of expenditure over time. Secondly, because of the finite nature of natural resources, a percentage of current earnings should be preserved for future generations to whom the resource may be lost. This is the heritage purpose.

ASSESSMENT OF PERFORMANCE

Fiscal Responsibility

The performance of the Trinidad and Tobago Government with respect to the fiscal responsibility criterion may be judged on the basis of three benchmarks. The first is the discipline to avoid windfall spending by basing the Budget on a conservative, agreed long run average price of oil and gas. Best and St Cyr and the Vision 2020 Macro-economic and Finance Committee recommended this approach, suggesting prices of US$25.00/bbl for oil and US$3.25/mmbtu for LNG .In recognition of the need to adjust these prices over time, Best and St Cyr recommended the use of a five-year rolling average price to determine the current year's Budget price. The Government of the day fully understood the need to use conservative oil and gas price assumptions in the Budget. In the presentation of the Budget for 2005–06, Prime Minister Manning noted:

> The reason behind these obviously conservative oil price assumptions is to maintain a disciplined expenditure profile and to avoid the need for expenditure cuts in the (admittedly unlikely) event that prices fall over the next year.

The concept of budgeting on an average long run price of commodity exports was partially incorporated within the rules of the Heritage and Stabilization Fund. One rule of accrual states that in determining the level of energy revenues, the price of oil and gas is based on an 11-year rolling average, comprising five years past, the current year and five years' future prices.[5] In practice, however, it is apparent that prices used in the Budget were set more in keeping with the next year's market expectations than any other variable. Table 3.11 compares the five-year rolling average prices with budgeted and estimated realized prices.

Throughout the period, budgeted oil prices were well above the suggested benchmarks. The average budgeted price of oil over the five year period was US$49.40.25/bbl, 36 percent above the five-year rolling average benchmark. The approach to natural gas prices appears to have been much more conservative. The average budgeted price is below or on par with the five-year rolling average, with the exception of 2008–09. In the latter year, the Government became more adventurous with its estimated gas prices as the markets, particularly in the USA, appeared to be more robust.

The second benchmark for assessing the fiscal discipline of the Government is the Expenditure-to-GDP ratio. The Vision 2020 Macro-Economics and Finance (MEF) Committee recommended an Expenditure-to-GDP ratio of less than 30 percent. Over the period 2002–2008, the ratio averaged 25.2 percent, well below the recommended benchmark. In contrast, in the last five years of the 1974–83 period, this ratio had exploded to average 41.3 percent, reaching a high of 49.8 percent in 1983.

The Government's fiscal discipline may also be measured by the Debt-to-GDP ratio. For the MEF Committee, this ratio should be kept below 50 percent. In the oil boom period, the Debt to GDP ratio averaged 12.7 percent. In the aftermath of the second boom, the Debt-to-GDP ratio declined from a

Table 3.11.   Oil and LNG Benchmark vs Budgeted Prices

	OIL (US$/bbl)			LNG (US$/mmbtu)		
	5yr. Rolling Ave.	Budget	Estimated Realized	5yr. Rolling Ave	Budget	Estimated Realized Netback
2004–5	23	32	46	2.14	1.50	3.05
2005–6	27	45	56	2.56	Not stated	4.36
2006–7	31	45	55	3.10	Not stated	3.68
2007–8	44	55	91	3.40	3.55	4.76
2008–09	54	70*	49	3.81	4.00	2.30
Ave.	36	49	59	3.00	3.00	3.63

*Budgeted prices were adjusted twice in response to the global financial crisis. In the final adjustment, oil was pegged at US$45/bbl and gas at $3.25/mmbtu

high of 34 percent in 2002 to 15 percent in fiscal 2009, well inside the suggested benchmarks. The Debt-to-GDP ratio had remained below 15 percent for the period 1974–1983.

Another benchmark is the size of the Non Energy Fiscal Deficit. An IMF staff paper had recommended that, in order to maintain expenditure at a sustainable level, the Government should restrain the non-energy fiscal deficit to between 8–10 per-cent of non-energy GDP (Velculescu and Rizanvi, 2005). The evidence shows, however, that the Government became increasingly dependent on rent proceeds from the energy sector. This is reflected in the explosion of the non-energy fiscal deficit, which moved from 8.61 percent in 2002 to a peak of 25.54 percent in 2006, before reverting to 18 percent of non-energy GDP in 2008. The decline in the latter years is due to rising non-energy revenue from the petrochemical sector which itself benefited from record high prices.[6] Over the period 2002–08 the non-energy deficit averaged 16 percent of non-energy GDP, 3 percent higher than during the period 1974–82.

In summary, while the Government demonstrated a greater degree of fiscal discipline in the second boom period (2002-2008) relative to the 1974–82 boom, several deficiencies endured. Both the Debt-to-GDP and the Expenditure-to-GDP ratio were, however, within recommended benchmarks. One important consideration in assessing these ratios is that this was a period of very rapid economic growth led by the explosive growth in energy GDP, derived mainly from the expansion of the LNG business. The apparent restraint may well have been unintended, due more to the rapidly rising GDP denominator that any deliberate attempt to restrain expenditure. However, the Government's approach to pricing became more adventurous in the last three years, suggesting an abandonment of its own "conservative pricing" stance in order to boost the level of revenue available to spend. The increases in expenditure relative to non-energy revenues is reflected in the size of the non-energy fiscal deficit which exceeded the recommended benchmarks.

Economic Transformation

Economic transformation is the second criterion for assessing Government's wealth management performance. Six years may be too short a period to judge the extent to which energy revenues have been used in the transformation of the non-energy sectors of the economy. In any event, the available fiscal data do not permit ready comparative analysis of the trends in Government expenditure directed towards this goal. However, a fair assessment of the degree of transformation experienced or the extent to which a foundation was built, may be gleaned from output trends in the sector, Government policy initiatives and the comparative business climate.

The data suggest that economic activity in the non-energy sector expanded over boom period. The Index of Domestic Production (excluding the energy sector) averaged 12 percent per annum, indicating that these sectors flourished in a booming economy.

Part of that growth, e.g. construction materials, was driven, no doubt, by energy sector expansion. The overall performance is commendable, particularly in the context of the policy decision to close down the sugar industry which resulted in a major fall in agriculture production. Non-energy exports also grew steadily over the period, averaging nearly 20 percent per annum. The share of non-energy exports in total exports declined from 20 percent in 2002 to 11 percent in 2008. However, in absolute terms non-energy exports increased by 273 percent between 2002 and 2008.

In recognition of the importance of diversification, the Government took several important initiatives in order to stimulate the development of the non-energy sectors of the economy.

Arising out of the Vision 2020 plan, ten sectors were targeted for attracting investment. These included: Financial Services, Tourism, Information and Communication Technologies (ICT), Food and Beverage, Printing and Packaging, Merchant Marine, Film, Entertainment, Fish and Fish Processing and Yachting. The reasons for, and the process used to select these sectors are

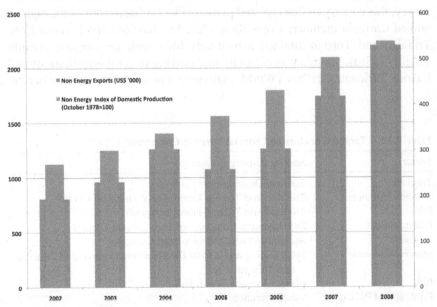

Figure 3.4. Non Energy Sector Performance Indicators.

not clear. However, strategic plans have been developed and, in some cases, special purpose companies were formed to facilitate industry development (see Table 3.12). In addition, the Government embarked on development of an innovation park—Tamana Intech Park—which had been earmarked to house the ICT and other innovative industries. The general thrust of these companies is to provide trade, market and business development services to the targeted industry clusters. The objective of placing the responsibility and impetus for plan implementation on a special purpose company outside of the public service was to provide each sector with a better chance of success. However, investigations reveal that the work of these companies was stymied by lack of funds and inadequate legislation. At least half of the targeted sectors required amendments to outdated legislation in order to make meaningful progress while in other cases, legislative amendments were not even drafted.

The State has played and should continue to play an important role in the industrial development of Trinidad and Tobago. Ultimately, however, significant private sector investment, both local and foreign, is vital, if any headway is to be made in the targeted sectors. Attracting investment to these and other areas depends, in part, on the overall competitiveness of the business environment. Unfortunately, over the last five years, Trinidad and Tobago has lost ground in the global competitiveness index.

The 2009–10 Global Competitiveness Report ranks Trinidad and Tobago 86th among 134 countries. Although moving up six places from the 2008–09 survey, this country trailed regional partners like Barbados (40th), the highest ranked Caricom member; Costa Rica, (55); Mexico (60) and Panama (59). Trinidad and Tobago attained a relatively high rank for macro-economic stability (23rd), but this was offset by low ranking under the Institutions and Labour Efficiency pillars (World Economic Forum 2009–2010). Specific

Table 3.12. Targeted Sectors and Special Purpose Companies

Sector	Special Purpose Company
Tourism	Tourism Development Company
Financial Services	Trinidad and Tobago International Financial Centre
Film	Trinidad and Tobago Film Company
Entertainment	Entertainment Company of Trinidad and Tobago
Seafoods	Seafood Industry Development Company
Merchant Marine	Shipbuilding and Repair Development Company of Trinidad and Tobago
ICT	eTeck (Tamana Intech Park)
Printing and Packaging	Sub Committee
Yachting	Sub Committee

areas of poor perception were Government bureaucracy, nepotism and favouritism in procurement, wasteful Government spending, high business costs of crime and violence, weakness in law enforcement, business impact of HIV/AIDS, low labour productivity and laws related to ICT (World Economic Forum 2009–2010).The underlying lesson is that it would require more than just sound macro-economic fundamentals to attract private sector investment and to achieve economic transformation.

Investment in Human Capital

As noted earlier, "developing innovative people" is one of the five development pillars detailed in Trinidad and Tobago's Vision 2020 Plan and has been the driver behind the state investment in human capital. The emphasis has been on four major areas:

1. Curriculum development for achieving a seamless education system from nursery to tertiary
2. The construction of a network of state-of-the-art modern Early Childhood Care and Education centres
3. Expansion of technical and vocational training, including special programmes for at risk youth; and
4. Boosting student access to tertiary level education by the creation of the University of Trinidad and Tobago and enhancing a system of scholarships, tuition financing and loans.

Over the period 2002–2008, Government expenditure on public education increased by an average of 16 percent per year, moving from TT\$ 2.3 billion in the 2002–03 fiscal year to TT\$5.0 billion in 2008. However, the share of education expenditure as a percentage of total expenditure actually fell from 16.6 percent to 14.5 percent, as increases in total expenditure (21 percent/annum) surpassed incremental outlays on education (Figure 3.5). The adequacy of Government investment in education can be assessed by cross-country comparison of the relative size of the education outlay and the quality of the education product. Two measures used when comparing countries' investment in education are the total education expenditure as a percent of GDP and education expenditure as a proportion of the national budget.

Statistics produced by UNESCO indicate that governments in North America and Western Europe (the industrialised countries) invested the highest shares of national resources in education: 5.6 percent of GDP (UNESCO Institute for Statistics 2007).That region is followed by the Arab States (4.9 percent) and sub-Saharan Africa (4.5 percent). By far the lowest level of

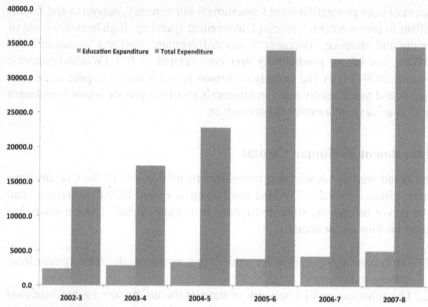

Figure 3.5. Expenditure on Public Education.

public spending is found in Central Asia, in East Asia and in the Pacific, all of which report only 2.8 percent of GDP.

Table 3.13 shows that Trinidad and Tobago trails selected countries in terms of education expenditure per unit of GDP, and is only ahead of Jamaica with respect to the share of education expense in total expenditure. The data suggest that while Trinidad and Tobago has increased outlays on education over the last decade, its expenditure to GDP ratio, at 3 percent, is below the global average and close to that of the world's poorest nations. Trinidad and Tobago needs to devote more of its resources towards human capital development. This conclusion is supported by the latest Global Competitiveness Report which places Trinidad and Tobago in 69th position for education expenditure as a percent of Gross National Income, compared with Barbados (9th) and Jamaica (28th).

Table 3.13. Comparative Education Outlays Select Countries

Country	Education/GDP (percent)	Edu.Exp/Total Exp.(percent)
Barbados	7.6	17.3
Jamaica	6.1	12.3
Malaysia	8.1	20.3
Norway	7.6	16.1
Trinidad and Tobago	3	14.0

Source: UNIDO Institute of Statistics

Government expenditure has been directed at increasing education opportunities for citizens with enrolment increasing at all levels of the system. However, there remains growing concern about the increasing numbers of young people who are not completing school, as well as the quality of some of those who do.

Investment in Public Goods

This criterion examines Government allocations to public goods (excluding education). Table 3.14 provides data on health and national security, two important public goods. Over the period, Trinidad and Tobago's expenditure on health services averaged 8 percent of total Government expenditure, equivalent to less than 2 percent of GDP. According to the World Health Organization, high and middle-income countries spent 11.2 percent and 6.3 percent of GDP, respectively, on health in 2006 (World Health Organization 2009). This data suggests that health outlays in Trinidad and Tobago fell short of what obtained in middle and high-income countries. In fact, Trinidad and Tobago held 166th place in a ranking of 188 nations by health expenditure as a percent of GDP in 2006.

The safety and security of citizens is of paramount importance and an obligation of the State. The data shows that national security spending increased over the period by 215 percent, slightly less than total expenditure growth of 225 percent (Table 3.14). This increase in security spending appears to have had little or no impact on a spiralling rate of serious crime in Trinidad and Tobago. Comparable cross-country data are not available. However, since the intent of spending on public goods is to improve the quality of life of all citizens, a fair assessment can be made of the impact of such expenditure by examining trends in key indicators of Human Development.

Table 3.14. Government Expenditure on Selected Public Goods

	2002–2003	2003–2004	2004–2005	2005–2006	2006–2007	2007–2008
Total Expenditure	14175	17317	22823	34053	32890	34623
Total GDP	71169	82652	100385	122108	137426	152115.2
Health	1259.8	1435.3	1995.7	1987.4	2371.4	2881.3
Health as % Total	8.89%	8.29%	8.74%	5.84%	7.21%	8.32%
Health as % of GDP	1.77%	1.74%	1.99%	1.63%	1.73%	1.89%
National Security	1651.9	1874.5	2215.2	2569	3158.5	3557.7
NS as % Total	11.65%	10.82%	9.71%	7.54%	9.60%	10.28%
NS as % GDP	2.32%	2.27%	2.21%	2.10%	2.30%	2.31%

Source: Central Bank of Trinidad and Tobago

An examination of the latest data on the Human Development Index shows that in 2009, Trinidad and Tobago was perhaps further removed from developed country status than in 2003, when it started the Vision 2020 journey. The most obvious areas of deterioration were crime, health and provision of public utilities, particularly water. For instance, whereas Trinidad and Tobago outperformed Barbados in GDP/capita, the latter retained its Human Development Rank 31, while T&T slipped nine places to 59 (UNDP 2009) In 2008, the infant mortality rate in Trinidad and Tobago was 23.59 deaths per 1,000,000 live births, compared with 11.05 in Barbados and just 3.65 in Singapore. T&T's growing reputation as a dangerous place is borne out by the data on homicides, which show the wide gap between this country and others. In 2007, T&T's homicide rate climbed to 43 per 100,000, compared with 10 in Barbados and less than 1 in Singapore (Table 3.15).

THE SAVINGS CHALLENGE

One of the major challenges faced by resource-rich countries in periods of resource boom is exactly how much of the windfall rents should be saved and how much should be spent. As indicated earlier in this chapter, the dilemma is perhaps greatest for those countries at a lower stage of development than

Table 3.15. Selected Human Development Indicators, Selected Countries

	2000	2004	2006	2008
GDP/Capita				
T&T	13,078	18,050	21,669	19,012
Barbados	15,494	15,720	17,297	13,356
Singapore	23,356	28,077	29,663	38,972
Infant Mortality Rate				
(# deaths/100K births)				
T&T	25.76	24.64	25.05	23.59
Barbados	12.37	12.61	11.77	11.05
Singapore	3.65	2.28	2.29	2.3
Crime (2008) Homicides (per100K)				
T&T				42.3
Barbados				10.4
Singapore				1
Human Development Rank				
T&T	50	54	57	59
Barbados	30	31	31	31
Singapore	24	25	25	25

Source: Human Development Report

it is for more advanced countries. Given vivid memories of the painful recession that followed the last oil boom (1974–82) and mindful of the "natural resource curse" that afflicts many resource-rich countries, practically every Government in old and emerging resource-rich countries have established Natural Resource Funds (NRF), otherwise referred to as Sovereign Wealth Funds, as part of their fiscal policy framework.

In general these Funds are deployed for two purposes; first, for revenue stabilization by smoothing the flow of revenue, given the inherent volatility of resource prices and the revenues derived therefrom; second, for heritage purposes, to ensure that future generations can benefit from today's depletion of natural resources to which they, too, have a claim.

In Trinidad and Tobago, Government's response to the challenge has evolved over the period of the two resource booms. During the first period (1974–89) it established Special Funds for Long Term Development with the apparent aim of sterilizing funds earmarked for capital projects pending implementation. This approach would allow the sequencing of projects consistent with the productive capacity as suggested by Best. However, allocations to, and withdrawals from such Funds were entirely at the discretion of the Government because no legislation was put in place or even contemplated to govern the management of the Funds. When oil prices collapsed in the early 1980s, the Funds were quickly drawn down to meet recurrent expenditure. By 1986, they were fully depleted.

In 1999, the Government of Trinidad and Tobago formally established the Interim Revenue Stabilization Fund, prompted, it seems, by two factors: the collapse of crude oil prices to US$14/barrel in 1998—the lowest level since 1986—following the Asian financial crisis; and the start of production from Atlantic LNG Train I in 1999 which was projected to give a major boost to Government revenue. These two dramatic swings brought into sharp relief the inherent volatility in prices of natural resource exports, and influenced the decision to establish the Revenue Stabilization Fund.

In 2003, the PNM Government added the heritage purpose to the Fund and it subsequently morphed into the Heritage and Stabilization Fund (HSF), which was legislated in March 2007.

As at March 2009, the HSF had a balance of US$2,916.6 million. This was equivalent to 17 percent of the total oil revenues collected since the inception of the Fund in 1999. While this may be a laudable accomplishment, several other questions need to be asked. Is there a target set for the optimal size of the Fund? How much do we need to save to get to the target in, say, 20 years?

In a speech to the Port of Spain Rotary Club in 2008, Central Bank Governor Ewart Williams suggested that at the current rates of deposits, and assuming no withdrawals and a real rate of return of 4 percent, the total

Table 3.16. Heritage and Stabilization Fund

Fiscal Year End Asset Balances (US$ Million)

Year	US$ Balance
2001	160.5
2002	162.6
2003	249.1
2004	449.2
2005	640.3
2006	1354.1
2007	1766.2
2008	2888.4
Mar-09	2916.6

Sources: Central Bank of Trinidad and Tobago Annual Economic Survey.

HSF Quarterly Investment Report

Fund balance would rise to a mere US$11.3 billion in the next 15 years (Williams 2008). He called then for a "more robust rate of accumulation" equivalent to about 20 percent of annual energy tax collections. Sadly, the approach of targeting a rate of savings does not appear to appeal to the Government. The Government's preference seemed to have been to allocate to long-term savings only that portion of income that exceeded the annual projected income on an annual basis. While laudable, this savings effort seems small in comparison to that of other small exporters. Countries like Kazakhstan and Timor Leste whose industries were relatively recent, seemed to accumulate oil wealth at a much faster rate than Trinidad and Tobago. Kazakhstan is said to have saved 75 percent of increased oil revenues over the period 2004–08 (Usui 2007) bringing its Wealth Fund, which was established in 2000, to $38 billion. In the case of Timor Leste, the Petroleum Fund established in 2005 had grown to $3.2 billion by the end of 2008[7]. A fundamental difference between these Funds and the Trinidad and Tobago HSF is that all revenues collected from the oil industry were paid into the Fund before allocations are made to the national Budget in accordance with the specified rules. In the case of Trinidad and Tobago's Heritage and Stabilization Fund, allocations are made only if actual revenue exceeds projected revenue.

However, direct comparisons of wealth accumulation to other oil producing countries may not be all fair. As shown in Table 3.17, the ratio of gas to oil in Trinidad and Tobago is much higher than in other oil producing countries. Rents derived from gas on a barrel of oil equivalent basis are much lower than those garnered from oil. Commentators on the rate of savings should, therefore, note this distinction.

Table 3.17. Gas to Oil Ratios in Selected Countries

	Oil Production	Oil Production	Gas Production	Gas Production	Gas/Oil Ratio
	000bbls/d	mmboe/d	bcf/d	mmboe/d	
Algeria	1993	1.993	8.3	1.511	0.76
Qatar	1378	1.378	7.4	1.347	0.98
Malaysia	754	0.754	6	1.092	1.45
Oman	728	0.728	2.3	0.419	0.58
Nigeria	2170	2.17	3.4	0.619	0.29
Trinidad &Tobago	149	0.149	3.8	0.692	4.64

Source: BP Annual Statistical Review

The central problem with the HSF as a means of providing for the future seems to lie in the rules established for the operations of the Fund. Several issues related to the rules of accrual and the rules of withdrawal required ventilation.

With respect to the rules of accrual, the HSF Act requires Government, as part of the annual Budget exercise, to make a projection of the petroleum revenues expected in the fiscal year. Where actual revenues exceeded projected revenues by more than 10 percent, the Minister must deposit all the excess to the HSF. Such calculations and deposits are to be made on a quarterly basis. In any fiscal year, the Minister must deposit a minimum of 60 percent of any surplus petroleum revenue to the Fund.

The first problem with the deposit rule summarized above is the narrow base for determining revenues that are subject to Fund allocation. The HSF Act specifically refers to revenues collected from the "Petroleum Business," that is, revenues collected under the Petroleum Taxes Act. The revenue base referred to does not include taxes collected and/or dividends received from the downstream energy sector, i.e. NGC, ALNG, the ammonia and methanol companies or other heavy gas-based industry at Point Lisas. These businesses are taxed under the Corporation Taxes Act and therefore do not fall under the ambit of the HSF Act. If the intent of the Act is to capture and save some windfall energy revenues for a rainy day and for future generations, then the exclusion of such an important sub-set of energy sector revenue is an aberration to be corrected. Essentially, the Act should cover all revenue from the energy sector, not only the Exploration and Production business (Mc Guire, 2008).

A second problem with the initial provisions of the HSF lay in the fact that the same rules for deposits governed both the stabilization and heritage purposes. In an environment of rising prices, deposits made to the Fund would, ostensibly, accumulate to provide funds for stabilization during periodic downturns in the short term, and to serve future generations in the long term. The problem with this, however, was that in periods of falling or weak prices, deposits were unlikely to be made to the Fund. For example no deposits were made to the Fund for fiscal 2009. As a result, no provision was made for heritage purposes in that year. A Heritage Fund is much like a company Pension Fund. In the case of the latter, a fixed percentage of salary goes into the Pension Fund regardless of the level of the employees' salary or company profitability. Similarly, it seems appropriate that provisioning for future generations cannot be dependent on the generation of a surplus. A more meaningful approach might be to make an annual allocation for the heritage purpose based on a fixed percentage (say, 5 percent) of the value of hydrocarbons produced. This was the approach taken in Oman where accumulation to the Oil Fund was made on the basis of the market value of 15,000 barrels of oil per day. This may require de-linking the heritage purpose from the stabilization purpose in both deposit and withdrawal rules.

Thirdly, the approach to determining the prices on which revenue projections were based has been questionable. The Act describes the mechanism for determining prices as follows:

> Estimated petroleum revenue shall be calculated on the basis of a unit price for petroleum derived from an eleven year moving average for prices of natural gas and crude oil. The 11 years comprised of five years prior to the current financial year and the current year plus five years following the current year.

Two problems arose. First, the mechanism used a forecast to make a forecast. The five years following any current year is itself a forecast heavily influenced by the current market psychology and would therefore be fraught with bias, rendering the forecast speculative and unreliable for the purposes of national budgeting. A simple, more conservative approach would be to use only the historic prices of the previous five to seven years. This approach was recommended by the Vision 2020 Subcommittee on Macroeconomics and Finance.

The rules of withdrawal have the potential to completely eliminate the heritage portion of the Fund. The legislation established strict guidelines for the annual withdrawal from the Fund. However, successive bad years could result in a complete depletion of the Fund to a floor of only US$ 1 billion. The existing rules of withdrawal permit the Minister to withdraw the lesser of 60 percent of his shortfall in revenues or 25 percent of the balance of the entire Fund, in order to make up a revenue shortfall. For example, assuming the Fund had a current balance of US$22 billion followed by a sustained period of falling prices and less than expected revenues, this balance may be cut to less than US$5 billion within five years and under

US$1 billion in 10 years. In short, the Act allows the current generation to consume the "wealth of future generations within a short 10 year period" (Mc Guire, 2008).

The withdrawal rules also gave the Government a free hand to withdraw within the statutory limits without linkage to any fiscal rules. A Government that chose to pursue an expansionist path could run too high a fiscal deficit and then finance it from the HSF. For this reason there seemed to be a need for additional withdrawal rules that would force the Government at least to seek Parliamentary approval and /or place a limit on the size of the deficit to be financed.

The rules applied well to stabilization but were flawed with respect to fulfilling the heritage objective. The two purposes, being mutually exclusive, should therefore not be governed by the same rules. Indeed, in the medium term there should be no withdrawals from the heritage portion of the Fund. The legislative provision dealing with the heritage aspect of the Fund was deficient and required urgent amendment if the Act were to operate in Trinidad and Tobago's best interest.

SUMMARY EVALUATION

The Government's performance with respect to managing the hydrocarbon wealth was examined under five criteria. The empirical evidence shows heightened consciousness with respect to the major challenges that hydrocarbon wealth brings. To varying degrees, a conscious attempt was made at improvement in all five areas. However, there was a tendency to surrender discipline in periods of extended prosperity. Moreover, the quality of the spending deteriorated and the priorities became increasingly questionable and out of sync with public needs and expectations.

Future Challenges: The Gas Economy and Its Implications

The energy sector—oil, gas and gas-based petrochemicals—has fuelled economic growth in Trinidad and Tobago over the second half of the twentieth century and into the first decade of the twenty-first century. During this time the economy and society experienced relative economic prosperity, apart from the 10 years of recession that followed the first oil boom. The productive base of the economy expanded markedly and, relative to its Caribbean neighbours, the Trinidad and Tobago economy was much more resilient. However, the economy remained highly dependent on the fortunes of the energy sector and thus continued to be vulnerable to external shocks.

Table 3.18 shows the striking similarity in the economy's energy sector dependence between the first and second boom periods under review. Oil contributed 41 percent of GDP in 1974–78 compared with 45 percent of GDP thirty years later. Similarly, the share of energy (oil) exports of total exports was 93 percent in 1974–78, compared with 87.3 percent in the second five -period, while the energy sector's contribution to Government revenue for 2004–08 was 57 percent, the same level as in the period 1979–1983. As the country moved into the future, therefore, its challenge has been to understand how this dependence, which has shifted from oil to gas, impacts on the fiscal account and, by extension, the economy.

As it moved into the twenty first century, the Trinidad and Tobago economy was emphatically a gas economy, producing approximately 115,000 barrels of oil per day and 4,100 million cubic feet of natural gas per day which, in barrels of oil equivalent (boe), represented a total of almost 800,000 boe per day. With oil production continuing to fall, the ratio of oil to gas—at 4.6:1 in 2011—will change, with gas becoming more significant.

It is very common for the word "petroleum" to be used to represent both oil and gas. In the USA petroleum means crude oil and not natural gas, whereas in Trinidad and Tobago, petroleum is defined in the Petroleum Act to mean both crude oil and natural gas. Commonly, therefore, the words petroleum, oil and gas are often used synonymously and sometimes even interchangeably. They are not—in terms of chemical composition, product potential or most importantly revenue or rent potential.

For Trinidad and Tobago, a key aspect of the economic transition was a full understanding of the implications of the differences between a gas and an oil economy in order to craft appropriate strategies and policies for transformation.

The growth of the natural gas industry has been well documented, particularly in Chapter 2. Given the considerable expansion of gas production, from less than 100 million cubic feet per day 30 years ago in 1978, to 4,100 million cubic feet per day in 2008 and the considerable capital invested in

Table 3.18.   Trinidad and Tobago Energy Dependence

	Oil GDP/Total GDP	Energy based Exports/Total Exports	Energy Rev/ Total Rev
1974–78	41.2	93.3	67.2
1979–83	33.5	93.9	57.5
1984–88	25.2	87.3	36.3
1989–93	26	79.2	35.6
1994–98	26.1	71.7	25.1
1999–03	29.2	79.4	29.3
2004–08	45.2	87.3	56.6

plant, property, manufacturing, utilities and associated services, the sector's dominance of the economy should be indisputable. Figure 3.6 demonstrates the extent to which gas was dominating the export earnings of Trinidad and Tobago by 2009.

The central import of this dominance of the natural gas industry is manifold.

The first- and perhaps the most important issue is that the levels of rent from a gas economy are much less than what may be obtained from oil. The following example numerically illustrates the difference.

In 2010, Trinidad and Tobago produced approximately 4,100 mmscf per day of natural gas, yielding an annual total of 1.50 trillion cubic feet (TCF). This gas was sold in the volumes of approximately 2,300 million standard cubic feet (mmscfd) to a Liquified Natural Gas plant (under different contracts), 1,520 mmscfd largely for methanol and ammonia production (under a multitude of varying contracts), and the remainder of approximately 280 mmscfd for generation of electricity. If reasonable annual average prices were assumed for these sales, then the annual weighted average wellhead price for natural gas would be US$3.30 (3.00) per thousand cubic feet (mscf). This amounts to total revenue at the wellhead of US$4.95 (4.5) billion. At an assumed 35 percent (33.33) effective tax rate[8] Government Revenue on a current year basis would approximate US$1.73 (1.5) billion from natural gas production alone.

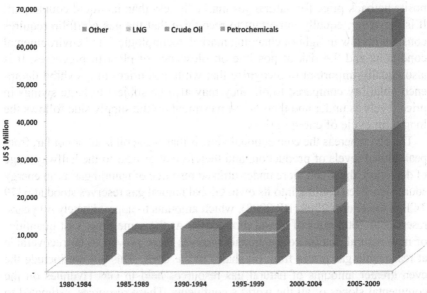

Figure 3.6.   Gross Forex Earnings 1980–2009.

Consider next if the 4,100 mmscfd were in barrels of oil- which would amount to approximately 683,000 barrels per day or approximately 250 million barrels per annum. At an estimated average annual price of US$120 per barrel for 2008, total revenue at the well head would approximate US$30 billion, and with SPT being levied on oil and an effective tax rate of approximately 60 percent, government revenue would amount to US$18 billion. This would be more than 1,000 percent greater than that provided by current levels of gas production. Hypothetically, such a level of oil production would therefore provide US$16.3 billion more Government revenue than its gas equivalent. This translates to an additional $TT100 billion more than the current annual budget of Trinidad and Tobago of TT$45 billion. While periods of high energy prices exacerbate this disparity, since oil prices attracts a substantial risk premium, a similar situation will prevail under most market conditions, as shown by the numbers in brackets above.

The differential between oil and gas prices can be expected to continue for some considerable time in the future, due largely to the cost of converting, shipping and transporting gas to markets in the temperate world. In fact, given potential projected surplus of LNG supplies and expansion of the global gas trade, natural gas prices could show an even more significant discount compared to oil prices over the second decade of the twenty first century.

A second important feature is the dampened volatility of gas pricing as opposed to that of oil. The diverse nature of gas utilization in Trinidad and Tobago—from petrochemical to power to steel and to LNG—results in a composite netback price for natural gas markedly less than its liquid counterpart. It is, however, equally important to recognize that the gas portfolio requires constant review in light of changing market, technological and environmental conditions and the risk of possible obsolescence of plant or processes. It is also equally important to recognize that while gas prices may exhibit dampened volatility compared to oil, they may also be subject to large swings in price levels as under and then over-investment on the supply side follows the long term cycle of energy prices.

Thirdly, whereas the conventional view is that crude oil is at, or not far, from peak global levels of production, and therefore at or near to the halfway stage of depletion, the much more under-utilized resource of natural gas as an energy source has been coming into its own. Global natural gas reserves stood at 6379 TCF at the end of 2008 (BP 2008), which amounts to approximately 60 years' reserves at 2008 rates of global production. At the same time, vast quantities of new natural gas (unconventional) reserves were proven to be recoverable at reasonable gas prices from oil shales in the USA. This did not include the even greater amounts of natural gas resources held in Gas Hydrates on the continental slopes of all the world's continents. These resources, estimated to be in excess of hundreds of billions of cubic metres, were considered by some more optimistic researchers to be technologically within reach by 2030. The implications for future gas prices were already evident, with high gas prices significantly improving the gas supply situation in the USA leading to a fall in natural gas prices as burgeoning shale gas supplies rapidly came on stream.

Fourthly, differing taxation systems are needed for gas and oil. A sound petroleum taxation system must discriminate in its application of windfall tax provisions. Larger oil fields can bear a higher tax take. However, the level of the tax take must be necessarily lower for larger gas fields. The tax system must also recognize that smaller, high cost fields cannot bear the same high levels of tax take if they are to become productive and not remain stranded. Getting the correct fiscal regime is, therefore, an essential prerequisite to getting an efficient allocation of acreage/bidding rounds and exploration activity, in particular where this acreage is in the deeper horizons offshore or in marginal or small fields. Almost a decade after becoming a gas economy, Trinidad and Tobago's tax system was still one devised for oil production, not gas.

The above analysis suggests that with respect to macro-economic management, the future will not be anything like the past. Industry dynamics suggest that future growth in volume, revenue and rents will be slow, at best, if not declining over the medium term. The changing gas to oil ratio may require an adjustment in the basis on which the Government budgets and sets targets for allocation to the HSF. As the energy sector becomes more integrated into global business, competitive pressures may force a review of the use of price subsidies as a means of sharing hydrocarbon wealth with citizens.

The Point Lisas strategy also needs to be reviewed. It was conceived in a different world, in terms of the size and diversity of markets, industry structure, technology, global trade, competitiveness and pricing. To continue to extract maximum value from the industry, the State or State agencies will need to participate directly in the value chain of the gas economy; downstream of f.o.b sales, in particular, cannot be ignored. Continued dependence on extracting maximum rents from upstream tax revenue could prove disastrous. Important strategic decisions need to be made on how the Point Lisas experience can be leveraged into capturing new opportunities both internal and external to Trinidad and Tobago.

Finally, greater emphasis needs to be placed on boosting the contribution of the non-energy sector in meeting the challenge of economic transformation. Significant steps have been taken in terms of targeting specific sectors and revising investment policy and legislation. However, the surrounding context also requires attention in terms of reducing crime, increasing transparency in Government procurement, and moving from general to sector-specific fiscal regimes.

NOTES

1. http://www.revenuewatch.org/about-rwi/index.php.
2. Report of the Vision 2020 Energy Subcommittee on Macroeconomy and Finance.
3. GOTT Ministry of Planning Vision 2020 Operational Plan 2007-10.
4. Corporation taxes paid by firms in the petrochemical sector are classified as non-energy taxation.
5. Certain inherent weaknesses of this rule are addressed later in this essay.
6. Corporation taxes paid by firms in the petrochemical sector are classified as non-energy taxation.
7. Sovereign Wealth Fund Institute; www.swfinstitute.org.
8. The Supplemental Petroleum Tax (SPT) is not applicable to gas.

BIBLIOGRAPHY

Auty, Richard. *Sustainable Development in Mineral Economies; The Resource Curse Thesis.* London: Routeledge, 1993.
Auty, Richard, and Alan Gleb. "Oil Windfalls in a Small Parliamentary Democracy. Their Impact on Trinidad and Tobago." *World Development* Vol 14, no. No. 9 (1986): 1161-1175.
Beblawi, H, and G.(Eds) Luciana. *The Rentier State.* London: Croom Helm, 1987.
Best, Lloyd, and Eric St Cyr. *Transforming the Plantation Economy. Economic Policy and Management Choices. Trinidad and Tobago 1950-2005.* Port-of-Spain: Lloyd Best Institute, 2012.
———. "T&T Choices for Our Economy in this Age of Plenty." *Trinidad and Tobago Review*, March 2005.
BP. "Statistical Review of World Energy." 2008.
Corden, W. M, and J.P Neary. "Booming Sector and Dutch Disease Economics. A Survey." *Economic Journal*, 1982.
Government of Trinidad and Tobago (GOTT). *Report of the Commmittee to Review Government Expenditure (Bobb Report).* Port of Spain: GOTT, 1978.
Lal, D, and H Myint. *Political Economy of Poverty, Equity and Growth.* Oxford: Clarendon Press, 1996.
Mc Guire, Gregory. "Heritage and Stabilization Fund: Did We Get it Right?" In *Guide to Monitoring the Management of Oil and Gas Resources of Trinidad and Tobago. A Report to the Trinidad and Tobago sustainable Development Network.* Cropper Foundation, 2008.
Mc Guire, Gregory. "Why Moody's is Wrong." *Trinidad and Tobago Review* 31, no. 2 (Feb 2009).
Sachs, J, and D Warner. *Natural Resource Abdundance and Economic Growth.* Cambridge, MA: Centre for International Development and Harvard Institute for International Development, 1997.

Sachs, Jeffery, M Humphries, and J Stilglitz. *Escaping the Resource Curse.* New York: Columbia University Press, 2007.

Seers, Dudley. "Mechamism of an Open Petroleum Economy ." *Social and Economic Studies* 13, no. No.2 (1964).

Stevens, Paul. "Resource Impact, Curse or Blessing? A Literature Survey." Dundee, UK: University of Dundee, 2003.

UNDP. *Human Development Report 2009.* New York : United Nations Development Programme, 2009.

UNESCO Institute for Statistics. *Global Education Digest 2007. Comparing Education Statistics Across the World.* Montreal: UNESCO, 2007.

Usui, Norio. *How Effective are Oil funds. Managing Resource Windfall in Azerbaijan and Kazakhstan .* ERD Policy Brief, Asian Development Bank, 2007.

Velculescu, Delia, and S Rizanvi. "Trinidad and Tobago:Energy Boom and P[roposals for a Sustainable Fiscal Policy." *IMF Staff Working Papers* (International Monetary Fund), 2005.

Williams, Ewart. *Understanding the Heritage and Stabilization Fund- Address to the Port of Spain Rotary.* 2008.

World Economic Forum. *Global Competitiveness Report.* Switzerland: World Economic Forum, 2009-2010.

World Health Organization. *World Health Statistics.* WHO, 2009.

Chapter Four

Natural Gas Market Structure, Contracts and Pricing in Trinidad and Tobago

Gregory McGuire

INTRODUCTION

The process of searching for and producing crude oil and natural gas are similar; however, their paths from wellhead to market diverge considerably. In the case of oil, an international market and means of transportation to such markets have been established for almost a century now. Any country or company finding oil in commercial quantities for the first time can produce and sell that oil to the market within a very short timeframe. Contracts, pricing and distribution channels are well established and continue to evolve. The situation with natural gas is quite different. The physical properties of natural gas place limits on the timing and reach of its production and distribution. A ready market must be available locally for early commercialization of a natural gas discovery. In temperate countries with their well-established transmission and distribution systems, winter heating demand usually provides the initial market to support natural gas commercialization. However, the dynamics of market development in a tropical island with a small population and limited industrial base are distinctively different.

There is a growing body of literature, published and unpublished, on natural gas development in Trinidad and Tobago. However, most have tended to focus on policy, output growth or the development of a particular sub-sector or company. Wendell Mottley provided a detailed account and interesting insights into industrial policy in Trinidad and Tobago since 1974, which may be considered to be the story of gas-based development (Mottley 2008). Parsan provided a rich analysis of the growth and development of the fertilizer industry of Trinidad and Tobago (Parsan 1981). Farrell examined issues of technology transfer and negotiations with multinationals during the first decade of gas-based development 1975–85 (Farrell 1987). James Ball examined the story of Atlantic

112

LNG which set new benchmarks for the industry (Ball and Sheppard 2004). At the first IGT Natural Gas in the Americas Conference (1994) Malcolm Jones provided an analysis of the factors that spurred growth in the Trinidad natural gas industry over the period 1974 to 1993 (Jones 1994). Professor Ken Julien, delivering the Dr Eric Williams Memorial lecture in 2005, traced the development of the industry, highlighting the major decisions and events that spawned an industry that had grown from infancy to world recognition over the course of thirty years. Boopsingh and Ramlal examined the relationship between gas prices, profit and taxes in the upstream and downstream to determine an optimal pricing regime to facilitate the development of the industry. Charles Baisden has written extensively on the development of the local industry and future gas-to-market options for increasing value-added in the industry (Baisden 2002). Boopsingh and McGuire incorporated the specific issue of the structure of natural gas pricing within a discourse on production integration in the CSME (Boopsingh and Mc Guire 2007). McGuire later traced the evolution of market liberalization in natural gas as part of a wider study on Competition in Energy Markets (Mc Guire 2007).

This essay aims to add to the literature by tracing the evolution of the natural gas market in Trinidad and Tobago in terms of its structure, contractual and pricing arrangements. The issues discussed are set in the context of the industry developments mapped out in earlier chapters.

The development of the natural gas industry in Trinidad and Tobago can be conveniently classified into three broad stages: 1974–1985; 1986–1999 and 1999 to 2010. The first period, from 1974 to 1985, was the embryonic stage, marked by the State's decision to use the newly found abundant supplies of natural gas in a deliberate strategy of industrial development. This strategy—which has come to be known variously as the Point Lisas strategy or Resource Based Industrialization strategy—was driven both by the presence of abundant reserves without an immediately available market and the accumulation of huge revenue surpluses in the State's coffers arising from then unprecedented increases in international petroleum prices as well as domestic production from the mid 1970s. The strategy featured State-led investment in infrastructure and direct capital investment in downstream natural gas-based industries. The period 1974–1985 saw the State investing in excess of US$3 billion in infrastructure and process plants. The industrial landscape was dramatically changed with the commissioning of new plants in ammonia, urea, methanol and iron and steel. The new infrastructure included natural gas pipelines, power generation, and industrial estate and port facilities.

The collapse of international oil prices and a change in Government ushered in the second stage—retreat and revival, 1986–1999. This was a period of two tales, one of retreat in the face of depressed economic conditions and another of revival. Although spanning three political administrations, a common feature during this period was a relative withdrawal of the State in its role as entrepreneur and an embrace of the State as facilitator. In fact, the Government divested its equity in several plants to foreign investors[1], while strategic changes in macro-economic and natural gas pricing policy saw renewed growth in the natural gas market, particularly after 1992. Although the State still made a few substantial outlays—PPGPL and Trintomar in particular—investments by the private sector in direct productive capacity exceeded that of the State during this period. Natural gas consumption nearly doubled, from 490 mmcfd in 1991 to 980 mmcfd in 1999, prior to the start-up of the first LNG plant. New plant capacity was commissioned in methanol, ammonia and steel in addition to ex-panded power generation, port and pipeline capacity.

The third stage, 1999 to 2010, marked the path towards global status. The dominant feature here was the start-up and rapid expansion of the LNG business in Trinidad and Tobago. However, LNG growth has often overshadowed the fact that continued investments in new plant capacity in the methanol and am-monia business contributed to Trinidad and Tobago's positioning as the world's largest exporter of these commodities. Overall, there was a three-fold increase in natural gas consumption, from 980mmcfd in 1999 to 4030mmcfd in 2008, with LNG accounting for 64 percent of the total increase. Each phase of development featured shifts in the degree of State participation, as well as changes in market structure, contracts and pricing arrangements. These issues will be dealt with in this essay, which proceeds in chronologic order, covering structure, contracts and pricing in each phase in the next three sections. The final section explores the key challenges likely to confront policy makers and the industry in the future.

THE EARLY YEARS, PRE-1974

In the early years of the industry, natural gas use was confined largely to pro-ducing companies' own use in their field operations. The introduction of gas injection into oil wells in the Forest Reserve area in the 1930s proved success-ful in improving oil recovery rates. Most of the natural gas produced then was associated gas. In the early 1940s, the Penal area, traditionally regarded as an oil zone, was the site of the discovery of the country's first large dry natural gas deposit on land. Other gas zones were discovered in the 1950s, including the Mahaica dry gas field and the Soldado associated gas fields. History records indicate that the first commercial gas sales contract was made in 1953 between Shell Trinidad Limited and the Trinidad and Tobago Electricity Company, when gas was used in the power generation plant in Penal. In 1958, Shell was contracted by the American multinational W. R. Grace for a gas supply for its ammonia plant—Federation Chemicals Limited (FEDCHEM)—built in the

Point Lisas area. Later, two other producers, Texaco and BP, also supplied natural gas for the Fedchem complex, which was further expanded in 1962. As gas production on land increased, Shell Trinidad Limited entered into a long-term contract with the Trinidad and Tobago Electricity Commission (T&TEC) in 1963. Under the terms of the contract, Shell agreed to build the pipeline and supply natural gas to T&TEC at a rate of TT$0.10 per thousand cubic feet. The royalty paid by Shell under the terms of the production license was TT$0.015 per mmcf. The discovery of a new hydrocarbon province off the east coast in 1968 provided the resource base for expanding the range of production possibilities during the following decade.

THE EMBRYONIC STAGE 1974-86

Market Structure

Arrangements for the transmission, distribution and pricing of natural gas lie at the core of any natural gas market. These mechanisms define the interaction among the various market entities i.e. sellers, buyers, transporters or shippers with a pipeline or pipelines, and a regulatory regime monitoring tariffs and contracts. Markets have varying degrees of competition dependent for the most part on the level of maturity and the number of sellers and buyers in the market.

In the pre- 1974 years, not much of a market for natural gas existed. As noted earlier, the few commercial arrangements were directly between the producer and the buyer which, in the case of T&TEC, was the State. Given the discovery of abundant supplies of natural gas over the period 1968–1973, the Government's deliberate decision to embark on the resource-based industrialization strategy perhaps required four important pre-conditions for successful strategy execution. These were:

• available markets
• appropriate gas infrastructure
• legislative/administrative framework
• mutually beneficial contracts

The State took full responsibility for satisfying these conditions. With respect to market development, in January 1975 the Government convened a special technical conference on Best Uses of Our Natural Gas Resources which led to the identification of several priority projects (Government of Trinidad and Tobago 1975).

These projects included:

- power generation
  modernization of the petroleum refinery
- aluminium smelter
- iron and steel
- expansion of ammonia and methanol production
- establishment of methanol plant
- LNG for export

A special high-powered technical committee, the Co-ordinating Task Force (CTF), was established to study and develop the proposed projects. This committee was the hub of the administrative machinery which was expanded, first in 1975 with the establishment of the National Gas Company of Trinidad and Tobago Limited (NGC), primarily as a pipeline and gas transmission company, and later, the National Energy Corporation as project developer and the sole buyer and seller of natural gas. No specific legislative arrangements were put in place for gas business. The Government at that time seemed satisfied that the existing provisions in the law governing oil were sufficient to satisfy its requirements for natural gas. The State undertook a slate of infrastructure investments that served to lay the foundation for growth and development of the industry. These included the development of the Point Lisas Industrial Estate and Port, and the building of a 24-inch cross-country gas pipeline. The CTF led negotiations to secure a gas supply agreement with Amoco, which was completed in 1976. The CTF also reached agreement with W. R. Grace for the establishment of a joint-venture company, Trinidad Nitrogen (TRIN-GEN), to build a modern world-scale ammonia manufacturing facility. The TRINGEN 1 plant began operations in 1977. The following year, the mandate of the CTF was transferred to the National Energy Corporation, which continued to pursue industrial development at Point Lisas.

The market structure in those embryonic years of the industry was very simple. There was a single supplier, Amoco, which was contracted by the Government to provide natural gas, first to T&TEC and then to the newly established firms in Point Lisas. The National Gas Company took over operations and maintenance of the new 24-inch cross-country pipeline as well as a 16-inch pipeline to the T&TEC facility in Port of Spain, which was part of the assets of Shell which had been acquired by the Government in 1974. By 1981 all pipeline assets had been transferred to NGC. In 1983, the Government negotiated a new gas supply contract with Amoco, which was to be supplied from a new field, Cassia. Against this background, all contracts, both purchase and sales, were transferred to the accounts of the National Gas

Company. By 1984, NGC became both monopsonist (sole buyer) and monopolist (sole seller) of natural gas, in addition to its ownership of the pipeline, a natural monopoly. It had fully entered the merchant/wholesaler business: buying in bulk and selling in smaller quantities to the large and small industrial users. The NEC's role was then narrowed to that of infrastructure and project development and management. Its assets included the port and marine piers at Point Lisas, the Trinidad and Tobago Methanol Company and the Trinidad and Tobago Urea Company.

Contracts and Pricing

Early natural gas supply contract arrangements were quite complex, reflecting in part the uncertainty about the respective roles of various state institutions. While Amoco was the only seller, the buyer varied. For example, in 1975 the Government reached agreement with Amoco for a supply of natural gas to T&TEC (basic contract). However, NGC was the buyer for a second contract signed with Amoco in 1977 for gas from the Teak, Samaan and Poui fields. When in 1981, the Government negotiated a second major gas supply contract with Amoco for gas from the giant Cassia field, NEC was named as the buyer. This contract was for an initial period of 15 years with 100 percent take-or-pay obligations. In 1981–82 NEC took over administration of the T&TEC contract between Amoco and the Government. However, there was no corresponding agreement between NEC and T&TEC. This incomplete arrangement would prove to be a burden on NEC's cash flow as a result of irregular payments by T&TEC. This ambiguity about which entity should be the contracting party seems to have stemmed from differences in the policy perspective of the Government. The White Paper on Natural Gas recommended NEC as the sole purchaser/reseller of natural gas and the NGC as a transmission company (GOTT). However, this approach was developed under the Chambers administration[2] (1981-86), and all contracts were transferred to the NGC in 1984.

Early consumer contracts followed the pattern set with upstream producers. Contracts signed with the major users were of 15- to 20-year duration for fixed supply and contained take-or-pay provisions. As stated earlier, T&TEC's contract was an exception.

The approach to natural gas pricing in Trinidad and Tobago is rooted in the Report of the Adams Committee on Natural Gas Pricing 1978, which made recommendations on the pricing mechanism for industrial sectors (Government of Trinidad and Tobago 1978). Table 4.1 shows the initial prices recommended for certain industrial customers. The pricing arrangements in the early years followed the classic model of cost plus pricing, with a base price

Table 4.1. Approved Gas Prices to Industrial and Commercial Users Based on Adams Committee Report 1978

Category #	Industry Type	Company	Base Price	Escalation Factor
I	Public Utility	T&TEC	16c/MCF (1978) Plus Transportation fee	As per existing Contract with Amoco
II	Miscellaneous Small Consumers	CDC, Lever Bros etc.	54 cents /MCF (1977)	7 percent per annum
III	New Metal Based Industries	Iron and Steel Mill	60 cents /MCF	6 % per annum
IV	New Chemical Industries	Tringen Fertrin	65.0 cents/MCF	As per existing contract
V	Own Users	Texaco, Trintoc	$1.10/MCF	Six (6) % per annum
VI	Prime Commercial	Fed. Chem	$1.20/MCF	Six (6) % per annum

and a fixed escalator. The negotiated base price in the first Amoco contract was US$0.36 per mcf, with a fixed escalator of four percent. Prices for downstream consumers were quoted in US dollars and carried a fixed escalator of six percent. Special provision was made for "small consumers," defined as firms that consumed less than one mmscfd per day. The majority of these firms were in the local non-energy manufacturing sector. The Committee strongly recommended that prices for small consumers should be in TT dollars and escalated at a rate of seven percent per year. Unlike the large firms, however, such consumers were to absorb the cost of connection although the facilities and equipment were to be owned by NGC. It was argued that low-priced natural gas would aid the competitiveness of these industries. Contracts were expected to be renewed annually. In the case of the larger consumers, the Government negotiated a price of around US$ 0.70/mmbtu, escalated at four percent per annum (Julien 2007).

The recommendations of the Pricing Committee were broadly accepted by the Government. However, Federation Chemicals lodged a formal protest on

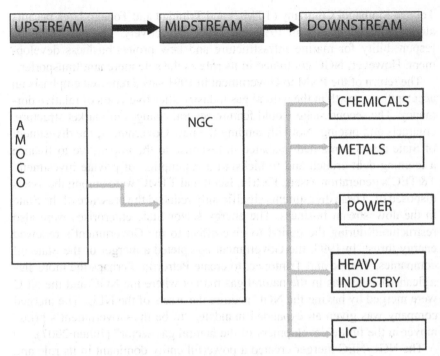

Figure 4.1. Trinidad and Tobago Process Map of Natural Gas Market 1984.

the grounds that the pricing proposals were a discriminatory attempt to subsidize the new industry at the expense of established firms. Fedchem argued the case for an equitable pricing basis, the same as the newly established Tringen and the proposed Fertrin. The Frank Rampersad Gas Pricing Committee, which was established to negotiate contracts and pricing arrangements on a case by case basis for new projects, was asked to review the Fedchem case and make recommendations. In the end, the Government retained its position and the Fedchem pricing proposal remained intact.

THE SECOND STAGE: RETREAT AND REVIVAL, 1986–1999

The change in Government in 1986[3] brought new directions to the NEC and, with it, the structure of the industry. Strapped for cash in the wake of a collapse of oil prices and a heavy debt burden, the Government, under the influence of the IMF, abandoned the role of the State as entrepreneur and sought to divest its holdings in the downstream business. The operations of the NEC were scaled down significantly and its subsidiaries, the Trinidad and

120 *Chapter Four*

Tobago Methanol Company (TTMC) and Trinidad and Tobago Urea became autonomous companies in 1998 and 1990, respectively. The NEC retained responsibility for marine infrastructure and new project/business development. However, NGC continued in its role as the sole merchant/transporter.

The return of the PNM to Government in 1991 saw a renewed emphasis on accelerating growth in the natural gas industry after five years of relative dormancy. The second stage would feature several changes in market structure, contracts and pricing. Notwithstanding the new Government, the divestment of State assets continued unabated in response to the imperative to finance a looming debt crunch and to kickstart a resumption of private investment. T&TEC's generation assets, Fertrin, Iscott and TTMC were among the assets disposed of. These divestments significantly reduced the presence of the State in the downstream business. The energy sector State enterprises were also restructured during the period to give effect to the Government's renewed energy thrust. In 1993, the Government completed a merger of the State oil companies, Trintoc and Trintopec, to create Petrotrin. Perhaps the more significant change was in the natural gas market where the NGC and the NEC were merged by having the NGC acquire the assets of the NEC. The merged company was given an expanded mandate: "to be the Government's prime mover in the future development of the natural gas sector" (Julien 2007).

The NGC/NEC merger created a powerful entity dominant in its role and influence in the natural gas industry. In the post-merger period, the NGC/NEC functioned in the following roles:

• The merchant aggregator. NGC purchased gas from upstream producers under individual contracts which was in turn sold to downstream industry.
• Sole transporter and distributor of natural gas. NGC owns an extensive pipeline transmission and distribution system and in the second stage retained its position as the sole transporter and distributor of natural gas. The distribution system that takes natural gas supply to over 140 customers is also owned and operated by NGC.
• Equity investor. In 1991, NGC held equity in Phoenix Park Gas Processors 51 percent, (PPGPL). It would later take up shares in Atlantic LNG, (10 percent Train I; 11.11 percent Train IV), offshore compression assets, and offshore producing assets. In addition, the NEC owned significant marine infrastructure at Point Lisas and La Brea.
• Business Developer. NGC/NEC has played a central role in developing the gas business, and downstream expansion in the petrochemical business continued rapidly in this phase. The number of petrochemical plants grew from seven in 1991 to 12 in 1999. Total gas consumption in the petrochemical business increased from 203 MMscfd in 1986 to 483 MMscfd in

1999. Newcomers included Caribbean Methanol Company (CMC), TTMC II and M IV, PCS Nitrogen 03 and 04 units, and Farmland/MissChem. Steel saw expansion by Caribbean Ispat and the introduction of Nucor and Cliff and Associates.

Towards the end of this period, the wide-ranging role and assumed powers of the merged NGC/NEC drew the attention of the World Bank, and international consultants Gaffney Cline and Associates, was hired by the Government to produce a Natural Gas Master Plan.

Among the concerns were the view that NGC's ownership and operation of the natural gas pipeline, its role as a gas merchant and aggregator and its contractual arrangements with the dominant supplier, were potentially conflicting and a hindrance to the further development of the market. Perhaps for the first time in Trinidad and Tobago, it was argued that as long as the transmission and distribution system was owned by NGC, it would not be possible to achieve any significant degree of competition in gas supply unless a regime of fair, transparent and non-discriminatory access was instituted. While recognizing that the sector was "too critical to warrant dramatic change but too important not to change, the consultants, GCA, recommended an evolutionary approach that would ultimately result in de-monopolization and liberalization of the market (Cline 2001).

On the upstream end of the industry, the second period witnessed the end of the Amoco supply monopoly. In 1991, the State-owned Trintomar commenced delivery of natural gas to NGC under a 120mmscfd contract. Trintomar's subsequent demise[4] opened the door for the introduction of a third supplier in the form of Enron Oil and Gas—later to become EOG Resources. Determined to introduce further competition in the upstream business, the Government, through the NGC, reached an agreement with British Gas in 1994 to purchase incremental supplies from its newly developed Dolphin Field. This was the first contract for natural gas produced under the Production Sharing Contract (PSC) in which the State took its taxes as a share of production. By the end of the second phase in 1999, there were three major suppliers of natural gas to NGC, with BP Amoco's share reduced to 59 percent of the total supply of 891 mmscfd, inclusive of supplies from NGC's gas compression platforms.

Contracts and Pricing

Given the changes in market structure described above, there were equally important shifts in contracts and pricing arrangements during the second period. State-owned Trintomar had been expected by contract in 1990 to provide NGC with 120 mmscfd beginning in 1991. However, when a drilling accident precipitated the decline of the Trintomar deliverability and recoverable reserves, EOG Resources (formerly Enron Gas and Oil) secured a 15-year agreement for a maximum of 150 mmscfd, as replacement for the Trintomar volumes. The Amoco Cassia contract of 1983 was renewed in 1991 for an additional 20 years. Amoco entered into another contract in 1997 for a total of 620 mmscfd, ramping up from the existing 350 mmcfd to full contract volumes by 1999, and by 2000 the volume contracted was 645 mmscfd, with the proviso that BP would have to supply up to 825 mmscfd, if required. British Gas' contract specified an initial minimum take of only 87 mmscfd in 1996 with a gradual seven-year ramp-up to 275 mmscfd in 2003. The relatively low start-up volume was an indication of the extent to which the Government was prepared to go to ensure that there were new supply options in the market.

Perhaps the most significant changes in the second phase occurred in the pricing arrangements for natural gas sales ex-NGC. A collapse of international market prices for oil and petrochemicals in the mid 1980s brought the fixed escalator pricing regime under severe challenge. In 1985, the average prices of ammonia and urea were US$160/MT and US$135/MT, respectively. By March 1986, these prices declined substantially, ammonia by 30 percent to approximately US$115/MT and urea by 34 percent to US$95/MT. In the wake of the price slump, the NEC noted that "several potential project sponsors have already withdrawn from further participation and others have singled out the fixed escalator rate in the gas pricing formula as the major obstacle in reaching agreement." The NEC argued that the price regime of the day had become a disincentive to investment.

Discussion on a new pricing regime then began in 1986. The Tringen II ammonia project, a joint venture between the Government and W. R. Grace which commenced production in 1987, was the first to benefit from a modification of the old pricing regime. The Tringen II pricing formula was as follows:

A base price (1985) of US$ 1.290 per MMBTU escalated at 6 percent per annum subject to a reduction from 1987 of US$0.1887 per MMBTU escalated at 6 percent per annum, to be applied against the gas price until the later of December 1994 or the date by which buyer repays indebtedness for the capital costs of buyer's plant (National Energy Corporation 1986).

This modification really made little difference to the overall problem, since the upstream producers continued to apply fixed escalator pricing. The NEC suggested a full-scale overhaul of the gas pricing policy in order to maintain T&T's competitiveness as an investment location for petrochemical plants. Five options were identified:

1. Renegotiate the Amoco gas supply contract
2. Natural gas pricing linked to the selling price of end products contemplated for the use of such gas
3. Natural gas price linked directly to gas prices in the United States
4. Creation of a buffer entity between NGC and production companies
5. Producers sell directly to end-users; NGC as a purely transmission company

With respect to Option 3 the report reasoned that "to stimulate new investments in Ammonia and Methanol, a change to a formula in which gas prices are linked directly to these products' prices has been advocated by project sponsors and lenders. It must be recognized "that without a floor, NGC could face a situation where it suffers a loss on the purchase and sale of natural gas" (National Energy Corporation 1987). In 1987, the NEC proposed a product-related pricing formula for a new methanol project under consideration.

The Government requested a review of the NEC proposal by the Standing Committee on Natural Gas Pricing chaired by Frank Rampersad (Rampersad 1987). The committee concluded inter alia:

- The introduction of product-related pricing when matched against NGC's purchasing arrangements exposes NGC to considerable risk.
- The generally depressed prices for the petrochemical products based on gas have resulted in downward pressure on gas prices. As a result of this, NGC's purchasing contracts with AMOCO need to be revised downwards, both with respect to the base price and especially the annual escalator.
- NGC has to take into account that the introduction of product-related pricing in the case of the new methanol plant will lead to demands for a similar pricing basis from the existing commercial customers. The approach to product-related pricing should, therefore, be taken with due circumspection.
- In the interest of supporting the Government's industrialization effort NGC should take the risk of entering into product-related pricing arrangements; however, at the very minimum, the floor price of such arrangements should cover NGC's cash costs and, over the term of the contract, the pricing arrangements should give NGC a realistic expectation of earning a rate of return of 10 percent on its equity base.
- As an alternative to the proposed pricing arrangements, Trintoc should consider paying NGC a transportation charge and supply the gas directly to the proposed methanol plant.

In summary, while the committee supported the concept of product-related pricing, it cautioned against a possible domino effect, increased risk to NGC-insofar as its own purchases were on a fixed escalator basis- and the level of the floor price. In proposing a completely new alternative to the current structure and pricing, the committee was essentially attempting to shield NGC while undertaking additional risk.

Concerned about the reservation of the committee, the NEC representatives submitted a minority report identifying those areas in which they did not see "eye-to-eye" with the committee. In particular, the minority report reiterated the case for acceptance of the product-related pricing formula.

New petrochemical investors will only be attracted, at this point in time, to a foreign location, if they perceive opportunities to guarantee their product supplies from a production facility capable of always operating at the lower end of the production cost spectrum. We cannot truly wish to resist the movement to product-related natural gas pricing, in the face of the otherwise inherent country-specific competitive advantages, which Trinidad and Tobago enjoys in relation to other gas-rich countries, who offer foreign investors such a basis, e.g. Chile. (National Energy Corporation 1987)

The Minority report also emphasized that "the product-related natural gas pricing must be the mechanism for spurring further industrialization of our economy" (National Energy Corporation 1987).

Although the specific project which prompted the new product-related pricing formula never materialized, this pricing basis was eventually accepted and introduced to methanol producers in 1988. The existing methanol plant, TTMC, and later CMC, were the first to benefit from the revised formula.

The key elements of the initial formula were as follows:

- A base price of natural gas of US$X per mmbtu tied to a Methanol Reference price of US$Y per tonne.
- The price of natural gas would change with the price of methanol on the following basis:
  (a) If Mb > M:
     Then G = Gb-.02*(Mb-M)
  (b) If Mb < M
     Then G = Gb+0.01 *(M-Mb)
  Where Mb = Methanol Reference Price
  Gb = Base Gas Price
  M   = Price of methanol
  G   = Price of gas
- In the event of a decline in methanol prices, the price of natural gas would not fall below a pre-determined floor.

Product-related pricing would become the new standard for pricing of natural gas to the petrochemical sector as a whole. The existing ammonia

Table 4.2. National Gas Company Gross Profit/Loss on Gas Sales to Small Consumers

Year	1986	1987	1988	1989	1990	1991	Total
Sm. Con.Price (US$/Mmbtu)	0.67	0.71	0.71	0.69	0.74	0.79	
Amoco Price (US$/Mmbtu)	0.66	0.72	0.74	0.77	0.78	0.84	
Margin	0.01	-0.01	-0.03	-0.08	-0.04	-0.05	
Volume(Mmbtu)	5,981,508	6,162,584	6,361,182	6,362,886	7,058,819	7,001,412	
Gross Profit/Loss (US$M.)	59,815.08	1,625.84	(190,835.46)	(509,030.88)	(282,352.76)	(350,070.60)	(1,334,100.46)

Source: McGuire, Gregory Policy Proposals on the Pricing of Natural Gas May1992, National Gas Company 1992

producers converted to product-related pricing in the early 1990s and it was adopted by all subsequent petrochemical plants. Ammonia producers benefiting were: Yara (formerly Hydro Agri, Fedchem), Trinidad Nitrogen 1 and 2; PCS Nitrogen (formerly Acadian Fertrin), Point Lisas Nitrogen (at that time, Farmland Misschem). The methanol producers benefiting were, Trinidad and Tobago Methanol and Caribbean Methanol Company. Despite the intent to have all players in the market benefit from an even playing field with respect to gas costs, there remained variations in individual contracts with respect to floor price, discount factors and destination markets and marker prices. Variations also occurred because the base price was related to the cost structure of the particular petrochemical plant and the share of gas cost in that structure.

This period also featured significant changes in the pricing regime for the group classified as "miscellaneous small consumers." The case for a revision of the pricing regime was made on two grounds (Mc Guire 1992). Firstly, the TT$ pricing structure put in place by the Adams Committee in 1978, remained in force without any adjustment for the impact of two devaluations since its inception. As a result, and notwithstanding the 7 percent escalator, the NGC's margin on sales decreased consistently as did its cumulative losses. For the period 1986 to 1991, NGC accumulated cash losses of $US1.3 million on its transactions with small consumers. This estimate does not take into account any transportation or distribution tariff and profit element. Secondly, the classification "miscellaneous small consumers" was apparently used as a catch-all category into which all consumers, not otherwise classified, were placed. As companies grew over time, there emerged some glaring aberrations in the small consumer grouping, such as Trinidad Cement Limited. Finally NGC was required to maintain metering stations and facilities which estimated costs of about TT$500/per month per station. This was not covered by the pricing regime.

An in-house policy document recommended the following:

- An increase in the price of natural gas from US$1.16/mmbtu to US$ 1.28/ mmbtu.
- A reduction in the annual escalator from 7 percent to 4 percent
- A switch to US$ denominated pricing, although payments were to be made in TT$.

The policy document also defined the small customers as those who used natural gas only as fuel, had total consumption of less than 500 mcf/d, and whose activity fell within the non-oil sector defined in the Trinidad and Tobago System of National Accounts. As a result of the new criteria three firms were recommended for reclassification, because their volumes or uses of gas were outside the newly established boundaries.

Further change was made to the Light Industrial and Commercial (LIC) pricing regime in 1995. By then, it was recognized that the cost of infrastructure was the primary constraint to market growth in this segment of the market. The NGC introduced a two-tier pricing structure with gave consumers an option of:

a. Paying for the cost of the pipeline and metering station and enjoying the benefits of a lower price, or
b. Requesting NGC to bear the upfront cost of the service pipeline and facilities with the customer repaying through a higher gas price. This adjustment proved very attractive to LIC customers particularly since even the increased gas price represented a substantial saving compared with the costs of alternative fuels. The number of LIC customers grew from 54 in 1994 to 78 in 1999.

TOWARDS GLOBAL STATUS 1999–PRESENT

The advent of LNG in 1999 marked the beginning of a new gas-based phase. LNG induced changes to all elements under review in this essay: that is to say, market structure, contracts and pricing. With respect to market structure, the LNG project broke from the tradition of purchases of gas and transportation services supplied by NGC. Atlantic LNG Train I purchased its supplies directly from the producer, Amoco/BP, which was also responsible for transportation to the plant through a new 36-inch dedicated pipeline. While the pipeline is owned by NGC, it was actually financed and built by Amoco due to the stringent guarantees required by the project financiers. Subsequently the pipeline was bought back and leased to Amoco/BP under an operating/maintenance agreement, with NGC retaining capacity rights for 400 million standard cubic feet per day.

The model of direct sales between producer and consumer was further modified as the LNG business model changed. Train II and III and Train IV have been set up as processing plants paid at a fixed utility rate to convert the natural gas to LNG. The plant, therefore, never holds the title to the gas which it processes into LNG and delivers to a subsidiary of the producer company. The change in the business model has had fiscal implications arising from the potential for indeterminate pricing facilitated by intra-company product transfers.

Contracts and Pricing

LNG contracts brought the first direct links between the Trinidad and Tobago natural gas industry and that of the industrialized markets. Under the Train I contract, netback pricing was introduced for the first time, linking the

Trinidad and Tobago natural gas market to those of the USA and Europe. The following are the key provisions in the LNG pricing arrangements for the US market:

1. Sales are made on a Free on Board (FOB) basis
2. The FOB price is related to the average monthly sales price received by the buyer or the buyer's affiliate in the market
3. The average monthly sales price (SP) is calculated by the formula: SP = TP/TN where:
   - TN is the total monthly mmbtu delivered
   - TP is the total proceeds received by the buyer with respect to LNG sales. The total proceeds are usually linked directly to prices in the market in New England which are linked to the Henry Hub price.
4. Calculations are made semi-annually reflecting different contract conditions.
5. The Semi Annual Contract Price (SACP) is calculated as Netback Fraction (NBF) of the Semi Annual Sales Price (SASP) as follows: SACP=SASP x NBF.
6. The Net Back Fraction varies from one contract to another, in the range of 72-76 per cent depending on the level of prices.
7. The Gas Price to the Producer is calculated as a netback faction of the FOB price.

In the case of sales to Enagas for the Spanish market with respect to Train I the following applies:

1. Gas is sold on an FOB basis
2. The Contract Price is linked directly to the price of alternative fuels, and determined by formula similar to the following:

$$P = P_0 (0.5 \ G/G_0 + 0.3 \ LF/LF_0 + 0.2 \ HF/HF_0$$

Where the base price (P_0) = XUS\$/mmbtu.
   G = the average price of Gas Oil for the relevant period
   LF = the average price of Low Sulphur Fuel oil for the reference period and
   HF = the average price of Heavy High Sulphur Fuel oil for the ref. period.

In the case of Trains II and III the gas price to the producer is the FOB price less the costs along the value chain .i.e. processing fee to plant, plant margin and pipeline tariff.

Notwithstanding the change in the LNG business model, netback pricing arrangements remained the order of the day for the LNG business. Further evolution in contractual relationships resulted from the presence of NGC-LNG as an equity holder with processing rights in ALNG Train I. Not having its own source of supply, NGC purchases supply from producers bpTT and EOG Resources in order to utilize its processing rights of 89MMscfd in Train IV.

Emerging trends in the international LNG trade also inspired changes in the pricing mechanisms in later LNG contracts. One such trend was the growth of arbitrage and cargo swaps. In its earliest days, the LNG business was a closed loop from wellhead through liquefaction, to re-gas, to consumer. However, later LNG contracts provided sellers with the flexibility to dispose its cargo to any buyer willing to pay a higher price. As a result Train IV agreements contained complex details on the determination of value from such transactions as well as from sales of natural gas liquids (NGLs).

The LNG Train I contracts set the precedent for a new contracting approach in the domestic market. Given the presence of multiple producers with gas reserves that they wished to monetize and the desire to have direct access to the markets, it became clear that one way to accelerate monetization of discovered reserves was to facilitate the direct supply arrangements with new projects. The result of the compromises made was that both EOG resources and BP (formerly Amoco) became involved in new downstream investment

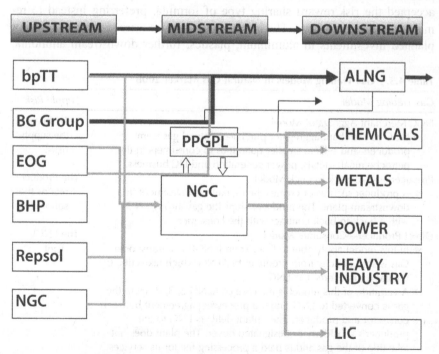

Figure 4.2. Trinidad and Tobago Process Map of Natural Gas Market 2003.

in ammonia and methanol respectively. EOG Resources was the first supplier
to hold the new form of contract. The 2000 agreement with NGC is a back-
to-back agreement with the Caribbean Nitrogen Company ammonia plant
(CNC) in which EOG holds 20 percent equity. A special tranche of natural
gas is supplied by EOG to NGC and from NGC directly to CNC. Two contracts were executed, NGC and EOG for the supply of gas and NGC/CNC for
the onward sales of that gas.

BP, which took over the Amoco assets in 1999, had a similar agreement
with Atlas Methanol, while EOG benefited from new agreements with
M5000 and Nitro 2000. In all cases the product-related dimension previously restricted to contracts between NGC and the petrochemical companies,
now extended to the upstream supplier. This was an important modification
because producers had been known to have stoutly resisted attempts to have
them adopt product-related pricing.

A bullish investment outlook in the period 2005-07, and an optimistic
shareholder led NGC to contract for new supplies in advance of firm commitments from potential new downstream operators. EOG, BHP and BG signed
new contracts from 2010 to 2011 for a term of approximately 15 years. The
pricing formula for BHP and EOG comprised a weighted fixed escalator and
product-related element. In 2010, BG remained the only supplier that had not
accepted the risk/reward sharing type of formula, preferring instead to remain with fixed escalator. The incremental supplies were secured to cater for
planned investments in aluminium, plastics, further downstream ammonia,

Table 4.3. Gas Trading Models in Natural Gas Market 2008

Gas Trading Model	Supply Risk
NGC Merchant Aggregator Model ⇒ NGC as merchant aggregator purchases natural gas from producers and sells in smaller quantities to consumers in the petrochemical, metals, power generation and LIC business.	NGC bears all the supply risks.
Producer—NGC Back to Back Model ⇒ A producer secures or creates the market via investment in a downstream plant. The producer ships the gas through NGC with a back-to-back contract with the consumer.	The Producer retains the supply risk
Direct Producer—Consumer Model ⇒ In this model applicable to LNG Train I; NGC is a transporter. Gas is sold directly from producer to ALNG which takes title to the gas and coverts it to LNG ⇒ A variation of this model is the case of ALNG 2, 3, 4. Here the gas is converted to LNG under a processing agreement between convertor and producer. The plant delivers LNG to the producer's subsidiary or designated buyer. The plant does not take title of the gas and is paid a processing fee for its services.	The LNG plant

gas to liquids and iron and steel. A portfolio of projects totalling in excess of 600mmscfd was anticipated to come on stream in the 2009–2012 time-frame. Unfortunately the onset of the global financial and economic crisis resulted in cancellations and/or deferral of most of these projects. The result was a mismatch between NGC's purchase and sales commitments thereby exposing the company to heavy Take-or-Pay obligations and potential cash flow problems. The situation raised the question of whether the arrangements were the most efficient for managing the supply and demand balance.

The cost plus pricing structure for the LIC customers was revised further in 2005, in response to pleas from the Trinidad and Tobago Manufacturers Association for price relief. The TTMA argued that it was unfair that local manufacturers were paying US$1.59/mmbtu for gas with an average escalator of 4 percent, while multinational clients were paying US$ 1.00/mmbtu, with an escalator of 2 percent. The TTMA requested reduction of both the gas price and the escalation factor. The TTMA case seems to have been based on the assumption that the floor price of gas sold under the product-related pricing formula was equivalent to the average price paid by those customers—mainly the petrochemical sector. This was an erroneous assumption since the actual price paid by the petrochemical sector as determined by the formula was highly volatile and a function of petrochemical product prices. In periods of high petrochemical prices, natural gas price to the petrochemical sector could soar to over US $3.00/mmbtu. Indeed, over the period 2004 -2008 the average price of gas sold by NGC to the petrochemical industry was US$ 3.12/mmbtu.

Nonetheless, recognizing the role played by the LIC sector in terms of employment creation, exports and output, NGC agreed to a conditional concession on price. By formal agreement effective December 1, 2004, NGC agreed to reduce the price of gas charged to the LIC sector by US$0.20/mmbtu, with the escalator remaining at 4.0 percent. NGC undertook further to transfer an additional US$0.20/mmbtu sold for a period of four years, to a special Fund for Industry Development. These arrangements appeased the local manufacturing sector for a few years. However, with the onset of the global economic crisis and the concomitant slowdown in the Trinidad and Tobago economy, local manufacturers were again arguing the case for a reduction of natural gas prices. The recurring pleas for price reduction suggests local manufacturers' lack of understanding of the pricing mechanisms used in the sector, as well as their over-reliance on cross subsidies in order to remain or achieve competitiveness. The case of the LIC sector provides some evidence of how contradictory national policy can hurt the NGC's merchant business in the long run. Two important issues arise. First NGC's margin on sales to this market is shrinking as a result of rising acquisition costs against mandated lowering of sales prices. Secondly, competitive edge of natural gas in the market is gradually being eroded as the gap closes between increasing gas prices and fixed/subsidized alternative energy prices.

This period also witnessed some evolution of the product-related pricing basis for downstream plants. As old contracts matured and new ones were negotiated, there was modification to the contract formulas to modify the distribution of rents collected in periods of high prices. In summary, some companies gave up more of their upside in order to benefit from a lower floor.

THE FUTURE

There can be no doubt that what has been termed the Trinidad and Tobago Model for gas-based development has been highly successful in monetizing the natural gas resources of the country. The State and State agencies—NGC/NEC—have played vital roles in the creation of industry. But this success seems to be the compost in which the seeds of change have been set. With success also came increasing reference to the Trinidad gas industry as being mature. This description stemmed in part from the country's century-long experience as an oil producer and the corresponding age and technical status of many of its oil-producing provinces. Maturing may also mean that growth has leveled off. This may be due to stagnating markets and/or a surplus of suppliers competing for limited opportunities. The gas industry is often labelled with the latter meaning. Whatever the driver, the definition of the industry as "mature" often evoked thoughts and proposals to reform the industry's structure along the lines of mature gas industries in North America and Europe. In these markets, the thrust has been towards encouraging more competition in natural gas markets. In most cases this is achieved by removal of monopoly positions, the introduction of open access transportation and distribution, the unbundling of services and the creation of independent regulatory authorities.

The appropriate structure for the further development of the natural gas market in Trinidad and Tobago was a key feature of the Natural Gas Master Plan (Cline 2001). The consultants felt that the structure of the industry was well-suited to the developmental phase but saw a clear need for separation of the commercial and regulatory functions, the removal of monopoly structures and the creation of a competitive environment. In its submission to the Gas Master Plan consultants, bpTT argued that the industry development was characterized by four distinct phases: embryonic, growth, maturity and deregulated (Figure 4.3). The role of Government changes at each stage—beginning with rent collection, industry promotion and direct investment and ending with free market and total divestment. Mottley placed Trinidad and Tobago at Stage III (Mottley 2008).

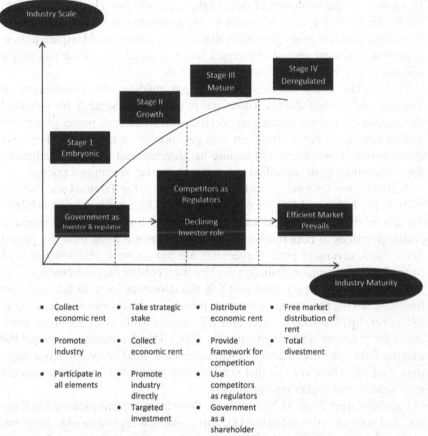

Figure 4.3. Gas Industry: Stages of Maturity. Source: Trinidad and Tobago: Gas Master Plan, Submission to the Ministry of Energy and Energy Industries by BP Trinidad and Tobago LLC, Sept. 2001.

When the issue arose in 1999, it was in part prompted by what was then perceived as the high degree of risk faced by NGC from margin compression, as well as the dual role of merchant and de facto regulator. Ten years later, the problems of a heavy supply overhang and consequent looming Take-or-Pay liabilities, coupled with the collapse of the petrochemical markets similarly exposed the vulnerability of NGC. In 2003, participants at a Vision 2020 Energy Workshop listed among its imperatives the need to "establish a regulatory framework that facilitates open access and pricing, within the context of a regional cross-border and interconnected network of gas pipelines (Energy Subcommittee 2004).

The fundamental question is this: Is a liberalized gas market with open access pipeline and market-determined pricing feasible in Trinidad and Tobago?

In some ways the evolution of direct sales contracts provides a glimpse into the future. While the full assessment of the proposition is beyond the remit of this essay, suffice it to say, however, that such an option would require policy-makers to surmount several challenges, some of which stem from the unique features of the Trinidad and Tobago gas market.

First, unlike many developed-country gas markets, the Government of Trinidad and Tobago utilized natural gas in a deliberate strategy for industrial development. This has meant that specific sectors, such as power generation and the LIC sector benefit from low-cost gas supplies. A move towards market liberalization, therefore, would require the development of some mechanism for transitioning from controlled low prices to market determined prices.

Secondly, multiple price mechanisms co-exist in the Trinidad and Tobago market. For instance, LNG prices are determined on a netback basis, while in the case of the petrochemical sector gas prices are linked to product markets. Although prices in both markets followed an upward trend over the period 2003–2008, divergent price movements are not unusual. Harmonization of prices becomes a major challenge for any market liberalization process.

Thirdly, on the supply side, bpTT is the dominant force in the upstream business, having the strongest reserves position and the largest market share. Moreover, bpTT operates under an E&P licence while other suppliers operate under Production Sharing Contracts (PSC). Despite attempts to "level the playing field," the E&P licence is still believed to hold economic advantages over the PSC. There is a risk that in a liberated market the low-cost producers may squeeze out higher cost producers.

Fourthly, apart from ALNG supplies, there is no explicit pipeline tariff associated with gas sales in the market. Part of the new regime would, therefore, require the unbundling of the NGC service to separate the transmission tariff from the cost of gas.

A fifth challenge relates to the cost of production and hence, the viable price of future supplies. The areas with the brightest prospects for new gas supplies are reserves of the deep and ultra-deep horizons and the cross-border reserves held jointly with Venezuela. Conventional wisdom suggests that the monetization of these reserves will be more amenable to a market-based pricing structure.

The above is by no means an exhaustive list of the number of challenges to be addressed in a move towards a more liberated market. It is clear that this is a matter that cannot be avoided for much longer. Policy makers will have at least two sets of recommendations with which to start the process. Consultants Gaffney Cline and Associates suggested an evolutionary approach consisting of three steps (Cline 2001):

• Creation of an independent regulatory authority to oversee the gas sector. The key issues to be addressed by the regulator will include transition of

NGC's role, related party transactions and management of anti-competitive behaviour)
- Separation of NGC into two distinct businesses: Transco and Gasco, with Transco as an open access non-discriminatory transporter with transparent tariffs determined by an independent regulatory authority
- Removal of NGC monopoly over gas purchase/sale rights.

An internal NGC study reached not dissimilar conclusions (Furlonge and Ransome 2002). The study examined four structures for the gas industry.

1. Option 1: The current structure with NGC as the monopsonist and monopolist (apart from the ALNG sales);
2. Option 2: NGC retains its current customers, but all new customers may purchase gas directly from producers and utilize the now open-access NGC pipeline;
3. Option 3: NGC relinquishes the merchant business but retains ownership and operation of the pipeline on an open access basis.
4. Option 4: Fully liberalized market with a privatized open-access pipeline and direct sale between producers and customers.

The study recommended Option 2 as the most desirable for the Trinidad and Tobago market. By this option NGC will own and operate the pipeline system on an open access basis, NGC would continue to purchase and sell gas but without the monopoly rights. Existing customers will have the option to negotiate with any supplier at the end of their contract term. This option was seen as yielding some key benefits, including encouraging more upstream and downstream investments, resulting in growth in revenue and employment; inducing NGC to be more competitive and business oriented in order to maintain its stake in the merchant business; establishment of appropriate legislation to better monitor and regulate the industry. The report further highlights two major risks associated with this option. First is the stagnation NGC could face if it failed to acquire gas supplies at a competitive price. Customers both old and new would prefer to go directly to a supplier. As well, NGC's profitability may be compromised if it was required to hold on to low-price sales contracts. Secondly, opening up the merchant business can lead to the dominant supplier becoming or at least exerting monopoly influence in the market. This suggests that provisions to keep NGC whole must be included in any legislation that accompanies the liberalization process. This means that consideration would have to be given to how unprofitable customers in the NGC portfolio were to be addressed.

An interesting feature of the Trinidad and Tobago gas market is the way in which it has evolved in response to market stimuli. This has been particularly evident in the case of contracts and prices, and it seems set to continue. There is reason to believe that the standard long-term gas contracts may not be the norm in the medium term. Parties on either side—producers and consumers—may have an interest in having greater flexibility in term and quantity. For example, producers with small fields may be unable to satisfy a 10- or 15-year contract but will be happy to do a five-year deal. Large producers may wish to exercise the option to send excess gas to the LNG market or the petrochemical market to take advantage of either spare capacity and or buoyant markets. Similarly, consumers with older, less efficient plant may wish to have the option to temporarily mothball those facilities when product prices do not support their continued operation. Others may be able to stretch capacity to take advantage of temporary market upswings. Existing long-term contracts, with high Take-or-Pay volumes, do not allow the industry to take advantage of such dynamic market opportunities.

The issue of price formation in a liberalized market is not addressed by the studies cited above. Whatever the structure that evolves or is administered, policy makers would need to address the question of price determination. The application of annual fixed escalators on price is a useful and pragmatic tool in the early stages of the development of a gas market, particularly where domestic demand is small and the country does not partake in international gas trade. However, as a major player in both the LNG and petrochemical markets, the Trinidad and Tobago industry may have moved beyond that stage. In addition, the international gas trade has grown rapidly since 1999. For example, global LNG trade doubled from 92 million tonnes/yr in 1999 to 180 million tonnes/yr in 2008. By 2010, the market had a growing volume of uncontracted supplies available for spot sale and for a way to earn the best netback prices for sellers/and traders. These trends are improving the correlation between gas prices in major markets and will before long lead to the emergence of internationally recognized natural gas price benchmark(s). The Trinidad industry is far too integrated with the global business to remain isolated from the trends. Prices in the petrochemical and LNG business are already market sensitive but the use of fixed annual price escalators continue upstream and in most fuel-use contracts downstream. This is gradually eroding the competitiveness of gas in both the domestic and export market. By the end of the first decade of the twenty first century, market developments suggested that a hybrid type of pricing may emerge as a workable solution in a liberalized market. This mechanism involved use of a volume-weighted average of netback prices from the petrochemical and LNG businesses. A T&T gas price could then be declared on a monthly basis by a designated authority. That gas price would be applicable to natural gas at the wellhead. This, plus the application of regulated transmission and distribution tariffs, would determine the gas price to customers currently on fixed escalators. However, a regime of market-determined gas prices should not co-exist with a regime of

Table 4.4. Evolution of NGC Gas Sales Contracts

Year	Parties	Volume	Term	Pricing Basis
1978	NGC/Fertilizers of Trinidad and Tobago Limited	72,000	20	Fixed price plus escalator
1992	NGC/Fertilizers of Trinidad and Tobago Limited	72,000		Product-related (tied to ammonia prices)
1994	NGC/Arcadian Trinidad Ammonia Limited			Product-related (tied to ammonia prices)
2000	NGC/PCS 01/02	125,000	19	Product-related (tied to ammonia prices)
1994	NGC/Arcadian Trinidad Ammonia Limited	25,000	15	Product-related (tied to ammonia prices)
1997	NGC/PCS Nitrogen Limited (03)			Product-related (tied to ammonia prices)
2004	NGC/PCS Nitrogen Limited (03)	42,000	15	Product-related (tied to ammonia prices)
1996	NGC/Arcadian Trinidad Ammonia Limited	65,000	15	Product-related (tied to ammonia prices)
1997	NGC/PCS Nitrogen Limited (04)			
1959	Federation Chemical			
	AMMONIA FEEDSTOCK			
1977	NGC/Tringen I			
1989	NGC/Tringen I			
1991	NGC/Tringen I	54,625	13	Product-related (tied to ammonia prices)
2004	NGC/Tringen I	56,000		Product-related (tied to ammonia prices)
1986	NGC/Tringen II			
1991	NGC/Tringen II	53,000	13	Product-related (tied to ammonia prices)
2004	NGC/Tringen II	30,000	13	Product-related (tied to ammonia prices)
1991	NGC/Hydro Agri	40,300	10	Product-related (tied to ammonia prices)
2004	NGC/Yara	64,000	20	Product-related (tied to ammonia prices)
1995	NGC/Farmland MissChem Limited	64,000		Product-related (tied to ammonia prices)
2003	NGC/Point Lisas Nitrogen Ltd (PLNL)	60,000	15	Product-related (tied to ammonia prices)
2000	NGC/Caribbean Nitrogen Company Ltd (CNC)	60,000	15	Product-related (tied to ammonia prices)
2002	NGC/Nitrogen 2000 UnLimited (N2000)	60,000		Product-related (tied to ammonia prices)
2006	NGC/Methanol Holdings Trinidad Limited (AUM)	87,000	22	Product-related (tied to ammonia prices), with discount fro downsteam product

State-controlled and subsidized liquid fuel prices. Energy prices liberalization must be across the board. Historically, there has been stout resistance to going that route primarily because the Government saw subsidized liquid fuels price as a means of sharing the hydrocarbon wealth with the population. Emerging trends suggested that the imperative to change in the gas industry may force reform in the entire energy market.

NOTES

1. ISCOTT was leased to ISPAT in 1989 and subsequently sold in 1993; The Fertrin Joint Venture was sold to Acadian, later to PCS Nitrogen.TTMC and TTEC were also divested.

2. Trinidad and Tobago's first Prime Minister Dr Eric Williams died in office in March 1981; however, the party he founded, the PNM continued in Government until 1986.

3. The National Alliance for Reconstruction (NAR) won the 1986 general elections, ousting the PNM after 30 years in power.

4. See case study in Chapter 1.

BIBLIOGRAPHY

Baisden, Charles. "Gas to Market Developments in Trinidad and Tobago." *GASCO News*, 2002.

Ball, James, and Rob Sheppard. *Liquefied Natural Gas From Trinidad: The Atlantic LNG Project.* Stanford University, 2004.

Boopsingh, Trevor, and Gregory Mc Guire. "Understanding Gas Pricing." *Production Integration in Caricom.* Kingston: Ian Randle, 2007.

Cline, Gaffney. *Trinidad and Tobago Natural Gas Master Plan.* GOTT, 2001.

Energy Subcommittee. *Vision 2020 Energy.* GOTT, Ministry of Planning and Development, 2004.

Farrell, Trevor. *Worship of the Golden Calf: An Oil Exporter's Industrial Strategy, Technology, Policy and Project Planning During the Boom Years.* Department of Economics, U.W.I, 1987.

Furlonge, Haydn, and Godfrey Ransome. *Options for Gas Transmission and Distribution in Trinidad and Tobago.* NGC, 2002.

Government of Trinidad and Tobago. "Best Use of Our Petroleum Resources." 1975.

Government of Trinidad and Tobago. "Report of the Adams Committee on Natural Gas Pricing." 1978.

Jones, Malcolm. "Development of Natural Gas Industry in Trinidad and Tobago." *Natural Gas in the Americas I.* Institute of Gas Technology, 1994.

Julien, Kenneth. "Emergence of the National Energy Sector." *GASCO News*, 2007.

Mc Guire, Gregory. *Competition in Energy Markets: Trinidad and Tobago Case Study.* Latin American Energy Organization, 2007.

Mc Guire, Gregory. "Policy Proposals on the Pricing of Natural Gas." 1992.

Mottley, Wendell. *Trinidad and Tobago—Industrial Policy 1959-2008.* Ian Randle, 2008.

National Energy Corporation. *A Proposal for a Flexible Gas Pricing Structure.* NEC, 1986.

National Energy Corporation. *Minority Report on Gas Pricing.* NEC, 1987.

Parsan, Elizabeth. "The Fertilizer Industry in Trinidad and Tobago." Msc. Thesis, 1981.

Rampersad, Frank. *Report of the Committee on Gas Pricing.* GOTT, 1987.

Chapter Five

Maximizing National Value— Ownership, National Participation, Local Content and Sustainable Development

Anthony E. Paul

INTRODUCTION

The concept of national sustainable development from natural resource exploitation has proven an elusive dream to many underdeveloped countries. In the 100 years of the oil and gas industry, Trinidad and Tobago, through a remarkable series of convergences of high oil and gas prices with high production levels, combined with visionary leadership and strong institutional capacity, has managed to capture and convert a lot of its value for the purposes of national development.

With the growth of LNG production in the late 1990s, there was widespread recognition that much more could be done, given the dramatic growth in natural gas production, consumption and prices. In 2003, this was translated into the Energy Sector's Vision 2020 Draft Plan, in support of the broader national objective of transforming Trinidad and Tobago into a developed country. A major factor that would contribute to the high level of national value capture was recognized to be the level, depth and breadth of local participation, specifically local participation, ownership and control (involving private equity, in addition to the State sector).

The Energy Sub-committee[1] sought to align the sector goals, objectives and targets with the overall national vision for Trinidad and Tobago to achieve developed nation status by 2020. The challenge was to determine which of the nation's goals are deliverable from the sector in its natural course of business, and how to leverage sector activities for maximum impact on the wider economy.

The energy sector is by far the largest economic sector in Trinidad and Tobago. Its overall goal must be to extract maximum value from the natural hydrocarbon resources in a manner that gives Trinidad and Tobago the capability to sustain itself beyond the life of the resources in the sector.

To avoid the "natural resource curse," the country must use the sector's outputs (raw commodities extracted, human capabilities and products created and financial revenues earned) in a manner that captures and transfers the factors of production needed for sustainability (capital, assets and capabilities) to other sectors of the economy.

By its nature, size and reach, the sector has an unprecedented opportunity to develop the people, businesses, technology and capital markets of Trinidad & Tobago. The industry's size and reach suggests that it could also have a significant impact on sectoral as well as national ethics. An important secondary goal of the sector should therefore be to establish and maintain a set of ethical values and governance for the hydrocarbon sector that sets Trinidad and Tobago as the desired standard in the developing world through its clear commitment to transparency and ethics.

To attain the vision of developed nation status, this sector, which engages developed country companies, people, behaviours and standards and which has a huge footprint on the nation, must leverage its personality to deliver on the nation's objectives of human and economic development.

Its overall goal must therefore be to extract and transfer from the energy sector to other sectors those human and economic characteristics that would benefit the nation as a whole.

To achieve these goals, the following overarching objectives have been identified.

1. Enhanced and accelerated economic development
2. Enhanced human development
3. Robust and respected institutional framework to manage the industry
4. High quality, transparent governance of private and public sector institutions
5. Well-developed private sector, including small and medium enterprise sector
6. The natural environment is protected and enhanced
7. Significant industrial development and diversification to high value-add service industries

Clearly, all of the goals are impacted to a greater or lesser extent by the level of local participation through ownership and control.

NATIONAL OWNERSHIP IN TRINIDAD AND TOBAGO

For small and emerging petroleum-producing countries, the concept of national ownership is synonymous with state ownership during the early stages of national development. Several implications arise from this, many of which are obscured by ideological considerations, particularly as promoted by international institutions which oversee funding and governance. In many regards, however, T&T could be considered unique. Its entrepreneurial beginnings half a century before its birth as a sovereign nation-state laid the foundation for a relationship in which the foreign private sector is accepted as essential to undertaking the exploration risk that precedes production.

BACKGROUND

Chapters 1 and 2 illustrated in some detail the progression to nationalisation of oil industry assets in T&T. Against the background of political independence from Britain in 1962, and the report of a government-appointed Commission of Inquiry into the domestic oil industry, the State made its first tentative steps into ownership as BP sought to relinquish its holdings in Trinidad to pursue its very prospective holdings in the North Slope of Alaska. Those assets were vested in the new Trinidad-Tesoro Petroleum Company Limited which was created as a joint venture with the Tesoro Petroleum Corporation of San Antonio, Texas in 1968.

With the advent of OPEC and the oil embargo in 1973/74, Shell Trinidad Ltd. recognized that its old refining assets at Point Fortin and declining land oil production were liabilities in the increasingly competitive global operations of a changing world order. Thus by August 1974, the newly formed Trintoc (Trinidad and Tobago Oil Company) became the first 100 per cent fully integrated State-owned oil company, complete with oil-producing assets on land and offshore, and with refining and retail marketing outlets. Four years later, in 1976, the State acquired Texaco's domestic retail operations and merged them with the marketing assets purchased from BP back in 1972, to create the National Petroleum Marketing Company (NPMC). The new NPMC became the sole retail marketing company for petroleum products with control over all the outlets of BP, Shell and Texaco. Not affected by these developments on land, the joint venture at Trinmar, (TNA) in the southern Gulf of Paria, continued operating under the same arrangements established in 1953. However, with both BP and Shell interests having been sold to the Government, this very productive set of marine oilfields became another joint venture, with the State having a majority stake as the majority owner (50.1 per cent) of Trinidad-Tesoro. In the early 1970s, the government announced its intention to form a national oil company but despite some early tentative steps, this did not come to fruition until much later.

In the meantime, the discovery and production of large gas reserves off the east coast of Trinidad became the focus of the Government's attention as arrangements were sought for the export of natural gas in the form of LNG, from Trinidad to the USA. A policy announced by Prime Minister, Dr Eric Williams early in the post-1974 era emphasised the Government's intention to use the country's natural gas resources for its own development rather than for export. To that end a large international conference—"The Best Use of our Petroleum Resources"—was held in January 1975 at Chaguaramas on Trinidad's North West coast. By April 1975, another new State enterprise was formed—the National Gas Company of Trinidad and Tobago (NGC) with the expressed purpose of purchasing, transporting and selling natural gas to the domestic market.

In 1975, W. R. Grace & Co., which had been manufacturing anhydrous ammonia at Point Lisas since 1959, was persuaded to enter into a joint venture with the State to construct a new world-scale ammonia export facility next to its existing facilities. Tringen 1 was commissioned in 1978. Amoco was also persuaded to build another ammonia/urea export facility in lieu of a legal "requirement" in its license to build a new refinery. By 1981, two other ammonia plants were commissioned as Fertilisers of Trinidad and Tobago Limited (Fertrin) began operations as a joint venture company (Chapter 1, Case Study 3 refers). The fully State-owned Iron and Steel Company (IS-COTT) and a 100 per cent State-owned urea plant at Point Lisas were commissioned in 1981. A first-time effort at methanol manufacture, Trinidad and Tobago Methanol Co. Ltd. (TTMC) was also commissioned as a 100 per cent State-owned venture in 1983/84.

By 1985, the State had extended its reach even more deeply into the petroleum sector with the sale by Texaco and Tesoro of much of their Trinidad and Tobago interests to the State in the first and last quarter of that year respectively. Texaco retained two important interests in offshore marine acreage, its one-third share of Trinmar and a 50 per cent share in some large gas fields held with Tenneco as the operating partner. Trinidad Tesoro became the Trinidad and Tobago Petroleum Company (Trintopec) which, in 1993, was merged with Trintoc, by then holder of both the Shell and Texaco refining assets, to become Petrotrin, the Petroleum Company of Trinidad and Tobago (Figure 1.1, Chapter 1 refers). In 2001, Texaco finally sold its one-third share in Trinmar to Petrotrin, thus making Trinmar a fully State-owned enterprise, becoming a subsidiary of Petrotrin.

Fuelled by the dramatic increases in the price of oil after 1974, the role of the State in the petroleum sector expanded, as did the sector as a whole, first through acquisitions of older producing entities and then with the establishment of the Pt Lisas Industrial Estate and its several gas-based industrial manufacturing plants. In the production sector, Amoco Trinidad reached a peak oil output of 140,000 bopd in February 1978. By the 1990s however, funds for energy sector expansion had diminished considerably and the State sector once more assumed the role of facilitator. New capital for exploration and production came with the entry of both British Gas and Enron, the latter in response to the failure of the State's effort at offshore gas production at Trintomar (Chapter 1, Case Study 5 refers).

Downstream assets, developed mainly by State capital in the absence of other takers, suffered with the economic downturn in the late 1980s which prompted the sale of Fertrin, TTMC and the power generating assets of T&TEC to fund other Government priorities. Later, with improved market conditions, this divestment resulted in the expansion of manufacturing and processing facilities as occurred at Fertrin's successor, PCS Nitrogen. With government now acting as a facilitator, rather than the primary investor, new private investment flowed in to fuel further expansion of methanol production with Atlas and later Titan, and to support the growth of the largely local, privately-owned TTMC into a global market leader in methanol. T&T's reputation as a world class natural gas processing and manufacturing centre attracted new investments by international companies in steel-making (Nucor) and ammonia (Farmland-Misschem). Gas output escalated sharply, moreso after LNG production came on stream in 1999 with increased investments in Trinidad and Tobago by international capital. In the meantime, the National Gas Company had to expand its pipeline capacity and other transmission infrastructure rapidly to meet the surging demand. Petrotrin also sought to rise to the demand for more oil and refining capacity. With the support of a US$450 million loan from the Inter-American Development Bank, the State oil company embarked on a major upgrade of plant and equipment at its Pointe-a-Pierre refinery while pushing its production effort both offshore and through new secondary recovery efforts on land.

LOCAL CONTENT AND PARTICIPATION: THE CHALLENGE

Typically, a developing country endowed with abundant natural resources of oil or gas recognises that its development is enabled by a wasting asset which belongs to all its citizens and which, once removed, cannot be replenished. As caretaker and manager of these assets, the government has an obligation to ensure that the exploitation of these resources is conducted in a manner that generates maximum benefit to all the people of the country, including future generations whose potential inheritance in being used up. In recognising the impact of resource depletion on opportunities for capturing future wealth, governments should assume the responsibility for ensuring that the exploitation of resources in the present is linked to the generation of wealth in the future.

The oil and gas business requires high input levels of capital, technology, know-how and experience. Given their limited human and capital resources, developing countries invariably have to engage foreign individuals, international businesses and organizations which have the required capabilities for exploring for natural resources and for exploiting and commercializing them.

Moving from a state of total dependency on foreign participation to self-reliance is an aspiration of all developing nations. In this quest, the participation of nationals and domestic firms becomes critical. A key element in making the transition is national control over decision-making.

For T&T, its 100 per cent ownership of key energy companies provided a nursery for developing the practice and habit of decision-making, not only through operational and management activities, but also through strategic business development, financial and leadership control.

However, while control over decision-making is a vital condition, it is not sufficient for ensuring sustainable development beyond a wasting natural resource. That requires a comprehensive development framework that includes an effective fiscal and regulatory regime and policies for local content, capacity development and participation through equity ownership.

AN ATTITUDE OF SUCCESS

In their anxiety to attract foreign investors, many resource-rich developing countries undervalue their own resources and over-value investors' inputs. This reflects a lack of understanding of the value of the resource to the investor, its support companies and its home country.

Developed countries and the mature developing ones that have done better at extracting balanced terms negotiate from the position of owners and controllers of their resources and destiny, rather than as recipients of reward or goodwill. For poor, developing countries, it is virtually impossible to negotiate as an equal, in the absence of self confidence, strong leadership and courage at the top, consistency, skilful analysis and high quality procurement skills and policies (including marketing, negotiating, contracting and contract management capabilities). Lack of experience at the operating levels and clearly articulated national objectives and rules of engagement across the board are vital, but often lacking . Required, but often absent, is a supportive role by the multilateral development and funding agencies, who have historically designed their programmes in ways that serve the needs of the developed countries that finance them.

In the absence of allies within the funding agencies, developing countries would do well to find ways to learn from the experiences of fellow developing countries and seek out, attract and contract investment partners who are the right fit for their national development goals. In T&T's case, for example, this played out to its benefit through the personal relationships that were developed at the highest levels between the Prime Minister of T&T, Dr Eric Williams and the chief executives of Texaco and W.R. Grace in the period just after independence in 1962 (and again in the 1980s and beyond).

As in the case of China's participation in natural resource development in Africa, the question of local content and value-add tends to be challenged, particularly on the grounds of cost and efficiency bases. In response, natural resource rich countries can relate this approach to their experience in military procurement, where, in exchange for transferring huge sums of national wealth overseas, they seek "offsets" that return value, directly or indirectly, to their country.

Offsets refer to "the entire range of industrial and commercial benefits provided to foreign governments as an inducement or condition to purchase military goods or services, including benefits such as co-production, licensed production, subcontracting, technology transfer, in-county procurement, marketing and financial assistance, and joint ventures." A brief discussion of the use of offsets is provided in Appendix 1[2]

MECHANISMS OF VALUE CAPTURE

Governments and countries with natural resources typically seek to maximize the value that is retained in-country or locally through fiscal measures (taxation and royalty policies and government expenditure). Other non-fiscal measures are available to support local value capture and retention through the participation of nationals and local businesses. Getting the most out of these requires local ownership and participation along as much of the value chain as is practical, both within and outside the host country/community. It also calls for local content policies that seek to maximize the use of domestic goods, services, people, businesses and financing, i.e. locally sourced factors of production.

In addition, more and higher value can be captured through on-going local capacity development. Local capacity—in individuals, institutions and businesses—can justifiably be built to support the sector's growth. Clear policy is needed for guiding the investment in developing capacity to embrace local participation in more of the value chain and for transfer to other sectors in order to support wider national development. Legislation and contracts need to factor in access, from the outset, to these opportunities which often arise late in the life of an asset or contract. This is important for investors who are concerned about the long term integrity of their business (often referred to as political stability) and about the impact of political and social fallout against deals considered by the public to be inimical to the interest of the host country.

The mechanisms for capacity development should be carefully identified, secured and contracted for. A key approach to capacity development is transfer of technology and know-how from international participants. Experience has shown that the alliances that have the best success at enhancing, deepening and broadening capability and international competitiveness of local people and businesses, are those partnerships that involve equity participation of locals (see Figure 5.1).

To achieve the widest possible benefit, opportunities should be identified for creating and supporting cluster developments with other industries with potential synergy with some aspect of the natural resource sector.

THE PROCESS OF MAXIMISING
LOCAL VALUE-ADD: FIRST THINGS FIRST

While there is no one size that fits all, and while all countries need to customise the approach to their own unique circumstances, experience indicates

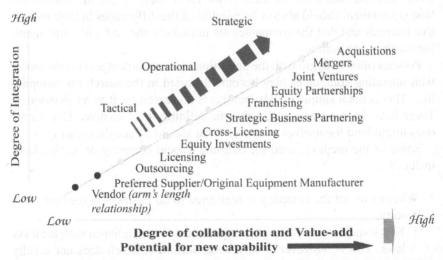

Figure 5.1. **Relationship between Transfer of Know-how and Technology and the Degree of Integration.**

that a staged approach helps to align the implementation strategy to national development goals.

The preliminary stage requires an analysis of the status quo and a mapping of the industry's requirements (inputs) and outputs against national development aspirations. To be effective, a detailed analysis of the industry value chain, including the country's capacity and the participating companies' strategies, will require expertise that may not be available to the host government in the early stages of resource exploration and/or production.

A difficult question faced by poor nations with low salary levels is "how do we justify paying the high costs required for these services?" An analysis of the converse, "what is the cost in lost value, of not having these skills available to us?" leads to an interesting discussion. The answer lies in the State's understanding of the value of investing in the development of people and by having nationals actually involved in the work—especially alongside experts and in-country, where the impact can expand to others and the business support environment can be implemented.

DEFINITION AND TARGET SETTING

Ideally, the issues of local content, target setting and measurement are best addressed at the outset to ensure clarity among all stakeholders. Operating companies, with a history of dealing in different territories, often know what works and does not work for them. Their input could be useful although the host government should always be mindful of the differences in their respective interests and that the companies are ultimately charged with implementing much of the policy.

Policies often struggle with the definition of local content and the discourse with operating companies may become distorted in the search for "simplicity." This is not a simple matter, but this is no reason for it to be abandoned. There have been several approaches to defining local content. The simple ones might lend themselves to abuse. What should be sought is clarity.

Some of the methods used for defining a local company or service have included:

1. Whether or not the company is registered to do business in the host community.
   - This sometimes comes with a requirement for compliance with local tax laws. This is, however, a very weak definition which does not usually address the use of affiliate companies to provide financing, goods and services, as well as the cost of these.

2. A requirement of local ownership—usually 50 per cent or more of its equity has to be held by nationals or legal entities which are registered to do business locally.
   • It is common for companies to abuse this through shareholder agreements that give decision-making or revenue/profit-sharing rights that are out of alignment with the shareholding, often favouring a foreign partner.
   • In some instances, the foreign partner may have other rights that effectively give it majority control, such as the right to buy out the local partner, at any time, for a nominal sum.
3. Majority of staff are national—usually 50 per cent or more of its employees and contractors must be nationals/locals to be considered a local entity.
   • This too, can be subject to abuse. For example, when the actual expenditure associated with foreign employees as compared to local employees far outweighs the ratio of numbers of employees and simply does not reflect the intent of local value capture.
4. Goods and services substantively produced locally—for example 50 per cent or more of its employees and contractors are nationals/locals (for labour intensive activity), 50 per cent of its raw materials are of local origin or 50 per cent combined goods and people of local origin.
   • Issues of numbers of employees, source of origin and cost of goods, in terms of numeric rather than value ratios, often arise with negative consequences.

These are flawed in one way or another and experience suggests that the definition of local content should carefully consider ownership, control and financing by citizens of the home country, even as it attempts to conform to internationally accepted norms and conventions and with issues of practicality.

The difficulty in definition is at its most acute in the setting of targets and measurement of outcomes. Again, companies can be great allies or can erode a lot of value by the effort they put into supporting or perverting the process. Because of the engineering orientation of projects and operations, companies often seek clear, measurable and reportable targets. Governments, on the other hand, often have less quantitative and clearly delineated targets.

Instead of defining fixed targets on a project-by-project or activity-by-activity basis, some countries or regions have found success by carving out selected activities, skills or clusters for focus and by measuring their achievements in ways specific to those. The level of granularity is best worked out by experts in the work processes and skills involved. In time, as capacity and demand change, new or revised targets can be introduced.

For consistency of application and clarity of reporting, an independently auditable system is desirable. This in turn requires consistency of definition and measurement. Complicated assurance systems require very strong and capable institutions, in the absence of which, they could lead to abuse. Where institutional capacity is immature, simple definitions may be appropriate for enforcement. In that context, the following approach is recommended:

- Contributions to local economic and social development can emerge from income to a variety of local factors of production:
  1. Land *(including resources below the surface)*
  2. Labour *(including entrepreneurial & non-manual inputs)*
  3. Capital *(equity & debt)*
- Local Content can therefore be described in terms of:
  1. income received by locals
     – revenues accrued by owners of land and resources
     – Income streams to local shareholders and creditors
- Local ownership of firms and assets is a contributing factor, but not the only contributor to true value-added Local Content.
- Local Content refers to the quantum/percentage of locally produced materials, personnel, financing, goods and services rendered to the oil and gas industry and which can be measured in monetary terms.
- For national development, implementing local content must consider Local Participation in the oil and gas industry with the objective of creating value and contributing to the economic and social development of the country.

For measurement purposes:

- Local Content can be defined as that portion of the sums expended that is retained in the local (T&T) economy.
- Local Participation refers to the level of local equity ownership.

THE CONCEPT OF LOCAL VALUE-ADD

While the concept of local content is well understood and dominates the host government/company dialogue, a more meaningful outcome may be achieved if the local aspirations were to be cast in the frame of Local Value-Add (LVA). This goes beyond local content by bringing to the fore the concept of local ownership and participation in different parts of the value chain.

This is not to be confused with nationalisation and does not imply 100 per cent local ownership of any aspect of the industry. The ability of locals to own some share of an element of the industry, whether as minority shareholder or controller, whether through the state or as private individuals, or whether as a primary operator or supporting services provider, brings a greater level of integration of the sector to the national economy, allowing for profits to flow back into the local economy and for business skills, systems, processes and standards to be developed in line with the requirements of the international partners.

LVA captures the inputs of local goods and services as well as the benefits of local ownership, participation and financing. This can in turn, address issues of local capacity development to meet current and future needs. Taking this approach to local content policies and strategies may create better alignment with the aspirations for national development.

ROLE OF THE STATE

In addition to promoting aggressively, and rigorously applying enabling policies wherever State-controlled resources are involved, the State has a role to:

- facilitate the development of local capability to enable local value added
- remove barriers to local participation
- set targets of local content and participation that will be assigned to individual projects, operations and/or operators and support these targets with appropriate contract terms, including activity obligations and reporting procedures
- ensure that the metrics for each target are appropriate for achieving the required objectives and are consistent with the current and future states of the industry and country
- measure and report on the performance of operators in the sector
- periodically compare the local content and participation performance amongst operators, between projects and operations and, with other countries, to establish benchmarks, targets and opportunities for improvement and for the transfer of best practices.

The approach used in this paper to describe the process of capturing maximum value from natural resources, through local value-add is summarised in Figure 5.2.

DEVELOPING THE POLICIES AND STRATEGIES

The intent always is to implement strategies that ensure delivery of the stated goals. Pragmatism is therefore advised. For maximum benefit, it is best to design the objectives, policies and strategies through:

- an in-depth analysis of the sector and country/region
  ◦ As this typically needs to happen before the start of production and associated revenue to the state, the ability of governments to access good advice is often limited at this critical stage.
- taking a long term view, with a clear understanding of the base line of local capacity and the building blocks/dependencies for each capacity targeted

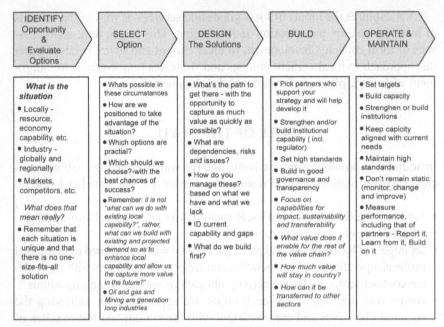

Figure 5.2.   A Systematic Approach to Capturing Local Value-add.

- focusing on the areas of maximum impact
- transparency and the involvement of civil society
  - Given that developing countries have limited human resource and expertise in the areas of interest, there are huge benefits to working in consultation with other local stakeholders, who may have different perspectives, aspirations, priorities, etc. This is important if the primary objective of addressing national and community priorities is kept in mind.
  - Procurement in the natural resources sector, being the biggest area of spend and occurring as frequently as it does across national borders, is notorious for corruption. Where state resources are involved, transparency of procurement procedures, tender awards and contracts, is important for achieving the best results, in terms of national objectives.
  - Transparency enables the involvement of civil society as both support to government and a check on government and private sector excesses.

The national development vision, into which the LVA approach is cast, should have clearly defined national goals and objectives that allow for developing policies that guide the behaviour towards achieving those goals.

In designing and implementing legislation and regulation to give effect to policies, national objectives remain non-negotiable. While companies at a local level acknowledge and often support the LVA concept, head office and regional procurement considerations often militate against such support. Regulation makes it clear whose objectives have priority.

A policy framework should articulate the guiding principles for determining:

- the major mechanisms for local content, participation and capability development
- where, how and by whom these will be delivered, including some key areas for priority focus, the performance measurement, assurance and reporting processes to be used.

In attempting to get the maximum multiplier effect, it is important to seek out and capture capacity that is transferable to other sectors of the economy. Building other sectors provides a road to sustainability that enables the benefits of the depleting resource to be passed on to future generations.

With all the goodwill, well-crafted policies provide no guarantee of delivering the objectives unless the requisite policies and strategies are adhered to. This is achieved only through regulating them and empowering the responsible institutions through:

- developing capacity for analysis (of the resource, industry, markets and investors), finance, procurement, negotiating, contracting and contract and project management
- implementing systems, tools and processes for metrics definition, target setting and data collection that are easy to implement and use
- reporting for accountability, performance measurement, continuous improvement and updating

At a national level, beyond policy and regulation, delivery has to be contracted and monitored. This is only effective if rewards and penalties are attached to compliance or lack thereof.

Bidding should include a requirement for plans to utilise local content and build local capability. These can be weighted to reflect the importance attached to the delivery of national/ regional objectives. Winning bidders should then be contracted to deliver on these promises.

Getting the desired results depends on the right partner, who is typically the operator and who will be at the front line of delivering local value-add, alongside the international contractors. In selecting that partner, and through the projects and activities in the operations, LVA experience and culture should be used as criteria for evaluation and selection of service providers and operator partners.

Even as legislation is essential and is being implemented (Brazil, Timor Leste, Nigeria, Ghana) conflict of interest may arise where a Government or NOC functions as the regulator while being a PSC/PSA partner. In such cases an independent agency, charged with overseeing the local content policy is required, so that 'commercial' interests do not override national interests, without being appropriately challenged. This independent local content agency must have the power of law to be effective (e.g. Brazil and Nigeria).

GETTING DOWN TO WORK—
THE LOCAL CONTENT BUILDING BLOCKS

Developing countries have some common history and situations. Typically, they have some natural resource (oil, gas, minerals, forestry, beaches, agricultural lands, water, etc.). Historically, they lacked the capacity to move these from resource to revenue stream and have been conditioned to use the same model for resource development:

1. Find an advisor (usually foreign, usually supplied by some aid agency, donor government or multilateral agency), who will:
   a. Evaluate the resource
   b. Conduct a market analysis
   c. Recommend a development strategy
2. Having identified a potentially viable business opportunity, the government, alone or in concert with a development partner, will then choose a business partner to:
   a. Design a detailed development plan
   b. Source and contract for markets and marketing support services including shipping, logistics, marketing, trading, distribution, etc
   c. Source and contract for financing, including possibly using the asset for equity and even sometimes raising debt against this
   d. Source and contract engineering, procurement and construction contractors, often from its home base
   e. Oversee the design of infrastructure, plants, etc., often at its home base
   f. Oversee the selection of equipment, etc
   g. Procure goods and services to build out the infrastructure, plants, etc.
   h. Manage the design and implementation of operations systems, procedures, etc.
   i. Manage the construction and commissioning
   j. Hire and train staff to operate the facility
   k. Operate and maintain the facility
   l. Market, transport, trade and distribute products.

Locals are typically involved only at the latest stages of this process, (i) to (k). All the initial work and (l), the commercial aspects of dealing with the produced resource are done at head office, outside of the host country. As the front end, "head office" work is typically only required for "new projects." There is no opportunity for locals to participate or to capture the knowledge needed to do so. The result is that these have always remained head-office skills, resulting in some developing countries stuck in a position where they are always dependent on external help to develop their resources, in spite of multiple projects being developed in a single locality or contract area over time. Even though commercial marketing activities go on for a long time, they continue to be done at head office, outside the sphere of influence of the host for reasons that have gone unchallenged, even as technology has evolved to make the need for location specific delivery of many of these services almost redundant. Figure 5.3 illustrates the scale of the capital expenditure that goes into a natural resource asset before production starts, compared to the on-going expenditure to maintain production.

To move forward, countries need to develop the building blocks that have the potential to get them to the point where they too, can possess those "head-office" skills. A major deterrent in trying to go after these is the lack of continuity of demand for new projects. Trying to get all the capability at once from a single project is not practical.

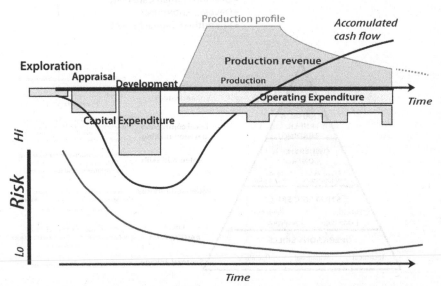

Figure 5.3.   Cash Flow/Activities during the Life Cycle of a Natural Resource Asset.

A far better approach is to put in place a system of building blocks, so that:

1. the basics are done in country and done well
2. sustainable skills and services are targeted from the outset
3. the highest value capabilities that are immediately accessible are secured
4. A plan is put in place to build on these to go after higher value, but with the implementation of sustainable capabilities around what is high value and what is sustainable should consider the multiplier effect of that capacity.
5. Cluster development, both among resource related services and with non-resources- related sectors. It should be sought and facilitated to ensure more benefit is captured.

One way of thinking about the building blocks, as used in the Trinidad and Tobago Framework for Local Value Add, is in terms of developing capacity in People, Businesses and the Capital Markets. This is illustrated in figure 5.4.

PEOPLE

Trinidad and Tobago built capacity in support of its development needs by focusing on the whole education system (including curriculum, teacher and

Figure 5.4. A Framework for Local Value Add, in Support of National Development.

trainer development, systems, processes, infrastructure and access) to meet industrial demand. But, not stopping there, the country leveraged the education infrastructure and systems to deliver training to other sectors and the broader community. This was augmented by development programmes that included on-the-job training, overseas assignments and specialist training by leading trainers in the world, locally and at best-in-class institutions internationally.

Recognising that the technical skills programmes were paying dividends, new and more specialist training programmes were introduced over time. Trinidad and Tobago became a leading exporter of technical experts in everything from drilling complex wells to commissioning and operating sophisticated chemicals plants.

As the industry became more mature and sophisticated, the training moved to degree programmes, initially engineering and geo-sciences then to business/commercial skills before moving to post-graduate research and development, for getting higher value from the resource.

For a long time though, commercial skills were ignored. So too, were design engineering skills, even though there were superb operations and maintenance engineers being routinely produced. Some of these technical skills were in the realm of "head office skills"—the ones that dealt with front-end planning, design procurement etc. Training programmes were augmented by, among other things, creating industry relationships with universities and technical schools and on-the-job training as part of education programmes. Recognising that existing engineering training was very theoretical and limited, changes had to be made to get more front-end design capabilities in the engineering programmes.

ENTERPRISE DEVELOPMENT

The next step was therefore to raise the technical training to another level, while developing programmes for commercial skills. These led, naturally, to business capacity development.

Aside from the commercial skills required to analyse, negotiate, procure, access finance, develop strategies, contract and project manage, a significant aspect missing from the local landscape was leadership development. Although management skills training has been part of the local landscape for many decades, the shortage of skilled managers is as chronic in T&T as it is in other parts of the developing world. Here, one underlying cause has been identified as the character of management in the country itself.

In the era of colonialism, the practice had been, for the home/head office to design strategies, change management programmes and develop and deploy the supporting work systems, tools and processes. Local managers got involved only after the management and operating systems/toolkits were developed and about to be implemented. They were required only to learn these and oversee their implementation. Simply put, they were given a detailed book of rules and only expected to learn how to apply them well. This worked very well in an operations environment, which is what is typically created in natural resource-rich developing countries. What was needed was a mechanism to ensure that as employees were promoted into more senior management and leadership positions, they could analyse an evolving situation and create appropriate "rule books/toolkits" of their own.

As elsewhere, the State oil and gas sector of T&T climbed the steep learning curve with the help of a cadre of competent, dedicated and nationalistic individuals, who were full of self-confidence and had been given the power to build and grow local companies. However, with time and the increasing growth and complexity of the industry, those who had been coping well found themselves ever more burdened and with less and less time to develop or mentor successors, unless a systematic method for doing so were introduced. At all levels and in all disciplines, the "master craftsman" class of business leaders runs the risk of disappearing. Deepening the scope of services in-country provides more opportunities for locals to own and lead oil and gas related businesses and to increase the pool of future leaders.

CAPITAL MARKETS

In Trinidad and Tobago, access to competitive financing has been a problem for companies trying to get into or grow in the oil and gas business. Even though this sector has been generating huge amounts of capital for the local economy, the vast majority goes to the Government. Local banks were awash in cash, but the cost of borrowing is very high. Banks take no risk and Angel and Venture financing are virtually non-existent. Local service companies have to rely on owners' private wealth to generate working capital. Not understanding the risk of the business, the risk assigned and high rates charged by the banks resulted in a cost of capital that eroded the local supplier's ability to be competitive.

Implementing venture capital schemes, providing opportunities for local investors to participate, including selected niche mature fields for development and small downstream plants, were identified as mechanisms to provide the kind of soft landing in which the unsophisticated investor class could feel comfortable in, to support the very competent technical class.

Assigning a portion of the State's share in joint ventures by placing some State companies on the local stock market was seen as an effective mechanism for allowing the wealth generated by the industry to be more widely distributed, through the holdings of pension and mutual funds and individual investors.

LEVELLING THE PLAYING FIELD

While governments can control local companies' access to upstream and downstream opportunities, it is the operating companies that determine where expenditure on goods and services go. It is important to emphasize the services sector in upstream oil and gas since these represent around 80 percent of all money spent by operating companies, for many years, far exceeding the amount paid in taxes and royalties to the host government.

Governments often have more than one opportunity to determine how locals are given access to providing services. Aside from policy and legislation, the government also contracts companies to operate and often, in the case of Production Sharing Agreements, has oversight of budgets and the procurement process.

The traditional approach of "giving preference to local suppliers if the cost, quality and timeliness of delivery of their goods and/or service are of equal quality to the international competitor" has not helped build local capability, as only those who are already globally competitive have a chance of engaging. In fact, this approach has served to hinder access by local suppliers, rather than facilitate it. There is no opportunity to become competitive if the local is not given a chance to do, learn and improve. For this reason "local capability development" must be an important part of any implementation strategy.

Companies may use the tendering process to give preference to local suppliers, for instance, by making local content and/or local capacity development a criterion for bid evaluation. The weight of this may be adjusted to reflect the importance of this capacity to industry or national development. Foreign contractors are therefore not disadvantaged as they are typically the ones with the ability to build capacity locally, through their partnering and sub-contracting strategies and their own local staff development approaches.

None of the benefits of capacity development will be secured unless locals have a fair chance to compete for services. Some companies can be very creative at engaging and enabling local suppliers, while others divert their creativity towards subverting the intent of sound government policy or regulation. Just as there are many examples of ingenious and successful approaches to developing the local supply chain, so too, abound examples around the world of methods used to disadvantage or hinder the participation of locals and overstate the actual quantity of local content. The onus is on the government and civil society to be alert and knowledgeable, so as to ensure that national policies are being effected.

Some ways of levelling the playing field to support local suppliers include:

- Ensuring access to opportunity in a timely manner (i.e. at the same time in a project life cycle as other suppliers—companies doing work at head office, tend to engage home-based suppliers at the front end stage and only invite local suppliers at the tendering stage, where they are disadvantaged, in terms of the required response time.
- No special treatment—bid documents are often designed to target specific suppliers or groups of suppliers and to exclude others.
- Unbundling contracts—companies use the "efficiency of managing less interfaces," as a reason for aggregating services, so that the ability to deliver far outweighs the competence of small, local suppliers. Often, locals are relegated to supplying labour and to competing on cost.
  - This leads to a situation where thin profit margins eliminate the potential for local companies to invest in growth and development, so the ability to compete becomes an illusion.
  - Using a work breakdown structure, governments, via National Local Content Boards or Authorities, or some such legal or regulatory device, may ensure that the contracting is broken up into its various component inputs, so that the strategically important capacity can be provided locally and/or by locals; any extra cost may be viewed by the government as an investment in the future;
  - Special focus should be placed on those skills or services that are deemed strategic to national interests, or which will result in reduced costs, if delivered locally, so that the initial "investment" in capacity development might be recouped.
  - Supporting capacity development institutions can then be shaped to deliver to the needs, while having a market to serve.
- Timely payment of invoices/re-imbursement for goods and services actually provided. Small local businesses have a harder time collecting and due to higher finance costs locally, they end up with reduced profit margins, which stifle their ability to grow and improve and may even cause them to go out of business.
- International service contractors may register a local affiliate, as required by law, but may deliberately leave it low on assets. From time to time, one of these would leave the jurisdiction, leaving local sub-contractors' invoices unpaid at the end of a project.
  - While the main operating company, with a license or contract with the State is held by performance or other bonds, these do not always extend to their contractors. Even though the Petroleum Act mandates contractors being licensed, this has never been implemented.

- Addressing barriers that currently prevent this from happening, such as:
  - bilateral trade treaties with investors' home countries, where foreign governments seek to deliberately exclude requirements for local content.
  - the cost of local financing
  - other procurement practices
    - access to project pipeline and front end work
    - tendering and bid evaluation criteria which give credit to local content or capability development (where current local content is limited).
- Creating and maintaining databases of:
  - projects and operations work programmes, including their needs for the provision of goods and services and their scheduling
  - local suppliers of goods and services
  - people development programmes and initiatives of the operators and their international contractors, including work permits awarded and the related commitments
  - business development programmes and initiatives that support the small and medium enterprises (SMEs) in the sector
  - the status of activities of in-country operators, State-owned companies and agencies and their contractors, including their:
    - local content and participation policies, strategies and initiatives
    - targets, benchmarks and performance metrics
  - appropriate legislation, regulations and contracts.
- Selecting, from time to time, specific goods or services for focusing the local content, participation and supply capability development efforts. Recognising that not all projects, activities, goods or services can be addressed immediately, nor can they all be delivered or sustained locally, the strategy employed should identify areas of focus and special treatment.
- Implement policies to ensure that specific opportunities or equity in projects are available to local private sector companies and investors.
  - Acreage management strategies that recognize the differences between land, shallow water and deep water exploration and production, to promote the development of local independent operators and suppliers.
    - Local operators utilize and support local services companies and ensure their sustainability. They also continue to produce older fields with lower margins after internationals leave.
  - Delineate midstream and downstream projects for favourable local treatment, so as to create and promote opportunities for local private investment perhaps alongside state participation in new ventures.
- Diluting the State's "carried participation" after the high risk exploration or project development phase, so that locals (funds or individuals) can access equity, while augmenting the State's ability to meet its project financing requirements. Care must be taken in these circumstances that the procedures for selecting the local investors are open, fair and transparent;

- Typically, the themes of "local content and participation" have focused primarily on the aspects of in-country activity. The oil, gas and minerals industries generate tremendous value in downstream parts of the value chain, which MNCs tend to break up and place outside of the resource rich country.
  - Skilful partnering can result in building local capabilities that are essential for the capture of further opportunities in the value chain that are outside of the country (shipping, processing, trading, distribution, marketing, etc.)
  - This potential is not achieved unless there are specific strategies for doing so;
- To address the issues of limited capacity and demand, regional collaboration among neighbouring producers may allow for creation of centres of excellence for training, fabrication, accounting services, maritime services, for example.
  - The countries of the Economic Community of West African States offer an example;
- Enshrine LC&P metrics and report on on-going operations, via annual reporting to State Company or Ministry, PSC Operating Committee meetings, etc.

SOME PITFALLS

Be cautious of bi-lateral treaties that promise trade and investment in exchange for "investment friendly" climate that eliminates local content and work permit requirements.

- Companies convince their home governments to put these in place to support their investments
- Companies' home country governments set up treaties that promise more trade and investment; in return the host country agrees not to introduce "investor unfriendly" legislation and to hold certain projects immune against local content and work permit requirements, for example.
- Governments are convinced that these are essential for further downstream, investments;
- Treaties can have the effect of diluting the intent of natural resource laws and/or contracts already in place, including local content and capacity development requirements.
- The host State often uses other tools to assist in capacity development and/ or local content (such as work permits). Bi-lateral treaties may remove the impact of these.

- A clear linkage must be articulated to those in other government agencies who manage these supporting tools/processes, so that the effective impact of LVA is not diminished.
- A country's lack of self-confidence and capacity to manage challenges with respect to WTO, bi-laterals, protectionism and internal corruption etc., present major limits to countries that are aggressively pursuing local value-add strategies.
- Companies have the capacity to either corrupt the process or improve it.
  - Their initial requirement is that any provider of goods or services must be competitive in cost and quality. This is not likely to happen at the outset but should not be a reason to eschew local capacity development, which is itself an investment paid for, ultimately by the host country, through cost recovery and/or tax write-offs.
  - Operating companies are very creative at finding ways around the reporting system, using a host of mechanisms which allow them, for example, to shift costs around different cost centres, which the local tax authority lacks the capacity to track.
  - They can also be very good at finding ways to develop the local supply chain, which they do routinely in their home countries.
  - Typically, companies will invoke "international best practice" or home country "standards" to ensure that locals are unable to compete, and bring in a preferred international partner. On occasion, this is the consequence of a range of situations, from as simple as personal relationships (at all levels, from design engineer, project manager or procurement professional, to senior executives), to as complex as moving costs or benefits across cost centres or tax jurisdictions.
- In one instance, a British company changed all the requirements for diving contractors to meet North Sea standards, in an environment where the conditions were nowhere near those of the North Sea. Local diving companies that had been operating for more than 30 years were immediately displaced by a British firm, who then promptly hired the local divers and re-certified them, with minimal training.
  - In other instances, HSE standards are applied without any attempt to get the local contractors up to speed. Here, as in the case above, the absence of local standards opens up the process to abuse, as governments are not likely to tell companies that their standards are too high.
  - The response includes having the companies work with local training institutions and contractors to build their capacity to be able to participate. In addition, the government or regulator, not companies, should set or ensure national standards exist or are observed. Again, the need for targets and penalties cannot be overstated. Companies having better negotiators than some developing countries, can—and do—claw-back gains made

by the state in upstream licences/contracts, through getting into new or downstream projects, for instance.
- Corrupt government and state company officials and IOC personnel could significantly affect the procurement process and the impact of LVA. Also, international companies and their contractors in the front line of procurement, have more opportunities for corrupt practices than local officials. Ultimately, the population pays the price of inefficient and/or corrupt procurement.
  - Governments are not likely to find out about internal company investigations of corrupt or unethical practices in IOCs.
  - Transparency of contracts and procurement procedures- including tendering and bid awards- are critical in mitigating this impact.
  - A deficiency of critical expertise in the start-up phase could expose governments to the risk of gaps in contracts and procedures that could seriously work against them later on;
  - Codes of practice for company and government personnel, with penalties for lack of compliance, could assist within an effective policing system;
  - Benchmarking of project and operating costs across multiple companies and jurisdictions/locations could be very helpful to governments. While often readily available these studies are not systematically used by governments who would benefit by adopting the practices of companies that submit their data to be collated and analysed for benchmarking purposes.

LEARNING FROM SOME
SUCCESSFUL IMPLEMENTATIONS

It Must be a National Priority—
Have a very high level champion

- Policies and objectives must be clear, consistent and connected to national development goals.
  National goals and objectives must be non-negotiable.
- Local content and knowledge and technology transfer should be regulated and not be left as optional for international oil and service companies.;
- Bi-lateral treaties that promise trade and investment at the expense of local content, work permit requirements and knowledge transfer opportunities should be avoided.

Figure 5.5 illustrates one approach to defining the priorities and strategies for successful implementation of a local content plan. Note the multiple opportunities for both State intervention as well as derailment of objectives. The imperative must be therefore for a coherent, strategic and well-executed and maintained plan.

Figure 5.5.   An Approach to Defining Priorities, Initiatives and Activities for Successful Local Content and Participation Implementation.

Think Strategically, Act Practically

- Set up a fair and realistic local content policy:
  - Adapting it to the existing skills base is a necessary, but not sufficient condition.
  - Focus on services
  - Disaggregate service contracts to give locals a chance to compete and build capacity but recognise that the global or regional procurement strategies of international companies might mitigate against this. (Remember "offsets.") Be selective, based on strategic value to stakeholders.
- Engage early in the life cycle and contract for it..
- Take a business-like and business-friendly approach:
  - It should be desirable and achievable
- Manage the programme of activities in the sector as a portfolio, so that project pace and scheduling allow maximum opportunity for developing and utilising local capabilities on an on-going basis.
- Target local capability development by increasing the number, depth and breadth of in-country activities, so as to encourage fuller participation of nationals and enterprises in the value chain:
  - "Do it in- Country" first, then "Do it with Locals" next.
- Give first preference to locally owned, controlled and financed enterprises, then to those that demonstrate a clear culture, commitment and capacity for maximising local value-added, participation and capability development, consistent with the country's aspirations and vision:
  - Focus on improving local technical and management skills, business know-how, technology, financing, capital market development, and wealth capture and distribution.

- Pick partners who support your strategy and will help to deliver it.
- Consider "regional centres of excellence" to build up critical demand mass.
  - Shared services, skills development, infrastructure, equipment
- Regulate local content and knowledge and technology transfer
  - Make it part of the legislation, as well as the contracts;
  - Despite all the goodwill in the host country, head office often has different incentives to use outside contractors;
  - International companies will always attempt to minimise their risk by using suppliers whom they know and trust, at the expense of the developing new suppliers including established local companies.
- Don't remain static (monitor, change and improve)
  - Measure performance. Report it. Learn from it. Build on it.
  - Set targets based on practical capacity development or usage goals.
  - Use these targets to determine appropriate metrics and then develop simple and clear systems and procedures for measuring and reporting.
  - Metrics should always be under review to remain relevant to changing circumstances.
  - Metrics may be combined, e.g. number of man-hours, with specific focus on some types of activities, plus the cost of local vs. foreign man-hours.

Analyze, Analyze, Analyze

- See capacity development as an investment
  - The question to be asked:
    - Not: "What can we do with existing local capability?"
    - But: "What can we build with existing and projected demand, so as to enhance local capability and allow us to capture more value in the future?
  - Identify current capability and gaps
  - Identify areas for focused effort
  - Set targets
  - Build capability
  - Strengthen or build institutions
  - Set and maintain high standards
  - Don't remain static but monitor, change and improve.

Appendix 2 lists some of the Local Content Best Practice & Recommendations from the comprehensive Chatham House Project Good Governance in National Petroleum Companies.[3]

CREATING SUSTAINABILITY FROM THE ENERGY SECTOR

T&T Lessons On Local Content And Capacity Development—The Generation Game

Ironically, some of T&T's better examples of national and local development, supported by human, institutional and infrastructural capacity enhancement took place in the middle of the 20th century, pre- and post-WWII, under a colonial government. Although the industry was owned and operated by foreign companies, activities involved in all aspects of operating the business were conducted within T&T and those conducting them spent most of their careers here. T&T was truly home for these expatriates and their companies.

This may not have been by choice, but of necessity at a time when travel and communication were so limited that oilfield operations caused entire eco-systems to be built around the fields—everything from technical and business support services, to social support services such as restaurants, schools, hospitals, churches, cinemas and cemeteries had to be built and maintained for the use of both expatriate and local personnel and their families (often separate facilities for different groups, but that is another story). Not only was travel to their home country limited to annual vacation, but even a day trip to the cities was out of the question since many of the oilfields, like the towns and cities, were not connected by access roads.

The result was congruence between the nature of the industry and the way it was managed, whereby the oil companies defined the shape and evolution of the communities in which they operated. To this day, people speak about the towns and institutions supported by Shell and Texaco (see Chapter 10), and aspire to recapture that spirit of community involvement instilled by the companies. Corporate Social Responsibility initiatives that are not grounded in an understanding of the oil community eco-system will find it difficult to achieve the social and economic peace within the communities in which the corporations operate. Worse, community sustainability beyond the life of the enterprise will be elusive with the attendant risk of boom towns becoming ghost towns once the oil and gas companies have left.

While T&T's past successes may be sustainable into the future, there remain areas for improvement. Communication technology and the culture of expatriate expertise stand in the way of attempts by developing countries to assert their sovereignty in serving their own best interests. The experiments on local content, capacity development and sustainability that T&T undertook between the 1970s and the beginning of the 21st century, suggest that such hurdles can be overcome. Inspired policies and strategies, combined with visionary leadership can, indeed, negotiate the space to ensure that international oil and gas companies accept responsibility for the development and sustainability of the national energy eco-system.

Towards the end of the first oil century, there were signs that the negotiating relationship between T&T and foreign oil and gas investors had begun to change. One hundred years in the business had given T&T a measure of self-confidence that laid the basis for more equitable negotiations. For one thing, T&T recognised that it held assets that were of great value to foreign companies and countries:

- Natural resources: oil and natural gas.
- People: skills and experience;
- Supporting environment: infrastructure, services, legal and fiscal regime, stable political and business environment, educational and government institutions.

T&T recognized too, that it wanted development on many fronts:

- National, regional, local/community
- Human: capabilities, know-how/experience in new and specialized areas
- Capital markets development and access to capital
- Technology
- Access to markets

From across the table, T&T was aware that foreign investors were bringing assets of their own that T&T needed:

- Capital
- Technology Know-How
- Strategic expertise in areas such as value chain analysis, financing, negotiating, contract management, risk management, procurement, project management, trading and marketing.

On some fronts, there was alignment of interests—investors wanted access to T&T's natural resources and businesslike institutional framework. On other fronts, there were clear conflicts. Driven by the need to create shareholder value, investors pushed for maximum profits and greater capture of resource value. Investors pushed to extract value as quickly as possible leaving little room for increasing local capacity to capture greater local value.

What differentiated T&T this time around was the confidence of its leadership as reflected in its surer sense of ownership and control of its resources, instead of subservience of a junior player standing cap-in-hand, requesting goodwill or reward.

Going forward, T&T, like other countries, will face new challenges. New opportunities will present themselves as well. As before, an approach, supported by deep and considered analysis, as taken in the 1990s will serve well. Countries pursuing policies for sustainable development will ask the following:

• How to get it quickly?
• How to translate the benefits from investment into development?
• How to sustain development?

Recognizing their limitations, they will seek out these investors who are most aligned with their objectives. Traditionally, multinational companies brought all the missing pieces of the puzzle for a country seeking development through natural resource exploitation. As aggregators of goods and services, they maximized their benefit from the natural resource by capturing value along the entire chain, including outside the host country. The traditional model also involved splitting the value chain so that value-adding processing and trading occurred outside the host country and often, without the involvement of the original owner of the raw material.

The marketplace has undergone significant change since those days. There are now two different types of players vying for the attention of resource owners. Smaller, nimble investors act as dis-aggregators, keeping their core business tight and narrowly focused and capturing value by bringing together the other pieces of the project with the support of specialists (in finance or technology, for example). The key to negotiating with these investors is to recognize that their business model hinges on having access to the natural resource. They have nothing without the resource which is what enables them to get finance, technology and skills to develop and monetize the resource. Once countries understand the value of their resource to such an investor, they will understand how much of an upper hand they have in the ensuing negotiations. This is a complete reversal of the days when countries "competed" for investors by racing to the bottom in giving away their resources faster and cheaper.

The second group of investors is, in a sense, super-aggregators, who provide services beyond the industry needs and which governments should provide, but often lack the capacity for doing so. These investors (usually state companies, supported by their home government) understand the political need for quick implementation of public works and services. Early in the development of a natural resource, they can provide access to finance, procurement and project management skills (often lacking in small governments) so that some aspects of development (such as major construction) that usually take a long time, given the nature of cash flow from natural resource projects, can be delivered in sync with the political elections cycle. There are however, several pros and cons to this approach, particularly involving good governance and transparency which are at the very heart of sustainable development.

One other challenge that T&T faced and others will, is the question of aspiration—pace and scale of growth. How much should be sought? How quickly? To these, the prevailing wisdom advises: "Don't try to do too much too quickly," "start small," and "manage expectations." A better way to approach this dilemma may be to ask another question:

- Which is better?
  ○ To over-aspire and under achieve, or to under-aspire and strive to over-achieve?
  ○ To "manage expectations" or to "aim high?"

APPENDIX 1: OFFSETS

- Common in military procurement contracts
- "Offset" means the entire range of industrial and commercial benefits provided to foreign governments as an inducement or condition to purchase military goods or services, including benefits such as:
  ○ co-production
  ○ licensed production
  ○ subcontracting
  ○ technology transfer
  ○ in-county procurement
  ○ marketing and financial assistance
  ○ joint ventures

(Defence Offsets Disclosure Act of 1999, Pub. L. 106-113, section 1243(3)).

- There are two types of offsets: direct offsets and indirect offsets.
  ○ "Direct offset" is a form of compensation to a purchaser involving goods or services that are directly related to the item being purchased.
- For example, as a condition of a US sale, the contractor may agree to permit the purchaser to produce in its country certain components or subsystems of the item being sold.
- Normally, direct offsets must be performed within a specified period.
  ○ "Indirect offset" is a form of compensation to a purchaser involving goods or services that are unrelated to the item being purchased.

- For example, as a condition of a sale the contractor may agree to purchase certain of the customer's manufactured products, agricultural commodities, raw materials, or services.
- Indirect offsets may be accomplished over an expected, open-ended period of time
- Valuation of offsets is an arbitrary process resulting from:
  - the perceived needs of the importing nation and
  - The negotiating skill of the US supplier.

APPENDIX 2

Chatham House Good-Governance in National Petroleum Companies—Local Content Best Practice and Recommendations:

Distortion in the procurement process

- The risk is that the distortion to the procurement process created by local content requirements could lead to delays and cost increases, and unnecessary tensions between the IOCs and NOC.
- For most countries, the rational solution should be to develop a local supply of some competitive goods and services required by the petroleum industry, but not to demand an indiscriminate use of local suppliers.
- In the case of minimum local content requirements, waivers will often be required because the local capacity is too limited. This may easily create a situation of bureaucratic delays as applications for exemptions are processed. It may also prepare the ground for increased corruption with the aim of avoiding such delays.

A Neutral and Transparent Local Content Policy

- Some countries such as Norway and UK have neutral organizations (Achilles, Offshore Supplies Office) to facilitate efficiencies in the supply chain management, and to provide objective information to the oil companies on potential and actual capabilities of suppliers and contractors, and to provide suppliers with consistent and up-to-date information on potential contracts and purchasers in the markets.
- In Nigeria, the oil industry has been arguing strongly for a similar system to ensure fairness and transparency, and the Nigerians have accepted the need for an independent body to register and pre-qualify the companies to avoid some of the pitfalls often linked to local content policies.

- Helpful processes may include:
  - ○ the introduction of tools to monitor national content or adherence to labour standards of supplies related to such new developments, and
  - ○ Other measures to maximize local/national value creation from local/regional oil and gas developments.
- The local supply chain will be more successful if combined with exposing local suppliers to the discipline of the market competition after a relatively short period of protection.

Key Questions for Local Content and Development Policies

- Are development requirements clearly specified?
- How is performance measured, and by whom?
- Is there a process for adjusting obligations in light of changed circumstances?
- Are development requirements public?

Toolbox for Local Content (Development) Commitments

- Public criteria for development commitments (e.g. minimize discretionary support for individuals, competitive processes for gaining support)
- Benefits of development programmes should be public (not private deals for political favourites)
- Special agency like UK OSO (Offshore Supplies Office) with knowledge of local development to:
- Advise on feasibility of requirements
- Monitor performance
- Adjust commitments
- Report to government and companies involved

NOTES

1. Vision 2020 Energy. Draft Report of the Vision 2020 Energy Subcommittee May 2004; Chapter 5.
2. For a brief discussion on the use of "OFFSETS" see appendix 1; See also US Government Offsets Disclosure Act of 1999, Pub.L. 106-113, section 1243(3).
3. See Report on Good Governance of the National Petroleum Sector April 2007. (http://www.chathamhouse.org.uk/research/eedp/current_projects/good_governance/).

Chapter Six

Trinidad and Tobago and Its Neighbours

Anthony T. Bryan

INTRODUCTION

As Trinidad and Tobago (T&T) celebrated 100 years of uninterrupted production in its oil industry, it would be wrong to assume that managing the industry implies autonomous choice and responsibility. For any developing economy dependent on a single export commodity, powerful economic and political forces, both domestic and external, qualify the choices open to governments and structure their incentives. How can governments strike a balance between internal structural forces, external constraints and daring initiatives, in order to influence positive development outcomes? If, as some critics insist, the geological wealth of T&T has turned out to be a mixed blessing for the country, it is tempting to put the blame on poor leadership and examples of questionable public policy. In the end, governments are the main recipients of oil revenues and decide how they are spent.

Oil exporting countries like T&T face two important challenges. First, oil is a wasting asset that eventually will be exhausted. It is not a permanent source of income. Revenues from oil must be used to create self-sustaining sources of wealth. Second, oil revenues are unstable and governments must negotiate what price level best meets their particular mixture of short- and long-term objectives. They must also take an interest in maintaining stability or, at minimum, a price floor. In meeting these challenges, how a country conducts its "resource diplomacy" becomes a critical measure of its ability to overcome constraints to its long-term economic potential.

In recent history, the most remarkable characteristics of Trinidad and Tobago's growth as a petroleum economy, and recently as a natural gas economy, have been the country's democratic political stability; the ability of successive governments to understand, drive and orchestrate the technocratic

human talent in the service of the energy sector; government policies that
have conferred a competitive advantage to projects (while balancing the long-
term benefits of a potentially successful project with the concessions needed
to implement the project); and the consistently positive attitude towards foreign investment. T&T's hydrocarbon resources and natural gas reserves have
made it the most industrialized country in the Caribbean, and it is, arguably,
one of the few oil exporting countries that has used its resources wisely.

The making of T&T's energy policy has been deliberate and consistent.
All political administrations have read from the same page. T&T is a stable
democracy where the institutions for upholding and enforcing international
commitments are strong and not severely politicized. Rarely has the politics
of making energy policy resulted in domestic strife. On occasion (as in the
case of Texaco Trinidad in the 1980s), there was some political and civil
disruption over an ideology that favoured divestment of the petroleum sector. Although the domestic politics of energy is almost tranquil in T&T, the
politics of regional energy cooperation is quite spirited.

The consistency of T&T's energy policy over time, despite changes in
political leadership, has underpinned its relations and diplomacy with its Caribbean and Latin American neighbours. The oil-based economy of the 20th
century presented the country with significant diplomatic challenges, as does
the gas-based economy of the 21st century. T&T's geopolitical and regional
influence in the Caribbean, because of its energy resources, have always
required formidable technical expertise, elements of pragmatism and the use
of significant political and diplomatic skill. Its "resource diplomacy" with
respect to countries such as Venezuela and the USA, and with regional group-
ings like CARICOM and PetroCaribe, is the main ingredient of the story.
Some other countries and institutions are also part of the mix (Bryan 2007).

T&T AND VENEZUELA

Because of proximity and the geological resource connection, the relationship
between Venezuela and T&T has been singular and, at times, intense. That
relationship began to accelerate during the boom period of the oil industry between 1914 and 1924. The considerable increase in production in these years,
the result of successful exploitation of Forest Reserve and many south-west-
ern fields by Trinidad Leaseholds Limited (TLL), Apex Trinidad Oilfields in
Fyzabad and Kern Trinidad Oilfields, served to consolidate foreign expertise
in the industry. The administrative and technical staff was mostly British and
European, the drillers tended to be American and the semi-skilled or unskilled
labour Trinidadian, or from smaller Eastern Caribbean islands. The social life

of the oilfield staff camps were organized on a "whites only" basis reflecting the larger societal structures in the country at that time. By the 1920s the oil companies had begun to train local blacks as technicians, but many of them, resenting the salary discrimination that favoured foreign drillers and technicians, left Trinidad for Venezuela to take advantage of the oil boom there. In Venezuela they were treated on an equal basis with other expatriates. It was not until the 1950s that significant numbers of Trinidadians entered supervisory positions in their country's oil industry (Brereton 1981).

Despite the fact that many T&T families settled in certain areas of Eastern Venezuela, there has always been a facility of movement of peoples between the southwest of Trinidad and proximate areas of Venezuela, and that many Venezuelans studied in Trinidad's "prestige" secondary schools, formal state relations between both countries were traditionally distant. Venezuela's claim to two-thirds of Guyana's territory, and the ongoing issue of T&T's fishermen being fined and jailed for fishing in "Venezuelan waters" have not inspired confidence at official levels in a strong relationship. But those very circumstances demanded that T&T maintain a close interaction with Venezuela. While formal diplomatic relations ensued, and there was constant interaction between both countries in regional multilateral organizations such as the Organization of American States (OAS), the Inter-American Development Bank (IDB), the Caribbean Development Bank (CDB), the Sistema Económico Latinoamericano (SELA) and the United Nations Economic Commission for Latin America (UNECLAC), it was at the level of Caribbean regional economics and politics that the relationship sometimes became disruptive.

Ironically, one of the early regional flash points between Venezuela and T&T was the result of an initiative undertaken by both Mexico and Venezuela with respect to Jamaica. In November 1974 Mexican president Luis Echeverría and Jamaican Prime Minister Michael Manley signed a formal Jamaica-Mexico agreement in which the two countries intended to undertake the joint production of alumina, aluminium, and aluminium manufactures in Mexico and Jamaica. It envisioned the construction of an alumina plant in Jamaica (JAVEMEX) having a capacity of 900,000 short tons per year and an aluminium smelter (JALUMEX) with an annual capacity of 120,000 tons sited in Mexico. The Mexican smelter would be supplied with Jamaican alumina. Each government would own 51 percent of the enterprise located in its territory, with 29 percent of the remaining shares going to the partner and the rest of the 20 percent divided between privately owned companies, other governments or foreign investors. Other joint enterprises between the two countries, particularly in maritime transport, were detailed. The plans did not come to fruition because Mexico withdrew from the projects in April 1978 under the new Mexican administration of Jose López Portillo, who shifted the Mexican foreign policy direction away from the regional leadership role envisioned by his predecessor.

The Jamaica-Mexico agreement, during its short shelf life, became a catalyst for regional controversy because of a side agreement between Jamaica and Venezuela in 1975. Jamaica agreed to supply Venezuela with 200,000 tons of alumina a year for 10 years and 400,000 tons of bauxite a year for three years, increasing to 500,000 tons for the remaining seven years. In return, Venezuela agreed to provide Jamaica with all the crude petroleum needed to satisfy its industrial requirements at a pre-1973 price, the difference to be deposited in the Central Bank of Jamaica and used for the financing of programmes and investment projects contributing to the development of natural resources and the promotion of exports. In a separate agreement, Venezuela agreed to hold 10 percent of the shares in JAVEMEX (Bryan, The Islands and the Littoral 1979).

The Mexican-Jamaican-Venezuelan projects with respect to bauxite and aluminium evoked heavy public criticism from T&T's Prime Minister, Dr Eric Williams, in 1975. He saw them as counterproductive to a proposed aluminium project agreed to by the governments of T&T, Jamaica and Guyana in June 1974. Most of Williams' accusations were directed toward Venezuela. The Prime Minister portrayed Venezuela as a neighbourhood giant attempting to "recolonise the Caribbean" through "petrodollar politics." His verbal attacks implied that he was concerned that both Venezuela and Mexico were attempting to play pivotal roles in the Commonwealth Caribbean region, a role that might have been reserved for T&T. He withdrew T&T's participation in the planned smelter project with Jamaica and Guyana.

The entire issue resulted in malaise in relations between Jamaica and T&T, and between the latter and its major partners in CARICOM, and raised what would become a perpetual regional debate about the effects of bilateral arrangements by CARICOM member states with non-member countries, on the integration movement and on regional coherence in the Caribbean (Bryan, 1979: 240). These Jamaica-Venezuela arrangements, which became the subject of much political controversy in the Caribbean at that time, were a prelude to much later controversies over PetroCaribe and ALBA.

In the relations between Venezuela and T&T there were also examples of cooperation in difficult times. Although at the rhetorical level in the 1970s relations with Venezuela seemed to have reached a very low point, at the functional level there were productive initiatives. Talks on fishing and maritime delimitation produced a Joint Fisheries Commission in 1977 (whose life was extended subsequently) as well as an agreement on the delimitation of marine and submarine areas in 1990. Notably, since the first global oil crisis in 1973 the oil exporters in the region implemented several financing mechanisms designed to ease the burden on less fortunate neighbours. Three such regimes existed prior to 2003. In 1980, T&T offered the CARICOM Oil Facility, which provided for the financing of incremental purchases of oil, fertilizer, and asphalt from T&T at 1979 prices. At about the same time, Venezuela and Mexico offered the region's oil importers special loan arrangements under the San José Accord. Both facilities lapsed when oil prices crashed in 1983. In the aftermath of the price spiral in 2000, Venezuela introduced the Caracas Accord, which was an extension of the earlier San José Accord. Under this agreement beneficiary countries are entitled to loans, with low interest and extended repayment terms, to help finance the cost of oil imports from Petróleos de Venezuela S.A (PDVSA), the Venezuelan State petroleum company. In 2004, T&T proposed its own oil facility which included a loan initiative to finance purchases of petroleum products above US$30per barrel oil price. It also financed a Trinidad and Tobago Petroleum Fund for providing annual economic development grants to CARICOM countries. The common weakness of all these facilities is that they transfer the burden of today's consumption and costs to tomorrow's generation. They are based on the assumption that oil prices will fall and therefore provide room for repayment in the future, when in fact there is no guarantee that this will indeed be the case.

PETROCARIBE

In July 2005, a dramatic change in petroleum supply to the Caribbean islands was initiated with the signing of the PetroCaribe agreement between Venezuela and a number of Caribbean countries. The agreement has provided budgetary and development options for some countries in the region suffering from the loss of their traditional export markets for agricultural commodities. It offers oil to its members at preferential prices. At first glance, the basic facts about PetroCaribe are straightforward. According to its framework agreement (PetroCaribe, 2005) each signatory agrees on how much oil or petroleum products it requires from Venezuela. Depending on the world price of oil, a fixed percentage is assigned to the recipient nation in the form of a soft loan. If oil is at $50 per barrel, the loan to the nation concerned will be set at 40 percent of the value of the overall purchase; if, for example, oil goes to $100 per barrel or beyond, a 50 percent loan will be provided over the agreed period. Financing is at 1 percent interest. There is a two-year grace period and an overall repayment period varying between 17 and 25 years. This structuring, it suggested, enables nations to continue to operate within conditions imposed by multilateral agencies such as the International Monetary Fund and World Bank.

The programme envisages that nations receiving refined products will see reduced prices per barrel. Among recipient nations, only the Bahamas, Jamaica, and Suriname have appropriate refineries. The regional scheme was extended to incorporate oil exploration, distribution and storage. There are separate agreements with Cuba for oil exploration and with Cuba the Dominican Republic, and Jamaica for the improvement and expansion of their refining capacity, designating them as refining centres to supply fuel and fuel products to CARICOM states. Under a deal struck in December 2006 between PDVSA and the West Indies Oil Company (WIOC) for the rental of fuel storage facilities, Antigua & Barbuda (which owns 25 percent of WIOC) became a collection centre and trans-shipment point in the distribution of diesel, jet fuel, and gasoline to Eastern Caribbean countries. The PetroCaribe programme also tries to address the problem of storage. Unused tanks located in Venezuela will be dismantled and shipped to CARICOM countries. The programme was extended to Haiti in January 2006 after the election of René Preval as president. In December 2006, Belize signed on to the deal. Honduras joined in December 2007. Guatemala and Costa Rica joined the grouping during 2008, bringing the membership to 18. Several Caribbean countries started to benefit (or expected to benefit) with supplies of crude or refined products through the arrangement. But by the end of the decade the results for PetroCaribe members were mixed. Jamaica benefited most from shipments, and PDVSA helped to finance development projects, such as a $500 million Jamaican refinery upgrade and expansion, under an agreement that would give the Venezuelan State oil company a 49 percent stake in the facility. Venezuela also took on the role of principal supplier, providing in 2007 almost 24,000 bpd out of the 28,000 bpd consumed in the country. There were also loans to help in the completion of major highway projects in Jamaica. Caracas also got involved in upgrading Cuba's Cienfuegos refinery and a refinery in the Dominican Republic.

However, all was not well with PetroCaribe. First, progress over implementing these projects was slow and PDVSA had serious problems in trying to deal with the management of such small quantities, particularly where the infrastructure for delivery had to be created. Only Jamaica and Cuba received regular (as opposed to sporadic) shipments. The Venezuelan oil minister, Rafael Ramírez, acknowledged in December 2007 that his nation was shipping far less oil than previously expected. PetroCaribe members received 145,000 barrels daily (rather than the 300,000 barrels initially planned), and of these, 95,000 went to Cuba under a more complex arrangement. Second, while there is little doubt that the PetroCaribe programme was an energy lifeline that prevented the region from going into economic free fall in a time of austerity, it also proved to be a great accelerator of debt for some Caribbean members. While the agreement offered concessionary financing to these heavily indebted nations, it placed them in a financial bind by allowing some to pay with agricultural goods (whose value fluctuated greatly from week to week) for part of their fuel bills. These nations ultimately take on more debt to pay these bills. Projections are that by 2015 more than one third of the external debt of the CARICOM members of PetroCaribe will be owed to Venezuela (Jessop 2011). Third, Venezuela's "oil diplomacy" through PetroCaribe depends on continuously high oil prices, and is possible only as long as such is the case.

REACTION TO PETROCARIBE

The issues surrounding PetroCaribe have posed diplomatic challenges for the CARICOM region as an entity. T&T and Barbados declined to sign the Petro-Caribe agreement. T&T was concerned that its Petrotrin refinery stood to lose about 30 percent of its product sales of petroleum products, fuel oil, diesel, and gasoline to the Caribbean. Approximately 56 percent of Petrotrin's product sales were in the Caribbean market. Phoenix Park Gas Processors Ltd., which traditionally supplied natural gas liquids to the CARICOM region, also suffered a decline in sales. The PetroCaribe arrangement undercut T&T's two regional initiatives: an oil facility to CARICOM countries that includes a loan initiative to finance purchases of petroleum products above the price of $30 a barrel of oil, and a Trinidad and Tobago Petroleum Fund (established in 2004 and ratified by CARICOM in 2005) that makes an annual grant to CARICOM member states to help them in developing their economies.

The Government of T&T was angered specifically by the almost total acceptance of the Venezuelan initiative by CARICOM members in preference to the regime of assistance being offered by T&T. Prime Minister Patrick Manning of T&T was critical from the outset about the rush to sign the agreement in spite of its apparent weaknesses. He indicated that the initiative would force out private oil firms, leaving the region dependent on a single State-run supplier—Venezuela's PDVSA. He also suggested that Petrotrin, the T&T State-owned refinery that was the traditional supplier to CARICOM, would be hurt financially and that T&T could stop selling its oil and petroleum products to its neighbours and seek extra-regional markets. In such a case, he noted, guarantees could not be offered to countries attempting to resume buying oil and petroleum products from T&T if the PetroCaribe agreement eventually faltered (BBC Caribbean, 2006). According to the Minister of Energy of Barbados, that country saw no need to sign on to PetroCaribe because its crude oil is already refined in Trinidad; PetroCaribe would not deliver discounted prices for petroleum products; petroleum products originating in Venezuela would attract the 20 percent CARICOM Common External Tariff (CET); and the agreement would result in debt accumulation at a tremendous rate (Wood 2005).

As of mid-2011, neither T&T nor Barbados had joined PetroCaribe; but over the years their positions had become more accommodative indicating an awareness of the serious economic circumstance of their CARICOM neighbours. Indeed, shortly after PetroCaribe was established, Prime Minister Manning of Trinidad and Tobago agreed to act on behalf of his CARICOM colleagues in negotiations with the Venezuelan government on the operational aspects of PetroCaribe. Increasingly, Venezuela was viewed as a trusted regional partner by energy-dependent CARICOM countries, and PetroCaribe projected itself as a real attempt to find a regional solution to the supply problems that they faced. But as each country reported its progress under the PetroCaribe framework agreement it became clear that there were variations between the individual country terms that were negotiated with Venezuela. Some countries, such as Jamaica and Antigua & Barbuda, were able to negotiate better side agreements than others.

Venezuela's financing arrangement as structured up to 2011 could cause problems for the emerging Caribbean Single Market and Economy (CSME), depending on the regulatory structures that are advanced by the latter. There has also been concern in regional political, business, and diplomatic circles that the PetroCaribe arrangement might have an impact on Caribbean diplomacy, in particular voting patterns in multilateral institutions and regional bodies such as the United Nations and the Organization of American States (OAS). In July 2006, such diplomatic concerns were put to the test when Venezuela lobbied and received bloc support from CARICOM leaders in its (failed) quest for a non-permanent seat on the United Nations Security Council. Despite pressure from the United States to support Guatemala, the CARICOM countries were quite disinclined to do so because of Guatemala's continuing antagonism toward Belize in its border dispute with that country. In fact, neither the Venezuela/Guyana border dispute nor Venezuela's claim to Bird Island (Isla de Aves) off Dominica were deemed by the CARICOM governments as sufficient reasons to deny support for Venezuela's campaign for the Security Council seat. Apparently, a long-term economic relationship that could compromise future independent action relating to border issues did not seem to be a concern for the CARICOM leaders. Despite the valid questions about the potential use of PetroCaribe as a political instrument, the arrangement did not appear at that time to give Venezuela any clear political advantage in the international arena.

ALBA (Bolivarian Alliance for America)

Oil diplomacy has been a constant feature of Venezuelan policy since the country became a founding member of OPEC in September 1960. In this regard, the existence of "petropolitics" in its external relations was nothing new.

But quite unabashedly the Chávez Government used oil to support ideological rhetoric, and as a foreign policy instrument, to an extent unprecedented in Venezuelan history. It would be difficult to find another example in Latin America of brandishing "resource diplomacy" so openly in the international political arena. The Venezuelan strategy has been either the projection of the power of oil wealth or the arbitrary use of oil wealth to influence the policies of other countries directly or through covert measures.

The formation of ALBA (originally called the Bolivarian Alternative for America but subsequently renamed as the Bolivarian Alliance for America) is one development that has raised suspicions of a new strategic alignment that responds to president Hugo Chávez's long term regional political objectives of "21st-century socialism" and an alternative to the proposed (but still moribund) Free Trade Area of the Americas (FTAA), as well as a weapon in his ideological war with Washington. However, ALBA is seen by its proponents as an attempt at regional economic integration that is not based primarily on trade liberalization but on a vision of social welfare and mutual economic aid. The ALBA was formed on December 14, 2004 with Venezuela and Cuba as its first members. Since then Bolivia, Ecuador, Nicaragua and Honduras have joined, (but Honduras formally withdrew in January 2010 after a new government came to power in June 2009 in a controversial coup d'etat). Dominica became the first CARICOM country to sign on to the agreement on January 15, 2008, and in April 2009 St Vincent and the Grenadines was accepted as the seventh member of ALBA. Antigua & Barbuda joined in June 2009, and Grenada has attended meetings of ALBA as an Observer.

Dominica's membership provided a diplomatic flashpoint for CARICOM. Although other CARICOM governments were sympathetic to Dominica's economic plight and efforts to improve it (See Bryan Case Study #1), Dominica's ALBA membership generated considerable debate in the region among both policy-makers and commentators, over CARICOM's inability to reach foreign policy consensus on Venezuela's initiatives in the region. In fact, both PetroCaribe and ALBA became divisive foreign policy issues (as did the question of the continuing recognition of Taiwan by some CARICOM states) within the region. Some prominent regional scholars and technocrats expressed the view that Dominica and others who supported ALBA regarded it as just another avenue for obtaining economic aid that is not available within the CARICOM regional integration grouping, and dismissed the arguments of others that ALBA could undermine CARICOM. The efforts of Jamaica and T&T to act unilaterally in the early 1990s to qualify for "NAFTA parity" treatment by the United States; the separate negotiations by CARICOM countries with the US on the drug interdiction "Shiprider" agreements; and T&T's agreement on a Free Trade Agreement (FTA) with Costa Rica, disallowed by COTED (The Council on Trade and Economic Development of CARICOM) and eventually negotiated as a CARICOM-Costa Rica FTA, were often cited as some of the actions of CARICOM member states that were at variance with regional commitments and responsibilities. Ironically, one of the most potent initiatives of the ALBA group could not be accessed by the CARICOM members of ALBA. The SUCRE (Spanish: Sistema Único de Compensación Regional, English: Unified System for Regional Compensation) is a regional virtual currency to be used in commercial exchanges between members of ALBA. It is intended to replace the U.S. dollar as a medium of exchange, in order to decrease U.S. control of Latin American economies and to increase stability of regional markets. In the case of ALBA members Dominica, Saint Vincent and the Grenadines and Antigua and Barbuda, the new currency posed a dilemma, as they are members of the Eastern Caribbean Currency Union and use the East Caribbean dollar.

In sum, PetroCaribe's regional impact and the membership of Dominica, Antigua and Barbuda, and St Vincent and the Grenadines in ALBA may have damaged the coherence and integrity of CARICOM. But the issue for the longer term was the extent of cohesiveness of CARICOM foreign policy as, globally, new configurations altered old allegiances and traditional diplomatic positions unravelled.

T&T, VENEZUELA AND CARIBBEAN RESOURCE DIPLOMACY

Under its PetroCaribe arrangement, Caracas provided almost all Caribbean nations and some in Central America with a concessionary financing framework for the purchase of Venezuelan oil. As indicated earlier, the scheme offered deferred payments, a fund for social and economic programmes and support for refining, storage and delivery systems. It cannot be denied that PetroCaribe provided a lifeline at the precise moment at which many Caribbean nations felt there was no longer any interest among traditional partners in supporting them. But whether it was good for regional integration was an open question. Despite the attraction of PetroCaribe, a six-member committee, appointed by CARICOM's Heads of Government in February 2003, was assigned the task of delivering a clear Regional Energy Plan utilizing the expertise of Trinidad and Tobago. Many analysts regard the plan as somewhat of an anti-climax since, even under the anticipated CSME, an energy policy document would be an umbrella that recognizes the right of individual states to pursue their own policies (Energy Caribbean Yearbook (2007/8)).

By 2010, PetroCaribe, even with its warts, posed a barrier to the implementation of a CARICOM regional energy policy. T&T's Petrotrin was an early casualty of the PetroCaribe initiative. The incursion of PDVSA into regional refining posed a direct threat to T&T's State company—the Petrotrin refinery that has traditionally serviced the CARICOM regional fuels trade. In order to survive, Petrotrin sought to more fully serve the US and other markets. But more importantly, PetroCaribe also caused a shift in the regionally dominant CARICOM energy supplier away from T&T to Venezuela. The PetroCaribe agreement is not in itself the model of regional energy cooperation that can serve the CARICOM region properly. The agreement is based primarily on the primacy of Venezuelan oil, high revenue stream because of global markets, and the export of commodities and minerals to continue profligate budgetary policies and social programmes. If by nature, or by force, Chávez left the scene and PDVSA and Venezuela had new presidents, what would happen with Cuba's oil debt and PDVSA's investments in the region and abroad?

President Chávez's capacity to use oil as an instrument in international relations depends on the quantity and quality of Venezuela's oil reserves, on the country maintaining a significant role as a producer and exporter of crude oil, and on the strength of the industry, which would have to continue to expand in a context of high efficiency, high investment and high prices. If these circumstances were not present, this capacity would be diminished. Chávez would have trouble maintaining his domestic social programmes, which could lead to growing social tensions. His grandiose economic aid promises abroad would be very hard to meet. In 2009, energy analysts estimated that Venezuela would need oil prices at $97 a barrel to balance its external accounts. Venezuela's main problem is that public spending has risen proportionately with the increases in oil prices. Also, the Chávez Government did not substantially increase its foreign reserves to save for a rainy day, and it could not increase oil production to make up for falling prices because many of the country's PDVSA oil monopoly's facilities were not adequately maintained.

As of May 2009, there were disturbing signs that Venezuela's declining oil output would sink to its lowest level in two decades. The Government's expropriation of the assets of some 60 oil service companies under a new law early that month, and their assignment to PDVSA whose revenues had tumbled, also raised concern about Venezuela's ability to increase its declining oil production at a time of low oil prices. PDVSA had hired the contractors to help it produce oil by operating drilling rigs, using technology to extract oil from ageing wells or moving personnel or equipment on boats, but was unable to pay the contractors regularly. By shifting its problems onto its suppliers, PDVSA stored up even bigger problems for the future. It lacks the ability to operate as efficiently as the service providers. Future oil production is under threat. The expropriations in the oil sector, as well as in broad areas of the economy, also sent a grim signal to companies considering investment in Venezuela (Mander 2009).

The personification of Venezuelan foreign policy in President Chávez raises serious concerns that certain bilateral and multilateral relations in the region could eventually be aborted. Within the context of resource diplomacy, a great deal depends on the capacity of Venezuela to deliver product effectively. Investment in and maintenance of Venezuela's oil fields have diminished as the Chávez administration forced PDVSA to give more money to the Government to finance social spending. Venezuela's crude-oil output has slid more than 700,000 barrels a day over the past decade. The production decline in Venezuela, which holds enough reserves to put the country into the same league as Saudi Arabia, has been primarily self-inflicted. Billions of dollars in profit from PDVSA have been diverted to a variety of domestic and international programs. The diversions have greatly hit the oil industry in Venezuela and PDVSA's ability to invest (Martin 2010).

In an effort to correct deficiencies in the petroleum production and supply chains, President Chávez also encouraged new players into the regional energy matrix. Starting from a tiny role in Venezuela's oil market when Hugo Chávez came to power, China has emerged as a major player, and has participated in the export, transportation, refining and distribution of Venezuela's heavy Orinoco crude oil through upstream operations, massive capital investments, strategic planning and long-term purchase agreements. The relationship has produced over 300 bilateral investment commitments, and China-Venezuela bilateral trade exceeded USD 10 billion in 2009, China edged out Colombia in 2009 to become Venezuela's second-largest trade partner (other than the US oil market). China has also become Venezuela's biggest foreign lender, and has agreed to provide more than $32 billion to be repaid in oil shipments. China's support of Venezuela, with financial aid and generous investment, has created an unsustainable cycle of indebtedness and dependence on China. Furthermore, there is scope for future crisis in the relationship since Chinese interests in Venezuelan commodities and markets may not fully coincide with the foreign policy objectives of the Chavista regime (Bryan 2011). The PetroCaribe model of regional energy cooperation is based on the primacy of Venezuelan oil, largesse, and the use of ideology as a strategy for regional cooperation. It is not a sustainable model for the future! Those Caribbean governments that have accepted the largesse should understand that eventually, they will have to increase their energy independence by strengthening regional energy cooperation and developing alternative sources of energy. A common approach by CARICOM, as envisioned in the formulation of a Caribbean energy policy, could help to transform PetroCaribe, as well as the region's relations with Venezuela, into approaches with less potential for politics to trump economics. The alternative scenario is one of heightened insecurity among regional consuming countries over access to supplies (Bryan 2009).

T&T AND CROSS-BORDER
COOPERATION WITH VENEZUELA

In spite of the PetroCaribe and ALBA controversies, the energy fortunes of both T&T and Venezuela are inextricable. Unitizing cross border gas reserves is a very complex issue and one that requires a careful weighing of logistical, economic and political considerations to arrive at the best possible formula for all parties involved. Such a formula has to take into consideration factors like price, supply-demand relationships and financing. The arrangement is all the more complex when one considers that while the MOU between T&T and Venezuela is essentially a government-to-government agreement, it must depend on the various multinational and State companies operating in the waters of both Trinidad and Tobago and Venezuela to implement the process.

Venezuela's Plataforma Deltana's blocks 1, 2 and 4 share borders with T&T offshore blocks. This includes bpTT's Kapok field, block 6 (d) and block (5b). The Loran field, where ChevronTexaco's discovery was made, straddles block 6 (d) on the Trinidad side of the border in which British Gas and ChevronTexaco are the operators, and Block 2 of the Venezuelan side, operated by ChevronTexaco. The Loran field is located in the north-eastern section of the Plataforma Deltana. In February 2003, PDVSA awarded ChevronTexaco and Statoil a 35-year license to appraise and develop two of its five offshore blocks located in the Plataforma Deltana. The Plataforma Deltana blocks are estimated to contain natural gas reserves up to 38 tcf. In December 2004, when President Hugo Chávez announced the Chevron/Texaco discovery, he noted that it would provide the impetus to accelerate Venezuela's own LNG ambitions which have been sagging for some time.

As of May 2009, Venezuela was producing 6.3Bf3/d (178Mm3/d) of natural gas, of which 4.3Bf3/d is re-injected in the course of oil production. The remaining 2Bf3/d is used to meet domestic demand. The country is working to increase natural gas production to reach output of 12Bf3/d in 2013. Venezuela expects to begin natural gas exports in 2014, according to the Minister of Oil and Energy, Rafael Ramírez. Colombia exports natural gas to Venezuela, but the bi-national pipeline between the two countries was developed so that Venezuela could reverse the flow and begin natural gas exports to Colombia in 2012. PDVSA has also signed agreements with a number of international firms to produce and export LNG. Ramírez, has, meanwhile, praised PDVSA's efforts on the Dragón block offshore Venezuela whose development is part of the country's Mariscal Sucre gas production programme. The first well drilled on the block tested at 70Mf3/d. PDVSA scheduled the drilling of eight more wells on the block before spudding wells on the Patao field in 2011. Infrastructure was developed so the offshore fields could begin adding 600Mf3/d of natural gas for domestic use in 2011. Total production from the four Mariscal Sucre blocks was expected to eventually reach 1.2Bf3/d. Some industry analysts have estimated a natural gas deficit for Venezuela of nearly 2Bcfd with the result that refiners and thermo-generators are forced to burn more expensive liquid fuels (Business News Americas 2009).

How best to commercialize large tranches of gas sitting in the Atlantic Ocean, hundreds of miles from landfall in Venezuela, with no pipeline infrastructure yet in place to carry it to any market on the mainland? Felix Rodriguez, president of PDVSA Gas, indicated in October 2007, that with an estimated investment of almost $4 billion, PDVSA intends to finish the LNG, SIGMA complex located in Güiria, Sucre State, by the end of 2013 (Petroleum World 2009). Given Venezuela's proximity to a well established LNG infrastructure in T&T, it may also one day make sense for Venezuelan gas to be monetized in T&T. The MOU for unifying of cross-border natural gas reserves at the Manatee and Loran marine fields indicates the willingness of the two governments to work together to get the best out of their respective oil and gas industries (GOTT 2010). T&T's share of the reserves has better positioned it to attract industries requiring natural gas, as well as energy-based companies. Much depends on the international economic situation and on the prevailing price structure. Furthermore, there is a very long distance between a government-to-government MOU and actual contractual terms to supply gas across a border to an LNG project.

As the Venezuelan LNG experience indicates, government-private company negotiations can become protracted, and agreements can be years in the making. Nevertheless, if T&T is to expand its LNG business, gas from Venezuelan fields may play a critical role in making this happen. But will Venezuelan politics continue to trump economics? The development of the CIGMA LNG facility has also been tied to the development of Caribbean gas markets, with the Caribbean Basin being identified as a "strategic" market, according to PDVSA. This presumably applies primarily to Jamaica, Cuba and the Dominican Republic, as other Caribbean markets are simply too small to make LNG a feasible option. Geo-politics appears to be playing a key role in the development of Venezuelan gas resources. It remains to be seen whether shifts in the regional and hemispheric geo-politics can influence Venezuela's decision-making regarding exploitation of their gas reserves.

T&T AND THE UNITED STATES OF AMERICA

Companies from the United States of America have played a long and pivotal role in providing investment, technology and expertise to the petroleum industry of Trinidad and Tobago. The advent in 1956 of self-government in T&T and the rise of a nationalist party coincided with the global expansion of the US oil industry. The arrival of Texaco and its negotiations for the assets of TLL and the relatively smooth transition to full operational status were partly due to an excellent relationship between the Texaco Chairman of the Board, Augustus Long, and the country's Prime Minister Dr Eric Williams. The 1970s were the watershed years for Texaco. In 1970, the year of the "Black Power" riots in T&T, the company significantly increased the number of nationals in its employ, presumably under pressure from the Government. By 1973, as OPEC shifted the balance of pricing power from the multinationals to the producer countries, the Trinidad and Tobago Government introduced new petroleum tax legislation establishing the Ministry of Finance as the entity to set Tax Reference Prices and Throughput fees. It also made the refining, producing and marketing divisions into separate taxable entities by law. During that period, Venezuela as a pivotal member of OPEC, started nationalizing the oil industry, created PDVSA, and Texaco soon lost control of its Venezuelan operations and its crude production in that country. In 1985, facing a different petroleum tax regime, opposition from the Oilfield Workers Trade Union (OWTU), changes in the international markets for oil that made the operations of an "offshore" refinery such as Texaco Point-a-Pierre less viable, and subjected to protracted negotiations, Texaco sold all its refining assets, its land holdings, properties and some of its offshore holdings in T&T for $US185 million. That same year, the Government also purchased the assets of another US company, Tesoro, by paying in fuel oil shipments the estimated approximate value of $US150 million. Over time and through several incarnations (Trintoc and Trintopec), the assets of both Texaco and Tesoro were eventually merged into Petrotrin by January 1994. The negotiations surrounding Texaco, Tesoro and the T&T Government set the tone for a range of possibilities to resolve such disputes (See Bryan, Case Study #2).

The exciting narrative of T&T's recent and current energy relationship with the United States is vested in the transition of T&T from an oil to a natural gas economy, and in the global politics of natural gas. T&T has several inherent advantages that allowed for a seamless transition from oil to gas. It is one of the oldest oil provinces in the world with a mature oil industry. As a result, the level of institutional knowledge of the oil industry ensured that the human resources necessary to effect this transition were available. Seasoned Government technocrats in the Ministry of Finance and the Ministry of Energy whose portfolios were petroleum made the transition to gas, and several were eventually recruited into top management in the private sector gas industry. Also in T&T's favour was its geographic location in the middle of the Americas, approximately 2,200 nautical miles from the nearest US port. Consequently, the cost of shipping ammonia, wire rods, methanol and

LNG were lower than from more distant locations. In the 1990s it made more economic sense for companies in the United States and Canada to produce ammonia and methanol in Trinidad and have it shipped back to the US market for sale to customers.

R. Shepherd and J. Ball in their 2004 detailed study of the development of LNG in T&T have identified several factors responsible for the success of LNG development in the country. T&T was able to develop its LNG industry before Nigeria and Venezuela, both countries with much larger proven reserves. The first LNG projects in Algeria and Libya, launched in the 1960s and 1970s, suffered a series of setbacks and market reversals, and every subsequent attempt to launch an LNG export project in the Atlantic Basin had failed. LNG export was a Pacific affair in which the Middle East had only a small role. The LNG project in T&T, however, had unique features both commercially and politically, which were more exceptional than in the 1960s and 1970s.

In 1992 Cabot LNG, a relatively small Boston-based LNG importer and owner of the Everett LNG receiving terminal just north of Boston, approached the Government of Trinidad and Tobago about developing a new LNG export project. Although three attempts had been made previously to develop LNG in Trinidad, nothing had come of them and the Government had largely concentrated on attracting intensive gas-based industries to the country. The industries had come but had not greatly prospered. Cabot's approach came soon after the Government had decided to liberalize its economic policy; new sources of revenue were badly needed. A memorandum of understanding (MOU) was signed by Amoco and British Gas (both had significant gas prospects in Trinidad) with Cabot and the National Gas Company of Trinidad and Tobago (NGC) to promote an LNG export project, and they launched a feasibility study in 1993. Atlantic LNG, the joint venture company eventually set up to own and run the project, was formed in 1995. Sales contracts were signed with Cabot and with Enagas of Spain in 1995 for a total of 3 million tonnes per annum (mtpa) of LNG. Construction started in 1996. The first cargo, bound for Boston, was loaded at the end of April 1999. Design work and sales negotiations for a two-train expansion with a further 6.8 mtpa capacity (Trains 2 and 3) were started in early 1999, and construction started in 2000. Train 2 started up in August 2002 and Train 3 in May 2003. Production from Train 4 began in December 2005.

Trinidad and Tobago's LNG success story was based on several factors. The T&T Government created a political and economic environment for the project that compared favourably with that faced by its would-be competitors, from its attitude towards outside investment to its political stability. Such ingredients were probably as important to the project's success as its commercial innovations. The two T&T Governments initially involved gave support when it was needed and T&T stood out as the most hospitable of the three (Algeria, Nigeria and T&T) competing for LNG investment. With respect to financing, T&T's democratic traditions and a track record of orderly change of government worked in its favour. Both US Exim Bank and the Overseas Private Investment Corporation (OPIC) were not averse to T&T risk. Between them they provided political risk cover for the bulk of the initial loan (US$571.4 million of US$600 million total debt). This aspect of T&T contrasted significantly with Nigeria, which attracted little political risk cover at the time. In addition, according to Shepherd and Ball, there was far more consistent Government support in T&T (in spite of some noise and hard negotiation) and encouragement, in contrast to Nigeria, which suffered from random and unhelpful government intervention, and from a government in Venezuela that had to struggle to gain internal acceptance of foreign involvement in the project (Ball and Sheppard 2004).

The combination of small scale, low cost, and capture of the vital US niche market were also factors in T&T's favour The Boston market was captured by a combination of Cabot's direct involvement, a more flexible deal than the one already negotiated by Cabot with Nigeria, and continuous difficulties with the Nigerian project. This all-important high-priced Boston market was quite small, and as a result it would only form a small portion of sales from the larger Nigerian and Venezuelan projects. These projects needed to find much larger additional sales that would take time to arrange, if they could be arranged at all, and which would inevitably be at lower prices. However, a small-scale project was likely to lose economies of scale, so cost reduction was very important for Atlantic, particularly as the economics for all projects in the Atlantic were quite marginal.

LNG projects are technically and logistically complex and present a challenge for the host government. LNG projects (particularly the first project) usually require preferential tax treatment compared with oil, and often compared with gas for local use, as well. Such concessions to multinational companies are politically sensitive and require skilled negotiation. In this context, there has often been public criticism that the government of the day practically gave away the natural gas for Atlantic-LNG Train I through a tax holiday. At that time Atlantic LNG saw it as a marginal project and, given the low price of gas then (US$ 2.50mmBTU), a substantial risk given the capital cost. In fact, since Train I there have been no further tax holidays for any of the subsequent trains, although duty free importation on equipment remains as an incentive (Andrews 2006). In the final analysis, there has been a remarkable level of policy consistency and political commitment by different T&T administrations to moving the energy sector forward.

In retrospect, the natural gas and LNG ventures were also a great risk for a small country. According to Professor Kenneth Julien, the "energy czar," who in various roles has overseen T&T's energy development since the late 1960s, the natural gas industry was not initiated with any national vision. Originally, it was developed with the single purpose of putting to use the gas that was being flared (flaring came to an end in 1982) while the producer companies sought to extract as much oil as they could in order to benefit from high oil prices in the 1970s. According to Julien, establishing the NGC was a pragmatic face-saving decision born out of necessity since there was as yet no vision, plan or strategy. The decision to pursue LNG in 1993 was a risky one that required dedicating a large percentage of the relatively small natural gas reserves (12tcf) at the time to an industry that was still in its early stage of global development and one that had no presence on either side of the Atlantic. Remarkably, T&T, a small country with less than 1 percent of global natural gas reserves, took a major leap and dragged the large multinationals BP (Amoco) and British Gas along for the ride (Julien 2007)!

While other energy experts agree that there was no alternative to the export of gas as LNG, after it became clear that there was more gas than could reasonably be used in the manufacture of ammonia and methanol, and the fact that the steel industry was in trouble, they also point to changes in Government policy that facilitated the growth of the industry. In my interviews with energy experts Trevor Boopsingh and Gregory McGuire, they point out that the People's National Movement (PNM) government specifically altered the policy originally laid down by Prime Minister Eric Williams on the absolute use of gas for local manufacture. During the period when it was out of office (1986-1991) the PNM included in its 1992 election manifesto the proposal that North Coast gas be exported as LNG. The reversal of the Williams position of "no LNG" was triggered by the availability of a sufficiently large reserves pool with limited market options, and the fact that LNG was the most attractive option for increasing market size while at the same time stimulating upstream activity. Consequently, the market need for gas was created. The introduction of the product-related pricing model for petrochemical plants, and the encouragement of private sector investment (as opposed to the traditional full State ownership), stimulated the exploration for gas. As a result by 1995 Atlantic LNG (ALNG) was established with Prof Kenneth Julien as its first Chairman. In essence, the actions taken in the 1990s were an extension of the deliberate decision taken in the 1970s to utilize the natural gas resources as a catalyst for industrial development in a "Resources Based Development Strategy." In the late 1980s, because of a serious recession, unavailable funds, and questions about the viability of existing plants during a period of depressed prices by the NAR Government, there was a hiatus.

THE T&T-US FUTURE ENERGY RELATIONSHIP

Although T&T's gas reserves are modest in comparison to some other countries, its resources have been well managed. Given its (2010) proven natural gas reserves (17 tcf), and natural gas production (4.2 billion cubic feet of gas per day) that facilitates inter alia downstream production of ammonia and methanol, iron and steel, direct reduced iron, power generation, urea and natural gas to liquids processing facility, and the export of LNG, T&T is now classified as a natural gas economy. The four LNG trains produce 2.4 billion cubic feet per day, just 0.3 percent of the world's proven natural gas reserves, and through proper management of the natural gas resources, T&T has become the seventh largest LNG exporter in the world. Until 2009, its Train 4 of Atlantic LNG with a production capacity of 5.2 million metric ton per annum (mmtpa), was the largest in the world. LNG cargoes go to all of the major markets, including Asia. Depending on future reserves, and the construction of more LNG plants, it is poised to play an even greater role in the global natural gas industry in the coming years. Like its oil-based economy of the 20th century, the gas-based economy of the 21st will present the country with significant opportunities, as well as economic and political risks.

Given the trend in the United States towards using natural gas to replace coal and oil in power generation, the LNG trade is likely to increase in the future. Natural gas provides a cost-effective bridge to a low-carbon future. Nearly every major energy company and many smaller ones predict that by the year 2020, the international market for natural gas will develop to rival that for crude oil, with US production and demand serving as a major driving force. By the middle of 2005, LNG from T&T had accounted for 77 percent of LNG imports into the United States. Its percentage was expected to diminish as more global suppliers come to market in the US. Moreover, by early 2011 it was clear that the increase in North American natural gas due to the shale gas boom, a projected increase in global gas demand although amid a decrease in domestic demand in the US between 1999 and 2010, meant that North America could become a liquefied natural gas (LNG) exporter by 2015 (Boman 2011). T&T's only option is to diversify its exports of LNG, globally.

The decision by the United States Department of Energy in May 2011 to give Cheniere Energy of Houston permission to export up to 2.2 billion cubic feet of LNG a day for 20 years to any country with which the US has signed a free trade agreement (FTA), could also threaten T&T producers of LNG such as bpTT, even in the Caribbean market. The US can now export LNG and compete with T&T. If bi-directional capability (i.e. to import and re-gasify LNG and to liquefy indigenous gas for export) becomes routine the LNG market in the Atlantic Basin region would be reshaped as the US would compete with traditional suppliers for market share (Furlonge 2011).

Cheniere Energy's Sabine Pass in Louisiana and Freeport LNG in Texas are two LNG re-gasification facilities that have liquefaction capacity added to allow for LNG exports from growing shale gas reserves in the US. Markets in the Dominican Republic and Puerto Rico supplied by T&T have already been penetrated by Cheniere (Renwick 2011). In the future, T&T must navigate a complex field of political concerns in order to secure its place in the US and elsewhere and to emerge as a global partner in setting the LNG agenda.

The T&T-US energy relationship is strong at a functional level. The US Department of Energy, along with the Departments of Homeland Security and Defense collaborated (in 2008) with T&T's Ministries of National Security and Energy and Energy Industries in evaluating the vulnerability of the country's energy infrastructure. The US and T&T have agreed to work together to ensure the safety of key local energy facilities and to lend their expertise to the wider Caribbean. At a high policy level, the top energy priority of the US administration of President Barack Obama for Latin America and the Caribbean is an "Energy Partnership of the Americas" that advances the idea of developing alternative fuels in the region. In addition to meeting the domestic goal of reducing US oil dependency and fighting global warming, the energy partnership would shift US policy away from its current narrow focus on free trade agreements and anti-drug efforts. Energy would open a new path to relations with the hemisphere, by emphasizing overall energy and climate change objectives, as well as the opportunity for job-creating investments, energy diversification, and the regional development of environmentally safe alternative energies. Brazil and Mexico would be key players in this partnership and T&T, with its diverse energy infrastructure, is well positioned to play a key role for the Caribbean in the emerging relationship.

T&T AND BRAZIL

T&T's relationship with Brazil is guided by the emerging status of the Brazilian state oil company Petrobras. The discovery of new deep-sea reserves, thousands of metres deep and under a salt layer, has raised expectations that Brazil could increase production to 3.1 million barrels per day by 2020. The Santos Basin "pre-salt" region of Brazil sits in waters more than 2,000 metres deep and beneath another 5,000 metres of rock and salt under the seabed. The pre-salt region runs about 800 kilometres off the coast of Rio de Janeiro and Sao Paulo. Expectations for this region were heightened in April 2009 when Petrobras reopened its first well in the Tupi field and found a strong flow. The Iracema well, which is 30 kilometres north of the first well and is part of the same structure, helped to confirm the Tupi field reserves. Tupi, whose discovery was announced in November 2007, contains an estimated 5 billion to 8 billion barrels of oil, making it the largest discovery in the Americas in three decades. The Tupi Pilot Project went online in late 2010, after an Extended Well Test (EWT) was completed. Once brought on stream, Tupi was expected to produce and process 100,000 barrels of oil and 4 million cubic metres of gas per day (Blount and Kinch 2009).

Petrobras has also been "re-testing" wells which it had previously considered dry or not commercially viable. It has also been building five oil refineries to increase its refining capacity to 3.2 million barrels per day by 2020. Brazil's deep-water oil and gas reserves, in the pre-salt area have changed the regional dynamics of the industry. The Brazilian potential was always there, but the global recession of 2008/2009 brought equipment costs down and technical and professional personnel, scarce until mid-2008, were once more available. The geological and geographic characteristics of the pre-salt call for sophisticated, high-precision equipment, and advanced exploration techniques. Brazil rapidly sourced the specialized personnel, techniques, and equipment needed to explore the region at reduced costs. Petrobras is the most progressive, best managed, and most technologically advanced petroleum company in Latin America. It also has the Brazilian Development Bank (BNDES) as a lender of last resort. As Petrobras continues its exploration of the pre-salt area, and expands its international capabilities, it will ensure Brazil's energy self-sufficiency and will strengthen its position as a world energy player. Brazil's rise as an oil and gas power will significantly realign the delivery of natural gas and LNG in Chile, Argentina and other countries, away from Bolivia and towards Brazil (Berliner 2009). The Bolivia-Brazil pipeline (GASBOL) is the longest natural gas pipeline in South America. The 3,150 kilometres (1,960 mi) long pipeline connects Bolivia's gas sources with the south-east regions of Brazil.

While Brazil continues to plan for future expansion of traditional fossil fuels like oil and gas, its energy policy remains two-pronged. The Government is overhauling the country's energy basket to place more emphasis on renewable resources. Seventy-five percent of Brazil's energy comes from hydroelectric power, and the Government intends to build more such stations, but without causing further deforestation in areas like the Amazon rain forest (CIGI Project Report, 2009). In April 2009, President Luiz Inácio Lula da Silva indicated that Brazil will invest more heavily in other renewable energy sources, like bio-diesel made from oil-bearing plants such as palm trees, sunflowers, castor beans and peanuts, and especially in expanding production of the bio-fuel most consumed within the country: ethanol, manufactured from sugarcane. About 46 percent of the Brazilian energy mix is already based on renewable sources, while ethanol accounts for 16 percent. In Brazil, 90 percent of new vehicles, which currently make up 25 percent of all cars in the country, have flex-fuel motors that can run on gasoline or ethanol or both (Frayssinet 2009).

The Brazilian promotion of ethanol has drawn criticism from those who are concerned about competition between planting crops for energy or food, and argue that using food grains for energy production could cause food to become scarce and expensive. But Brazil uses sugarcane for methanol production. The supposed benefits of bio-fuels for the environment are also questioned in some quarters that suggest that bio-fuel production may increase, rather than reduce, global warming. But Petrobras' main focus in this area is to develop technologies for producing second and third generation bio-fuels on an industrial scale. Second generation bio-fuels can be obtained from the cellulose of any plant, using the whole plant and not just the grains, and thus reducing water consumption. For the third generation, algae and other organisms from which bio-fuels can be extracted can even be grown in extreme environments such as deserts, frozen regions or the sea. In the view of Petrobras President José Sergio Gabrielli, the important thing is to increase exports to make Brazil one of the top players in the world ethanol market. "We want to increase our refining capacity in order to become a large producer of refined products. We aim to make Petrobras not only a major exporter of crude, but also of oil by-products" (Frayssinet 2009).

While the relationship between T&T and Brazil in the energy sector is relatively recent, Brazil's exponential growth in the ethanol production sector, as well as in other alternative fuel processes, would have important lessons for T&T as it also moves in those directions. The potential for collaboration in energy, the environment and agriculture is significant. Business relationships between the two countries are becoming more frequent with T&T exporting LNG to Brazil. Any deepening of the relationship would have to be based on investment opportunities that take into account a role for both countries in the exploration, production, and refining of petroleum, the production of ethanol and the provision of energy services for promising offshore fields in Guyana, French Guiana, and Suriname. While Venezuela continues to occupy T&T's cross-border aspirations, Brazil is the low profile elephant in the T&T energy future.

T&T AND CARIBBEAN NEIGHBOURS

As described earlier, T&T's energy policy was always seen to be instrumental in ensuring that the energy requirements of its CARICOM neighbours were met through the CARICOM Oil Facility, or regional programmes such as the CARICOM Petroleum Fund into which Trinidad and Tobago puts approximately US$80 million annually of grant funds for the assistance of partners in the Caribbean Community. However, at times more ambitious objectives have fallen prey to inter-governmental misunderstandings and diplomatic faux pas or slow political processes. The provision of LNG from T&T to Jamaica, and the delay in the construction of the Eastern Caribbean Gas Pipeline are two such examples.

Since 2003, Jamaica has been exploring the feasibility of importing natural gas from T&T, either in small LNG carriers or via pipeline. By November 2004, T&T and Jamaica had agreed on the outlines of an agreement under which T&T would supply Jamaica with LNG on a "competitive and predictable" basis. A Jamaica/T&T government partnership would build a re-gasification plant at Port Esquivel on Jamaica's south coast and a US/French consortium signed an agreement for the front-end engineering and design (FEED) study for the re-gasification plant. Under an MOU between the Jamaican and T&T governments, T&T was to supply 1.15 million tons of LNG per annum to Jamaica at "competitive prices" and on a preferential basis for 20 years. The National Gas Company of T&T and the Petroleum Company of Jamaica were to partner on the project. Its financing would be 50/50 by both governments. The US$240-million storage and re-gasification facility initially scheduled to start at the end of 2006 and completed in 2008 has been delayed.

The politics surrounding the project were problematic from the beginning. Initially, agreement to go ahead was delayed because the Jamaicans were insisting that under the imminent CARICOM Single Market and Economy (CSME), Jamaica is entitled to "national treatment" in the purchase of LNG. In essence, Jamaica argued that LNG should not be treated as a separate product from natural gas and that, except for transportation and other specific costs, it should purchase the commodity at the same price at which the NGC in T&T purchases natural gas. At one point the Jamaican Government indicated that it would take the natural gas issue before the Caribbean Court of Justice in order to resolve fundamental disputes over the interpretation of the treaty establishing the CSME.

The process remained stymied until both sides eventually agreed to put Jamaica's court challenge, and its argument for "national treatment," on the backburner after the visit to Port of Spain by Jamaican Prime Minister P. J. Patterson in November 2004. Subsequently, during an official visit of the new Jamaican Prime minister, Portia Simpson Miller to Port of Spain in April 2006, T&T Prime Minister, Patrick Manning, announced that a long-term supply of natural gas would be made available to Jamaica, starting in 2009, at a negotiated pricing arrangement that would be mutually acceptable. He stressed that in arriving at a price, "we are recognizing that Jamaica is a CARICOM partner and therefore different from all the other countries that we now supply with (natural gas), and giving effect to a long standing policy of the government of Trinidad and Tobago to have virtually most favoured nation arrangements with respect to CARICOM countries." In an obvious reference to the possibility of profiteering on the preferential price, he also emphasized that the collaboration should ensure that "third parties do not benefit at the expense of us both." The supply still had not commenced by mid-2011.While the T&T Government gave a commitment to facilitate Jamaica, the invest-ment decisions by both countries, the supplier and the pricing mechanism, were yet to be decided. Gas supply options for T&T include CNG and LNG from Train IV, in which the NGC has an 11 percent stake.

A final resolution to the terms of the T&T supply of natural gas to Jamaica is a matter of technical and business negotiation, but some other issues would have to be considered. First, the T&T Government has no LNG to offer until Atlantic LNG Train IV could give additional gas supply; alternatively T&T could postpone supply and await the arrival of the next LNG train (Train V). Second, the Jamaican contention that a domestic pricing mechanism should apply, rather than T&T's insistence that there has to be a Caribbean gas price that bears relation to Henry Hub (the US benchmark for natural gas), should be laid to rest. In a competitive world, such a subsidy for a highly marketable, extremely valuable and fungible commodity (even to a CARI-COM neighbour) would be a serious regional geopolitical action with global consequences. The values and quantities concerned might not be much by global standards, but T&T's domestic buyers and other foreign LNG custom-ers would challenge such a move, as would the LNG energy companies. It is unlikely that the T&T Government would ever agree to a pricing and supply structure that would question the global energy economy and challenge the private sector dynamic. Jamaica remains very interested in securing imports of LNG. In early 2007, the government signed a memorandum of understand-ing with Venezuela for the delivery of LNG by 2009, after T&T indicated that it was unable to meet Jamaican demand (given the decision to pause on the development of further LNG trains in the absence of significant new gas reserves). Since the Venezuelans are targeting first delivery of LNG in 2014, the Jamaicans are forced to look elsewhere (including floating LNG re-gasification platforms) for gas to meet their short-term needs. They are also investing heavily in alternative energy sources such as solar, wind farms and hydroelectric.

The Eastern Caribbean Gas Pipeline project that is designed to transport gas from T&T to the islands of the Eastern Caribbean, serving Guade-loupe, Barbados, Martinique, St Lucia and Dominica, is moving ahead. The delay in its construction was the result of slow political processes in the intended consumer countries. Originally conceived by the T&T Gov-ernment, it was turned over to a group of international investors. The project is feasible, economically viable, and commercially sustainable. It will provide an energy source that is more predictable and at far less volatile prices than diesel or fuel oil. It is possible that the long-term solution to the energy deficiency problem in these islands resides with a gas pipeline from T&T, given that the main energy-consuming sectors are power generation, transportation and manufacturing. However, the main challenges are finance, management of the adjustment to gas, internal bureaucratic delays, and the willingness of the receiving countries to make the appropriate business arrangements.

The strength of the Caribbean gas pipeline project is based on the pricing and its reliability. The project will provide the Eastern Caribbean islands with gas at a stable and competitive price, relative to oil alternatives. The major clients are expected to be the regional power companies. The first gas is scheduled for delivery in 2014. It will be 25 million cubic feet a day (mmcfd) to Barbados (Energy Caribbean 2011). However, its main challenge could well be the distribution of small scale LNG by barges or ships.

T&T AND WEST AFRICA: NEW INITIATIVES

Global energy relationships do not necessarily respect geographical boundaries or hemispheric divides. In this context, the initiatives by T&T to identify areas of co-operation in the energy sector with African countries is a significant extension of T&T's "energy neighbourhood." This has been in effect commercially through the operations of both Shell and Texaco since the first half of the last century, as crude oil production from West Africa was imported into Trinidad for refining. The refined petroleum products were then exported from Trinidad via smaller tankers to the eastern seaboard of the USA and to Europe. Having discovered oil and gas in Equatorial Guinea, Marathon (the operator) encouraged the President of that country to visit Trinidad and Tobago to see how the latter had monetized natural gas and particularly, the first Atlantic LNG Train that was then operating. Noticing the similarity in size, population and colonial history between the two countries, President Obiang was so impressed with the tremendous strides that had been made, he took on the challenge of mirroring T&T's achievements. One of the first things he reputedly did was to request that the LNG train in EG be built "exactly like the one in Trinidad." Subsequently, Minister of Energy Ela Ntugu Nsa led a delegation to T&T to study and understand the structure and functioning of the State agencies in the sector. Soon after, SONAGAS was formed to replicate the role and functions of the NGC. One of the first activities of the Executive Director, Dr Ndong Ondo and his management team was to pay a visit to T&T in June 2006, where they engaged local experts in understanding the workings of the natural gas industry. On that visit, the delegation paid a courtesy call on Prime Minister Patrick Manning after which the latter pledged to provide technical cooperation to Equatorial Guinea at no cost. This became the genesis of what is now called the African Initiative.

At the eighth African Union Summit in Addis Ababa in January 2007, the Prime Minister stated that Trinidad and Tobago would make expertise available free of charge to certain African countries, viz. Chad, Nigeria, Cameroon, Equatorial Guinea, Gabon, The Republic of Congo (Brazzaville), and Angola. Since then, several missions have travelled back and forth—technocrats, businessmen and educators from T&T to East, West and South Africa; from Africa—Presidents (including those of Nigeria, Ghana and Uganda), Energy Ministers and technocrats from several African governments and State companies, often accompanied by business leaders ("Energy Study Visits") and an ECOWAS High-level Energy Mission. T&T's diplomatic missions, headed by the High Commissioner in Nigeria, became the focal points for facilitating these exchanges. Several experts from T&T state enterprises as well as from the Ministry of Energy and Energy Industries visited Chad, Gabon, Nigeria and Benin in 2007 to have preliminary discussions with members in the energy sector. Following this mission, a Nigerian delegation came to Trinidad in 2007 to meet with state and private energy stakeholders as well as to visit the Petrotrin oil refinery, industrial estates and plants. T&T has also received missions from Uganda, Cameroon, Angola, Gabon, Ghana, South Africa and Tanzania. The Economic Commission of West African States (ECOWAS) has facilitated meetings between Trinidad and Tobago and West African nations. Member states of the ECOWAS also facilitated hosting of the Ministerial Conference of African Energy Ministers in Trinidad and Tobago in May 2009. At a political level the Prime Minister of T&T saw it as a concrete way of strengthening the historical ties between T&T and the continent of Africa, and as an example of South-South co-operation for developing nations (Manning 2009).

The relationship should yield dividends for T&T energy services companies in Ghana, which began producing oil in late 2010, and in Nigeria which does not have the infrastructure to get the natural gas product to end users. Among the areas in which West African nations are expected to benefit from T&T expertise are oil and gas exploration services, drilling, logistics and design, construction of production platforms, reservoir engineering and enhanced recovery, pipeline design and construction, plant maintenance and operations and consulting services (Webb 2009). T&T business persons have been invited to take advantage of a US$3–5 billion oil and gas investment in Nigeria; and the Energy Chamber of Trinidad and Tobago led an Energy Services Trade Mission to Ghana, Gabon, Equatorial Guinea and Nigeria during September and October 2009 to facilitate business-to-business matchmaking with T&T companies, market briefing and meetings with government officials.

The initiatives with African nations will rely more on taking advantage of potential business opportunities. The T&T government has provided strategic interventions, established contacts, and paved the way for private sector involvement. Only time will tell if this is a new and fruitful dispensation for a small but energy-mature oil and gas economy.

CONCLUSION

If past events are any guide, the energy future of T&T with its neighbours will demand even more technical expertise, pragmatism and significant resource diplomacy. Regional energy security is an important factor, but its traditional focus on procurement and market stability has been bolstered by politics and strategic calculations. The interconnectivity of the global oil and natural gas markets means that decisions made by producer or consumer countries will affect the energy security of others. The structural shifts in global energy markets and political alliances are also manifested in displays of "petro-politics" and the use of resource diplomacy as we have seen in T&T's relationship with its neighbours.

The T&T relationships with Venezuela, the United States and Brazil have their own dynamic. Cross-border exploration, production and refining will continue to characterize relations with Venezuela. Ensuring that T&T continues to be a reliable and secure provider of crude and LNG to the US but with the ability to leverage for improved market access for non-energy manufactured items will be an ongoing process. Working closely with Brazil on investment opportunities in the exploration, production, and refining of petroleum, the production of ethanol, and the provision of energy services for French Guiana's massive Zeadyus field discovered in 2011 and promising offshore frontier fields in Guyana and Suriname will cement that budding relationship. However, it is in the relationships yet to be forged with the entry of other potential regional energy actors in deeper oil and gas provinces in the neighbourhood, such as Cuba, Guyana and Suriname, that strategic objectives with respect to regional energy security and resource diplomacy must be devised. T&T must continue to play a leadership role in the CARICOM region by continuing to influence co-existence with the PetroCaribe regime for as long as the latter survives. Similarly, it should continue to pursue with its CARICOM neighbours the development of an effective regional energy policy that includes the use of alternative and renewable sources of energy. The CARICOM countries need a clear vision of regional energy cooperation or integration. At its best such a policy would integrate the region's energy policy into trade, economic, environmental, security and foreign policies, and broaden dialogue with producing and consuming nations alike. Adherence to national, regional and international mandates on protection of the environment will be one of the main challenges for the next 100 years. T&T must take a leadership role in all of these initiatives and policies.

The petroleum sector will continue to be of significance to Trinidad and Tobago for the foreseeable future. Despite its "mixed" blessings, no other industry and its downstream offspring has offered more promise, opportunity, and the potential to spur investment, job growth and diversification during the past 100 years. Specifically, Trinidad's adherence to hydrocarbon-based industries has deeply influenced the politics, economics, culture, social mores and the labour environment in the country. But ironically, the poverty level is significant in some of those regions of the country that are hosts to the extractive industries. Trying to gain fundamental and lasting benefits from oil and gas development, in order to improve life for future generations of citizens is a laudable objective for the next 100 years. As we have stressed, risks, leadership and resource diplomacy are important pathways. There are roadmaps but no easy solutions.

CASE STUDIES

Case Study 1—Dominica, Caricom and Alba

Since his election to office in 2004, Prime Minister Roosevelt Skerritt of Dominica has forged a relationship with Cuba's Castro and Venezuela's Chávez, which has resulted in Dominica (population 72,000) receiving substantial aid from both countries. About 1,000 Cuban and Venezuelan experts in energy, education, health care, agriculture, tourism, housing and other construction are working in Dominica. Under the PetroCaribe agreement, crude oil from Venezuela is stored in huge amounts in Dominica for distribution to other Caribbean countries. An $80-million-dollar oil refinery will also be constructed on the island with Venezuelan cooperation. Dominica pays for 40 percent of its PetroCaribe oil imports—that is about 900 barrels a day—with its main export, bananas. The Venezuelan Government said it has given Dominica a $10.1 million grant to expand the Melville Hall Airport; forgiven the island nation's $1.5 million debt and assisted in restoring the sight of some 500 blind Dominicans, in either Cuba or Venezuela. In education, about 2,000 Dominican students enjoy Cuban and Venezuelan scholarships in Computer Science, Medicine, Engineering, Sports, Physics, Math, and Agriculture.

Case Study 2—T&T and TESORO

The Tesoro case has the distinction of having been referred to the International Centre for Settlement of Investment Disputes (ICSID). ICSID, an affiliate of the World Bank created by treaty in 1964 which provides arbitration and conciliation services to facilitate the settlement of investment disputes between host countries and foreign investors. The dispute arose out of a joint venture which the two sides established in 1968, each with a 50 percent interest, to develop and manage oilfields in Trinidad. By their joint venture contract and subsequent agreements, the two partners developed a complex arrangement on the extent to which profits would be paid as dividends or reinvested to develop additional oil properties. By 1983, following the rise of oil prices and continued turbulence in world petroleum industry, Tesoro and the Government of T&T were embroiled in a conflict over whether and, to what extent, to use accumulated profits for payment of dividends to themselves or for reinvestment to develop new oil properties. Finally, Tesoro decided to sell its shares and, pursuant to the agreement, offered them first to the T&T Government. The two parties then began to negotiate a possible sale, but appeared to make little progress. In August 1983, Tesoro filed a request for conciliation with the ICSID Secretary-General, claiming that it was entitled to 50 percent of the profits as dividends, and that the Government had breached the joint venture agreement on dividend payments. Tesoro and the Trinidad and Tobago Government agreed to a single conciliator (instead of a commission of three or more conciliators as the Rules allow) and through direct negotiations chose Lord Wilberforce, a distinguished retired English judge, in December 1983 to serve as their conciliator. Following receipt of the report, Tesoro and the Trinidad and Tobago Government began negotiations, and by October 1985 they had reached a settlement by which the joint venture company would pay dividends to the two partners in cash and petroleum products totaling $143 million. The conciliation thus helped the parties reach an amicable settlement of their dispute with minimum cost, delay, and acrimony. The whole conciliation process from start to finish took less than two years to complete, and administrative costs and conciliator fees amounted to less than $11,000. Equally important, conciliation preserved the business relationship between the parties. Had the matter proceeded to arbitration, without conciliation, the case would have lasted several years, cost many hundreds of thousands of dollars and perhaps more, and would have resulted in a complete rupture of business relationships between Tesoro and the Government (Salacuse 2003).

BIBLIOGRAPHY

Andrews, John, interview by Anthony Bryan. *Chairman, Atlantic LNG* (March 9, 2006).
Ball, James, and Rob Sheppard. *Liquefied Natural Gas From Trinidad: The Atlantic LNG Project.* Stanford University, 2004.
Berliner, Maria Velez de. "Latin America 2009: Opportunities and Challenges." London, January 27, 2009.

Blount, Jeb, and Diana. Kinch. "Petrobras 'Very Secure' on Tupi Output Expectations." Bloomberg.com, April. 30, 2009.

Boman, Karen. "Shale Boom , Gas Demand to Make North America LNG Exports Reality." *Rigzone.* 2011.

Brereton, Bridget. *A History of Modern Trinidad and Tobago.* Heinemann Educational Books Limited, 1981.

Bryan, Anthony. "PetroCaribe and CARICOM: Resource Diplomacy and its Imapct on Small State Regional Cooperation." In *The Diplomacies of Small States: Between Vulnerability and Resiliance*, by Andrew, F Cooper and Timothy M.(Eds.) Shaw. London: Palgrave Macmillan, 2009.

Bryan, Anthony. "The Islands and the Littoral." In *The Restless Caribbean: Changing Patterns of International Relations*, by Richard Millet and Marvin.W. Will, 234-247. New York , 1979.

Bryan, Anthony. "Trinidad and Tobago." In *Energy Corporation in the Western Hemisphere*, by Sidney (ed) Weintraub, 366-404. Centre for Strategic and International Studies, 2007.

Bryan, Anthony. "What is China Doing in Latin America." *Business Journal*, December 2011: 1163.

Business News Americas. *Venezuela's Natural Gas Output reaches 178Mm3/d. Exports targeted for 2014.* May 14 , 2009.

Energy Caribbean. "Gas will Flow by 2014." February 2011.

Energy Caribbean Yearbook(2007/8). "Is an Energy Plan for the Caribbean Still Relevant." MEP Publications, 2007.

Frayssinet, Fabiana. "Energy-Brazil: Two Pronged Policy." Inter Press Service News Agency , May 6, 2009.

Furlonge, Hayden. "Trials of a Small Hydrocarbon Rich Country." *International Energy: A Professional Online Forum.* June 17, 2011.

GOTT. *Unitization Agreement.* 2010.

Jessop, David. "Energy Dependency and President Chávez," *The View from Europe.* July 17, 2011.

Julien, Kenneth. "Emergence of the National Energy Sector." *GASCO News*, 2007.

Mander, Benedict. "Chavez seizures fuel Venezuela Oil Fears." *Financial Times.* May 10, 2009.

Manning, Patrick. *Address by the Honourable Patrick Manning , Prime Minister of Trinidad and Tobago at opening of the African Ministers Conference,.* Port of Spain, May 11, 2009.

Martin, Jeremy. "Latin America's Oil Power Transition." *Business Journal*, December 2010.

Petroleum World. *Venezuela moves ahead wuth 28.8 trillion gas project.* March 9, 2009.

Renwick, David. "The Start of Demand for LNG in the Caribbean." *Business Express.* CCN, Trinidad Express, June 8, 2011.

Salacuse, Jeswald W. *"Mediation in International Business."* The Fletcher School of Law and Diplomacy, Tufts University,, 2003.

Webb, Yvonne. "US$5 Billion in Oil and Gas Investments." *Trinidad Guardian.* May 11, 2009.

Wood, Anthony. "The Case Against PetroCaribe- Statement by the Minister of Energy ." *Barbados Nation .* Sept 18, 2005.

Chapter Seven

Future Hydrocarbon Resources

Anthony E. Paul

INTRODUCTION

The precursor of the first 100 years of commercial production is characterised by exploration based on easy-to-find oil. It seeped at the surface, at and
around the Pitch Lake in La Brea and in the Guayaguayare forests, among
other places in South Trinidad. Obviously, it was coming from somewhere
below the surface. Intuitively, the first entrepreneurs and engineers in the
hydrocarbon business in Trinidad recognised that there was an active "petroleum system" in the southern basin of Trinidad. Their search for oil led to
the understanding that we have today of the system. So new was the science
of oil exploration that the pioneers not only discovered the system but were
also forced to invent many of the tools and processes that are now taken for
granted in the industry.

Innovation (the design, development, early adoption, or customisation of
tools, systems or procedures) has always been a part of the Trinidad oil and
gas landscape. Innovation drove hydrocarbon exploration and production not
only in Trinidad, but also in other parts of the world. It has involved aspects
of the industry as far apart as micro-palaeontology, electric well-logging,
directional drilling, marine field development, offshore 3D seismic, refining,
natural gas pricing, downstream natural gas portfolio design, LNG, iron and
steel, concession models, fiscal terms, education and value-chain trade-offs.

The history of innovation in Trinidad and Tobago in the first 100 years
might, by itself, be deserving of an entire book. Fortunately, the stories of
those honoured by the 100th anniversary celebrations will document a few of
these major breakthroughs.[1]

As Trinidad and Tobago moves into the second century of oil and gas
production, the search for new reserves will demand a continued culture of

innovation and enterprise. As before, the very acts of observation, analysis, decision-making and participation in the industry will require technical, commercial and social interventions in new and different ways.

Oil at the surface, it came to be understood, had actually been generated in rocks below the surface and worked its way upwards, via some migration pathway, into a suitable state of equilibrium. Where there was no mechanism to keep it underground, the oil reached the surface. One stunning example was the creation of one of the world's largest oil seeps of around 100 acres at La Brea in Trinidad. Unfortunately for those seeking to extract high value fuels from this oil, the effects of bacteria and evaporation removed many of the lighter components of the oil, leaving instead that most remarkable road surfacing material, Trinidad Lake Asphalt.

The search, therefore, required an understanding of how the sub-surface looked and behaved. The scientific method, so often the tool of first choice in Victorian times, had a field day in Trinidad. Innovation in the oil industry in Trinidad at the end of the 19th and beginning of the 20th centuries, became the order of the day as men and women lent their minds to creating solutions for problems and challenges. In so doing, they gathered as much information as was available, found ways of getting and sharing new data and collaborated with other interested parties in creating an enabling environment to get to their shared goals. Business, private individuals, research and teaching institutions as well as the State all played their roles.

Standing at the dawn of the second century, as we are, with so much more information and so many more tools available for collaboration, opportunities flourish for that spirit of shared goals to lead to new discoveries. This is the single most important factor in finding, developing and producing new hydrocarbon resources today. This chapter examines the following:

1. Increased opportunities for enhancing the capital worth of Trinidad and Tobago by adding to its hydrocarbon resource and reserves base.
2. Pursuing and banking them.
3. The stakeholders and their roles .
4. Quantifying resources and reserves and 5 key initiatives for securing new and sustainable reserves and production.

WHY DO WE BELIEVE THERE ARE SIGNIFICANT NEW RESERVES TO BE FOUND AND PRODUCED?

All of the activities that go into, as well as the products that are derived from the oil and gas industry, flow from the initial processes of data gathering, analysis and interpretation that constitute the discovery and assessment of resources in the ground. That process is initiated only if there is a suitable geological environment; it goes no further than enquiry unless the geology is supported by an amenable fiscal, legal and political/social environment designed to attract capital and know-how. Even so, nothing is achieved in the absence of enabling and cost-efficient technology.

The first half of Trinidad and Tobago's oil century led to the truism that "Trinidad is the graveyard of geologists." It is a description of the complex geology of the island, sitting as it does at the boundaries of three major tectonic plates (Atlantic, South America and Caribbean), with relative motion, changing in both speed and direction over time. As if that were not challenging enough, sediments come from different directions and sources, including one of the fastest depositional rates in the world for a major river system, causing distortion to the continental shelf, while these sediments are themselves penetrated from below by mobile shale masses, moving in pulses!

The resulting variety of structural and stratigraphic features presents a swathe of petroleum trapping styles, sometimes in adjacent geographical location, at other times vertically superposed in the same place by the change in earth processes over geological time.

Figure 7.1 shows the range of tectonic styles, from extension to compression and lateral displacement, all within the relatively small space of onshore southern Trinidad and extending into the offshore terrains.

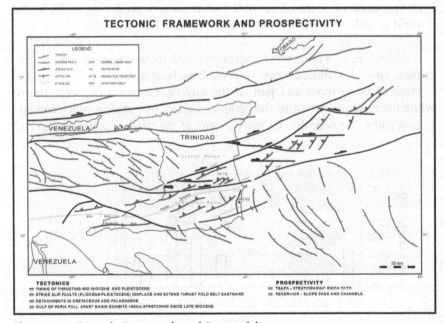

Figure 7.1. Tectonic Framework and Prospectivity.

This presents a double-edged sword. The very complexity of the geology makes it difficult to find and produce new reserves. Data collection, analysis and interpretation, field development and production, are all more difficult and costly. The complexity introduces risk into any prospect, which in turn reduces the allocation of resources and has an impact on the fiscal terms to be applied.

On the other hand, the complexity drove rigour and discipline (sometimes even conservatism!) into the culture, allowing new and adventurous thinkers plenty running room to apply different ideas and approaches. The results were spectacular and include:

- The continuous rebirth of the basin, with new fields being discovered throughout the century, as the exploration push is made in support of some major national objective or driven by major new technological break-through (see Figure 7.2).
- The presence of all the leading international oil companies at one time or another in T&T.
- The development of some of the largest oilfields in the world, many of which have produced over 100 million barrels (despite the complex geology).
- The production to date of over 3 billion barrels of oil .
- The discovery of several billion barrels of oil equivalent which remain to be monetized (gas, heavy oil and oil sands included).
- The presence of some of the oldest continuously producing wells in the world as well as some of world's largest producing gas wells.

Over time, as new areas were understood, new technologies applied or new markets opened, significant new reserves have been added.

Trinidad is on trend and part of the prolific Eastern Venezuela Basin. While the tectonics provided the complex variety of trapping styles and migration paths, the depositional mechanisms of the shallow water (delta) and

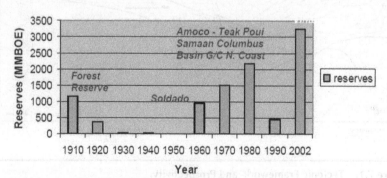

Figure 7.2.   Reserves Added through Time.

deeper (turbidite) extensions of the fluvial river systems produced the major reservoir and seal rocks. Underlying all of this are the world-class Upper Cretaceous source rocks—equivalent to La Luna and Querecual in Venezuela.

A few key facts provide reason for confidence that new areas will yield major new resources:

- The rich Cretaceous source rock, even though variable in composition and richness across the basin remains in the oil- and gas-generating window, even though buried at great depths (< 40,000 feet), sits below one of the coolest basins in the world. Off the east coast, Pliocene and Pleistocene depositional rates in the Orinoco River system were so great that the source rock has not yet attained the temperatures to make it barren. This means, therefore, that, with the "plumbing" system in place, the oil and gas that are currently being generated, or which have been generated while the basin was developing, may have moved from the source and still be trapped in deep prospects and in new areas.
- The greater part of Trinidad and Tobago's sovereign territory remains unexplored, in spite of it still being within the hydrocarbon system. This is mostly so in the deep and ultra deep areas (> 1,000m) off the east coast (Figure 7.3).

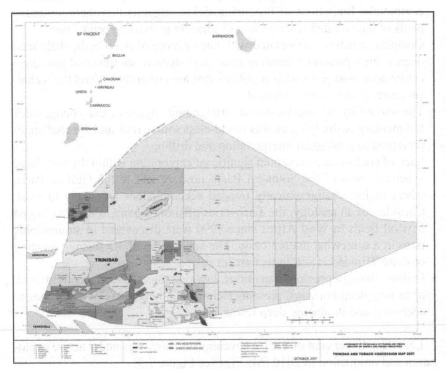

Figure 7.3. Trinidad and Tobago Exploration and Production Concession Map.

- A thick sedimentary pile of Pliocene and Pleistocene rocks (>40,000 feet, in places) presents a range of reservoir and trap opportunities, not yet fully understood. These younger sediments provide a rich biogenic source for natural gas, which augments the bounty of the Cretaceous across the off-shore provinces.
- Miocene and older Tertiary sediments contain reservoir quality rocks in several parts of the basin, but their distribution remains poorly understood.
- Cretaceous reservoir quality and distribution, from sandstones to fractured mudstones, remain poorly understood. There is almost no understanding of the distribution or reservoir characteristics of shelf edge carbonates of Cretaceous age, equivalent to the El Cantil in the Venezuela border area.
- The mix of migration, trapping and sealing mechanisms and the impact on them of tectonics are not yet fully understood—source maturity, migration paths, traps and seals have been dynamic throughout the course of the basin's evolution.
- Over the course of the 100 years of commercial oil and gas production, the complex geology has yielded several small fields, in addition to the many large ones. A normal distribution of field sizes suggests that there are many more small ones to be found, as well as several large ones.
- An understanding of the geology, production history and technical and commercial limitations of producing fields, suggests that there are many pools of unexploited reserves in and adjacent to existing production.
- Complex structures, associated with one or more of steep beds, shale/mud diapirs, high-pressure transition zones and shallow and residual gas, present imaging and processing problems that are currently beyond the technical limits of the seismic method.
- The variability of structural and stratigraphic styles in the young, thick sedimentary basin, lying on this world-class source rock and the challenges presented to geological interpretation and drilling.
- Lack of control data prevented significant exploration within the very large synclinal areas of the Southern Basin onshore and in the Gulf of Paria, where major, stratigraphically trapped accumulations are likely to exist. Consider, as an analogy, the discoveries offshore Ghana, where the largest new oil fields in West Africa since 1990 were discovered in stratigraphic traps in a somewhat mature basin. The application of 3D seismic imaging onshore Trinidad is still in its nascent stage.
- Drilling through pressure transitions, low pressure/depleted gas fields and/ or to very deep horizons, presents technical and commercial challenges to accessing and producing deep resources.

Less than 40 per cent of T&T's sovereign territory was under active exploration and production in 2010 (MEEI) (See Figure 7.3).

WHERE ARE THE RESOURCES AND HOW ARE THEY TO BE FOUND?

Figures 7.4, 7.5 and 7.6 illustrate the regional setting of the Trinidad and Tobago petroleum sub-basins to the greater Eastern Venezuela Basin, the areas under active exploration and production, some of the major regional influences on structure and sedimentology and a stratigraphic chart, highlighting some aspects of the complexity as well as the reservoir-bearing formations.

SOURCE ROCKS

The Upper Cretaceous source consists of black shale of high Total Organic Content and is thermogenic across the basin, except that it is eroded in the Northern Gulf of Paria, the Northern Basin (onshore) and the Northern Basin East Coast Extension. This source is thought to be absent on the Caribbean Plate but present on the northern part of the South American Plate.

The following description is taken from the Geological Society of Trinidad and Tobago[2]

- Rich Type II marine oil source of the Upper Cretaceous Naparima Hill and Gautier Formations (approx. 5,000 ft thick).

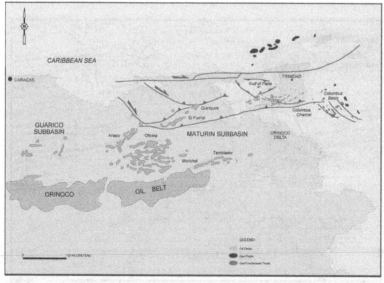

Figure 7.4. Major Oil and Gas Fields of the Eastern Venezuelan Basin.

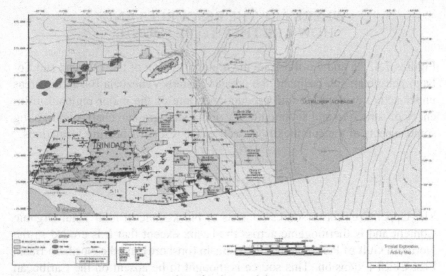

Figure 7.5.   2010 Exploration and Production Activity.

- Biogenic, hemipelagic mudstones and shales, deposited on prograding continental slope of the Upper Cretaceous passive margin.
- Shelfward (south) and basinward (north), the source rocks appear to be leaner and more gas prone
- Age equivalent to the prolific source rocks of the La Lune, Querecal and San Antonio Formations of Eastern Venezuela.

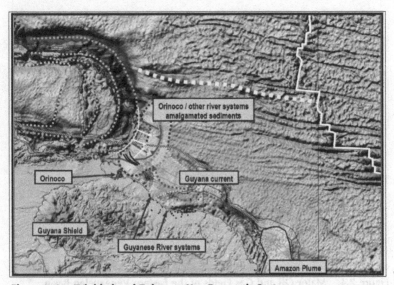

Figure 7.6.   Trinidad and Tobago—Key Reservoir Systems.

- Source rock facies, maturation levels and oil quality vary extensively across the basin, due to depositional and structural complications (i.e. mature source is not ubiquitous).

All the gas in the NCMA area is dry and from a biogenic, or younger source. The Eastern Offshore (Columbus Basin area) is thought to have a mix of thermogenic (Upper Cretaceous) and biogenic (Tertiary and younger) sources (see Figures 7.7, 7.8 and 7.9).

TRINIDAD AND TOBAGO SUB-BASINS

The nomenclature of the various sub-basins or petroleum provinces in Trinidad and Tobago is evolving, so although there are some common terms used, they may not be consistently applied. For the purposes of this chapter, we shall refer to the sub-basins/provinces by their geographical locations:

1. Gulf of Paria: North and South
2. Land: Northern Basin, Central Range Thrust Belt, Southern Basin, Southern Range
3. Columbus Channel: offshore south coast
4. North Coast Marine Area: shallow and deep water
5. Central Range Extension (also called the Angostura trend): extends to Barbados

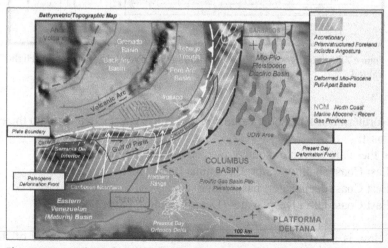

Figure 7.7. Major Sub-Basins Configurations and Petroleum Provinces.

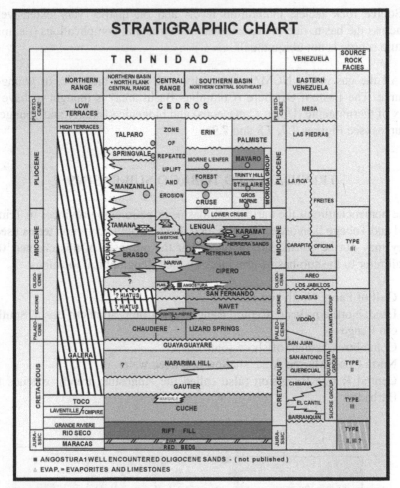

Figure 7.8.   Stratigraphic Chart of Trinidad with Producing Formations Highlighted.

6. Northern Basin offshore extension and North coast extension into the east coast:
   • these are barren of source rock, so are not mentioned further
7. East Coast shallow water: Columbus Basin, shelf
8. East Coast deep water: basin slope
9. East Coast Ultra Deep Water (Deep Atlantic): basin floor

Below is a list of the fields in the major sub-basins with some of their characteristics, along with some of the play concepts that may drive future exploration.

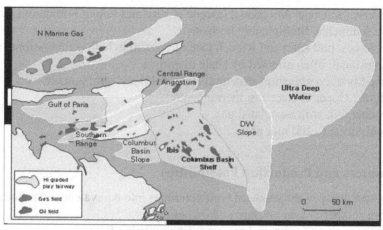

Figure 7.9. Trinidad-Major Sub-Basins.

GULF OF PARIA (GOP)

North GOP

- Fields: Couva Marine (oil), Iguana and Manicou (gas)
- Source: Upper Cretaceous, thermogenic in CM area
- Field Sizes: small

Resources and Production Possibilities

PetroCanada's discoveries confirmed the availability of new opportunities. Small gas fields may find markets locally, so look-alikes may be attractive, once infrastructure to take the gas ashore is in place.

Intriguingly, the Couva Marine crude is somewhat of a mystery, as is the Cretaceous source rock. The sub-basin also has the only significant evaporate (anhydrite) occurrence near to oil production. Neither the petroleum system, nor the disposition of the anhydrite or sediments below it is properly understood. Major advances in sub-salt seismic imaging at the beginning of the 21st century has promoted the case for better understanding of the geochemistry and sedimentology of this area, so as to get a better handle on the petroleum system. On the negative side, the high thermal gradient created by the presence of the anhydrite introduces challenging circumstances for oil and gas generation.

South GOP

- Fields: Soldado Main, Soldado East, Soldado Northwest, North Marine, Point Ligoure

- Reservoirs: Upper Miocene–Pliocene (Cruse and Forest Formations), deltaic sediments. Multiple pay horizons
- Tectonics: pull apart and wrench tectonics result in both compressional and extensional, often affected by shale diapirism
- Trap Style: combination structural (fault/fold) and stratigraphic
- Source: Upper Cretaceous, thermogenic
- Product: oil, with associated gas
- Field Sizes: 0–200 mm bbls

Resources and Production Possibilities

- Prospectively in the southern Gulf continues into equivalent environments, from southern basin onshore and includes:
  - Extension and enhanced recovery from existing fields.
  - Recent economic and technology improvements have not been applied as robustly since the 1990s, as they once were, to the existing fields. These will benefit from an injection of new ideas, technology and capital to enhance production and increase reserves.
- There is a tradition of ending drilling when "economic basement" has deemed to reach at the Top Lower Cruse (Mid Miocene). Deeper reservoirs and stratigraphy are not fully understood, but known to have reservoir qualities in parts of the basin. Deeper drilling will require better seismic imaging and better understanding of the reservoir distribution.
- Cretaceous reservoir distribution is also not well understood, although there are several Cretaceous penetrations in the sub-basin, some with reservoir quality rock.
- Heavy oil is known to exist in large volumes, but has not been quantified or fully valued, although they are known to exceed 2 billion barrels of oil in place. There has been strong interest in exploring for, and developing these at times when the price of oil has been high. Project economics can be greatly improved by reducing risk through a concerted exploration and appraisal programme. The resources can be moved, with relative ease into the proven category, given good prices and by applying the technology and experiences of Eastern Venezuela, for example.
- Seismic quality is poor, due to complex geology, mud diapirism, surface hazards and acquisition geometry challenges, among other things. New acquisition and processing will be applied in the future to release these resources, which may to be in the order of billions of barrels.
- Stratigraphic traps within the basin, downdip of faulted or anticlinal closures.
- The age of the fields in Trinmar, as onshore, combined with the rich nature of the source rock and the dynamic nature of the seals and migration pathways open up the possibility of reservoirs being recharged following

slowdown or termination of production. There is a case for an analysis of this, to determine whether well recompletions or redrills might produce new reserves.

• Enhanced recovery programmes will add reserves, given the low levels of primary production from the fields.

• Horizontal drilling, supported with better quality seismic data, will add recovery to existing reservoirs.

• Mapping of closure of traps alongside or below mud diapirs will require special seismic imaging, as has been done to uncover the salt-related resources in the Deep Water Gulf of Mexico, Angola and Brazil.

LAND

Northern Basin

1. Small gas fields (e.g Mahaica) and gas shows. No evidence of oil. Cretaceous source probably eroded.
2. May contain other small gas fields, close to infrastructure, but hampered by culture (social and industrial infrastructure).
3. Evaluation of organic rich shales, including those within synclinal areas, for gas generating and fracturing potential here and in other parts of Trinidad, will give an understanding of the shale gas opportunity. Existing horizontal drilling capacity, infrastructure and markets for natural gas can improve project economics.

Southern Basin

1. Western Fields: Forest Reserve, Palo Seco, Grand Ravine, Point Fortin, Guapo, Cruse, Vessigny, Cedros, Quarry, Coora, Erin
2. Central Fields: Oropouche, Barrackpore, Penal, Rock Dome/Moruga, Catshill/Trinity/Inniss, Carapal Ridge, Balata, Los Narajos, Mandingo
3. Eastern Fields: Goudron, Navet, Beach, Guayaguayare

Resources and Production Possibilities

There are parallel opportunities to the southern Gulf of Paria. The opportunities are just as significant:

• Cretaceous reservoirs—many penetrations, with turbidite reservoirs in several wells. Depositional and structural settings are poorly imaged and understood. These leads have the potential for turning up fields of several hundred million barrels size.

- Lower Tertiary reservoirs, similarly, are penetrated and have produced in many wells, but remain poorly imaged and understood. As with Cretaceous prospectivity, deep drilling will need to support the imaging and interpretation. As above, the prize here is a field of several hundred million barrels.
- Mid-Tertiary and younger reservoirs (of similar geological age to those currently producing, at greater depths, in other parts of the basin). With the complex structuring, several reservoirs are buried below traditional drilling depths and, often, under complex, thin skins. Of the 13,000 or so wells drilled on land, only a handful have penetrated below 5,000 feet, with the vast majority being less than 3,000 feet. A first look at a well map suggests dense drilling; however, a distribution map showing well depths would illustrate the sparsity of deep drilling onshore Trinidad.
- Shallow: oil sands and extension and enhanced recovery from old fields. Improved contractual terms, economic (fiscal) conditions (to mitigate the impact of the high cost of importing oil for the local refinery) and technology are yet to be applied in any coherent way to the existing fields. It is common knowledge that the land fields have been largely ignored over the past 20 years or so. Attempts to inject new ideas, technology and capital to enhance production and increase reserves have not progressed as would have been anticipated, especially during the high oil-price scenarios of the first decade of the 21st century.
- Improved reservoir and structural understanding from 3D seismic imaging. Up until 2008, or thereabouts, no oil on land in Trinidad was discovered using seismic imaging, due to poor quality seismic data and the gross under-imaging of the basin. In contrast, the successful offshore discoveries depended heavily on quality 3D seismic imaging.
- The age of the fields onshore, more so than in Trinmar, combined with the rich nature of the source rock and the dynamic nature of the seals and migration pathways open up the possibility of reservoirs being recharged since production ended or slowed down. There is a case for an analysis of this, to discover if well recompletions or re-drills might produce new reserves.
- Enhanced recovery programmes will add reserves, given the low levels of primary production from the fields.
- Horizontal drilling, supported with better quality seismic data, will add recovery to existing reservoirs and make newly discovered ones more attractive.
- Stratigraphic traps within the basin, downdip of faulted or anticlinal closures are to be expected and will likely be large. Reservoirs will be less fractured, moving away from the anticlines or major fault systems, providing for better development economics.
- Closure alongside or below mud diapirs, requiring special seismic imaging.

At 2005, the audited reserves for Trinidad and Tobago reflected 2.7 billion barrels of proven, probable and possible (3P) oil. These did not include the heavy oil in Soldado and the SW Peninsula oil sands. The heavy oil and oil sand potential are already proven in reservoirs in the Gulf of Paria and the southwest peninsula.

These are two opportunities with great upside potential but which require very high capital and high technology (R&D) projects. On the other hand, these projects have very long life spans and produce at a relatively high sustained level (estimated in one study to have the potential of up to 100,000 bpd for the Soldado heavy oil and up to 50,000 bpd for the onshore southwest peninsula oil sands and heavy oil). The nature of these reservoirs and production techniques means that the plateau production level may be maintained for up to 20 years. Of course, particularly with the oil sands, there will be environmental and social (land use) issues to be addressed, beyond the norm. The volume and value of resources involved would suggest that addressing these issues should be a priority.

Additional benefits to be derived from their development include:

- high levels of local value-add as a result of high potential for local content and participation and high employment levels (in project construction and operations), translating into high in-country spend
- downstream value-add from the produced liquids (refining, manufacturing and marketing)
- short time for bringing to production (relative to deep water, for example)
- low investor risk, as resources and technology are already largely proven.

Many of the opportunities on land are attractive to smaller, low-cost operators, as indeed the pioneers were a century ago. Creating opportunities for these players have, globally, proven to be an effective means for increasing field life and production, while developing capacity and using local services. As at 2010, about a third of all Petrotrin's land production came from operations by these small businesses. Maximizing production from T&T's resources requires the creation of a niche for small, low-cost, independent operators and a feeder chain to ensure that acreage is continuously available to utilize their resources and assets. This in turn requires an institutional capability and systemic processes for identifying and making these opportunities available within the appropriate legal and fiscal framework.

Figure 7.10 illustrates the general disposition of these exploration and production opportunities.

As the maps in Figure 7.11 and 7.12 illustrate, the land area of Trinidad is poorly imaged by 3D seismic technology, a method that has been widely credited with the major discoveries of the 1990s and later, in the offshore

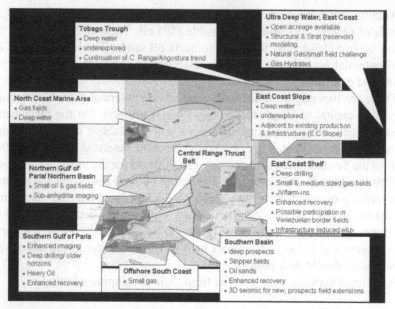

Figure 7.10. Exploration and Production Opportunities in Trinidad and Tobago Sub-Basins.

eastern areas. The widespread use of high quality 3D acquisition and "fit-for-purpose" processing propelled Trinidad and Tobago into one of the leading players in the world natural gas markets. On the other hand, oil and gas fields onshore Trinidad and, to a lesser extent, in the Gulf of Paria, have been discovered and developed almost entirely on well-to-well correlation, based on palaeontology and well logs, supported mainly by limited 2D seismic technology.

Southern Range/South Coast

The complex Southern Range/South Coast area represents the eastward extension of the Pedernales Field of Eastern Venezuela. The key attractiveness of this province lies in the deeper reservoirs that are covered by shallow sediments that are highly complex in structure. Poor quality seismic imaging continues to make exploration difficult because of the steep dipping beds near the surface, rugged topography and thick vegetation of the range. Special seismic imaging, however, might uncover closure alongside or below mud diapirs.

Target reservoirs will include Cretaceous age clastics that are caught up in the fold belt below existing fields. Some estimates put field size potential at 300 million barrels. As with the Columbus Channel and the Southern Basin,

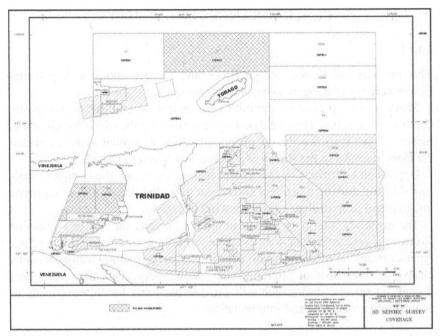

Figure 7.11.   3D Seismic Coverage in Trinidad and Tobago.

the key risks involve reservoir character and the ability to capture quality seismic or other sub-surface imaging data.

High resolution aeromagnetic data and the evolving wireless 3D seismic technology could reduce acquisition costs and environmental challenges. Exploration will have to include data collection and analysis on the flanks, including the transition zone in the Columbus Channel to the south.

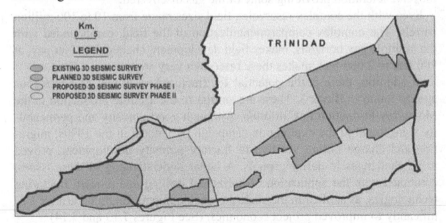

Figure 7.12.   3D Seismic Holds the Key for Land Exploration.

CENTRAL RANGE THRUST BELT

Land

This includes the Central Range Block and Eastern Block with potential Lower Tertiary (Paleogene) deep-water reservoirs.

Shallow plays present opportunities but tend to be compartmentalized by complex structuring. The likelihood is for smaller fields, which are oil prone. Seismic data quality is poor, but the opportunities are similar to those pursued for many decades in the Rocky Mountains and Western Canada.

Opportunities include deeper prospects that lie below the complex, shallow skin and may be much less structured, providing larger plays. Improved imaging and deep drilling capability will be required.

The exploration foray by Talisman did not uncover the Lower Tertiary or Cretaceous reservoirs that were estimated to hold 800 million barrels of oil. An understanding of the reservoir depositional and structural history remains elusive, as does that of migration and charge story. Talisman did collect decent 3D seismic data which will provide the basis for improvements in acquisition, processing and interpretation.

Angostura/East Coast extension

The recent (1990s) discoveries by BHP Billiton and its partners proved up the elusive Oligocene reservoirs of submarine fan and delta systems that had been tested onshore. As with the land extension, the trap style is a combination of stratigraphic and structural features in this compressional fold belt. The oil and condensate source is the Upper Cretaceous, with possibly some biogenic alteration providing some of the gas discovered.

Even with the complex reservoirs, field sizes range from 10 to 100 million barrels. The complex compartmentalization of the field, compounded with the multiple pay horizons, makes field development challenging. Net pay, at 100 feet to 2,000 feet, makes these reservoirs very attractive.

In addition, there is the potential for fractured reservoirs of Cretaceous age, as found in Block 3. These are similar to the argillite production in the Monterrey Formation in California. Although good porosity and permeability were found in the exploration campaign by Unocal in the 1990s, migration and charge timing, relative to fracture porosity development, proved to be challenges in defining pools. A better understanding of these issues, combined with the application of horizontal drilling and modern fracturing technologies, as applied in the shale gas developments, might contribute significantly to improved project economics. (See Figures 7.13 and 7.14)

The Angostura trend extends through the deeper water blocks 23 and 24, into Barbados, and may provide opportunities for deep-water exploration.

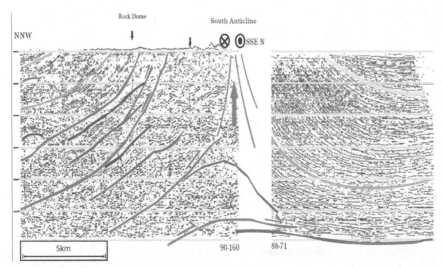

Figure 7.13.   Southern Range Anticline Prospectivity.

The source is known to be oil-prone in the Barbados area, so the risk of bio-genic gas only is not as large as in other areas off the North Coast of Trinidad and Tobago. See Figure 7.15.

SOUTH COAST (OFFSHORE, COLUMBUS CHANNEL)

Resources and Production Possibilities

- This gas-prone part of the basin has been tested and proven to be gas bearing on both sides of the TT/Venezuela border. As markets evolve

Figure 7.14.   Onshore Cretaceous Plays.

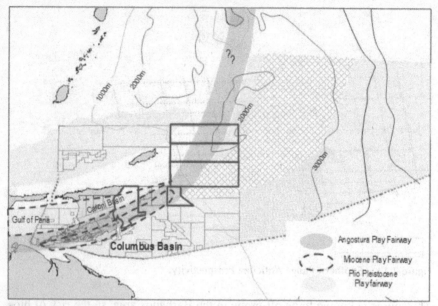

Figure 7.15. Angostura, Eastern Offshore Thrust Belt Play Fairway. Subsurface & Wells Forum, Toronto 2004.

and infrastructure improves, there could be increased exploration and production from these fields. Small fields should attract niche players who may be contented with short-term contracts of a mature natural gas market. Proximity to land and shallow water depth reduce infrastructure cost, compared to similar small gas discoveries off Tobago and in Block 4 (Red Snapper).

• With a commercial arrangement in place, Trinidad and Tobago can capture some Venezuelan gas to monetize in T&T, which might open the door for exploration on both sides of the Channel.

• Aside from Cretaceous clastics, similarly aged shelf edge carbonates of the El Cantil Formation (Figure 7.16) equivalent are thought to underlie the border area at depths of around 20,000 feet. These may provide reservoir quality rocks and an exploration target not yet explored in T&T.

Although this area is not nearly as complex as the Southern Range (Figure 7.13), imaging at depth will also be critical; so too will be reservoir and charge/migration modelling. The good news is that gas reservoirs have been encountered on both sides of the border.

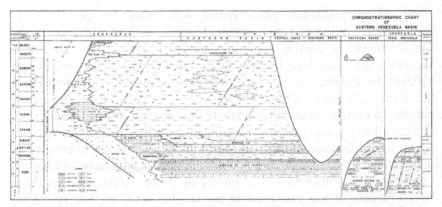

Figure 7.16. Cross Section, Cretaceous Stratigraphic from Venezuela across the Columbus Channel to Southern Basin.

EAST COAST

The East Coast, by virtue of its size and the thickness of the sedimentary basin, contains the major new areas/concepts for additional resource potential. As the geology and drilling and development challenges change with water depth, the EC area will be treated as three separate sub-basins/provinces.

Analysis of a distribution curve of fields discovered to date suggests that there remain considerable new fields to be discovered, both large and small. So far, mainly large fields have been developed, as would be expected in a new basin. As markets and infrastructure become ubiquitous, small oil and gas fields could become very attractive. See Figures 7.23 and 7.24 for an illustration of the field sizes in T&T.

Shallow Water Shelf (Columbus Basin)

This area contains some of the "giant oilfields of the world"; formed along major extension faults, which get younger towards the Atlantic, trapping oil and gas in Pliocene and Pleistocene age deltaic sediments. A key characteristic of the basin is the multiplicity of stacked pay horizons which present large reserves in a relatively small area.

The sub-basin is characterised by large fairways, with clean sands that provide good reservoir continuity in pool sizes of 10 to 200 million barrels, trapped in broad anticlines, associated with the extension faults. Net pay varies between 100 feet and 3,000 feet. The stratigraphy and structuring are locally complex and require significant effort in biostratigraphy, sequence mapping and seismic processing to overcome the effects of shallow gas and subtle lithology changes.

Oil, gas and condensate are abundant, with Upper Cretaceous thermogenic source, influenced by younger, biogenic sources and/or evapora-
tive fractionation, causing a complex mix of phases in field area, with
variations occurring both laterally and vertically. One school of thought
believes that the thick sedimentary cover centred over the Columbus Basin
has, locally, pushed the Cretaceous source into the gas-generating window,
although it remains in the oil window to the East and North. This suggests
that the oil discovered on the shelf was generated in Plio/Pleistocene times
which would indicate more oil at depth. This provides an alternative to
the fractionation theory (a view that oil and gas are migrating up from the
source and the lighter ends have moved up faster) which ascribes about
50–70 percent of the gas found in the sub-basin to biogenic (younger)
sources. Both agree that deeper drilling will more likely produce oil rather
than gas. See Figure 7.17

Challenges remain in understanding reservoir continuity and pressure
influence on seismic, especially at depth. Although pressure gradients are
normal, there are significant regional overpressure areas at depth.

East Coast Shelf Fields include:

• Western, Oil Prone Fields: Teak, Samaan, Poui, Galeota, Mora, Osprey,
  East Manzanilla, Ibis, Pelican, Oilbird;

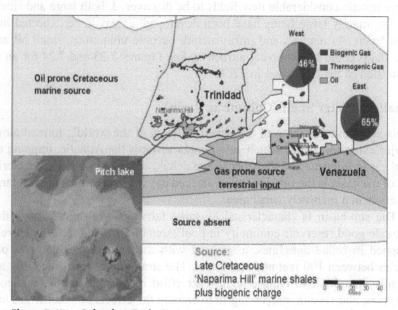

Figure 7.17.   Columbus Basin Source Types.

- Eastern, Gas Prone Fields: East Queens Beach, Mahogany, Coralita, Chachalaca, Manatee, Manakin, Dolphin, Dolphin Deep, Starfish, Kiskadee, Cassia, Mango, Kapok, Amherstia/Parang, Immortelle, Flamboyant, Cashima, North East Queens Beach.

Figures 7.18, 7.19 and 7.20 illustrate some of the characteristics of the East Coast fields.

Resources and Production Possibilities

There exist a range of prospects for new reserves and production in the East Coast offshore shallow (shelf) areas, with various challenges and issues to be addressed:

- Deeper drilling below current production (drilling technology has progressed significantly since the original fields were developed, so that, despite traditional challenges, reaching deeper reservoirs should become routine).
- Extensions of existing fields
- Small or more complex pools or other exploration that may tie back to existing infrastructure or which does not meet the capital efficiency hurdles or other portfolio considerations of existing licence holders, but might be

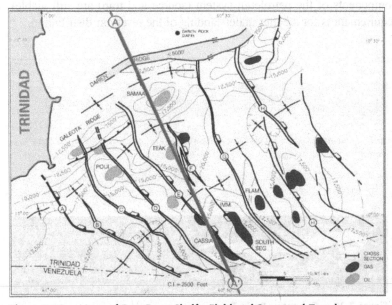

Figure 7.18. Maps of East Coast Shelf—Field and Structural Trends.

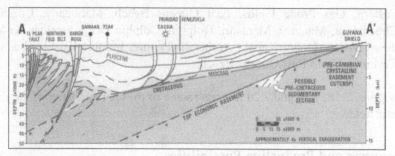

Figure 7.19. Cross Section Across East Coast Shelf Fields, showing regional trends.

attractive to a different operator. The T&T laws and contracts envisaged this situation and made provision for the Minister of Energy to require that existing licensee either diligently explore or exploit the resources, or return the acreage to the Minister.

- New seismic technology (acquisition, processing and interpretation/visualization) will allow better imaging, especially below shallow and residual gas and mud diapirs.
- Bigger, less deformed structures, with the likelihood of larger field sizes and simpler depletion plans are expected at depth, below the thin-skin complexity.
- Deep Ibis (BPTT) failure due to missed reservoir at the drilled location; other components of the petroleum system (source and trap) are still viable—the requirement is for a better understanding of the reservoir distribution.

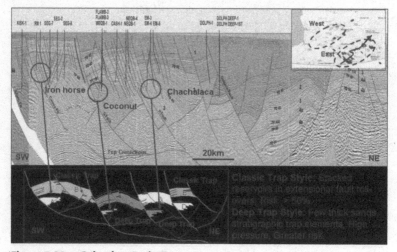

Figure 7.20. Columbus Basin Traps.

- Stratigraphic traps within the basin, downdip of fault induced anticlinal closures.
- Reservoirs are likely to be more oil than gas-prone at depth, although this depends on many criteria, including location in sub-basin, relative to source.
- Follow-up of the discovery in the older Tertiary reservoirs of the fold and thrust belt (Angostura Trend) to the south of BHP Billiton's acreage.
- Infrastructure usage will change with maturity, resulting in more shared facilities.
- Increased gas reserves become available as development costs are reduced with improved infrastructure availability (pipelines, processing facilities and compression) and market maturity. In this way:
  ○ Smaller gas fields will become economic.
  ○ Smaller reservoirs will become suitable recompletion candidates.
  ○ "Stranded" reservoirs will be accessible via sub-sea completions, with tieback to nearby infrastructure.
  ○ Small gas fields could be developed as T&T's gas business becomes more mature and plants require shorter gas supply contracts, thereby removing the need to have dedicated reserves for a new plant and which can only come from large fields.
- Dedicated low pressure infrastructure (either purpose built or derived from older, underutilized pipelines and facilities) will facilitate the booking of reserves in depleted reservoirs and smaller pools that are currently considered as "stranded" gas to be booked.
- Offshore processing (by using floating or fixed plants) should become economic as technology advances.

Whereas the early discoveries in the shelf were driven by seismic and, later, by Direct Hydrocarbon Indicators (DHI) for gas, the new exploration success will require a better imaging and understanding of the deeper reservoirs and structures, with potential challenges around the high pressure ramp and reservoir quality. To overcome the imaging challenges, a step change in seismic (acquisition, processing and analysis) is required. One can choose to await that breakthrough or to be a part of it.

BP's Deep Ibis play tested the deep reservoir and structural concept. This was just one of several deep structures seen on seismic images (see Figures 7.17 and 7.18) and illustrated by BPTT's mapping of prospects and leads in the basin (Figure 7.21). Penetrating the high-pressure transition, which occurs below 18,000 feet on the shelf, required high pressure drilling, an expensive undertaking especially since BP had diagnosed a high temperature environment, although there was no indication that this was a character of the Columbus Basin.

Aside from the drilling and seismic issues, other issues to be overcome include the lack of rock property control for seismic modelling and the poor understanding of the stratigraphy and reservoir characteristics (including porosity, permeability and cementation) of this deeper water equivalent of the Cruse and Gros Morne Formations.

Still, there has not been much effort or success in pursuing pure stratigraphic plays in the Columbus Basin. Given the stratigraphy, petrophysics and petroleum system, these may provide huge potential, but will require new research.

Shelf exploration success, therefore, will depend on addressing the challenges of imaging presented by residual and shallow gas, pressure transition and complex structures. These, in turn, will require an understanding of the mechanisms for residual gas formation and new approaches to seismic data collection, processing and analyses (such as wide azimuth, bottom cable and shear wave acquisition and pre-stack depth migration). A significant R&D effort in this direction will be required if the resource potential of deeper gas in the shelf area is to be unlocked. Figure 7.22 illustrates the exploration and production of these, in the context of the phasing of gas development in T&T.

East Coast Slope/Deep Water

Resource and Production Possibilities

The Orinoco Delta hosts the most prolific oil and gas basin in the world—the Eastern Venezuelan Basin. This results from the overlap of the very rich

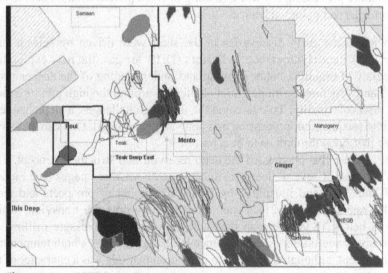

Figure 7.21.   BPTT Deep Prospects.

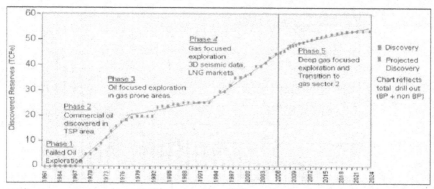

Figure 7.22. Progressing East Coast Provinces with Technology.

and massive source rock (Cretaceous shales) and a massive delta deposition system.

1. Most of the major oil and gas discoveries of the last two decades of the 20th Century were in deep-water basins around the world, associated with major river delta systems. On the Atlantic margin, the Gulf of Mexico, West Africa and offshore Brazil have their equivalent in offshore Trinidad, where there has been drilling only in the inner part of the slope with a bypass of reservoir rocks, heading to deeper water accumulations. This area (referred to by the Ministry of Energy as the "ultra-deep," although it in a water depth of only 4,000–7,000 feet) has only recently acquired 2D seismic data and will likely not be drilled before 2013.
2. Oilfields in deep water have tended to be extremely large (of the order of several hundred million barrels) and very highly productive (wells make in excess of 20,000 bopd and fields produce in the order of 300,000 bopd). The deep-water Caspian fields of Azerbaijan are said to have more reserves than Kuwait, for example.
3. The expectation is that T&T will discover several oil and gas fields in deep-water areas, with three to five giants and a few smaller ones which, together, have the potential to deliver a country production of as high as 1 million bopd, assuming the timing of exploration and discovery are fortuitous.
4. Advancements in technology and markets would allow for deep-water gas to become commercial as a result of high production levels (2–5 bcfd), from gas associated with oilfields as well as predominantly gas fields. This will, of course, require an appropriate fiscal regime and market conditions.
5. Large volumes of gas hydrates have been found in the shallow sediments of the deep-water areas. These have not been adequately mapped or quantified, as they await the development of appropriate technology to make their exploitation commercial.

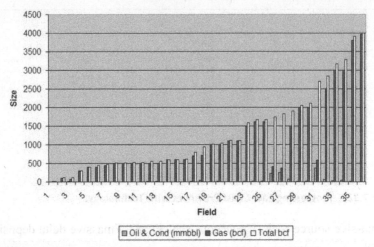

Figure 7.23.   Columbus Basin Oil and Gas Field Size Distribution.

   This area includes Blocks 25(A) & 25(B), Block 26 and Block 27, which were explored in the late 1980s to early 1990s by Shell, Exxon and Arco/bpTT. The programme involved 3D seismic coverage of all blocks and exploration wells (Hayden, Pepper Sauce, Adelpha, Catfish, etc.).

   To date, no commercial hydrocarbon has been found. The data revealed Plio-Pleistocene confined slope channels and ponded, intra-slope mini-basins

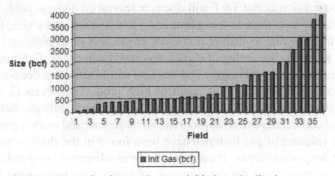

Figure 7.24.   Columbus Basin Gas Field Size Distributions.

with combination stratigraphic/structural traps. Block 25(A) revealed a compressive play to the west. Because of the risk of the presence and effectiveness of the reservoir, which appears to have by passed the drilled zones, (see Figure 7.25) the area remains largely under-explored.

Ultra-Deep Water (Deep Atlantic) Province

Beyond the by-pass zone of the slope, sediments found their way to the basin floor and formed into fan systems which provide better reservoir distribution in deeper waters. These Plio-Pleistocene, base-of-slope and basin-floor submarine fan systems were potentially formed into large, gently folded traps by the compressive structures that are related to the Atlantic plate subduction (See Figures 7.26 and 7.27). Mud diapirism would also have assisted in forming traps.

Underneath all of this is the Upper Cretaceous oil-prone source rock, which gets richer to the North. "Piston core data confirm the presence of thermogenic gas and oil," indicating that the "UDW province has generated and expelled hydrocarbons—viable working source system" (MEEI). Geochemistry of samples confirms the similarity to Trinidad Cretaceous oil source.

These will be very deep water, complex fields with the potential of very big reserves (several hundred million barrels), with high well productivity similar to deep-water fields on the Atlantic margin. Large structures have been mapped from the seismic coverage. There is a sense that the sub-basin can yield over 2.5 billion barrels of oil.

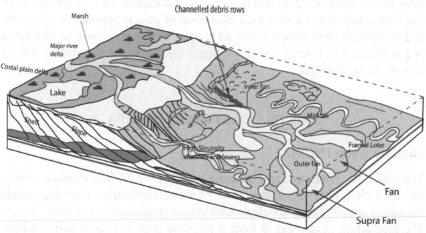

Figure 7.25.   Deep Water/Slope By-Pass Zone leading into Ultra Deep Fan System.

Reservoirs are likely to be Late Miocene to Early Pliocene turbidites of slope and basin fan origin, while seals would have been provided by the intra-basinal mudstones. This stratigraphic complexity will be compounded by the mix of structural styles that were produced over time as the plates moved—early compression- followed by strike-slip, then uplift caused by more recent compression.

As in other places in T&T, seismic imaging, drilling and, in this case, production challenges, remain. Closure alongside or below mud diapirs will require special seismic imaging, as has been done for salt intrusions, to uncover the resources in the Deep Water Gulf of Mexico, Angola and Brazil.

T&T stands at the gateway of one of the last unexplored deep-water extensions of a major river/delta system in the world. Added to this is the fact that it is the one with the most prolific hydrocarbon systems. T&T stands to benefit from the experiences of other deep-water developments around the world, so that development cycles and costs should be lower than benchmarks around the world, provided especially that goods and services return to pre-2004 rates. By not being at the leading edge of deepwater exploration and production, two major hurdles have already been cleared by other countries (the cost of developing and improving new technology and understanding the geological setting) and will benefit T&T.

Fiscal reform to address deep water gas and small fields should go a long way towards addressing these risk factors. T&T can get a better deal than some early entrants, depending on how well it manages the offsetting risk considerations that impact investment decisions and engages potential investors.

One independent industry estimate puts the prospectivity of the Deep Atlantic at over 5,500 million boe, unrisked (~800 MMBOE, risked), with pool sizes in the order of 72 MMBOE (P50) with a median of ~50 prospects. In one case, analysts put a very high likelihood of gas, as opposed to oil, as the hydrocarbon to be discovered. Not all agree with this prognosis, as illustrated by the Ministry of Energy's research that is quoted above, suggesting that oil is more likely than gas.

NORTH COAST MARINE AREA

Shallow water (NCMA)

The Chaconia, Hibiscus and Poinsettia fields in the NCMA produce natural gas for LNG. They are made up of Pliocene age marine shoreface sands trapped in simple, broad anticline combination stratigraphic and fault closure. The production of dry gas is from a biogenic source. Liquid hydrocarbons production during the Drill Stem Test of the discovery KK-2 well, drilled in the 1970s remains an enigma.

The simple structures in the NCMA provide for excellent seismic data quality, so that the fields with net pay, ranging from 20 feet to 100 feet in pool sizes of 20 to 1,000 bcf are quite attractive, in spite of their relatively thin sands. New blocks are available for exploration and are expected to turn up new reserves.

The proximity to the Dragon and Patao fields of Venezuela also raises the possibility of infrastructure development that might encourage smaller field development.

Further to the east, the "stranded' Onyx field, offshore Tobago, might be a candidate for some type of floating production/conversion facility, such as small scale LNG.

Deep Water NCMA

To the north and into the deeper water blocks of the NCMA, the Cretaceous source rock re-appears and provides a thermogenic source for oil. The biogenic source may also continue, so that both oil and gas are likely.

Blocks 21 and 22, for instance, have the potential for Miocene and Pliocene plays, although the lithologies are not well understood in the absence of well penetrations. The structures are large and simple, making seismic mapping relatively simple.

Block 22 has turned up gas discoveries for PetroCanada and was still under appraisal at the end of 2010.

Tobago Trough

Lying north and east of Tobago (see Figures 7.5, to 7.7 and 7.28), this sedimentary basin includes Blocks 23(A&B) and 24. To date, there has been no

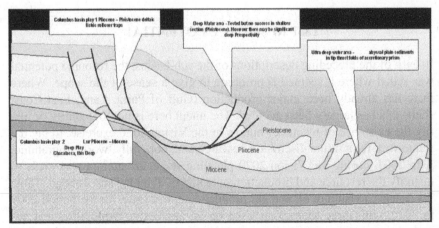

Figure 7.26.   Structural and Stratigraphic Character of Ultra Deep Province.

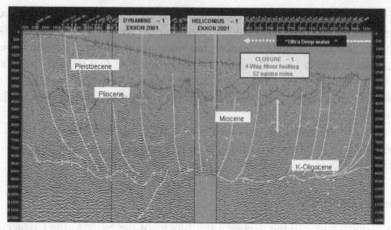

Figure 7.27.   Slope to Ultra Deep Regional Seismic Line.

exploration drilling, but 2D seismic surveys have been shot over the area as far back as 1980. The trend of the Angostura extension passes through the trough as it heads towards the Barbados accretionary prism and alongside this is the eastwards extension of the NCMA. The simple geology of the latter paves the way for large structures.

The Cretaceous source rocks are thought to be rich and oil-prone. With water depths ranging from 1,000–2,000 m, exploration and development will be difficult and expensive. Reducing the technical risks (better data and modelling) and enhancing the commercial terms could make the venture more attractive.

Figure 7.28 illustrates the structural trends along the north of Trinidad and around Tobago.

T&T RESOURCE POTENTIAL

In each of the preceding descriptions of the sub-basins, the resource potential was stated where it seemed appropriate to give a sense of the scope. Where there has already been major production (Gulf of Paria, Land, East Coast shelf) this has largely been avoided. The intent here is not to quantify or justify the existence of resources but, as in the Vision 2020 exercise, to lay the framework for a future discussion, research and, hopefully, work programme.

In 2004, during the Vision 2020 planning stage, an attempt was made to quantify the resource and production potential of Trinidad and Tobago. Table 7.1 reflects a vision of oil and gas production at that time, for the period 2009 to 2020, with three scenarios, based on an aggressive exploration and appraisal programme, as was then on track:

Table 7.1.   Resource Potential—A 2004 Perspective

Year		2009	2015	2020
Oil and Condensate(bopd)	Low	201,000	250,000	200,000
	Medium	250,000	350,000	500,000
	High	350,000	600,000	1,000,000
Natural Gas (bcfd)	Low	3.9	5	6
	Medium	6	7	10
	High	7.8	10	15

1. Low case: only a handful of "new" discoveries.
2. Medium case: a few of the "new provinces" pan out partially.
3. High case: most of the "new provinces" pan out successfully.

The report noted that "these estimates had not been subjected to rigorous geological or risk procedures, but were back-of-the envelope numbers, estimated on the basis of limited data points without any judgment about accuracy." However, the conclusions were "intended to stimulate discussion in the absence of any published data that consider the upside."

The main message is that there was "a reasonable probability that Trinidad and Tobago's production levels, high as they are, may go even higher after the current phase of growth. Nevertheless, this growth will always be finite and for a limited period. This presents opportunities as well as dangers. The biggest danger is complacency, which allows a tremendous opportunity to slip as we fail to prepare Trinidad and Tobago and its future generations for long-term competitiveness."

The reality is that neither the aggressive exploration and appraisal programme, nor the rate of discovery anticipated, was accomplished. In fact, the effect of slow pace of new licensing and fiscal reform, combined with increasing operating and capital costs and the faltering global economy, have resulted in the outlook becoming bleaker, certainly in terms of timing. In 2009, the reality was that the figures were at the low case for gas and significantly below (~110 bpd) for oil production.

These numbers are seen as overly optimistic by external observers, when one considers the views of Gaffney Cline, Wood Mackenzie and earlier USGS analyses. BPTT, the major producer, is on record as saying that smaller, more expensive oilfields will be found. Some observers interpret the low response to the 2005/2006 bid-round for the Deep Atlantic blocks to be an indication of their prospectivity, relative to the "aggressive fiscal terms" (according to some potential bidders) then applied.

The 1999 US Geological Survey (USGS) review of the oil and gas potential of Trinidad and Tobago was conducted before some major and significant new studies and discoveries were made in the basin. The review

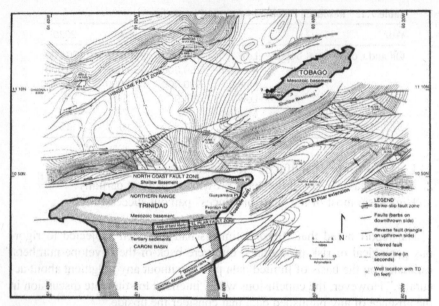

Figure 7.28.   Structural Trends, North Coast Marine Area and Northern Range Extension.

was, therefore, not as up-to-date with the deep water, deep drilling or gas stories. It is reflected here, in any case. From Figures 7.29 to 7.31 the USGS suggested that there was a mean of 21 new oil and 104.7 gas fields yet to be discovered. Respectively, the minimum field sizes were 4 MMBO and 24 BCFG. At the time, there were 40 oil and 24 gas fields already discovered, larger than these minima.

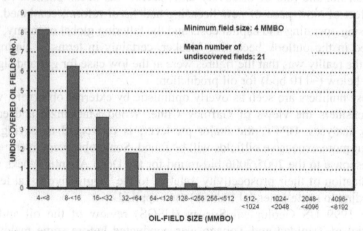

Figure 7.29.   Trinidad Basins – Undiscovered Oil Fields (USGS, 1999).

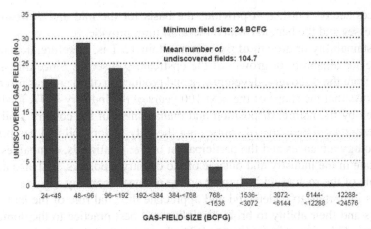

Figure 7.30. Trinidad Basins—Undiscovered Gas Fields (USGS, 1999).

HOW DO WE GO ABOUT FINDING AND MONETISING THESE?

Towards an Exploration Strategy for Trinidad and Tobago

The upstream energy industry is a significant contributor to economic growth in T&T. On its own, it provides the most revenue from oil and gas through taxes, royalties and revenue shares from the operators, as well as taxes and employment and the concomitant multiplier effect from the very significant

CHARACTERISTICS OF ASSESSMENT UNIT

Oil (<20,000 cfg/bo overall) or Gas (≥ 20,000 cfg/bo overall):.....   __Oil__

What in the minimum field size?.............   ___4___ mmboe grown (≥1mmboe)
(the smallest field that has potential to be added to reserves in the next 30 years)

Number of discovered fields exceeding minimum size:................   Oil: __40__   Gas: __24__
  Established (>13 fields)   X   Frontier (1-3 fields) _____ Hypotetical (no fields) _____

Median size (grown) of discovered oil fields (mmboe):
  1st 3rd __52.1__   2nd 3rd __22.2__   3rd 3rd __32.4__
Median size (grown) of discovered gas fields (bcfg)
  1st 3rd __622__   2nd 3rd __314__   3rd 3rd __151__

Assesment-Unit Probabilities:
  Attribute   Probability of occurance (0-10)
1. CHARGE: Adequate petroleum charge for an undiscovered field ≥ minimum size..........................   __1.0__
2. ROCKS: Adequate reservoirs, traps and seals for an undiscovered field≥ minimum size...............   __1.0__
3. TIMING OF GEOLOGIC EVENTS: Favourable timing for an undiscovered field≥ minimum size.....   __1.0__

Assesment-Unit GEOLOGIC Probability (productof 1, 2, and 3):................................   __1.0__

4. ACCESSIBILITY: Adequate location to allow exploration for an undiscovered field
≥ minimum size...   __1.0__

Figure 7.31. USGS Perspective of Characteristics of Undiscovered Fields in T&T (1999).

services sector. Further, it provides the basis for the mid and downstream businesses and the benefits which these, in turn, provide.

Sustainability or growth of the sector within T&T is, therefore, dependent on the sustainability or growth of the upstream sub-sector. Since this is derived from the discovery, development and production of oil and gas reserves, it follows that the shape of the next 100 years of the industry in T&T will be defined by the nature, disposition and management of the country's oil and gas resources. These are, of course, not the only factors; oil and gas prices, technology advances and the participation of T&T nationals, companies and the State in the industry and outside of the country's borders, will also affect the role of the sector and its impact on the national economy.

It is important to understand and appreciate the vital role of the large operators and their ability to bring discipline and best practice to the domestic industry. This cannot be understated. The importance of their role in unravelling the complexities of the basin is unchallenged. Even so, all companies make discoveries that are considered un-economic or sub-economic, based on several factors, not only their own internal considerations. In T&T, there have been many such discoveries that are not booked to the national reserves and which may be so converted. Similarly, there are very many "leads" that have not been pursued by existing licencees. In the twenty years on either side of the millennium, there was a trend of major oil and gas discoveries being made by smaller, independent companies that were able to attract innovative geologists and work in ways that did not fit with the model of the bigger, less risk-averse multinationals. The key to entry for these small, nimble explorers is access to data and acreage. T&T management of both of these will have to be significantly adjusted to attract these companies. Having done so, T&T must make sure that those that are attracted are in fact well qualified to conduct the necessary operations and that the appropriate institutional capacity required for managing them is put in place.

The diverse range of the potential opportunities requires, in other words, a portfolio of operators to be identified, attracted, contracted and managed effectively.

Key Success Factors

A few key areas of focus have been identified time and again, for accessing the resource potential of the individual sub-basins. These, combined with the lessons of the first 100 years, should provide the basis for defining priority areas of focus for a sustained resource management programme. Primary among the requirements are:

a. An implementable and appropriate exploration and acreage management strategy.

b. A data acquisition and management strategy that seeks to reduce the risk involved in working this complex basin, while making data widely available, so that innovation and new ideas—the key elements of past success—can be accessed as widely as possible.

c. A seismic imaging capacity development strategy. Complex areas, including thrust and wrench fault areas, mud diapirs and steeply dipping beds, are common in T&T and notorious for being difficult for seismic imaging, while harbouring or lying above oil and gas fields. Subtle lithological changes within the sand and shale sequences hold the secrets to stratigraphic traps. There is a treasure chest of research crying out to be opened.

   Building capacity in both R&D and services contractors will flow from the data management strategy and into the local business and support development that were so much a part of the early landscape.

d. Development of a local drilling capacity strategy that will utilise local expertise that has been honed over many decades to become today's standard of world leader in every corner of the earth. Such a strategy would create readily available expertise and assets for meeting the needs of a pipeline of projects, assuming such were kept full by the acreage management strategy.

   A strategy that builds local companies to pursue the many small opportunities on land, by providing continuous access to drilling opportunities, linked as it were to a T&T branded drilling school, will further enhance our national education capability, while keeping fields active. With good management, such a company could grow to assume more complex operations, offshore T&T and overseas, while allowing T&T nationals to survive slowdowns at home.

e. A flexible and responsive fiscal regime. Given the multiple complexities and facets of each individual opportunity, commercialisation must be at the forefront of E&P activity. Far too many "discoveries" lie fallow because they are either non-commercial or sub-commercial. In a world of ever-changing technology, costs and product prices, it is important that the regulator retain capacity to be nimble and responsive, not just to technical matters that affect the industry's health, but to commercial ones as well.

   The results of the 2006 deep water licensing round do not simply reflect the prospectivity of the basin, but also the timing and terms requested at a time of an abundance of competing opportunities available around the world. Each of the various opportunities highlighted and discussed here come with its unique risks and challenges (e.g. high cost technology, high operating costs, coupled in some cases with low value of heavy oil, market risk, etc). The one thing that the government has within its own control is the nature of fiscal terms. Agility in addressing this area will provide the framework for determining its commercial reward of these plays.

f. Institutional capacity, systems and processes for transparent, predictable and nimble acreage management. Understanding and responding to the challenges raised above require a capacity to access information, analyse it in the context of national objectives and develop appropriate responses.

As T&T crosses this bridge from the first to the second century of oil and gas, it is remarkable how much has changed and how much remains the same. The attributes that helped T&T to become a success story from a resource rich country over the twentieth century are the same ones that are needed in moving into an era of sustainable development.

Innovation, collaboration, leadership, clear thinking and alignment with national objectives are the key elements of our past success and will remain so. Nationals, individuals and businesses, working in concert with the world's best in developing local capacity, took on and conquered the world of oil and gas.

Extracting from an extractive industry is what we have done well and what we will continue to do. How well we do will depend on our attitude and the choices we make.

NOTES

1. Trinidad & Tobago: Celebrating a Century of Commercial Oil Production. Official Centenary Publication of the Ministry of Energy & Energy Industries (available online at time of writing at http://energy.gov.tt/energy_industry.php?mid=3)
2. Source: http://gstt.org/Geology/source.htm)

Chapter Eight

Sustaining and Leveraging the Energy Sector Portfolio over the Next 100 Years

Baajnath Sirinath

INTRODUCTION: CONSISTENT REINVENTION

The Trinidad and Tobago economy has consistently reinvented itself over the last several hundred years with the oil and gas industry having made several significant contributions to the global energy industry over the course of the twentieth century. This chapter offers an overview of the options for maintaining and extending the competitive advantage of Trinidad and Tobago in the global oil, gas and related industries. It examines improvements in the discovery and use of resources, accessing the best markets and using the most efficient value chains and processes. Leveraging the oil and gas industry to expand the services sector and create new knowledge-based industries is also explored. Some of the opportunities for establishing renewable energy industries at scale, using our developed energy markets, are described. Finally, the evolution of institutional arrangements to support the growth and development of these options are briefly reviewed.

Oil and gas have dominated the economic landscape for the last 100 years. During this time we have witnessed the transition from land-based oil production to marine oil production, gas production for the petrochemical industry and most recently gas production for the LNG industry.

If we look back even further at the principal economic activities over the previous 400 years, as shown in the Figure 8.1, Trinidad and Tobago demonstrates an impressive series of relatively seamless transitions in the commanding heights of its economy. As we contemplate the next century, insights from our economic history provide us with ready constructs for creating the future. The figure which is a depiction of the trajectory of its economy over the last 400 years is a testament to the creativity and vision of the people of the twin-island

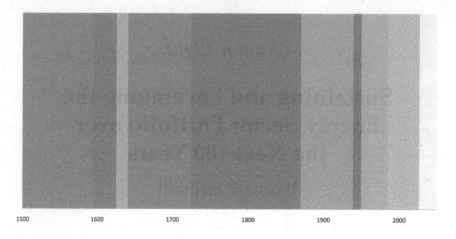

■ Subsistence farming ■ Tobacco ■ Cotton ■ Sugar Cane ■ Cocoa ■ Oil ■ Petrochemicals ■ LNG   ?

Figure 8.1.   Consistently Reinventing the Commanding Heights.

state and gives hope that the new sources of economic activity will be created to support the continued development of the country.

From this figure, it is clear that the local economy has been on a path of continuous growth and development for centuries. The first few centuries after the arrival of Europeans were marked by a variety of agro-based industries. Since then its peoples have demonstrated ability to consistently reinvent them by leveraging human and other resources to meet world demand for desirable goods and services. The pace of development post-independence has been particularly impressive. Over this period, sugar cane gave way on the centre stage to oil, then oil gave way to gas-based petrochemicals and gas-based petrochemicals to liquefied natural gas.

The transition from oil to gas is a particularly impressive story, not for the gas industry it created, but because the strategy of creating the next engine of the economy even while the current one is growing, can be a model for creating the next transition. Figure 8.2 depicts the transition from oil to gas, starting in the 1970s. With the oil economy in early ascendancy with no end in sight, a visionary decision was taken to develop gas-based industries. History bears out (in the shaded area) the creation of a world-class gas economy as the oil economy entered into an unexpected early decline. The foresight in starting the process of creating a new industrial base whilst the existing economic basis was in early ascendancy has to be recorded as one of the more significant achievements of this tiny nation State. To persist in the development of its gas reserves by pursuing LNG as a viable export product was an equally spectacular achievement.

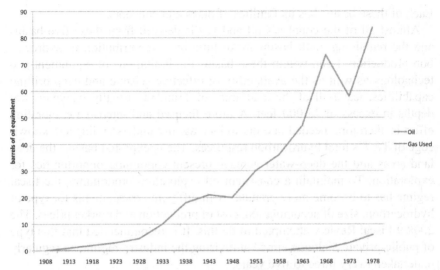

Figure 8.2. Gas Industry Started before Peak of Oil Industry.

This construct of moving to the successor phase of economic development while still in the predecessor stage of high activity is of enduring value and may actually be of greater importance than the gas economy that was created in the last several decades and which is the usual focus of attention. This idea is critically important for survival in a world with accelerating rates of change and relentless competition. In this regard, initiatives such as the Vision 2020 exercise are important in transforming the economy even as the peak of the gas industry is yet to be determined.

OIL INDUSTRY

Finding New Resources

Geologists acknowledge 13 oil- and gas-prospective basins in Trinidad and Tobago (Tobago is not known to have hydrocarbon resources onshore). Five of these produced the majority of the country's hydrocarbons:

1. The Southern Gulf of Paria Basin
2. The Southern Basin (on land)
3. The Columbus Basin Shelf
4. The Offshore Extension of the Central Tectonic Zone (the Angostura discovery in the Lower Oligocene horizon Block 2c, now joined by another one in Block 3a)
5. The North Coast Marine Area (NCMA)

Each of these basins has its families of plays and concepts.

Almost all of the country's oil and gas is derived from these five basins and the remaining eight basins make little or no contribution to hydrocarbon production. Even within these basins the limitations of equipment and technology as well as the availability of effective seismic and deep drilling capabilities, leave all of the land areas of Trinidad virtually unexplored at depths in excess of 12,000 feet. A more focused and intensive exploration effort is, therefore, needed in order to increase our understanding and knowledge of T&T's total hydrocarbon resources. The unexplored basins, the deep land areas and the deep-water acreage present continuing opportunities for exploration. To maintain a consistent oil exploration programme, the fiscal regime has to become more granular with different arrangements for type of hydrocarbon, size of accumulation, cost of production and market prices. The 2008/9 Fiscal Review attempted to do this. It is recommended that this type of public-private dialogue aimed at revising the industry regime be regularly undertaken every three to five years.

Improved Recovery from Existing Resources

In addition to finding new resources, there are many options for improving the recovery from existing resources. In the 1980s a lease operatorship and farm-out programme was started. This programme needs to be significantly expanded. Many of these initiatives have shown that smaller operators with idle equipment, lower overheads, less bureaucracy, new ideas and a more entrepreneurial culture are able to keep smaller fields going for longer, actually adding to the recoverable reserves. The Exploration and Production arm of state oil company, Petrotrin, is well positioned to place its considerable portfolio of mature fields for lease operators and farm-outs in the near term. This could substantially expand the number of locally owned businesses involved in oil and gas production and will more efficiently pursue the decline phase of the mature fields now under Petrotrin's stewardship. This approach should also include the mature offshore oilfields at Trinmar and Galeota which can be joint-ventured so as to retain access to equity crude. This will increase both production and ultimate recoveries from these fields. Finally, this would allow state capital to be re-deployed to other areas where private capital may not be forthcoming.

It is a well-known fact that primary oil recovery only recovers a portion of the oil in place in any given reservoir. There are many methods of enhanced oil recovery, some of which the industry is already familiar with. One area that needs to be examined further is the capture and use of the considerable emissions of carbon dioxide in enhanced oil recovery. Pursuing this now may provide another avenue for mitigating the ill effects of climate change, a factor that was not previously a major consideration in using carbon dioxide for enhanced oil recovery.

Another secondary recovery mechanism, which arises from the interconnection with the gas industry, is the use of depleted oil reservoirs to store gas. This will serve dual purposes. For the oil industry, the re-pressurising of old reservoirs will increase oil recovery. For the gas industry it will provide "capacitance," allowing withdrawal from storage of richer gas when needed by the industry that may be much more cost-effective than maintaining high-cost spare upstream capacity for occasional production upsets. This type of project is also amenable to private local capital as requirements are much lower than that typically needed for new oilfield development projects.

The taxation regime for these projects and other types of improved/secondary projects should focus on increasing absolute taxes rather than on extracting a large percentage share of nothing as sometimes seems to be the case.

Unconventional Resources

Development of the country's abundant heavy oil resources in both the land and marine areas requires appropriate special-purpose fiscal regimes, new technologies and, perhaps, even institutional arrangements, as well as invitations to experienced companies (e.g. operators familiar with the experiences of Canada) in heavy oil and tar sands so as to accelerate the development of these resources.

Accessing Premium Markets

Much more attention needs to be paid to the marketing of crude oil and refined products. As at 2011, T&T produced approximately 90,000 barrels of oil per day. It is important to start this process by segregating products, such as condensate from black oil, so that the optimum price for each stream can be obtained. This may require, for example, new/upgrades of the liquid pipeline infrastructure from the east coast to Pointe-a-Pierre. Along with pipeline infrastructure upgrades there is the need for establishing a separate world-class oil terminal facility on the west coast, at Pointe-a-Pierre, for example, to take full advantage of the multiple synergies available from aggregating in a more favourable location. This would improve economies of scale and allow closure of the small high-cost east coast liquid export facilities.

The refining industry is handled in a subsequent section but with respect to refined products the same type of initiatives need to be explored. The upgrade of the refinery to access metropolitan markets needs to be combined with other initiatives described later to regain control of the premium regional markets.

Conservation and Efficiency

There are many opportunities for conservation and efficiency improvements in the oil industry. A significant amount, ca. 25,000 barrels per day or the equivalent of 25% of production, is sold at subsidised prices in the domestic market. There are many avenues to reducing the amount of petroleum products used and much work needs to be focused here in the near term. For example, car-pooling, staggering work hours, higher usage of public transportation and more fuel-efficient vehicles are a few of the options available. Fuel substitution is another approach.

A massive programme of conversion of public transportation and government vehicles to CNG will displace a considerable amount of liquid fuels (gasoline and diesel) for export to premium markets at market prices instead of low subsidised prices. Part of the savings in petroleum products subsidy can be used to fund this conversion exercise, including the gas distribution and fuelling stations infrastructure.

An appropriate social safety net and tax incentives followed by a reduction of the petroleum products subsidy will cause a significant conversion of private vehicles to CNG. As described later, renewable transportation fuels (bio-fuels and electricity) would allow the eventual removal of the petroleum products subsidy which, among other impacts, will lead to further reduction in the domestic use of liquid fossil-based fuels, thereby creating another increase in the volume of transportation fuels for premium export markets.

REFINING INDUSTRY

Two significant injections of capital, the first in 1991–1996 (approximately US$500 million) and the second in 2005, via the Gasoline Optimization Program (estimated for completion at more than US$1,200 million in 2010), provides the refinery at Pointe-a-Pierre with significant modern and new equipment and instrumentation. If these assets are combined with new initiatives in the areas of inventory management, refining losses, working capital and administrative and labour costs, then the refinery could stand a chance of improving its performance. However, it is the change of ownership from state to the ordinary citizens via the Stock Exchange that is likely to have the largest sustained positive impact. It is recommended that a separate refining company be created and privatized via public offerings on the local stock exchange on a phased basis over, say, the next five years. This would increase the capitalization of the stock exchange significantly. As private ownership increases, the efficiency of the refinery will increase whilst each subsequent sale of shares will bring increasing value to the government for use in creating new economic activities and repeating the now familiar process of re-inventing the commanding heights of the economy. This allows the country to retain and improve the productivity of economic activity while simultaneously creating the next generation of industries. It should be pointed out that the life of the refinery is not tied to local production of oil but can continue to operate long after on the basis of importing its entire requirement of crude feedstock. Consequently, its connection with the domestic upstream sector is simply a temporary arrangement of convenience.

GAS INDUSTRY

Future Shape

In much the same way as oil peaked in the 1970s, declined and then levelled off at about half the peak rate, it is quite likely that the future of the known gas province will be broadly similar. The Trinidad and Tobago Chamber of Industry and Commerce's Long Range Gas Industry Depletion Planning Model depicts a long future for gas on a volumetric basis built on a wide range of assumptions. It is estimated that beyond the plateau of the gas industry, a long second-half of more than 50 years could be expected. Figure 8.3 shows the

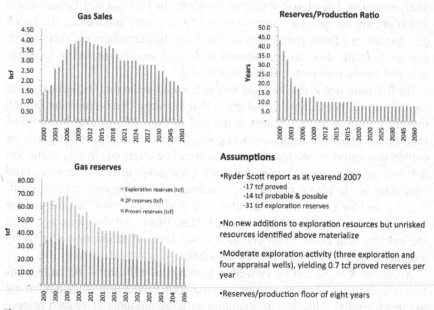

Figure 8.3. Long Range Gas Industry Forecast.

output from the model for gas production to 2060. After coming off the current plateau of circa four Billion Cubic Feet per Day (BCFD), and assuming a modest replacement of 0.7 TCF per year based only on what is known of reserves today, a level of circa two Billion Cubic Feet per Day (BCFD) (half the current rate) can be sustained thereafter for almost 50 years. Aggregate resources consumed under this scenario are approximately fifty Trillion Cubic Feet (TCF), within the boundaries of audited resource estimates (2010). This assured base economic activity is significant in its own right and, additionally, is a springboard for many other activities.

The model has some historical data as noted in the figure 8.3 and an assumed production profile. It also assumes that no new additions are made to the exploration resource base but that all of the un-risked reserves and resources identified so far are found. These assumptions allow us to draw down these "known" resources along various profiles as shown in Figure 8.3. The model allows an updating of views of the forward gas industry profile as often as is required.

It is important to briefly touch on R/P ratios. A high R/P could mean that a country has not yet started its resource development i.e. that is the "P," production, is low. It could also mean that a country is preparing to develop its resources and is creating the bank of proved reserves needed to approve projects for further development. It could also act as a disincentive to further exploration as an R/P number over 20 indicates that the gas may be effectively stranded. The high R/P ratio of the 1990s in Trinidad and Tobago acted as a stimulant for the establishment of an LNG industry and thereby increased gas demand at a faster pace than possible from the petrochemical sector. This expansion in the downstream assured no loss of momentum in the Exploration and Production sector during that period.

An R/P ratio that is too low, say below 5, could mean that the industry is at the tail end of its life. Or it could mean that the stage of development is such that the contracts are all almost at the end of their life, so that less proved reserves are needed to back contracts going forward. In that case, a significant exploration effort is needed if contracts are to be renewed. In this event, the R/P will go back up and then saw-tooth back down after the reserves (and contracts) are in place; production continues and the process repeats itself. It is a cause for concern and can also be a leading indicator that the current level of production cannot be sustained. Note this is not the same as saying the industry will come to an end as a lower level of production effectively lengthens the useful life of the resource base.

A ratio of 8 to 12 can be viewed as healthy and efficient—indicating sufficient time to pull through resources to maintain production while not having too much capital lying idle in maintaining large amounts of proved reserve inventory. However, the front end of the resource progression hopper (bid round, licensing, exploration) needs to be efficiently working to maintain this ratio or it could quickly fall.

Figure 8.3 depicts that, for the specified set of assumptions, the industry has a sales profile of over several decades starting with some incremental growth, a plateau, then a period of decline, and finally a long "tail." This is typical of individual reservoirs and likewise of entire hydrocarbon provinces. It is expected and inevitable that the gas industry will decline; just as the oil industry has over the past several decades. Notwithstanding this, it is also possible that if the markets for gas are not retained in the face of increasing global competition, that the gas province's decline could be sharper and the lifespan shorter than that of oil. It is impossible to predict its exact trajectory with certainty but the long range forecasting model allows us to regularly refresh our views of the future using a variety of input parameters.

It is likely that the gas industry will have a long life in Trinidad and Tobago, and probably will be longer than we can predict today. Looking closely at the picture, one will see that T&T eventually comes off the plateau (assuming no new reserve additions) and at this point industry sustainability (industry as we know it) is under threat because of an expected decline of ability to produce enough gas to meet the industry demand.

Clearly, the first decades of the new century in the hydrocarbon history of Trinidad and Tobago will belong to gas. During this period it is expected that the industry will become increasingly efficient and innovative as the world's new gas economies start up and attempt to compete with Trinidad and Tobago, the first gas economy in the world. The domestic gas industry started off with many first-mover advantages: a ready supply of relevant human capital from the oil industry, low cost gas, shared infrastructure such as ports and industrial estates and a visionary government with an enabling institutional and fiscal environment. In the coming years, opportunities need to be pursued that will access new hydrocarbon provinces, new technologies for mature and small reservoirs, leverage already built infrastructure, already built and fully paid for gas conversion capacity, facilitate and promote industry consolidation and efficiency improvements, and ensure that the best pool of intellectual capital is at hand to meet these challenges. While growing the contribution of the gas economy by increasing the volume of gas may be challenging in the coming years, there are many sources of significant value growth yet to be explored. The latter part of this section explores other value creation concepts. The lowest cost of gas production and conversion and the highest value added to gas will be twin pillars of competitive advantage in the next era of the gas economy.

Finding New Resources

The shape of the industry described above in Figure 8.3, is based on the known resources in the areas under licence or contract. Proper industry planning and the appropriate enabling framework will undoubtedly yield new provinces in the deeper waters offshore and deeper horizons on land. When combined with access to cross-border reserves, extension of the industry plateau and even further growth may be possible. One of the key enabling factors will involve shifting of inappropriate rents from the relatively low risk and well-established downstream sector. Failure to do this will dampen the development of the higher risk upstream activity needed to supply the downstream.

Improved Recovery From Existing Resources

While finding new resources as described above is not assured, increased recovery of reserves from known resources is much more likely and is influenced by proper industry planning and oversight, technology development and deployment and appropriate targeted fiscal regimes. The low hanging fruit includes small pools of gas that are close to existing infrastructure. The planning framework and fiscal arrangements need to be reviewed and enhanced to assure the progression of these resources to actual production in the available windows of opportunity.

The introduction of compression for lower pressure gas resources holds the potential to create new reserves from known accumulations of gas. Again, the appropriate enabling fiscal regimes and infrastructure developments hold much promise for future activity.

Unconventional Resources

There has been an upsurge in reserves added from unconventional sources such as shale gas in other mature hydrocarbon provinces, most notably the US where as much as 600 TCF of unconventional gas resources are claimed to have been added in recent years. It is clear that this is an area on which the country has yet to focus attention to determine if there is any potential locally in these resource categories.

Accessing Premium Markets

The pricing of gas relative to oil has traditionally been at a discount. Recent lows in gas prices below US\$3.00/mmbtu is equivalent to less than US\$20/barrel of oil equivalent at a time when oil prices are over US\$70/barrel. For a country that produces roughly 700,000 barrels of oil equivalent in gas every day, parity of pricing with oil at these levels represents an annual prize of approximately US$13 billion. This presents a large incentive to close the gap.

Trinidad and Tobago already benefits to some extent from access to premium markets for LNG. As competition in this sector increases, improving the flexibility to take advantage of these markets will become increasingly necessary in assuring optimal returns. Similar studies of opportunities in methanol and ammonia need to be undertaken to explore the potential upsides in these products.

Efficiency and Conservation

Empty infrastructure from upstream production to port capacity downstream will provide a new source of competitive advantage in the future. Upstream platforms with spare processing capacity will enable production from proximate small pools of stranded gas, for example via tiebacks to subsea completions. Unitization and joint development of marginal fields will bring new resources into production. Many other opportunities are likely to be explored in the future, such as third party use of spare pipeline capacity, joint pipeline developments and shared onshore processing, compression and transmission facilities.

In addition to the physical infrastructure, commercial arrangements such as the predictable requirement of around 1.5 TCF of gas every year at known pricing bases will be another competitive advantage. This factor is not yet present in the emerging gas economies where there is no established demand or pricing for gas.

A new and emerging source of value is accessible from the coordination of scheduled maintenance activities and, thus, better integration of upstream and downstream industries to remove the need for capital-intensive excess upstream production capacity with low utilization rates. This will ultimately reduce the cost of gas production.

Consolidation of similar activities within the downstream sector has been generating incremental value. This is a long practised avenue of value creation dating back to the operation and management of the Tringen plants by Fedchem in the 1970s. More recently, MHTL's (Methanol Holdings) outsourcing of plant management and operations activities to IPSL (Industrial Processing Services) is a prime example. The consolidation of plant management and operations across their five methanol plants has reduced the cost of operations significantly. This base has allowed IPSL to expand its plant management and operating services in the local and internationally petrochemical industry. The recent consolidation of the operations of Atlas Methanol and Titan Methanol and the subsequent deepening of this integration by creation of a common control room points to further opportunities. At Atlantic LNG there is the opportunity for further integration of operations through unitization of the separate ownership structures and consequent deepening and simplification by the operation of this site as one large virtual LNG train.

One estimate for the US says that it could save 23 percent of its non-transportation energy consumption by energy efficiency alone. In Trinidad and Tobago, by upgrading the electricity generation system from simple cycle to combined cycle generation efficiency could be improved by as much as 40 percent. This could be the cheapest way to "add" gas reserves in the country. Though this is probably the largest opportunity, many other opportunities could be pursued to bring significant savings.

Downstream Industries

The gas industry has a long future and with increased levels of efficiency this future may be sustained in the face of increasing global competition. Rationalization of old or inefficient plant capacity over time will lead to the creation of new industrial estate space at a relatively cheap cost creating another factor advantage. Much value can then be obtained by investing in new less gas-intensive industry, downstream integration and by migrating to higher value propositions. This has been demonstrated in the AUM (Ammonia, Urea and Melamine) complex with its five downstream plants. As primary and/or inefficient plants are rationalized, the industry can proceed down the value chain by adding downstream units to the remaining primary production. This creates new less gas-intensive industrial activity.

KNOWLEDGE-BASED INDUSTRIES

Services

In addition to plant operations and management services, other knowledge-based industries are possible e.g. maintenance, plant turnarounds, design, construction, etc.

Consulting

Trinidad and Tobago, long a contributor to the world's oil industry, has now started to systematically market its expertise in gas-based development to the emerging gas economies, particularly in Africa. This is the opportunity for the creation of many new consulting companies.

Education

T&T can be the training ground for the emerging gas economies of the world. The proximity of the UTT campus to Point Lisas makes it an ideal candidate to go beyond local training to become the premier international institute for training in the oil and gas industry. A unique advantage of Trinidad and Tobago is the very varied oil and gas industry that exists in a very compact geographical space. This can create new sources of revenue and intellectual capital generation, creating rivals to or joint venture arrangements with, executive education programmes from institutions such as Thunderbird, postgraduate training similar to that offered by IHRDC, undergraduate degrees similar to Texas A&M, Colorado School of Mines, Pennsylvania State University, University of Texas and University of Oklahoma. The capability to provide industry exposure and industry trained professionals for programmes such as these in Trinidad and Tobago provides a singularly unique opportunity. Similarly, an industry conference location rivalling Houston could be developed combining Caribbean expertise in tourism with high-end technical educational products.

RENEWABLE ENERGY

Case for Renewable Energy

Trinidad and Tobago's abundance of oil and gas would suggest that there is no need for renewable energy. However, this is not the case, as the significant production and use of fossil fuels actually means that renewable at scale is possible. Additional revenues can also be obtained by displacing hydrocarbons into the higher value export markets. Significant volumes of natural gas can be displaced by renewables and directed to higher value markets. In Trinidad and Tobago approximately 1 gigawatt (GW) of electrical generating capacity uses 260 million cubic feet of gas per day (MMCFD). By 2020 the consumption of electricity is expected to double. If one assumes that by this time all the generating capacity has been replaced by more efficient combined cycle plants, instead of the existing simple cycle plants, then instead of requiring double the amount of gas of 520 MMCFD, only 320 MMCFD of gas will be needed. Table 8.1 shows the amount of gas reserves that will be consumed by varying amounts of electrical generating capacity over different time periods. If we assume that 1000 MW of power is displaced, for example by hydroelectric power from Guyana for a period of 50 years, then the table says that 2.9 TCF of gas would be saved. Similarly, twice that amount of electricity (2000 MW) over twice as long a period (100 years) would result in a displacement of 11.7 TCF. This is more than half of the entire proved reserves of the country.

Table 8.1.   Gas needed for Combined Cycle Electricity Generation, TCF

Power	Daily Gas	Term			
MW	MMCFD	25	50	75	100
500	80	.07	1.5	2.2	2.9
1000	160	1.5	2.9	4.4	5.8
1500	240	2.2	4.4	6.6	8.8
2000	320	2.9	5.8	8.8	11.7

Source: Author's estimates

This is not the only major displacement opportunity. Currently the LNG industry uses some 250 MMCFD of natural gas as fuel. If the natural-gas-fired compressors are replaced by electrically driven compressors and these switched to power from a regionally available renewable source such as hydroelectric power, then gas can be displaced for the life of these facilities. If we assume 25 years, then a further 2.3 TCF of gas can be displaced.

In general, gas used in electricity generation is sold at the lowest price, circa US$ 1/MMBTU. If the gas displaced by renewables is then sold into higher priced markets, considerable profit can be generated which, in effect, can be considered surplus or can be used to subsidise the cost of renewables. This alone would make renewables a value-creating proposition. Table 8.2 allows us to look at the value of displaced gas depending on the amount of gas displaced and the extra value obtained for the gas. For example, if 1000 MW of generating capacity, using 160 MMCFD in combined cycle mode, is displaced, then annually U$60 million extra would be earned for every US$1/MMBTU of additional value that is obtained by selling the gas into a higher priced market.

The resources so displaced extend the life of the industries to which the gas is diverted. This generates additional value from the continuation of gas conversion activity. Bearing in mind that the conversion capacity in Trinidad and Tobago would be fully paid for by that time, the value generated from conversion activities in the future will also be significant. Consider the case

Table 8.2.   Annual value of Gas Displaced, (US$Million)

Power	Daily Gas	Value of Gas, US$MMBTU			
MW	MMCFD	1	2	3	4
500	80	30	60	90	121
1000	160	60	121	181	241
1500	240	90	181	271	362
2000	320	121	241	362	483

Source: Author's estimates

of circa 500 MMCFD of gas now used for power generation, and gas fired compression service being diverted to a train of LNG or other value added use.

Trinidad and Tobago produces a large amount of LNG, petrochemicals and steel for the global market. Given that the starting point is natural gas, on a unit of production basis, these needed products are produced at the lower end of the environmental impact to the world. Production of these materials elsewhere via oil or worse yet coal is many times more harmful. However, our large carbon dioxide emissions from these activities is beneficial to the world, it does provide significant opportunity for reduction. Switching from liquid transportation fuels to CNG, bio-fuels and electricity from renewable resources will decrease the local consumption of over 1.1 billion litres of gasoline and diesel used annually. Switching from natural gas for electricity to renewable sources of electricity, from gas-fired compression to electric drivers as described above, and the other options to be described later, will all result in a significant reduction in absolute greenhouse gas emissions. The ability to get credits for this, while not guaranteed, is possible and could provide even more financial incentives for renewable industries.

Finally, the introduction of renewable energy industries signals a sustainable future for Trinidad and Tobago. It holds the promise that ultimately even after the hopefully distant time when oil and gas is finished that new energy sources would be in place to assure the continuation of economic activity and the quality of life. It is difficult to quantify the impact on financial and intellectual capital flight, except to say that the result of progress on this front is likely to be positive.

With the abundance of oil and natural gas, there has been little impetus to pursue renewable energy in Trinidad and Tobago to date. However, this is now changing. The Government has completed draft policy guidelines for renewable energy and has convened a committee to formulate a Green Paper. In the coming decades hydro-electric power from Guyana on a large scale and solar, wind and ocean currents may all become part of the energy portfolio. In the transportation sector, ethanol and bio-fuels could join liquid petroleum products and CNG. The remainder of this section explores some the renewable options for Trinidad and Tobago in some more detail.

Hydroelectric Power

Hydroelectric power can be brought to Trinidad from neighbouring countries. For example, Guyana is believed to have 7GWH of raw hydro potential, some of which can be marketed to Trinidad and Tobago through the use of submarine High Voltage Direct Current (HVDC) cables. The geography allows the cable to be run from Guyana to Trinidad without encroaching upon Venezuela's territory. This project would not call for any new technology, as sub-sea HVDC is already widely used to transport hydro power from one country to another, such as from Italy to Greece, and Canada to the United States. HVDC is the preferred technology for long haul transmission systems as it results in lower line losses than AC. Power is controlled rapidly and accurately. Sub-sea cables have also proven to be secure and reliable. This project would require the construction of a dam and power plant and a HVDC cable.

In the Trinidad and Tobago context, the potential benefits of the use of hydropower go way beyond the environmental impetus and the simple substitution of a non-renewable resource. Hydroelectric power promises significant economic benefits to the country. Firstly, the use of hydropower for electricity generation "frees up" gas for alternative uses in Trinidad and Tobago, thus prolonging the life of the local gas industry. More importantly, it provides a savings because of more lucrative high-margin use of natural gas. As an illustration, consider the case of a 500MW power plant run on combined cycle using about 80mmscfd of gas. Over 50 years this amounts to 1.5tcf gas reserves saved. For every dollar extra earned from the sale of this displaced gas, the annual additional revenue generated would be US$30 million.

Economic benefits also flow in terms of reduced government expenditure. The gas fuel used by the Trinidad & Tobago Electricity Commission (T&TEC) is currently provided by the Government at lower costs than to other industries. This gas can be diverted to higher value end uses. If sold on the global market, this gas could be generating much valued foreign exchange. Over the five-year period 2000–2004, T&TEC and its customers effectively received US$800 million worth of subsidies when the price of gas is compared with LNG netback pricing.

Switching to hydro avoids the capital cost of converting simple-cycle plants to combined cycle as is currently expected for the next 10 years. Instead, it would allow less efficient gas-fired plants to be shut down at the end of their economic life, making way for the new power source. Hydroelectric power also forms a sustainable platform for electricity-based industrialization in the metals sector, (steel and aluminium, in this case) and in the plastics processing sub-sector. Marginal power-intensive projects would become more economic, and global competitiveness would increase as these industries migrate from gas-fired electricity generation supply to hydro. Industries such as smelters would be brought in line with world practice and would not have to rely on cheap gas—a potential harbinger of anti-dumping charges. It would also provide security of electricity supply as well as stability in the price of electricity. T&TEC could secure long-term prices, sheltered from the vagaries of fluctuating world oil/gas prices. This would ultimately benefit consumers. Finally, hydroelectric power would diversify the country's energy portfolio. Follow-on projects may unlock remaining hydro and other potential in the country and region.

This hydro project would be a sustainable form of co-operation between Trinidad and Tobago and Guyana. More importantly, it would be mutually beneficial, making it a sound profitable long-term investment. A project of this kind would bring sustainable economic activity in country (hydro projects are known to have a 50 -100 year lifespan). The hydro project will generate jobs for CARICOM nationals in the construction of the dam as well as the operation of the plant. Increased economic activity is certain to bring improvement in living standards in Guyana. More strategically, the hydro project would create an opening for other investment opportunities in Guyana. Trinidad and Tobago and Guyana can together take the lead in bringing

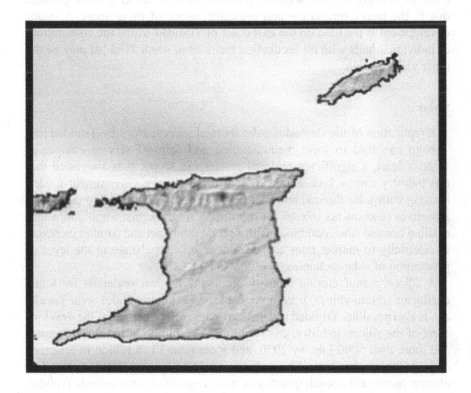

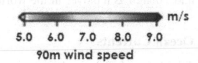

m/s

5.0   6.0   7.0   8.0   9.0

90m wind speed

Figure 8.4.   Wind Resource Map of Trinidad and Tobago.

the Caribbean onto the world stage in the development of alternative power sources. Such a project could also be a platform for energy integration across the Caribbean. It would also bring opportunities for export of electricity to Northern Brazil, Eastern Venezuela, and the Eastern Caribbean.

Wind

The Wind Resource Map of Trinidad and Tobago, Figure 8.4, shows that Trinidad and Tobago does have some wind resource potential that is amenable to exploitation for the generation of electricity. Wind farms can be located along the northern, eastern and southern coastlines.

While there are better wind speeds at the Northern Range and on the Main ridge in Tobago, the development potential there is unlikely to be pursued due to the heavy forestation and protected nature of these areas. A major development is possible on the east coast of Trinidad whilst the co-mingling of individual units with oil production facilities in south Trinidad may be the other viable option.

Solar

The replication of the Barbados solar thermal success story by Trinidad and Tobago can lead to local manufacturing and spin-off service companies with, at least, a significant regional geographic scope. It is suggested that this industry can be kick-started by out-fitting all new Government-funded housing with solar thermal and solar PV. Changes to the building codes and incentives (such as tax rebates for retrofitting solar thermal installations into existing homes) when combined with a social safety net and parallel increases in electricity to market rates can cause a significant change in the level of penetration of solar technology locally.

A silicon manufacturing industry producing the raw materials for semiconductor (micro-chips), fibre optic cables and (photovoltaic) solar panels, etc. is also possible. Trinidad and Tobago's aggressive pursuit of the development of the silicon industry, can result in TT$2 billion in industry revenues and more than 5000 jobs by 2020, and more than TT$5 billion in revenues and 20,000 jobs by 2030. This industry could be based on imported hydroelectric power and a small quantity of natural gas, and can establish Trinidad and Tobago as a player in the world of solar technology.

Ocean Currents

Trinidad and Tobago has some strong steady currents, one to the south through the Columbus Channel and the other between Trinidad and Tobago in the Galleon's Passage. Power generation from ocean current is at an early stage of development. However, some countries have significant potential. For example, the UK hopes to generate, eventually, as much as 10 percent of its electricity from tidal power. It is recommended that the University of Trinidad and Tobago and the University of the West Indies start the appropriate research programmes to collect the requisite data and pilot studies to foster development of this local renewable resource.

CONCLUSION: INSTITUTIONAL ARRANGEMENTS

Speed and Quality of Decision-Making

Over the years the Energy Sector has benefited from visionary leadership and relatively quick decision-making. This has given Trinidad and Tobago many first-mover advantages in the creation and evolution of the industry. Having created such a large and successful industry, there is a continuing need for proper sectoral planning. Planning is now more difficult given the increased rate of global change and the difficulty of attracting and retaining staff in the Ministry of Energy in part due to the significant discrepancy with private sector compensation.

To develop and maintain its capacity, the Ministry of Energy can consider non-traditional options. A possible source of personnel could be wider use of staff seconded from the State enterprises to the Ministry. The reverse practice could also be more widely used to give Ministry staff industry experience. A system of staff rotation could result in the development of a significant cadre of energy sector professionals to support many of the initiatives described above.

Another resourcing option is to co-opt industry stakeholders into the national planning process in a structured routine manner, such that the Government has access to the considerable resources of the private sector while it retains the final say in all matters. A possible execution mechanism is to include all the stakeholders via annual conferences and workshops to build the one- and five-year industry plans and to set robust strategies for the 10- to 20-year horizon. Mechanisms to manage the performance of these plans, as well as to revise them on a regular basis, also need to be put in place. The annual workshops could be a useful forum for planning plant turnaround activity in the entire industry and creating significant value by eliminating inefficient practices. Medium-term workshops could focus on ensuring that plans are in place to replace the circa-1.5 TCF of gas currently being produced so that the base market of continuity of supply is assured. The long-range workshops could focus on issues like renewable energy and subsidy reduction.

Role of Government as Shareholder

The Government of the Republic of Trinidad and Tobago has consistently exercised great vision and stepped in to establish new industries in the energy sector when private equity has been slow in coming forth. To continue extending the frontiers of economic activity, as described above, the Government does not only have to depend on private capital. Having created a State enterprise, the jobs have been created, a tax stream has been created and all the other economic linkages are established. To leave the Government's equity stagnant is to stretch the already beleaguered State apparatus to efficiently manage this enterprise and, more importantly, it denies the economy the further use of this capital in the creation of another enterprise that is needed to advance economic development. As in the past, the Government can divest already established enterprises to the more efficient private sector and re-use the capital to drive the execution of some of the options articulated in this chapter. This recycling of public capital is an important concept as it both assures the health of existing enterprises and the creation of new economic entities, which in turn creates jobs and generates significant tax revenues for the country.

Heritage and Stabilisation Fund

The Heritage and Stabilisation Fund established by the Government of Trinidad and Tobago is an important new development in the Energy sector. It has created a new avenue for inter-generational economic justice. Whilst the one-off benefits of extracting oil and gas cannot be shared with all subsequent generations, the financial proceeds from extraction activity is much more amenable to the requirements of inter-generational economic justice. From a depleting oil and gas resource an evergreen asset has been created so that succeeding generations could potentially have access to the benefits from the oil and gas industry, even after it is no longer part of the economic landscape. The Fund has at least two significant characteristics for the extension of the energy sector in non-traditional ways. The Fund itself can be a catalyst for the further growth and development of the Financial Services Sector as managing the Fund itself becomes a new economic activity for that sector. One could easily imagine that each tranche of the fund is managed by a separate locally-based entity. As the Fund evolves and develops, there is another less tangible but perhaps even more important benefit. It offers a positive sign to future generations. Likely they will perceive its development as a bond of trust, as a sign of sustainable development, and react to this development by slowing the pace of intellectual and financial capital flight. Their confidence in the future of the country will initiate its own virtuous cycle development.

Sustaining and Leveraging the Energy Sector Portfolio over the Next 100 Years

Trinidad and Tobago has many options for creating value and extending the life of its hydrocarbon-based energy sector. With proper management, the hydrocarbon sector could be a significant part of the next 100 years. The country has been a leader in oil, gas and related industries such as petrochemicals and LNG. It has many options to add new resources and to ensure efficient and timely progression of resources to the market. It has an already-built infrastructure that will offer low conversion costs in accessing premium markets. The country has huge untapped potential in the areas of conservation and efficiency that will make material contributions to extending the life of the industry. Where private capital is lagging in extending the economic frontiers, the country has a large store of stagnant capital in state enterprise equity waiting to be redeployed.

Many new industries are possible based on the well-established energy sector. These include support services, consulting, and education and training to the international community. The large energy sector provides an excellent springboard for the establishment of renewable energy at scale, and the savings in subsidies on petroleum products provide a unique source of funding for this activity. The financial surpluses from the industry can generate increased activity into the financial services sector and can, through the Heritage and Stabilisation Fund, create a renewable resource out of what is classified as a depleting resource, as future generations choose to use only the interest from the fund and preserve the principal for successive generations.

Having crossed the 100th anniversary of the oil industry, Trinidad and Tobago seems well positioned to take the lead activities that will initiate positive cycles of development and which will earn it a leadership position in the world. These initiatives will be the main engine of development that will take it to developed country status in the coming decades.

Chapter Nine

Energy and Development—
Realizing the Vision

Kerston Coombs

THE VISION IN 2003/04

Trinidad and Tobago has, over the last 25 years, succeeded in creating a world-class, globally competitive natural gas industry. The policy approach outlined in the country's "Energy Vision 2020" paper proposed that in crafting an overall Vision for development, Trinidad and Tobago should leverage the strengths of that existing world-class energy sector to efficiently diversify and strengthen the relevant non-energy sectors which either source, supply or are intrinsic to this stellar sector of the economy (Vision 2020 Energy Subcommitteee 2004). In the context of the multi-sectoral planning exercise which resulted in the national 2020 Vision for Trinidad and Tobago, the Energy Sub-Committee thus presented a vision that focused on the primacy of the energy sector to the sustainability and development of the local economy on its path to the year 2020. More specifically, the Sub-Committee saw the industry as progressing to become "sustainable, operating transparently with the full support of the government through effective governance and the people of Trinidad and Tobago . . . including locally owned and managed energy-based companies that participate throughout the complete value chain in projects and operations that are both local and global in scope and scale."

The vision also saw Trinidad and Tobago's energy sector bringing excellence to the Caribbean region through energy production, supply and use. The vision saw the sector's success driving the rest of the economy to produce the necessary pillars, such as world-class education institutions, energy services and a vibrant capital market which would support and foster innovation and entrepreneurship in and beyond the energy sector.

The composition of the Energy Sub-Committee spanned the full range of disciplines which are required for energy activities, i.e. a mix of upstream, midstream and downstream managers and professionals, including the electricity and service industries. The stakeholders were from the public and private sectors, multinational and State enterprises and professional organizations, and included trade union representatives. The original Energy 2020 vision was, therefore, a national consensus created by knowledgeable personnel familiar with the energy sector, rather than that of the Government or an institution. The Draft Vision 2020 Energy plan was accepted by the Government of Trinidad and Tobago and incorporated as part of the overall National Vision 2020 plan.

VISION 2020: KEY OBJECTIVES

The Energy Sub-Committee accepted that energy would remain the major source of economic activity, foreign exchange earnings and Government revenues for some considerable time. As a consequence, the Sub-Committee decided that for the visioning exercise to be meaningful, a total and holistic methodology should be employed in its deliberations. In essence this meant that all aspects of the energy sector had to be considered, including its sustainability and the best possible approaches to extracting maximum value for the country over the medium and long terms.

Therefore, in the context of Vision 2020 the focus had to be on ensuring sustainable long-term development of the energy sector and, by extension, the country. There are several goals critical to achieving this vision:

- To extract maximum value from the hydrocarbon resource in a manner that supports national sustainability beyond the life of the domestic energy sector;
- To sustain a competitive world class energy sector with a high level of local involvement in deeper, broader, more complex and environmentally responsible industries, making Trinidad and Tobago a recognized leader in key sectors such as:
- Finance: Trinidad and Tobago will be a regional financial and energy trading centre, supported by a strong and vibrant capital market.
- Education: Trinidad and Tobago will have world renowned educational institutions to support the development of highly skilled and competent personnel.
- Outsourcing: Locally-owned companies will provide services to both energy and non-energy industries locally and internationally in areas such as IT, HR, accounting, maritime services and engineering.
- Technology and Innovation: Trinidad and Tobago will be a renowned centre of innovation and technology development advanced by strong linkages between the private sector and academia.

- To increase the share of benefits accruing to Trinidad and Tobago from the value chain through the strengthening of the linkages between the energy sector and the rest of the economy;
- To develop a robust framework of governance that establishes and maintains a clear commitment to transparency and ethical behaviour;
- To further support sustainable development through the definition and enforcement of high standards for health, safety and environmental practices, as well as to contributing to the development of the communities in which they operate.

ISSUES AND PRECONDITIONS

To achieve the goals identified above, the Energy Sub-Committee recognised that it would be necessary to manage the natural resource endowment skilfully and strategically. In particular, the proper management of the exploration portfolio, including the timing and quantum of new lease acreage and the timely development of the necessary infrastructure needed to support it. Indeed, it appeared evident that the future of the industry would depend on its ability to sustain and even enhance current levels of oil and gas reserves and that this would, in turn, require intensive exploration efforts in all provinces onshore and offshore including the deep water basins.

The Sub-Committee anticipated an active and urgent exploration strategy with several bid rounds attractively packaged, thereby creating and maintaining investor interest. The reality has, however, been one of delays and uncertainty in the fiscal regime and eventual finalization retroactively, with an emphasis on increasing tax revenues as well as long delays in the award and finalization of successful bidders.

The significance of this issue should not be underestimated since the choices available to the country for downstream activities would depend to a large extent on the results of activities in the upstream. As an example, the choices to be made among petrochemicals, metals, power and LNG would be greatly influenced by the location and extent of any new gas finds.

Among the areas identified as having potential for future discoveries are:

Onshore: Deeper horizons using 3D seismic data
Offshore—Gulf of Paria: Deeper horizons using 3D seismic data
Offshore—East Coast: Offshore shallow water acreage, and Offshore deep-water acreage
Offshore—South Coast: Columbus Channel and Platforma Deltana

Given the level of uncertainty usually experienced in these undertakings, the report listed three possible outcomes for oil and gas production from 2009 to 2020. These were described as follows:

Base Case: only a handful of "new" discoveries
Medium Case: a few of the "new" provinces pan out partially
High Case: most of the "new" provinces pan out successfully

The low case of 3.9 billion cubic feet per day of natural gas production was achieved one year before its projected realization in 2009. However, from 2004, oil production fell to levels of one half of the projected low case level of 210,000 barrels of oil per day in 2009.

The report also emphasized that in addition to the need for sustained exploration, it would be necessary to strengthen the institutional and administrative apparatus of government to properly manage and direct the future of the sector. In particular the Ministry of Energy and Energy Industries (MOEEI) would have to be reorganized and strengthened to be able to deal with the emerging issues of resource allocation and enhanced value capture while ensuring that exploration activities including field and infrastructure development were performed to the highest standards of human welfare, safety and environmental care.

Maximizing country value also requires the most efficient use of capital and constant commercial diligence. In particular, the Committee was of the view that among other issues to be considered were the expansion of local content throughout the sector, and the capture of greater value by the private sector through direct equity investments. In addition, it urged the deliberate and concerted thrust for diversification within the energy industry and externally by forging linkages with the non-energy sector.

PROGRESS TO DATE

In order to put matters into context, it is important to recall that gas-based development started with the construction by W. R. Grace (USA) of the Federation Chemicals Ltd. fertilizer complex at Point Lisas in 1959/1960. A strategic decision was subsequently taken to produce ammonia for export using refrigerated tankers. This was a pioneering effort in long distance sea transport of ammonia and set the stage for the global, modern export-based ammonia industry. It was not until the mid 1970s however that the State flush with surplus revenues from the run up in oil prices, embarked on a deliberate strategy of heavy industrialisation based on natural gas that saw the expansion of petrochemical and other energy intensive industries so that by 2004, the Point Lisas Industrial Estate included nine ammonia plants, five methanol plants, one large urea plant, one large iron and steel complex and a gas processing facility.

The report of the Vision 2020 Energy Sub Committee also envisioned continued growth in petrochemicals with the addition of ethylene and polyethylene manufacturing as well as the start up of the country's first aluminium smelter. By 2010, the ammonia sector had grown by one additional plant, and methanol by two mega plants—the largest such facilities in the world. Atlantic LNG has also brought on line a fourth train fed by gas from new fields located off both the south-east and north-west coasts of Trinidad. In an effort to drive further downstream development, the Government has taken a decision that it would no longer approve any stand-alone methanol or ammonia projects, but only those projects that included significant downstream activity. This objective, while very laudable, has proven far more difficult to achieve, particularly in a situation of rapidly escalating costs for capital equipment, basic construction materials such as steel, and rising project management and construction costs. As an example, an ammonia/urea project that was estimated originally at circa US$650 million in 2006, was ultimately estimated at US$ 900 million by 2008.

Several proposed projects were either delayed or grounded including the Alutrint aluminium smelter, the Essar steel complex and the Westlake ethylene project. Indeed, the only major new processing facility under construction as at November 2008 was the Methanol Holdings ammonia urea and melamine project (AUM). Having therefore outlined the goals of the Vision and the overarching issues, it would be useful to examine what progress has been made towards the realization of these ideas.

PROGRESS TO DATE

Value Maximization

This is largely envisaged as the means whereby the country obtains the maximum value from its depleting resources either directly through taxation or other revenue generating mechanisms, or indirectly through active involvement of its citizens in all aspects of the sector's activities. In this regard the Energy Sub-Committee recommended that the Government seek to ensure national involvement throughout the value chain, particularly in the case of LNG and that local participation should be encouraged in ownership of assets in the energy sector with the Government leading the way by listing shares in key State enterprises on the local stock exchange.

The growth of LNG production and the profound effect it has had on gas production and utilization has already been noted. Also noted were the run-up in oil and gas prices and the resulting enhanced revenues accruing to the Government. However, the early LNG contracts were predicated on much lower gas prices and therefore the Government signalled its intention to press for a renegotiation of the original contracts in order to increase its take during higher price periods. The Government has also formed the LNG Company of Trinidad and Tobago with a mandate to expand the country's activities along the LNG value chain, including shipping, trading and investment in re-gasification facilities.

This is the first step in attaining the goal of increased local involvement in the LNG side of the business. However, while this is a necessary step, a consistent and sustained effort will be needed to achieve this goal. The decision on constructing a fifth LNG train will depend to a large extent whether new gas finds can support such a facility and on whether the country will have access to gas from the Loran-Manatee field jointly held by Trinidad and Tobago and Venezuela.

With regard to allowing access to equities of energy companies, the Government established National Enterprises Limited (NEL) which held part shareholding in Tringen, Atlantic LNG Train 1 and PPGPL (via NGC), TSTT and National Flour Mills Ltd. NEL was subsequently listed on the Trinidad and Tobago Stock Exchange. Notwithstanding these efforts, the national community as a whole still feels much removed from the activities of the energy sector. This is a long held position that must change if the country is to avoid a permanent cleavage between the "modern" energy sector and the more "traditional" non-energy sector. The Sub-Committee was of the view that wider participation by citizens through direct shareholding in the energy companies, starting with the State enterprises, would assist in bridging that gap by allowing for greater transparency and understanding of the energy companies' operations and, by extension, the sector as a whole.

With regard to direct revenue capture, the Government modified the tax regime for petroleum in June 2006 retroactive to January 2005. Coupled with the prevailing high prices, this resulted in much enhanced revenues to the Government. However, there was a downside to this since the Exploratory Bid Round of October 2006 attracted only one bidder for the marine blocks on offer. This was followed by a further review of the taxation regime. The sensitive work of seeking to renegotiate the terms of the Atlantic LNG Trains I, II and III agreements to ensure the State receives a larger take from the

LNG business requires a delicate touch since an onerous tax regime could be a disincentive to further investment.

LOCAL CONTENT AND ENTERPRISE DEVELOPMENT

In 2004, the Energy Sub-Committee on Vision 2020 stated, "the goal of increased local content will remain elusive unless supported by positive action on the part of Government and the firms that account for most sector expenditure." The committee recommended that a policy declaration on local content and sustainable development be part of every major energy sector project and that the policy should ensure that:

- The local content definition is communicated and applied widely
- The local content measurement system can be applied by independent auditors
- A certification process for local companies, goods and services is developed and implemented
- Major energy sector companies should be encouraged to issue their individual local content or sustainable Development Charter in keeping with the national vision
- Specific targets should be set establishing ratios of nationals to non-nationals in energy sector employment; percentage of in-country expenditure for all operators and third party expenditure and targeting of specific skill sets for nationals

In 2005/06 the Government with the involvement of many industry stakeholders, developed a Local Content and Local Participation Policy Framework. Its stated intent was that "Trinidad and Tobago will maximize the level of participation of its national people, enterprises, technology and capital through the development and increasing use of locally owned businesses, local financing and human capabilities in the conduct of all activities connected with the energy sector, along its entire value chain, within and outside of Trinidad and Tobago" (Ministry of Energy and Energy Industries 2004).

The Policy Framework stressed that the main emphasis would be on:

- Local Participation: maximizing the depth and breath of local ownership, control and financing, in order to increase local value capture from all parts of the value chain
- Local Content: maximising the level of usage of local goods and services, people, businesses and financing

- Local Capability Development: maximizing the impact of ongoing sector activity, through transfer of technology and know-how to deepen the international competitiveness of Trinidad and Tobago's people and businesses
- Create and enhance capabilities that are transferable to other sectors of the economy
- Create and support cluster developments with other industries that have a natural synergy with the energy sector
- To ensure implementation of the policy, a Permanent Local Content Committee (PLCC) was to be established

The experience with regard to local content was mixed. By the end of 2010 the PLCC had not yet got off the ground. In the meantime, several foreign service companies had followed their multi-national clients into the Trinidad and Tobago market. In some cases they made joint venture arrangements with smaller local players in the interest of being considered "local." As a means of bringing more skilled work onshore the strategy appeared to be working. This development forced other local companies to improve their levels of performance, especially in the areas of health, safety and environmental care. A few also began to venture beyond Trinidad and Tobago in search of new opportunities.

A similar situation existed with regard to the goal of deepening local involvement in the sector. There was a dramatic and hugely successful intervention by the local conglomerate C. L. Financial in ownership of methanol and ammonia plants. There was also significant success in heavy steel fabrication and erection by at least one local company as described in detail in Chapter 1. The period has also seen the establishment of two local companies which have been successful in securing contracts for operations and maintenance of plant facilities, both locally and internationally. These were significant pillars to be built upon to secure a larger slice of the pie for local entrepreneurs. Unlike in the past, financing of medium-sized projects was no longer a major obstacle with local banks and other financial institutions willing to lend or invest in projects considered feasible with sound fundamentals.

LINKAGES WITH THE ECONOMY

For the Energy Sub-Committee, enhancing the linkages between the energy sector and the rest of the economy was a burning issue. While it was clear that the energy sector would continue to dominate the economy for years to come, it was also important that steps be taken to promote the development of other sectors through a strategy of economic diversification. Applying the skills and knowledge gained from the successes of the energy sector to the wider economy as a whole was therefore a priority. To deepen the linkages between the energy and non-energy sectors, the Government encouraged downstream spin-offs that could be more readily handled by small and medium sized industrialists.

This was not the first time that downstream activities were being promoted as spin offs from energy projects. Great expectations of downstream expansion in the steel industry from ISCOTT/ISPAT never materialised. The hope that this round would be more successful would be realised only if firm preconditions for downstream activity were built into the contracts, with timeframes and enforceable penalties for non-compliance.

By 2010, there were some positive indicators, including the construction of seven offshore platform topsides at the La Brea Industrial Estate. One facility constructed at that site included a significant amount of engineering which was executed locally.

Among the areas identified by the committee for linkages with the energy sector was academia. A start was made by way of funded research on specific topics, although there was still a long way to go. In Trinidad and Tobago, research spending by both the private sector and the Government is approximately 1.2 percent of GDP (2003) compared with levels of 2 to 4 percent elsewhere. Opportunities for research abound. For example, there must be very few locations in the world with 17 synthesis gas operations of varying ages and technologies in such close proximity as exists in Point Lisas. This could be the subject of an important study if properly conceived and financed. Similar possibilities for research exist in other aspects of plant operations and processes, such as new or improved catalysts or materials.

Another priority area of linkage was food security. Through the use of fertilizers, crop yields can be greatly enhanced. Trinidad and Tobago produces nitrogen fertilizer (urea) which can be blended with potash and/or phosphate to make the appropriate blends of mixed fertilizer that would be the most effective plant food. There are other opportunities that can be explored going forward.

Perhaps the best contribution, still to be realised, is the possibility of infusing the rest of the economy with the discipline, systems thinking and global approach and attitudes developed in the energy sector.

OTHER ISSUES AND CONCERNS

Sustainability vs. Obsolescence

The question must be asked: to what extent have the goals of the Energy Vision been met and are they sustainable? With regard to the goal of extracting maximum value, it is clear that the taxation policies adopted in 2006 and came into effect January 1, 2005; seek almost exclusively to maximize the tax take to the Government from oil and gas production. Further, one can argue that the pricing mechanism adopted by the National Gas Company (NGC) has allowed the Government to realize a significant portion of the upside run-up in the prices for methanol and ammonia with relatively little downside risk. Simply put, this pricing model enabled the NGC to reduce its price for gas to a floor price when the price of the commodity (ammonia or methanol) fell below an agreed index price, and to increase its price when the commodity price rose above an agreed price. Obviously during a period of rising commodity prices, the NGC gains substantially since there is no ceiling on the gas price.

The question of sustainability over the medium to long term, however, is more problematic. Two issues need to be considered. First, is the need to eventually replace ageing plants due to obsolescence and/or safety conditions. The second issue concerns the availability of gas at a price that will continue to make production of these commodities competitive over the medium term. In a sense, both issues are connected since rising gas prices could lead to premature closure of some plants, as has happened elsewhere. For example, one ammonia plant has been in operation for over 40 years, another for over 30 years and two others for over 25 years. Clearly, some thought must be given by both the companies and by Government concerning the future of these facilities. Closure without replacement would have serious implications not only for Government revenues, but also for both direct and indirect employment.

It is to be expected that as exploration efforts move into the more expensive deeper horizons off shore, gas prices will increase. Companies in Trinidad and Tobago will face stiffer competition as lower cost sources come on stream in areas like West Africa and Venezuela. With the new trend of using larger ships for transportation, any freight advantage that Trinidad and Tobago might otherwise have could be more than offset by the cheaper gas price in the "new" exporting countries. This is brought into much sharper focus during periods of reduced prices for these commodities in the major markets when the companies' revenues are reduced and, consequently, their tax payments to the Government.

On the other hand, it is certain that some of the facilities are nearing the end of useful, efficient and safe operations. Clearly, a process plant built 30 or 40 years ago will not have the capacity or gas conversion efficiencies of a modern plant. For example, the first methanol plant built in Trinidad and Tobago and started up in 1984 had a capacity of 1,200 metric tons per day. The plants built later at Point Lisas are of 5000+ metric tons per day capacity. In the case of ammonia, the conversion efficiencies range from approximately

50 mmbtu/metric ton for the oldest plant to approximately 35 mmbtu/metric ton for the newest ones. As the price of gas increases, the less efficient plants will become uneconomic to operate even though they would not have to bear a capital charge. A decision to locate the replacement facilities in Trinidad and Tobago will be made in the boardrooms of the parent companies in Oslo or Houston. That decision will take into account the issues raised above regarding gas pricing and availability and, as such, there is no guarantee that Trinidad and Tobago would remain the preferred location. The country has already seen the painful and very expensive cost of delays in decision-making in such circumstances. The unwillingness to treat with two obsolete refineries that had become irrelevant to the global trade in oil after the shift of power to OPEC and the producer countries in 1973–1974, was outlined in detail in Chapter 1 in the Case Study on Texaco. As noted, final closure of the obsolete Point Fortin refinery took place in 1994 at a cost of approximately US$1 billion in subsidies from the productive sector in the last decade of its existence.

It is, therefore, essential that a strategic approach be taken, for example, in company negotiations with the NGC for renewal or extensions of gas supply contracts, to ensure as far as possible that gas is allocated preferentially to the most modern and upgraded of these facilities to allow for an extended operating life. Nevertheless, unless there are major new gas finds, it is prudent to plan for the eventual reduction in production of these commodities. It is for precisely this reason that Trinidad and Tobago should strive to become a location of excellence in gas-based research and development; it appears to be an option that should be actively encouraged and pursued. As has happened before, there is no reason to prevent Trinidad and Tobago pioneering this new thrust in gas-based activity and thereby ensuring its future place in the industry. While the Vision Sub-Committee envisaged a Centre for Enterprise Development which has got some initial funding and has made some serious start-up efforts, the creation in 2006, of the Natural Gas Institute of the Americas, as part of the University of Trinidad and Tobago, is very encouraging.

Wendell Mottley, in his book on Industrial Policy in Trinidad and Tobago, published in 2008 spends some time in Chapter 9 on the stages of Gas Industry development as outlined by BP. He expresses the view that Trinidad and Tobago is now at end of Stage II of an evolutionary process where the industry develops and is about to enter Stage III, where competition develops and where the Government should be providing the framework for that competition to help make commercial choices. Table 9.1 of his book outlines in tabular form some of the essential elements that he has identified as representative of each of the four stages of growth. It is noteworthy that the issues of transparency and Governance are critical towards a successful entry to this third stage, and countries such as Germany, Italy, Japan, Spain and the Netherlands are at this stage in their gas industrial development (Mottley 2008).

Human Resource Development

A feature of the Point Lisas story that is often overlooked is the learning that has occurred over time. Starting with Federation Chemicals and continuing through Fertizers of Trinidad (Fertrin) and Trinidad and Tobago Methanol Company (TTMC), there developed a cadre of trained, capable and experienced technologists and managers who have been able to provide the expertise needed to safely and efficiently manage the new production facilities as they came on line. Some serious thought should be given to harnessing and preserving this collective institutional memory for the future, possibly through university assignments or recording of individual experiences. Over the years, the manpower requirements to satisfy repeated expansion of production facilities at Point Lisas were met by a combination of hires from existing plants and an intake of trainees. However, by the year 2003/04, with the very rapid build up in new facilities both at Point Lisas and at Atlantic LNG, the serious deficiencies which had already appeared only worsened. Add to this the expansion of upstream activity by the oil and gas majors which also attracted some of the available manpower, and one gets a picture of the very difficult situation being faced by all industry participants.

The industry responded by increasing its internal training programmes, as well as sponsoring trainees to attend courses at San Fernando Technical Institute and the newly established Trinidad and Tobago Institute of Technology (TTIT). The latter institution in particular developed specific courses for plant operators and electrical and instrumentation technicians that were approved and accepted by the companies. All surveys at that time indicated a serious shortage of skilled manpower throughout the range of disciplines required by the sector. There were increasing calls by industry for more to be done to bring the skills of the employee population up to the appropriate levels. In response, the Government established the University of Trinidad and Tobago (UTT), with its first campus incorporating TTIT, one of its main objectives being to provide specialist training needed for engineers and technologists required for the industry. One feature of some of the offerings at UTT was an emphasis on a "sandwich type programme" that involved students spending part of their course on the job in an operating facility. UTT also embarked on developing a programme of marine and maritime studies as proposed by the committee. In addition, there was a major thrust towards increased offerings in tertiary education by State sponsorship of free tuition in approved institutions.

As a result of these and other initiatives, the percentage of students in all institutions of tertiary education has grown dramatically from under 5 per cent in 2001 to 10.7 percent in 2005 and estimated to be over 30 percent in 2010. This is a solid base to build on for the future, particularly by accelerating the knowledge of new supervisors and senior engineers. Many of them, due to rapid industry expansion, were placed into positions for which they were not fully prepared. In response to this, many companies supported their newly recruited engineers by providing them with the opportunity to attend MBA courses. This was not an unqualified success, given that for many engineers it became an avenue for avoiding the tough engineering problem-solving that was a prerequisite for the job. However, exposure to studies in behavioural and financial matters helped broaden the perspectives of many new managers. More should be done, however, to spread the experiences gained by the various parties throughout the industry as a whole. While there are many conferences and seminars held annually, they tend to focus on broad issues of policy, finance and investment. However, apart from the meetings of the Society of Petroleum Engineers and the Geological Society of Trinidad and Tobago, there are few opportunities for dissemination of technical knowledge and experience among industry practitioners.

Governance Issues

In commenting on issues of governance in the sector, the Energy Sub-Committee pointed out the need for structures to be put in place both within the Ministry of Energy and State companies to ensure transparency, objectivity and fairness in their dealings with the public. Areas of particular interest are procurement, award of contracts, project approvals and raw material pricing. Underpinning these, however, must also be proper internal practices in the respective organizations.

The passing of the Freedom of Information Act and the mandatory publishing of the annual reports of the State energy companies are major advances over the previous situation. Now, at least, the financial performance of the companies can be reviewed by the public on an annual basis.

A continuing problem, however, has been the difficulty often experienced in getting timely decisions from the respective Government departments. Part of the reason is systemic, in that there may be different departments in the same Ministry dealing with the same matter, but with conflicting positions. There is also an overlap in regulatory functions between the Ministry and, for example, the NGC. These matters need to be properly examined and solutions found if the pace of development is to accelerate.

A particularly contentious issue surrounds the opaqueness of the gas pricing arrangements for both the petrochemical and LNG companies. This is particularly frustrating when trying to understand the meaning of prices quoted by Government officials e.g. in the Budget presentation. The reason usually quoted for refusal to disclose prices is the confidentiality clause contained in the gas supply contracts. However, some of these claims ring hollow since most of the listed parent companies of the local subsidiaries are required to disclose these prices in their annual reports, either to their shareholders or to the respective Stock Exchange Commissions.

One is left to wonder whether this issue of undisclosed gas pricing had any bearing on the initial lukewarm approach towards the Extractive Industries Transparency Initiative (EITI). This particular effort is supported by various governments, NGOs and companies, with the aim of strengthening governance structures in resource-rich countries. The main objective of the EITI is to have companies reveal how much money they pay to governments and for the governments to state how much revenue they receive from the companies, and to validate those claims. This issue of governance remains problematical. For example, several years have passed since the extensive discussions held among a wide range of stakeholders about a Gas Master Plan (Cline 2001). To date nothing has been placed in the public domain.

Among the matters raised during discussions of that plan were the role of the National Gas Company (NGC) as purchaser, seller and transmitter of gas and the lack of transparency flowing from such an arrangement. An opposing view at the time was the existence of the NGC as a monopoly intermediary between the gas producers and the user companies. It was suggested that it was the best way to ensure that the State obtained maximum value from the gas supplied to the plants at Point Lisas. Earlier in this chapter in the section on Sustainability vs. Obsolescence, the critical importance of transparency and governance was highlighted.

Health, Safety and Environment

In general, the gas-based industries at Point Lisas have adopted internationally recognized standards for health, safety and environmental protection. Their policies and procedures can withstand the most severe scrutiny and are in large part a reflection of the HSE policies pursued by their parent companies in their home jurisdictions. This is shown by the relatively few accidents and fatalities that are recorded. However, this situation is not universal. HSE problems persisted in at least one facility on the estate including serious and frequent accidents and fatalities. There were also occasional unacceptable levels of particulate emissions that affected nearby operations. Attainment of global standards throughout the energy sector would not be achieved if these conditions were allowed to exist. It would appear that there is need for stricter enforcement of the laws embodied in the OSH legislation. The Energy Sub-Committee, recognizing the importance of this issue, recommended the creation of a Statutory Agency to ensure the recruitment of a high level of competent personnel and to assist in achieving the global aspirations of this entire sector.

Environmental/Social Impact Issues

In the absence of a clearly defined strategy and a coordinated, proactive approach to treating with the social impact of rapid industrial expansion, a lot of anxiety and tension has developed between energy companies and the communities in which they operate. Occasional flashpoints erupt and escalate, especially when the issues attract the attention of environmental and community activists. This has been particularly evident where some of the smaller and more rural communities reacted angrily to perceived threats to their existing ways of life, whether real or not. This issue surfaced with preliminary attempts to create the first new industrial estate at Union Estate where the clearing of forested lands led to the loss of habitat for some of the indigenous wildlife. It was exacerbated with the efforts of ALCOA to create a large global-scale aluminium smelter in the remote agricultural community of Chatham. Out of these experiences has come greater awareness of the need for sustained communication.

Priority should be given to more effective strategic planning, especially with regard to communication and community relations. The implementation of modern change management strategies is also critical so as to effectively handle the complex people issues that will arise when small, rural communities are buffeted by industrial development. The pace and magnitude of the changes that such communities will experience could lead to significant conflict if the issues are not proactively addressed.

A relatively new feature of the industrial landscape is the requirement for all new or expansion projects to obtain a Certificate of Clearance (CEC) from the Environmental Management Authority (EMA) prior to the start of any construction works. In most cases an Environmental Impact Assessment must be carried out which would include extensive discussions with nearby communities, neighbouring facilities and interested professional bodies, prior to approval. This has brought Trinidad and Tobago in line with practice in most developed countries. Notwithstanding these provisions, there have been some apparent failures of the authorities and, in some cases, prospective investors, to properly inform and assure community residents about new industrial estates or sensitive industries planned for construction in their communities. This has led to demonstrations and protests by residents and significant delays in project execution. This question of greater transparency and a more sensitive approach to residents' concerns must be a top priority.

A planned approach to other outstanding environmental issues is also quite urgent now. These include the clean-up of old land fields (wells, facilities and pipelines) and the decommissioning of marine platforms and pipelines and old/obsolescent plants and machinery.

In this regard, greater resources must be allocated by the relevant authorities to the monitoring aspect of the environmental management portfolio. As an extension of concern for the environment, most companies have, however, sought to interact with the communities in their immediate vicinity through initiatives in sports, education, health and small business, especially those involving the youth of the respective areas. These activities have helped to foster relatively smooth and calm relations with residents in or near the areas of company operations.

Energy Vision 2020 had proposed a more enlightened approach to building relationships between corporation and community in the energy sector. Traditional public relations practices were felt to be inadequate to fulfil the legitimate aspirations of the various communities and to maximize the available resources, both technical and financial. Since then many of the large energy companies have launched major initiatives in an effort to build more meaningful and sustainable partnerships with their neighbouring communities. Some of them are: In Mayaro, bpTT introduced its MIPED project; in Toco BHP-Billiton initiated its Village Turtle Trust; and BGTT continues with its very popular Energy Challenge, as well as its Science Bus and youth cricket activities. The National Gas Company has its "pipeline" communities programme and companies at Point Lisas such as Yara has its associated agricultural support systems. Methanex, Methanol Holdings (Trinidad) Ltd and PCS Nitrogen have also responded to the need for meaningful community partnering. State-owned Petrotrin, which spans almost all the communities across southern Trinidad, has continued the focus of its predecessors, Shell, Trinidad-Tesoro and Texaco, on sport, education and culture as mechanisms for community development.

While the Vision 2020 group did not highlight the issue, one of the major consequences of the energy sector's success is the widening gap between the sector and the rest of the population. It is now clear that a more concerted effort must be made to manage this growing chasm, which again highlights the need for effective change management strategies. There are considerable challenges ahead for the energy sector and the country as the process of industrialization and modernization continues. However, there are significant opportunities for human development and enhancing the quality of life but it will require a more sensitive, responsive and imaginative approach in dealing with the social and environmental impacts of industrial expansion.

WHAT'S NEXT?—SOME IDEAS ON THE WAY FORWARD

It is extremely clear that the national economy continues to be dominated by the fortunes of the energy sector. Nowhere is this as vividly demonstrated as in the dramatic growth in Government revenues and budgetary allocations over the period 2003-2010. This dominance can be expected to continue for an extended period, notwithstanding the widespread discussion and debate on the position of the nation's oil and gas reserves and how long these will last. The fact remains, however, that our hydrocarbon resources are finite and will be economically exhausted at some time in the future. Therefore a major objective of any visioning exercise must be to sustain the industry as long as possible while taking those steps necessary to transform the economy for a future where oil and gas will no longer be its main drivers.

In that context, the initiatives to greatly enhance access to tertiary education are a welcome move in the right direction, however there needs to be a much more aggressive approach to spreading the use of ICT throughout the community including the Government and business community. Indeed, Government may well be ahead of the private sector in this instance which might imply that the two parties do not agree on where the priorities should be for future growth of the economy.

Going forward, there will be need for an ever-increasing participation of the private sector in the business activities that will be required for the new economy. The current, very low, equity participation in the energy sector must change, especially as new opportunities arise through downstream and spin-off possibilities from the new plants. The objective must be the development of a diversified economy that can survive well beyond the era of oil and gas.

The crucial matter of improving the competitiveness of the economy as a whole cannot be overemphasized. Inordinate delays by the bureaucracy in making key decisions are matters of serious concern for the efficiency of private businesses. In that regard, the establishment of the National Productivity Council, which includes representatives of Government, unions and the private sector, will go a long way towards realizing that goal.

More than ever before, the fortunes of the country are inexorably linked to the fortunes of the energy sector. A properly thought out road map for the future of the energy sector that is understood and accepted as the way forward in the short to medium term is now a necessity. Such a document should include positions on the following as a minimum: resource allocation, reserve generation, gas consumption versus production, replacement of obsolete plant, energy conservation, alternative energy, reduction of subsidies, safety and environmental protection and enhancement. Additionally, the Government had signalled its intention to examine the establishment of a single National Petroleum Company that will subsume some of the functions of the entities and enterprises in the public sector such as the Ministry of Energy and Energy Industries, the National Gas Company, The National Energy Corporation, Petrotrin, National Petroleum and perhaps T&TEC. There is no doubt that the roles and functions of the various entities need to be streamlined and rationalized.

As important as the above, is the need to strengthen and or modernize public institutions to cope with the great changes that have overtaken the industry in the last decade. For example, the reform under way at the Ministry of Energy and Energy Industries should result in an institution that is efficient, flexible and responsive to the needs of all the actors in the industry. In addition, its research capability should be greatly enhanced.

The energy sector remains largely unknown to the general public except for the occasional discourse on export gas pricing or whenever there is an increase in the price of gasoline at the pump. The initiative by UTT to provide a programme on energy matters specifically designed for practising journalists is, therefore, highly commendable. The committee has recommended that the Government consider placing a portion of its holdings in companies such as Petrotrin, NP, NGC and NEC directly on the stock market. This will provide the market with a boost at a time of very flat trading and encourage small investors to take a greater interest in the activities of these State enterprises and, by extension, the sector as a whole. The push for greater local content in the industry appears to have stalled. The significant gains made in certain areas point to the very real possibility of Trinidad and Tobago eventually becoming a serious exporter of a wide range of energy services especially to emerging oil and gas economies in Africa. For this reason, it is imperative that the local content initiative be aggressively pursued, as it is the foundation for the development of future service providers. It is also necessary for local equity to be given an opportunity, where possible, to participate especially in downstream operations. This should not only be encouraged but also facilitated on mutually acceptable terms by Government. In order to encourage direct linkages between the products of the energy sector and the rest of the economy, an annual monetary award and other incentives should be given to all firms that can demonstrate such a linkage.

SOME CONCLUDING ISSUES

The increases in natural gas production and usage in Trinidad and Tobago in the first decade of the twenty first century have been astounding. However, at approximately 4,000 mmscf per day, gas production, barring several major discoveries, can be said to have "peaked" or "plateaued," depending on one's point of view. Several scenarios can be developed of how the gas future might look depending on the rate and timing of new exploratory drilling, size and frequency of finds and quantum of any additional consumption. Thus, a critical issue that has been delayed is the adoption of an appropriate set of policies that will better define the future gas resource position of the country. This will entail getting the correct fiscal regime so as to ensure the development of, in particular, deep-water acreage and smaller and marginal pools of both oil and gas. Oil production, in serious and continuing decline since the 1980s, (the BHP-Billiton output being the sole significant new output in that timeframe), can most likely be enhanced if recognition is also given to the additional need to launch a serious attempt at bringing onto production the very large heavy oil deposits that exist both onshore and offshore in the Gulf of Paria. This has been an outstanding omission in policy and practice since the 1990s and it is now critical that it be addressed.

In respect of natural gas, the variability and volatility of prices and the emergence of large, new 'shale gas' supplies in the USA suggest the need for a clearer definition of the markets to which natural gas should be directed in Trinidad and Tobago, and under what terms and conditions. These are crucial elements that upstream investors in high risk exploration projects will wish to have some clarity about, prior to exploration. In order to encourage exploration especially offshore, the future taxation regime will have to be reviewed. This will of course impact the price of gas sold to NGC by the producers and subsequently the price of gas charged by NGC to downstream petrochemical and metals producers.

However unless that encouragement is given the rate of exploration in the near/midterm could be well below the requisite level to meet current market needs, far less meeting future prospects, or determining the correct replacement type policies that should be adopted.

Therefore, one picture that cannot be ignored is one of gradual decline in production over several years. The decline may be reduced or even arrested for a while if the country was to have access to cross-border gas from Venezuela or large new fields were to be found. Note that any reduction in gas production will also result in a reduction in output from the consuming industries. The situation, therefore, is such that the country must now begin a serious look at developing an alternative energy strategy. This will include studies of the various sources of alternative energy most appropriate for Trinidad and Tobago and also those businesses that are much less energy intensive that can be readily established here. This is absolutely necessary if the country is to cope successfully with a future of declining gas supplies.

With regard to alternative energy, one possibility lies in assisting in the development of hydro-electricity in Guyana and importation of electric power by Trinidad and Tobago via submarine cable. The concept is not new; however, a more recent attempt at developing such a project appears to be making some headway to the extent that Brazil is showing interest in it. This could be an opportune time for Trinidad and Tobago to become involved.

One of the outcomes of Trinidad and Tobago's successful gas-based development has been a significant increase in the emission of greenhouse gases, in particular carbon dioxide (CO_2) from the 10 ammonia plants. As a result, the country is a major contributor to greenhouse gas emission on a per capita basis. Although a large portion of the CO_2 is used as process feedstock in five of the seven methanol plants, much of this gas is vented to the atmosphere. Recently there has been a proposal to collect most of the CO_2 for use in secondary recovery in depleted oilfields. This and other methods of carbon sequestering should be encouraged as they could provide a means for the country to gain carbon trading credits and improve its profile as a greenhouse gas emitter.

Recent events in world economy have clearly demonstrated the interconnectedness of global financial, market and commercial activities. The widespread collapse of the international financial markets coupled with the subsequent contraction in global economic activity underscores the potentially destabilizing effect of too great a reliance on commodity exports as a means of sustainable economic growth. It also suggests as an imperative that, in the future the country must be prepared to accept that more of the financing of its energy activities will have to be sourced locally as against through direct foreign investment. For this to happen in a meaningful way, innovative methods must be found to safely and effectively harness the pool of available local funds held by the country's institutional investors.

Given Trinidad and Tobago's location, the Vision 2020 Sub-Committee saw a clear role for the country as the premier regional supplier of quality petroleum products, as well as natural gas and associated products. However, the advent of Venezuela's PetroCaribe and ALBA strategies has posed challenges for Petrotrin's retention of its regional markets in petroleum products, and has impacted Trinidad and Tobago's relationship with CARICOM. This has severely challenged the ability of the sole refinery in Trinidad and Tobago, at Pointe-a-Pierre, to operate at an internationally competitive level. Notwithstanding these developments, Petrotrin's refinery began another upgrade at an estimated cost of US$ 1.2 billion, to meet the challenges posed by the demanding environmental standards of the premium US markets for gasoline.

The committee also envisioned Trinidad and Tobago as a conduit for regionally sourced natural gas to the region, the USA and elsewhere, recognizing that US demand for gas will be managed through strategies that facilitate
the USA's security requirement for diverse supply sources. In this regard
there are many opportunities available for partnering with Venezuela, Brazil
and Western Africa that could result in the trade of energy services and products both regionally and internationally and provide mutually beneficial and
profitable partnerships for the country.

As Trinidad and Tobago moves into the second decade of the twenty first
century, it is well-positioned to build on the successes of the past in shaping
its future. It has the expertise and experience in energy to define its interest
and pursue them; and it enjoys a reputable and unique standing that opens
doors for it in the emerging energy markets in the world,

Strategically pursued, the second decade could be the one that finally meets
the challenge of creating linkages within the energy sector, and between
energy and the other sectors of the national economy. If this succeeds, Trinidad and Tobago would have solved the problem of how to utilise its energy
resources to transform the national economy.

BIBLIOGRAPHY

Cline, Gaffney. *Trinidad and Tobago Natural Gas Master Plan.* GOTT, 2001.
Ministry of Energy and Energy Industries. *Local Content and Participation Policy
   Framework.* GOTT, 2004.
Mottley, Wendell. *Trinidad and Tobago—Industrial Policy 1959-2008.* Ian Randle,
   2008.
Vision 2020 Energy Subcommitteee. *VISION 2020 Energy* . GOTT, 2004.

Chapter Ten

The Social Impact

Richard Braithwaite and Trevor M. Boopsingh

INTRODUCTION

"We Are Not Shell!"

During a heated discussion between residents of south-west Trinidad and one of the more recently established energy-sector companies, a senior executive responded emphatically that "we are not Shell." The company's pledged philanthropy was deemed to be insignificant and a trifle when compared to the benevolence to the community from Shell Trinidad Limited during its glory days. Since the inception of the oil industry in Trinidad and Tobago over 100 years ago, the oil and later on, natural gas sector has considerably configured the economic, social, political and cultural environment of south Trinidad. This wide-ranging significance is aptly encapsulated in the reference to Point Fortin as "the town that oil built."

Several "new" petro-chemical entities have subsequently emerged during the post Shell/Texaco era of industrial expansion in south-west Trinidad. Most of these companies subscribe to the modern mantra of Corporate Social Responsibility and repudiate the role of "community godfather" that Shell, Texaco and later on, Trintopec and Trintoc had dutifully performed. Many older residents still recall with great affection the era of Shell and Texaco. They itemize the many roads, houses, schools and hospitals that were built and the benefits that accrued not only to employees, but to the wider community. Likewise, the residents recount Shell's contributions to sport and culture and the proud legacy that "south" was known for in both spheres during this era. Ironically, at the same time, they also bemoan the present state of dilapidation of many of the once pristine sporting and cultural facilities.

Even young residents of Point Fortin who have no personal experience of Shell, still romanticize about what is known as the "Shell era" of corporate patronage which the oil windfall readily afforded. This saga of Point Fortin originates in 1907 when Trinidad Oilfields drilled its first exploratory well on the La Fortunee Estate in Point Fortin. The success of this well ushered in the establishment of oil exploration and production operations in Point Fortin, and consequently the community's evolution into the nation's key oil-based location. Trinidad Oilfields was subsequently acquired by United British Oilfields of Trinidad (UBOT) and eventually incorporated as Shell Trinidad Limited in 1956.

Apart from the Point Fortin area, the oil industry has made major contributions to the development of southern Trinidad since its inception. Historical accounts show that the Pitch Lake generated great interest with the possibility of extracting oil from the pitch. As a result, the Merrimac Company established small-scaled operations to obtain oil by distilling the pitch in 1857. In this same year, the Merrimac Company drilled what is considered to be the world's first oil well, in La Brea—although it was a dry hole. Even though the Merrimac Company collapsed shortly thereafter, a few years later, the Trinidad Petroleum Company drilled a successful well at a depth of 250 feet in La Brea. However, no further exploration activity in La Brea would ensue until the following century.

In the early half of the 1900s, La Brea emerged as a centre of rapid industrial and community development, thus briefly earning the reputation as "the industrial capital of the Caribbean." It is reported that while other towns and villages were still using kerosene or "pitch oil" lamps, La Brea already had electric street lighting generated by the small oil refinery in the area. American diplomat Baker, highlighted the relative modernity of La Brea at that time. He remarked that "the houses are most commodious and equipped with sanitary and electric lighting facilities. At night the brilliant illuminations can be seen from great distance" (Baker 1924).

Likewise, he went on to recount the establishment of New Jersey, a new housing community in La Brea specifically for the employees, which was constructed by the Trinidad Lake Asphalt Operating Company. Baker noted that "this new village will when completed house nearly 3,000 persons and is equipped with a piped water supply, sewerage and electric lighting." This increase in economic activity in La Brea attracted jobseekers from all over the country as well as from the neighbouring islands such as Grenada, St Vincent and the Grenadines. Moreover, because of its natural deep-water harbour, La Brea also emerged as a major hub for shipping and maritime activities. Baker also remarks that the social life of La Brea was well reputed especially when "large entertainments are given, which are attended by rank and fashion, youth and beauty from all Trinidad." As such, La Brea rose to prominence as an important centre of socio-economic development in the early half of the 20th century, as commercialization of the Pitch Lake as well as oil production and refining activities ensued.

In 1902, the first successful oil well was drilled in Guayaguayare. Even though eight other wells were sunk, operations were eventually abandoned in 1911 as conditions were hazardous and funding scarce. Higgins reports that although the Guayaguayare operations ended, "three fine bungalows had been built on the beach, the railway was well established and a stores shed, barracks and commissary had been built." In spite of limited success, the prospect of oil exploration and production remained at the forefront of the minds of the oil pioneers who eventually directed their efforts on Point Fortin. As such, the first commercially viable wells were drilled by Trinidad Oilfields Limited in the Parry Lands area in Point Fortin. As a result of this success, exploration activities picked up in nearby locations. And so, by 1912, Trinidad Lake Petroleum Company also reported successful operations in the vicinity of the Pitch Lake, as well as in Vessigny.

In addition to constructing industrial plants, residential facilities and providing ancillary services, the pioneer oil companies also contributed significantly to the construction of access roads throughout south Trinidad. Undoubtedly, the construction of roads and railway was in the interest of the furtherance of oil development, but even when the government proposed major development for agricultural and oilfield roads in 1911, in the end, these roads were constructed by the oil companies. The road from Brighton to Point Fortin, the road from Fyzabad to Guapo as well as the road from Rio Claro to Guayaguayare was either "started but not completed" or "planned but not built" by the Government. Over the years, more than 320 km of access oil field roads have been cleared, laid and maintained by the oil companies in the southern districts.

Admittedly, the community's economic transformation and infrastructural development was most significant, albeit most visible, during the period of the pioneer oil companies, primarily because they were Greenfield developments which required the construction of enabling facilities. Notwithstanding this fact, it needs to be determined if the new interaction between community and the neo-corporations is less altruistic as it is approached within the context of Corporate Social Responsibility which seeks to engender autonomy and sustainability at the individual as well as organisational level. Under this latest business administration trend of Corporate Social Responsibility, the new energy corporations advocate the practice of "teaching a man to fish rather than giving him a fish."

THE SHELL ERA IN THE TOWN THAT OIL BUILT

Dr Bridget Bereton in *A History of Modern Trinidad: 1793-1962,* provides
the following narrative:

> Point Fortin became the first centre of oilfield operations as a port and a de-
> veloping town ship. In 1907 Trinidad Oilfields Ltd. set up base at La Fortunee
> Estate, Point Fortin, in what is now Trintoc's Industrial Area, and buildings
> and clay roads were built in a region that had been wild bush and abandoned
> estates. After UBOT took over in 1913, a refinery, a jetty, houses, railways and
> pipelines were constructed and a crude but flourishing town sprung up. Point
> Fortin was, in fact, 'the town that oil built', growing up in the space of fifty
> years from a forest clearing with a few rough huts to a modern town of about
> 30, 000 people. (Brereton 1982)

The British engineer Arthur "Beeby" Thompson who was commissioned
in 1906 to explore for oil in the British colony, recounts that the "first efforts
to get going were seriously hindered by an outbreak of malaria together with
vampire bats which sucked blood from men while they were asleep" (Higgins 1996). A yellow fever outbreak was reported to be so severe that only
a "dozen or so men" of a labour force of several hundreds reported for work
during the epidemic. Conditions were miserable, living quarters consisted of
mud and carat houses on the village outskirts and auxiliary facilities were
non-existent. It is, therefore, understandable that labour was scarce and unwilling. As such, workers migrated from the neighbouring islands particularly
Grenada and St. Vincent and the Grenadines. However, with the commercial
success of Trinidad Oilfields Ltd. (TOL) in Point Fortin, the community
emerged as the key oil-exporting operation throughout the British colonies,
as well as grew in importance as a port-of-call for ships to refuel, especially
for the British navy. As a result, these events advanced the construction of
dwelling facilities, clay roads, tanks, pipelines and railways. Workers were
keener to come to Point Fortin and their families were more predisposed to
accompanying them. Shortly thereafter, amenities such as a post office, police station and banks, as well as government agencies, were set up. As such,
labour was not only required for the oilfields but also for support services
within the community.

The rapid expansion of the Point Fortin area was so evident that in 1911,
less than five years after the commencement of operations, it was reported in
The Mirror by a visiting journalist, "that it is difficult to discover how Point
Fortin got its bad name so far as health is concerned. There are not here those
horrible mosquitoes and sandflies . . . there are no swamps around. Much of
the uncultivated land is cleared to make room for the working of the wells,

and with a medical man on the spot to direct sanitary improvements; Point Fortin stands as good a chance as Panama of getting rid of its fever reputation." The development of Point Fortin so greatly impressed this reporter that he concluded thus, "I have heard that much work had been done by the Trinidad Oilfields Ltd. at Point Fortin but I had no idea that so much had been accomplished" (Higgins 1996).

The influence of Shell in Point Fortin officially started in 1913 when United British Oilfields of Trinidad (UBOT), the local subsidiary of Shell, purchased all the assets of TOL and assumed full control of the operations in Point Fortin. Over time, UBOT purchased the Clifton Hill estate and leased the La Fortunee and Adventure estates from the British Crown. In effect, this conferred legal title and control over practically all of the land in Point Fortin. The "Company," as UBOT was referred to in Point Fortin, accelerated infrastructural development with the construction of a 7,000-foot pier, electricity and water stations, a refining plant and road works. Simultaneously, UBOT introduced a training programme to equip workers with the required skills to operate and maintain the new machinery. Retirees of the Shell era remark on the sophisticated training that numerous local workers received, either via in-house training programs or overseas (Campbell 2008).

On the topic of training, the first trade school in Trinidad was established by Trinidad Leaseholds Limited in 1946. What would evolve as the country's leading establishment for practical training and technical education of oil workers started in an unassigned canteen building and by practicing with machine tools that were not being used by the main workshops. Over the ensuing years, the concept of training young boys in-house for the majority of skilled tradesmen positions became so prevalent that it was not only adopted by other oil employers but by the sugar and other light manufacturing industries. The oil industry, through the training and apprenticeship scheme has produced internationally sought-after technicians and drill men.

However, UBOT's continued expansion created acute housing shortages. As a result, in 1938 UBOT with some persistence by the labour union, commenced the construction of residences for employees. The three housing zones that were built were differentiated according to employment status and grade within UBOT. As such, Clifton Hill was designed with recreational clubs, a swimming pool, tennis courts and a golf course for the white expatriate executive staff; Mahaica was reserved for monthly paid local middle managers while Techier Village was developed for the weekly and hourly paid workers. In effect, Point Fortin came to be regarded as Shell's oilfield camp.

By 1946, Point Fortin had become a flourishing town with an average of 14,651 persons (12,206 directly employed and 2445 employed by contractors) employed daily in the petroleum industry. For these Point Fortin residents,

UBOT was many things: boss, service provider, landlord, judge and de facto governor, as the affairs of Point Fortin were basically overseen by UBOT (Campbell 2008). In addition to building recreational facilities on each housing zone, a commissary, a cinema and sporting facilities were also established communally for residents. Additionally, social services such as schools, a hospital as well as the provision of water, electricity, sanitation services, fire services and roadways were supplied by UBOT. A local government official and resident during the Shell era commented that "Point Fortin was the envy of south Trinidad," because not only did most people have pipe-borne water, gas and electricity in their homes, nearly everyone had a recreation club to attend "regardless of their class" (Campbell 2008).

Many residents still reminisce on Point Fortin as being the "sport and cultural capital of Trinidad and Tobago" during the Shell era, and indeed, sporting activities were crucial to the Point Fortin persona during the Shell glory days. In addition to building the Mahaica Oval to specifically host sporting and cultural events, Shell also sponsored a football team, athletics, cricket clubs and a variety of sporting activities in Point Fortin. The company's football team dominated the local southern league for many years, and a large part of this success has been attributed to the sponsorship and support provided by Shell. It is reported that in addition to being coached by expatriate staff, "Shell bought your socks and shoes, provided bus transport to games, and allowed you to miss work" (Campbell 2008).

As a result, Shell's influence pervaded every facet of the lives of the residents in Point Fortin. The "company" undertook this responsibility even when Shell Trinidad Limited acquired its subsidiary, UBOT in 1956. However, with independence[1], the Government assumed full responsibility of the UBOT-developed infrastructure, including the provision of public utilities, the hospital, schools, recreational facilities and more importantly, the governance of Point Fortin in the 1960s. However, the combination of an upgraded refinery and dwindling onshore exploration activities necessitated a reduction in the labour force by the end of the 1960s. To this end, Shell collaborated with the new self-governing administration on a number of initiatives such as: 1) encourage early retirement; 2) convert some staff positions to contract positions; 3) encourage Dunlop Tires to establish a factory in Point Fortin in 1968; 4) launch a relocation programme that transferred employees to other Shell operations in other parts of Trinidad or around the world and 5) support alternative business ventures, such as agriculture. And in the wake of its departure, Shell also set up a financial programme to assist employees to acquire the houses that they were renting from the company. However, the eventual exodus spiralled into such a severe retraction of local businesses and ancillary services that the curtailment of Shell's activities in Point Fortin was said to have "cast a gloom over the community" (Lewis 1980).

TEXACO TRINIDAD IN POINTE-A-PIERRE

The island's other oil refinery located at Point-a-Pierre was owned and managed by the local subsidiary of the Texas Company—Texaco Trinidad (Textrin). Akin to the pre-Shell era in Point Fortin, living accommodations in Point-a-Pierre were also minimalist. However, when Textrin commissioned a new processing plant in 1939 to produce high-grade diesel oil to fuel the high-speed automotive diesel engines being used in heavy transport vehicles, the company also authorized an extensive construction plan which included a new hospital, a communal dining hall and residential facilities. This was the largest construction undertaking in Pointe-a-Pierre to date and therefore necessitated a large pool of construction specialists, engineers and support staff. For the first time in the history of the country, professional and ancillary staff was sourced from Canada. As a result, not only was a new fully-outfitted refinery built, but also a new modern hospital with air-conditioned wards and operating theatre, a bachelors' mess hall and surrounding bungalows to house bachelor staff, as well as two-story brick homes for married staff and sports facilities, including a golf course, and a school. Moreover, this project proved to be an extensive training agenda for the local workforce as the Trinidadian tradesmen were unfamiliar with most of the modern construction techniques being used. As such, expatriate staff was recruited from the UK to work on the project, as well as impart skills in brick-making, brick-laying, plumbing, plastering, painting and decorating, carpentry and joinery and electrical technology.

To the residents, the Pointe-a-Pierre camp was an "extremely pleasant place in which to live and work and, as oil camps go, there can have been very few, if any, that could better it" (Higgins 1996). Maintenance costs were significant but a senior official is recorded as saying, ". . . we know our salaries were low, so let's make it a nice place to live in." Beautification of living quarters and camps were encouraged in this "garden city." Houses were well maintained, lawns, hedges, flowering and vegetable gardens were kept trimmed, while native and foreign fruit and flowering trees were planted. The Anglican Church which was built in the early 1940s, as well as the older Catholic Church which was previously independently built, were both fully supported by Textrin. In addition, water, electricity, sanitation services, pipe-borne gas and access roadways were supplied throughout the residential camp by Texaco.

Textrin also instituted the very successful low-cost finance plan to enable workers to build their own homes on available company lands located at Pointe-a-Pierre, Guayaguayare and Brighton, on land owned by the employees or on long-term lease land. Textrin guaranteed the access to credit for employees under the Textrin plan by maintaining adequate deposits with local Trinidad banks.

The health, welfare and housing of employees in the oil industry were deemed as matters of paramount importance. As such, the two largest companies, Trinidad Leaseholds Limited (TLL) and United British Oilfields of Trinidad (UBOT), had up-to-date hospitals with qualified medical officers. During the embryonic years of the industry, anti-malaria and other prohibitive programmes were carried out by the oil companies and eventually resulted in the eradication of these diseases in the oil production zones. Today, Petrotrin owns and operates the Augustus Long Hospital and seven medical centres located at Pointe-a-Pierre, Penal, Guayaguayare, Forest Reserve, Brighton, Point Fortin and Santa Flora. The Augustus Long Hospital provides full medical services inclusive of surgery to employees, and houses the only specialized burns treatment unit (albeit on a small scale) in the country. The Medical Centres at Pointe-a-Pierre are fully functional facilities and are the sentinel station for the collection of epidemiological data in certain infectious diseases and occupational diseases[2].

TRINTOC/TRINTOPEC

In 1974, the Government acquired the assets of Shell Trinidad Limited and established the first State-owned oil company, the Trinidad and Tobago Oil Company Limited (Trintoc). In 1985, the Government further expanded its role in the petroleum sector through the acquisition of Trinidad-Tesoro and the establishment of the Trinidad and Tobago Petroleum Company Limited (Trintopec). These acquisitions involved not only the assets and infrastructure of the predecessor companies but also, in a less formal but equally critical manner, the expectations and aspirations of the surrounding communities.

When the Government acquired the assets of Texaco Trinidad Inc., almost the entire southern portion of Trinidad from Mayaro in the East to Point Fortin in the west came under direct national control. At that time, it was perceived by many as a case of the sardine swallowing the shark, as State-owned Trintoc emerged as the new heavyweight on the local petroleum scene. In the early 1980s when the oil price was plummeting and there was a mandate to cut operating costs, Trintoc's Managing Director, Walton F. James, the first local chief executive of any major oil company in Trinidad and Tobago, insisted that Trintoc maintain its extensive community development portfolio. He is remembered as saying that "it is in times of difficulty that sport and culture become even more important since they build morale and community spirit and inspire hope for the future." It was during this period that the Trintoc football team emerged from being a minor league team in 1980 to become national champions in 1987. This success was attributable to significant corporate support. The team's sobriquet "Pride of the South" was proof of its widespread popularity and recognition throughout south Trinidad. Trintoc's philosophy was not merely based on good public relations but also on sound business strategy, as in communities like Point Fortin and the many other "oil towns" in south Trinidad, employee relations and community relations were indistinguishable. Most of the workforce lived with their families in the surrounding communities and as such, any goodwill and support within the community automatically translated into positive employee relations.

Trintoc also resurrected the popular Southern Games which had gone into limbo with the departure of Texaco. The newly branded Trintoc International Invitational Games signalled a revival of sporting activities throughout south Trinidad. At Palo Seco, Trintopec had inherited a stadium, complete with cycling velodrome, from Trinidad Tesoro. The J. P. Shmalz Velodrome was an important regional venue for sporting events, and the annual Palo Seco Games continues to be a stage for showcasing local athletes and cyclists.

Apart from sport, the era of Trintoc and Trintopec saw a continuation of significant funding for cultural groups, especially the steel band. Trintoc sponsored the popular Trintoc Invaders based in Port of Spain, the Trintoc Sun Valley orchestra which resided in Point Fortin, as well as the Trintoc Tobago All Stars across in the sister isle. Trintopec sponsored the Deltones Steel Orchestra of Siparia and the Starlift Steel Orchestra, another popular Port of Spain steel band. Trintoc also sponsored the Point Fortin Cultural Workshop while Trintopec supported the Boodoosingh Trace Tassa Group. It was during the Trintoc era, through significant technical and financial support, that the Point Fortin Borough Day celebrations gained national prominence.

PETROTRIN

In 1993, Trintoc and Trintopec were consolidated under a single umbrella: the Petroleum Company of Trinidad and Tobago (Petrotrin). The merger of these two national oil companies with several different predecessors and corporate philosophies was a herculean task involving not only a rationalization of assets and personnel but also the integration of numerous communities and community initiatives. As part of its merger strategy, the newly appointed

Board of Directors established a merger sub-committee to manage the communications and community relations aspects of the new company.

As such, a new corporate monthly newsletter entitled *One Voice* commenced publication. The name was devised to signal that Trintoc and Trintopec were no longer separate entities but was now a united company. It was a message that had to be communicated throughout numerous production fields on and offshore as well as to the operating areas across south Trinidad. It was then that the historical role and popularity of sport, particularly football, was exploited in an effort to expedite the merger process. At the time, both Trintoc and Trintopec sponsored powerful rival football teams, with Trintoc having won several national titles in the preceding years. The idea of merging these two top teams with their array of national stars was irresistible and so the "Oil Squad" was born. The combined team played several exhibition matches throughout south Trinidad and won loyal supporters within the various "fence-line" communities and even further afield.

Eventually, the teams were officially merged and the United Petrotrin football team was established as a tangible symbol of unity and cooperation between two former competitors. Until 2009 United Petrotrin continued to be one of the country's premier football teams. Today Petrotrin, to a large extent, also seeks to uphold the traditional relationships between the company and the communities in which it operates.

OIL AND SPORT

Since the early days of the petroleum industry, the marriage of oil and sport produced many outstanding sporting personalities and championship teams. Higgins (1996) constantly refers to the focus on sport during the embryonic years of the oil sector. One theory is that sport was used as a mechanism to curtail the heavy drinking and gambling among workers during their downtime in the remote oilfields of the southern region of the island.

The extent of this relationship was manifested in the very names of the major sports clubs which emerged from the "oil belt." In north Trinidad names such as Maple, Malvern, Colts and Casuals were used. In contrast, in south Trinidad the top sports clubs assumed the identity of the oil companies: UBOT, TPD, Shell, Texaco, Forest Reserve, Tesoro, Trintopec and Trintoc. This was not mere coincidence but a reflection of the importance of sport in the corporate philosophy at the time. Higgins (1996) recounts that when the new oilfield at Groudon in southeast Trinidad was developed in the 1930s; several facilities were constructed including "three-storied offices, five barracks for forty employees, eight large two-storied bungalows, a fully-equipped mechanic's garage and a playing field." He further records that "every encouragement both financial and otherwise was given to sports. Sport grounds, sports equipment and club facilities were provided." Throughout the history of the development of the sector, wherever the companies established their operations, a sports ground was always close at hand.

As a result of this corporate philosophy, the petroleum industry eventually owned and maintained the finest and most modern sporting facilities in the English-speaking Caribbean. This collection included several football fields, turf wickets, squash courts, basketball courts, swimming pools, and golf courses. Whether it was an impeccably maintained Mahaica Oval in Point Fortin, or the premier cricket facility at Guaracara Park in Pointe-a-Pierre, or the famous "Acre" at Goddard's Park in Forest Reserve, the sporting facilities which were built and maintained by the energy sector were second-to-none in the Caribbean at that time.

It was no surprise therefore, that, these facilities nurtured an abundance of sporting talent in various disciplines. Many of the sportsmen have excelled at both national and international levels. In cricket, Raphick Jumadeen from Texaco Pointe-a- Pierre and Augustine "Gus" Logie from Texaco Brighton in La Brea are two of the more recent players to have emerged "out of the oil" to represent the West Indies Cricket Team. Earlier, legends such as West Indies fast-bowlers Prior Jones and Jaswick Taylor, the great Sir Learie Constantine and spin legend Sonny Ramadhin were some of the few who passed through the "oil" on their way to international glory. The list of sporting icons would also include golfer Stephen Ames who learnt his craft on the golf-course at Pointe-a-Pierre.

On the football field, players like Ahamad Charles who played for Apex Fyzabad and Aldric "Son" Baptiste who represented Trinidad Petroleum Development Company (TPD) are but a few exemplars. There were also popular teams like United British Oilfields of Trinidad (UBOT) and the championship Shell Squad of the 1950s which included Hall-of-Famers Delbert Charleau, Doyle Griffith and Rawlins "Cax" Baptiste. Shortly after the Shell era in Point Fortin, an exciting Point Fortin Civic Centre team emerged featuring some of the best players to have ever worn national colours. Among them were Warren Archibald, Wilfred "Bound to Score" Cave and the skillful Leroy De Leon. While "Civic," St Benedict's College and the national football team all benefited from these talented players, it was mainly due to the "Shell Colts," a Shell youth development programme in Point Fortin, that they were first unearthed and nurtured for top-class international football.

In Palo Seco, a powerful British Petroleum (BP) Palo Seco team enjoyed considerable popularity throughout the surrounding communities. Likewise, this team boasted some outstanding individuals such as Bobby Sookram,

Aldwyn Ferguson and Edgar Vidale who went on to become a successful national coach.

Apart from providing venues for some of the most memorable sporting achievements at events, such as the world-renowned Texaco Southern Games, the company's sports clubs also developed many of the country's greatest athletes and cyclists, the most successful of them being Olympic gold medallist Hasely Crawford. His rise from poverty to international acclaim as the world's fastest human is testimony to the profound and positive influence that the oil industry has had on sport throughout Trinidad and Tobago. The substantial support of the oil companies did not cease at the provision of sporting facilities and equipment but many of the top sportsmen were also afforded permanent jobs within the oil companies while they were training. This assured their livelihoods even after their sporting days were over. Today some of our current and former top sporting personalities like Darren Ganga and Clayton Morris throughout the energy sector and hold leadership positions within the various sporting organizations and NGOs.

ALL ARE EQUAL—WITHIN THEIR LEVEL

In spite of its substantial support for community development in the fence-line communities, the pioneer oil companies established a rigid social stratification that was judiciously maintained. Company employees were segregated in accordance with organizational levels of senior staff, junior staff and hourly/ weekly workers. The senior staff levels were confined mainly to expatriate personnel and a few select locals. Junior staff and the hourly/weekly workers comprised nationals, all of whom had separate bargaining units. This labelling dominated every social aspect of the employees' lives. As described earlier, the Point Fortin residential camps were segregated according to this organizational status. So profound was company position that employees were identified within the community as a "monthly man" and even further, his wife would be referred to by her husband's position. Similar to the Point Fortin residential area delineation, Pointe-a-Pierre adopted a "totem-pole" housing policy. As such, the Pointe-a-Pierce Staff Club and swimming pool, golf course and yacht club and yachting facilities were reserved exclusively for senior staff employees, their families and friends, while non-eligible employees were accommodated at the comparatively limited facilities at the nearby Guaracara Park.

Another reason for this arrangement was the adoption of a military-type management philosophy in which hierarchy, rank and status were sacrosanct. Consequently, the location and size of company housing, the size of office, brand of company car and even access to company private schools were carefully assigned to reinforce this management ideology, which also reflected the colonial and social values of the time.

It was anticipated that the transition to fully State-owned enterprise would dismantle these social barriers and corporate symbols. Although some initial efforts were made, the early attempts were met with vociferous resistance from many of the local managers who were now the decision makers and beneficiaries of these company "perks." Although several company clubs have since been "desegregated" and are now all-embracing, the Petrotrin Pointe-a-Pierre Club still maintains a membership policy which bears little difference from that of the era of foreign ownership and management.

Concomitantly, some former workers perceive that Shell's "godfather policies" were not totally benevolent but were part of a masterful strategy to optimally organize the workforce for maximum efficiency and productivity. As such, nearby company-sponsored living quarters ensured a ready complement of staff "on demand," even during after-work periods and on public holidays. As such, the construction of oil-field camps can also be seen as serving the production companies' interests.

100 YEARS HENCE—THE COMMUNITIES TODAY

The Kairi Report (2005) reveals an overall decline in poverty levels in Trinidad and Tobago, down from 24 percent in 1997/98 when the last survey was conducted. (Kairi Consultants 2005) 15.5 percent of the population was characterised as poor while 1.2 percent was indigent[3]. Table 10.1 shows the poverty, indigence and vulnerability estimates by island, as provided by the report.

The report noted that the "geographic distribution was highly unequal with the poorest areas being geographically concentrated into a band that extended

Table 10.1. Poverty Estimates 2005

Population		Percentage of Individuals		
		Trinidad %	Tobago %	Trinidad & Tobago Total %
Socio Economic Status	Indigent	1.2	–	1.2
	Poor	15.4	19	15.5
	Vulnerable	9.2	3.2	9.0
	Non Vulnerable	74.1	77.7	74.3
Total (%)		100	100	100
Total (n)		14524	694	15218

Source: "Analysis of the 2005 Survey of Living Standards," Kairi Consultants

from the north-east along the east of the country and then across its south."
Among the regions of highest poverty were the borough of Point Fortin (24.6
percent), Mayaro/Rio Claro (26.6 percent), and Siparia (27.7 percent) all of
which had poverty levels of over 20 percent. What is noteworthy here is the
fact that this poverty band is consistent with the main energy sector areas
of operation in Trinidad. As such, the incidence of the highest and most
persistent poverty in Trinidad occurs within the heartland of the oil and gas
operations. The report also states that "as much as 30.6 % of the population
sampled had not passed any exam above the primary level." By contrast, educational qualifications increased across the socio-economic status.

In another study, UWI economist Dr Sandra Sookram alluded to the
fact that "although Trinidad and Tobago was classified as a high income
country by the World Bank[4], it has pockets of extreme poverty" (Sookram
and Kedar 2005). That is to say, that there is a gross disparity in economic
wealth in the society, and the majority of poverty in Trinidad and Tobago is
concentrated in the south and south-east regions of the country which is the
core of the energy sector operations. In reality, many residents not only live
on the fence-line of the lifeblood of the country's economy but also exist in
close proximity to the well-paid employees of the profitable energy industry. The unemployment rates[5] for 2005 show that Point Fortin (15.1percent)
and Victoria (which includes Penal, Debe and Princes Town: 10.0 percent)
were not only the two administrative districts with the highest unemployment rates, but were also well above the national unemployment average of
8 percent (Central Statistical Office 2005). Therefore, the highest poverty
and unemployment levels in the country exist within the districts of operation of the energy companies.

At the 2008 launch of an Economic Survey for the Caribbean[6], the Foreign Affairs Minister Paula Gopee-Scoon noted that "Trinidad and Tobago
had not only met the (MGD) goals, but had exceeded them." But Dr Johann
Hans Geiser, International Development Expert and former UN Resident Co-
ordinator for Trinidad and Tobago, contends that the challenge for Trinidad
and Tobago, "given the country's rich resources, should be to re-estimate
the TT$600 per month which is used as a marker for poverty and establish
a new one which will be a truer reflection of the number of people living in
poverty." Ralph Henry states that no matter how it was looked at, the poverty
level was extremely high and something should be done to deal with it (Allaham 2008). However, there are two urgent concerns to be addressed: 1) the
reality that the nation's most acute poverty, unemployment and illiteracy levels exist within the areas of operations of the energy sector; and 2) the grave
economic and social inequality within the country which boasts of a GDP of
US$16,900 per capita.

The figures all demonstrate the fact that the model of community development adopted by UBOT, Shell and Petrotrin in the "oil communities" such as Point Fortin, Fyzabad and Siparia, was unsustainable and self-defeating as it perpetuated a culture of dependency on "handouts" from the energy companies operating in the locale. The communities were supported by the "*de jure*" energy company and flourished as long as the company maintained operations. Although there was substantial investment in infrastructure, sporting and cultural activities, expenditure did not meaningfully contribute to the economy or development of the communities. As such, when the company ceased operations in the community, the social and economic fabric of the community disintegrated. La Brea and environs is a casualty of this unsustainable development model. Increasingly, this model has spilled over into the national development strategy where the Government has become overly dependant on hydrocarbon rents and has, therefore, exacerbated the nation's vulnerability to the vagaries of the energy sector.

The Vision 2020 Sub-committee for Poverty Alleviation and Social Services seeks to achieve the following objective as articulated in its mission statement: "the reduction of poverty to 5 percent or less by 2010, and the development of social service delivery programmes to manage social and economic vulnerability such that there is the total elimination of the incidence of chronic poverty or indigence by that date." The report states that poverty encompasses much more than the conventional definition as provided by the World Bank, "the inability to attain a minimal standard of living" but incorporates issues such as the "vulnerability to poor health and education, deprivation in knowledge and communication, inability to exercise human and political rights and the absence of dignity, confidence and self respect" as proposed by the UNDP (Vision 2020 Subcommittee 2004). As such, we turn to the Human Development Index (HDI) which is promoted by the UNDP. Although it is not an all-inclusive gauge for human development, it is considered to be a "broadened prism" for ascertaining development.

The 2005 HDI ranks Trinidad and Tobago 57th out of 179 countries. (UNDP 2005) Table 10.2 compares the standing of several Caribbean countries based on the Human Development Index.

Trinidad and Tobago which boasts of being the region's leading natural gas and petrochemical exporter, as well as having the only liquefied natural gas plant[7,8] benefited from unprecedented high global energy and downstream commodities prices and as of 2008, experienced 15 consecutive years of positive economic growth. Yet still, the country ranked considerably lower than Barbados and the Bahamas on the Human Development Index. Likewise, Trinidad and Tobago placed slightly higher than Antigua and Barbuda and St. Kitts and Nevis. Undeniably, the poverty and

**Table 10.2. Human Development Index;
Ranking for Selected Caribbean Countries 2005**

Rank	Country
37	Barbados
49	Bahamas
57	Trinidad and Tobago
59	Antigua and Barbuda
60	St Kitts and Nevis
66	St Lucia
77	Dominica
86	Grenada
87	Jamaica

unemployment levels, as well as internationally recognized indices denote that, despite hydrocarbon wealth, successive governments in Trinidad and Tobago have all failed to deliver effective sustainable social and community development programmes in Trinidad and Tobago.

The Sectoral Report for Regional Development and Sustainable Communities (Vision 2020 Subcommittee on Regional Development 2004) seeks to address two issues:

- Transformation and renewal of society at the level of the 14 municipal and regional corporations and Tobago; and
- The creation of sustainable communities whose residents are able to access their needs for adequate housing, social facilities, physical infrastructure, recreation and employment opportunities either within or in close proximity to the community.

Inter alia, this committee envisions:

- A strengthened role and significance for citizen involvement and participation in promoting regional development, community identity, and in decision-making at regional and community levels;
- Considerable improvement and expansion of basic needs and amenities to include food, security, housing and shelter, water, safety and security, health, employment and wealth creation, infrastructure, transport and education;
- Improved access to, and improvement in the provision of, quality goods and services;
- Strengthened regional and community links to industry; and
- Enhanced role for the private sector.

The enhanced role for the private sector is critical to the sustainable development of the communities and the wider society of Trinidad and Tobago. Within the social sciences discourse, there is considerable agreement that monopolistic State service delivery and development initiatives are "unfeasible, undesirable or simply rather old fashioned," and there is increasing movement toward "diversity, experimentation and multi-actor arrangements such as inter-organizational partnerships, between state agencies and either commercial enterprises or civic organizations (Joshi and Moore 2004). In Trinidad and Tobago the closest semblance of private sector participation in social and community development activities is now conducted within the context of Corporate Social Responsibility (CSR). However many CSR initiatives are merely a regurgitation of traditional PR programmes,

According to the World Bank, CSR can be defined as "the commitment of business to contribute to sustainable development by working with employees, their families, the local community and society at large to improve their quality of life, in ways that are good for development." The underlying tenet of CSR is the notion that it is about "promoting responsible business practices which benefit business and society, and help achieve social, economic and environmentally sustainable development by maximizing the positive impact business has on society as well as minimizing the negative" (International Business Leaders Forum 2010). CSR is differentiated from philanthropy, charity, sponsorship and even public relations. Philanthropy relates to "donations or charitable giving from which companies do not necessarily expect any direct positive impact on their business activities." Public relations focus on activities which can reap a financial return for the company. Although CSR appears to be an appealing intervention for social and community development in Trinidad and Tobago, the World Bank cautions that worldwide "the implementation and impact of CSR are still patchy and the agenda still immature." The international NGO, Christian Aid argues further that CSR can simply become public relations as the boundary between CSR and Public Relations can be very blurred (Christian Aid 2004). The Vision 2020 Sectoral Report on Energy agrees that it is the "resort to patronage over sustainable development programmes [which] has conspired to place some of the communities with long-standing relationships with energy sector companies among the most depressed in Trinidad and Tobago, with poverty and unemployment levels more than double the national average" (Energy Subcommittee 2004).

A report on CSR in Trinidad and Tobago conducted by the UNDP in conjunction with the South Trinidad Chamber of Industry and Commerce (STCIC) states that in Trinidad and Trinidad, *inter alia*:

CSR is still at early stages of development and is primarily driven by foreign companies;

The focus is on philanthropy and public relations—it was noted that although all of the companies interviewed engaged in some social programme during the 2001–2006 period, only few of them actually engaged in CSR. A large number of companies disbursed their contributions in an *ad hoc* manner, generally as requests arise. As such, companies still perceive philanthropy as their main social objective:

• Geographic saturation and duplication of CSR activities are prevalent as the geographic spread of social programmes in the country tends to be in their fence-line communities. As such, communities such as Mayaro (bpTT and Petrotrin), Couva (Point Lisas Industrial Estate), Tabaquite (Petrotrin), Talparo (Petrotrin), Port of Spain (head offices of all energy companies are located in the capital city) and Point Fortin (Petrotrin, ALNG) are the major beneficiaries of social spending in Trinidad and Tobago. Companies from the Energy and Related Industries sector, as a result of their geographic-specific operations, are engaged in similar types of activities in the same communities, thus duplicating efforts;
• Corporate spending is heavily concentrated in education and sports and, to a lesser degree, in community development, arts and culture. The high PR mileage attached to sport and entertainment activities attracted the majority of funding.

The Energy and Related Industries Sector is the CSR leader in Trinidad and Tobago with the key players being the foreign companies. It should be noted that only four of the interviewed companies[9] accounted for over 30 percent of the total monies spent in social and environmental programmes, thus confirming a high concentration of development programmes in the hands of a few players (UNDP; STCIC 2007).

Both the Vision 2020 Sectoral Report for Regional Development and Sustainable Communities and the Mapping CSR Report conclude by underscoring the "great potential of the private sector to play a key role in the national and social development of Trinidad and Tobago." Christian Aid[10] also contends that multinational corporations are powerful drivers of international trade and investment, and have a critical role to play in upholding and advancing social and environmental standards, especially in developing countries'.

It is not coincidental that the majority of social community development programmes have been spearheaded and continue to be carried out by the Energy Sector companies and, more specifically, by the locally operating MNCs. Foremost is the fact that this is the sector with disposable income for development programmes. Former Minister of Finance, Wendell Mottley underscores a "dualism" in the economy by categorizing the energy sector and energy services sector as being "first world" and "second world" respectively (Mottley 2007). The rest of the economy is characterized as being "third world." The main provider and in most cases, the monopolist of public goods and services—the public sector—exists in this "third world." He asserts that the energy sector is highly competitive and efficient because of foreign investment as well as the application of worldwide standards to technology, capital and labour, while spillover effects have permeated the energy services sector. Unfortunately, the two sectors are "de-linked" from the rest of the economy which "remains untouched by modernizing influences of the energy sector," regardless of the rapid rate of growth, application of world class practices or technological advancements in the energy sector. Correspondingly, the "Third World" sector is "irrelevant to its first world cohabitants." This concurs with the previously stated verity that abject poverty can and does exist on the fence-line of the economically dominant "first world" energy sector.

As described previously, the pioneer oil companies not only developed Greenfield exploration, development operations and refining plants but also constructed residential estates which were self-serviced with electricity, water, security, garbage disposal and road maintenance. Although the scope of service delivery has been reduced, production and operations facilities as well as employee residential camps at Point Fortin, Pointe-a-Pierre and Guayagayare are still self-sufficient as Petrotrin and BP continue to distribute self-generated electricity, gas and water to all residential camps and operating zones at a high service quality with minimal service interruptions. Energy sector service delivery can provide numerous instructive examples for the "Third World" in the areas of health services, utilities provision, apprenticeship and training, sport and cultural development, infrastructure development and facilities management, community participation and programme management.

Although development initiatives often disregard the importance of synergistic relations between the state and society, these relations at the local levels are "often critical to successful development strategies" (Evans 1996). While it may seem unconventional and contrary to standard operating practices of public sector service delivery, the concept of private sector participation, referred to as co-production is not a new or novel one. This notion of "institutionalized co-production" refers to "organizational arrangements, which implicate clients in effective service delivery, on a sustained, regular basis in the provision of public services through regular, long-term relationships between state agencies and organized groups of citizens, where both make substantial resource contributions" (Joshi and Moore 2004). These unorthodox arrangements such as The Citizen–Police Liaison Committee (CPLC) in Karachi and The Ghana Private Transport Union (GPRTU) seek to foster synergistic cooperative behaviour "that improves the overall quality of service delivery."

It is because the energy sector possesses the capital, technical competency, administrative know-how and hands-on knowledge of the fence-line communities that the sector is best poised to implement effective value-added development programmes. In spite of pockets of success, particularly in sport and training and development, the current approach of operating within clearly defined spheres has not realized the potential of the social or human capital of the oil communities nor that of the society in general. This very conventional and non-committal participation of the energy sector has not effected real human development. This is a clarion call to action for the energy sector companies to forge lasting development throughout the communities by fostering meaningful partnerships with the State for the development of fence-line communities.

In reality, these relationships between different agencies are usually "undefined, informal, and renegotiated almost continuously." As such, institutionalized co-production involves the blurring of the lines of the bureaucratic Weberian state apparatus in which the role and function of public and private are clearly defined and separate. Within a co-production arrangement, power, authority and control of resources are likely to be unequally and ambiguously divided between the state and non-state actors. However, as successful examples have illustrated, this fuzziness in boundary lines may be the price for effective service delivery.

This phenomenon of "ties that cross public-private boundaries" is paramount to China's transformational story. Likewise, the vast research on the East Asian Tigers all chronicle state/society linkages that span public/private boundaries. In addition, the ties between officials in organizations such as Taiwan's Industrial Development Bureau, Japan's MITI, or Korea's Ministry of Communications and those that manage private industrial corporations have been attributable to the "joint project" of industrial transformation (Evans 1996). However, researchers on this topic concede that social capital, which is most critical to the outcome, is formed in "spaces" that are neither public nor private but "fill the gap between these two spheres." Therefore, the communities are essential to provide the "glue" in this suggested co-production arrangement. As such the triad—state, community and company—is essential for the development of the communities and ultimately, the nation.

THE NEW MANDATE—CORPORATE SOCIAL RESPONSIBILITY VS PUBLIC RELATIONS

The Vision 2020 Report of the Energy Sub-Committee articulated a similar decisive role for the energy sector: "the energy sector has a vital role to play in the social and community development of Trinidad and Tobago; with their direct and indirect access to human development expertise, energy companies can creatively assist in redressing the many social ills affecting the national community."

Unlike the pioneer oil companies of yesteryear, some of the more recent entrants into the local energy sector landscape have adopted seemingly conflicting philosophies in terms of social and community development. One school of thought advocates an almost exclusive focus on the company's "core business" and a rejection of the role of community "godfather." This view is based on the principle that the companies pay significant taxes and royalties to the Government which has the ultimate responsibility for developing the various communities. Many of the former company-owned sporting and cultural facilities which were subsequently donated to either the state or local government agencies now lie in a state of significant disrepair.

The irony is that the southern region has a large youth population, with approximately 55 percent under 25 years old. While many of them currently lack the educational background for gainful permanent employment, they have a natural aptitude for sporting and cultural activities. This may explain why Point Fortin, for instance, has produced more national "Road March" champions than any other town or village in Trinidad and Tobago. There are even some cultural historians who argue that the steelband originated in south Trinidad where the oil drums were readily available. A senior police officer recently bewailed the latest crime statistics and declared that currently many of the youths are "graduating to the gangs" upon completion of the mandatory secondary school tenure. More than ever, these facilities should be available to harness their innate sporting and artistic talents, both in the facilitation of human and social development, and more importantly, as a deterrent to the pernicious effects of drug trafficking. Commonwealth Secretary-General Kamalesh Sharma recently highlighted[11] the importance of sport as "an effective instrument for community and youth development, building character, discipline, tolerance and friendship, promoting fair and open sporting competition, protecting the integrity of young athletes, besides creating broader opportunities for socio-economic development in the Commonwealth." He went on to state that sport not only promotes learning and is a means to develop a healthy lifestyle but it also embraces everyone, including those who might otherwise be excluded. He pointed out that sport can bring people closer to others whom they would know better, and advances respect and understanding.

In describing what he terms as the "Dark Side of Trinidad and Tobago's Industrialization," Wendell Mottley warns that "young people are the most vulnerable. Most of them resign themselves to unfulfilled lives. Many of them give themselves to a life of crime." Statistics on the socio-economic conditions of young people from communities surrounding the energy sector reveal above national-average drop-out rates and very low levels of academic achievement. Mottley posits that "this group, many of them are barely socialized and emotionally disturbed is large enough to turn their youthful energy into generating considerable problems for the wider society" (Mottley 2007).

As economic challenges deepen, any disengagement by the energy-sector from a more meaningful role in the wider society can exacerbate a potentially volatile situation. In this context the adoption of the Corporate Social Responsibility concept as a tool for managing the company/community interface can be a launch pad for sustainable development. Unfortunately, as the South Chamber CSR Mapping Report suggested, the current approach to CSR is largely a "rehash" of traditional public relations practice with its heavy emphasis on publicity. When asked to list their CSR initiatives, the companies repeated many of the old public relations "image-building" activities with little indication that they were modified to comply with the new imperatives of social responsibility or the realities of the current environment.

One plausible reason for the change in the relationship dynamics could be the physical relocation of the head offices and hence, decision-makers, of the neo-corporations to Port of Spain, the capital city. This has created a psychological distance and disconnect with the communities in which the industrial plants operate. In this regard, the pioneer oil companies could justifiably claim to be more *au courant* with the concept of CSR given their "embeddedness" and substantial investments in community development initiatives.

There are, however, some innovative new initiatives emerging within the energy sector which are demonstrating a greater awareness of the need for relevant and sustainable community development programmes. Such examples include:

- BHP Billiton's Turtle Watch project in the coastal villages of Matura, Grande Riviere and Fishing Pond, whereby the company assists the resident turtle-watching groups to work collaboratively to promote nature and community-based tourism for these villages;
- PCS Nitrogen agricultural project in central Trinidad which consists of six greenhouses, four acres of land dedicated to demonstrating new technologies and modern farm management techniques, an agricultural resource centre for the training of small farmers and 50 acres of land for cultivation for food crops, all in an effort to ensure food security and lower food prices;
- bpTT Mayaro initiative for private enterprise development (MIPED) programme, which is the country's first micro-finance lending organization to be sponsored by a private non-financial company. In addition to providing credit facilities, the programme also extends to training in marketing, accounting and management to support small and micro enterprise business development.

- In sport the National Gas Company (NGC) has introduced a 'Right on Track Programme for youth athletic development. NGC has also financed the training and development of coaches to create a local pool of coaches, who assist in the training of young athletes within the school and community environments.

CSR within the energy sector also offers the possibility of a more creative and indigenous approach to human, social and community development without the need for any significant increment in funding. For example, steelband sponsorship amasses into millions of dollars annually, with the majority of these funds being allocated to a single event—the Panorama Competition. A more 'socially responsible' approach would focus on programmes in music literacy and the application of modern marketing techniques for the promotion of the art form, both locally and internationally.

CSR must also eschew the tokenism that accompanies many corporate social investment programmes. The Vision 2020 Energy sub-committee acknowledges that "the challenge facing the sector is to use its considerable financial, technical and managerial resources to implement sustainable community development programmes." The sectoral report illustrates the inherent dichotomy between the traditional approach and the new mandate by explaining that "moving communities to a path of sustainable development is a long-term process and does not easily comply with the short-term need for PR mileage and publicity. However, if the sustainability is an imperative, then programmes must be designed accordingly with an emphasis on expanding the human and social capital within the communities." In addition priority should be given to the institutional strengthening of community groups and organizations so that they can better withstand changes in the fortunes of the sector.

Drucker remarked that "a healthy business and a sick society are hardly compatible" (Drucker 1993). As such, the "new" community development enterprise must now focus on "people-centred development" whereby economic growth serves to enhance the well-being of the majority (Ul Haq 1995). As such, the critical factor resides in the effective use of the hydrocarbon wealth. That is, "the use that people make of their wealth, not the wealth itself." In this regard, the approach to development should be holistic and consider economic growth as being essential for human development but not the principal determinant of development. The existing model of development is shown to be lacking and in need of change.

Despite the economic challenges now confronting the sector, the "considerable financial, technical and managerial resources" would be still available if a more collaborative approach is adopted. The state-owned sector with the cadre of local executives at the helm should be at the forefront of exploring and exploiting the new possibilities of co-production relationships, strategic alliances and development programmes. The Minister of Energy and Energy Affairs announced in 2010 that CSR would be one the criteria used in the evaluation of new industrial projects in the energy sector.[12] This should encourage a more strategic and comprehensive approach to the design and implementation of CSR programmes. It should also promote a deeper analysis and understanding of local realities, an awareness of the legitimate aspirations of local communities and a commitment to meaningful consultation and public participation.

NOTES

1. Trinidad and Tobago became an independent country in 1962.

2. http://www.petrotrin.com/Petrotrin2007/MedservHospital.htm.

3. Indigence line (Annual in local currency- TTD) $3,060.0. Poverty Line (Annual in local currency—TTD) $7,980.0.

4. The World Bank classifies a high income country as having a GNI per capita of US$11,456 or more. The entire country classification list can be found at: http://go.worldbank.org/K2CKM78CC0.

5. Continuous Sample of Survey, Labour Force Report 2005, Central Statistical Office, Trinidad and Tobago. The unemployment rate is calculated as the number of persons unemployed as a percentage of the total labour force.

6. Launch of the Global MDG Report and the ECLAC Survey of the Caribbean, 2007/2008 at Normandie Hotel, St. Ann's, on 03 October 2008.

7. Atlantic LNG Train 4 plant is the world's single largest production facility.

8. Trinidad and Tobago is the largest single supplier of LNG to the United States; providing two-thirds of all LNG imported into the U.S. since 2002 (U.S. Department of State).

9. Ninety companies participated in this study. These comprised of small, medium and large locally-owned, as well as foreign-owned, companies in all major sectors of the economy.

10. Christian Aid (2004) Behind the Mask: The real face of corporate social responsibility.

11. 4th Commonwealth Sports Ministers Meeting in Beijing, China, on 9 August 2008.

12. Address by Minister of Energy and Energy Affairs Carolyn Seepersad-Bachan at the Prize Awards ceremony of the Energy Sector Corporate Social Responsibility Task Force. Petrotrin Staff Club May 2011.

BIBLIOGRAPHY

Allaham, Aabida. "A Quarter of Trinis Living in Poverty." *Trinidad Express.* November 26, 2008.

Baker, Dean Henry. "The Asphalt Lakes of Trinidad and Venezuela as natural wonders of the World." 1924.

Brereton, Bridget. *History of Modern Trinidad and Tobago 1783-1962*. New Hampshire: Heinemann, 1982.

Campbell, Jacob. "Technologies of Governance in a Trinidad Company Town." School of Antropology, University of Arizona, 2008.

Central Statistical Office . *Continuous Sample Survey, Labour Force Report 2005*. GOTT, 2005.

Christian Aid. "Behind the Mask: The Real Face of Corporate Social Responsibility" *St Andrews*. 2004. http://www.st-andrews.ac.uk/~ (accessed June 2012).

Drucker, Peter. *Management; Tasks, Responsibilities Practices*. HarperBusiness, 1993.

Energy Subcommittee. *Vision 2020 Energy*. GOTT, Ministry of Planning and Development, 2004.

Evans, Peter. "Government Action, Social Capital and Development; Reviewing the Evidence on Synergy." *World Development* 24 (June 1996): 1119-1132.

Higgins, George. *A History of Trinidad Oil*. Port of Spain: Trinidad Express Newspaper Limited, 1996.

International Business Leaders Forum . *IBLF*. 2010. http://www.iblf.org/en/about-iblf/corporate-partners/affiliates.aspx (accessed 2012).

Joshi, A., and M. Moore. "Institutionalised Co-production: Unorthodox Public Service Delivery in Challenging Environments." *Journal of Development Studies, 40(4)*, 2004: 31-4.

Kairi Consultants. *Analysis of the 2005 Survey of Living Conditions*. Port of Spain: Kairi, 2005.

Lewis, Ellis. *Inauguration of the Borough of Point Fortin*. San Fernando: Rahaman Printery, 1980.

Mottley, Wendell. *Industrial Policy in Trinidad and Tobago 1959-2006*. Kingston: Ian Randle, 2007.

Sookram, Sandra, and Abbi.M. Kedar. *Poverty and Household Welfare in Trinidad and Tobago; Evidence from the Survey of Living Conditions* . SALISIS, 2005.

Ul Haq, Mahbub. *Reflections on Human Development*. Oxford University Press, 1995.

UNDP. *Human Development Report 2005*. New York: United Nations Development Programme, 2005.

UNDP; STCIC. *Mapping Corporate Social Responsibility in Trinidad and Tobago* . South Trinidad Chamber of Industry and Comerce, 2007.

Vision 2020 Subcommittee on Regional Development . *Report on Regional Development and Sustainable Communities* . GOTT, 2004.

Vision 2020 Subcommittee. *Vision 2020 Poverty Alleviation and Social Services Sectoral Report*. GOTT, 2004.

Chapter Eleven

Hydrocarbons and the Environment in Trinidad and Tobago

An Emerging Legal Relationship

Rajendra Ramlogan

INTRODUCTION

Trinidad and Tobago provides a prime example of a single commodity-based developing economy, illustrated by its dependence on sugar in an earlier era and now, on hydrocarbons. In its quest for development, however, it holds an interesting stance on environmental protection as it relates to its largest foreign exchange earning sector—the energy sector, as typified by oil and gas exploration and exploitation. The legal environmental regime is of much concern, therefore, both to proponents of sound environmental management and to the entities engaged in hydrocarbon exploration and exploitation.

Trinidad and Tobago, a former British colony, inherited a common law legal system. In reviewing the legal environmental regime of Trinidad and Tobago, what emerges is the emphasis on statutes in regulating activities that affect the environment. Indeed, there is very little by way of judicial pronouncements to show a trend in the development of legal norms through this mechanism. The conservative interventionist attitude of the courts minimises the potential role of the common law; nevertheless, the position adopted by the courts of Trinidad and Tobago is to be expected. The extremely technical and scientific nature of environmental problems renders it unlikely that the courts would be able to develop case law as a tool for protection of the environment. The common law doctrines that have emerged through judicial activism are mainly manifested in the articulation of general principles for governing behaviour. In dealing with environmental issues, the need for specific standards and codes of behaviour, and the knowledge required to fulfil this need, make it unlikely that the courts would be able to satisfy this need.

Before examining the legal environmental regime of Trinidad and Tobago as it applies to the hydrocarbon sector, it is necessary to ascertain the nature of the country's environmental laws. Trinidad and Tobago's legal structure for the protection of the environment may appear somewhat chaotic. There are numerous government-related agencies that are involved in activities which, in varying degrees, may affect environmental elements of the hydrocarbon operations. These agencies can be placed into several broad categories. First, there is control at the ministerial level with the Ministry of Energy being directly responsible for some aspects of hydrocarbon operations. Second, participants in the hydrocarbon sector are also subject to the jurisdiction of departments of government, such as the Factory Inspectorate which examines issues, such as working conditions. Third, the hydrocarbon sector is subject to the authority of certain statutory bodies (boards, tribunals, authorities and commissions, such as the Environmental Management Authority (EMA). Finally, there are the municipal corporations, made up of elected local government officials, which also perform certain environmental functions under several laws. The hydrocarbon sector is subject to some of the requirements of the municipal corporation's local government authority over the area where operations are located.

The environmental legal regime of Trinidad and Tobago can be divided into two eras: the pre-Environmental Management Act 1995[1] (*"EM Act"*) era and the post-*EM Act* era. It can be demonstrated that while in the past there was no shortage of legal norms for protection of the environment, the enforcement rate was nonetheless dismal. The enactment of the *EM Act* in 1995, and its subsequent re-enactment in 2000, was intended to usher in a new era of environmental management. It is, therefore, important to discern the critical changes in the legal environmental regime that are expected as a result of its restructuring, in particular, with reference to the hydrocarbon sector.

THE HYDROCARBON SECTOR AND THE ENVIRONMENT

Given the extreme importance of the hydrocarbon sector to the economy, the attitude of (energy) policy makers to environmental protection is rather interesting. While both pre- and post-independent budget speeches were significantly shaped by the obvious dependence on the hydrocarbon industry, there was little attempt to formulate a policy concerning this sector. Even despite the passing of the *Petroleum Act* of 1969, the first policy paper only appeared some twenty years afterwards. It was not until the change of government in 1986, when the National Alliance for Reconstruction (NAR) came into office, that the policy paper was written. As the 1986 Energy Policy states: "This Paper is a first step towards documenting a comprehensive Energy Policy for Trinidad and Tobago. It involves consolidation of previous and existing policies, updated and articulated into a more fully integrated energy policy document..."[2]

Given the NAR administration's concerns about environmental issues, the policy included a theoretical commitment to safeguard the environment. The policy, however, stated no actual prescriptive measures on sustainability[3] or pollution prevention, nor did it set any deadlines for implementing any such measures. Nevertheless, it did acknowledge that "the disposal of wastes from energy will continue to degrade the environment..."[4] The policy vaguely stated that its two main goals were to:

Provide adequate energy for the country's needs...in the most efficient and economical way, while ensuring that . . . the long term quality of the environment is maintained at an acceptable level, and . . . enable Trinidad and Tobago to fulfil its obligation to several UN organisations to which it has pledged to contribute to the solution of environmental problems . . .[5]

"*Acceptable level*" needs to be clearly defined. There need to be specific measures to ensure efficiency. There is also need for precision in terms of the country's ability to fulfil its international environmental obligations. This first policy left much to be desired for environmental concerns.

The 1992 Energy Policy offered no more commitment than the first. This particular policy stated that "the Government will place further emphasis on environmental considerations and the promotion of the use of environment-friendly energy substitutes as alternative transportation fuels."[6]

This was imprecise and offered no suggestions as to how such environmental considerations would be achieved. In detailing the parameters for formulating an energy policy, out of eleven concerns expressed, environmental concerns were the tenth mentioned. Although it was not expressly stated that the measures appeared in order of priority, it was assumed that the order in which the measures were presented reflected the importance attached to environmental policy in 1992. The situation remains largely unchanged in the 1994 Energy Policy.

The United National Congress administration (UNC 1995-2001) also appeared concerned with the phenomenon of environmental degradation and, as such, endeavoured to include environmentally friendly practices in its policies. The 1998 Energy Policy also made sweeping statements: "The national drive for efficiency, effective management, environmental preservation, sustainable development and a total quality nation must be reflected in the country's energy policy."[7] This policy considered environmentally cleaner fuels and supported the use of compressed natural gas (CNG) as a vehicular fuel. The policy was implemented but hampered by an inadequate distribution of CNG outlets throughout the country. The result was that only a small population of drivers made the conversion to CNG. This policy made mention of sustainable development; yet, there were no practical measures in place to support this.

It is also interesting to note that the section on environmental matters, which appeared in the 1998 policy, was the last section of that policy, consistent with all previous policies where the environment receives last mention. This, along with the lack of clarity, vision, and clearly-defined steps for achieving sustainability and pollution prevention, would suggest that the 1998 policy, like all others before it, did not have the required commitment to environmental protection in the interest of development. The conflict between environment and energy and the difficulty of reconciling both is aptly illustrated in the position adopted by the then Minister of Energy in 2000. While espousing a philosophy that indicated the "ministry's policy was zero tolerance for environmental damage caused by energy sector companies," the Minister simultaneously conceded to the enormity of the challenge by admitting that "while the sector was the major contributor to the nation's development and to the national economy, it was also the biggest contributor to environment degradation."

THE PRE-EM ACT ERA AND THE HYDROCARBON SECTOR

Common Law

It is generally accepted that the common law functions to protect personal interest and is not extended to the more esoteric concept of environmental rights. It creates the right for plaintiffs to be protected against losses suffered, such as financial loss or enjoyment of property. The reason for the inability of the common law to protect environmental rights is rooted in its philosophical approach. Pollution can only be dealt with effectively by numerical standards and scientific monitoring, while, generally, the common law is based upon imprecise standards unrelated to numerical levels.[8] In attempting to balance competing interests, the common law looks to reasonableness of actions rather than restricting conduct to specific levels. This approach of reasonableness makes it difficult to simulate identical results, as reasonableness is largely based on the circumstances surrounding individual cases. In addition, as the common law is based on balancing competing rights, it stands to reason that the right to take action would be vested only in those directly harmed. Moreover, there are problems with proof, as in pollution cases, for it is not always easy to establish the causal element. The presence of a high level of a particular substance in water may be due to natural as well as man-made factors. In many instances, the common law requires some element of fault with respect to the person causing the pollution and, as most acts of pollution are not due to deliberate acts, the hurdle of establishing fault can become insurmountable. Finally, the common law is

mainly reactive and is seldom capable of being used to facilitate prevention of
environmental harms.

Private Nuisance

The law of nuisance addresses the unlawful interference with a person's use
or enjoyment of land, or of some right over or in connection with it. The
unlawful interference, however, must be balanced with the manner of use of
the defendant's premises, whether it is being used in a reasonable manner
or not. Thus, the balance lies between the reasonableness of the defendant's
activity and the impact on the plaintiff's proprietary rights.[9] In the field of
environmental protection, the common law action of nuisance is the primary
mechanism for private action. The important issue is with whom liability
rests for a nuisance. The general rule is that a person is liable for a nuisance
who either creates or causes it, or continues or adopts it, or who authorised
its creation or continuance.[10]

Of much interest to the hydrocarbon sector is the question of liability for
harm done by previous occupiers of lands. In Trinidad and Tobago, the hydrocarbon sector has emerged largely on the foundation of several successor
companies and there is always the issue of liability for historical harm. It
would appear that an occupier of land is liable for a nuisance even though
it was not created by the present occupier, if such occupier continued the
nuisance while in occupation of it, or if the occupier had knowledge, actual
or constructive, of its existence. In Broder v. Saillard, it was held that the
occupier of a house was liable for allowing the continuance on his premises
of any artificial work which caused a nuisance to a neighbour, even though
it was put there before he took possession.[11] The defining presumption is
whether the person knew of the nuisance and did nothing to prevent it.[12] In
the case of Cushing v. Walker & Son,[13] the Court was very clear in stating
that a defendant who did not know of a nuisance caused by a third party and,
with reasonable efforts could not have discovered such a nuisance, cannot be
held liable for damage caused by the nuisance. This principle was re-stated
in British Road Services Ltd. v. Slater and Another,[14] where the Court held
that the liability of an occupier of land for failing to remedy a nuisance which
he inherited did not arise although the source of the nuisance was plain to be
seen, until the occupier became aware of its being a nuisance or, with ordinary and reasonable care, should have become aware of the nuisance.

An interesting aspect of this liability pertains to the cost of removing the
risk of the nuisance. In Leakey and Others v. National Trust for Places of
Historic Interest or Natural Beauty,[15] it was held that:

....under English law there were both in principle and on authority a general duty imposed on occupiers in relation to hazards occurring on their land, whether the hazards are natural or man-made. A person on whose land a hazard naturally occurred . . . and which encroached or threatened to encroach onto another's land thereby causing or threatening to cause damage, was under a duty, if he knew or ought to have known of the risk of encroachment, to do what was reasonable in all the circumstances to prevent or minimise the risk of the known or foreseeable damage or injury to the other person or his property, and was liable in nuisance if he did not. Where a substantial expenditure was required to prevent or minimise the risk of damage, the occupier's financial resources assessed on a broad basis, were a relevant factor in deciding what was reasonably required of him to discharge his duty . . ."

This decision seems to suggest a limit on what a person is required to do when he inherits a nuisance, in terms of the allocation of resources, to alleviate the nuisance before it causes damage.

Finally in the area of private nuisance, the latest English pronouncement on this matter, with respect to environmental issues, is most instructive. It would seem that the law has firmly come down on the side of having the issue of foreseeability present in its deliberations and if the problem giving rise to the nuisance was not foreseeable when the causal events occurred, the Court would generally reject the claim in nuisance. In the case of Cambridge Water v. Eastern Counties Leather,[16] the defendant operated a tannery that used chlorinated solvents that were not easily soluble in water. The defendant used these solvents from the early 1950s to 1991. There was evidence of some spillage in the 1970s. At the time of use, it was legal to use the substances and there was no evidence to suggest that, in 1976, when the spillage occurred, it would have remained in the water and contaminated the waterworks of the Plaintiff. Lord Goff noted that "the development of the law of negligence in the past sixty years points strongly towards a requirement that such foreseeability should be a prerequisite of liability in damages for nuisance, as it is of liability in negligence."[17] One can argue, therefore, that if the original party could not have foreseen that an act would have led to a nuisance, the present occupier cannot be held liable in nuisance.

Public Nuisance

Mention must be made of public nuisances, which arise when an act or omission materially affects the reasonable comfort and convenience of an entire group of people. It is recognised that a class must be a definable section of the public in the area affected by the alleged nuisance. A requisite number are affected if the nuisance is so widespread in its range or so indiscriminate in its effect that it would be unreasonable to expect one person to take preventive legal measures, as opposed to the community at large: A-G v. PYA Quarries Ltd.[18] A public nuisance may become a tort where a member of the public suffers damage over and above that suffered by others. In such circumstances, an individual can bring a private suit to recover any loss.[19]

Rule in Rylands V. Fletcher

This principle, as originally enunciated in the case of Rylands v. Fletcher,[20] stated that the "person who for his own purposes brings onto land and collects and keeps there anything likely to do mischief if it escapes, must keep it at his peril, and if he does not do so, is prima facie answerable for all the damage which is the natural consequence of its escape." Like nuisance, therefore, this principle tends towards strict liability and is more common in dealing with environmental matters. Many acts of pollution are caused by materials and/or substances which are brought onto land and then escape.

There are several important constraints on the use of the Rule in Rylands v. Fletcher. First and foremost, the use must be non-natural. This has been expanded to mean that the use had to be some special use, bringing with it increased danger to others, and must not merely be the ordinary use of the land, or such a use as is proper for the general benefit of the community.[21] Second, there is the requirement that the substance must escape from the land where it is kept. Third, the principle applies specifically to protect land owners and, therefore, it is generally accepted that there are no actions for personal injuries received from the escape of substances from a non-natural use of land.[22] A turning point in the Rule in Rylands v. Fletcher came in the case of Cambridge Water v. Eastern Counties Leather that was discussed above under nuisance. This decision seems to have extended the doctrine of forseeability in the application of the Rule and, as stated by Lord Goff, "it appears to me to be appropriate now to take the view that foreseeability of damage of the relevant type should be regarded as a prerequisite of liability in damages under this rule."[23] It can be argued, therefore, that if the original party could not have foreseen that an act would have later led to an escape of a non-natural user and the resulting damage, the current occupier cannot be held liable.

Interestingly, in the application of the Rule, case law does not seem to offer instances of a person coming into possession; the Rule speaks of a person bringing or collecting the dangerous thing on the land but not of instances where a third party, in the past, had brought the dangerous thing to the land. Following the case law on nuisance, however, the courts may be prepared to consider imputing the bringing and collecting to a successor in possession.

Negligence

The law of negligence is generally seen as less effective in dealing with environmental matters. Negligence may constitute the majority of civil claims but in environmental litigation it is rare. An action for negligence may be the only remedy available to a person who cannot sue for nuisance or under the Rule in Rylands v. Fletcher. While an action in nuisance can be considered quite strict, in terms of liability the law of negligence is fault-based. It is unlikely, therefore, that where nuisance is irrelevant that negligence would succeed. It is not the intention of this opinion to review the law of negligence; suffice it to say, the three main principles of negligence are that there must be a duty of care owed to the plaintiff; the defendant has breached that duty; and there has been foreseeable damage resulting from the breach. There is no need to have a proprietary interest to bring an action based on negligence; therefore, it widens the potential class of claimants. In one of the few instances where a negligence action succeeded, the defendants discharged a chlorinated solution into a river that was in drought and there was insufficient water to dilute the pollutant. The plaintiff, who abstracted water from the stream to irrigate crops, suffered damage to crops because of the high level of pollutants. One of the defendants in the matter, the regional water authority, was held liable in negligence for failing to advise the plaintiff of the potential danger from the condition of the water he was abstracting.[24]

If a present occupier of lands, through its own act or omission, causes foreseeable damage to a party to whom it owes a duty of care, then there can be liability. Nonetheless, in the case of liability of the present occupier for personal or property harms suffered by a person as a result of the occurrence of an environmental event arising from past activities conducted by parties other than the present occupier, the issue of proving fault can become quite difficult for a plaintiff.

Trespass

A simple tort is that of trespass which involves direct interference with personal or proprietary rights without lawful excuse. This action has not been well developed in environmental matters but, in theory, can arise, for example, by making someone inhale toxic fumes. The difficulties in employing trespass as a common law mechanism for dealing with environmental claims are due to several factors. First, the restriction of directness, as the interference with the personal or proprietary right must be direct rather than consequential.[25] Second, the act of trespass must be intentional or negligent.[26] Third, there must be established a causal link between the directness of an act and the inevitability of its consequences.[27]

Use of the Common Law in Hydrocarbon-Related Matters in Trinidad and Tobago

A review of the judgements from the courts of Trinidad and Tobago does not reveal the use of common law devices such as nuisance, negligence, Rule in Rylands v. Fletcher and trespass in claims for harm due to environmental events, with the exception of one occasion where an interesting decision was rendered. One of the major pollution problems in Trinidad is contamination of land and water by oil. This matter has been of some concern to farmers as oil companies traditionally opt to compensate farmers voluntarily rather than improve their operations. This is largely attributable to the relatively low levels of compensation paid and the adverse media reaction to court proceedings by multinationals. At the end of the oil boom in Trinidad and Tobago in the early 1980s, the State oil companies were handling the bulk of oil production on land. These companies were reluctant to pay compensation at the levels previously paid by the multinationals. This led to confrontation with farmers and, in 1988, a High Court action was filed, alleging that one of the State oil companies had engaged in acts of negligence and nuisance, resulting in pollution of agricultural lands. The 1988 case of Ramcharan Mongru v. Trintoc was dismissed in 1991 on a preliminary objection that jurisdiction for oil pollution cases was properly vested in the Oil and Water Board. The court held that it had no jurisdiction in spite of such a Board not being appointed for over 30 years. The Oil and Water Board should have been appointed under the Oil and Water Board Ordinance (1950) and this would have provided a forum for private action to be taken against parties causing pollution by the discharge of oil. This right of recourse is non-existent, however, due to the failure to appoint a board; this failure bars the pursuit of common law remedies in oil pollution matters. This Oil and Water Board Ordinance has since been repealed and replaced by regulations made under the Petroleum Act (see Petroleum (Pollution Compensation) Regulations, 1997 (Legal Notice No. 134 of 1997). These Regulations preserve the common law remedies, except they can only be pursued after exhaustion of the dispute-resolution procedures outlined in the Regulations.

STATUTORY LAW

This section addresses some of the key elements of the statutory regime for protection of the environment as it applies to hydrocarbon operations. As a preliminary observation, there are numerous pieces of legislation capable of protecting the environment although, as seen below, deficiencies in these pieces of legislation (such as vagueness of language, non-passage of subsidiary legislation, lack of punitive sanctions, and absence of precise standards) and institutional weaknesses, rendered enforcement non-existent.[28] The hydrocarbon sector benefited from this malaise and, as a result, was allowed to prosper in a legal framework that eschewed sound environmental management.

AIR POLLUTION

At the onset, it must be emphasised that there is no existing legislation that identifies specific air pollutants. There are several pieces of legislation in place, however, that can be used in varying degrees, to deal with the problem of air pollution, either by facilitating the enforcement measures, or by introducing regulatory provisions.

One mechanism that can be used to address air pollution is the law pertaining to nuisance. The essence of the tort of nuisance is that a plaintiff or claimant has had his use or enjoyment of property adversely affected by the conduct of another. Accordingly, smoke, smells and fumes, have been held to constitute an actionable nuisance when it interferes with the use and enjoyment of property. The Public Health Ordinance,[29] Section 69, imposes a duty on the part of local authorities to initiate action to abate nuisances. Similarly, by virtue of Section 221(1) of the Municipal Corporations Act,[30] councils are provided with the authority to enact regulations for the suppression of nuisances, but this provision has not been employed.

The next tool for addressing air pollution is through the use of industry or activity specific legislation. Section 29 (1)(j) of the Petroleum Act[31] provides for the issuance of regulations to prevent air pollution by those engaged in petroleum operations. Regulations in this area are quite scanty with only Regulation 43(s) of the Petroleum Regulations[32] making mention of the need for a person granted a licence to conduct petroleum operations to be required to take all reasonable precautions and safety measures to prevent the liberation of gas, causing pollution of surrounding air.

WATER POLLUTION

Fresh Water

The regulation of water pollution operates on different levels. First, there is the level of industry. The most important in this area is the petroleum sector. Water pollution is an imminent risk in a country dominated by energy sector activities. Accordingly, Section 29(1)(j) of the Petroleum Act[33] provides

for the making of regulations to prevent water pollution and for compensation caused by any such pollution. The Petroleum Act (Petroleum (Pollution
Compensation) Regulations)[34] was passed to address the problem of water
pollution and said compensation.

The situation with respect to tidal rivers is separately covered by Regulation 42(2)(c) of the Petroleum Regulations.[35] This requires a licensee to ensure that precautions are taken to avoid pollution of tidal rivers.

Moving away from specific industries, there is a plethora of laws that can
be used to address the issue of water pollution. A useful starting point is the
Litter Act[36] which creates the principal offence of littering. As per Section
3(1), this offence occurs when "a person who without reasonable excuse—
(a) deposits any litter in or on any public place other than (i) in a receptacle
placed for the purpose of collecting it; or (ii) in or at any approved site..."
Litter is defined in Section 2(1) as "any solid or liquid material or product
or combination of solid or liquid materials or products including but not limited to any bottles, tins, logs, sawdust, derelict vehicles, cartons, packages,
packing materials, paper, glass, food, animal remains, garbage, debris, sand,
gravel, stone, aggregate, dirt, waste (including any human and animal waste)
or any other refuse, or rubbish or waste material, and any other material or
product that is designated as litter..." Waste is defined in Section 2(1) as
including "domestic waste, industrial waste or commercial waste." A public
place is generally defined as everywhere that the public has access to, or areas
owned by the State and includes ". . . (iii) any waters to which the public has
access without payment of any fee for bathing or for other recreational purposes; (iv) every wharf, pier, or jetty (whether under the control of the Port
Authority or not) to which the public has access..." As per Section 2(1) of the
Litter Act, premises include natural watercourses and drains.

Protection of water resources can also be found in Section 18(1) of the
Waterworks and Water Conservation Act,[37] which prohibits "the throwing
or depositing of any tree, log, branches, brushwood, stone, gravel, soil, or
other refuse in any watercourse or in any channel, drain or outfall for water
constructed or maintained by or on behalf of the State." Section 15(1) of the
Waterworks and Water Conservation Act provides for the making of regulations for the governance of Water Improvement Areas and regulations have
been so made, such as those concerning the Caroni River and the Water Improvement Area (Caroni Irrigation) Regulations.[38]

It is also a criminal offence to commit certain acts of water pollution. Section 73(1) of the Summary Offence Act[39] creates liability even for owners of
land who cause water pollution affecting other lands.

By far, one piece of legislation that provides extensively for water pollution is the Public Health Ordinance.[40] Section 54(1)(c) of the Public Health

Ordinance vests power in local authorities to make regulations for keeping drains clean and in repair. This is an important power as drains frequently feed into watercourses; however, this power is yet to be exercised. These local authorities are also required by Section 56C to maintain, cleanse and empty all public drains under their control. Specific requirements for prevention of water pollution are contained in Section 57(1). This section prohibits "the disposal in any drain of any matter likely to injure the drain or to interfere with the free flow of its contents, or to affect prejudicially disposal of its contents; any chemical refuse or waste stream, or any liquid of a temperature higher than one hundred and ten degrees Fahrenheit, being a liquid which when so heated is, either alone or in combination with the contents of the sewer or drain, dangerous, or the cause of a nuisance, or prejudicial to health; and any petroleum spirit, or carbide of calcium." Section 68(1) addresses the deposit of offensive matter in any river, drain, or watercourse.

The Public Health Ordinance also employs nuisance to address water pollution. Under Section 70(1)(j), it is a nuisance to have the refuse, or washings of any town, village, or building falling into any harbour, river, watercourse, ravine, pond, or ditch or on any foreshore. Finally, Section 90 provides general power over water resources in districts falling under the jurisdiction of local authorities. It is stipulated that "a person is liable who defiles or pollutes any well, watercourse, stream, lake, pond, or reservoir forming part of the water supply of the district of a local authority, or permits or suffers drainage or refuse from his land or premises to flow into or be deposited in such well, watercourse, stream, lake, pond or reservoir." According to Section 92, the local authority shall be deemed to have control over all wells, watercourses, streams, lakes, ponds, and reservoirs within their district.

The concept of the right vested in local authorities to assist in combating water pollution is extended in the Municipal Corporations Act.[41] As per Section 232(e), municipal corporations are responsible for the construction and maintenance of all drains and watercourses, except main watercourses and highway watercourses. Section 145 of the Municipal Corporations Act renders liable anyone "who impedes the free flow of water in any ditch, drain or water-course in or adjoining any street within a Municipality or into any ditch, drain or water-course on any land into or through which water from any such street flows, or any ditch, drain or water-course under any such street."

Not only does the law cover the actual deposit of foreign matter into water sources but also the alteration of watercourses. One example of such legislation is the Malaria Abatement Act.[42] Section 9 of the Malaria Abatement Act deals with the situation where someone damages or injures, or, in any manner, blocks or obstructs or diverts the bed or the flow of any main drainage channel. The Malaria Abatement Act empowers the Minister to make detailed regulations to manage watercourses and to prevent the deposit of rubbish or filth. No such regulations have been made.

Another piece of legislation that can be used to address physical alteration of watercourses is the Highways Act.[43] Section 36(3) of the Highways Act provides liability for any person who, without the consent of the highway authority, alters, obstructs or interferes with a ditch, gutter, drain, watercourse, bridge, culvert, tunnel, pipe or barrier which has been constructed, laid or erected by the Authority or which is under the control of the Authority.

No discussion can be complete without mention of the role of the Water and Sewerage Authority ("WASA") of the Republic of Trinidad and Tobago. Section 42 of the Water and Sewerage Authority Act[44] places responsibility on WASA for maintaining and developing the waterworks and other property relating thereto; for administering the supply of water thereby established; for promoting the conservation and proper use of water resources; and for providing water in the Republic of Trinidad and Tobago. The power to protect water resources extends to the making of necessary regulations for protecting water resources from pollution, as contained in Section 51(1). Byelaws have been made to prevent pollution of two water systems, the Courland Waterworks and the Quare River of Valencia. These are known as the Prevention of Water Pollution (Quare River, Valencia) Bye Laws[45] made under Section 51(1) of the Water and Sewage Act Chap 54: 40. Liability for acts of water pollution is provided for in Section 53(1) which ascribes liability to any person who allows to be polluted any spring, well or adit, the water from which is used or likely to be used for human consumption or domestic purposes, or for manufacturing food or drink for human consumption.

Marine

There are many pieces of legislation that could potentially impact on hydrocarbon activities in the marine areas of Trinidad and Tobago.

Section 2(2) of the *Oil Pollution of Territorial Waters Act*:[46] "The waters to which this Act applies are the territorial waters of Trinidad and Tobago and the waters of the harbours therein." *Section 3(1)*: "If any oil is discharged, or allowed to escape into any waters to which this Act applies from any vessel, the owner or master of the vessel from which the oil is discharged or allowed to escape is liable on summary conviction to a fine of ten thousand dollars and to imprisonment for twelve months."

As per Section 232(I) of the Municipal Corporations Act,[47] Municipal Corporations are responsible for the "maintenance, control and enhancement of the physical environment including monitoring water-courses, beaches and water-front areas, swamps, forests, game sanctuaries, savannas, parks and other open spaces."

Section 12(2) of the Archipelagic Waters and Exclusive Economic Zone Act:[48] "The passage of a foreign ship shall be considered prejudicial to the peace, good order or security of Trinidad and Tobago where it engages in the archipelagic waters in the following activities . . . (h) any act of wilful and serious pollution contrary to the Convention..." Section 19: "Trinidad and Tobago in the exclusive economic zone has (a) sovereign rights over—(i) the exploration and exploitation, conservation and management of the living and non-living resources of the waters super adjacent to the sea-bed and of the sea-bed and its subsoil . . . (b) jurisdiction over— . . . (iii) the protection and preservation of the marine environment . . ." Section 22: "No States, international organisations, nor person shall without the consent in writing of the President . . . engage within the exclusive economic zone in any of the following activities—(a) the exploration and exploitation, conservation and management of living and non-living natural resources . . . (f) the protection and preservation of the marine environment . . . " Section 32: "The President may make regulations for implementing the provisions of this Act for . . . (a) protection and preservation of the marine environment, and the prevention, reduction and control of pollution of that environment arising from—(i) land-based sources including rivers, estuaries, pipelines and outfall structures; (ii) sea-bed activities under the jurisdiction of Trinidad and Tobago and artificial islands installations and structures under its jurisdiction . . . "

Section 3(1) of the Continental Shelf Act:[49] "Any rights exercisable by Trinidad and Tobago outside territorial waters with respect to the seabed and subsoil and their natural resources are hereby *vested* in the State. (2) A person who conducts or attempts to carry out any activities...without first having obtained a licence from the Minister, shall be deemed to have infringed these rights . . . " Section 7(1): "If any oil is discharged or escapes into any part of the sea in a designated area—(a) from a pipe-line; or (b) (otherwise than from a ship) as the result of any operations for the exploration of the seabed and subsoil or the exploitation of their natural resources in a designated area, the owner of the pipeline or, as the case may be, the person carrying out the operations is guilty . . . " Section_13 gives the Minister the right to make regulations to carry out the Act —none has been made.

Section 21 of the Harbours Act"[50] "Any person who throws any ballast or any stones, sand, gravel, dirt or rubbish into the Gulf of Paria, at any place where there is less depth of water than eighteen meters, is liable . . ." Section 24: "No sand, shingle, ballast, stones, gravel, coals, bricks, tiles or loose earth shall be deposited so as to be within three meters of the edge of any wharf . . ."

Section 3(1) of the Marine Areas (Preservation and Enhancement) Act: "The Minister may by Order designate any portion of the marine areas of Trinidad and Tobago as a restricted area where he considers that special steps are necessary for—(a) preserving and enhancing the natural beauty of such areas; (b) the protection of flora and fauna of such areas; (c) the promotion of the enjoyment by the public of such areas; (d) the promotion of scientific study and research in respect of such areas." Section 6(1): "The Minister may make regulations generally for the purpose of giving effect to this Act, and in particular . . . provide for . . . (a) the protection of the flora and fauna in restricted areas and the establishment of offences in connection therewith; (b) the care, control and management of the restricted area; (c) the regulation of the use and enjoyment of such areas . . ."

As noted, the Litter Act[51] creates the principal offence of littering in public places. A public place is generally defined as everywhere that the public has access or area owned by the state and includes ". . . (iii) any waters to which the public has access without payment of any fee for bathing or for other rec-reational purposes; (iv) every wharf, pier, or jetty (whether under the control of the Port Authority or not) to which the public has access . . ."

Section 70(1) of the Public Health Ordinance "A licensee shall ensure that operations do not unreasonably interfere with other activities in the area and, in the case of operations in submarine areas, care shall be taken to avoid pollution of the seas, beaches or tidal rivers to ensure that navigation, agriculture, fishing, authorised scientific researches, and conservation of the living resources of the sea are not unjustifiably hindered, and likewise that no damage is caused to submarine cables and pipe-lines . . . " Section 70(2): "For the purpose of this Ordinance the drainage, refuse, or washings of any town, village, or building falling into any harbour, river, watercourse, ravine, pond or ditch or on to any foreshore so as to be a nuisance or injurious to health shall be deemed to be nuisances liable to be dealt with summarily in manner provided by this Ordinance."

Section 29(1)(j) of the Petroleum Act,: "The President may make any such regulations...for the prevention of pollution of . . . water . . . and for com-pensation thereof . . . " Regulation 42(2)(c) of the Petroleum Regulations, "A licensee shall ensure...in the case of operations in submarine areas, care shall be taken to avoid pollution of the seas, beaches or tidal rivers to ensure that navigation, agriculture, fishing, authorised scientific researches and conser-vation of living resources of the sea are not unjustifiably hindered . . . "

Regulation 42(2) (c) of the Petroleum Regulations: "A licensee shall ensure that operations do not unreasonably interfere with other activities in the area and, in the case of operations in submarine areas, care shall be taken to avoid pollution of the agriculture, fishing, authorised scientific researches, and conservation of the living resources of the sea are not unjustifiably hindered, and likewise that no damage is caused to submarine cables and pipe-lines."

Regulation 9 of the Petroleum (Testing, Storage, etc.) Regulations:_"The following rules in respect of the unloading or loading or transhipment of petroleum, crude petroleum or dangerous petroleum within any declared Harbour of Trinidad and Tobago or within the territorial waters of Trinidad and Tobago shall be observed . . . (b) No petroleum, crude petroleum or dangerous petroleum shall be discharged or allowed to escape into the waters of any declared Harbour of Trinidad and Tobago or into the territorial waters of Trinidad and Tobago."

Mines, Borings and Quarries Act,[52] Drilling Regulations Section 21: "Whenever any well is found to be in such a condition that, in the opinion of the Engineer—(a) water may have access to oilsands; (b) seepage of oil, water, mud, or pitch from either inside or outside and string of casing in the well may cause pollution to land, watercourses, foreshore or sea; (c) the mechanical condition of the well or any surface fitting is dangerous, the Engineer may by notice in writing to be served on the owner, agent or manager require him to carry out such measures as [he] may direct to repair, partially plug or completely abandon the well within a period of time to be specified in such notice. Should the requirements of any such notice not be complied with the Engineer or any other person authorised in writing by the [Minister] may enter the property and take all measures necessary to carry out the requirements of such notice . . . " Regulation 20(4):, "Whenever any well is found to be in such a condition that, in the opinion of the Engineer— . . . (b) seepage of oil, water, mud or pitch from either inside or outside any string or casing in the well may cause pollution to . . . foreshore or sea . . . the Engineer may . . . such measures . . . to repair, partially plug or completely abandon the well . . . "

BIOLOGICAL DIVERSITY

Flora and Fauna

There are several pieces of legislation in Trinidad and Tobago that address the protection of sensitive species. Section 3(2) of the Conservation of Wildlife Act[53] provides for the establishment of game sanctuaries. Section 5(1) states that "Except as provided by section 10, no person shall hunt or shall be a member of a party engaged in hunting any protected animal . . . " The Minister with responsibility for wild life can make regulations under the Conservation of Wildlife Act to add or delete from the schedule of protected animals. Section 7(1) states, "no person shall hunt or be a member of a party engaged in hunting any animal during the close season." Section 18(1) provides that "No animal shall be exported or carried coastwise without the written permission of the Chief Game Warden."

It is also a criminal offence to kill, maim or wound species of fauna. Section 16 of the Summary Offences Act[54] mandates, "Any person who unlawfully and maliciously kills, maims or wounds any dog, bird, beast or other animal is liable . . . ."

Turning to flora, there is limited statutory protection. The Forests Act[55] creates certain offences with respect to the protection of trees on state lands (this has now been extended to private lands). Section 8 states, "Any person who—(a) pastures cattle or permits cattle to trespass; (b) fells, cuts, girdles, marks, lops, taps, bleeds any tree or injures by fire or otherwise any tree or timber; (c) causes any damage by negligence in felling any tree by cutting or dragging any timber; (c) kindles, keeps or carries any fire except at such seasons and in such manner as the Minister may from time to time notify; (e) subject to any manufacturing process or transports or removes any forest products; or (f) enters a prohibited area, is liable . . . "

There is also criminal liability pursuant to Section 19 of the Summary Offences Act: [56] "Any person who steals, or unlawfully and maliciously roots up, destroys or damages the whole or part of any tree, sapling, shrub or underwood, wheresoever growing . . . shall be liable . . ."

Town and Country Planning could also play a role in protecting flora as per Section 20(1) of the Town and Country Planning Act,[57] which states: "If it appears to the Minister that it is expedient in the interests of amenity to make provision for the preservation of any tree, trees or woodlands in any area, he may for that purpose make an order . . . (a) prohibiting . . . the cutting down, topping, lopping or wilful destruction of trees . . . (b) for securing the replanting . . . of any part of a woodland area that is felled in the course of forestry operations . . . "

In providing development permission under Second Schedule, Part IV, Section 5 of the Town and Country Planning Act,[58] Town and Country Planning may make provisions for the "preservation or protection of forests, woods, trees, shrubs, plants and flowers." These statutory provisions have had little effect on the hydrocarbon sector and, therefore, awareness of the hydrocarbon sector to sensitive species is almost non-existent.

ECOSYSTEMS

Because Trinidad and Tobago is an island, sensitive areas will, of course, include marine, wetlands, and land areas. This article does not propose to address these different sensitive areas, but merely to look at one such category, namely the inland ecosystem. There are many statutory provisions that affect land management. A few will be mentioned for illustrative purposes.

Section 17(1) of the Agricultural Fires Act,[59] states "the period commencing on the first day of December in any one year and ending on the thirtieth day of June in the next succeeding year shall be for the purpose of this Act be deemed to be the fire season." Section 18(4) mandates "no person except the holder of a permit issued under subsection (2) shall set fire during a fire season for any purpose except cooking." The Forests Act[60] creates certain offences with respect to the protection of state lands which are deemed to be Forest Reserves. Section 2 of the Forests Act states, "in this Act 'prohibited area' means a specified area being part of a Forest Reserve or State lands declared by the Minister by Order to be a prohibited area." Section 6(1) of the State Lands Act[61] states: "The Commissioner shall have the management of all lands of the State, and shall be charged with the prevention of squatting and encroachment upon the same and of spoil and injury to the woods and forests on such lands . . . and shall superintend the settlement and allotment of State lands and the laying out of village lots . . ."

Section 5(2) of the Town and Country Planning Act[62] requires that "Not later than seven years after the commencement of this Act . . . the Minister shall submit a development plan . . . indicating the manner in which he proposes that land in Trinidad and Tobago may be used . . . (3) A development plan . . . may in particular—(a) define the sites of proposed roads, public and other buildings and works, airfields, parks, pleasure grounds, nature reserves and open spaces; (b) allocate areas of land for agricultural, residential, industrial or other purposes . . . " Section 20(1) of the Town and Country Planning Act states: "If it appears to the Minister that it is expedient in the interests of amenity to make provision for the preservation of any tree, trees or woodlands in any area, he may for that purpose make an order . . . (a) prohibiting . . . the cutting down, topping, lopping or wilful destruction of trees . . . (b) for securing the replanting . . . of any part of a woodland area that is felled in the course of forestry operations . . . " In providing development permission under Second Schedule, Part IV, Section 5 of the Town and Country Planning Act,[63] Town and Country Planning may make provisions for "preservation or protection of forests, woods, trees, shrubs, plants and flowers."

Section 16 of the *Petroleum Act*[64] provides that "Within two months after the expiration or sooner determination of an Exploration and Production (Public Petroleum Rights) Licence, as provided for in the Regulations . . . the licensee shall . . . (c) to the like extent restore, as far as may be possible to their natural and original condition the surface of the licensed area . . . " *Section 29(1)(j)* states that "the President may make any such regulations . . . for the prevention of pollution of land . . . and for compensation thereof

. . . " *Petroleum (Pollution Compensation)_Regulations, Regulation 3* states that "for the purposes of these Regulations, land is deemed to be polluted as the result of petroleum operations if it is polluted by—(a) the escape of oil or salt water or any solid or liquid matter, whether of a nature similar to oil or water or not . . . "

Regulation 18(1) of the Drilling Regulations,[65] made pursuant to the *Mines, Borings and Quarries Act,* provides for approved precautions to be taken to prevent any uncontrolled flow of oil or gas during drilling. *Regulation 20(4)* states: "Whenever any well is found to be in such a condition that, in the opinion of the Engineer— . . . (b) seepage of oil, water, mud or pitch from either inside or outside any string or casing in the well may cause pollution to land . . . the Engineer may . . . (take?) such measures . . . to repair, partially plug or completely abandon the well . . ."

Again, despite the presence of many pieces of legislation that seek to protect land resources in Trinidad and Tobago, there has been little application of them to the hydrocarbon sector.

HAZARDOUS SUBSTANCES

In Trinidad and Tobago, the sparse legal regime for dealing with hazardous substances concentrated on the presence of chemicals and pesticides. The principal piece of legislation for addressing the issue of chemicals is the Pesticides and Toxic Chemicals Act.[66] This Act was intended to establish a specific regime to deal with chemicals and pesticides. Section 4A(1) of the Pesticides and Toxic Chemicals Act states "that no person shall manufacture, import, sell, use, store in marketable quantities, or transport a controlled product unless the product is registered and that the person does so in the prescribed manner." Section 2 of the Pesticides and Toxic Chemicals Act defines a "controlled product" to mean any pesticide or toxic chemical. The Pesticides and Toxic Chemicals Act is, more or less, a framework piece of legislation and Section 12(1) empowers the Minister to make regulations for carrying into effect the provisions of this Act. By Legal Notice 225 of 1987, regulations were made to provide for the registration and import licensing requirements for pesticides. Further, Legal Notice 226 of 1987 provides specific pesticides importation regulations, and Legal Notice 227 of 1987 addresses licensing of premises requirements. It is worth noting that while a regime is being developed to deal with pesticides, nothing is being done with respect to chemicals.

It is entirely feasible for trade laws to be used to control the importation of chemicals. Section 44 of the Customs Act[67] provides the authority for the President to prohibit importation of any goods whatsoever. Authority is vested by the Trade Ordinance[68] for similar restrictions. Section 4(2) of the Trade Ordinance provides the authority for prohibiting the importation of any goods or class or description of goods.

NOISE POLLUTION

There are several bits and pieces of domestic legislation that can be used to address the problem of noise pollution. The general law of nuisance is of some value. Public Health Ordinance,[69] Section 69, makes it incumbent on every local authority to ascertain nuisances and take steps to have them abated. Noise is a well-known nuisance in the common law and, therefore, this provision can make some inroads in dealing with the problem of noise pollution. Similarly, Section 221(1) of the Municipal Corporations Act[70] provides for the making of byelaws, rules and regulations for the prevention and suppression of nuisances. Municipal Corporations, therefore, can provide specific rules to deal with noise pollution, but this has not taken place.

WASTE

Hazardous Waste

There is really no legal regime in the Republic of Trinidad and Tobago for dealing with hazardous waste, although some pieces of legislation exist. In dealing with specific industries, some legislative support can be found. As an example, there are some controls in place for pesticides and toxic chemicals. According to Section 12(1) of the Pesticides and Toxic Chemicals,[71] the Minister may make regulations with respect to "the types of packages in which controlled products may be imported, transported or sold, and as to the disposal of such packages after use, and as to the disposal of unwanted stocks of controlled products and of waste materials containing controlled products." Although no regulations have been made with respect to chemicals, Regulation 4(1) of the Pesticides (Registration and Import Licensing) Regulations[72] requires information on methods of safe disposal of waste pesticide and any containers in which pesticide was stored, while Regulation 16 of the Pesticides (Licensing of Premises) Regulations[73] requires that facilities for the disposal of empty packages and containers for waste and spilled or waste pesticides and toxic chemicals shall be such as to avoid contamination of the environment. Further, according to Regulations 16(2), covered dustbins and other receptacles for waste and spillage shall be made of materials able to resist corrosion by pesticide waste and shall be made sufficiently secure to discourage the removal of waste material by unauthorised persons and to prevent spillage of pesticides.

Moreover, Section 26(2)(d) of the Petroleum Act[74] provides that where any facility, right or privilege is required in order that petroleum operations may be properly and conveniently carried out, such ancillary rights include a right to dispose of water or other liquid matter obtained from petroleum operations or any by-product works. In addition, Regulation 18(2) prohibits the waste of petroleum products. This principle is extended by Regulation 43(s) of the Petroleum Regulations,[75] made pursuant to the Petroleum Act,[76] which mandates the taking of all reasonable precautions and safety measures to prevent all waste.

Non-Hazardous Waste

There are several pieces of legislation dealing with non-hazardous waste. The Litter Act,[77] discussed above, creates the principal offence of littering. Littering, to some extent, is also controlled by Section 47(c) of the Highways Act[78] which prohibits the deposit of anything whatsoever on a highway which may damage the highways. Further, according to Section 54(1) of the Highways Act it is an offence for any person to deposit anything whatsoever on a highway; or to allow any oil or corrosive matter or any filth, dirt, lime, or other offensive matter or thing to run or flow onto a highway from any adjoining premises.

PLANNING PROCESS

The planning influence on the hydrocarbon sector was limited, in the main, to two pieces of legislation. First and foremost, control over petroleum operations was vested in the Ministry of Energy and Energy Industries. The Petroleum Act,[79] Section 6(1) states, *"no person shall engage in petroleum operations . . . unless he first obtains a license . . . "* Section 9(1) states, "where the Minister . . . decides to grant a license, he shall grant a license . . . upon such terms and conditions he considers appropriate." Section 2(1) states, "Petroleum Operations means the operations related to the various phases of the petroleum industry . . . and manufacture of petrochemicals." The other piece of legislation having some limited impact was the Town and Country Planning Act.[80] The Town and Country Planning Division has some input in the establishment of industrial undertakings. What is important to note is that none of these pieces of legislation expressly provided for the environmental impact assessment process as a tool for ensuring that developments in the hydrocarbon sector posed no significant threat to the environment.

REMEDIES IN STATUTORY LAW

Remedies in statutory law for personal or property harms suffered by a person as a result of the occurrence of an environmental event arising from past activities conducted by parties other than the current occupier are somewhat limited. The first area of interest is created under the Petroleum Act.[81] By virtue of the Petroleum (Pollution Compensation) Regulations,[82] Regulation 4 creates a right of complaint for pollution caused by petroleum operations and the Regulations go on to establish an alternative dispute resolution procedure for having the claim settled.

SPILLS, RELEASES AND OTHER INCIDENTS

There is no specific legislation dealing with record-keeping and monitoring; however, in the hydrocarbon sector, the Ministry of Energy has been quite pro-active in this area. The situation was addressed through the inclusion of conditions contained in the license, even though there existed no legislation to expressly compel notification of spills, releases and other incidents. The Petroleum Act,[83] Section 6(1) provided that "no person shall engage in petroleum operations . . . unless he first obtains a license . . . " It is normal for the Ministry to use the licensing regime to stipulate a course of action to deal with spills, releases, and other such incidents.

RECORD KEEPING AND MONITORING

In Trinidad and Tobago, there exists no legislation to expressly compel record-keeping and monitoring. This does not mean, however, that record-keeping and monitoring were, of necessity, not required. Due to the fact that petroleum operations were vested in the Ministry of Energy, it insisted on record-keeping and monitoring as part of its licensing regime. As noted above, the Petroleum Act,[84] Section 6(1) provided that "no person shall engage in petroleum operations . . . unless he first obtains a license . . . " Section 9(1) provides "Where the Minister . . . decides to grant a license, he shall grant a license . . . upon such terms and conditions he considers appropriate."

It was also possible that conditions of record-keeping and monitoring could be attached to approvals granted under the Town and Country Planning Act.

PUBLIC NUISANCE

As mentioned previously, public nuisances carry civil, as well as criminal consequences. Section 70 of the Summary Offences Act[85] states that "Any person who causes a nuisance to the public, and any person who at any time takes any part in causing such a nuisance, and any person occupying or having control over any house, yard or premises of whatever nature, who permits such nuisance, is . . . liable on summary conviction . . . ."

THE POST-EM ACT ERA AND THE HYDROCARBON SECTOR

The EM Act did not remove any of the common law rights that existed prior to its enactment so the various common law actions, described in Section 3.1 above, continue to exist unhindered. Further, the EM Act did not repeal other statutory laws discussed in Section 3.2 above, although, in many instances, there is significant legislative overlap. This, of course, creates potential for much chaos as, for example, a person may obtain a permit to discharge pollutants into a water course, but this can then lead to liability under one of the several other pieces of legislation dealing with water pollution.

The EM Act established a new legal and institutional framework for the protection of the environment. The EM Act was a revolutionary piece of legislation in that it established the EMA and made it the primary state agency responsible for enforcing environmental laws and standards. This represents a major departure from the historical position, which saw the Ministry of Energy being the dominant party responsible for all hydrocarbon issues, including those dealing with the environment.

In terms of legal norms, the EMA was mandated by the EM Act to develop rules addressing certain key environmental sectors, namely, water pollution, air pollution, planning and development, noise pollution, sensitive areas, sensitive species, wastes and hazardous substances. The EM Act also made provisions for enacting rules to promote proper record-keeping and monitoring. In addition, the EMA was mandated to ensure spill contingency plans were part of the requirements of doing business in Trinidad and Tobago. Thus, arguably, the EMA and its statutory mandate represent the biggest challenge to the hydrocarbon sector. Analysing the environmental challenges to the hydrocarbon sector demonstrates how critical the emerging role of the EMA is proving to be.

AIR POLLUTION AND THE EM ACT

The role of the EMA in dealing with air pollution is of great significance. Section 49 of the EM Act empowers the EMA to "investigate the environment generally and such premises and vehicles as it thinks necessary for the purpose of—(a) ascertaining the extent of air . . . pollution and the significant sources of pollutants which by their release cause or contribute to such pollution . . . " Section 50(1) prescribes that the EMA may "require a facility to apply for and grant permits to authorize any process releasing air pollutants subject to such terms and conditions as it considers appropriate." This section mandates the EMA to develop standards for emission of air pollutants by identifying the characteristics of air pollutants and permissible release limits. Section 51(1) stipulates that "No person shall release or cause to be released any air pollutant into the environment which is in violation of any applicable standards, conditions or permit requirements under this Act." Rules for managing air pollution have been drafted and submitted for public comment, pursuant to the requirement of the EM Act. The draft rules have identified a specific number of air pollutants and the limits for stack emissions.

WATER POLLUTION AND THE EM ACT

As is expected, the most prominent role for the control of water pollution is now vested in the EMA. The EMA has been given the widest possible mandate to deal with water pollution and, based on its legislative-derived authority; it is possibly, the agency with the single largest responsibility for water pollution. According to the EM Act, Section 52(1), the EMA shall "investigate the environment generally and such premises and vehicles as it thinks necessary for the purposes of ascertaining the extent of water pollution and significant sources of water pollutants and characterizing or describing that pollution." This section goes on to require the EMA to maintain a register of water pollutants as prescribed by the rule which must contain data identifying the quantity, conditions, or concentrations relevant to the identification of each pollutant. Based on its research, the EMA is required to develop and implement a programme for the management of such pollution which shall include the registration and further characterisation of significant sources of any ongoing or intermittent releases of water pollutants into the environment.

In 2001, the Water Pollution Rules, 2001[86] were laid in Parliament by the Minister responsible for the Environment, subject to the negative resolution of Parliament, and have subsequently become the law of Trinidad and Tobago. The overall objective of the Water Pollution Rules, 2001 is to improve and preserve water quality in Trinidad and Tobago. The Water Pollution Rules, 2001 identify specific water pollutants and create a requirement that entities register with the EMA if their discharge of these water pollutants is above a certain limit. The Water Pollution Rules, 2001 then create an upper limit where a permit would be required if any person is desirous of discharging water pollutants above the maximum permissible discharge limit. The Water Pollution Rules, 2001 have, however, only been enforced by the EMA from 2007.

NOISE POLLUTION AND THE EM ACT

There is clear authority vested in the EMA to solve the problem of noise pollution. Noise is considered a pollutant under Section 2 of the EM Act. The specific management of noise pollution is subsequently provided for in Section 49(1) of the EM Act which stipulates that the EMA "shall, as soon as practicable after the commencement of the Act, investigate the environment generally and such premises and vehicles as it thinks necessary for the purpose of ascertaining the extent of noise pollution and the significant sources of pollutants which by their release cause or contribute to such pollution." Further, the EMA is required to create a register of noise polluting sources and to implement a programme to manage such pollution. The specific offence of noise pollution is covered by Section 51(2) which states that "no person shall emit or cause to be emitted any noise greater in volume or intensity than prescribed in rules made under Section 26 or by any applicable standards, conditions or requirements under this Act." The Noise Pollution (Control) Rules[87] are now the law of Trinidad and Tobago and a precise standard for industry of 75 decibels for non-impulse sounds has been stipulated. A variation, which functions like a permit, is required if a facility exceeds the prescribed standards due to its normal operations.

BIOLOGICAL DIVERSITY AND THE EM ACT

Environmentally Sensitive Areas

Section 41 of the EM Act provides for the designation of environmentally sensitive areas. The Rules for Designation of Sensitive Areas (Legal Notice Number 64 of 2001) are now the law of Trinidad and Tobago. There are two major concerns that participants in the hydrocarbon sector may have with respect to these Rules. First, Rule 4(1)(c) provides for limitation on the use of the designated area and Rule 4(1)(d) provides for the taking of appropriate mitigation measures. If hydrocarbon activities are being conducted in an area that is deemed designated, or is subsequently designated, the operators may find themselves having to operate against a different criteria than non-designated areas, especially with regard to potential environmental threats to the area. Moreover, stricter standards are emerging for sensitive areas and these are reflected in the water pollution and noise standards.

Environmentally Sensitive Species

Section 41 of the EM Act provides for the designation of environmentally sensitive species. The Rules for Designation of Sensitive Species (Legal Notice Number 63 of 2001) have been enacted and can potentially affect the hydrocarbon sector. Rule 4(1)(d) provides the basis for prohibiting activities for the protection of environmentally sensitive species and Rule 4(1)(f) provides for the taking of appropriate mitigation measures. Thus, if a species is designated as environmentally sensitive and it is discovered in the vicinity of existing or proposed hydrocarbon operations, it could be that those operations might be significantly restricted or even prohibited. Further, *Rule 4(1) (f)* provides for the taking of appropriate mitigation measures and this may translate into higher costs of operations.

HAZARDOUS SUBSTANCES AND THE EM ACT

According to the EM Act, Section 26, the Minister may make rules subject to negative resolution of Parliament, "for the designation of hazardous substances or categories of hazardous substances and the performance standards, procedures, safeguards and licensing or permitting requirements in accordance with which such hazardous substances shall be handled . . ." Section 59 of the EM Act provides for the development by the EMA of a programme for the designation of specific hazardous substances. Section 60 goes on to create an offence of handling hazardous substances without the grant of a licence or permit by the EMA. To date, no rules have been made with respect to the management of hazardous substances.

HAZARDOUS WASTE AND THE EM ACT

Parliament clearly contemplated that the EMA would be responsible for the development of a hazardous waste regulatory body in the Republic of

Trinidad and Tobago. According to the EM Act, Section 26, the Minister may make rules subject to negative resolution of Parliament, "for... the definition of various categories of waste, the requirements with respect to the handling and disposal of such categories of waste, and the licensing of facilities at which such wastes are handled or disposed; and the design, construction, operation, maintenance and monitoring of facilities or processes for the control of pollution and the handling of wastes."

The management of waste is provided for in Section 55(1), which requires the EMA to investigate the environment, generally, and such premises and vehicles as it thinks necessary for the purposes of ascertaining the volume and nature of wastes which are handled and disposed of into the environment. The EMA is also responsible for identifying and characterising the different categories and the significant sources of such wastes. Pursuant to this undertaking, under Section 55(2), the EMA is required to develop and implement a programme for the management of such wastes, which may include the registration and further characterisation of significant sources of wastes being disposed of into the environment.

As part of its management function, under Section 56, the EMA is required to submit to the Minister of the Environment a programme to define those wastes which should be deemed "hazardous wastes"; to establish requirements for the handling and disposal of hazardous wastes; to establish appropriate standards and design criteria for hazardous waste handling and disposal facilities; and to establish licensing and permitting requirements with respect to such wastes. In addition, by virtue of Section 57(1), the EMA may require and grant permits to authorise any person's waste disposal activities, or licenses for the operation of any waste handling facility, subject to such terms and conditions as are suitable. In 2008, the EMA submitted draft hazardous waste rules for public comment.

RECORD-KEEPING AND MONITORING UNDER THE EM ACT

Section 47 of the EM Act specifically authorises the EMA to develop rules for operations, such as the hydrocarbon sector, to sample and analyse pollutants that are released or hazardous substances that are handled. The scope of these rules includes the installation of appropriate monitoring equipment and the keeping of appropriate records. No rules have yet been made in this area. It is expected that the hydrocarbon sector would be particularly affected by any rules that may be promulgated.

NOTIFICATION OF SPILLS, RELEASES AND OTHER INCIDENTS UNDER THE EM ACT

The EMA, pursuant to Section 61 of the EM Act, is required to "investigate and designate categories of circumstances involving accidental spills or other releases of pollutants, or other incidents with respect to hazardous substances, which may present a risk to human health or the environment." The EMA shall then develop appropriate rules to handle such spills, releases and other incidents, if and when they occur. No rules have yet been promulgated in this area; however, it is anticipated that rules will appear in the near future and that the hydrocarbon sector will be a prime target, as most spills are hydrocarbon related.

REMEDIATION AND THE EM ACT

The EM Act also gives the EMA the authority to intervene and remedy any environmental problem. Section 25 states:

Whenever the Authority reasonably believes that a release or threat of release of a pollutant or hazardous substance, or any other environmental condition, presents a threat to human health or the environment, the Authority may, after consultation with the Minister and in co-ordination with other appropriate governmental entities, undertake such emergency response activities as are required to protect human health or the environment, including—(a) the remediation or restoration of environmentally degraded sites; (b) the containment of any wastes, hazardous substances or environmentally dangerous conditions; and (c) such other appropriate measures as may be necessary to prevent or mitigate adverse effects on human health or the environment.

The EM Act is silent as to recovery of cost for the actions of the EMA from the person causing the environmental problem or the occupier of the land from which the problem emanates. The EM Act does, in fact, provide for use of monies from an environmental trust fund to pay for remediation works. Section 72 states that:

> . . . there is hereby established an Environmental Trust Fund which shall be used to fund the operations of the Authority and for other purposes authorised under this Act, including— . . . (c) emergency response activities to address actual or potential threats to human health or the environment, including remediation or restoration of environmentally degraded sites, containment of any wastes,

hazardous substances or other environmentally dangerous conditions, or other appropriate precautionary measures to prevent significant adverse effects on human health or the environment . . .

Having discussed the reluctance of the common law to intervene directly in a situation like this, it may not be likely that the EMA could sustain a common law attack to recover remediation costs. While the *EM Act* is silent on recovery of costs from the private party, it is expected that this situation will not remain static. One can anticipate that regulations may be introduced to provide for the recovery of such costs, especially as, thus far, the environmental trust fund has not proved to be viable.

PLANNING PROCESS UNDER THE EM ACT

The EM Act has established an entirely new regulatory framework for approving projects in the hydrocarbon sector. Section 35 of the EM Act provides that any new or significant modification of an existing designated activity shall require a Certificate of Environmental Clearance ("CEC") to be applied for pursuant to the Certificate of Environmental Clearance Rules ("CEC Rules").[88] The CEC Designated Activities Order of 2001[89] identified several activities pertaining to the hydrocarbon sector that would require a CEC:

- establishment of the manufacture of petroleum products, petrochemicals or petrochemical products (Activity 19);
- exploration for crude oil and natural gas (Activity 24);
- establishment of a facility for primary or secondary production of crude oil, condensate or associated gas (Activity 25);
- establishment of a facility for natural gas or condensate production (Activity 26);
- establishment of infrastructure for pipeline systems (Activity 27);
- establishment of infrastructure for crude oil refining (Activity 28);
- establishment of infrastructure for the storage of petroleum or liquid petroleum gas or their derivatives (Activity 29);
- establishment of infrastructure for marine transportation (Activity13 and Activity 34).

The statutory requirement with respect to fees associated with the grant of a CEC is contained in the CEC (Fees) Regulations[90] which provide for a standard application fee of US$81.00.[91] If an Environmental Impact Assessment is required, payment of charges ranges from US$807.00 to US$96,775.00. Most of the activities associated with the hydrocarbon sector can be found in the upper range: US$16,129.00 to US$96,775.00. It should be noted that the EMA is required to identify cost items resulting in charges exceeding US$16,129.00 and must deliver a statement of expenses to the party concerned.

The administration of the CEC process is governed by the CEC Rules.[92] These rules establish the procedure for applying for, obtaining, or appealing decisions with respect to the grant of the Certificate. It is clear, therefore, that the law provides for significant environmental impacts of hydrocarbon activities to be addressed prior to the grant of planning permission to engage in such activities.

CONFRONTING THE FUTURE

Public Participation in the New Environmental Legal Regime of Trinidad and Tobago

Perhaps the greatest challenge to the hydrocarbon sector raised by the EM Act is the ushering into law of a legal regime that mandates public participation. The hydrocarbon sector generally functioned under the regulatory guidance of the Ministry of Energy and in that regime there was no requirement for public participation. The situation has now been dramatically transformed. It is not surprising that the hydrocarbon sector has been involved in two of the three cases filed, thus far, against decisions of the EMA to grant approval for specific projects and, in these cases, public consultations were very much central to the proceedings.

The Preamble to the EM Act sets out the spirit of the legislation and its intended objectives. The preamble makes it quite pellucid that public concerns are critical to the development of an effective legal regime for the protection of the environment. The Preamble to the EM Act states:

> WHEREAS, the Government of the Republic of Trinidad and Tobago (hereinafter called "the Government") is committed to developing a national strategy for sustainable development, being the balance of economic growth with environmentally sound practices, in order to enhance the quality of life and meet the needs of present and future generations... And Whereas, management and conservation of the environment and the impact of environmental conditions on human health constitute a shared responsibility and benefit for everyone in the society requiring co-operation and co-ordination of public and private sector activities . . . And Whereas, in furtherance of its commitment, the Government is undertaking the establishment and operation of an Environmental Management Authority to co-ordinate, facilitate and oversee execution of the national environmental strategy and programmes, to promote public

awareness of environmental concerns, and to establish an effective regulatory regime which will protect, enhance and conserve the environment . . .

The EM Act continues to emphasise the general principles articulated in the Preamble and the objects of the Act emphasise the public role in terms of awareness and participation. Section 4 of the EM Act states: "Objects of the Act (a) promote and encourage among all persons a better understanding and appreciation of the environment . . . (c) ensure the establishment of an integrated environmental management system in which the Authority, in consultation with other persons, determines priorities and facilitates coordination among Governmental entities to effectively harmonise activities designed to protect, enhance and conserve the environment . . ."

The general functions of the EMA also include the role of fostering public awareness and public participation. Section 16 of the EM Act states: "(1) The general functions of the Authority are to . . . e) promote educational and public awareness programmes on the environment; (2) In performing its functions, the Authority shall facilitate co-operation among persons and manage the environment in a manner which fosters participation and promotes consensus, including the encouragement and use of appropriate means to avoid or expeditiously resolve disputes through mechanism for alternative dispute resolution."

It is necessary now to see how the environmental legal regime has emerged, with respect to public participation, in the two main areas of regulatory concern, namely, the regulation of new and significantly modified activities through the CEC process and the reduction of the pollution inventory of Trinidad and Tobago through the use of the permitting mechanism.

PERMITTING PROCESS

Making of Regulations to Grant Permits

The right to grant permits has been vested in the EMA under the EM Act in several key areas, including waste,[93] water,[94] air,[95] noise,[96] hazardous substances,[97] sensitive species,[98] and sensitive areas.[99] To facilitate the management of these key environmental areas, the Minister with responsibility for the environment is required to make rules pursuant to the EM Act to provide for the specific regulation of these areas and the right to grant permits.

The EM Act provides that the making of the required rules to facilitate the granting of permits must contemplate public participation in the rule-making process. It is stated, in Section 27(1) of the EM Act, that "(1) In the course of developing rules, the Minister shall—(a) submit draft rules for public comment in accordance with section 28; (b) consider the public comments received and revise the rules as he thinks fit . . ." Section 28 of the EM Act goes further and explains how compliance with receipt of public comments must operate:

> (1) Where a provision of this Act specifically requires compliance with this section, the Authority shall—(a) publish a notice of the proposed action in the Gazette and at least one daily newspaper of general circulation—(i) advising of the matter being submitted for public comment, including a general description of the matter under consideration; (ii) identifying the location or locations where the administrative record is being maintained; (iii) stating the length of the public comment period; and (iv) advising where the comments are to be sent; (b) establish and maintain an administrative record regarding the proposed action and make such administrative record available to the public at one or more locations. (2) The administrative record required under subsection (1) shall include a written description of the proposed action, the major environmental issues involved in the matter under consideration, copies of documents or other supporting materials which the Authority believes would assist the public in developing a reasonable understanding of those issues, and a statement of the Authority's reasons for the proposed action. (3) The Authority shall receive written comments for not less than thirty days from the date of notice in the Gazette and, if the Authority determines there is sufficient public interest, it may hold a public hearing for discussing the proposed action and receiving verbal comments.

The EM Act, therefore, built into its statutory regime the need for public participation on rules that would vest power in the EMA to grant permits to facilitate continuing pollution within a legal framework.

GRANTING PERMITS

The EM Act makes no provision for public participation in the granting of permits. Rules have been made to deal with water pollution, sensitive areas and sensitive species; however, these rules fail to provide any avenue for the public to comment on the grant of a permit to any particular entity. This is of much concern, as Trinidad and Tobago follows a pattern of mixed development and it is not unusual for a heavy polluting industry to be in close proximity to residential communities. Despite this, the public has no means of expressing its view on the grant of a permit during the permit application process and must resort to judicial review if there is disagreement with the terms and conditions of the permit granted by the EMA.

It is noteworthy, however, that, with respect to noise, there is provision for public participation in the granting of a permit for the emission of noise. Rule 10 of the Noise Pollution Control Rules[100] states:

"(1) An application for a variation with respect to an event or activity shall . . . (d) be placed in one national daily newspaper in a form prescribed by the Authority for a period of at least two (2) consecutive days and at least one calendar week before the submission of the application for a variation; (2) An application for a variation with respect to a facility shall: (b) be placed in one national daily newspaper in a form prescribed by the Authority for a period of at least two (2) consecutive days and at least one calendar week before the submission of the application for a variation . . . " Rule 11 provides for affected persons: "(1) The Authority may, during the determination of an application under these Rules, request oral information or additional written information from—(b) a person who is directly affected by the application . . . "

Granting the right to the public to comment on the granting of variations for the emission of noise is commendable but somewhat strange in light of the refusal to grant a similar right with respect to the granting of a permit for water pollution.

THE CEC PROCESS

The CEC process allows the EMA to control the environmental impacts associated with new developments or environmental impacts associated with the significant modification of existing developments. The CEC is intended to ensure that there is no or limited environmental consequences of development activities occurring in the post-EM Act era. It is necessary to review how the CEC process works and how it has captured the ideal of public participation in the environmental decision-making process, as, once an application for a CEC is determined to have environmental impacts, the person seeking the CEC ("the Applicant") may be required to provide additional information. Where the impacts are significant, this will often cause the initiation of the environmental impact assessment ("EIA") process. This is a critical process and it is necessary to test the role of public participation in this process.

TERMS OF REFERENCE ("TOR")

The first stage in the CEC process, as it applies to the requirement for an EIA, deals with the terms of reference ("TOR") for the EIA. The EMA prepares the draft TOR and forwards same to the Applicant who is then made

responsible for obtaining comments from stakeholders and other members of
the public. This is a critical function as the quality of the TOR often determines the quality of the EIA. Rule 5(2) of the CEC Rules provides that "(2)
the applicant shall, where appropriate, conduct consultations with relevant
agencies, non-Governmental organisations and other members of the public
on the draft TOR and may, within 28 days after notification under subrule (1)
(c), submit written representations to the Authority requesting that the draft
TOR be modified and setting out a.) the manner in which he proposes that
the TOR should be modified; b.) a reasoned justification for the proposed
modifications; and c.) a report of the consultations with relevant agencies,
non-Governmental organisations and other members of the public on the
draft TOR."

The EMA has interpreted Rule 5(2) of the CEC Rules to mean that the onus
rests with the Applicant to determine who are the appropriate stakeholders
and the manner of undertaking the consultations. The result has been varied,
with some stakeholders being invited to comment on TORs while others with
seemingly equal standing, are ignored. Additionally, some Applicants have
opted for public meetings where comments can be offered on the draft TOR,
while others elect to receive comments only in writing. By not laying down
a set procedure for facilitating public comments on draft TORs, the EMA
has unwittingly allowed a system to emerge that is totally dependent on the
integrity and willingness of the Applicant to engage in the widest possible
public consultation in the review of draft TORs.

WRITTEN PUBLIC COMMENT PERIOD

Once the EIA is completed and submitted to the EMA, it is placed into the
public domain for written comments. There are two issues associated with
the written public comment period, namely, the duration of the period and the
documents that are made available for public comment.

With respect to the duration of the written public comment period, the *EM
Act* establishes a minimum period but sets no outer limit for such period.
Section 28(3) of the *EM Act* states, "The Authority shall receive written com-
ments for not less than thirty days from the date of notice in the Gazette . . . "

It would appear to be the trend for the EMA to set the time for receipt of
written public comments at the minimum of 30 days. Given the fact that many
of the projects in Trinidad and Tobago are energy based (petroleum and petrochemicals), it is difficult to have large and complex EIAs reviewed within 30
days. Moreover, there is a paucity of technical expertise in Trinidad and Tobago
available and willing to review these EIAs and, therefore, significant time is

spent trying to obtain such resources. Additionally, the EMA often adopts the position that EIAs are copyrighted material and, therefore, only allows 10 percent of the EIA to be photocopied according to copyright legislation. Any further information required must be read at the Library of the EMA. The situation is exacerbated by the fact that the review period is 30 calendar days, as opposed to 30 working days, thereby reducing the number of days that the public may access the documents.

The issue of the duration of the written public comment period was raised in the first environmental public interest litigation launched in Trinidad and Tobago. This case involved a decision by bpTT to expand its deliverability and transportation share in the Atlantic LNG Trinidad and Tobago Limited ("ALNG") liquefied natural gas project. The main components of the project included the installation of two new drilling platforms, upgrade of one existing platform (Cassia A), installation of two infield submarine pipelines (26" and 6"), and installation of a 48" main trunk pipeline. Due to the perceived adverse environmental effects on the lives of many residents of Trinidad and Tobago, the application for a CEC by bpTT was opposed by Fishermen and Friends of the Sea ("FFOS"), a local non-governmental organisation (NGO). It was argued on behalf of FFOS that, due to the complex nature of the proposed activities and the voluminous documents which the public was required to peruse in order to comment properly on the EIAs, the EMA owed a duty to the public to provide a longer period for public comment than the statutory minimum period of thirty (30) days. FFOS was not successful in its judicial review application as the matter was filed outside the date for submitting such an application. The Courts refused to exercise their discretion to extend time for filing of the application for judicial review outside of the statutory timeframe.[101]

The second issue that goes to the heart of the integrity of the written public comment period is the availability of all relevant information to allow for meaningful public participation. As stated in Section 28(2)(1) of the EM Act, "(2) The administrative record required under subsection (1) shall include . . . copies of documents or other supporting materials which the Authority believes would assist the public in developing a reasonable understanding of those issues . . . "

It is now accepted that there is a clear duty on the part of the EMA to provide sufficient information to allow for meaningful public participation.

PUBLIC HEARING

Perhaps the main and most significant pillar of the public participation process is the discretion vested in the EMA to hold a public hearing where there is sufficient public interest. *Section 28(3)* of the *EM Act* states, "... if the

Authority determines there is sufficient public interest, it may hold a public hearing for discussing the proposed action and receiving verbal comments."

The EMA has made sparing use of this power and it is certainly the exception for a public hearing to be held rather than the norm. The failure to hold a public hearing in the *BP Matter* constituted one of the grounds for judicial review, but this was not addressed due to the dismissal of the application on the grounds of undue delay and substantial prejudice and hardship to third parties.

The issue of the public hearing was also questioned in the second environmental public interest litigation to be filed in Trinidad and Tobago. In a case involving an appeal over the decision of the EMA to grant a CEC to ALNG for the construction and operation of a Fourth Train for the Liquefaction of Natural Gas,[102] the EMA held a public hearing pursuant to Section 28(3) of the EM Act to receive verbal comments. The EMA, however, took the position that this section only required them to host a single meeting to hear the views of the public and that there was no requirement to have any further meetings to discuss with the public how their views were addressed by the EMA. Justice Stollmeyer, in the ALNG Matter, agreed with the views of the EMA and noted:

> The EMA has a broad discretion in determining whether and when to hold public hearings. There is no express provision requiring follow up public hearings before granting the CEC. That is left up to its discretion, and will depend on the circumstances of the case and the severity of the concerns . . . The rules of natural justice do not necessarily require that there be a formal, oral, hearing in public. It is sufficient if those affected, or likely to be affected, are put into a position that allows their views and opinions to be heard, to be ventilated fully, and that those views and opinions be considered properly in the decision making process. There is no requirement for ongoing public debate.[103]

While the decision of Justice Stollmeyer is the current position of the law as it stands at the first instance level, it is hoped that this limited view of the public hearing, that by and large excludes any follow-up meeting to discuss how the public views were addressed prior to the taking of a decision, would not endure. Environmental democracy based on public participation and effective public consultation cannot be fulfilled with a single perfunctory meeting by an authority without engaging the public in a meaningful debate to demonstrate that their views were considered and addressed in any final decision.

CITIZEN SUITS

One of the innovations contained in the EM Act that has been used to challenge companies is the right of citizen suits or direct private party action as it is deemed in the EM Act. This represents a landmark departure in traditional environmental legislation, as it provides for direct private party action. Section 69 of the EM Act stipulates that "(1) any private party may institute a civil action in the Commission against any other person for a claimed violation of any of the specified environmental requirements identified in section 62 . . . ." This is an important provision as it provides for an aggrieved private party to have a matter brought before the Environmental Commission where there is a perception that the EMA is not living up to its statutory responsibility under the EM Act.

Section 62 of the EM Act defines an environmental requirement as including the requirement upon a person to:

(a) comply with the procedures for the registration of sources from which pollutants may be released into the environment; (b) comply with the procedures and standards with respect to permits or licences required for any person to install or operate any process or source from which pollutants will be or may continue to be released into the environment . . . (e) comply with the performance standards, procedures, licensing or permitting requirements established for the handling of hazardous substances; (f) apply for and obtain a Certificate of Environmental Clearance; (g) comply with the conditions and mitigation measures in any such certificate; (h) comply with the procedures and standards with respect to the periodic or continual monitoring of pollution or releases of pollutants or conditions required under a permit or licence; (i) provide timely and accurate notification with respect to an accidental or unauthorised release of a pollutant, or other incident with respect to a hazardous substance; (j) control the release of pollutants in such a manner as to comply with any permit or licence granted under section 50(1), 53(1), 57(1) or 60(1); (k) submit timely payment of required fees or charges payable to the Authority.

The sections that are omitted are those where no direct private party action can be taken. What is clear is that a participant in the hydrocarbon sector can only be liable in direct private party action under the EM Act where there is a pre-established relationship with the EMA through permits, licenses, or orders. ALNG has already faced the challenges being posed by citizen suits. ALNG was granted a CEC, No. CEC0114/2002, for the establishment of a Fourth Train (Train IV). This CEC has attracted the attention of private citizens with two actions already being filed before the Environmental Commission of Trinidad and Tobago alleging non-compliance with the terms of the CEC. The first action alleged the non-implementation of a Community Awareness and Emergency Response Program as required by the CEC.[104] The second action questioned the establishment of a buffer zone by ALNG pursuant to the CEC.[105] These actions against ALNG suggest that private citizens are prepared to challenge companies that they believe are not conforming to permit conditions or environmental requirements as contained in the EM Act. The failure of the EMA to enforce environmental laws, which was a feature of the complaints against other enforcement agencies prior to the enactment of the EM Act, will not benefit companies, as the right of citizen suits will ensure that compliance occurs.

A NEW REGIME IN SANCTIONS

Civil Liability

The EM Act contains an entirely new regime for punishing environmental infractions, both in civil and criminal law. This new regime is certainly more punitive than what obtained in the past and can ensure that environmental management is given greater significance. Section 62 of the EM Act creates the notion of environmental requirements, the breach of which will trigger the various sections dealing with compliance and enforcement.

Upon committing a breach of an environmental requirement, a person may, according to Section 63 of the EM Act, be issued notice of a violation. This notice may require a person to make necessary amendments or to make representation to the EMA with respect to the stipulations of the EMA. If the matter is satisfactorily resolved, the notice may be cancelled or the matters specified in the notice dismissed. In addition, the agreed resolution may be reduced in writing into a Consent Agreement.

Failing agreement, the next stage is the issuance of an administrative order as per Sections 64 and 65 of the EM Act. This administrative order can carry several sanctions including a directive to stop the conduct complained about; a directive to remedy any environmental damage; a directive to conduct an investigation; a directive to perform monitoring and record keeping activities; and civil assessment.

According to Section 66(1) of the EM Act, a civil assessment can involve:

(a) compensation for actual costs incurred by the Authority to respond to environmental conditions or other circumstances arising out of the violation referenced in the Administrative Order; (b) compensation for damages to the environment associated with public lands or holdings which arise out of the violation referenced in the Administrative Order; (c) damages for any economic benefit or amount saved by a person through failure to comply with applicable environmental requirements; and (d) damages for the failure of a person to comply with applicable environmental requirements, in an amount determined pursuant to subsections (2) and (3).

According to Section 66(3) of the EM Act:

The total amount of any damages under subsection (1)(d) shall not exceed—(a) for an individual, five thousand dollars for each violation and, in the case of continuing or recurrent violation, one thousand dollars per day for each such instance until the violation is remedied or abated; or (b) for a person other than an individual, ten thousand dollars for each violation and, in the case of continuing or recurrent violations, five thousand dollars per day for each such instance until the violation is remedied or abated.

In addition to the civil remedies outlined above, Section 68 of the EM Act provides additional remedies to the EMA as it stipulates that:

...whenever the Authority reasonably believes that any person is currently in violation of any environmental requirement, or is engaged in any activity which is likely to result in a violation of any environmental requirement, the Authority may in addition to, or in lieu of, other actions authorised under this Act —(a) seek a restraining order or other injunctive or equitable relief, to prohibit the continued violation or prevent the activity which will likely lead to a violation; (b) seek an order for the closure of any facility or a prohibition against the continued operation of any processes or equipment at such facility in order to halt or prevent any violation; or (c) pursue any other remedy which may be provided by law.

An example of the increased punitive nature of civil assessments being imposed by the EMA is illustrated in the case of the Tarouba Stadium.[106] The Urban Development Corporation of Trinidad and Tobago ("UDECOTT") applied for a CEC to carry out the development of the Tarouba Stadium but commenced work prior to the granting of the CEC. UDECOTT was fined US$16,328.00 for carrying out work at the stadium without approval.[107] The ability of the EMA to impose draconian civil assessments would certainly operate as a constraint on participants in the hydrocarbon sector where, in the past, such sanctions were not a major consideration in its environmental decision-making process.

Criminal Liability

The EM Act also creates the criminal offence of knowingly and recklessly endangering human health and the environment or any sensitive species or sensitive area by virtue of Section 70. This section carries a fine of TT$100,000[108] and imprisonment for two years. Section 2 of the EM Act makes it clear that "person" includes a company or firm. It is possible, therefore, for criminal action to be taken against participants in the hydrocarbon sector on the basis of Section 70. Indeed, this almost became a reality in 2006 with respect to an offshore incident. In March 2006, a canister was discovered at Mayaro Beach and radiation level tests revealed that it contained an iridium-192 source shielded with 16 kg of depleted uranium. A newspaper quoted the EMA as indicating that the purchaser of the device in Trinidad had been identified.

The newspaper report further went on to state that the device was believed to have been dumped into the sea and washed ashore on the high tide from one of the many offshore oil platforms off the coast of Mayaro. Moreover, the report indicated that the EMA found that the discarded equipment is used by the petroleum industry to establish the integrity of welded joints and that it was "not to be opened or tampered with." Additionally, it was stated that the EMA would conduct an investigation to determine whether any offence was committed when it was discarded and that a TT$100,000[109] fine and two years in jail can be imposed on anyone who releases a pollutant or hazardous substance and knowingly or recklessly endangers life or health, according to the EM Act.[110]

Personal Liability

A major innovation in the EM Act is the creation of personal liability for company officials for violations, creating civil liability through the use of the responsible corporate officer doctrine. Section 71 states:

> . . . where a violation of any environmental requirement has been committed
> by a person (other than an individual), any individual who at the time of the
> violation was a director, manager, supervisor, partner or other similar officer
> or responsible individual, or who was purporting to act in such capacity, may
> be found individually liable for that violation if, having regard to the nature of
> his functions in that capacity, the resources within his control or discretion, and
> his reasonable ability to prevent the violation—(a) the violation was committed
> with his direct consent or connivance; or (b) he, with knowledge, did not exer-
> cise reasonable diligence to prevent the commission of the violation.

The notion that company officials can be held personally liable will certainly serve as a warning to them as they conduct their business in Trinidad
and Tobago.

Public Interest Litigation

One of the major developments in 21st century justice in Trinidad and Tobago has been the introduction of public interest litigation. Access to justice has often been linked to the concept of public interest litigation, which can sim-ply be defined as litigation filed in a court of law for the protection of public interests in areas such as the environment. Hershkoff presents a succinct ex-planation as to the theoretical bases of public interest litigation:

"Public interest litigation on behalf of marginalized groups and interests rests
on three related theoretical accounts of law. First, public interest litigation draws

from an anti-positivist perspective that questions the inevitable legitimacy of majoritarian outcomes. Judicial intervention in this view may be justified by process-defects in the enactment process that structurally work to exclude or dilute the interests of affected groups. In addition, legislation may be suspect because of an inadequate deliberative process that ignores, distorts, or misstates the concerns of outsider groups; judicial review solves a public choice problem by ensuring due regard for those who would otherwise, to borrow from Mancur Olson, 'suffer in silence.' Majoritarian laws may also be distrusted because they deviate from national normative commitments (whether constitutional or statutory) or because they lack what U.S. constitutionalists call 'minimum rationality.' Second, public interest litigation rests on a view of law that acknowledges the gap between 'law on the books' and 'law on the ground.' Even after a legislature or regulatory agency has adopted protections or proscriptions affecting a particular group, the formal provision may not be given effect because of evasion, indifference, or hostility. Judicial intervention is warranted on this basis to secure compliance with existing rules and standards. Public interest litigation does not inevitably bridge the gap: court decrees may go unenforced because of political decision; failure of will; or a kind of slippage between text and action different from that found in the legislative arena. Third, public interest litigation recognizes the expressive value of law and its constitutive relation to the customs and discourse of a civil society. Public interest litigation on this view is part of what sociologists call the 'new' social movements in which participants contest the terms of public meaning. The very act of litigation affords a juridical space in which those who lack formal access to power become visible and find expression. Moreover, because courts are only one means for the enforcement of law, reform can be sustained only when it becomes second-nature and interwoven into discourse, low-level discretionary acts, and market exchanges. Lawsuits can give what Professor Dan M. Kahan in a different context describes as 'gentle nudges' for the internalization of changed social values by altering the terms of public discussion and giving voice to reform goals."[111]

The council for public interest law, which was established by the Ford Institution in the US, opted for the following definition of public interest law:

Public interest law is the name that has been recently given to efforts to provide legal representation to previously unrepresented groups and interest. Such efforts have been undertaken in recognition that the ordinary market place for legal services fails to provide such services to significant sections of the population and to significant interests. Such groups and interest include the poor, environmentalists, consumers, racial and ethnic minorities and others.[112]

Public interest litigation is a mixture of constitutional reform and non-constitutional statutory provisions. It has also emerged as an attempt by judges to consider the intent of the public at large. As such, civil society action is a very powerful tool and is a fundamental aspect of any public participation programme. While success in the area of public interest litigation is often hinged on the capability and independence of the judiciary, it ensures that citizens are guaranteed a voice in the judicial system. Undoubtedly, the judicial system itself will inevitably be strengthened, thus ensuring that issues pertaining to the establishment of sustainable development practices are adequately addressed.

In Trinidad and Tobago, the passage of the Judicial Review Act, No. 60 of 2000 ("JR Act") heralded the entrance of public interest litigation onto the judicial landscape. Section 5 of the JR_Act states:

(1) An application for judicial review of a decision of an inferior court, tribunal, public body, public authority or a person acting in the exercise of a public duty or function in accordance with any law shall be made to the Court in accordance with this Act and in such manner as may be prescribed by rules of court. (2) The Court may, on an application for judicial review, grant relief in accordance with this Act— . . . (b) to a person or a group of persons if the Court is satisfied that the application is justifiable in the public interest in the circumstances of the case.

The passage of the JR Act was quickly felt in the hydrocarbon sector with the filing of the BP Matter by the NGO, FFOS. Although unsuccessful, this was followed by the ALNG Matter involving the same NGO. It was, perhaps, not surprising that the Government moved swiftly to limit public interest litigation. The Judicial Review (Amendment) Bill 2005 ("the Bill") was introduced by the Government in Parliament in 2005, with the express aim of limiting the categories of persons who might apply for judicial review by repealing Section 5(2)(b) of the JR Act which vests jurisdiction in the Court to deal with public interest litigation. Due to the proroguing of Parliament, in September 2005, the Bill effectively lapsed;[113] however, during the time between the laying of the Bill in Parliament and its lapse, a challenge was launched by another NGO attacking the decision of the Government to remove public interest litigation.[114] Justice Gobin, in her decision on the challenge, noted:

I consider that the role of the bona fide public interest litigant in a relatively young democracy such as ours is critical to the maintenance of the rule of law. This is more so at a time when for the most part the population is crippled and consumed by fear for personal safety, protection of family and property. When in this environment there are still to be found persons who are genuinely public-spirited who can emerge out of the state of paralysis to act with the intention to promote the rule of law, they ought to be encouraged. If they are shut out either on technicalities by judges or by overstepping of the executive, we may as well pave the road to tyranny. The public interest litigant is the watchdog that may yet prove to be more valuable to us as a society than the one that actually barks.

The decision of Justice Gobin was reversed at the level of the Court of Appeal in the case of the Attorney General of Trinidad and Tobago v. Trinidad and Tobago Civil Rights Association, C.A. Civ. 149/2005. According to Warner JA:

"33. Public interest litigation in its purest form entered the Indian judicial process in about the year 1970. The disenchantment with the formal legal system's impact on the underprivileged led to the development of the jurisprudence of public interest litigation. 34. The genesis of that class of litigation is explained in the case of Guruvayur Devaswom Managing Committee and another v C K Rajan and others [2003] INSC 375 (14th August 2003)The Courts exercising their power of judicial review found to its dismay that the poorest of the poor, deprived, the illiterate, the urban and rural unorganized labour sector, women, children, handicapped by 'ignorance, indigence and illiteracy' and other down trodden have either no access to justice or had been denied justice. A new branch of proceedings known as 'Social Interest Litigation' or 'Public Interest Litigation' was evolved with a view to render complete justice to the aforementioned classes of persons. It expanded its wings in course of time. The Courts in pro bono publico granted relief to the inmates of the prisons, provided legal aid, directed speedy trial, maintenance of human dignity and covered several other areas. A balance was, therefore, required to be struck. The Courts started exercising greater care and caution in the matter of exercise of jurisdiction of public interest litigation. The Court insisted on furnishing of security before granting injunction and imposing very heavy costs when a petition was found to be bogus. It took strict action when it was found that the motive to file a public interest litigation was oblique." 35. In Canada, the concept of public interest standing originated in such cases as Thorson v Canada (Attorney General), [1975] 1 S.C.R. 138, Nova Scotia (Board of Censors) v McNeil, 1975 Canll 14 (S.C.C.), [1976] 2 S.C.R. 265, Canada (Minister of Justice) v Borowski, 1981 CanLII 34 (S.C.C.), [1981] 2 S.C.R. 575 and was further explained in Finlay v Canada (Minister of Finance), 1985 CanLll6 (S.C.C.), [1986] 2 S.C.R. 607. It originated to allow individuals to sue to prevent illegal government action, or the operation of invalid legislation, even though the litigants could not demonstrate that they had a private right that was being interfered with, or that they were suffering damage peculiar to themselves, different from that of the public generally. (See Maurice v Canada Minister of Indian Affairs and Northern Development 1999 Can Lll 9147). 36. Public interest legislation was introduced in this jurisdiction by the Judicial Review Act 2000. Standing, though relaxed after the decision in IRC v National Federation of Self Employed and Small Business 1982 A C 617 is still a prerequisite. An applicant does not need to show a direct financial or legal interest to succeed, but must show a sufficient interest. 37. Counsel for the respondent's arguments that the Bill prohibits public interest litigation are self-defeating when viewed against the background of the authorities he cited. These authorities demonstrate that claimants of limited means as well as other activists do have access to the courts. (See R (Corner House) v Trade Secretary of State for Trade and Industry—claimants were an educational research and campaign organization; [2005] 1 WLR 2600 and R v Lord Chancellor ex parte Child Poverty Action Group 1998 2 ALL ER 755—applicants were a registered charity whose objects included promotion of action for relief of poverty among children; R (on the application of England) v Tower Hamlets London Borough Council and others 2006 EWCA—claimant an active campaigner for the industrial heritage of Tower Hamlets. The respondents cannot therefore complain that the bill if enacted would prevent them from setting foot in the 'court room door'. (See Matthews v Ministry of Defence (2003) 2 WLR 135 Paragraph 29.) 38. The protection of the law that the respondents enjoyed was the right to apply to a court for such remedy (if any) as the law of Trinidad and Tobago gives to them. 39. In the result, I have found no violation of threatened violation of the respondents' constitutional rights. The appeal is therefore allowed and the decision of the judge is set aside."

The decision of the Court of Appeal was based on the fact that the Court seemed inclined to adopt the position that while the Bill may have the effect of limiting the statutory right to public interest litigation, this right exists independent of the Bill in the judicial practice of Trinidad and Tobago.

DEVELOPING NEW TECHNIQUES OF AGENCY MANAGEMENT

The hydrocarbon sector had a peculiar history in terms of its management by the Ministry of Energy. This Ministry is the government agency charged with the responsibility of executing the Government's policy on the hydrocarbon sector. As such its responsibilities include the granting of licenses for hydrocarbon activities. The Ministry also directly receives financial benefits from the hydrocarbon sector, including scholarships and other awards for its employees and the payment of a special tax for the running of the Ministry's operations.[115] Yet, the Ministry was traditionally the enforcement agency charged with environmental management of the hydrocarbon sector through the monitoring and enforcement of the licensing regime. This structure led to a fair degree of cynicism as to the Ministry's ability to impartially establish and enforce proper environmental standards. There is a common perception that a very good relationship exists between participants in the hydrocarbon sector and the Ministry of Energy to the point that it undermines the ability of the Ministry to perform its statutory obligations. Whether this perception is accurate or not, the new environmental legal regime creates an entirely new structure for the development and enforcement of environmental standards in Trinidad and Tobago.

The EMA is a body separate and apart from the hydrocarbon sector; there is a great degree of uneasiness in the relationship between the hydrocarbon sector and the EMA as both sides adjust to each other. The EMA's management structure, as determined by the EM Act, is intended to create an impartial broad-based agency focused on environmental management in Trinidad and Tobago. It is instructive to note the manner in which the Board of Directors of the EMA is appointed.

Section 6 of the EM Act: (1) There is hereby established a body corporate to be known as the Environmental Management Authority, which shall be governed by a Board of Directors consisting of the persons appointed in accordance with this section. (2)The President shall appoint—(a) a Chairman; (b) nine other Members drawn from the following disciplines or groups, namely, environmental management, ecology, environmental health, engineering, labour, community-based organisations, business, economics, public administration, law and non-profit environmental non-governmental organisations.

The governance of the EMA is, therefore, intended to be placed in the hands of persons who represent a cross-section of the community and professionals, including those with environmental skills. This governance structure represents a marked departure from the straightforward, politically-controlled governance structure of the MOEEI and the impact on the hydrocarbon sector was felt quite early as one of the participants in the hydrocarbon sector felt the heavy hand of the EMA. This lent credence to the perception in the hydrocarbon sector that management of the relationship with the EMA was fraught with challenges.

Talisman (Trinidad) Petroleum Ltd. ("TPL") applied for a CEC to conduct a seismic survey within the Nariva Protected Area in Trinidad for the purpose of ascertaining the hydrocarbon potential of the area. The EMA wrote to TPL, by letter dated 06 August 2002, refusing to grant the CEC to TPL. The refusal by the EMA to grant a CEC to TPL was appealed and it is instructive to note comments attributed to key stakeholders in the decision-making process prior to the hearing of the appeal by the Environmental Commission. In an article written by Mark Meredith for the *Trinidad Express* newspaper, the issue of the appeal by TPL over the EMA's refusal to grant a CEC was discussed. It was reported that "veteran Nariva campaigner Molly Gaskin had submitted a list of comments to the EMA . . . in her capacity as President of the Pointe-a-Pierre Wildfowl Trust . . . The Trust's opinion that no CEC should be granted . . ."[116] At the time of the submission of these comments, Ms Gaskin was the President of the Pointe-a-Pierre Wildfowl Trust and a member of the Board of the EMA, a scenario that creates, at the very least, an apparent conflict of interest. Mark Meredith went on to discuss the views of the Chief Executive Officer of the EMA, which, as reported, would appear to continue the approach of Ms Gaskin. According to Dr. Dave McIntosh, "It brings one of our most cherished possessions up against the interests of an oil company . . . it puts something like Nariva which is at the top of the list, against oil and gas production which is at the top of the list of our economic activities. This is a heavyweight battle."[117] Indeed, Dr McIntosh, in his reported comments in response to a question as to the significance of TPL being successful in the appeal, sought to put pressure on the Environmental Commission by stating in the same article, "The people would understand that the Commission has no objection to these activities taking place in highly sensitive areas."[118]

Notwithstanding the comments of Dr McIntosh, the Environmental Commission was not persuaded by the attempt of the EMA to ignore appropriate principles of public law. Section 36 of the EM Act gives discretion to the EMA to issue a CEC but only "after considering all relevant matters, including the comments or representations made during the public comment period." Section 36 imposes a duty upon the EMA, after it considers all these matters and it decides to grant a CEC, to impose such terms and conditions in granting the CEC as it thinks fit. Justice Zainool Hosein made it clear that the EMA had a duty of fairness which required it to at least provide TPL with the opportunity to show that it could carry out the seismic without damaging the Nariva Swamp:

> I think it is right that I should indicate a few of the relevant aspects of the principles of natural justice, which are applicable in this matter. The right to a fair hearing is a principle of natural justice and has been applied as a base on which to build a kind of code of fair administrative procedure. The courts took their stand several centuries ago on the broad principle that bodies entrusted with legal power could not validly exercise it without first hearing the person who was going to suffer. This principle was applied very widely to administrative as well as to judicial acts, and to the acts of individual Ministers and Officials as well as to the acts of collective bodies such as justices and committees. Even where an order or determination is unchallengeable as regards its substance, the court can at best control the preliminary procedure so as to require fair consideration of both sides of the case. Thus the law makes its contribution to good administration . . . overlooking it is one of the most common legal errors to which human nature is prone. When a Lord Chief Justice, an Archbishop of Canterbury, and a three-judge Court of Appeal have strayed from the path of rectitude, it is not surprising that it is one of the more frequent mistakes of ordinary mortals.

See page 469–470, Administrative Law by Wade & Forsyth, 8th Ed.

It is important to note that the significance and universality of the principle "make it applicable to almost the whole range of administrative powers, however silent about it the statute may be" (See page P. 474 op cit.). The duty to act fairly and to observe the rules of natural justice involves "giving to the person whose activities are being investigated a reasonable opportunity to put forward facts and arguments in justification of his conduct of these activities before they reach a conclusion which may affect him adversely" per Lord Diplock in Hoffman La Roche (f) & Co. vs. Secretary of State for Trade and

Industry (1975) A.C. 295 (368 D-E). That a decision-making body should not see relevant material without giving those affected a chance to comment on it and, if they wish, to controvert it is fundamental to the principle of law (which governs public administration as much as it does adjudication) . . . see Sedley J., R. London Borough of Camden ex.p Paddock (1995) COD 130. See also *Judicial Review Handbook* 3rd Ed. By Michael Fordham at Para 60 5.5. Indeed the Appellant complains that he did not see or know of the material or documents upon which the Respondent had based its decision until the hearing of the Appeal. In A.G. vs. Ryan (PC) [1980] ac 718 at page 730, per Lord Diplock at P. 730: "It has long been settled that a decision affecting the legal rights of an individual which is arrived at by a procedure which offends against the principles of natural justice is outside the jurisdiction of the decision-making authority." These principles *mutatis mutandis* may be applied to the method by which the Respondent arrived at its decision to issue the Refusal. When these principles of fairness are taken into account, it is clear that the Appellant, having been denied the opportunity to persuade or to show how it would be able to carry out the proposed activity without damaging the Swamp (especially in the absence of a prohibition against such activity), the decision to refuse in the circumstances would be fundamentally flawed."[119]

The situation of the unfair treatment of TPL points to one of the challenges in dealing with an entirely new regulatory regime. Yet, this case has been quickly followed with some suspicions that the response of the business community in dealing with the EMA has been to seek to manipulate the agency. The Chairman of the EMA is reported to have made a plaintive cry against pressure from what he deems big business:

Chairman of the Environmental Management Authority, Dr John Agard, on Thursday said the authority is pressured by big business to back off on enforcing its policies. "Frequently no one will be happy . . . but it is an odd situation and we have to be dispassionate," he told journalists at an EMA seminar on environmental journalism at the EMA's Elizabeth Street, St Clair, offices. "It is very stressful around here because industry believes that the EMA is giving them a hard time. I would be bold enough to say that one of the stresses of a regulatory organization is you end up pleasing no one."[120]

While there is no evidence that the Chairman was speaking about the hydrocarbon sector, his remarks certainly must be considered by all stakeholders, including the hydrocarbon sector. The interaction between participants in the hydrocarbon sector and the EMA is an evolving one and will certainly require changes from the way in which the participants in the sector had dealt with the Ministry of Energy when it was primarily responsible for regulating the environmental behaviour of companies through the licensing regime. It is expected that the hydrocarbon sector's conduct will be different within the confines of the new legal environmental regime being promoted by the EMA and based on the EM Act.

Working with Precise Environmental Standards and the Permitting System

Participants in the hydrocarbon sector are accustomed to dealing with a legal environmental regime based on general requirements, rather than on precise environmental standards. As an example, the Petroleum Regulations, as they apply to marine areas, speak of the need to avoid marine pollution. Regulation 42(2)(c) of the Petroleum Regulations:[121] "A licensee shall ensure that operations do not unreasonably interfere with other activities in the area and, in the case of operations in submarine areas, care shall be taken to avoid pollution of the agriculture, fishing, authorised scientific researches, and conservation of the living resources of the sea are not unjustifiably hindered, and likewise that no damage is caused to submarine cables and pipe-lines."

The immediate question that arises is: what constitutes pollution? It is generally accepted that pollution ought to be defined within specific parameters and that the absence of such parameters creates an absolute obligation not to introduce any substance whatsoever into the environment, a position that is unrealistic and unenforceable. The rules and regulations being made, pursuant to the *EM Act*, are establishing precise environmental standards that must be met. Standards have already been promulgated for water and noise and standards for air have been submitted for public comments. It is expected that entities in the hydrocarbon sector will comply with the standards and will develop management structures to ensure compliance.

Related to precise environmental standards is the permitting system. When persons are unable to meet the required environmental standards, such persons will be required to obtain the relevant permit. Permits will come with terms and conditions and, therefore, there will be the need to ensure that such terms and conditions are met. This will require an environmental management system to ensure that persons do not breach the terms and conditions of their permits. Failure to comply with the terms and conditions of a permit can also result in the filing of a citizen suit, thus making it imperative that entities in the hydrocarbon sector ensure compliance with terms and conditions of any permit which they may be granted.

ADDRESSING HISTORICAL ENVIRONMENTAL HARM

Trinidad and Tobago has a long history of continuous hydrocarbon operations being conducted by successive companies. A major question in environmental law treats with the passing of the affected property or the contaminating source through the hands of a succession of innocent owners: where is liability to be now placed? To quote the eminent environmental law scholar John D. Leeson: "The simplistic approach is doubtless to say, as the law does, that a prospective purchaser has the responsibility to make any necessary inquiries and investigations to satisfy himself of the condition of the property he is buying, and is not therefore, at least in law, innocent."[122] This position was reviewed by a leading law firm in Singapore, a country with a similar legal tradition as Trinidad and Tobago, and it is instructive to note the perception of a leading expert.

Where the environmental legislation imposes liability for the present consequences of past activities, the current owner may be held liable for all civil and potentially criminal consequences of the past activity. Since the person or company that undertook such past actions is frequently no longer around, the liability scheme established was intentionally cast very broadly. The position is simple. The owner or occupier of the premises is deemed responsible for the clean up of any waste generated at the premises, whether the waste was discharged prior to the party entering into occupation of the premises or after such entry. In other words, the owner of a facility today can thus be held liable for the cost of cleaning up hazardous substances buried there, even if they were buried long before that owner acquired the property, simply by virtue of having the status of owner. The actual party causing the discharge would always remain liable if he were locatable. For instance, a company (or its corporate successor) that disposed of manufacturing wastes at a facility decades ago and then sold it, may be liable for the cleanup that the present owner undertakes. In either case, the acquirer of a business today can find itself paying for the consequences of actions taken long ago, and for which it received no direct benefit.[123]

Thus, issues such as abandonment of oil wells that have been inactive prior to assumption of licence rights by a new company will become relevant as Trinidad and Tobago attempts to grapple with the issue of liability for past environmental harms.

CONCLUSION

It would appear that, although historically there was a plethora of environmental laws in Trinidad and Tobago, enforcement was quite limited. Within such a scenario, the laws dealing with protection of the environment in Trinidad and Tobago had little impact on hydrocarbon operations. This situation would appear to have changed dramatically with the introduction of the EM Act which has introduced specific management regimes for dealing with areas such as planning, noise pollution, water pollution sensitive areas and sensitive species. Additionally, the EM Act contemplates the development of specific management regimes to address air pollution and waste management. Draft subsidiary regulations have already made their way into the public domain to satisfy the statutory requirement for public comments. It is contemplated that subsidiary regulations for hazardous substances, information gathering and spills would evolve over a period of time.

The significance of developments through the EMA and the *EM Act* cannot be understated in the context of the hydrocarbon sector. It is expected that current and future developments would pose significant challenges to this sector, leading to a revolution in corporate behaviour that could engender a more proactive and responsible approach to environmental management. It is early yet. The EMA is now acquiring its regulatory personality and it is, therefore, difficult to gauge its success.

NOTES

1. The Environmental Management Act, No. 3 of 1995, repealed and replaced by The Environmental Management Act, No. 3 of 2000, now Ch. 35:05, 2004 Rev.

2. Ministry of Energy and Energy Industries ("MOEEI"), Draft: An Energy Policy for Trinidad and Tobago (Port of Spain. MOEEI, 1986), p. 4.

3. Sustainability is interpreted to be the exploitation of the hydrocarbons in a manner that enhances both current and future potential to meet human needs and aspirations.

4. MOEEI, Draft: An Energy Policy for Trinidad and Tobago, p. 71.

5. Id.

6. MOEEI, Green Paper for Proposed Energy Policy for the Republic of Trinidad and Tobago (Port of Spain: MOEEI, 1992), p. 27.

7. MOEEI, Green Paper for Proposed Energy Policy for the Republic of Trinidad and Tobago (Port of Spain: MOEEI, 1998), p. 7.

8. Simon Ball and Stuart Bell, Ball and Bell on Environmental Law (Oxford: Blackstone Press, 1997) p. 129.

9. Saunders Clark v. Grosvenor Mansion Limited [1900] 2 Ch. 373.

10. Radstock Co-operative and Industrial Society Ltd v. Norton-Radstock UDC [1968] Ch. 605.

11. Broder v. Saillard [1876] 2 Ch. 692.

12. Sedleigh-Denfield v. St Joseph's Mission [1940] 3 ALL ER 349.

13. [1941] 2 All ER 693.

14. [1964] 1 All ER 816

15. [1980] 1 All ER 17.

16. [1994] 1 All ER 53.

17. Id. at 72.

18. [1957] 2 QB 169.

19. Castle v. St Augustine's Links [1992] 38 TLR 615.

20. [1865] H&C 774.

21. Rickards v. Lothian [1913] AC 263.

22. Read v. Lyons [1947] AC 156.

23. Cambridge Water v. Eastern Counties Leather [1994] 1 All ER 53 at 76.

24. Scott-Whitehead v. National Coal Board [1987] 53 P&CR 263.

25. Reynolds v. Clarke [1725] 1 Stra 643.

26. McDonald v. Associated Fuels [1954] 3 DLR 713.

27. Jones v. Llanrwst UDC [1908] All ER 922.

28. Rajendra Ramlogan & Natalie Persadie, *Developing Environmental Law and Policy In Trinidad and Tobago* (San Juan, Trinidad: Lexicon Press, 2004), pp. 28–32.

29. The Public Health Ordinance, (CAP.12/4), 1950 Rev.

30. The Municipal Corporations Act, Ch. 25:04, 2004 Rev.

31. The Petroleum Act, Ch. 62:01, 2004 Rev.

32. See subsidiary legislation to The Petroleum Act, Ch. 62:01, 2004 Rev.

33. The Petroleum Act, Ch. 62:01, 2004 Rev.

34. See subsidiary legislation to The Petroleum Act, Ch. 62:01, 2004 Rev.

35. See subsidiary legislation to The Petroleum Act, Ch. 62:01, 2004 Rev.

36. The Litter Act, Ch. 30:52, 2004 Rev.

37. The Waterworks and Water Conservation Act, Ch. 54:41, 2004 Rev.

38. See subsidiary legislation to The Waterworks and Water Conservation Act, Ch. 54:41, 2004 Rev.

39. The Summary Offences Act, Ch. 11:02, 2004 Rev.

40. The Public Health Ordinance, (CAP.12/4), 1950 Rev.

41. The Municipal Corporations Act, Ch. 25:04, 2004 Rev.

42. The Malaria Abatement Act, Ch. 28:50, 2004 Rev.

43. The Highways Act, Ch. 48:01, 2004 Rev.

44. The Water and Sewerage Authority Act, Ch. 54:40, 2004 Rev.

45. See subsidiary legislation to The Water and Sewerage Authority Act, Ch. 54:40, 2004 Rev.

46. The Oil Pollution of Territorial Waters Act, Ch. 37:03, 2004 Rev.

47. The Municipal Corporations Act, Ch. 25:04, 2004 Rev.

48. The Archipelagic Waters and Exclusive Economic Zone Act, Ch. 51:06, 2004 Rev.

49. The Continental Shelf Act, Ch. 1:52, 2004 Rev.

50. The Harbours Act, Ch. 50:06, 2004 Rev.

51. The Litter Act, Ch. 30:52, 2004 Rev.

52. The Mines, Borings and Quarries Act, Ch. 61:01, repealed and replaced by The Minerals Act, Ch. 61:03, 2004 Rev.

53. The Conservation of Wildlife Act, Ch. 67:01, 2004 Rev.

54. The Summary Offences Act, Ch. 11:02, 2004 Rev.

55. The Forests Act, Ch. 66:01, 2004 Rev.

56. The Summary Offences Act, Ch. 11:02, 2004 Rev.

57. The Town and Country Planning Act, Ch. 35:01, 2004 Rev.

58. The Town and Country Planning Act, Ch. 35:01, 2004 Rev.

59. The Agricultural Fires Act, Ch. 63:02, 2004 Rev.

60. The Forests Act, Ch. 66:01, 2004 Rev.

61. The State Lands Act, Ch. 57:01, 2004 Rev.

62. The Town and Country Planning Act, Ch. 35:01, 2004 Rev.

63. The Town and Country Planning Act, Ch. 35:01, 2004 Rev.

64. The Petroleum Act, Ch. 62:01, 2004 Rev.

65. See subsidiary legislation to The Minerals Act, Ch. 61:03, 2004 Rev.

66. The Pesticides and Toxic Chemicals Act, Ch. 30:03, 2004 Rev.

67. The Customs Act, Ch. 78:01, 2004 Rev.

68. The Trade Ordinance, No. 19 of 1958.

69. The Public Health Ordinance, (CAP.12/4), 1950 Rev.

70. The Municipal Corporations Act, Ch. 25:04, 2004 Rev.

71. The Pesticides and Toxic Chemicals Act, Ch. 30:03, 2004 Rev.

72. See subsidiary legislation to The Pesticides and Toxic Chemicals Act, Ch. 30:03, 2004 Rev.

73. See subsidiary legislation to The Pesticides and Toxic Chemicals Act, Ch. 30:03, 2004 Rev.

74. The Petroleum Act, Ch. 62:01, 2004 Rev.

75. See subsidiary legislation to The Petroleum Act, Ch. 62:01, 2004 Rev.

76. The Petroleum Act, Ch. 62:01, 2004 Rev.

77. The Litter Act, Ch. 30:52, 2004 Rev.

78. The Highways Act, Ch. 48:01, 2004 Rev.

79. The Petroleum Act, Ch. 62:01, 2004 Rev.

80. The Town and Country Planning Act, Ch. 35:01, 2004 Rev.

81. The Petroleum Act, Ch. 62:01, 2004 Rev.

82. See subsidiary legislation to The Petroleum Act, Ch. 62:01, 2004 Rev.

83. The Petroleum Act, Ch. 62:01, 2004 Rev.

84. The Petroleum Act, Ch. 62:01, 2004 Rev.

85. The Summary Offences Act, Ch. 11:02, 2004 Rev.

86. The Water Pollution Rules, Legal Notice No. 230 of 2001.

87. See subsidiary legislation to The EM Act, Ch. 35:05, 2004 Rev.

88. See subsidiary legislation to The EM Act, Ch. 35:05, 2004 Rev.

89. See subsidiary legislation to The EM Act, Ch. 35:05, 2004 Rev.

90. See subsidiary legislation to The EM Act, Ch. 35:05, 2004 Rev.

91. A rate of US$1.00 to TT$6.30 was used.

92. See subsidiary legislation to The EM Act, Ch. 35:05, 2004 Rev.

93. Sections 55-58 of The EM Act, Ch. 35:05, 2004 Rev.

94. Sections 52-54 of The EM Act, Ch. 35:05, 2004 Rev.

95. Sections 49-51 of The EM Act, Ch. 35:05, 2004 Rev.

96. Sections 49-51 of The EM Act, Ch. 35:05, 2004 Rev.

97. Sections 59-60 of The EM Act, Ch. 35:05, 2004 Rev.

98. Sections 41-46 of The EM Act, Ch. 35:05, 2004 Rev.

99. Sections 41-46 of The EM Act, Ch. 35:05, 2004 Rev.

100. Legal Notice No. 60 of 2001.

101. Fishermen and Friends of the Sea v. The Environment Management Authority and BP Trinidad and Tobago LLC, Privy Council Appeal No. 30 of 2004 ("the BP Matter").

102. Fishermen and Friends of the Sea v. The Environmental Management Authority and Atlantic LNG Company of Trinidad and Tobago, H.C.A. Cv. 2148 of 2003 ("the ALNG Matter").

103. Id. at 53.

104. Michelle Dove v. Atlantic LNG Company of Trinidad and Tobago, DPA No. 001 of 2006.

105. Vijay Sookdeosingh v. Atlantic LNG Company of Trinidad and Tobago, DPA No. 002 of 2006.

106. "UDECOTT Pays for Building Without Approval," *Trinidad Guardian*, 22 November 2005. Available at http://legacy.guardian.co.tt/archives/2005-11-22/business2.html.

107. The fine was TT$102,865 converted at a rate of US$1.00 to TT$6.30.

108. US$15,873.00 (Converted at a rate of TT$1.00 equivalent to US$6.30.

109. Id.

110. Richard Charan, "Depleted Uranium Washes Ashore in Trinidad," 07 March 2006. Available from Internet: http://www.ttgapers.com/Article1438.html.

111. H. Hershkoff, "Public Interest Litigation: Selected Issues and Examples," (n.d.), pp. 7-9. Available from Internet: http://www.siteresources.worldbank.org/INTLAWJUSTINST/Resources/PublicInterestLitigation%5B1%5D.pdf. [accessed 08 November 2008].

112. A. Mohapatra, Public Interest Litigation and Human Rights in India (New Delhi: Radha Publications, 2003), p. 70.

113. Legal Notice No. 219 of 07 September 2005.

114. Trinidad and Tobago Civil Rights Association v. Attorney General of Trinidad and Tobago, HCA No.1070 of 2005. The Trinidad and Tobago Civil Rights Association was successful at the First Instance but the decision was reversed at the Court of Appeal. See Attorney General of Trinidad and Tobago v. Trinidad and Tobago Civil Rights Association, C.A.Civ. 149/2005.

115. Oil Impost imposed on oil producing companies paid in accordance with production levels to fund the operations of the MOEEI. Under Production Sharing Contracts, the MOEEI charges an administrative fee to assist in running of the operations of the MOEEI.

116. Mark Meredith, "Talisman's Tour—An Explosive Issue," *Trinidad and Tobago* Express, 10 November 2002. Available from Internet: http://www.trinidadexpress.com/index.pl/article_archive?id=29546154.

117. Id.

118. Id.

119. Talisman (Petroleum) Limited v. The Environmental Management Authority, EAP No. 3 of 2002, pp. 20-22.

120. Jada Loutoo, "EMA cries pressure from big business," *Trinidad Guardian*, 31 May 2003.

121. See subsidiary legislation to The Petroleum Act, Ch. 62:01, 2004 Rev. Emphasis added.

122. John D. Leeson, *Environmental Law* (London: Pitman Publishing, 1995), p.36.

123. Kala Anandarajah, Partner and Head, Knowledge Management, Rajaj & Tann.

Chapter Twelve

Petroleum Taxation in Context

The Role of the State

Trevor M. Boopsingh

INTRODUCTION

Small petroleum-based economies face a range of unique challenges, including the size of the State in comparison to the global petroleum giants who outrank them in terms of accumulated and available capital and hard-won specialist knowledge. This knowledge includes technical know-how, risk management and marketing capabilities. Accordingly, most small States seek to use their sovereign power to offset these inherent disadvantages while utilizing, in particular, the risk capital available from international petroleum companies for most of their exploration activities. In negotiating the way forward, a critical management instrument is the contract by which the parties determine the share of rewards that will flow to the company and the State from successful discovery of petroleum. Much has been written on the subject and opinions on the various areas of contracts are widely available.

BACKGROUND

Petroleum Taxation and Contracts 1956–2002

In 1956, Trinidad and Tobago achieved the status of a self-governing colony within the British Commonwealth. This was about half a century after the beginning of commercial oil production in Trinidad in December 1907. In 1962, the country relinquished the colonial status in favour of Independence. One of the first priorities of the new government of Dr Eric Williams was the establishment in 1964 of the Mostofi Commission of Inquiry into the Trinidad and Tobago petroleum industry. From this inquiry flowed the Petroleum Act and accompanying Regulations which were introduced and enacted over the course of 1968 to 1970. Until then, the form of contract for all oil companies had been the Exploration and Production License.

The new Act, along with the modified Income Tax Acts which applied to all businesses prior to Independence, governed the petroleum business through to the last quarter of 1973 (Boopsingh 1990). Of particular relevance was the Submarine Well Allowance, a fiscal incentive dating back to the late 1950s. This allowance was introduced to encourage investment in platforms and other facilities for marine exploration and production in what would eventually come to be regarded as one of the giant oilfields of the world— Soldado. The consortium to which this area in the southern Gulf of Paria was assigned included Shell, BP and Texaco operating under an Exploration and Production License called Trinidad Northern Areas (TNA).

After the October 1973 oil embargo, instituted by the OAPEC (Organisation of Arab Petroleum Exporting Countries), new petroleum tax legislation was introduced and enacted in March 1974. (Trinidad and Tobago Parliment 1974) Among the critical changes were:

1. For tax purposes, oil company businesses were separated into three different taxable entities: exploration and production; refining; and marketing
2. Exploration and production entities were required by law to compute their income for tax purposes by using the Tax Reference Prices which were posted (established) by the Minister of Finance. A Petroleum Profits tax (PPT) at a new rate of tax was also introduced
3. Certain limitations on deductions and costs applicable in determining taxes were introduced
4. Refinery throughput taxes were levied on each barrel of crude processed
5. The Petroleum Levy and Subsidy Act was enacted with the aim of preventing increases in the price of petroleum products being fully passed onto the domestic consumer and
6. The Production Sharing Contract (PSC) was introduced as the preferred method (as opposed to the E&P Licenses) by which new acreage would be made available to international petroleum companies.

An Oil Audit Division under the supervision and direction of an Assistant Commissioner of Inland Revenue was established with responsibility for monitoring matters arising from items 1 to 5 above. Production Sharing Contracts (PSC) were issued and overseen by the Ministry of Energy which signed four contracts in 1974 (Boopsingh 1990). The Petroleum Act was later amended to accommodate changes arising out of the introduction of the PSC.

These PSCs were of the Peruvian type, which required that production sharing between the State and the company be done on the basis of defined percentages written into the contract. These percentages varied depending on production levels, with the State taking its share in lieu of royalty and tax payments and the company's share covering the cost of exploration and development of the given fields. Thus, the State would not lose income through cost escalation while the company would bear no risk of losing income through tax increases.

Tax Reference Prices posted by the Minister of Finance continued to be used as the basis for petroleum taxation for all E&P licensees until 1981 when, as a result of approaches made by the various oil companies including State-owned Trintoc (formerly Shell Trinidad Ltd. whose assets had been purchased by the State in 1974), the Government changed the system of taxation retroactive to January 1st 1980 (Ministry of Legal Affairs 1981). The new fiscal regime for E&P licensees required the use of fair market values for crude oil sales and transfers, but all companies were subject to the new Supplemental Petroleum Tax (SPT) before computation of Petroleum Profits Tax.

The SPT was established as separate rates for land and marine areas at the rate of 35 percent and 60 percent respectively. The separation of the refining and marketing businesses from exploration and production continued for the purposes of taxation.

By that time, natural gas had been discovered in the acreages covered by each of the four Production Sharing Contracts signed in 1974. However, because there was no readily available market, no PSC came into operation and none was therefore relevant for taxation purposes. The natural gas produced fell under E&P licenses and was therefore taxed on the basis of the prices realized from sales contracts to the National Gas Company (NGC) and the Trinidad and Tobago Electricity Commission (T&TEC). No SPT was levied on income derived from natural gas. Condensates produced from natural gas-producing fields were also not subject to SPT because of allowances for smaller fields with low oil production.

As crude prices went into decline after 1981, the Government relaxed the tax regime. The applicable SPT rate on land-based crude oil was lowered to 15 percent in 1983 while the SPT rate for marine crude was reduced to 55 percent in 1984, with income from both being granted additional deductions prior to computation of SPT. With the global collapse of crude oil prices in 1986, the new Arthur N.R. Robinson administration further lowered the rate of taxation in 1988, dropping the rate for land crude to 5 percent and marine crude to 20 percent. In addition to other changes, it enacted sunset legislation with the requirement that a review of the petroleum taxation system be completed within five years.

Thus in 1992, the new Patrick Manning government enacted new legislation which, in essence, introduced a variable rate of SPT as laid out in an accompanying Schedule to the Amendment to the Petroleum Taxes Act (Ministry of Legal Affairs 1992). While maintaining different rates for land and marine operations, the schedule introduced variations under which the SPT rate rose and fell with the price of crude oil. Fair market values continued to be the basis for establishing crude oil prices with the separation of the three businesses continuing as a feature of petroleum taxation. The only company to be affected was Trintoc, by then the sole refiner in Trinidad and Tobago after Texaco sold most of its Trinidad assets, including the Pointe-a-Pierre refinery to the Government in 1985. Income from natural gas and condensates from gas-producing fields remained not subject to SPT.

As outlined earlier, much of the energy sector development of the 1990s in Trinidad and Tobago focused on gas development and, in particular, the development of LNG, with Atlantic's Train 1 producing its first cargo for sale in mid-1999. Of particular importance were the fiscal incentives provided to Atlantic, which facilitated the establishment of an LNG plant in Trinidad, the first to be built in the Western Hemisphere for over two decades. Incentives included pioneer tax status for Train I and accompanying facilities for 10 years, and the offsetting of construction costs for the gas supply pipelines to the new plant, against income from the producing operation.

Apart from a spike related to the second Gulf War, annual crude oil prices remained relatively stable in the US$15–$25 range through the 1990s into 2003 with the exception of 1998/99 when the Asian financial crisis took its toll on Japanese energy consumption, among others, pushing oil prices to severe lows.

Designed as it now was, the system of petroleum taxation in Trinidad and Tobago required little attention or modification, particularly as LNG brought new petroleum output (both gas and condensate) rapidly into production, with commensurate revenue increases for the State.

The Governments of the nineties had also taken aggressive approaches towards leasing new acreages and establishing new gas-based industries. By 1996/97 the country's natural gas production had overtaken the national output of crude oil on a BTU basis. Gas production, pricing and taxation, which had not featured as a source of government revenue except in the development of domestic gas-based industry, were beginning to attract increased attention from tax authorities. In 1994, for the first time, British Gas operating under a PSC of 1974 vintage, brought on stream natural gas from off the east coast. In response, the Government modified the contract to take development cost into account, thereby recognizing the concept of cost recovery and, thus, the Indonesian type PSC.

This new development triggered sharp differences between the Board of Inland Revenue and the contractor regarding the computation of taxes under the tax laws for E&P licensees as well as the application of the principle of cost recovery to natural gas production, using low-priced domestic gas sales as the basis for income. Not surprisingly, tax payable was often greater than the total share of gas contractually allocated to the Government for meeting the combined royalty and petroleum profits tax payments to the State. Temporary solutions were instituted but the discrepancy persisted given low gas prices and the fact that the SPT/PPT system had been designed for oilfields.

A new model PSC was issued by the Ministry of Energy which recognized cost-recovery clauses while maintaining the basic principle of Government recovery of royalty and tax payments through its share of production as defined in the contract. BG and its partners offshore the North Coast (NCMA) of Trinidad (including Trintoc) then converted its licences into the new PSCs so as to supply natural gas for the expansion of Atlantic LNG by the addition of two new trains.

PETROLEUM TAXATION: 2003–2009

Over the period 2001 to 2003, as the second and third trains of Atlantic LNG were being built and brought into production, three general elections were held in Trinidad and Tobago. The hectic political environment provided little space for dealing with policy matters, especially those considered non-critical. Petroleum taxation fell into this category, given the rapid increase in crude oil and natural gas output, and the prospect of further increases from new oil and gas finds by BHP-Billiton off the north-east coast of Trinidad. With the election of a new Government in 2002, new priorities were established including the development of a national plan titled Vision 2020— Achieving Developed County Status.

By 2004, as the planning process got underway, LNG Train 3 was in full operation with new oil production expected from the BHP-B fields by the end of the year. Of equal importance, however, was the phenomenal rise in oil prices that began in that same year, as shown in Figure 12.1.

The impact of increases in the price of both oil and gas, coupled with the growing domestic output of natural gas, served to focus attention on the increasing revenues being generated by hydrocarbons and the developing global trade in LNG. By late 2006, the trade press reported that LNG was being sold for as much as US$15 per mmbtu in Far East markets

These developments were already under review by the new Government as it scrutinized trading arrangements under the contractual agreements for building Trains 2 and 3. These arrangements had been signed by the previous Government in the context of oil and gas prices during the Asian financial

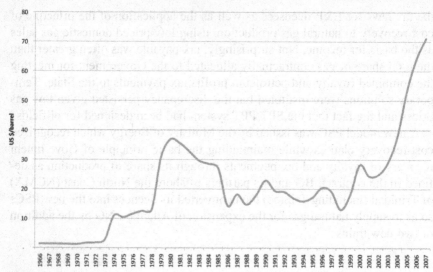

Figure 12.1. Oil Prices.

crisis of 1999. Unable, and perhaps unwilling, to change the contractual arrangements for these three trains, the Government opted to expand output with an additional train, Train 4, in order to take advantage of improved trading conditions and to enhance T&T's share of the benefits of the rapidly developing global trade in LNG. Atlantic LNG Train 4 was an expanded and modified version of its predecessors. It was designed to process 800 mmscfd of natural gas with a scheduled launch date of 2007.

The Government also signaled its intention to introduce new petroleum tax measures in 2004/05 to deal with revenue losses resulting from transfer pricing and the sale of Trinidad LNG on the international market, from which the country gained no income. Meanwhile, the growing role of natural gas and the need for appropriate taxation for larger producers became a point of focus for the authorities. In delivering his 2006 Budget statement in October 2005, the Minister of Finance repeated the call for new tax measures. In June 2006, new measures retroactive to January 1, 2005 eventually came into force without much consultation, focused largely on improving revenue collection in the short and medium term (Ministry of Legal Affairs 2005). The Government's petroleum revenues climbed astronomically from TT$7.641 million in 2004 to TT$13.360 million in 2005, and to over TT$20 billion in 2006 and 2007, continuing at these higher levels to 2008 (See Table 2.5 in Chapter 2).

Thus, the retroactive changes in petroleum taxation were established with a high price, high revenue scenario, with little consideration of the possibility of protracted and unsettling negotiations for new acreages as well as little recognition that natural gas development, both upstream and downstream, could not be treated for tax purposes in the same manner as crude oil production. Further, with increases in output from Train 4 scheduled to take LNG production up to 2500 mmscfd and total gas production to over 4000 mmscfd by the end of 2007, gas reserve depletion became an issue for the first time since the early 1990s.

As noted earlier, the 2006 tax legislation was retroactive to January 1, 2005 and contained the following significant new changes:

- Only royalty was now a deduction prior to SPT
  Under the PPT, all first-year allowances were removed
- Tax liabilities for exported gas were to be computed using Fair Market Value
- SPT on oil remained as a price variable tax rate along the following lines:
- Marine: 0—42%; Land: 0—35%; Deep Water: 0—18%

Deep water was a new category for acreage in water of over 1,000 metres deep.

A deep water block was defined as an area of which more than 50 percent was in deep water. The following applied if a deep water block was awarded under either licence or contract:

- E&P Licence
- 40 percent capital uplift for exploration well expenditure
- SPT payable as per the schedule listed as Class D
- Production Sharing Contract
  1. Contractor pays PPT & UL
  2. 40 percent capital uplift for exploration well expenditure
  3. Consolidation of exploration well costs among deepwater PSCs

Thus, for the first time, PSCs awarded after January 1, 2008 would have the contractor's share of production, subject to petroleum profits tax and unemployment levy.

In this scenario the new tax legislation of 2006 introduced for the first time, probably worldwide, the Taxable Production Sharing Contract. Thus, when a further bid round was closed in the last quarter of that same year, only one bid was received by the Ministry of Energy for one block out of the four blocks in the bid.

THE ROLE OF THE STATE

The Vision 2020 Energy Committee noted the following in its submission to the Government:

The State's dominant role in the sector over the past two decades, both in terms of providing seed capital for industry, as well as creating an appropriate incentive infrastructure for its eventual development, suggests a continuing role in the eventual attainment of the sector's vision.

The sub-issues outlined in Figure 12.2, create a framework for the fashioning of such a role.

The Vision 2020 Energy Committee Report proposes a number of prescriptive measures for dealing with such issues in such a way that the overall objectives are met in a cost effective manner with maximum impact on the sector and the country (Energy Subcommittee 2004).

Some of the issues detailed in figure 12.2 deliberately overlap with the infrastructural issues already outlined (in the Report) and the issues pertaining to Human Capital and Institutional capacity mentioned below. The State's role can be either one of direct intervention or facilitation in order to achieve sector vision and goals.

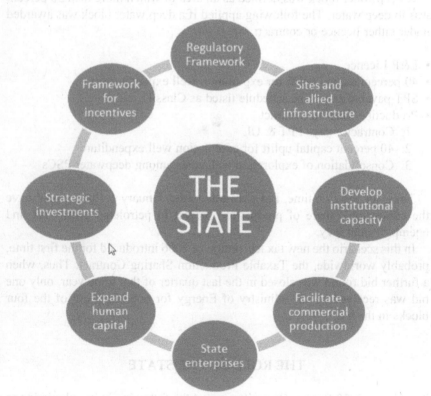

Figure 12.2.   Energy Sector Issues Pertaining to the Role of the State.

With the large revenue increases in hand, the State opted for a plethora of objectives, almost all of which required direct intervention rather than facilitation. It invested in the development of a new industrial estate at La Brea with allied infrastructure; it approved Petrotrin's investment in a large refinery upgrade, a gasoline optimization programme, as well as the development of a gas-to-liquids plant at Pointe-a-Pierre; it announced a series of new strategic investments in an aluminium smelter with downstream aluminium manufacturing facilities, an ethylene complex, a new steel complex, and a novel methanol-based polyethylene complex, in addition to adopting a position that no new ammonia/methanol plants would be approved unless they were supplemented by downstream value-added product output. Additional plans were drawn up for other new industrial estates and ports.

Further to these initiatives in which State equity was a major requirement, the Government also expanded its programme for the development of human capital with the establishment of the University of Trinidad and Tobago (UTT). Among UTT's objectives were the development of entrepreneurial skills, industrial human resource capacity and the increase of the national pool of tertiary graduates from less than 10 percent to more than 30 percent.

The State invested in a large new non-energy industrial development, Tamana InTech Park, to promote the diversification of the economy towards a knowledge-based economy.

Meanwhile, the upstream sector attracted little attention except as a supplier of natural gas for LNG Train 4 and its revenue flow. Fiscal incentives for upstream and downstream energy projects were, it would seem, assumed to be sufficient and in place, given the price of energy and energy-related products on the global market.

Taken as a whole, it would seem that the attitude of the Government of Trinidad and Tobago was one of Resource Nationalism, as it is termed in the literature. In this, Trinidad and Tobago was not much different from much of the oil-producing world during the five year period 2004-08, particularly Russia and Venezuela.

Pete Stark, Vice President of Industry Relations, IHS Inc. noted the following:

> The oil and gas industry is in the midst of a critical transition driven by a series of factors, including the Asian energy-demand crunch of 2004, the 2005 hurricanes in the Gulf of Mexico, and recent low discovery rates. These factors, coupled with political uncertainties, threats to petroleum infrastructure, production disruption resulting from civil unrest, and limited access by international oil companies (IOCs) to giant resources in the Middle East and the former Soviet Union, have ushered in what has been referred to as the 'Age of Energy Supply Anxiety' (Stark 2007).

In addition, higher oil prices and mounting political pressures, combined with a bit of anti-Americanism and rapidly growing demand for energy in the Asian market (particularly in China), stimulated producing countries to increase control of their oil and gas resources and move toward resource nationalism. The resulting global scramble by both IOCs and national oil companies (NOCs) to secure hydrocarbon resources altered the industry's competitive landscape significantly, which in turn caused a major shift in the balance of power favoring the NOCs, mandating new perspectives on nego-tiations and partnerships.

No longer are NOCs managing only state-owned hydrocarbon resources to their nation's long-term benefit, they are also expanding internationally to secure the additional energy resources necessary for sustainable economic growth for their countries. In other words, NOCs are becoming international exploration companies, competing with IOCs at home and in the world mar-ketplace."

Interestingly his next paragraph in that editorial noted, almost presciently, the following:

> Considering that governments and NOCs control more than 80% of the world's remaining oil reserves, are expanding and upgrading refineries and infrastruc-ture, and are developing gas resources, the effect is considerable. But that has not always been the case. In the past, when oil prices were low, investments in exploration dropped, and governments were eager to create incentives to attract investments—including reducing tax rates and state participation, or providing royalty relief.

This impact of resource nationalism was perhaps better reflected in Trini-dad and Tobago in other ways, such as the failure of several bid rounds to reach any meaningful conclusions as negotiations dragged on for the award of new blocks in the 2003 bid round. In addition, instead of majority participa-tion or even total control, as in the case of Venezuela and Russia, Trinidad and Tobago's demands for greater State participation came in the form of an increased role for State-owned Petrotrin in the award of new exploration acreage. Further, the scope for greater local content in the energy sector was enhanced, further fuelling the growth of domestic industry.

CURRENT ISSUES

With the global financial and credit crisis making its impact in the USA and spreading to Europe before enveloping the global economy in late 2008 and 2009, a dramatic slowdown in economic activity led to a rapid decline in demand for oil and gas. The fall in demand for oil in particular was most marked in the USA where oil consumption fell to its lowest level since 1998.

The precipitous decline in oil prices from the heady heights of US$148 per barrel in mid 2008, was accompanied in Trinidad and Tobago by the slow rate of acreage allocation. The resulting low level of exploration activity fell well below the requirements of the much higher gas reserve replacement rate. Annual gas production in 2008 in the post-LNG production era was at the much higher rate of 1.4 TCF. It had therefore become very evident that the 2006 changes in petroleum taxation which were already inadequate to the demands of 2006/07, would clearly not satisfy the post-2008 world of oil and natural gas in Trinidad and Tobago, particularly in the context of the global economic crisis that had enveloped the developed world.

Falling oil prices were followed by falling demand for natural gas and after a lag of some two years, by falling prices for both ammonia and methanol. Figure 12.3 shows the trend in natural gas prices in the USA as illustrated by the NYMEX Natural Gas Futures over the period July 1, 2008 and July 23, 2009.

With 85 percent of the country's hydrocarbon output now being natural gas, and with almost 90 percent of that output being sold in the form of either LNG (60 percent), ammonia (circa 15 percent) and methanol (circa 15 percent), the impact of the fall in the price of natural gas on Trinidad and Tobago's economy was bound to be significant.

By July 2009, oil prices had rebounded to the $65–$75 per barrel range without indications of a similar trend by natural gas. Four factors served to

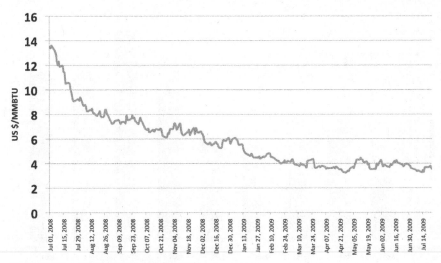

Figure 12.3. NYMEX Natural Gas Futures.

modify gas prices in the USA and Canada. The first was the significant new sources of natural gas being produced from unconventional sources such as shale gas, coal-bed methane etc. These have proven to be both economic to produce at natural gas prices of $4–$6 per mmscf, and far more productive than previously thought. At mid-2009, an industry-related group estimated the USA's total natural gas resources at 2,074 trillion cubic feet, an increase of 542 trillion cubic feet from two years before. Of this amount, 238 trillion cubic feet were estimated to be proven gas reserves.

The other three factors operating to keep US natural gas prices non- resurgent in the short term were:

1. 2009 was a record year for new LNG production capacity around the world at a time of low global gas demand.
2. US energy policy sought to bring on-stream energy from "greener" sources and from conservation measures, and
3. The shift from coal to gas-fired generation in the USA did not occur as rapidly as expected since the coal industry preferred to absorb the environmental costs rather than close their existing coal-fired generation capacity.
4. Nevertheless, it should also be noted that according to the Energy Information Administration, USA, the prices for LNG imports from Trinidad and Tobago were relatively high, as shown in Figure 12.4. The prices used in this figure are those quoted for December of each year so as to show the trend since 2001 and to reduce the impact of annual seasonal

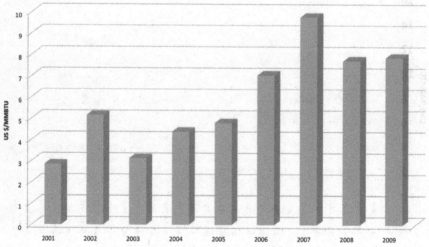

Figure 12.4.   US LNG (TT) Import Prices (Dec).

volatility. Of equal importance is the trend in LNG imports into the USA since December 2008 which shows LNG from Trinidad and Tobago falling from almost 60 percent of total US LNG imports in that month, to 36 percent in April 2009, while LNG imports from Egypt increased by approximately 250 percent, actually surpassing the volume of LNG imports from Trinidad and Tobago for the first time in April 2009. However, while LNG exports from Trinidad and Tobago to North America fell from 13,314 million cubic metres in 2007 to 8,559 million cubic metres in 2008, exports to OECD-Europe increased from 2,551 to 5,323 million cubic metres from 2007 to 2008 (Data Source: EIA, US DOE). Corresponding data for exports from Trinidad and Tobago into the Far East was not available.

The charts in Figure 12.5 from the BP Statistical Review 2009, shows the decline in petroleum product prices in both the Gulf Coast and Rotterdam markets.

Falling petroleum product prices, as shown in Figure 12.5, led the way for falling oil prices as product prices impact and respond quickly and directly to market conditions. Thus refining margins fell even more sharply, from more than $12 per barrel in mid 2008 to a little over $2 per barrel by January 2009. Additionally, rising prices for steel and for large project management which carried new investments uncomfortably close to non-viability had created major capital cost over-runs in a number of projects in Trinidad and Tobago, such as the gasoline optimization programme and gas-to-liquid projects at the Pointe-a-Pierre refinery. Petrotrin thus suffered an immediate double

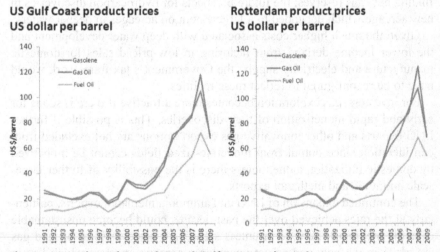

Figure 12.5. Chart of Rotterdam and Gulf Coast Product Prices.

whammy from refining margins that had dropped into the very negative range and from large capital-cost overruns in the construction of the two projects. Exacerbating its financial position was the high cost of labour due to the country's extensive construction programme.

As steel prices cooled in the post-2008 world of decreased demand, the shortage of readily available finance from the global market began to affect all the projects contemplated by the Government. On the other hand, the National Gas Company (NGC) had an over-abundance of gas on its hands, having entered into contracts with BGTT, EOG Resources and BHP-Billiton for the purchase of all available natural gas for a slate of assumed new domestic industrial projects. Like all other gas contracts, these three had take-or-pay provisions and were to come into effect for supply starting in 2008/09. Whereas BG and EOG Resources had ample supply stakes in providing gas for LNG, BHP Billiton was a first-time gas supplier which had been fortunate in bringing its new oil fields into production in 2005 at a time of rising oil prices. Thereafter, however, it had been hit hard by much faster decline rates and much fractured geology, with smaller-than-expected oil fields. It was probably anticipating sales to the then more lucrative LNG markets rather than to NGC, whose contracts came with a composite pricing mechanism for purchasing natural gas that included low-cost buyers such as the domestic manufacturers and Trinidad and Tobago Electricity Commission (T&TEC).

The gas supply overhang had therefore now arisen in the context of falling natural gas reserves and limited exploration activity. However, exploration activity in Trinidad and Tobago was dependent on three factors: the much greater likelihood of finding new gas as opposed to oil; the after-tax-cost of finding new gas reserves; the future prospects for hydrocarbon discoveries in new acreage which depended to a large extent on acreages in deeper waters.

Given the much higher costs associated with deep water development and the lower income derived from factoring in low-priced sales for domestic manufacture and electricity supply, the Government's tax framework would have to be reconfigured to reflect these realities.

For investors, gas exploration becomes more attractive if there is scope for early and rapid monetization of their discoveries. This is possible if further LNG exports and other innovative gas export options are not excluded from consideration since output from moderate-sized fields cannot be monetized by domestic utilization alone, unless there is the possibility of further large-scale ammonia and methanol exports.

The continued expansion of LNG and ammonia/methanol exports, particularly at the rates achieved over the past decade, could become unsustainable over the medium-to long-term unless significant discoveries of oil and gas are made in the new and as yet unexplored acreage, most of which lies in water depths in excess of 1,000 metres. Further, there was the matter of the 2006/05 petroleum tax revisions having been made in conditions of high prices for both oil and natural gas. High prices had been accompanied by higher development costs, and little account had apparently been taken of the need to structure the system to support the development of smaller and/ or higher cost discoveries.

In January 2008, the Minister of Energy (2007-2010), Conrad Enill, announced the following requirements for revision of petroleum tax legislation:

- Review of fiscal incentives for deep water
- Review of supplemental petroleum taxes to small petroleum operators
- Review of incentives for marginal or small fields, drilling activities, enhanced oil recovery and heavy oil
- Review of the structure of the production sharing contracts (PSCs)
- Review of the taxation regime for downstream projects, and
- The development of a special fiscal regime for downstream projects

He stated further: "The aim... is to ensure that the taxation legislation continues to be relevant to the changing energy sector needs and contributes in a positive manner to its sustained growth and development" (Rampersad 2008).

The consultant who had assisted the Government in the 2006 revision of the petroleum tax regime was further enrolled, and submitted his report to the Government in the last quarter of 2008.

By the beginning of 2010, the proposed revision of the petroleum tax regime faced at least three constraining factors:

1. The sharp fall in Government revenue as a result of the fall in prices for crude oil, petroleum products, ammonia and methanol and, most importantly, natural gas well head prices based on global prices for LNG. Government revenue from petroleum which exceeded TT$20,000 million for 2006, 2007 and 2008 was likely to decline by more than 25 percent below those levels for the years 2009–2012. The ability to provide adequate fiscal incentives for upstream petroleum development activity in particular, (e.g. smaller or marginal fields) was therefore limited.
2. Limited capacity for providing fiscal incentives for the upstream also extended to the ability to provide incentives for new downstream activity and to use low-priced natural gas for feedstock for these plants, as previously done. Without these two incentive schemes, raising external debt finance on the international capital markets was very challenging.
3. Generating exploratory activity of the level required to expand natural resource output or even to sustain current output levels, require the following:
   - Expeditious acreage-award practices
   - Attractive contract terms for natural gas, in particular, and moreso in expensive deep water areas

- Sharing of production which recognizes that natural gas may be the likely hydrocarbon to be found
- Defined and transparent gas sales capacity within those contracts, and
- A policy position re the development of new LNG exports, and the allocation of such exports to new and successful exploratory contractors, as well as existing producers

Taken together, this strongly implies that the PSCs may, in most instances where natural gas is the form of hydrocarbon to be produced, require a separate petroleum tax regime. Where exploration and production licences are the contract form, incentives to promote the development of smaller gas fields will be required if they are not to continue as "stranded" gas reserves.

THE ROLE OF THE STATE—TWO OUTSTANDING ISSUES

Among the persistent and unsettling issues for the State in a small petroleum economy is the need for adequate capital and expertise for treating with international petroleum companies in the intricacies of exploration, development and reward sharing in ways that serve and protect the national interest. However, there are some negative implications for the national well being.

a. The Role of Domestic Private Capital. Domestic private capital becomes secondary to state capital, especially if domestic capital is expected to act as a service provider for larger capital interests and more so if it does not have the technical, risk management and specialist expertise that is required. Thus, unless the State makes a special effort to facilitate domestic private capital it is unlikely that domestic capital will play any major role except via services of a limited nature.

In this context, two approaches may be considered. First, a deliberate policy of public/private partnership for certain strategic investments as outlined in the Vision 2020 Energy Sub-Committee Report. The State may, for example, seed investments and nurture them to maturity before divesting to the domestic private sector. Second, a means must be found for private domestic capital to safely and securely utilize the accumulated savings of private individuals for enterprise development in the country. This would be an acknowledgement that State capital and foreign direct investment alone cannot provide either all the funding requirements or the entrepreneurial drive necessary for taking the economy further.

b. Governance. The lack of access to information held by the State hampers the ability of non-governmental interests to contribute effectively towards ensuring that strategic decision-making by the State is apolitical and based on positive project economics. Even more important are the governance issues that arise from the combination of the State's limited capacity and the private sector's weak competitive capacity. International petroleum companies and service providers are both likely to accommodate dubious and non-transparent practices by the State which wields significant power.

When the ability to provide patronage is enhanced by the accrual of large revenue flows to the State, autocratic decision-making by the State undermines the scope for meaningful consultation.

As the environmental agenda comes into conflict with the demand for resource exploitation, the role of public education will become increasing important. As key stakeholders in the debate, the public will require information with integrity if social peace and national consensus is to be built and maintained.

BIBLIOGRAPHY

Boopsingh, Trevor. *Oil Gas and Development—A view from the South* . Longman Trinidad, 1990.

Energy Subcommittee. *Vision 2020 Energy*. GOTT, Ministry of Planning and Development, 2004.

Ministry of Legal Affairs . *Act # 15 of 1996—An Act to Amend the Petroleum Taxes Act of 1994*. Port of Spain: Government of Trinidad and Tobago, 1992.

Ministry of Legal Affairs. *Act No.2 of 2006. An Act to ammend the Petroleum Taxes Act of 1974*. Port of Spain: Government of Trinidad and Tobago, 2005.

———. *Act.NO. 5 of 1981, An Act to Amend the Petroleum Taxes Act of 1974*. Port of Spain: Government Printery, 1981.

Rampersad, Curtis. "Experts points to new oil and gas environment." *Trinidad Express Newspaper*. Caribbean Communications Network, April 16, 2008.

Stark, Pete. "The Winds of Change; Resource nationalism Shofts the Balance of Power to National Oil Companies." *Journal of Petroleum Technology*, 2007: 34-36.

Trinidad and Tobago Parliment . *Act No.22 of 1974. The petroleum Taxes Act* . Port of Spain: Government Printery, 1974.

Chapter Thirteen

Taking Trinidad and Tobago Forward and Abroad

The Technical Challenges

Anthony E. Paul and Trevor M. Boopsingh

INTRODUCTION

Even though Trinidad and Tobago is a small energy player, producing less than 1% of world output, the oil and natural gas industry is one of the oldest in the world, predating even Venezuela and Saudi Arabia. Today, Trinidad and Tobago is the world's fifth largest exporter of liquefied natural gas and a leading producer of methanol, urea and ammonia. Since the commercialization of oil deposits in 1908, the energy sector has gone on to become the principal export earner and major contributor to Government revenue and gross domestic product (GDP). The sector provides a unique case, as there are few other countries that benefit from such a wide plethora of energy-related activities at all positions of the value chain—upstream, midstream and downstream—in both the oil and natural gas industries, occurring concurrently and concentrated within such a small geographic area. To a large extent, this is due to the long history of the petroleum industry, the depth and scope of knowledge along the value chain, the maturity of the local industry and the physical characteristics of Trinidad and Tobago (geology and geography).

The maturity of the industry as well as its successes in developing a world-class natural gas industry can position Trinidad and Tobago as a global energy player and serve as a launch pad for the energy sector to become an exporter of energy services, business development competencies, equity investors and strategic business partners. The maturity and distinctiveness of Trinidad's energy sector provides some unique challenges, which must be addressed and overcome if the vast overseas opportunities are to be realised. Ironically, the major issues to be dealt with concern the management of the industry here at home, where investors and services companies need an on-going portfolio of opportunities to be able to grow and sustain their offerings. Without the

378

nurturing of this home-based incubator, and the supporting eco-system, locals will struggle to maintain their base, far less expand their horizons.

In this chapter, we shall look at the nature of the current thrust to go overseas and then at the challenges that we are facing to keep the home fires alight, including:

- ensuring the sustainability of the energy sector through a well thought-out and implemented upstream development strategy
- instituting an appropriate and equitable mix of fiscal and other incentives to encourage the participation of diverse operators
- encouraging local content and participation within a context of limited local capital capacity, risk averseness, low opportunity and variable and weak Government support
- maintaining an amicable equilibrium among all energy-related sub-sectors and players
- effectively managing dominant international operators within the context of foreign relations and diplomacy, geo-politics and bi-lateral treaties
- creating an active and innovative downstream sub-sector which guarantees the efficient monetization of reserves and exerts healthy demand pressures on the upstream sub-sector
- Maximizing the export potential of key success elements of the "Trinidad Model" in an attempt to diversify the economy and markets
- Understanding the new role and evolution of the State to actively promote the energy sector as a major part of its trade portfolio.

As with all mature industries, the greatest challenge lies in sustainability and growth. In the case of the energy sector in Trinidad and Tobago, this challenge originates firstly in the upstream sub-sector, from which flows the mid and downstream activities and businesses. The section on managing the challenges will therefore focus strongly on this sub-sector.

In 2006, the Geological Society of Trinidad and Tobago (GSTT) conducted a five-day workshop in 3-D seismic interpretation for 23 senior Cuban geologists and geophysicists, in Havana, on the invitation of the Cuban Geological Society, the Latin American Centre for Physics and the Cuban Geophysics Division. The workshop was developed, designed, put together and presented entirely by the members of the GSTT, using our own experiences, skills and training. As a direct consequence of this workshop, many opportunities for collaboration in science and technology, particularly as they relate to the earth sciences and the petroleum industry were identified. So impressed were the participants and their organizations with the level of skills and experience available in Trinidad and Tobago, that "the Minister of Basic Industries of

Cuba, indicated that he will communicate directly with our government, to initiate, facilitate and improve cooperation between Cupet (the Cuban State Oil company) and Petrotrin, the University of the West Indies and its Cuban counterparts. He also expressed his desire to host a delegation of Trinidad and Tobago institutions and companies, who might be interested in participating in the Cuban oil industry." [1]

This was by no means the first such initiative and positive response. Sadly, however, the infamous US Helms-Burton Act, which imposed personal sanctions on officers and directors of companies, even non-American ones, doing business with Cuba, prevented most local businessmen from following up at that time.

This Chapter tries to capture a few key points to illustrate the cause and nature of T&T's unique position in being so regarded and the current opportunities with which we are faced.

TAKING THE LESSONS LEARNT ABROAD

Trinidad and Tobago's energy-based industrialization has, for the most part, and especially in the LNG and petrochemical business, been successful. Trinidad's approach to monetization of the natural gas resources is internationally acclaimed and is commonly referred to as the "Trinidad model." What is seen is the end result of many years of trial and error, through periods representing all segments of the spectra of the oil and gas business features—high and low levels of skills, prices, production, reserves, investment, taxes, local capital and State ownership—during times of global booms and recessions. If a situation is likely to occur, T&T has experienced it, made decisions when it happened and has the scars or jewels to show for those decisions. What is more, much of this happened within the last generation, when leaders in the developing world remember T&T at being just another newly independent nation, starting out, just like them. In other ways, T&T feels familiar to them and its achievements don't seem beyond their reach, given that the T&T experience offers a point of reference and example for their own development initiatives.

The "Trinidad model" is sufficiently matured to allow T&T to leverage its long and deep history of expertise to project itself as a facilitator for people and institutions in developing countries to design, build, operate, manage and lead their natural gas sector. As such, there is vast potential to train and build new gas industries in, and to create a foundation for future cooperation with, other gas-based developing countries. To retain the model's marketability however, the people of T&T have to be aware that they have to be continuously learning from their past and current situations and continue to do the things that brought them to where they are now, improve on them and be seen to be moving forward, while not repeating the mistakes of the past. A tarnished image is much harder to sell.

In almost every aspect, history shows how the petroleum industry evolved—political, legislative, fiscal, policy, E&P technology and business development model—as it responded to the challenges and growing sophistication in drilling technology, geological environments, the ever-changing global politics and economy and commodity trading markets. Lessons have been obtained at every epoch and aspect of the energy sector. However, as intimated above, the key lessons reside at the leadership level from where strategy, policy and oversight for the sector emanate.

The Trinidad and Tobago model demonstrates that the entire business development strategy must start with a thorough understanding of the resource potential in terms of the proven, probable and possible size, quality, and geological characteristics of the catchment area and, therefore, the technology required for exploration and production. Although new discoveries are pertinent and must be pursued through an active exploration programme, an awareness of the core resource potential is key to the development of a national vision, development objectives and ultimately the development of policies and legislative framework that determine the scale and scope of refinery and downstream industrialization as well as the usage, pricing methodology and sales strategy of the oil and gas reserves. Clarity and consensus on the national vision and objectives among the various government agencies are crucial; their commitment is critical to the implementation and management of the process. Moreover, knowledge of the hydrocarbon supply determines the balance of power in the approach and negotiation of production contracts and other agreements for the commercialization of the petroleum reserves.

Additionally, an understanding of the reservoir—geology, risk and technology requirements—enables the negotiating government to propose a relevant and targeted mix of fiscal and non-tariff incentives to stimulate interest among E&P companies of all sizes and derive maximum returns for the country. Of utmost importance to the success of the commercialization of the hydrocarbon resource is the selection of an appropriate partner. That is, the company chosen as the "business partner" must be complementary to national development objectives. In addition to having a business partner with a strategic fit, the balance of power should not be overwhelmingly in favour of either partner. Furthermore, this relationship must be enforced by a legally binding contract that is managed and overseen by a relevant government agency which has the institutional capacity and legislation to administer the operations of multi-national companies, in an environment of healthy tension, where the investors feel that decisions and actions by the regulators are firm and strong but consistent and fair.

It may seem far-fetched or presumptuous for a developing country to conceive that it can effectively collaborate with multinational corporations and negotiate a contract with favourable conditions and benefits to the host country, but this control is derived from knowledge of the country's hydrocarbon potential and, hence, bargaining power. In the case of Trinidad and Tobago, knowledge of the proven, probable and possible natural gas reserves off the east coast of Trinidad facilitated the feasibility of the Atlantic LNG project. Later, it allowed for the construction of a four-train facility to increase economies of scale and engender the required cost competitiveness to enter the US market.

Thus, assessment of the full hydrocarbon potential and the formulation of a national development strategy and objectives are critical and overriding inputs in developing national energy policy. The Trinidad and Tobago experiences (good and bad) show that, inter alia, the critical success factors of an energy-based industrialization initiative are:

- political will and leadership
- clarity, communication and consistent application of policy
- communication and feedback on implementation effort
- effective data collection and analysis
- maximum participation of locals
- empowered and effective oversight institutions
- collaboration and constancy of behaviour across state agencies
- maximum participation of civil society.

An understanding of the resource potential, based on proper research, evaluation and analysis, is required for the start-up of the industrialization efforts while factoring in technological changes in the future. Continuous exploration and production is required to maintain the potential resource base at its optimum level. It is during the "mature" stage of the industry cycle that the appropriate mix of policy, fiscal incentives, taxation regimes and production contracts become even more pertinent for ensuring the longevity and sustainability of the energy sector. Globally, Trinidad and Tobago now has to compete with countries that have recently discovered oil and gas deposits. Many of these new entrants are located in low-income developing countries that are willing to compromise labour, environmental, profit-sharing and contract conditions in the effort to attract investors to monetize their hydrocarbon assets. By contrast, Trinidad and Tobago can be branded as a country with a stable and peaceful democracy, the relevant enabling business environment along with oil and gas laws, and policies and human resources to militate against this "scramble for the bottom."

One hundred years of energy experience has now positioned Trinidad and Tobago as a global energy player and a potential partner, investor and pool of expertise and services for new energy players. In this regard, the approach to supporting governments in Africa (commonly called the "Africa Initiative"), provides some detail on the value of the Trinidad and Tobago experience to newly emerging producers of oil and gas in the developing world.

IMPLEMENTING THE AFRICA INITIATIVE

Earlier, in Chapter 6, it was noted that at the 8th African Union Summit in Addis Ababa in January 2007, the Prime Minister of Trinidad and Tobago stated that T&T would make expertise available at no cost to certain African countries, viz. Chad, Nigeria, Cameroon, Equatorial Guinea, Gabon, The Republic of Congo (Brazzaville) and Angola. Several missions have since travelled back and forth across the Atlantic: technocrats, businessmen and educators from Trinidad and Tobago to East, West and South Africa; from Africa: Presidents (including those of Nigeria, Ghana, Uganda and T&T), Energy Ministers and technocrats from several African governments and state companies. The African delegations are often accompanied by business leaders ("Energy Study Visits") and an ECOWAS (the Economic Community of West African States) high-level energy mission. Trinidad and Tobago's diplomatic missions in Africa, headed by the High Commissioners in Nigeria and Uganda, became the focal points for facilitating these exchanges.

As these countries found oil and natural gas and sought to use it to benefit their national development, it became commonplace for them to ask Trinidad and Tobago to assist in developing or implementing natural gas policies and master plans. By sharing the experiences of T&T in moving towards a more developed status by, *inter alia*, leveraging its oil and natural gas endowments, an opportunity is provided to deliver very tangible results for all parties. This is an enormous undertaking that poses significant challenge and delivery risk, given the size of the task, the limitations of the Trinidad and Tobago state sector and the urgency of the request. Thus it appears clear that a collaborative effort, involving the Trinidad and Tobago Government, state companies and the energy private sector, will have the greatest chance for success in the initiatives required to pursue any opportunities that might arise out of, or supplement this support.

Trinidad and Tobago's experiences over the entire oil and gas value chain cover all aspects, from policy formulation, through strategy, planning, business development, project management, start-up and operations to business exit. This country has built its own training programmes to develop capacity in the energy sector. Aside from sharing the skills, Trinidad and Tobago can also share the evolution of the "ecosystem" of the energy sector that supports its growth. That is, how the country reacted to different circumstances and how the pieces fit together and support each other. The organisms in this ecosystem include education programmes, infrastructure, policies, legislation, institutions, governance and decision-making processes.

In the services sector, collaboration with newly developing and expanding sectors of Africa provides opportunity for local companies to access new markets at a time when domestic demand has become lean, as a result of the global economic slowdown. Private-public collaboration will be an important factor in Trinidad and Tobago's ability to extend its current oil and gas business beyond its shores, allowing a deepening of its participation in the industry. Trinidad and Tobago participants may engage in many parts of the oil and natural gas value chain, by pursuing any of several opportunities, such as:

1. Acquisition of licenses over acreage in appropriate African countries for access to reserves and/or production, through:
   a. Exploration, and/or
   b. Development, and/or
   c. Production management.
2. Provision of services to the oil and gas sector including:
   a. Upstream & downstream operations and production support
   b. Capacity development, including skills training and mentoring
   c. Infrastructure development (ports, pipelines, etc.)
   d. Facilites management (ports, industrial estates, etc.).
3. Accessing of raw materials and/or product:
   a. oil and natural gas for manufacturing and/or trading and distribution;
   b. participation interests in downstream processing and/or manufacturing plants
      i. petroleum products and natural gas derivatives;
      ii. pipelines and utilities;
      iii. electric power plants and transmission and distribution systems;
      iv. industrial estates/exports.

   The above provide opportunities for a range of Trinidad and Tobago companies—from business developers and financiers of plant and facilities operators, to participation in the mid- and downstream natural gas sectors and infrastructure development and operations.
4. Accessing markets for Trading and Distribution of commodities/products.
   This will allow these companies to deepen participation in the natural gas sector, outside of Trinidad and Tobago, by leveraging knowledge gained from its own partnerships and downstream activities in these areas.
5. Providing liquidity for trading in T&T or International (T&T and partner countries) Commodities Exchanges, this may be developed over time.

For trading exchanges to start, develop and succeed there must be significant access to one or more of the major components: supply, demand, capital and risk management capability. The liquidity of supply, provided by product in 3 above, allows Trinidad and Tobago and their international partner companies to undertake the activities in 4 above, through the exchange of their choice.

6. Provision of training, research opportunities and services to African companies and government by working in conjunction with the University of the West Indies, and the University of Trinidad and Tobago, technical and vocational schools and other tertiary education institutions.

Trinidad and Tobago's biggest asset is its people. Already many of its citizens are in Africa, working in almost every country in the oil and gas sector. They are largely employed with multinational exploration and production companies or oil service companies. What is missing from the African landscape is Trinidad and Tobago companies. It is incumbent on the Chambers of Commerce and the Government to assist this process by making readily available to local companies the basic information that would allow them to penetrate international markets.

There is an ongoing scramble for African resources by the superpowers and their major oil and gas companies as well as by the leading emerging nations and independent private companies. There is no doubt that the African nations that have been exposed to the 'Trinidad experience' are overwhelmed by T&T's achievements. This country has proven to the African countries that it is capable of transferring know-how for development, and is further aligned with these African countries by historical, developmental and cultural similarities. Several African countries see T&T as a preferred model for developing their oil and gas industry. This has created unique opportunities for Trinidad and Tobago, not only to lead others along its development trajectory, but to help them to understand the pitfalls along the way, so that they could chart their own path and develop even faster and better.

The African Initiative of taking the "Trinidad and Tobago Model" beyond our shores presents a unique opportunity to deliver the long sought-after and ever-elusive promise of enhanced south-south cooperation among nations that can identify with each other.

In its quest to export the Trinidad and Tobago model to other developing countries, T&T can benefit from several competitive advantages, not the least of which is historical solidarity, small size and non-threatening presence. Africa and Trinidad and Tobago share a history of colonialism, slavery and culture, as well as the pursuit of post-independence resource-based industrialization in collaboration with some resource-rich developing countries. As such, former colonized countries in the continents of Africa,

Asia and South America are able to relate to and embrace T&T's model of economic and industrial development. The model is particularly relevant to other resource-rich developing countries for a number of reasons: it was indigenously developed within a holistic framework for national development; it institutionalizes an effective legal and regulatory framework; it offers successful commercialization and downstream business development strategies as well as pricing and fiscal methodologies, education and training systems and investment policies.

More importantly, these relationships create openings for south-south collaboration and alliances between developing countries for monetizing energy resources and getting involved in downstream industrialization. All this augurs well for T&T's energy services sector since its indigenous services companies will have access to other markets. But more importantly, south-south collaboration would facilitate aggregation of energy reserves, capital, technological know-how and human resources to build world-class manufacturing industries that produce value-added, cost effective and competitive downstream products to international standards. This development of competitive and viable energy products through a south-south partnership would give developing countries the necessary leverage to negotiate favourable conditions effectively for other treaties and agreements such as agricultural and manufactured products, as well as production sharing contracts and equitable trade regimes with the developed countries of the north.

THE ENERGY SERVICES SECTOR

Undoubtedly, the energy sector remains the major productive sector of the T&T economy in spite of the various industrial diversification policies and instruments undertaken over the last 50 years. However, the sector's major activity is concentrated in primary extraction of a non-renewable resource, which means that most of the industries engage in activities in the early stages of the value chain and as such derive few economic linkages. While energy-based production accounted for over 90 percent of foreign exchange earnings in 2008, the sector employs only 4 percent of the labour force. Moreover, due to the dominance of foreign direct investment and services companies in the energy sector and overseas value-added, the majority of energy earnings are repatriated to or retained by foreign-based parent companies. The Trinidad and Tobago government has recognized these challenges and is seeking to reduce dependency on oil and gas through a two-pronged approach of 1) deepening downstream industrialization and 2) a non-energy sector economic diversification strategy.

The Vision 2020 sectoral report on Industry and Entrepreneurship stated that "for industry and entrepreneurship development in Trinidad and Tobago, it is critical to promote and encourage the non-oil manufacturing sector. New industries in this sub-sector are earmarked for special emphasis in terms of investment promotion and strategic alliances through joint ventures" (Ministry of Planning and Development 2004). These industries were:

- food and beverage
- chemicals including plastics
- metal processing
- leisure marine
- information technology/electronics
- printing and packaging
- construction
- exportable services

Diversification in the context of the Vision 2020 Plan seeks to engage in non-energy-related areas of business in an attempt to reduce the dependency on the energy-based exploration and production sector, and lessen the economic effect of oil and gas price volatility. The wisdom of policy makers and advisors has been to use the receipts from the energy sector for diversification and non-energy enterprise development projects. This, however, begs the question: does policy aimed at facilitating economic diversification simply require a deliberate plan where resources are diverted into the non-energy sector, namely the manufacturing sector? In other words, can meaningful and sustainable economic diversification in Trinidad and Tobago be achieved by isolating the energy sector? The dichotomous nature of the proposed diversification strategy can stymie the real potential of economic diversification. This is not to suggest that initiatives to develop the non-energy sector should be abandoned, but that the local energy services sector is the most competitive of the Trinidad and Tobago economy and, as such, presents the best launch pad for economic diversification. Even in its embryonic stage, the domestic energy services sector has never been protected by trade barriers or supported through Government incentives as was extended to the local manufacturing sector during the "Import Substitution" and "Export Oriented" eras of industrialization. Apart from work permit restrictions there have never been any entry barriers against foreign energy service companies setting up in T&T. In fact, local content policies were introduced only in 2004, and these are yet to be fully enforced through legislation and regulatory agencies.

As such, since inception, the domestic energy service companies have been compelled to compete with international energy service companies in a free and open domestic market in providing services to large global companies such as BP, Conoco Phillips, BG, BHP Billiton, Norsk Hydro, Methanex, PCS Nitrogen, and the indigenous companies such as Petrotrin and NGC. It is no coincidence, therefore, that a competitiveness assessment conducted for the Ministry of Trade and Industry identified the energy service industries as the only internationally competitive service section of the Trinidad and Tobago economy (Minstry of Trade and Industry 2006).

The large multinational companies which dominate the energy sector in Trinidad and Tobago implement and adhere to international best practices in business administration, finance, technology, occupational health and safety and environment, and therefore, maintain a highly competitive "world class" local energy sector. Former Finance Minister, Wendell Motley, refers to the local energy sector as being "modern, wealthy, technologically sophisticated and First World" (Mottley 2007). By contrast, the "Competitiveness of the Services and Non-oil Manufacturing Sectors of Trinidad and Tobago" survey classifies all of the non-energy sectors of the economy as being either "some-what competitive" or "uncompetitive," thus creating a "dualism" in the local economy. However, it is because of the energy multinationals' insistence on first-world standards, that the local energy services sector was compelled to become competitive in order to win contracts from these large global companies and compete with global energy service companies operating in the T&T market.

The prominence of local service providers can be traced back to World War II when tight foreign currency and import controls forced Halliburton to abandon business in Trinidad. Holbrook and Devenish, in their recount of the history of oilfield services wrote that "Trinidad is remarkable for the way that local companies, using local finance, management and staff were able to establish and offer keen and effective competition to those overseas compa-

Table 13.1.   Competitiveness Assessment for Selected Service Industries

Rating	Industries
Competitive	Oil and Gas Services
Somewhat Competitive	Engineering and Architectural Services
	Professional Business Services
	Information Technology Services
	Film and Video
	Entertainment
	Yachting and Leisure Marine Services
Uncompetitive	Merchant Marine

Source: Minstry of Trade and Industry. *Competitiveness of the Services and Non-Oil Manufacturing Sector of Trinidad and Tobago.* GOTT, 2006.

nies" (Higgins 1996). This resulted in Schlumberger and the locally-owned Trinidad Oilfield Service being the only two energy service companies operating in Trinidad during World War II. Moreover, Trinidad Oilfield Service was the only company to offer cementing services to the local petroleum industry at this time. This is very significant, as Trinidad and Tobago was the only oil-producing colony during World War II. As such, the local petroleum sector was of strategic importance to wartime efforts in providing refuelling facilities for the Royal Navy as well as petroleum products for the United Kingdom.

World War II also precipitated the advance of new technology that was developed specifically for the armed forces. However, by 1947 these technological developments were applied to the petroleum industry. As such, innovations such as the shaped-charge or jet-perforator for well perforating were introduced in various forms and sizes for a wide range of services including down hole cutting of tubing, drill-pipe and casing. Of critical importance was the fact that the two service companies in operation in Trinidad at that time were able to compete effectively by providing all these new innovations locally within a short time after they were made available in the US.

While it is argued that the potential of the energy services sector is heavily dependent on the economic performance of the energy sector, deepening of the sector can:

1. lessen the economy's vulnerability to commodity price shocks;
2. generate increased employment within the energy sector—the country's highest paying sector but also one of the country's lowest employers (only 4% of employment is directly attributable to the sector, despite its high contributions to exports, foreign earnings, and GDP;
3. ensure longevity beyond the depletion of local energy reserves in the long term; and
4. ensure local content and participation.

More importantly, the wide range of services enlisted under the "Energy Services Sector" makes this sector inherently diversified, as many of the services are not energy-sector specific. Well-developed and competitive local energy service companies stand to take full advantage of the opportunities afforded as the major multi-national energy companies increasingly outsource non-core activities. Many of these services must be performed even during recessionary periods or plant shut-downs. In all cases, the local companies and people doing the work must achieve a level of competence that will allow them to launch onto the international arena. Furthermore, the liberalization of global marketplaces, especially in other resource-rich developing countries (e.g. Africa, South America and South East Asia) provides export potential for local energy service companies. For these reasons, a case can be made for the prioritization of the energy services sector as a means of economic diversification.

There are numerous foreign companies operating in the energy service sector in Trinidad and Tobago. These companies include global energy service giants Schlumberger, Baker Hughes, Global Santa Fe and Halliburton. There have been several joint venture arrangements between local entities and these international service companies. Through these partnerships, local firms seek to benefit from the world-class experience and skill sets of their foreign associates. As seen in Chapter 5 on "Maximising National Value," the degree of value-added gained through knowledge transference correlates strongly with the degree of integration. As such, it is critical that firms in the host country forge deep equity relationships at every level of the value chain in order to achieve effective transfer of knowledge and technology. Although most business arrangements still operate at the lower levels of integration and collaboration, many major spill-over effects exist within the general industry as skill certification and international health, safety, and environmental standards have become basic contract requirements within the domestic industry.

As such, the energy services sector benefits from transference of developed-world practices and knock-on effects of the domestic activities of energy sector companies and their internal linkages and synergies, while promoting local content and participation. The development of a robust energy-services sector opens up the opportunity for the sector to evolve into an export-oriented value-added services sector whereby a wide range of energy skills become export commodities. But a focus on developing the entire energy services sector is now critical to foster the competitiveness of the sector within the domestic market and, ultimately, to nurture a globally competitive sector. It would be judicious of the Government to provide an enabling framework through the establishment of:

- relevant local content and participation policy
- taxation and non-tariff incentives
- the building of intra-sector linkages and systemic improvements to other sectors of the economy
- showcasing energy services competencies as an integral part of the nation's energy and trade portfolio most importantly, bi-lateral trade agreements with other investor-friendly developing countries such as in Africa and Latin America which would provide to local service companies, preferential access to markets, and even local content accreditation in countries involved in natural gas industrialization.

HUMAN CAPACITY DEVELOPMENT—
EDUCATION & TRAINING

Trinidad and Tobago nationals have a long-standing reputation in the global energy sector, especially in services related to engineering and drilling. Oscar Prieto, Atlantic LNG's CEO acknowledged the technical abilities and competitiveness of the human capital in T&T's energy sector, by conceding that "with the global LNG industry stretched thin for resources, some countries such as Qatar have been advertising in the media in Trinidad and Tobago for experts and have even visited the Caribbean island to headhunt" (Jaffar 2007). BP Chairman, Lord Brown reiterated this in May 2004 by recognizing that, ".....we (BP) have an excellent team of people—including 650 Trinidadians, 35 of whom are already working internationally and lead other BP business activities around the world" (Browne 2004). BP is emulating Schlumberger some 30 years after it was reported that Schlumberger had, by the 1970s, more Trinidadians in supervisory positions globally than any other nationality, except Americans.

The education system of Trinidad and Tobago has been systematically realigned over the past six or seven years to the industrialization strategy of the country and has evolved to support the growing sophistication and maturity of the domestic energy sector. The system has been built on a foundation provided by the church-run schools of the colonial era and has progressed from one of an MNC-administered apprenticeship scheme for semi-skilled craftsmen, to support industrial activity, to certifying tradesmen to operate and maintain the new industries as well as process and design engineers for conceptualizing and developing future industries and, ultimately, to training strategic business managers to chart and control the destiny of T&T's energy industry.

The higher level technical competency of local nationals can be attributed to the engineering and energy industry-related undergraduate and graduate programmes offered at the University of the West Indies and later, the University of Trinidad and Tobago. Lord Brown admits that BP "benefits from (y) our education system" (Browne 2004). These courses illustrate successful examples of educational institutions partnering with the relevant industry to create and deliver "industry relevant" academic training in the development of "industry ready" human resources. The University of the West Indies boasts of a long history of successfully administering quality engineering degree programmes that have equipped professionals with the necessary skills to play critical roles in both of the energy industrialization waves in Trinidad and Tobago, as well as for leading overseas operations. The University of Trinidad and Tobago has distinguished itself by focusing on a practical "co-operative" element as a major component of course content. That means that it is compulsory for students to earn credits by engaging in a managed work programme in a relevant industry or organization.

The local training institutions and undergraduate/post-graduate programmes have provided the backbone for the success of the oil and gas industry in Trinidad and Tobago. For new entrants to the international gas industry, educational institutions and apprenticeships in Trinidad and Tobago can be an attractive option.

In addition to being cost effective, Trinidad and Tobago provides the following competitive advantages for students from other developing countries such as in Africa, Asia and Latin America:

- International recognition. The undergraduate engineering programmes at The University of the West Indies are all internationally accredited by the Professional Engineering/Surveying/Geosciences Bodies of the United Kingdom. Likewise, the University of Trinidad and Tobago has collaboration agreements with several top international engineering schools and executed a Memorandum of Understanding with the University of Texas at Austin for the development of petroleum engineering programmes.
- Mild climate. Trinidad and Tobago enjoys a tropical climate, while its southern location in the Caribbean Sea puts it out of range of the hurricane belt.
- Language of instruction. Trinidad and Tobago is an English-speaking country. As such, all courses are delivered in the dominant language of the international energy sector;
- Political stability. Unlike many other resource-rich countries, Trinidad and Tobago is a peaceful, stable democracy. Each political transition has been peaceful and via free and fair elections;
- Favourable economic conditions. e.g. low and stable exchange rates, a comparatively low inflation rate, low unemployment rates and one of the lowest cost of living conditions in the Caribbean.
- Immigration laws. Student visa and visitor entry requirements are lower than those of the United States and United Kingdom. This is particularly relevant for students from Middle Eastern and African countries (where most of the world's oil and gas reserves are located), as more stringent controls have made entry into North America, the UK and most of Europe difficult;
- Commuting. The well-developed network of roads and the small size of the country make in-country commute easy. As such, travel to and from production fields (even offshore facilities) and downstream industries for research and hands-on training can be completed in one day. This accessibility also provides for a focus on on-the-job training modules—a component that is not possible at many other locations because of distance, safety and climatic conditions.

INSTITUTIONAL CAPACITY DEVELOPMENT—
GAS INDUSTRY KNOWLEDGE, EXPERIENCE
AND INVESTOR POTENTIAL

The National Gas Company has export potential in terms of gas-business expertise and resources. This agency has been spearheading and managing the gas industry in Trinidad and Tobago since 1975 and can be considered a global pioneer in the business. This long and deep history of the gas industry coupled with the fact that the NGC has been accredited with an investment grade rating by international rating agencies makes it a prime option to develop business opportunities in fledgling gas-based economies.

During visits to Trinidad by African diplomatic missions, the NGC has been showcased as the business model for natural gas monetization. This provides potential for NGC to undertake services or even take equity positions in approved enterprises in these countries, should host governments so desire. As business developer, NGC stands to gain from profits, but more importantly, would be able to secure downstream marketing positions to supplement its T&T portfolio, as well as open up export markets for the local energy-services sector. However, this calls for the deliberate intervention of the Government to provide the required launch pad via the promotion of the capabilities of the energy sector as an export commodity, and the supporting mechanisms such as bi-lateral trade and investment agreements that cover intellectual property agreements, double taxation treaties and the free movement of professional human resources.

Financial Services

Trinidad and Tobago is the only resource-based industrialized economy in the Caribbean. The economies of most of the other islands depend primarily on agriculture, tourism and in some territories, offshore banking. However, the tourism sector of most of the islands is dominated by international hotel chains and, as such, most of the proceeds of the industry are collected offshore via international booking agencies and do not accrue to the government or citizens of the host island. By contrast, the vibrant energy industry in Trinidad and Tobago has provided local and locally-operating banks with excess liquidity which is collected onshore due to the active participation of the State and national energy companies such as Petrotrin and NGC. Therefore, Trinidad and Tobago has maintained, and will continue to maintain the position of both financial capital and financier of the Caribbean region.

Local institutions have financed projects such as government infrastructure, energy and electricity generation, tourism and entertainment and financial investments throughout the Caribbean. The State-owned First Citizens

Bank has been pursuing an energy-based portfolio and currently holds equity position at a regional electricity generating plant and has financed other electricity-generating facilities throughout the region. It currently has a mutual fund whose portfolio consists primarily of energy-based assets. The regional investment base of the local financial institutions has been so extensive that many offer specialized investment instruments such as Caribbean-based investments, real estate investments and other energy mutual funds, all of which contain sizeable regional investments within their portfolios.

Trinidad and Tobago can consolidate this regional financial leadership position as industrialization efforts ensue and as liquidity and funding capacity increases. Concomitantly, there is little industrialization potential regionally as no other island has any significant proven hydrocarbon reserves. Initiatives such the strengthening of the CSME[2] and the establishment of a single economy will further strengthen Trinidad and Tobago's regional potential within the financial services sector. In light of the fact that local financial institutions do not have the capital or the risk appetite to solely finance or syndicate any of the major billion-dollar energy projects in T&T, the regional financial market presents a logical and viable alternative. However, in an effort to compete effectively with international banks operating throughout the region, local financial houses must become sophisticated with their product offerings especially in the areas of capital markets, stock markets, commodity trading, venture capital and derivatives.

Domestic Private Sector Participation

Another critical issue is that of the domestic private sector involvement in the energy sector. This is a vital requirement in order to achieve the optimal level of equity participants, service providers and local content and participation within the energy sector. Although local conglomerate, CL Financial was the majority shareholder[3] of the methanol plants in Trinidad and Tobago, the energy sector is dominated by international companies. This can be attributed to several factors:

- Government's perceived reluctance to involve the domestic private sector in the energy sector.
- Lack of capital or access to capital of the magnitude required by the local private sector, given the risk averse nature, lack of industry sophistication and high interest rates and charges of the local financial sector.
- lack of technical knowledge to make informed business decisions
- lack of opportunity afforded to local private sector to participate
- risk aversion.

Once again, effective government policy through fiscal measures—taxation and royalty policies to encourage and build local involvement and capabilities—as well as non-fiscal measures such as the stipulation for a required percentage of local participation and preferential quotas for the use of local goods, services, labour and capital, as well as access to the database of projects in the pipeline can increase the depth and breadth of local ownership along the energy value chain. In the long run, this would augment local capabilities nationwide, as there can be spill-over effects of technology and business knowledge to other sectors, as well as business development through cluster industries. All of this would undoubtedly contribute to development and overall increased international competitiveness of the people and businesses of Trinidad and Tobago.

EXPLORATION STRATEGY

As mentioned earlier, the upstream energy sub-sector is the most significant contributor to the economy of Trinidad and Tobago. Singularly, it provides the most to Government revenue through oil and gas production, in the form of Petroleum Profits Tax, Supplemental Petroleum Tax, royalties, revenue shares from Production Sharing Contracts, and personal taxes, as well as the concomitant multiplier effect from the very significant energy services sector. Furthermore, it provides the raw material for the mid and downstream energy businesses and the revenue they, in turn, generate.

Sustainability or growth of the Trinidad and Tobago energy sector is, therefore, directly dependent in the short- to medium-term on the sustainability and growth of the upstream sub-sector. Since this is contingent on the discovery, development and production of oil and gas reserves, it follows that the outlook for the future of the energy industry in Trinidad and Tobago will be defined by the nature, disposition and management of the country's oil and gas resources. Of course, other factors such as international oil and gas prices, technological advances and the participation of Trinidad and Tobago nationals, companies and the State—locally or beyond the country's borders—will also directly affect the future of the sector and ultimately its contribution to the national economy.

At home, the country stands to capture maximum value from upstream activity through the efficient and sustainable exploration and exploitation of Trinidad and Tobago's petroleum resources. Therefore, sustainability of the resource rests largely on the country's ability to *strategically manage its acreage* in a manner that:

- encourages an optimal mix of E&P companies to ensure long-term development of the resource;
- understands the exploration and production project life cycle and global market conditions and is able to time the allocation of acreage to coincide as closely as possible with projected optimum conditions of demand, cost

and price at the respective stages in the project life cycle. This may be an elusive dream, of course, but is an aspiration worth pursuing.

- recognises the impact of industry and global technology trends on the timing of acreage access and the composition of acreage offered for release;
- takes into consideration global energy trends, geo-politics and the competition for international investors throughout the developing world and by new entrants;
- ensures an increasing level of local content and participation through legislation and oversight;
- is guided by judicious strategic leadership that aligns the national vision with commercial realities, and is sufficiently flexible to constantly adapt to the demands of the dynamic global environment; and
- facilitates and enables increased data acquisition, research, analysis and access to inform and encourage future development.

The current acreage release strategy appears to favour larger companies that have access to the required funding, skills and the technology to undertake exploratory activity in primarily frontier areas. While this approach may have been successful in the past, it may no longer be optimal, as:

- attracted players are primarily majors and larger independents, resulting in a reduced scope for participation by smaller and local players, who, in mature basins/plays, tend to bring creativity and innovation to exploration and exploitation as they go after smaller prizes, thus extending basin and field life-span and potential;
- smaller wells and oil or gas fields may not be optimally developed, even though they may be economically viable, because of the high hurdle rate and overhead costs to larger multinational firms;
- the current licensing regime grants exclusive access to seismic and well data of the large acreage blocks to the operating company. Under this agreement, only the licensee and the Ministry have access to data related to the productivity or potential of the licensed and, by extension, adjacent acreage. As the Ministry is bound by archaic legislation designed to keep much of the data confidential, any clear understanding of the regional picture and areas of known, smaller deposits which would be ignored by these large companies are unavailable to small operators; and
- the participation of small local operators can be the catalyst for the development of the country's future local energy players as E&P activity on the smaller reservoirs can provide them with the requisite skills, technological knowledge and capital generation for larger undertakings.

In light of this, the objective should be to develop a country acreage management strategy that will create an environment which:

- supports equitable and sustainable E&P activity, thus creating a continuous demand for upstream services, education, training, innovation and R&D, and hence support local institutions (schools, universities, service businesses, banks, etc.) and generate employment
- manages the pace of exploitation to accelerate small field development and extend field life
- maximises the level of recovery
- increases local participation
- encourages further upstream investment and production; and
- encourages downstream activity and local value-add

It is important to note that discoveries may be considered sub-economic for a variety of reasons e.g.:

1. Small volumes that do not meet minimum economic field size based on current costs, price forecasts or fiscal terms;
2. High development costs, associated with several factors, including:
   a. structural or stratigraphic complexity, requiring high numbers of wells and/or low well recoveries
   b. mixed phase hydrocarbons requiring oil rims be produced through horizontal wells, prior to gas blow down
   c. shallow depth of reservoirs
   d. low initial pressures
   e. secondary and/or tertiary recovery methods
   f. the type of reservoir drive mechanism
   g. water depth
   h. drilling depth to reservoir
   i. drilling complexity (pressure variation considerations)
3. Access to infrastructure and markets
   - distance and access to infrastructure and facilities, especially for new, offshore/distal or smaller fields and heavy oil
4. Inappropriate or excessively high tax regimes

KEY SUCCESS FACTORS

The conversion of concept to resource, resource to reserves and reserves to production is only realised through geological mapping, technical and commercial evaluation and drilling. The key components of resource evaluation through to value realisation are managed through the various phases of exploration, appraisal, development and production. This requires meticulous management of the processes that convert real estate into geological concepts, then into exploration programmes, and ultimately into reserves. The lesson of the first 100 years of energy development in Trinidad and Tobago is that a strategic approach to resource management which supports national economic development, is required at every stage of the E&P process so that depleted reserves are constantly replaced by new discoveries, which in turn are fed from new resources that are discovered by the use of new concepts and evaluation. The natural gas development model is, of course the prime case in point.

In Trinidad & Tobago's case, these were underpinned by an agile and responsive fiscal regime that was conversant with the variables and their movements, because of the skills, experience and collaboration of the technocrats influencing and managing the tax system (Board of Inland Revenue, Ministry of Finance and Ministry of Energy), while having the confidence of the political directorate and the population.

In an effort to maintain this flow, the following are some key areas to which urgent attention is now required:

1. Access to data. As articulated under the current terms and conditions of their E&P license, BPTT and Petrotrin control most of the acreage and, therefore, most of the geological and petroleum engineering data. As such, the Petroleum Regulations need to be updated to reflect current global industry practice in respect of data release in the best interest of Trinidad and Tobago.
2. Seismic. Facilitate in-country and national capability development in seismic services, so as to develop a contracting service capacity and an in-country research capability. e.g. land 3D acquisition and Depth Migration.
3. A flexible & responsive fiscal regime that is user-friendly and easy to understand. One of the major challenges is that there are many operating variables and a wide variety of different economic permutations within Trinidad and Tobago e.g. heavy oil development, deep-water exploration and development, marginal oil and gas fields in all areas, including stripper oilfields and stranded natural gas. This is further complicated by higher E&P costs as low-cost fields become exhausted.
   • Other factors which make for real challenges in the area of cost control will also have to be considered, including:
     i. higher exploration risks and increasing write off exposure
     ii. Drilling deeper, higher pressure and higher angle well bores
     iii. increasing reservoir complexity
     iv. high inflation
     v. petroleum subsidy and other miscellaneous taxes or levies that have been added to upstream producers over time
4. Institutional Capacity. The current industry requires strategic and oversight bodies, regulatory agencies and systems and processes that effectively and efficiently allocate and manage acreage in a transparent, predictable and flexible approach that is consistent with international standards and conven-

tions. The State and State agencies must also have the expertise and acumen to regulate an industry whose players are predominantly multinational companies that singularly have more assets, capital, technical competence, access to markets and information, global reach and influence than the host government.

5. Continuous Boundary Scanning and Strategic Leadership. The dynamic nature of the energy industry as well as the global environment as a whole necessitates unceasing monitoring and evaluation of trends, global events, new global hydrocarbon discoveries and technological advancements. Acreage allocation and management do not only have commercial implications but can also influence and be influenced by diplomatic relations, trade, taxation treaties and migration laws with other countries. Moreover, competent leadership that embodies the long-term vision of the country and the energy sector is critical.

NATURAL GAS

The current gas supply overhang co-exists with falling natural gas reserves and limited exploration activity. As noted in earlier chapters, natural gas exploration activity in Trinidad and Tobago is impacted by three factors:

1. future prospects for hydrocarbon discoveries in new acreage are largely in deeper waters or at greater depths;
2. these have much higher development costs;
3. lack of an open market for gas sales and pricing.

What may be needed for gas exploration to be promoted is an undertaking that provides assurances:

- that the market will be flexed to reflect the country's reserves position in a timely manner;
- that a policy of reserves to production ratio levels be set and managed through judicious and complementary exploration and market development programmes;
- that production levels give due consideration to conservation and cash flow issues that, as in the past, can distort the economy;
- that markets provide a return on investment that allows for more difficult and expensive gas to be developed;
- that market development will reflect exploration and production realities and investment risk;
- that the portfolio of gas leads, plays and fields be managed as such, with development considering the life of complex issues, so that, for instance,

more expensive fields may be brought on at times of higher profits, supplemented by lower cost fields;

• that emphasis be placed on smaller fields near to existing infrastructure and a marketing strategy that reflects and/or facilitates a more open market than the current long term contracts in the domestic market;

• that a portfolio of markets be established, in line with the strategic exploration and business development programmes, so that all players understand the pricing mechanisms into which they are playing;

• that gas pricing be open and transparent and reflect the market in T&T, perhaps via some basket of the different sales opportunities available locally, which is determined by the business development programme and which, in turn, will drive the gas exploration programme;

• that the country's acreage management strategy include the ability of the Ministry to re-allocate acreage or assets that are under-utilised or under-explored or whose development is delayed by a license holder, where the asset does not currently match portfolio considerations, but are misaligned with national strategic interests;

Thus high value exports, such as additional LNG, ammonia or methanol exports and other innovative and rapid gas export options can be considered, as appropriately sized field discoveries are made and where these cannot be monetized by domestic utilization only and higher value-added usage. The expansion of exports of LNG, ammonia and methanol, particularly at the rates achieved over the past decade, is not sustainable over the medium- to long-term unless very large discoveries of oil and gas are made in the new and as yet unexplored acreage. In any case, such expansion must involve higher value capture for T&T and its nationals, through more local participation along the value chain, both within and outside T&T.

The 2006/5 petroleum tax revisions were made under conditions of high prices for both oil and natural gas which are unlikely to persist for natural gas, in particular, in the medium term. Increasingly higher development costs had accompanied these rising prices, suggesting the need to restructure the system to facilitate the development of smaller and/or higher cost discoveries as well as the unique characteristics and complexities of the gas industry as opposed to oil.

Generating exploratory activity of the level required to expand natural resource output or to even sustain current output levels, will require the following:

1. appropriate contract terms and conditions for natural gas exploration and development, with particular reference, as noted above, to the costly deep-water areas.
2. sharing of production that recognizes the difference between oil and natural gas and the likelihood that one or the other will be found.

3. well defined and transparent gas sales management and capacity included within those contracts.
4. a policy position regarding the development of new natural gas markets, including increased LNG exports and the mechanism for the allocation of access to such exports to new and successful exploratory contractors as well as existing producers.

This strongly implies that for Production Sharing Contracts, where natural gas would be the hydrocarbon likely to be produced, the institutionalization of a separate petroleum tax regime may be more appropriate. In such instances where exploration and production licenses are the contract form, incentives or acreage management strategies to encourage the development of smaller gas fields will be necessary if they are not to lie idle as "stranded" gas reserves. Consideration should always be given first to T&T's strategic interests, even within a win-win outcome.

Conservation, Efficiency and Rationalization

As mentioned earlier, the production rate in T&T for oil and natural gas needs to take consideration of an appropriate reserves to production ratio that considers the important and relevant factors of growth, development, sustainability, possible economic distortions due to excessive State expenditures as a result of high revenues and the heritage of future generations.

In addition to the challenges listed above in respect of further development of the natural gas industry in Trinidad and Tobago, several changes regarding efficiency and rationalization were outlined in Chapter 4. Two of the more demanding ones are critical to the further development of the industry, particularly if it is to remain globally competitive. These are:

- the need to facilitate the closure of old and inefficient gas-consuming plants and enhance the quality of plant replacement, by providing conditions for the establishment of new plants that increase added value to, and utilise more efficiently, the depleting natural gas reserves of Trinidad and Tobago;
- the importance of managing excess capacity within the gas industry so as to maximize the use of capital across the entire value chain from upstream through transmission and consumption.

Transitioning from Petroleum to Renewables

One of the more entrenched policy positions in Trinidad and Tobago is the pricing of energy for domestic use in the country. This applies to natural gas, gasoline, diesel oil, kerosene, LPG and electricity. Subsidies are provided at various levels within enterprises, as well as by the State in its fiscal and tax policies. The result is two-fold. The subsidies can be large and are usually not reviewed or altered over periods of up to 10 years. Secondly, prices to the consumer can be so low that they act as a significant disincentive for competing fuels, especially if those competing fuel forms are not supported by fiscal incentives. Thus, a real challenge for the future is to move domestic energy prices to levels nearer to world market prices, and to provide incentives for available alternative energy forms to displace these depleting fuels. The displaced fuels can then be exported into higher value markets.

SUMMARY

With less than 0.5 percent of the world's total energy reserves, Trinidad and Tobago is now an established gas-based economy. In 2008, it is the fifth largest producer of LNG and the largest single exporter of ammonia and methanol in the world. In order to optimize the benefits along the entire value chain, Trinidad and Tobago must now consider further deepening its activities, not only into the downstream business where there are expanded product opportunities and value-added benefits, as well as scope for diversifying and expanding markets globally, but also to the upstream sector and its services.

However, in order to optimize the full benefits of the energy value chain and to ensure the sustainability of the energy sector as a whole, increased exploration and production activities must be pursued in order to supplement proven reserves. This requires innovative and flexible policies, appropriate incentives and attractive production contracts in order to stimulate participation of large international players as well as smaller local operators. Most importantly, the polarity posed by the need to have exports of natural gas as a firm option within the exploration contracts/licenses that will be needed for deep water blocks and that of the need to continue to allow for the further development and expansion of downstream industries based on natural gas, must be accommodated at the earliest opportunity.

With the recent discovery of oil and gas reserves in several African countries, Trinidad and Tobago is now faced with increasing competition that would woo E&P multinational companies away from its shores. Within the Latin American region alone, there are offshore blocks in Argentina, Colombia, Cuba and Uruguay. However, these pose higher operational and sovereign risk than the Trinidad and Tobago fields. Although Brazil's Santos basin is touted as being the world's leading oil and gas potential, the high cost of deep-water exploration and production could prohibit the participation of medium-sized companies. As such, this presents vast opportunities for Trinidad and Tobago as a viable investment alternative. Already, T&T is challenged to attract even the majors that are here into the deep water acreage, as their recent massive discoveries in Brazil, Angola, Venezuela and other places will require huge capital funds and pull investment away from Trinidad and Tobago. Ironically, the greatest challenge might be those that have invested heavily in T&T in the recent past and are in "harvest" mode, reducing their operating costs and improving efficiency so as to realise the returns promised to shareholders on those investments.

Both the upstream and downstream gas industries in Trinidad and Tobago are oligopolistic in character with a noticeable control being exercised by the multinational corporations. The upstream industry is dominated by bpTT which currently controls 62 percent of gas volumes traded. In addition to bpTT possessing legal title for over 60 percent of the country's natural gas reserves and 30 percent of the total offshore block leases, BP also has equity investments in Atlantic LNG, the principal power generation company (Powergen) and in two large methanol plants. Other upstream players, BG and Repsol, are also shareholders in Atlantic LNG. EOG Resources also has equity investments in the ammonia industry. Likewise, the downstream industry comprises a few large international firms controlling over 95 percent of the total output and more than 100 smaller customers with a combined market share of natural gas less than 5 percent.

In light of the above, regulatory State agencies with the requisite institutional capacity and legislative mechanisms to manage and regulate MNCs, are vital. The administration and management of gas-based industrialization, especially downstream activities, is more complex and requires a thorough understanding of international relations and geo-politics, trade policies and dynamics, adherence to principles of good governance through robust systems and procedures, and standardized and transparent decision-making. However, this must be balanced by quick turnarounds in decision-making in order to maintain the global leadership position within the natural gas economy.

Furthermore, many challenges exist and must be successfully resolved in order for the existing gas industry to thrive and grow in a sustainable manner by:

1. becoming more efficient
2. treating with the social and environmental impact of energy and industrial activity
3. capturing and exporting the ready range of highly developed energy services which now exist
4. converting our varied and extensive acquired knowledge into marketable high end advisory services and educational products
5. marketing/branding Trinidad and Tobago as an "all inclusive" destination for energy related services and solutions
6. Transitioning into certain renewable sources of energy in the future

Now, more than ever, with the great opportunities ahead, the technical challenges of the energy sector in Trinidad and Tobago demand astute leadership and effective communications.

BIBLIOGRAPHY

Browne, Lord John. "Trinidad and Tobago in the Global Energy Outlook." *BP Website.* may 2004. http://www.bp.com/genericarticle.do?categoryId=98&contentId=2018437 (accessed April 20, 2012).

Higgins, George. *A History of Trinidad Oil.* Port of Spain: Trinidad Express Newspaper Limited, 1996.

Jaffar, Linda Hutchinson. "Atlantic LNG Wedded to T&T." *Newsday.* Jan. 4th, 2007. http://www.newsday.co.tt/businessday/0,50164.html (accessed April 20, 2012).

Ministry of Planning and Development. *Trinidad and Tobago: Vision 2020 Industry and Entrepreneurship.* GOTT, 2004.

Minstry of Trade and Industry. *Competitiveness of the Services and Non-Oil Manufacturing Sector of Trinidad and Tobago.* GOTT, 2006.

Mottley, Wendell. *Industrial Policy in Trinidad adn Tobago 1959–2006.* Kingston: Ian Randle, 2007.

NOTES

1. GSTT Geonotes, July 2006.www.gstt.org.
2. Caribbean Single Market and Economy.
3. In a multi-billion dollar financial bailout in January 2009, the assets of CL Financial—inclusive of the methanol plants—were transferred to the Government of Trinidad and Tobago.

Chapter Fourteen

The Communication Challenge

Richard Braithwaite

INTRODUCTION

Following a presentation at an energy conference hosted in 2008 by the South Trinidad Chamber of Commerce (now the Energy Chamber), Herman Acuna, a Senior Vice President of Ryder-Scott expressed some surprise at the widespread misinterpretation of a recently published Ryder-Scott Oil and Gas Auditing Report. He became further dismayed when a local reporter implied that the Ryder-Scott Report had predicted the "collapse" of the Trinidad and Tobago oil and gas industry within 12 years.

Following Mr Acuna's interview, another senior energy company executive shared his concern and remarked privately, "Imagine after two hours of detailed presentations by international experts, someone could still talk about a collapse of the gas industry." A few weeks prior to this conference, in an article in the bpTT Insight magazine, then CEO of bpTT, Robert Riley, talked about the misconceptions concerning a so-called "boom" in the energy sector and suggested that "some serious misunderstandings about the Ryder-Scott report have not made the delivery of the message any easier." The misunderstanding that surfaced around the issue of oil and gas reserves and the Ryder-Scott audit is not unique and it is not a modern phenomenon, although it is becoming increasingly intractable.

Over 50 years ago, the Governor of the then British colony of Trinidad and Tobago, Sir Hubert Rance, bemoaned the lack of public understanding about the indigenous oil industry and its important role in the local economy. In a December 1952 letter, he wrote: "The Trinidad oil industry plays such an important part in the economy of the colony that every responsible citizen should not only be aware of the activities of the industry but also should appreciate something of the complexities and difficulties that confront the industry today." The Governor also noted that citizens often ignored the fact that the local sector had to compete in the sometimes unforgiving, international market. He continued, "It is perhaps true to say that very few inhabitants of the colony apart from the 17,000 employees in the industry realize the varied and complex activities carried on daily, nor is the highly competitive world in which Trinidad oil strives to hold its place appreciated." The complexities within the modern Trinidad and Tobago energy sector pose greater challenges than during the days of Crown Colony Government, and the communication gap between the sector and the public seems just as wide.

It is somewhat ironic that after 100 years of commercial oil production and the heavy socio-economic dependence on oil and gas, there continues to be so much ignorance about the energy sector. One explanation is that the sector has evolved into a very sophisticated and high-tech entity while the approach to communication remains as it was decades ago. On the other hand, the old energy sector was viewed as a foreign "enclave" and only craftsmen and second- and third-tier employees were involved directly in the sector, whereas today nationals at every level and from every discipline command almost the entire sector. Additionally, because the energy sector is one of the few high-performing sectors, and is the fulcrum of the country's economy, it is a natural breeding ground for political agendas.

While in past decades the traditional public relations approach to communication was fairly effective, many of the more popular techniques are useless and irrelevant in today's environment. In many respects the old PR techniques are incapable of "making the delivery of the message any easier." First of all, the media, both print and electronic, have expanded rapidly, and the internet, in particular, has made the transfer and retrieval of information instant and widely available to all. Information moves more quickly via social media networks than the traditional media, and 'breaking news' sometimes appears on Facebook and Twitter before it hits the daily press.

Audiences have changed and now span the spectrum from the knowledgeable and discerning to the cynical and uniformed. The public is also at the receiving end of thousands of sometimes conflicting messages on a daily basis. In this fast-paced environment where there is constant competition for viewership and listenership, the "sound-bite" has become the preferred style of communication. Thus a complex and multi-dimensional issue is often reduced to a 30-second quip that has been lifted out of its context and selected primarily for its sensationalism. This superficial approach is all the more evident when dealing with state companies and agencies, as it is perceived that their directives and efforts at communication result from political authorities.

In such an environment, trivial and uninformed statements are inevitable, as persons seek to capture media attention and communicate narrow, self-serving perspectives and opinions. However, many of the issues in the energy sector cannot be debated via sound-bites, sensationalism or trite slogans. For instance, the discussion of proven, probable and possible reserves and the calculation methodology, the dynamism involved in the annual changes which occur, as well as the appropriate use of the reserves-to-production ratio, cannot be fully articulated in a full-page advertisement or a 30-second clip.

A major challenge, therefore, is to implement comprehensive communication programmes that are more long-term, and seek "to get the right message, through the right media, to the right audience, at the right time and with the right effect." This requires reviewing old concepts of public relations and insisting on research, analysis and a greater emphasis on strategic communication.

In the final analysis, the essence of effective communication is credibility—not visibility—and it is the most potent weapon in the armoury of the modern communications specialist. The correct information provided by the wrong source is often perceived as incorrect. Having the right messenger is sometimes more important than having the right message. Trinidad and Tobago celebrated "100 years of oil" in 2008- which is a much longer period than for most other oil-producing countries in the world. Given the enormous influence that the energy sector has on the daily lives of citizens, it is important that serious, persistent and deliberate efforts are made to inform and educate the public and to clarify any misunderstandings and/or misinterpretations.

INDUSTRIALIZATION AND CHANGE

As the process of industrial diversification continues, the necessity for effective change management will also become more critical. Rapid industrialization means rapid change, not only within the energy sector, but also throughout the surrounding communities and the wider national community. Whether it is a polypropylene complex, a steel plant or a new refinery, the "people" issues will persist on the front burner and inevitably on the front pages. During the impasse arising from attempts to build the Alcoa smelter in south Trinidad, a local Roman Catholic priest called for greater "empathy" in dealing with the social impacts that arise from industrialization. It is a valid recommendation, and reflects the tension, anxiety and uncertainty that usually accompanies periods of transformation. The lack of information and dialogue further exacerbates this anxiety and apprehension.

Effective communication is therefore necessary for successfully managing change. Poor communication practices can sometimes have the opposite result, generating resistance to change and destroying credibility in turbulent and uncertain times; when people are nervous about the changes churning around them the best solution is to "communicate, communicate, communicate!"

Admittedly, the State-owned energy sector has been tardy at times in keeping up with modern communication trends, and has been remiss in communicating vital information, but there have been a few good examples of a pro-active, strategic approach. In the early 1990s the merger of Trintoc and Trintopec into a new State entity, Petrotrin, provides a useful case study.

From the inception of the merger exercise, the Boards of Directors of both Trintoc and Trintopec understood the important role that communications would play in the period of transition. Subsequently, a merger communication sub-committee of the board was established with the specific mandate to design and implement a plan that facilitated the change management initiatives. Apart from the conventional newsletters and PR publications, the plan introduced a series of interactive "deep cut" sessions that brought senior executives in direct contact with employees throughout the company.

The newly appointed CEO, the late Keith Awong, joined with board members and other senior executives in meeting employees throughout the company's widespread operations, from Guayaguayare to Palo Seco to Point Fortin and at the headquarters in Pointe-a-Pierre. That level of direct personal involvement by senior executives is rare in the energy sector, especially in state-owned companies where communicating with employees is perceived as the sole responsibility of the Corporate Communications or Human Resources departments. It is partly due to this myopic management style that trade unions and various workers' representatives emerged as key information brokers within the energy sector. The historical evolution of the oil industry with its rigid social stratification generated an adversarial and sometimes antagonistic relationship between employee and manager. This has become the framework within which the communication process is often trapped. The reluctance to communicate with employees and other stakeholders also stems as well from a narrow perception that the "people issues" are relatively unimportant and that resources and time are better used in the pursuit of technical or financial objectives. Unfortunately, this attitude only serves to create even more conflict and turmoil as both community and industry continue to see each other as adversaries.

In a 1995 speech, former World Bank official Dr Michael Cernea commented that ". . . every project is a social process, not just a commercial intervention, and brings into play an array of different actors. Yet for a long time the traditional approach was to treat projects as only economic or technical interventions." If large industrial projects are to be seen as having significant social impact, then effective communication has to be a major part of any such intervention.

In south and central Trinidad, the National Energy Corporation (NEC) has embarked on a programme of diversification which includes the development of several new industrial estates. These include the Union Industrial Estate in La Brea, the Point Lisas East Industrial Estate and the construction activity at Galeota in Guayaguayare. In each circumstance, the industrial sites are in close proximity to relatively small communities where the advent of heavy industry is likely to raise valid concerns and anxieties. Traditional ways of life are perceived to be under threat and residents are uncertain about the impact on their way of life and future livelihoods.

On the other hand, project developers sometimes disregard the legitimate concerns of the local communities, deeming them to be irritants and unnecessary obstacles on the road to industrial and economic progress. In the midst of all this is the usual cadre of political opportunists with various agendas. Unfortunately, as the issues become more politicized and emotionally charged, the facts become less evident and pertinent. To its credit, the University of the West Indies at St Augustine, in keeping with best traditions of research and scholarship, published a book entitled Aluminium Smelting—Environmental, Health and Engineering Perspectives in an effort to bring some objectivity to the debate on smelters (Knare, et al. 2006). In his opening address at the 2006 symposium which preceded the publication of the book, then campus principal and pro Vice-Chancellor Dr Bhoendradatt Tewarie stated that "the crux of the problem, in terms of the current debate, has to do with environmental, ecological, health and safety concerns on the one hand, and quickening the pace of development with the prospect for more jobs and better incomes on the other." He also explained the rationale for the symposium, emphasizing that "we expect in a university that arguments and perspectives will be evidence-based and that conclusions will be drawn and recommendations made on the basis of thoughtful, insightful scrutiny of available information, and careful, objective analysis of the facts." The need for "thoughtful, insightful scrutiny" and an "objective analysis of the facts" extends beyond the confines of the university, and is even more critical for those engaged in communicating to the 'man-in-the-street' the main issues within the energy sector.

IMPACT ON COMMUNITIES

The communication issues arising from the Ryder-Scott report are symptomatic of the wider challenges confronting the process of industrial expansion in Trinidad and Tobago. On the one hand, there is an increasingly cynical public demanding more information, and on the other hand there are the technical people who are solely concerned with plant and equipment.

This dilemma is perhaps best illustrated by citing a public meeting at the Vance River Community Centre in La Brea in 2006, when a "project developer" sought to engage the local community in dialogue. After repeated complaints from residents that they were unaware of the project details, an increasingly exasperated engineer pointed to a massive folder on a table in the corner of the room and blurted out, "but we left that for you all to read!" The project developer appeared not to have considered the ability of residents to read and understand a technical document filled with charts, graphs and industry-specific jargon. As far as he was concerned, the mandate to "communicate with the project-affected communities" had been fulfilled. At best, this attitude reflects an inability to understand the key elements of the communication process. At worst, it illustrates contempt for the views and opinions of supposedly uneducated residents in a "backward" community.

It is perhaps ironic that both sides of the industrialization debate seem to share a common arrogance when attempting to engage the ordinary "man in the street." Persons have been labelled "stupid" or "stooges" for showing support for industrialization, while equally offensive descriptions have been used against those who are genuinely concerned about the negative impacts on their communities and the environment. Both sides would fare better if greater attention were paid to objective analysis and, more importantly, to the views of the actual residents themselves and the conditions in which they live. The reluctance to give credence to the opinions within remote communities may also be a reflection of the social stratification of the society, where the urban, upper middle-class perspective is often perceived as the only one that matters.

In recognition of the need for more effective communication between project developers and project-affected communities, the Environmental Management Authority (EMA) includes a programme of public consultations as part of the requirement for the issuance of a Certificate of Environmental Clearance (CEC). The rationale for hosting such consultations is that "people should have a say in decisions about actions which affect their lives."

The concept of using public consultations to enhance communication is internationally accepted, although its effectiveness is coming under increasing scrutiny. In the United States, for instance, the administration of President Barack Obama faced an uphill battle in its early efforts to achieve health care reform. Much of the opposition to Obama's plan emerged at public consultations or "town hall" meetings where officials met with members of the public to discuss the "pros and cons" of the proposal. The meetings often descended into emotional outbursts and political mudslinging with some extremists even turning up with high-powered weapons. In a July 2009 article in USA Today, then Democratic Speaker of the House, Nancy Pelosi, openly criticized the behaviour at the public meetings as "un-American." She wrote: "The dialogue between elected representatives and constituents is at the heart of our democracy and plays an integral role in ensuring that legislation we write reflects the genuine needs and concerns of the people we represent. However, it is evident that an ugly campaign is underway not merely to misrepresent the health insurance reform legislation but to disrupt public meetings and prevent members of Congress and constituents from conducting a civil dialogue." She continued further on in the piece: "These disruptions are occurring because opponents are afraid not of differing views, but of the facts themselves." And in words that should resonate within corporate communication departments throughout the local energy sector, Speaker Pelosi added, "Healthcare is complex. It drives our economy. People must be allowed to learn the facts."

Facts may, indeed, be "stubborn things," as John Adams stated back in the 18th century, but in the highly charged, emotional atmosphere that pervades many of these consultations one wonders if "the state of facts and evidence" is not completely ignored in favour of demagoguery and "theatrics."

In Trinidad and Tobago, the EMA's mandate is usually for the developer to host two such consultations within the communities prior to the start of construction. While public consultations can be useful in the hands of a skilled moderator, they are only one step in establishing effective two-way communication. As an industrial project progresses through its various stages from pre-construction to start-up, the need for effective communication becomes even more critical.

Several issues are likely to arise that require ongoing dialogue between developer and community. For instance, the migration of workers from outside the immediate community can trigger considerable tension, especially if the "outsiders" are from different backgrounds. This is further exacerbated in a situation where the local residents have been promised employment as part of the "benefit package" to be derived by the host community. In the early 1990s, following the closure of the Trintoc refinery, the construction of Train I of the LNG facility in Point Fortin ushered in high expectations of resurgence in employment and commercial activity. Residents consistently complained that they were regularly overlooked for jobs on the project. On the other hand, the project developer pointed to the hundreds of workers on the construction site as evidence that the promise of employment was being kept. The reality was that while approximately 3,000 people were employed during the construction period, the majority of jobs went to people who lived outside the Point Fortin area and were "bussed in" by sub-contractors. An analysis of employment data for Point Fortin during this period suggests only a marginal increase in local employment, indicating that local residents had a legitimate complaint.

The subsequent destruction of the popular Clifton Hill beach further exacerbated the growing distrust and suspicion within the local community. It was, therefore, not surprising that the antagonism eventually erupted into industrial action that required the intervention of the Prime Minister before it was eventually resolved.

The strike by workers at the LNG facility received considerable support from the local community and it is a reminder that in relatively small communities, employee relations and community relations are often synonymous. In such circumstances, the line between internal and external communication is very thin since, in practical terms, they both share the same audience. Another important issue is the fact that many of the communities like Point Fortin and La Brea, have been "oil communities" since the inception of the petroleum industry over100 years ago, and have been predisposed to the vagaries of the socio-economic conditions that accompany the presence of the oil and gas companies. To a large extent, the communities have come to realize that socio-economic prosperity prevails as long as the companies are present in their communities. The Environmental Management Agency also requires that a Social Impact Assessment (SIA) is included in the overall Environmental Impact Assessment (EIA). The International Association for Impact Assessment defines Social Impact Assessment as "the processes of analyzing, monitoring and managing the intended and unintended social consequences, both positive and negative, of planned interventions (policies, programmes, plans, projects) and any social change processes invoked by those interventions" (International Association for Impact Assessment 2010). The issue of managing change is once again highlighted as a key component in successfully dealing with "intended and unintended social consequences" arising from industrial development. In an article in the IAIA's May 2002 newsletter, Ross Marshall of Scottish Power wrote that, "Social Impact Assessment (SIA) has become one of the most challenging aspects of current practice. While experience and the use of accepted methodologies have taught practitioners how to handle many of the issues and controversies linked to physical environmental impacts, social aspects are more subjective, controversial in nature and tend to polarize opinions. Insensitive or unsympathetic approaches can jeopardize the likelihood of any future objective communication with stakeholders" (International Association for Impact Assessment 2002). This suggests that those who are charged with "communicating" on behalf of project developers must exhibit a broad understanding of the issues and a deep appreciation for the legitimate concerns and realities confronting stakeholders.

This disconnect in understanding and awareness at the community level is clearly evident in the notion by some companies, especially the multinational companies (MNCs), that information and updates to the communities should be done primarily via the Internet and cyberspace. The Internet statistics for Trinidad and Tobago for 2008, as reported by the International Telecommunication Union, show a national usage of 17.3 percent (ITU 2009). A discerning practitioner would be aware that Internet penetration and literacy rates are appreciably lower at the community levels and hence e-services are not an appropriate medium for communication. The mismatch is illustrated by the practice adopted even by local agencies of informing communities of public meetings via the national newspapers and then bemoaning the low attendance at these events. Again, more appropriate media should be used, such as roaming loud speakers, which although frowned upon by more sophisticated communicators are still commonly used with great success in these communities for death announcements and to advertise cultural and sporting events.

Another contributory factor of the communication dilemma is the one-size-fits-all approach that is often adopted by the MNCs. Many of these corporations perceive that they will encounter the same community aspirations, concerns and demands in any developing country, regardless of the geographical location, history, culture and stage of economic and human development. As such, many international investors adopt the same approach that they have used in Africa or Latin America to the local context. Unfortunately, many companies have belatedly had to learn that this wholesale "cut-and-paste" strategy does not address the idiosyncrasies within the modern, plural Trinidad and Tobago society. Moreover, strategies that may address the needs of one community may not be appropriate for another, as each community has different ethnic, religious, educational and social components which account for wide-ranging and sometimes conflicting aspirations and needs.

Apart from the communities, three groups of stakeholders appear to be of singular importance. They are, firstly, the employees and separately from them, the representative trade unions. Next are the owners of the energy enterprises, which may be the State or a foreign-owned international company or some hybrid ownership structure. The third critical stakeholder is the Government and its many regulatory bodies (not including its equity ownership role) which may be either Ministries, State enterprises or agencies such as the Environmental Management Authority.

With respect to employees within the sector, many of whom may be either unionized or operating within company-specific employee associations, a serious effort should be made by management to communicate with them on a regular basis. This effort must be deliberate, continuous, focused, and in line with the company's strategic communication plan which is closely linked to the business objectives. When significant change is necessary, extraordinary strategies need to be implemented to treat with the changes expected and their impact on employees and the corporation. None of this replaces or excludes the regular contact and meetings that must be carried out in parallel with these efforts to ensure that employees and the representative unions are fully informed. Their role in the communication process will be ignored at the risk of precipitating industrial relations mis-steps and crises.

The main oil workers' trade union in Trinidad and Tobago, the Oilfields Workers Trade Union, is almost national in geographic scope, covering not only oil production, refining and marketing—both domestic and international—but also electricity and some of the smaller gas-based industries. The union was established in the first quarter of the twentieth century and was at the forefront of the early battles against colonial authority in the oilfields in South Trinidad, taking much pride in its role in the worker demonstration led by its leader Tubal Uriah 'Buzz' Butler in 1937. As such, it has always adopted a fiercely pro-worker attitude, often at times, in a direct adversarial stance towards management, particularly in respect of wages, salaries and working conditions. Over the years, it has been effective in identifying critical bottlenecks in either the supply chain of energy to the domestic consumer or within the key State enterprises, such as Petrotrin or T&TEC. The OWTU has also been quite willing to use whatever political leverage it has to ensure that the Government of the day hears and understands its views, not only on worker issues such as safety and wages, but also on ownership and management choices. The OWTU has also developed a very effective communication strategy that often pre-empts the more lethargic and sterile approach of corporate communicators. It is based on immediate and direct communication with its primary audience, its membership. The communication challenge here is the establishment of more cordial and productive working relationships between company and union.

The international nature of the energy industry also introduces another polarity that will challenge the management in any energy sector company, but more so in State-owned enterprises. Energy plays a key role in the economic life of most countries and the following issues are likely to engage decision-makers for some time to come and to exacerbate the communication challenge:

1. Oil and gas will still be dominating the world's energy market in terms of percentage share in 2030 and maybe even well into 2050.
2. Global geopolitics is undergoing a fundamental shift as Asia and the Far East become the largest market for energy in the World, surpassing the demand of Europe and North America combined.
3. The impact of energy and environmental policies adopted by international agencies, the USA, Venezuela, Brazil and other states in the Western Hemisphere on Trinidad and Tobago's energy policies.
4. The impact that continued unabated increases in global demand for fossil fuels will have on the global climate patterns.
5. The complexity of the oil and gas industry and as such, the difficulty for the average person to understand without expert analysis and breakdown.
6. The development of the leadership cadre required to manage these global and regional issues.

In the final analysis, the greatest communication challenge lies with the energy sector companies—both private and State-owned—as they co-ordinate seemingly conflicting efforts among stakeholders within a complex and turbulent global environment. This situation necessitates astute leadership that is committed to the achievement of long-term national development goals which are sustainable and people-oriented, strategic in approach and committed to the principles of transparency and accountability. Effective 'two-way' communication is a pre-requisite in developing appropriate policies.

The Vision 2020 Energy Sub-Committee Report highlights the need for "the support of a robust and over-arching communication strategy" and emphasizes that "a fundamental requirement for success is the communication of established priorities and management of the many other desirable demands." Moreover, the report aptly concludes by affirming that "preparing the country for accepting and shouldering its regional and Western Hemispheric responsibilities may well be the touchstone in the demand list of leadership issues" (Energy Subcommittee 2004). In so doing, it reiterates the advice given by Sir Hubert Rance in 1952 that "Oil plays such an important part in world affairs today that every citizen of oil producing countries should be aware, not only of the benefits which oil production can bring, but also of the dangers which can arise if wise control of the industry is not maintained."

In a September 2010 address, the then Minister of Energy and Energy Affairs, Hon. Carolyn Seepersad-Bachan reaffirmed the importance of effective communication stating that "consultation with stakeholders and the wider national community must necessarily form part of how we approach the work of Government so as to ensure the views of the people are considered in the formulation and implementation of policy." As the local energy sector continues to evolve into an even more complex and diversified entity, it is imperative that, in the words of Sir Hubert Rance "every responsible citizen should appreciate something of the complexities and difficulties that confront the industry today."

BIBLIOGRAPHY

Energy Subcommittee. *Vision 2020 Energy.* Ministry of Planning and Development, GOTT, 2004.

International Association for Impact Assessment. *IAIA.* March 12, 2010. http://www.iaia.org/iaiawiki/sia.ashx (accessed February 3, 2012).

International Association for Impact Assessment. "It's Good to Talk: The Importance of Consultation in SIA." *IAIA Business and Industry Series*, 2002: 5–6.

ITU. "ITU Statistics." *International Telecommunications Union.* 2009. (http://www.itu.int/ict/statistics).

Knare, Mukesh, Clement, K. Sankat, Gyan, S. Shivastava, and Chintanapalli (Eds) Venkobachar. *Aluminium Smelting, Health, Environmental and Engineering Perspectives.* Kingston: Ian Randle Publishers Ltd, 2006.

Chapter Fifteen

The Leadership Challenge

Kermitt W. Walrond

INTRODUCTION

This chapter addresses the key question: how well have we done over the years in developing the technical and leadership talent critical to our growing energy business space? Let me state at the outset that the views expressed herein are my own and are gleaned from my almost 50 years in the energy business both in Trinidad and Tobago and elsewhere in the world. Furthermore, much of it is based on my experiences in Trinidad and Tobago and is anecdotal at times. The limitations of obtaining relevant data are a significant drawback in supporting my conclusions. Insofar as such data have been obtained, it is used to illuminate these conclusions.

The country's traverse over the past 100 years in the energy space provides the opportunity for distilling some conclusions about our performance in this arena, both successes and performance gaps. Some perspectives on the possible root causes for these results are offered. Some indication of how we may use these experiences and the lessons learned, are also presented to suggest improvements in the way we may develop our personnel going forward.

Even the most cursory review of how well we have done in the area of developing top-notch skills and competencies in the energy business in Trinidad and Tobago shows that we have produced some excellent examples of top-ranking personnel in virtually all the traditional disciplines employed in our industry. In moving around the global energy business I have been extremely proud to run into fellow nationals, virtually on every continent, who have made a great name for themselves and their native land by dint of their highly regarded skills. Trinidad and Tobago geologists, engineers of every kind, drillers, production operators, refinery operators and managers at many levels are commonplace in most of the countries where the oil industry exists. So clearly, to the question of whether Trinidad and Tobago nationals can develop into world-class professionals in every discipline, in the energy space, the answer is a resounding yes.

There are two thornier questions. The first and more fundamental question is how did we develop these skills in the past? The second question which follows naturally from the first is, have we as a country been developing these talents in sufficient quantity to meet the evolving and growing needs of our local industry, now and in the future. These two questions provoke an over-arching and very important follow-on challenge which has to do with how we integrate these world class skills into our national institutions, both public and private, to transform them into world class institutions themselves.

To address the first question, what were the conventional methodologies for training and development of local talent in the energy space over the past 50 or more years? The answer comes from a personal retrospection of my own experiences during my career journey in the energy business which began a little over 50 years ago. That retrospection has led me to the view that the methodologies used for developing local talent in our energy business in Trinidad went through four primary phases. As will become evident, these phases were largely reactive to evolving circumstances rather than proactive according to some grand design of an envisaged future. The titles I have used for these phases are entirely my own:

1. The Colonial Phase
2. The Spot 'em and Train 'em Phase
3. The "Work Permit" Phase
4. The Sustainable Development Phase

THE COLONIAL PHASE

In the Colonial Phase (CP), the approach was similar to the approach adopted in the civil service during colonial times, and it was ending just at about the time I entered the industry as a fresh engineering graduate in 1962. This phase was responsive to where the required skills could most easily be sourced. It took the form of a three-layered hierarchy of staffing. Simply stated, this approach was that all senior positions were filled by expatriate staff (in those days, mostly from the UK), with mid-level positions filled by so-called "local whites" and all lower level personnel were drawn from the local "non-white" population. In the case of the upstream part of the industry, examples of the mid-level positions which were reserved for the "local whites" were drillers, tool pushers, production supervisors (as distinct from superintendents, who were part of the expatriate senior staff level), warehouse supervisors, administrative supervisors and so on. In the case of refinery positions, examples of these midlevel positions included refinery operators, pipeline supervisors and so on.

The result of this three-layered form of staffing based on social rather than purely merit criteria is that the training of local staff was designed to provide them only with the skills to do the narrow range of jobs reserved for their social status. Such limited training served the purpose of constraining them to that predetermined staffing layer in the organization. In short, and from the perspective of the local staff, the training was both of high quality, but limiting at the same time. One side effect of this strategy was that it helped to reinforce the stratification of the society which spawned it. In fact, it was during these early days in the business that the practice of a layered approach to employee fraternization was further reinforced in the form of the "senior staff club" reserved for the most senior staff who in those days were almost entirely expatriate staff; the "junior staff club" reserved for the mid-level personnel; and at the bottom of the ladder, the so-called "sporting club." Not surprisingly, the golf club was a subset of the senior staff club. It is easy to envisage how ring-fenced the training for each of the respective staffing levels became.

During this period though, it is important to highlight and underscore a major positive contribution to local training made by the operating companies of the day. At its cornerstone was the initiation of the so-called company trade school. These schools did an outstanding job, in my opinion, of training local crafts-workers such as mechanics, electricians, instrument fitters, machine shop fitters, pipe-fitters, welders, joiners, carpenters and so on. Graduates from these programmes were of world-class competence and a few of them were even able to move on to great craftsman careers in refineries overseas like in Antigua, the US Virgin Islands and Texas City, Texas, for example. It was a source of great pride for me to occasionally run into these graduates of this system overseas later on in my career. I have tried unsuccessfully to get some statistics of how many graduates these trade schools turned out each year during their existence. I think that data would tell an amazing success story in itself, certainly for those who were fortunate enough to have been the beneficiary of this phase of training.

THE SPOT 'EM AND TRAIN 'EM PHASE

The Spot 'em and Train 'em Phase (STP) was one which began to flourish towards the end of the 1950s. Essentially, this method was evidenced by the selection of "trainees" from the few top secondary schools that existed at the time, based on their academic performance and tuned to the specific training programme to which the selectees were targeted. The intent was to train locals to populate the junior staff levels of the organizations and, for an even more select few, to enter the senior staff levels after successfully completing a specific course of study at the university level, usually in the UK. In this latter case the training was provided as full scholarships. In the case of training for entry into the junior staff levels of the organizations, this was provided in-house at company training centres using very well designed curricula of lectures, course work and hands-on practical experience, both in trainee workshops and on the job. In principle, this STP method resulted in the training of the carefully selected few for specific job levels to meet internal company needs. In fact, the vernacular in those days was that the trainee was often referred to as a "Texaco" trainee or a "Shell" trainee or a "TPD" (Trinidad Petroleum Development Company) trainee and so on, but not as an "Energy" trainee or an "Oil Industry" trainee. The reference was always company-specific. Indeed, these company-based references were worn with pride.

Another important aspect, probably the most important aspect in the long run, of this STP approach was that the careers to which the approach was targeted were specifically technical in nature, e.g. drilling, tool-pushing, plant operatorships, instrument technicians, mechanical technicians, electrical technicians, warehouse administrator, and all the conventional engineering disciplines; and in very rare cases, accounts training locally. This narrow and largely technical training had serious consequences, as I will discuss later in this chapter when I discuss the talent gap and use the acquisition of the Shell and Texaco refineries by the Government as an illustration.

An interesting question I have pondered for many years was what drove the evolution from the CP to the STP approach to training? Remember, the transition to this strategy started while the country was still a British colony. So the achievement of independence was not the driver. Independence had not yet happened. My own view, based on a unique perspective, being a product of this STP approach myself, was that the driver for this phase was also reactionary in nature. In the 1950s, the industry was not only growing in size but also in strategic importance to the United Kingdom. Consequently, the expatriate staff was now becoming increasingly younger men who were academically well trained in the technical disciplines, but with limited industry experience. As a result, the arrival of this new, younger expatriate demographic to the workforce in Trinidad naturally begged the question: why not take advantage of the few high-quality secondary school graduates in Trinidad and train them just like the young expats were trained, in UK tertiary level academic institutions and world-class in-house training schools installed locally, but similar to the ones owned and operated by the same companies in their homeland? I certainly was not aware at the time of any significant, formal and concerted effort on the part of the Trinidad and Tobago Government to foster this evolution to the STP phase—although, I would readily admit that there were muted comments from among members of the local community at large and especially among my many friends at my equivalent level in the Ministry of Petroleum and Mines, as it was called at the time. Those comments essentially questioned why there were not more locals doing these entry-level professional jobs in the technical disciplines.

THE WORK PERMIT PHASE

The third phase, the one I call the Work Permit Phase (WPP) of training was the one where we saw the first concerted effort by the Government to take an influencing role in fostering the training and development of nationals in the energy business. The transition to this phase began around the mid-1970s. This phase was largely driven by the evolving political imperatives of a newly born republic seeking to assert its national pride and its germinating independence. This was a time when the country was just beginning to recover from the serious political and social upheavals and turbulence of the events leading up to and following the attempted coup of 1970. It was a time of rapidly increasing social consciousness, exacerbated by a growing lack of the skill sets necessary to more fully assume the ownership at all levels of our own destiny. The social tensions of this time are excellently documented by Dr. Selwyn Ryan (Dr. Ryan 2009). It did not help that in our energy industry, the staff layering described earlier in my discussion of the CP phase, still dominated the scene in spite of the efforts of the STP phase of training.

This was about the time when the newly established Work Permit Committee of the Labour Ministry really seemed to flourish. It was through this committee that the development of local talent came under the Government's oversight and direction, and this new thrust entered into the consciousness of the leadership of the expatriate operating companies of the day. The essential way in which this was manifested was by the requirement for the respective oil company to make the case for the need for each expatriate. It also became critical that the company demonstrated that it was making clear, meaningful and sustained progress in developing nationals to be able to replace the expatriate under consideration for a work permit in a timeframe acceptable to the Government. As the Work Permit Committee grew in its ability to more fully exercise its authority in accordance with its mandate, they began to require that companies seeking work permits to bring in expatriate staff must identify nationals on their staff who would be trained to become candidates for assuming the responsibilities of the new expatriate entrant by the time that expatriate's work permit expired—usually in two years, unless an extension was specifically granted. Such extensions were usually predicated on the committee's judgment that acceptable progress was being made in the training and development of a suitable national.

With this focus in mind, it should not be surprising, however, that some of these companies initially sought to game the system by only paying lip service to the principles involved, except when forced to show tangible evidence of good-faith efforts in training. That said, over time there was clear evidence of an evolving aggressive training of nationals in all areas of the operations. Speaking from experience with my employer of that time, Amoco, (by far the most commercially successful expatriate oil company in the country of the day), I was tasked under the executive sponsorship of the company's president himself, to embark upon an aggressive recruiting and training programme for engineers, geoscientists, and drilling and production personnel. I was given carte blanche to be as aggressive in this effort as possible, with the only proviso that the result should be a staff capability second to none. My progress in this effort was closely monitored by the President of Amoco Trinidad. He also invited key leaders in the Ministry of Energy and the Work Permit Committee to participate in monitoring this effort with formal presentations to them at least annually. To be completely candid, I know that the President of Amoco was moved to volunteer these formal reviews by the Government primarily because he saw it as a good way to convince the Work Permit Committee that the company was serious about developing local talent in the company.

All this was complemented by the Government itself taking action to do its part in training of nationals. In 1974, the Prime Minister of the day, Dr. Eric Williams declared that year the "Year of Petroleum," and initiated the practice of awarding many "Petroleum" scholarships. In 1976 the University of the West Indies initiated a one-year diploma course in Petroleum Engineering to supplement the conventional programmes of Chemical, Civil, Mechanical and Electrical Engineering which had first been introduced in the Caribbean at the St Augustine campus of UWI in 1962. The Diploma in Petroleum Engineering was intended for first-degree engineering and science graduates as a conversion programme to this discipline. It is a tribute to that university's support that this programme quickly morphed into a full Bachelor of Petroleum Engineering degree programme within a few years. Later, the course was supported through additional M.Sc. teaching programmes in Petroleum Management at the postgraduate level. Although that programme has since been discontinued, it has been replaced by a Bachelor of Science degree in Geosciences and Petroleum which is now highly regarded in the local industry.

THE SUSTAINABLE DEVELOPMENT PHASE

This fourth phase, the Sustainable Development Phase (SDP), is the phase that came into full bloom in the early 1990s. I give it this name not to suggest that it is already sustainable; it being quite possible that this phase may turn out to be not so. I will say more about that later. Suffice to say for now that this phase should, and with a little focus could, easily become sustainable. It is the phase in which not only are the companies and the Government of one mind as to the importance of a concerted set of programmes for the development of our national talent, but in which these two categories of players become increasingly integrated and collaborative in their approaches. Although this is clearly happening, I fear that it is more because of serendipity rather than design. Before I develop this theme, let me give more texture to this phase.

Two key drivers of this phase are, on the one hand, the recognition by the operating companies (and indeed by the service companies as well, led by the larger expatriate service companies), that the development of a highly skilled national staff was good business; and on the other hand, the recognition by the Government and the Ministry of Energy in particular, that a competent, world-class national staff in the energy field was not going to be built without a clear and firm Government steer.

Some additional and critically important new drivers for this phase have come into play as well. The new drivers stem largely from the rapidly evolving global geopolitics. Not the least of these is the fact that major so-called "National Oil Companies" are rapidly transforming themselves into a new and yet largely unrecognized breed of companies which I call "International National Oil Companies," INOC's if you will. This new breed of INOC is being driven by their political masters, their respective Governments, to avail themselves of access to new reserves wherever in the world they may be acquired. They serve and represent countries whose need for energy is growing rapidly as they seek to fast-track their own transformation to fully developed status. The national energy companies of China, Norway, Brazil, Russia and India are a few examples. Therefore they are the new competitors of the existing International Oil Companies, previously referred as "the majors." As this competition for access to reserves grows, it behooves niche country players like Trinidad & Tobago to acquire the skills not just to play but to win in this evolving, more competitive game. More on that later.

During the "Work Permit Phase" a set of parallel, even complementary, but not necessarily interlocking and collaborative initiatives were at work. Some of these initiatives were developed and managed by the private sector and some developed and managed by the public sector. These separate but parallel initiatives were not intrinsically sustainable because they were incubated and nurtured in individual crucibles which could not contain the critical mass necessary for sustainability. Each of these initiatives was susceptible to the level of economic stability of each respective company working in a distinctly cyclical business.

My sense was that only as the idea of sustainability of development in all its various and many dimensions came into vogue and as vigorous conversations began to swirl around this idea, that our industry began to ask the more fundamental questions about national training. This was when a transformational shift occurred in how we looked at the issue. This was when we shifted from talking about training as a "cost of doing business," a short term approach, to talking about the need for "investing" in training, a longer term perspective. This was the paradigm shift that got everyone talking about investing in our human capital as being an investment in the company's and/ or our country's future.

It was in this phase that we really began to see the proliferation of overseas assignments, usually by way of cross-postings, i.e. a national would be assigned to one of the company's other international operations while a correlative expatriate would be posted to Trinidad and Tobago for a similar period in exchange. It is important to appreciate that, contrary to appearances at first, this practice was not driven by a desire to curry favour with the Government or the Work Permits Committee, although it did find such favour.

The real drivers for this practice were twofold, at least. First, by this time international oil companies were rapidly evolving from being simply large oil companies with some of its operations being conducted outside of its home country, to large oil companies operating in a large number of countries; in other words they were becoming truly global companies with a culture that was global and diverse rather than having the single culture of its home country. It was with this more global mindset, that these oil companies began to realize that to have a truly enduring competitive edge in the global marketplace, they had to be able to think globally. Therefore, they had to have a leadership that was truly acculturated to think and manage with global sensitivity. Thus, cross-postings of this nature served the company very well indeed, while at the same time expanding the career horizons of the local professional. The real value added by this practice really escalated as these individuals began to ascend to the more senior and more influential ranks of the corporate ladder, and thus began to positively affect the corporation's capacity to think globally.

The second driver was that the energy industry in Trinidad and Tobago was now well on the road to becoming world-class. Thus, it naturally became, by that fact, an invaluable training ground for young professional staff from the company's home country, as well as from everywhere else in its global operations. Cross-postings were therefore, a natural outcome of this evolving stature of Trinidad and Tobago's energy industry in the world.

Much as this new practice was of immense value to the mission of developing our local professionals, it also brought some unique and new challenges, not the least of which was the fact that it opened up and substantially expanded the marketplace for home-grown talent. It simply placed local professionals in the global market place. I do not for one minute lament this eventuality, but simply make the point that it challenged the conventional way in which these careers are managed. For one thing, it threw the spotlight on such important issues as how to move compensation programmes from the locally-based market to the globally-based compensation market; which skills and competencies should be subject to this transformation; and how our management of attrition and retention should be adjusted to deal with "internal" attrition within the global company itself, or between national and global companies within Trinidad and Tobago. My intent here is not to suggest that cross-postings should be resisted for these reasons. Far from it. My intent is to applaud the fact that we must face these challenges bravely and with resolve. We fail to do so to the detriment of our Republic, in my view. It is this potential to lose fervour for this sort of training because the attending challenges are thorny, to say the least, that could threaten its potential to achieve sustainability. This is the threat to which I alluded at the beginning of this section.

IS THERE A TALENT CHALLENGE?

In the opening paragraphs of this chapter I posed two questions. The first was about how we developed local talent in our energy industry. Having briefly reviewed that historical development we can turn to the second question, which was about whether, as a country, we have been developing these talents in sufficient quantity to meet the evolving needs of the local industry, now and in the future. In other words, with our current training and development practices, have we been meeting our talent needs, and are we on track to continue to meet our future needs excellently? To put it bluntly, do we have a talent problem in our industry? Before launching into a discussion of this topic, I should state that I am keenly aware that there have been, and indeed will continue to be, short term perturbations of over and under supply of talent caused by short term economic perturbations in the nation's economy. Some of the events which trigger these short term spurts of layoffs and hirings are sharp cyclical swings in oil and gas prices, spurts of capital expenditure for new plants, platforms or major expansions of infrastructure, dramatic evolutions of new technology and significant changes in government policies and so on. That said, the following discussion has to do, not with these short term trends which are inevitable and certainly need to be managed, probably better than they have been in the past, but more so with the macro trend of long term expansion of our energy industry. I assume, of course that we will do all that is necessary to ensure the sustainability of our nation.

To address this issue, first let us look at Figure 15.1. It shows the output of engineering graduates from the University of the West Indies over the past 40-plus years, separated by discipline. Overall, the number of engineering graduates has been increasing over these years. This is as it should be, given the overall increase in industrial development of the Republic. The question the graph begs, however, is whether this growth in engineering graduates has been meeting the demand in Trinidad & Tobago at large and the demand of the energy sector in particular; keeping in mind that these figures include graduates from other West Indian countries, many of whom return to their homelands. Unfortunately, this question cannot be answered by this graph alone, but it does provide some interesting pointers to the answer and suggests the direction we should take to further define the answer, which I will now outline.

I start with the admittedly approximate assumption that the growing development of the energy industry along the entire value chain during these years would require a significant growth in engineering talent of all disciplines, but especially in the petroleum and chemical engineering disciplines. This highlights the first area of concern illustrated by this graph. It shows that the growth of chemical engineering graduates over the last

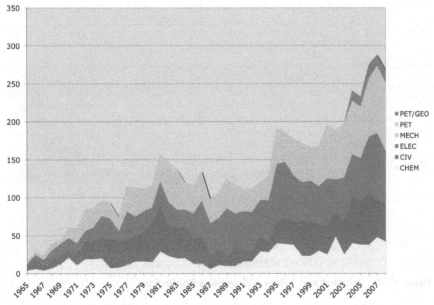

Figure 15.1. UWI Engineering Graduates 1965–2008.

40 years has been quite small. Furthermore, the number of graduates of petroleum engineering from our only local institute of engineering training over most of this period has been essentially negligible, and began only during the 1980s. Note also that the number of graduates in petroleum geosciences from the recently minted undergraduate programme at UWI has also been relatively very small.

For further clarification, I think it would be instructive to contrast the picture portrayed by this chart with data over the same period of the revenue stream to the national treasury from the E&P sector, the petrochemical industry and the gas export industry. Since this data is not easily available in the public domain, we may use Figure 15.2, Trinidad and Tobago's annual hydrocarbon production history (in barrels of oil equivalent per annum) as a proxy for the growth of our energy industry over the same period, and to explain the overall upward trend shown in Figure 15.1.

While, parallel with the growth in production shown in figure 15.2, there is a clear upward trend in the talent pool of nationals in the technical skills categories, the data seems to indicate (but admittedly does not prove) that the energy sector may have been growing faster than the locally grown engineering talent, especially since 1997. This suggests that an obvious and rather foreboding gap between the technical skill level required by the country and the skill level possessed by the country may be growing; not to mention the gap in commercial and managerial skills being developed versus what is needed.

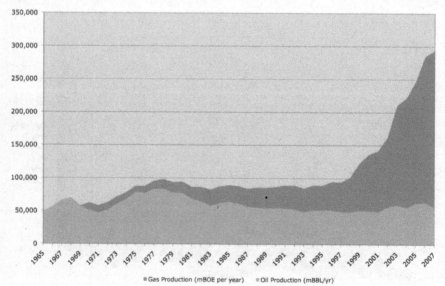

Figure 15.2. Trinidad and Tobago Oil and Gas Production.

I would suggest that whatever we are doing to close the gap is simply not keeping up with the expanding demand for talent by the expanding industry.

Further, crude price trends over the same period as shown in the Figure 15.3, indicates that the rapid ramp-up of production, especially since 1997, is complemented by a concurrent rapid ramp-up in crude prices. So one can hardly argue that the slow rate of closure of the talent gap is due to a lack of available funds.

To be clear, I would make two postulations which I will seek to develop in the following paragraphs. First, we have done a reasonable job in developing the talent needed in the more technical areas. Nevertheless, we have not closed the gap. I need only to point to the continuing strength of our expatriate technical population to make this point. Second, I suggest that we have done a very poor job in developing our leadership talent. The leadership skills I am talking about here are the kinds of enterprise leadership skills and talent required to lead a complex energy-based enterprise through an increasingly competitive and turbulent global business environment. I make an important distinction between that and the skills required to manage the complex operations in our energy business. The latter has to do largely with technical training underpinned with operations management training. The former is about being able to manage the enterprise itself, in all its many facets: commerce, negotiations, contracts, finance, law and global marketing. This is the kind of leadership now becoming known, especially in the world's business schools as Executive Leadership. Let me be clear. I am convinced we have developed outstanding leaders in our energy industry in the past. The point I am making is that we are now way short on the required quantity of outstanding leaders and the gap will widen considerably in the near and medium term. Let me develop these two challenges.

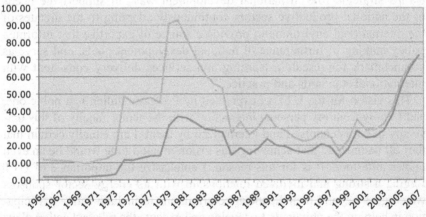

Figure 15.3.   Crude Oil Price (1965–2007) $/BBL.

THE TECHNICAL TALENT CHALLENGE

This is the easier of the two challenges to address but a very critical one nonetheless. The good news is that this shortage of technical talent is widely recognized both within the public and the private sectors. There is no doubt that the competition for this talent is keen. Indeed, one can argue that over the past few years, the recruiting efforts of all employers in this industry have simply resulted in moving the vacancies around from company to company with very little actual shrinkage in the overall number of vacancies. Another piece of good news is that the graduation rate from tertiary educational institutes has been increasing. The bad news, however, is that the growth in the supply of talent has not been enough to keep up with the growing demand. That said, I am of the view that the major steps already taken by the Government with the active and tangible support of the private sector, to wit, the advent of the University of Trinidad and Tobago in 2004, and the efforts of the University of the West Indies to meet the challenge posed by this new entrant, will contribute significantly in the long run to expanding the pool of technical expertise. The increase in the funding of scholarships in the relevant fields is also a major step in the right direction. The assumption here is that these steps will be sustained.

In this regard it is worth taking note of the underlying principles of The University of Trinidad and Tobago. In the first annual report of this university in 2005, in his "President's Report," then President, Professor Kenneth Julien, noted that UTT was intended to expand the opportunities for the nation's youth for university-level education and learning in applied sciences, engineering and technology (Julien 2005). He went on to say that UTT's strategic role in national development was "to support the needs of the national productive sectors continuously adapting to the dictates of the international environment; provide a source of expertise that informed policy making in furtherance of national development goals; and serve as a benchmark for research, learning and services delivery consistent with international standards and practice."

This vision for the UTT as expressed by Professor Julien is a noble one, and I know from my personal interaction with the senior faculty of this university that it is endorsed and internalized by them. I am equally certain that they all understand that achieving this vision in good time would be an even nobler milestone. It is for this reason, I emphasize the importance of UTT forging a strong and involved relationship with its energy sector sponsors which goes beyond their financial contributions to include active participation in helping the university to develop and execute the relevant action plans to achieve this vision.

In terms of opportunities for further key improvements, there is a need for a more assertive and focused effort in steering bright young high school minds into careers in the energy field. Discussions with scholarship administrators in the relevant Ministries and with personnel at tertiary level education institutes indicate a number of areas for improvement in the administration of scholarships:

1. The degrees pursued by scholars appear to be driven more by the wishes of the scholar and less by the needs of would-be employers. The problem with this bias is that without a well-structured career guidance programme, these choices may not be appropriately tuned to fill the skill gaps expected to exist when these scholars graduate. This points to a need for greater involvement by the industry's human resource leaders to ensure that the selection of degree disciplines is a more informed one.

2. Where expatriate corporations contribute financially to the funding of energy-based scholarships, they should be encouraged to take a more active role in assisting the relevant Ministries in providing summer job training for university students, as well as entry-level employment to new graduates. It should be deemed unsatisfactory for graduates with degrees relevant to the energy industry to end up working outside of the industry simply because of a lack of interest and/or commitment by industry to help new graduates secure initial "graduate engineer-in-training" positions in the energy sector.

3. There is considerable room for improvement in the collaboration between the administrating ministries and private industry in forecasting human resource needs in technical disciplines. This information is critical to making informed decisions relative to recruitment into tertiary level institutions, both in-country and overseas. There is an abundance of anecdotal evidence that this collaboration is sadly lacking, notwithstanding the many public utterances of industry leaders. Unfortunately, those words are not supported by actual practice in the trenches.

THE LEADERSHIP TALENT CHALLENGE

As indicated earlier, I am convinced that Trinidad and Tobago's energy industry has a significant lack of well qualified executive leaders to meet current and future demands. There are a number of ways in which this challenge could be easily quantified. I will cite just two examples.

First, data exists which would show the percentage of expatriates in the top three levels of leadership in all foreign companies in T&T's energy industry. This data could be collated for the last ten years or so. Expatriate construction companies should be excluded to make the data reasonably independent of the ramp up or ramp down of plant construction during the period.

Second, we should look at the data of the number of work permits granted on an annual basis for both short-term and long-term postings in the country, collated over the past 10 years or so. Again expatriate construction should be excluded for the same reason as expressed above.

Now it is easy to appreciate just how these two categories of data would illuminate the issue. Also, I know from my own experience in the industry that this data does exist in some form or other. Even more illuminating is the difficulty one encounters in trying to acquire this sort of data. It turns out that the acquisition of work permit information is not easily done. Furthermore, our efforts to collect data on the make-up of the top three levels of leadership in private companies in the industry were futile. Nevertheless, I remain persuaded that the evidence to support the contention about a leadership gap does exist. Of course, what is important is not that this information was not accessible to this author. What is really important is that this information should be available to, and be under constant analysis by those who are responsible for assessing whether these efforts are achieving our goals of nationalizing our key leadership positions.

An even more telling illustration, anecdotal though it is, of the slimness of our leadership ranks, can be gleaned from the age profile of the current leadership ranks and the lack of succession capability. Consider for example the demographics (e.g. age, years of service in the industry, years of service in current position and years to retirement) of the leadership ranks of energy sector State enterprises and the Ministry of Energy; then consider the nature of succession practice within these organizations and one quickly grasps the point that in a few years there will be a serious leadership vacuum.

IS THE TALENT GAP REALLY A PROBLEM TO SOLVE OR SIMPLY A TENSION TO MANAGE?

We need now to ask another question. Is the existence of a talent gap really a problem? In other words, does this gap cause an adverse effect in performance in the industry, and if so what exactly are those performance deficiencies. I think this is a critical question to answer since it may be that this gap is simply providing the industry with the kind of performance "tension" which ensures that our deployment of scarce talent is well optimized. This can be an important benefit of not having a surplus of talent. It simply forces us to use it well. On the other hand, if the use of this scarce talent is grossly inefficient, then we may be predisposed to making mistakes which in the worst case may be catastrophic. I suspect the latter is the case although I would be happy to be proven wrong.

To address this question it would be instructive to look at some of the previous key energy-based decisions our country has made and evaluate how well those decisions have turned out. Unfortunately, that sort of data is not easily available in the public domain. Not having that information, I must therefore resort to some anecdotal and probably very incomplete data to illustrate this theme.

First I cite two examples which I offer together since viewed in contrast one with the other, they also illustrate the distinction I sought to make earlier between technical competence and enterprise leadership.

The first example, drawn from the midstream sector of the energy value chain, is the case of the Government's acquisition of the Texaco and Shell refineries. At the time of the Shell acquisition in 1974, the conventional wisdom in the land was that for years these refineries were "run" by Trinidadians and that there was no doubt that we could take over and operate these refineries at least as well as they had performed in the past under expatriate leadership. We were soon to learn two important lessons from this example.

The first lesson was that conventional wisdom was absolutely correct, i.e. that we Trinidadians were quite capable of "running" the refinery. This is a tribute to the excellence of the STP phase of technical training described earlier in this chapter. It was the very narrow view of training of those early days (i.e. focused on technical training) that caused us not to recognize our blind spot in training for leadership in our energy industry—which sets up the second important lesson.

This lesson, which I believe took many by surprise, was that there was a whole different skill set which was supplied in the past by the expatriate senior staff, almost invisible to the local staff, and which was critical to the management of the enterprise. I am referring here to the enterprise leadership skill-set mentioned earlier, required to lead a complex energy-based enterprise through an increasingly competitive and turbulent business environment. These skills were exercised largely by the leaders of the Shell staff based at their home office and involved the kinds of high-level global contract negotiations, the keen understanding of global marketing forces and trends, financial and commercial oversight and strategy-setting activities which underpin the successful running of the enterprise.

It turned out that the new national oil company had to scramble to rapidly acquire that expertise "on the run," so to speak. It is a tribute to them that this was accomplished in relatively short order, largely because the company happened to have available at the time, the kind of talent that was capable of quickly assimilating this kind of "sink or swim" training successfully. Without good pre-planning, serendipity can be a useful substitute, it seems. So when the refinery assets of Texaco Trinidad were acquired in 1985, it was no surprise that the decision-making capacity of the former Shell employees, now Trintoc, showed far greater capacity to exercise commercial leadership than the former Texaco employees, though the latter knew only too well "how to run" the Pointe-a-Pierre Refinery.

The other example I cite is the case of the Government's acquisition of Trinidad Tesoro in November 1985 under terms that triggered questions about whether or not we had struck the optimum deal. The facts show that the transition into the new national oil company was handled much more smoothly. The fundamental reason for this is that Tesoro, and at least as importantly, its forerunner BP, had done a much better job of developing local enterprise leaders in its ranks in this upstream sector of the energy value chain.

During the late Sixties and early Seventies, we made some major decisions which have driven rapid and highly successful growth in the energy industry, to the extent that we have enjoyed a quite impressive and competitive position in several aspects of the business. Our LNG business and the business elements comprising the Point Lisas industrial complex are excellent cases in point. One cannot but wonder whether the extraordinary and visionary leadership of that time happened by design or merely as a matter of serendipity.

One classic and very instructive illustration of this challenge in monetizing our assets at a pace which keeps up with our exploration success has been our experience in bringing the substantial gas discoveries of the Sixties and Seventies to market. During the earlier part of these years, discovering gas reserves was seen as a failure to find oil. The gas reserves discovered in those years were simply booked and considered "stranded" gas, i.e. gas for which no market existed.

In those early years of our offshore east-coast exploration activity, even gas produced in association with our rapidly increasing oil discoveries, so-called "associated" gas, was seen as an unfortunate and valueless by-product of a successful oil development programme. A small percentage of this associated gas was used domestically where this was easy to do (for example, for power generation or as a way of augmenting depleting reservoir energy to produce more oil), and the rest was flared. In the case of our "stranded" gas reservoirs discovered in those early years, the producing companies with these reserves, predominantly Amoco, had their limited personnel fully deployed in maximizing the development of the comparatively more lucrative and more easily monetized oil reserves. The newly discovered gas reserves were "stranded" simply because the transportation facilities and markets were not yet developed.

Attention to these stranded gas reserves was quite limited and driven primarily by the Ministry of Energy. The Ministry's efforts in this regard were later enhanced by the country's rather persistent energy czar, Professor Kenneth Julien. At the risk of putting words in his mouth, I venture to suggest that his experience in pushing for a development of the vibrant gas-based industries known today as Point Lisas and the gas export hub in Point Fortin, at a time when such initiatives were considered maverick in the extreme, must have been very frustrating, to say the least. Insofar as his achievement in forging these new industries has been spectacular (and they certainly are), it should be seen as a tribute to his persistence much more so than to any abundance of talent in this area of the workforce.

Wendell Mottley (Mottley 2008) describes Ken Julien's essential role in the early stages of the country's industrial development as chairperson of a number of state corporations critical to the accomplishment of the State's industrialization objectives. He highlights Julien's effectiveness in providing "inspired leadership" to a cadre of young professionals to whom he delegated tremendous authority and executive responsibility. Mottley's description of Julien's role is on point. He argues that Julien's accomplishments could not have been achieved by the "typical state bureaucracy," and further suggests that the Prime Minister of the day, Dr. Eric Williams, "insulated the energy investments from the hassles and delays that might ordinarily be expected in a programme of such size, complexity and duration."

Acknowledging the obviously significant success in the use of a so-called energy czar in fostering the considerable energy industry development of the last few decades, the implication and question for the future is whether or not further developments in the energy industry will require the use of such a role, or whether the Governmental infrastructure could be enhanced to allow these developments to take place by direct leadership of Government through its established organizational leadership. Best practices in the most admired developed countries would suggest that the use of an energy czar should be seen at best as a temporary fix to expedite development while the bureaucratic infrastructure is developed to world-class status. At best it is a model for use at a certain stage of development. Thus, the continued use of the role of an energy czar in the future should be seen as a failure to develop our bureaucracies to world-class standards. Such a failure would come with attendant dire consequences for our nation's future. It is also worthwhile noting here that the continued use of an energy czar comes with an undesirable optic, since as a device to circumvent an inefficient and burdensome bureaucracy to expedite execution of projects; one may unintentionally give the impression of opaqueness rather than transparency in how decisions are made. Addressing our leadership talent gap and thereby upgrading the

performance of the Government civil services in all its critical dimensions
needs to be taken seriously and head-on.

Let us now look at another illustration of our leadership gap based on some
historical data. Figure 15.4 shows our annual natural gas production levels over
the period 1990-2007. On the surface, this chart shows a track record of which
we should all be very proud. Over the last 10 years alone our natural gas production has more than quadrupled; and since gas is not easily stored, this is monetized production, so to speak. It represents substantial revenue to the Treasury.

Lest we lapse into complacency fuelled by this stellar statistic, let us look
deeper and consider the data which underlies this production. The next chart
(Figure 15.5) is a view of our gas reserves at the end of each year over the
same period. This is the proven gas reserves which have been identified as
being in the ground and are yet to be produced. We should think of this as
our "in-the-ground gas bank account." It is from this account we produced
the gas represented by Figure 15.4. With this mental model, we could say
that when our "bank account" of gas in the ground, our reserves, is growing,
our future production of gas is more secure than when our reserves are decreasing. Against this background, and looking at these two charts together,
an interesting and worrisome picture emerges. Note that our reserves were
growing between 1994 and 1999.

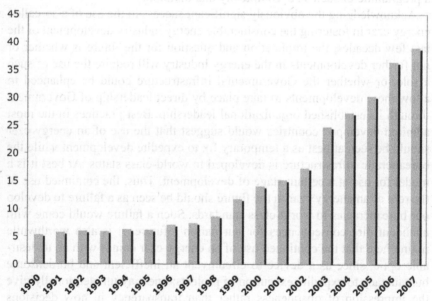

**Figure 15.4.   Trinidad and Tobago Natural Gas Production (bcm). Source: BP Statisti-
cal Review of World Energy June 2008.**

These were the years of very successful exploration activity when substantial new gas reserves were discovered. Note also that during these years, our gas production was essentially flat and only began to increase slightly towards the end of that period. The simple explanation for this is that there is a lag of quite a few years between discovering new reserves and bringing those new discoveries to market. The rapid ramp-up of gas production in the years 2000 to date is a direct result of bringing to market the reserves discovered in our halcyon years of exploration, 1994 to 1999.

Here, now, is the worrisome part. Again, looking at Figure 15.5, our gas reserves (our bank account in the ground, remember) has been trending downwards since 2000. Why? The simple answer is that we have been producing more gas than we have been discovering, comparing Figure 15.4 of our annual production with Figure 15.5 for the same period. In other words, we have been making more withdrawals from our bank account than we have been depositing. This is not a good situation to be in.

The next chart (Figure 15.6) is simply a way of combining the two previous slides into one. It is derived by dividing the reserves at the end of each year by the production of that year. This gives us the number of years of production one could expect if we were to (a) continue to produce gas at the same rate (usually does not happen) and (b) fail to add new reserves, by making more

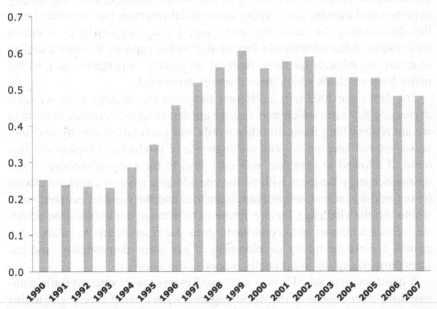

Figure 15.5. Trinidad and Tobago Proven Natural Gas Reserves, (tcm). Source: BP Statistical Review of World Energy June 2008.

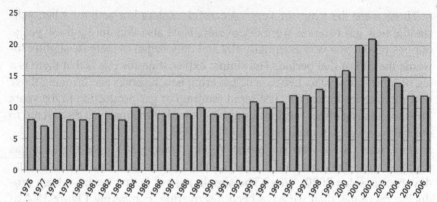

Figure 15.6. Reserves to Production Ration (years).

discoveries of gas, (a failure one hopes will not happen). Just to be clear, the R/P ratio, although a very simple-minded measure based on very gross assumptions, is quite a useful tool for assessing how well we are balancing the natural tension between the rate of discovery of new reserves on the one hand (making deposits into our gas account), and the rate of monetizing these reserves by production and sales (making withdrawals) on the other.

The growth in Reserves/Production (R/P) ratio during the 1990s clearly illustrates our successes in opening up exploration acreage, attracting quality explorers and thereby discovering commercial reserves. On the other hand, this data (during the '90s) may also suggest a lagging ability to monetize these assets, either because of a lack of skill and/or capacity to either establish or create the markets for these reserves or, equally importantly, to land the major business deals which these reserves demanded.

The data since 2002 tells a different and more urgent story. Here we see a decreasing R/P ratio which says that we are depleting our reserves faster than we are replenishing them. In other words, our exploration activity and successes are not keeping up with our high rate of production (depletion). This trend, if allowed to continue, will only lead to the eventual demise of our upstream energy business with all the considerable adverse knock-on effects on our midstream and downstream industries and the national economy as a whole. So the challenge for our future is to manage our exploration activities in such a manner as to continue to grow our reserves and to balance that growth against the timely development of gas usage domestically, and gas sales through exports to optimally monetize our reserves.

A question often asked is how does our Reserves to Production Ratio compare with other regions of the world. Figure 15.7 is offered in response to this question. It shows that on a worldwide basis, R/P ratios are of the order of 60 years for more than 20 years now. Not surprisingly the Middle East Region,

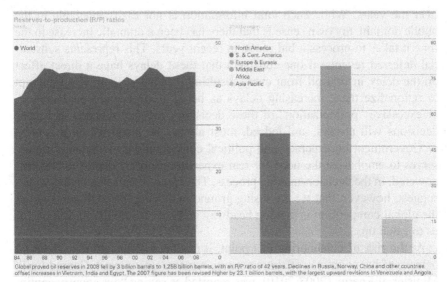

Global proved oil reserves in 2008 fell by 3 billion barrels to 1.258 billion barrels, with an R/P ratio of 42 years. Declines in Russia, Norway, China and other countries offset increases in Vietnam, India and Egypt. The 2007 figure has been revised higher by 23.1 billion barrels, with the largest upward revisions in Venezuela and Angola.

Figure 15.7. Reserves to Production Ratio 2008 by Region. Global proved reserves of natural gas increased by 7.97tcm in 2008, and the R/P ratio increased to 60.4 years. Increases in Turkmenistan and Iran accounted for most of the growth.

at the high end of the spectrum, has R/P ratios in excess of 200 years. The North American Region is at the low end of the spectrum at about 10 to 15 years. The South & Central America Region (to which T&T belongs) has an R/P ratio of around 48 years. Our R/P ratio as shown in Figure 15.6 is about 12 years. This is too low for a country whose economic viability is expected to continue to be heavily dependent on its energy sector for many more years than that.

Those who seek solace in the fact that the R/P ratio of the US is on average of the same order of magnitude as ours (theirs vary widely across the full spectrum of their producing provinces) should note that the US imports over 50 percent of its petroleum requirements from a range of countries, not all of which can be considered allies or politically stable, and many of whom are already significantly expanding their own local consumption of energy. So the US is already wrestling with the formulation of its own national energy strategy. For Trinidad & Tobago, what is even more worrisome is that our R/P ratio is on a downward trend. Altering this trend poses an enormous leadership challenge in not only developing the right long term strategy but in executing that strategy. To do this, T&T will need to dramatically increase its leadership capacity.

Another indicator of the adverse effect of the skill gap is the time it takes between inviting, processing and awarding bids in our successive bid rounds over the years. While such vital information is not easily available in the public domain, my own sense is that there has been a dramatic increase in the time it takes to process a bid round in recent years. This represents substantial deferred revenue if one considers that these delays have a direct effect on the delay in first oil from every resulting discovery. Even if we attempt to rationalize these increasing delays as being "Government bureaucracy" or excessive "politicization" of these decisions, the fact remains that these decisions will always, and indeed, must always be made within a context of Government bureaucracy and political considerations. This point merely serves to emphasize the need for real expertise, properly deployed and empowered, in the decision-making process. The fact of increasing delays would suggest, however, that we are losing ground in closing this skill gap even as the global competition is making headway and not standing still, waiting for us to catch up.

At the risk of belabouring this point, it has been estimated that about 60 percent of the country's offshore acreage remains unexplored. Conrad Enill, Minister of Energy (2007-2010), was reported as saying "our country continues to receive proposals from various companies wishing to invest across the spectrum of the oil and gas value chain" (Chan Tack 2009). Without a more expeditious license award process for dramatically increasing exploration activity, T&T's reserves/production ratio is likely to continue to languish.

A more current illustration of the critical nature of the gap in operational, project management and leadership skills and how serious the consequences can be involves state-owned Petrotrin. It was reported that Petrotrin has encountered serious problems with its billion-dollar refinery upgrade projects (Shah 2009). One key project cited as experiencing serious delays in completion and cost overrun was the design, engineering, and construction of a new Gas to Liquids (GTL) plant. While then President Kenneth Allum rightly observed that there were several reasons for the cost overruns and completion delays, it is instructive to note that the referenced report includes some telling conclusions. One was that in the case of the GTL Plant, "the wrong choice of contractor" was blamed for the project delays and cost overruns. The report said in part:

With specific reference to the GTL plant, a joint venture involving Petrotrin (49 per cent) and World GTL (Trinidad) Ltd, and which ought to have come on stream by the end of 2008, Jones said there were additional problems. "That project holds great promise of fantastic returns on investment. But it was badly handled almost from the beginning," he said. "The plant was based on World GTL's technology of using mothballed methanol plants, refurbishing and reconfiguring them, and using cheap, flared gas to make a high quality product. However, the contractor who handled the assembly, Ventech, an American company, lost its way in the technical designs and engineering."

Notwithstanding the numerous extenuating circumstances which could be cited as contributing to this failure to adhere to minimum standards in the execution of these projects, as the President of the corporation rightly stated, one must also admit that this episode provides a powerful teaching/learning opportunity through the post-appraisal process. Post-appraisal might well illuminate the issue of inadequate due diligence in the process leading up to project approval including, but not limited to:

- The proper assessment of the intended alliance partner's competence in the areas relevant to the project
- identification of the risks (including technical, commercial, financial, project management, and markets over the project life, etc.) to the project
- Designation and use of proper contractor selection criteria

Such a careful and objective post-appraisal might well conclude that there was indeed a crucial lack of the appropriate technical and leadership skills within the corporation for embarking on such projects without acquiring these requisite skills. Even more alarming to contemplate is the possibility that these critical skills may also have been absent in the eventual expatriate partner as well. Seeking the answers to such questions could be very enlightening for Petrotrin. What would a thorough root cause analysis yield?

Taking an overarching view of T&T's track record in developing technical and leadership talent in the energy sectors, we can conclude that we have done very well on average. We have achieved some stellar results that are the envy of the international energy business world, especially in the LNG and gas-based energy businesses in which we are now very active. That said, we have, however, not done too well in recent years in some other areas which provide us with some key opportunities for improvement. This is especially so in the area of managing our reserve growth necessary to keep pace with our production levels, both in oil and gas.

My blunt answer to the question of whether this is a problem to solve or simply a tension to manage is that it is a problem urgently in need of a solution. In the early years, it was viewed as a tension to manage with very good results. In recent years, however, it has become a serious problem to solve. When we consider the rapidly increasing competitiveness of the global energy business, the rapid intensification of the global search for clean energy-especially gas, the rapidly evolving technology in LNG and LNG transportation, the increased intensity with which the US (our major and closest gas export market) is seeking to grow its domestic supply of gas—when we consider all this and more, we cannot afford to blink lest we prematurely lose our pre-eminence in this business. We cannot afford to rely on serendipity to see us through in the future, much as it has served us well in the past. Our nostalgia and pride for our considerable experience should not lull us into the debilitating trap of complacency about our future.

To put into perspective the challenges that Trinidad and Tobago will face in the energy sector over the next few years, we need only to look at our gas R/P ratios in recent years. The BP Statistical Review of World Energy of June 2008 (see Figure 15.4 earlier in this chapter) quoted T&T's gas production over the eight year period 2000 to 2007 as growing fairly steadily from about 14 billion to about 38 billion cubic meters per annum. During this period, proven natural gas reserves showed a slow but steady decline from about 0.55 trillion cubic meters in 2000 to about 0.46 trillion cubic meters in 2007 (See Figure 15.5). During this period, we have talked constantly about our need to (a) become more aggressive at picking up the pace at which new acreage is awarded for exploration and (b) make serious progress in our stated desire to improve the fiscal regime under which further exploration can be encouraged. Action on both have been repeatedly delayed.

One has to wonder to what extent these delays have been caused by the lack of the appropriate level of leadership and project management skills in the Ministry of Energy for handling the workload involved in moving these processes forward. In this regard, a cursory assessment of the number of so-called "energy gurus" active in the Ministry and their average age will convince us of the inexorable greying of the energy executive leadership in Government. A review of the number of candidates currently available and being groomed as their replacement would, in turn, indicate the great need for a more focused and intensified effort at succession planning and execution to develop the appropriate level of leadership "feedstock" at the highest levels of governance of the energy industry. It bears repeating that our past practices in training and development of leadership talent, while having served us well back then, will simply not be good enough for maintaining and improving our great standing in the world energy space, especially as that space becomes ever more integrated, competitive and complex. As Wendell Mottley points out, "Trinidad and Tobago is under international scrutiny to see how it adapts its systems of governance to rapid growth and increasing complexity" (Mottley 2008). This key point applies just as well to training and development as it does to good governance. In fact, a case can be made that the latter depends on the former.

RAPID GROWTH AND INCREASING COMPLEXITY

It is worth taking the time to examine whether rapid growth and increasing complexity of the energy space is real or sheer hyperbole. To give some texture to this, I have chosen a few markers to illustrate the trends in growth and complexity in T&T's energy business space. These are:

- The diversity of businesses
- The spread of activity disciplines (e.g. marketing, petrochemical industries, fabrication of physical facilities)
- In diversity of commercial agreements and the multilateral negotiations associated with landing these agreements.

Figures 15.8 and 15.9 and associated discussion will illuminate this evolving complexity.

Figure 15.8 shows that some significant and dramatic changes took place in the Exploration and Production business over the 31 years between 1978 and 2009. Although the number of onshore oilfields decreased markedly, it was more than offset by a significant increase in offshore oil and especially gas fields, for a total growth of about 26 percent.

Figure 15.9 looks at the offshore facilities growth over the same period and reveals substantial growth in oil and gas platforms and the emerging growth on the north coast. It's worth noting that the technical skills required in the engineering, procurement, construction, installation and operation of these offshore facilities are significantly more complex than for onshore production and processing facilities. The complexity of these offshore facilities are evolving at an increasingly rapid rate as E&P efforts move into deeper and deeper waters.

The question which arises from these two graphs is whether this amazing increase in activity and the obvious transformations from onshore to offshore, and from oil to gas are anomalies or sustainable. The answer, either way, will have a transformational impact on how we plan for future leadership demands in many dimensions.

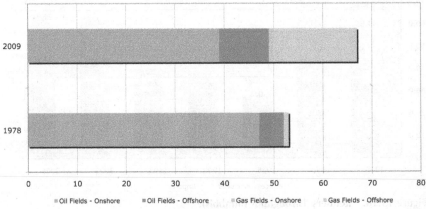

Figure 15.8. No. of Oil and Gas Fields (onshore/offshore).

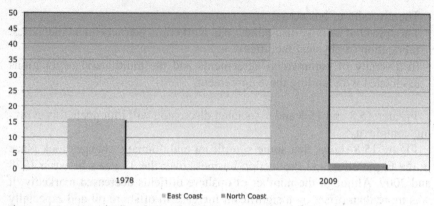

Figure 15.9. No. of Oil and Gas Platforms.

The picture for the midstream of T&T's energy space is illustrated by Figure 15.10. Here too, is an interesting transformation over the same period 1978–2009, even if deeper digging is required to discern its true significance. Suffice it to make just a few points from this one graph. Notice that the portion of refinery throughput sourced domestically has long ceased to grow. A case can be made that domestic onshore production has peaked, unless something substantial happens soon by way of new discoveries or a transformational new crop of secondary recovery reserves.

Furthermore, it appears that the sustainability of T&T's refinery operations is becoming increasingly dependent on imported crude. This then raises the

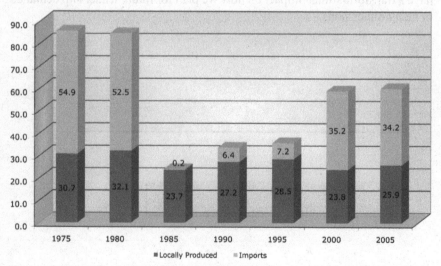

Figure 15.10. Refinery Throughput (mmbbls).

question of the margins on profitability from refining imported crude. There is also the question of the quality and sustainability of the arrangements for importing crude to the refinery—arrangements on which the refinery is becoming increasingly dependent. Again, this is an issue of sustainability. It suggests that this large enterprise can no longer be managed in a reactive manner. Trinidad and Tobago would need to get very aggressive about deciding what kind of future it wants for its refining business, if any, before seriously tackling the most effective methods for creating the desired future. Within the context of the local business and social environment, the implications for the kinds of unique leadership skills that will be required to take on this daunting but critically essential task are enormous.

Turning to the downstream end of the energy business (See Figure 15.11), not surprisingly, the picture is similar to—and obviously driven by—the rapid ramping up of exploration and production of offshore gas (See Figures 15.8 and 15.9). Except for the ammonia plant which preceded the period of review, all the downstream plants (units) were commissioned during the last 32 years. Here, too, the question of sustainability arises. This is not the time to rest on our laurels. While T&T's performance over this period can be judged as nothing short of extraordinarily great, greatness will not endure without the necessary steps to ensure it endures. Again, the implications for, and challenge to, the energy sector's leadership resources are enormous.

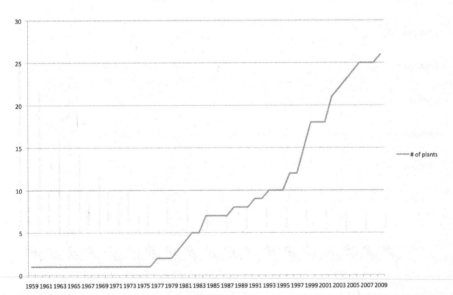

Figure 15.11. No. of Various Types of Processing Units – Downstream Energy Space.

No review of the evolving rapid growth and increasing complexity of our energy space, no matter how cursory, can be complete without a quick look at some of the support businesses critical to sustaining it. The following three supporting components are selected to make the point.

First is in the area of communications. Figure 15.12 illustrates the trends over the last 20 years. Note that the growth in telephone landline services, both for residential and commercial/industrial use, has become virtually negligible in the last five years for which data was available, i.e. up to 2006. In contrast, however, and as pertains elsewhere in the world, cellular phone usage in T&T has undergone a dramatic expansion. The implications for the technical and leadership skills required to support and lead our charge into this more sophisticated, rapidly changing and evolving technology is dramatic and critical. I suggest that here too, we cannot afford to be simply reactive to the revolution in communication technology, if we are to be serious about maintaining our hard-earned competitive edge in the energy business.

Next is the issue of electricity generation (See Figure 15.13). Here, too, we see a rapid and dramatic increase in T&T's electricity generation capacity commensurate with the rapid expansion in the energy business. This is not surprising in itself. The question, however, is whether we have the technical and leadership capacity (in all its myriad facets) to be able to grow this capacity in a manner that is truly supportive (i.e. in volume, cost and in timeliness) of our future in the energy business as planned. The key here is our capacity to deliver these support services on time.

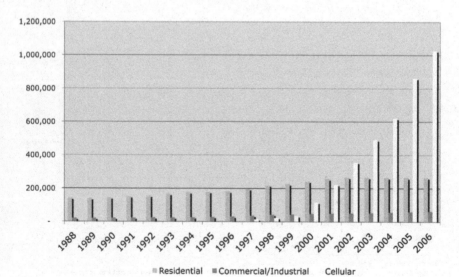

■ Residential ■ Commercial/Industrial Cellular

Figure 15.12. Telephone Access by Type.

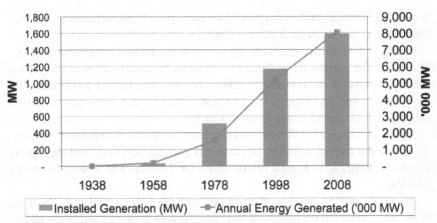

Figure 15.13. Electricity Generation (T&TEC).

The third and final illustration of trends in the businesses that support our energy space is water production. Figure 15.14 shows T&T's water production history for the 40-year period ending in 2005, the last year for which data was available. This data shows substantial growth in T&T's water production capacity over the review period. This chart is remarkable more for what it does not show, but what any water customer in Trinidad and Tobago would know only too well. It is that in the area of our water production, supply has seriously lagged behind demand for many years. There is an abundance of anecdotal evidence suggesting that the gap continues to grow. In this context it is worth noting the following quote taken directly from the website of the

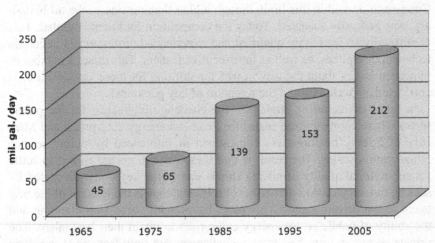

Figure 15.14. Water Production (WASA)

Water and Sewage Authority (WASA) which most likely pertains to the year 2006 (Water and Sewage Authority 2009).

Today, the Authority produces approximately 210 million gallons per day. The estimated current daily demand, however, stands at 270 million gallons per day, a gap of some 60 million gallons per day. In addition, to the disparity between demand and supply, it is estimated that WASA loses between 40% and 50% of its treated water through leakage.

Some have suggested that the real bottleneck is in our distribution capacity. Whatever the reason, a failure to close this gap can seriously and negatively affect our ability to capture a bright future for Trinidad and Tobago's energy business.

Obviously, there are many other support services to be considered. There are many ways in which we could cut and slice the data to more completely understand the challenges posed by the need to ensure the availability of the support services critical to a sustainable and bright energy future. I have attempted to make the point by this brief look at only three of the critical services.

THE INCREASING GLOBALIZATION
OF TALENT MARKETPLACE

Finally, I offer some perspectives about the evolving nature of the talent marketplace. Over the years, T&T talent in the energy business was perceived to be playing in a local marketplace where the competition was distinctly local. Up to about the early 1970s, one could convincingly argue that this talent marketplace was distinctly within the oil sector, as it was typically labeled. Compensation within this limit, though higher than outside of the oil boundary, was generally accepted. Today the competition for talent is global. This is especially so for highly qualified and experienced professionals in certain technical disciplines, as well as for executive leaders. This raises a number of important issues about the way in which recruiting for these key positions is conducted, as well as about the retention of key personnel.

In terms of recruiting strategies, the challenge is greatest for the public sector where compensation scales for State-run energy enterprises and Ministry of Energy positions are constrained or influenced by public service remuneration scales. The result is that these institutions are forced to settle for sub-optimal quality of talent. This is one of the key under-discussed issues on this subject. Another effect of this challenge is the leakage of the best talent to the private sector. This plays havoc with succession planning and the ability of public sector energy enterprises to retain their best talent. The private sector, in turn, has its own challenges, not only from rival domestic private sector companies but also from their global sister-companies and inter-corporation competition globally. To limit the impact of talent leakage, companies should design their training programmes for executive leadership with due provision for attrition of all sorts which, depending on the discipline, could be considerable.

On the topic of executive leadership training of nationals, it should be noted that executive training cannot be conducted exclusively in a classroom. This is the fundamental fallacy of many business school MBA programmes which cater to bright young students with no practical experience but who graduate with the mistaken perception that their classroom training has prepared them for senior executive leadership positions. As Professor Chandrabhan Sharma of the University of the West Indies put it to me in a personal communication: "An MBA without reference is worth nothing."

Two points can be made in dealing with this training challenge. The first is that we need to do a much better job of leveraging the presence of expatriate executive leaders employed in the Trinidad and Tobago energy industry. These professionals should be granted work permits not only because of their "know-how" but also their "show-how" ability. The Government should take a more aggressive role in ensuring that their stay in the country is conditioned on an additional mentoring responsibility for at least one, and preferably more, high-potential nationals carefully identified as such. This responsibility should be subject to regular and formalized oversight by the Government. The second point is that, as a country, we need to do a better job of leveraging our relationship with expatriate joint venture partners for well-designed cross-postings not only of high-potential nationals working within the JV company, but also a selected few high-potential nationals who are seconded from State-owned energy enterprises, and even Ministry personnel. In this regard, the identification of high-potential nationals, whether in private or public sector, should be in accordance with well-designed and formalized criteria. Excellent models for doing this already exist in the worldwide industry.

SUMMARY AND A PROJECTION INTO THE FUTURE

I hope this chapter has made the case that our history in the energy business has shown that, overall, Trinidad and Tobago has done an excellent job of developing highly competent national personnel in the technical and executive leadership disciplines, even though we got off to a slow start in the early 1950s. I have sought to highlight some stellar examples of decisions which were facilitated by this competence. That said, hopefully we can learn from the recent examples of results which suggest that, in recent years, the supply of such talent has not been keeping up with demand. I have pointed to some of the ways in which we could begin to address these shortcomings in training and development in a more formalized and state-of-the art manner. At a minimum, hopefully this overview will stimulate some worthwhile discussion which would lead to innovative new actions in addressing these serious issues.

Fundamentally, our future is likely to bear no resemblance to our past. In the early years of our energy industry's development, change took place at a relatively slow, even leisurely pace, especially given the prospect of a far more hectic future. The slow pace allowed the luxury of being reactionary in the approach to change and was driven largely by the need for solutions to problems as they arose. We had the luxury to actually see competition coming and to react to it in timely fashion. In that more tolerant and forgiving environment, even sub-optimal strategies for the development of required technology, talent and particularly executive leadership skills were possible, with the possibility of improving those strategies "on the fly," so to speak. I think the reader would agree that the four phases of development of local talent described earlier in the chapter were evolutionary in nature and took place over a number of years. Over the last 10 years however, the rate of energy development has accelerated rapidly. The level of gas output has quadrupled, the number of world-scale energy-based plants has doubled, and supporting manufacturing, services and logistics have more than doubled. Thus the systems of ten years ago are creaking to deliver expectations of acreage allocation, permitting processes and gas reserve generation, of at least twice their previous demands.

Our future will be very different both in substance and in dynamics of change, that is, in the nature of the change as well as in the rate at which change occurs. In addition, the changes we are likely to experience will, in substantial measure, be imposed on us by outside forces. Increasing complexity of our business environment and much greater external influences will be the order of the times. Competition will be fiercer and more diverse. In such a world, we will need a leadership marked by innovation, unconventional thinking and unique abilities to identify and solve problems which are currently unknown and even inconceivable. In such a world, the challenge is how we will adapt our techniques and strategies for developing our pool of leaders. We will surely require a much more focused and organized approach than we have used in the past. John Cooper Ramo more bluntly opines, "Whether they are running corporations or foreign ministries or central banks, some of the best minds of our era are still in thrall to an older way of seeing and thinking. They are making repeated mis-judgments about the world. In a way, it's hard to blame them. Mostly they grew up at a time when the global order could largely be understood in simpler terms" (Ramo 2009). I think this sentiment could easily be applied to Trinidad and Tobago's energy world as we consider the issue of developing future leaders who are capable of designing and thereby capturing a unique future for ourselves, in a world in which petroleum market forces will be changing rapidly, almost on a daily basis, with growing revolutionary complexities. I daresay we will be challenged to match this with training strategies which are equally revolutionary in nature. Whereas in our earlier years our evolving environment defined our training strategies, today I would argue the converse is true; our training strategies will define our future.

As one example of unique innovation, I cite the approach being taken by the University of Trinidad and Tobago in its structure and design for delivering more "fit for purpose" technical qualifications for our energy industry. I urge UTT and the energy industry to work at strengthening their partnership in this effort. The industry partners are making substantial financial contributions to the work of this university. We need to do all we can to strengthen the non-financial collaboration between the university and its partners so that the evolving curricula and its delivery are enriched by enlightened collaboration.

Similarly enhanced levels of collaboration involving industrial players, both private and public, and the relevant Ministries of energy, education, tertiary education, finance and the professional organizations within the energy space hold enormous potential for greater good.

BIBLIOGRAPHY

Chan Tack, Clint. *Newsday*, April 22, 2009.

Dr. Ryan, Selwyn. "The Roaring Seventies." In *Eric Williams, the Myth and the Man*, by Selwyn Dr. Ryan, Chapter 17. 2009.

Julien, Kenneth Professor. "President's Report, 2005 Annual Report of the University of Trinidad and Tobago." 2005.

In *Trinidad and Tobago Industrial Policy 1958–2008*, by Wendell Mottley, Capter 9, Page 174. Ian Randle Publishers, 2008.

Ramo, John Cooper. *The Age of the Unthinkable. Why the New World Disorder Constantly Suprises Us.* Little, Brown and Company, 2009.

Shah, Raffique. *Trinidad Express*, August 26, 2009.

Water and Sewage Authority. *WASA.* 2009.

Index

ABN Amro, 46
accelerated housing development
    programme, 85
Acuna, Herman, 405
Adams, John, 411
Adams Committee, 126; Report of the
    Natural Gas Pricing, 117, *118*
Addis Ababa, 198
Adventure Estate, 287
aeromagnetic data, 219
Africa, 146, 252, 279. *See also specific*
    countries
Africa Initiative, 383–86
African Union Summit, 198
Agard, John, 354
agency management, 351–55
Agrico Chemical Company, 23
Agricultural Fires Act, 325
agriculture, 21, 68, 393; roads for, 285;
    sugar industry and, 95; sustainability
    of, 29
agro-based industries, 242
A-G v. PYA Quarries Ltd., 314
air pollution, 317, 331
AISC. *See* Amoco International Sales
    Company
ALBA. *See* Bolivarian Alliance for
    America
Algeria, 45, 47, 188, 189

Allum, Kenneth, 438
ALNG. *See* Atlantic LNG
alternative energy, 196, 281
aluminium, 22, 175–76, 266
Aluminium Smelting—Environmental,
    Health and Engineering Perspectives
    (UWI), 409
Alutrint aluminium smelter, 266
Ames, Stephen, 293
Amherstia platform, 57
ammonia, 252, 265–66, 271, 371,
    374, 400; Arcadian Partners and,
    28; average prices of, *24*, 25–26,
    28, *28*; Fertrin and, 22–24; KAAP,
    29; natural gas and, 17–18; Point
    Lisas and, 22, 143; product-related
    pricing and, 124–25; Tringen and,
    22, 122; W. R. Grace & Co. and,
    143
ammonia, urea, and melamine project
    (AUM), 252, 266
Amoco, 10, 15–21, 36, 116–17, 143,
    421, 432; BG and, 46; Cassia
    contract, 122; compressor platforms
    and, 31; oil and gas output of, *17*;
    Peoples Gas of Chicago and, 18, 42;
    Petroleum Levy and Subsidy Act
    and, 13; tax reference prices and, 9;
    Trintomar and, 32

451

Trinidad Oil Syndicate, 3
Trinidad Petroleum Company, 284
Trinidad Petroleum Development Co. (TPD), 5, 293
Trinidad Tesoro Petroleum Company Ltd., 54, 142
Trinity Power Management Ltd., 39
Trinmar Ltd., 53, 214, 216
Trintoc. *See* Trinidad and Tobago Oil Company Ltd.
Trintoc Invaders, 291
Trintoc Sun Valley orchestra, 291
Trintoc Tobago All Stars, 291
Trintomar (Trinidad and Tobago Marine Petroleum Company Ltd.), 26, 32–39, 114, 121–22
Trintopec. *See* Trinidad and Tobago Petroleum Company Ltd.
T&TEC. *See* Trinidad and Tobago Electricity Commission
TTIT. *See* Trinidad and Tobago Institute of Technology
TTMA. *See* Trinidad and Tobago Manufacturers Association
TTMC. *See* Trinidad and Tobago Methanol Company
TTUC. *See* Trinidad and Tobago Urea Company
Tucker Energy Services, 30, 64
Tupi field, 192–93
Turtle Watch Project, 304
Twitter, 406
2D seismic technology, 218, 229

UBOT. *See* United British Oilfields of Trinidad
UDECOTT. *See* Urban Development Corporation of Trinidad and Tobago
Uganda, 198, 383
UK. *See* United Kingdom
UN. *See* United Nations
undergraduate degrees, 253
UNECLAC. *See* United Nations Economic Commission for Latin America

unemployment, 69, 76, 87
Unemployment Relief Programme (URP), 81
UNESCO, 97
Unified System for Regional Compensation, 182
Union Industrial Estate, 63
United British Oilfields of Trinidad (UBOT), 3–5, 284, 287–88, 290, 293
United Kingdom (UK), 171, 259, 389, 392, 419
United National Congress, 310
United Nations (UN), 180
United Nations Economic Commission for Latin America (UNECLAC), 175
United Petrotrin (football team), 292
United States (US), 180–81, 186–92, 199, 371–72, 439; Customs, 16; health care reform in, 410–11; natural gas in, 19; R/P ratio of, 437; shale gas in, 280
unitization, 251
University of Oklahoma, 253
University of Texas, 253, 392
University of the West Indies (UWI), 409, *425*, 425–26, 428, 447; African Initiative and, 385; Cuba and, 380; degree programmes of, 391–92; petroleum engineering course of, 421; research programmes at, 259; Vision 2020 and, 84
University of Trinidad and Tobago (UTT), 97, 273, 279, 369, 392, 428, 449; African Initiative and, 385; degree programmes of, 391–92; Point Lisas and, 253; research programmes at, 259; TTIT and, 51; Vision 2020 and, 83–84
Upper Cretaceous source rocks, 207, 209
Urban Development Corporation of Trinidad and Tobago (UDECOTT), 346
Urban Development Programme, 85
urea, 18, 22, 24–28, 143, 252, 266

URP. *See* Unemployment Relief
 Programme
Uruguay, 402
US. *See* United States
US Geological Survey (USGS), 235,
 237
UTT. *See* University of Trinidad and
 Tobago
UWI. *See* University of the West Indies

value capture: enhanced, 265;
 mechanisms of, 146–47
Vance River Community Centre, 409
Venezuela, 44, 174–77, 189, 271,
 280–82, 369–70, 403, 414; cross-
 border cooperation with, 185–86,
 199; cross-border reserves in, 134;
 Cunningham-Craig in, 3; Dominica
 and, 200; Eastern Venezuela Basin,
 206, 209, *209*, 228; Guyana and,
 175–76, 180; Lake Maracaibo, 15;
 LNG and, 186, 188, 196; PDVSA, 8,
 177, 182–83, 186; Pedernales Field,
 218; PetroCaribe and, 177–82, 281;
 resource diplomacy and, 182–84;
 TNA and, 6
Venezuelan Oil Company, 5
Ventech, 438
venture financing, 158
Vidale, Edgar, 294
Village Turtle Trust, 277
Virgin Islands, 418
Vision 2020, 51, 95, 97, 100, 234,
 243; Draft Plan, 140; education
 and, 83–85; Energy Committee,
 367–68; Energy Workshop, 133;
 housing programme of, 85; Industry
 and Entrepreneurship Report, 387;
 Macro-economic and Finance
 Committee, 92, 93, 104; National
 Development plan, 81; Sectoral
 Report for Regional Development
 and Sustainable Communities, 298,
 300; Sectoral Report on Energy,
 299; Subcommittee for Poverty

Alleviation and Social Services, 297;
 Subcommittee on Macroeconomics
 and Finance, 71–72. *See also* Energy
 Subcommittee
vocational skills training, 84, *85*, 97

Wall, Georges Parkes, 1
Wall Street Journal, 19, 44
Warner, Andrew M., 67
WASA. *See* Water and Sewage
 Authority
waste, 318; hazardous, 327–28, 333–34;
 non-hazardous, 328
Water and Sewage Authority (WASA),
 320, 446
Water Improvement Area Regulations,
 318
water pollution: fresh water, 317–20;
 marine, 320–23
Water Pollution Rules (2001), 331–32
water production, 445, *445*
Waterworks and Water Conservation
 Act, 318
Wealth Fund, 102
Weldfab Ltd., 60–64
welfare expenditure, 75
West Africa, 197–99, 208, 229, 271,
 282
West Indies Cricket Team, 293
West Indies Federation, 15
West Indies Oil Company (WIOC), 178
Westlake ethylene project, 266
WHO. *See* World Health Organization
Williams, Eric, 143, 146, 190, 361, 421,
 433; Long and, 7, 187; Mexican-
 Jamaican-Venezuelan projects and,
 176; PNM and, 138n2
Williams, Ewart, 101
Wimpey. *See* George Wimpey
 Caribbean Ltd.
windfall revenues, 68, 74, 92
wind power, 255, *257*, 258
WIOC. *See* West Indies Oil Company
withdrawal rules, 104–5
Wood Mackenzie, 235

CPSIA information can be obtained
at www.ICGtesting.com
Printed in the USA
LVHW031253291021
701914LV00004B/22

9 780761 863281